D0849928

BIOGRAPHIES OF ENGLISH CATHOLICS

IN THE

EIGHTEENTH CENTURY

Biographies of English Catholics

In the Eighteenth Century

BY THE

Rev. JOHN KIRK, D.D.

Being part of his projected continuation of
DODD'S CHURCH HISTORY

EDITED BY

JOHN HUNGERFORD POLLEN, S.J.,

AND

EDWIN BURTON, D.D., F.R.Hist.S.

London:

BURNS & OATES, 28 Orchard Street, W.

—

1909

BX 4676
K5
1968

S.B.N. - GB: 576.78526.1

Republished in 1968 by Gregg International Publishers Limited
1 Westmead, Farnborough, Hants., England.

Printed in England

Contents.

Introduction.

FOR those who are at all familiar with the history of the English Catholics in the early years of the last century, there will be little, if any, need of a formal introduction to the Rev. John Kirk. All our larger Catholic Archives preserve papers from his pen, his manuscript collections have been cited by numerous authors, and but for the almost insuperable obstacles of his times, the great history which he projected might have been carried out, and his name as an author might already have been notable for nearly a century.

From about the year 1776 (*see* p. 145), when as a student in Rome, he discovered a copy of Dodd's *Church History* among the books of the English College, his ambition was to continue that great work from 1688 to his own time. With this object in view he laboured for more than fifty years to gather together from all sources information as to the history of the Catholic Church in England during the eighteenth century.

He wrote and copied, he bound up loose papers, and his MS. series of volumes entitled *Collectanea Anglo-Catholica* grew to considerable dimensions. Yet he was never able to complete the undertaking he had projected in his youth. He grew old in collecting the material, and the history of the English Catholics in the eighteenth century remains unwritten.

Yet his labours have not been unproductive of result. To say nothing of his large manuscript collections, an invaluable source for future historians, which but for his industry might have been lost, we have the collection of Lives now given to the public. Dodd had included in his *History* chapters on the " Lives of Bishops," " Lives of Peers," " Lives of the Secular Clergymen," &c., and Kirk had not only accepted and somewhat amplified the idea, but actually carried this part of the plan into execution, and was able to write on the last page " FINIS, April 7, 1841."

Here too, however, one feels that he was regarding rather an end which circumstances had forced upon him, than the conclusion which corresponded with his conceptions. The *Lives* without the *History* were essentially incomplete, and we cannot but see that at that early date, before any other supplementary publications or a single Catholic book of reference was available,

no collection of Lives could have been truly complete. The work
is essentially that of a pioneer. It is inevitable that it should be
rough-hewn, and that sundry mistakes and numerous deficiencies
should be observable in it, which could now have been avoided.

Nevertheless, the book is one which will be more than welcome
to all lovers of English Catholic history. In the first place it
contains a considerable mass of new facts. Compared with
Mr. Gillow's invaluable *Bibliographical Dictionary of English
Catholics*, we find that the number of new lives which it adds is
most considerable. More than half the persons mentioned by the
historian of the eighteenth century have been passed over by the
collector, who had to take three and a half centuries into consideration, and to handle matters bibliographical with a thoroughness
to which the older writer made no pretensions. Kirk, moreover,
is in many points a final authority. It is impossible for us at
present to get beyond what he has to say on these little known
matters. The scientific historian can never feel satisfied until he
has such a text, whether faulty or faultless, as its author wrote it.

Finally, to pass over various other reasons which are not without their weight, the points in which Kirk is strong are points
which are every day growing in importance. There is no period of
Catholic history which is at present more obscure than the
eighteenth century. We know more, far more, about the thirty
years that succeeded the landing of Father Campion in England
than we do about the hundred and forty years that passed between
King James' flight from Whitehall and the Emancipation Bill.
Our Martyrs and other notable heroes of the early period have
attracted writers and historians by the score. The inconspicuous
church in the catacombs of the eighteenth century has hitherto
enkindled but little enthusiasm. But the period of neglect is
passing away. It is recognised that we are allied more closely
to the latter period than to the former. Whenever we try to
investigate the history of some existing Catholic mission,
institution or family, we find but little initial difficulty in following
up the desired track until we come to that obscure time, and then
again and again the clue is lost. The darkness that hangs over
those years is a puzzle to many, and a constantly increasing
number of enquirers are searching for guides and teachers who
will throw fresh light on the period. To them, Kirk's *Biographies* should be especially welcome. There was probably
never yet an historian who had a more intimate acquaintance with
this period (especially in what regards the Midlands and Lancashire) than Kirk ; and though he does not profess to have
thrown all his knowledge into these Lives, they remain, in spite
of all deficiencies, errors, inaccuracies and *want of author's
revision*, a solid and very valuable contribution to the history
of an interesting period.

As to the general history of those times, which, as we have shown, would have been fully treated in Kirk's contemplated work, a few broad ideas only can here be given. As has already been indicated, the period was one which differed considerably in character from the ages which preceded and which followed it. With the flight of James II. and the coming of William III., Catholics saw the ruin of their hopes for the restoration of England to the ancient faith. It is true that for a time they trusted to the prospect of a Restoration. On the death of Queen Anne in 1714, the succession of Prince James Francis by constitutional methods seemed for a moment possible ; a year later, in 1715, it proved to be utterly impracticable when attempted by force of arms. From that time Catholics lost hope, and even the brilliant but futile effort of 1745 did not convince them that the Stuart cause retained any chance of success. Possibly they had even ceased to desire it. For a silent revolution was gradually taking place among them; and whereas in 1715 they were all loyal Jacobites, in 1778 none found it impossible to take the Oath of Allegiance to King George. Early in the century they were still of political importance. This is indirectly proved by the persecution and the fresh penal statutes which signalised the accession of William III., and marked the whole of his reign. But before the same century closed the ministers of George III. were able with almost contemptuous tolerance to afford them the relief granted by the Acts of 1778 and 1791.

The eighteenth century, then, was for English Catholics a time of depression, of lost hopes and discouragement. Their numbers steadily, if slowly, dwindled away, and there seemed no future but one of gradual extinction. The policy of the Government was successful. There was no longer the persecution which is made glorious by martyrdom. No blood was shed after the Revolution, but the penal code, strengthened by new statutes in 1695, 1699, 1715, and 1722, lay like a dead weight on those who held to the ancient faith. Under every kind of civil and social disability they were excluded from public life and rendered powerless ; and in this way the Government effected its purpose of keeping them impotent and subdued. So long as they were submissive and quiet there was no active persecution by the Government, but, when it needed funds, fines, imposed on Catholics under the provisions of the existing laws, proved a convenient way of raising money. Sometimes private interest, whether of informers or others, set in motion the machinery of some persecuting statute. But in general such attempts were viewed with dislike by the civil authorities and courts of laws, and judges strained every point in favour of the victims.

Yet the lives of the English Catholics, if dull and uneventful, were by no means altogether miserable. The nobility and gentry, excluded from the public service of the State, did their duty upon their estates within the narrow limits allowed them by the law. At least in one instance, those who were not allowed to hold the

King's commission, raised at their own expense regiments for the King's service. George III. and his Queen welcomed at Court peers who were excluded from Parliament, and their friendly relations with the Howards, Petres, Jerninghams, and Welds—to name no others— showed that the King himself valued his Catholic subjects at their true worth.

In truth, the Catholic body, small as it was and ever growing fewer in numbers, was by no means lacking in distinction. Rarely if ever has the proportion of titled aristocracy and of great county families in the Church stood higher than during the early part of the eighteenth century. In the following pages there will be found accounts of the Dukes of Norfolk, Earls of Abergavenny, Ailesbury, Cardigan, Derwentwater, Lichfield, Newburgh, Nithsdale, Peterborough, Rivers and Shrewsbury; Viscounts Dunbar, Fairfax, Fauconberg, Molyneux and Montague ; Barons Abergavenny, Arundell of Wardour, Aston, Audley, Carrington, Clifford of Chudleigh, Dormer, Dover, Gerard, Langdale, Petre, Teynham, Stourton and Waldegrave ; besides families so well known as the Actons, Bedingfelds, Cliffords, Constables, Dicconsons, Englefields, Eyres, Eystons, Fitzherberts, Gages, Gascoignes, Gerards, Giffards, Haggerstons, Hornyolds, Jerninghams, Langdales, Lawsons, Mannocks, Mostyns, Sherburnes, Smythes, Stanleys, Swinburnes, Tancreds, Throckmortons, Tichbornes, Townleys, Vavasours and Webbs.

Another characteristic of the time was the nature of ecclesiastical government. During the short reign of James II. the Pope had restored episcopal government to the English Catholics, dividing the country into four districts, each governed by a Vicar Apostolic in direct dependence upon the Congregation of Propaganda. This put an end to the chaotic state of affairs which had existed for the previous century. The bishops who ruled these districts were without exception men of deep holiness of life and imbued with a profound sense of their responsibility. Among them were men of marked individuality, such as Bonaventure Giffard (Midland District, 1688-1703 ; London, 1703-1734), who suffered frequent imprisonment for the faith ; John Talbot Stonor (Midland District, 1716-1756) ; the venerable Bishop Challoner (London, 1759-1781), whose long, active episcopate was one of the glories of the times ; Dr. Walmesley, Benedictine monk and mathematical scholar (Western District, 1763-1797); and Bishop Milner (Midland District, 1803-1826). And round these were grouped other prelates who all did honour to their office.

It was well that men of such integrity and self-sacrifice filled the positions they did, for the situation was one which demanded the utmost prudence, and they were called upon to face problems of intricate and delicate character. The religious orders and communities which had done such splendid service during the long persecution had made for themselves a position which showed how well they could adapt themselves to altered circumstances. The Society of Jesus was indeed in its element amid the difficulties of the penal times, and carried on its work with remarkable success (*see* p. 279). Dominicans and Franciscans too, could thrive as preaching friars amid the chequered fortunes of missionary life (*see* p. 278). Perhaps even more remarkable is the way in which the Benedictines, whose history is so bound up with the fortunes of the Church in this land from the very beginning, rose to the occasion. Abbeys and priories had been swept away, monastic observance was no longer possible in England, but the Benedictine monks continued their work for souls, scattered up and down in private houses, deprived of that community life and environment which their Rule would ordinarily demand. They were forced to begin a new tradition, which ever continued one in spirit with the old, and in this way they, too, faced missionary enterprise with unconquerable courage (*see* p. 278).

Yet the very achievements of the Regular Clergy led to some difficulties, when the Vicars Apostolic were instituted to resume the episcopal office in England; and the constitutional settlement of the questions which arose, gave rise to a steady development of ecclesiastical legislation during this period.

A series of papal enactments marks the gradual stages of growth in that ecclesiastical organization which was to last in England until the Restoration of the Hierarchy in 1850.

By a decree of Propaganda under Pope Innocent XI. in 1688, supplemented by letters Apostolic, four Vicars Apostolic were appointed for England instead of one. In 1696, Innocent XII issued a decree declaring that by his predecessor's appointment of Vicars Apostolic all jurisdiction of Chapters or Vicars Capitular, both secular and regular, had been abrogated, and that all regulars were subject to the Vicars Apostolic, both as regards approbation for hearing confessions and other offices touching the administration of the Sacraments. In 1745, Benedict XIV. issued a fresh decree to settle questions which had arisen, and as this led to representations, both by the Regular Clergy and the Vicars Apostolic with regard to the difficulties of the situation, he finally issued the " Rules of the English Mission " in 1753, which successfully solved all problems, and proved to be a satisfactory constitutional basis on which to work for the future.

Some traces of the questions thus solved by Benedict XIV. will be found in the Biographies as well as occasional references to controversies regarding Jansenism and Gallicanism. As the colleges and religious houses were all situated abroad, owing to the penal laws which made such establishments impossible in England, those dwelling therein could hardly fail to be interested, and even at times involved, in these fierce theological controversies, and this reacted in some degree on Catholics at home. Yet with regard to Jansenism, for instance, there was no direct controversy in

England on the point.   No one was openly maintaining Jansenistic
doctrine.   The dispute here took the form of a discussion as to
whether there was or was not any Jansenism in England at all.
The brunt of the attack was borne by Douay College, which
ultimately secured for itself a triumphant acquittal from the charge
of heterodoxy.

On the whole, we may see in this epoch of Catholic history in
this country an obscure period, when men were called on to endure
rather than to achieve.   Under every discouragement Catholics
clung to their faith with tenacious loyalty.   The current of their
spiritual life ran all the deeper because it could not be expansive.
Their devotion was solid and silent, not running to any extravagance, incurring no suspicion of Quietism, tending to a stern
simplicity of life, and showing itself only by much unostentatious
charity.   Their homely lives were dull and uneventful, perhaps,
yet honest and honourable ; marked by some human weakness
indeed, but God-fearing and true to principle.

Above all, it should be remembered that they handed down the
faith loyally through a depressing and gloomy period, and Catholics
should never forget all they owe to the noblemen and gentlemen
who in their houses maintained the chapels which were the centres
of Catholic life throughout the country, at a time when that life was
well-nigh extinct in the towns.   Through those narrow channels
ran the sap which was to bring about the Second Spring.

John Kirk, who devoted so much of his time to gathering details
of lives which otherwise would have been forgotten, was a man of
his period, with the virtues and the limitations of his environment.
He was proud of his fellow Catholics and grudged no labour in
patiently gleaning every fact about them.   Possibly, indeed, all the
circumstances of his education and environment considered, it may
have been well that the opportunity failed him of carrying out his
early design, for though laborious, painstaking and conscientious,
he had not that literary training, that broad outlook or keen
insight, that the historian should possess.   His judgments, as
expressed, often betray the fact that he had not surmounted the
prejudices of his upbringing, and he was not qualified by his tem-
perament to be a final judge of controversies.   In his pages, the
past would not have lived again, and it may be feared that all
his care would only have resulted in a dry and lifeless collection
of facts.

One of the subjects which he would hardly have treated in a
satisfactory manner was the suppression of the Society of Jesus.
In the Lives before us the matter is rarely alluded to (*see*, however,
Cordell and Plowden, Charles), and the unsympathetic tone of these
references when they do occur reminds us that the years of his
education had been the very time when the Bourbon courts
combined to flood Catholic Europe with libels against the Jesuits,
and that his early manhood had been impressed by the violence

of the suppression. The arbitrary transfer of the Jesuit property, schools and colleges from hand to hand naturally caused heart-burnings and suspicions without number, both in those who suffered (to say nothing of their sympathisers) as well as in those who profited by the confiscations. These feelings are here and there faithfully represented by Kirk, a man only little in advance of his age. That he was somewhat more moderate and balanced than his contemporaries may be shown by comparing his relatively restrained tone with what Cardinal Pacca tells us of the education of that excellent Pontiff, Pope Pius VII. :

" The Pope had had anti-Jesuit masters and teachers, who had inculcated maxims and opinions altogether opposed to those of the Society, and everyone knows how deep are the impressions made by early teaching. I, too, had been taught in my youth to nourish against the Order feelings of aversion and hatred which amounted even to fanaticism. Suffice it to say that I was given Pascal's famous *Provincial Letters* (with the notes of Nicole under the name of Wendrock), both in French and Latin, to analyse and take notes from ; I had been given Arnauld's *Morale Pratique du Jésuite*, and other books of a similar kind. I was in perfect good faith about these books, and had not the shadow of a doubt as to their truth and accuracy " (*Mémoires*, 1832, ii. 182, 183). He then goes on to dwell on the providential and complete change of mind which time and experience brought both to himself and to the Holy Father, and which led to the restoration of the Society.

Kirk's education was liable to the same sinister influences which affected the early life of these representatives of pious Italian homes. Can we wonder if the smaller-minded man, though not a violent enemy, was never able to shake off altogether the evil influences of his early surroundings ? His fault was the fault of his age, and upon the whole his quarrels were few in number.

One of them needs a word or two of comment, for Kirk repeats it again and again, and evidently thinks the complaint unanswer-able. It regards the entrance of students from the English College at Rome into the Society. There were abuses in this matter, no doubt ; but Kirk does not see how they arose, nor how they were reformed, nor how we are to tell whether the College administration was good or bad.

The English College, then, was founded in 1579, before there was a single English house or novitiate of those Orders which had in the past done (as they do in the present) so much for the benefit of the Church. The Popes naturally wished that state of things to cease, and, in founding the College under the Jesuits, they put no hindrance whatever to the entrance of a cleric who wished eventually to enter an Order. In the Bull of the German College, which followed soon after the Bull for the English College, the intending religious is if anything welcomed to the Seminary, and (what removes all doubt) in the case of the Benedictine vocations the Roman Congregations decided clearly, and more than once, that a known vocation to that Order was no bar to admission to the Pontifical Seminaries.

But this decree was abused, and for a few years the English College was half filled with youths who meant eventually to become Jesuits. This was the less excusable, because by that time there was an English Jesuit novitiate, and there were houses into which the candidates for other religious Orders might be received.

No sooner was this pointed out to the Pope than, in a comparatively short time, considering the importance of the principle involved, the "Oath of the Mission" was imposed, by which the scholars were bound to declare under oath that they had already made their choice of a state of life and were resolved to cast in their lot with the Secular Clergy. This oath was exacted of all the students on the Papal funds, but there was a foundation established by Bernardino Lippi after the new decrees, and as he did not wish the oath to be exacted of the student he supported, there was still room for one scholar at Rome who had not fully made up his mind.

After this the number of scholars who, with Papal dispensation, became quite small, though Kirk seems always ready to resent the action of the Pope in granting any dispensation at all from the oath of the mission. Yet this attitude is indefensible, for the Popes had themselves founded and endowed the college, and it was for them to lay down conditions as to the manner in which it was to be conducted, both in general and with reference to particular cases. It cannot be denied that the college was managed substantially to the satisfaction of the Popes, seeing that it was carried on under their eyes, was freely criticised by countless visitors to Rome, and was regularly inspected by Papal deputies.

Apart from his prepossessions on this point, Dr. Kirk is a very impartial chronicler. He admits men of all kinds to his pages, recording their doings with friendly simplicity and usually refraining from unfavourable comment. Much information, which would otherwise have perished, he has successfully preserved, and though constant care must be exercised in making use of his biographies, they remain of unique importance for the history of the eighteenth century.

Of his own life there is no need here to speak in detail, especially as with naïve frankness he has already included his own biography in his collections. To the facts he has there set down it may be well to add some mention of another episode in his life. This is his connection with the "Staffordshire Clergy," a group of priests who early in the century gained an unenviable reputation. Their leader was the historian, the Rev. Joseph Berington, and they had the full approval of his cousin, Bishop Charles Berington, the coadjutor to their own Vicar Apostolic. Their published writings, however, as well as their action in opposing Dr. Walmesley, V.A.

Western Dist., laid them open to the charge of Cisalpinism, and the were suspended. Party feeling in those days ran high, and sundry hard things were said of Dr. Kirk and his friends. Nevertheless, we can now see that the unorthodoxy of the "Staffordshire Clergy" has been much exaggerated ; and when, after the death of Bishop Berington, Dr. Gregory Stapleton became Vicar Apostolic of the Midland District, he had no difficulty in persuading the few survivors of the group to sign a formula which he considered a sufficient test of their orthodoxy. Dr. Kirk long survived these controversies, and in his honoured old age he received a well-merited recognition of his labours, when in 1841 Pope Gregory XVI. made him a doctor of divinity. He died 21st December, 1851, in the ninety-second year of his age, and on the sixty-seventh anniversary of his first Mass, having lived to see the Restoration of the Hierarchy and the beginning of a new era in the history of the Church in England.

There are two manuscript copies of the Lives, the one being the draft of the other. The draft consisted of a large collection of small leaves, generally about six inches by four, in size. They were in fact blank sheets of large quarto note paper torn in half. They have now been arranged in alphabetical order, and are bound in three volumes, with the title *Kirk's Biographies*. After passing through various hands, they came to the Library of St. Francis Xavier's, Liverpool, and thence to the Library of *The Month*, at 31, Farm Street, W.

The fair copy is in the Archives of the See of Westminster, and the most sincere thanks of the Editors are due to His Grace the Archbishop for giving them every facility for transcribing and collating. The pains that have been taken in preparing the text have been very considerable, much more than any casual reader would imagine. Kirk's hand, though not a very bad hand, had its difficulties, and these difficulties became very considerable indeed over certain proper names. By carefully comparing the draft with the fair copy such doubts were in most cases solved, but not always (*see* p. 211 *note*) ; and sometimes by the insertions of query signs, etc., it has been necessary to indicate that the reading remains doubtful. It may also be (in the absence of the Author's revision) that we have, in spite of all our care, in some places inadvertently read him wrong, or not noticed slips, which he would have corrected, when reading the proofs. That Kirk was not a very accurate copyist was long since noted by Dr. T. F. Knox.

Kirk's drafts were generally rather fuller than his fair copies, and it was thought necessary at first to institute a careful collation, and to insert into the text in square brackets the matter contained in the draft but omitted from the finished text. But as time went on, it was recognised that these additions added hardly anything of value, and at the end they were no longer inserted. At the same time it may be added that there are mixed up with the drafts a few original letters of some value, for instance, a series of twenty letters from Thomas Berington (*below* p. 21) (dated 1731 to 1753) to Mr. Brockholes, of Chillington Hall, Wolverhampton, which contain a good many particulars about contemporary Catholic life.

Also one may note that the half sheets on which Kirk made his drafts frequently retain the dates of the original letters. These dates begin with the year 1813, and continue to the year 1836, being most frequent between the years 1815 and 1820. The conclusion would seem to be that the bulk of the Lives were written before 1820, and that the fair-copying was undertaken not later than the year 1836.

Kirk's plan, as has been said, was to follow Dodd, and to arrange his biographies under "Lives of Peers," "Lives of Baronets and Gentlemen," and "Lives of the Clergy." This order is preserved in the fair copy of the Biographies. This copy is written upon 54 small cahiers or gatherings of blank halves of quarto note-paper, folded into octavo size. But such an arrangement, though it may have commended itself to the public of Dodd's day, would certainly not suit ours, and the multiplication of series frequently led to over-lapping, and deflections from the alphabetical order, especially where a family name could be spelt in various ways, according to the then still semi-fluid state of our language in that respect. Accordingly it was thought best to rearrange all the lives in one alphabetical series, which is by far the most useful for the general student.

To facilitate reference, classified lists of biographies have been added at the end. The student will find these very useful if he wishes to follow out inquiries which cannot be satisfied by a single biography. For instance, the interesting subject of the so-called Chapter is touched upon in many of the Lives, but by having recourse to the series, "Capitulars and Church Dignitaries," a much fuller account—probably the best account yet printed—of its progress and functions may be obtained. Another interesting list is that of the places mentioned in this book, where Catholic house-holds—or presumably Catholic households—have lived. As it was quite common for priests in those days to visit Catholic houses of every sort, and to say Mass in them, this list will also be of the greatest use in tracing out the obscure history of our Catholic Chapels.

In conclusion, the Editors wish to thank all friends who have helped them in their work, and especially Father Patrick Ryan, S.J., and Miss A. M. Stearn, to whose care and patient labour it has been chiefly due that the text has been satisfactorily settled by collation, and that the proofs have been brought into strict accord with that text.

J. H. P.
E. H. B.

BIOGRAPHIES OF
ENGLISH CATHOLICS
OF THE EIGHTEENTH CENTURY.

ACTON, SIR RICHARD, of Aldenham Hall, in the county of Salop, Baronet. Only son of Sir Whitmore Acton, 4th Bart., by his wife Elizabeth, daughter of —— Gibbon Esq. Born Jan. 1, 1710 [1711], O.S. He was sent to one of our Universities, and Sept. 21, 1744, he married Anne, daughter of Henry, Earl of Stamford, by whom he had Francis, who died unmarried in 1762, and Elizabeth, who married Philip Langdale, of Houghton, and Sancton, Co. York, Esq. Sir Richard was High Sheriff for Salop in 1751. Some time after this he became a Catholic, and was received into the Church by Father Blythe. [I think] Mr. Philipps, the author of the *Life of Cardinal Pole*, was his first Chaplain. Sir Richard died at Aldenham, November 26 [Nov. 20], 1791, and was succeeded in his title, and also in his estates after the death of Mr. Langdale, by Sir John Francis Edward Acton, Bart., great grandson of Walter Acton, second son of Sir Walter Acton, the second Bart.—*Betham* ii. 13.

ADAMS, JOHN.—He was born in Staffordshire in September, 1709. When young he went over to Bornheim, a house of the English Dominicans, where he studied his humanity, and in 1729 was admitted into the English College where he was ordained priest, Feb. 13, 1735, and the same year came on the Mission. He died in London, Oct. 13, 1757.

ADAMS, THOMAS, a secular Priest, lived many years in the Fitzherbert family at Swinerton, and attended the Catholics at Oulton, near Stone. From about the year 1720 his sight was so much impaired that he was unable to say Mass. He died Jan. 29, 1732.

ADDIS, JOSEPH, was Chaplain at Arundel for several years. The first entries in the Baptismal Register are by him. I think he came to Arundel in June, 1745. [M.A.T.]

ADDISON, WILLIAM.—William Addison, *alias* Hildreth, Secular, lived at Dalton Hall, near Wycliff, in Yorkshire, a seat of a branch of the Meynells. He afterwards resided with Mr. Meynell at Aldborough, and died there, very old, April 28, 1736. He was much esteemed by his brethren in Yorkshire and was the administrator of their fund till 1730.

ALICE, DAME.—See *Catholic Magazine*, p. 476, Vol. ii.

ALLEN, HENRY, was admitted at Douay College where he defended his Divinity under Mr. Mayes in July, 1704, and was much applauded. He resided at Durham with Mr. Witham and assisted the Catholics about Hartlepool. On the death of Mr. Wilkinson he succeeded him at Sunderland, about 1732, but did not long survive him, dying in 1733. He had been much afflicted with the stone, and "after his death five were taken from him that weighed as many ounces," says Mr. Andrew Giffard, his contemporary.

ALLEN, JEROME.—Ob. Lisbon, 1814.

ALLIBON, JOB.—Job Allibon, a Missionary in Yorkshire, where he was chosen in 1676 to assist Mr. Franks, the Archdeacon in that county. On the promotion of Dr. Giffard he succeeded to his Canonry and was in such estimation with his brethren that in the General Assembly of the English

2

Chapter he was proposed by the Dean, Dr. Perrot, as a fit person to be the Sub-Dean, but was not taken to fill that post till Dec. 1706. His brother Richard was a Counsellor of Gray's Inn and was much employed by the Clergy in their temporal affairs. Was knighted by James II. and made a King's Counsel and then a Judge. Mr. Allibon died Dec. 11, 1707 or 9.

ALLOWAY, JOHN, of the Society of Jesus, was the third son of William and Catharine Alloway. He was born in Oxfordshire in April, 1743, and on January 7, 1755, was sent to Rome, where Father Sheldon, the Rector, placed him on one of the Free Funds which did not require the Alumnus to take that part of the oath of Alexander VII. which forbade him to enter into any Religious Order. Here he remained till Oct., 1766, when, having received the Minor Orders, he was admitted into the Noviciate of the Jesuits at Monte Carvallo, and in Sept., 1767, left Rome for Flanders. Some time after he was ordained Priest and came on the Mission. He resided in the family of Sir T. Stanley at Hootten in Cheshire, and died there, as he had lived, much respected, [15 Mar., 1808].

ANDERSON, SIR WILLIAM, made his theological studies at Valladolid. He assisted the Catholics at and about Stockton for some years after 1726, and was also Priest at Sunderland. He died suddenly in the street in London, Aug. 28, 1759. In the *Gentleman's Magazine* for Sept., 1759, he is called Anderton. (In the Clergy Obituary I find a *George* Anderson in this year.) Was he not brother to Sir James [Francis] Anderton, of Lostock, Bart., who married Margaret, daughter of Sir Henry Bedingfield, of Oxborough [who died without issue]?

In the MS. cases at Ushaw, p. 1074, I find the following account : "William Anderson, of Craythorne, was brought the 27th Dec., 1745, before R. Robinson and M. Consett, two Justices of the Peace, as a Popish Priest, and on his examination, confessing himself to be such, and refusing to take the oaths, was committed that day by them to York Castle, and afterwards the Jurors for our Lord the King upon their oaths presented William Anderson and John Rivett (being a Popish Priest), and little regarding the laws and estates of this realm, and not fearing the pains and penalties contained therein after the 25th of March, 1700, to wit the 18th of Sept. in the 19th year of George II. did say Mass at Craythorne and Ugthorpe, and that office of function of a Popish Priest did use and exercise, in contempt of the said Lord, the King and his laws."—See Art. *Rivett* and *State Trials.*

"Sir William Anderson came from town to Ugthorpe on Friday, 5th of Oct., 1739. He went away from Kendal, in Westmorland, Nov. 28, 1739, to Mr. Anderson at Sir John Fleetwood's, at Newton, near Chester."—Copied from an old Breviary at Mrs. Williams', Northumberland Buildings, Bath.

ANDERTON, BRUNO.—He was the nephew, I believe, of Roger and Christopher Anderton. At the age of 20 he was admitted into the College at Rome by his uncle Christopher, in Oct, 1663. Being ordained, he left the College for the Mission on April 23, 1669. He returned to Rome for the Jubilee in 1700, and died May 19, 1723, leaving to the Clergy agent at Rome 400 scudi.—*Annals of the College.*

ANDERTON, CHRISTOPHER, S.J.—Christopher was the second son of Christopher Anderton, of Lostock, Esq., Co. Lancashire, and his wife Alathea, daughter of Sir Francis Smith, of Wootton Wawen, in Warwickshire. His elder brother, Francis, born in 1628, was advanced to the degree of Baronet by Charles II. Christopher became a Jesuit, and was Rector of the College at Rome from 1663 to 1667, and again from 1673 to 1682. Father William Morgan succeeded him.—*English Baronetage,* 1741, Vol. iv., p. 633.

ANDERTON, SIR FRANCIS. — Francis Anderton, of Lostock, Bart. Was 4th son of Sir Charles Anderton, of Lostock, Bart., by his wife, a daughter of —— Ireland, of Lidiate, Lancashire. (Mr. Nicholls, iii., 29, says Sir Francis was son of Christopher Anderton, who married Alethea, 4th daughter of Sir Francis Smith, and son of the first Lord Carrington.) Sir Francis possessed an estate of 2,000 or 3,000 per annum. He joined the Prince and was taken prisoner at Preston in 1714. His counsel endeavoured to quash the indictment on the plea that his brother, who was a Priest, and still living, and not he, was the Bart. This not being admitted, he endeavoured to prove at great length that he came to Preston on his private affairs, that he knew nothing of the Rebellion till his arrival, that he attempted to get out again but was prevented by the guards and barricades. The evidence of the Crown on the contrary asserted that in their opinion any person might have got out any time before the King's troops. Several witnesses deposed that he was a very peaceable Roman Catholic. He was, however, found guilty, and received sentence of death, but was afterwards pardoned. (*Faithful Register of the late Rebellion*, 1718.)

Sir Francis had three brothers : Charles, James, and Laurence, who all succeeded to the title, and all died without issue. Laurence became a Benedictine, and on the death of his two elder brothers, Sir Charles and Sir James, without issue, succeeded to the title and estates. He died in London on Sept. 20, 1724, and was succeeded by his brother, Sir Francis Anderton. (*Engl. Baronetage* iv., 633.)

ANDERTON, ROGER, son of Roger Anderton of Birchley, Esq,, Co. Lancaster. At the age of about eighteen years he was admitted into the College at Rome, in Feb., 1639 by Father Fitzherbert, the Rector ; where he was ordained priest in June, 1645, in the following Sept. came on the Mission (*Annals of the College*). He resided in his native county, and on the death of Mr. Richard More succeeded him as Archdeacon of Lancashire and Westmorland and in that capacity assisted at the General Assembly of the Chapter in 1674. At this Assembly Dr. Perrot, the Dean, presided ; 5 Vicar-Generals, 19 Archdeacons, and 8 Canons attended, but 6 of them by their deputies. The General Assembly was opened on the 10th of April by a Mass of the Holy Ghost. All the members made the profession of Faith of Pius IV. It is well known that after the death of Dr. Smith, the last Bishop of Chalcedon, the Dean and Chapter exercised Episcopal Jurisdiction, until the appointment of Vicars Apostolic. Acting then in this capacity, the Assembly resolved that the *Monita* of the Bishop of Chalcedon, the *Legatum* of Dr. Champney, and the *Little Ritual* should be printed, after the latter had been revised and corrected by Dr. Ellice and Dr. Perrot ; that the Superiors of Douay and Lisbon Colleges be desired to take care that all they send on the Mission be well instructed in the Administration of the Sacraments, and make a spiritual retreat of at least seven days immediately before they leave the College. That some neighbouring Bishop, in case none be appointed by Rome in a reasonable time, be requested to come over to administer Confirmation throughout the kingdom. That a list be kept by the Dean of all Clergy Priests that come on the Mission, and of their qualifications, as far as can be learnt, and that country superiors give an account yearly of all their subjects, studies, and comportment ; all in order that fit elections of superiors be afterwards made : that in consequence of information from Mr. Franks, Archdeacon of Yorkshire, that " the Regulars generally allowed eggs on Fridays," the Superiors of Regulars be moved to endeavour to promote a conformity to the ancient custom of abstaining from eggs on Fridays and in Lent in the northern parts of England beyond the Trent. That the VV. GG., and Archdeacons call their brethren of their districts together yearly, appoint officers of their funds, and acquaint the brethren of their respective districts with the management and settlements of such funds ; that the respects of the General Assembly be humbly presented to the Cardinal (Howard) of Norfolk, with many thanks for all his kindness shown to the body of the clergy, and likewise that a prudent intimation be inserted of their hope that, in case it fall in with his Eminence's power, he will now, or at some time as it appears feasible hereafter, endeavour to procure the restitution of the College at Rome to the Clergy's government, as formerly ; and lastly, in consequence of Dr. Ellice's infirmities, Dr. Perrot was chosen Vicar-General, *in solidum*, to assist the Dean in the discharge of his various duties. The Acts were then signed in the 4th and last session, and that Assembly closed on the 13th of April. (Minutes of John Serjeant, Secretary of the Chapter in the Archives of ditto). Mr. Anderton assisted also at the General Assemblies held in 1684 and in 1687, and by deputy in that of 1694. He died in the following year, aged 74. Bishop Smith, V.A. of the Northern District, had a great respect for him, and desired Mr. Barlow, his V.G. in Lancashire, "to defer to his years and judgment." Bishop Leyburn made him Rural Dean for Westmorland, and Bishop Smith continued him in the same situation.

ANDERTON, THOMAS, born in Lancashire. At the age of 24 went to Rome, and admitted into the College Sept. 12, 1699; he was ordained Priest June 10, 1702, and in the following May left the College for Paris (*Annals of the College*). He was a member of the English Chapter and an Archdeacon. He lived many years at Townley, in Lancashire, where he died July 13, 1741.

ANGEL, JAMES, a native of Essex. He studied at Rome, where he was admitted as Alumnus in 1733, and received Priest's orders, Feb. 24, 1745. On the 16th of May following he left the College and came on the Mission, which he served many years at Fawley, in Berks. He afterwards lived in the family of Mrs. Eyston, of East Hendred, where he died May 18, 1775.

APEDAILE, GEORGE.—Born in the Bishopric [*i.e.* of Durham], and educated at Douay. Soon after his ordination he was made Confessor to the Poor Clares at Dunkirk. Here he lived happy, he said, till the ill-planned attack upon that town by the Duke of York in 1793, when he and all the other English in the town were arrested and kept in confinement until his removal to Arras, where he suffered greatly from the narrowness of his cell and the scantiness of his allowance. In May, 1794, he was removed to the citadel of Dourlens, in Picardy, together with the masters and scholars of St. Omers. Here he found the President, seniors, etc., from Douay, and remained with them until about October, when he was sent back to Dunkirk and allowed to accompany them to England in 1796. Having found a place of settlement at Church Hill, near Worcester, Mr. Apedaile accompanied them thither and continued to be their director till the time of his death, which took place February 26th, 1799, rather unexpectedly.

APPLETON, JAMES.—He studied and was ordained priest at Douay. Soon after he came on the Mission he accompanied the sons of Sir William Jerningham, Bart., in a tour on the Continent. On his return he lived some years as Chaplain in the family of Michael Blount, Esq., at Mapledurham, then in that of Thomas Giffard, Esq., at Chillington; next at Mawley, the seat of Sir Walter Blount, and lastly he settled at Stafford in 1804, where he continued till his death, March 2, 1814, aged 71.

He wrote: (1) *Sermons*, in 3 vols. (2) *Theophilus, or The Pupil Instructed, etc.*, 8vo., 1794; from the *Doctrine Chrétienne* of L'Homond. (3) *An Analysis of the Gospels through the year;* a posthumous work, published by Rev. F. Martyn.

ARCHDEACON, ROBERT.—Robert Archdeacon, *alias* Smelt. He was born in London of Catholic parents, Jan. 16, 1746, and was sent to Rome in 1763, and admitted into the College Jan. 13, under the Rector, Father Charles Booth. He was ordained priest Dec. 23, 1769, before he had completed his 23rd year, which probably was the cause of his remaining in the College till April 3, 1771. In what part of the London District he exercised his faculties does not appear, but on the death of Dr. Whittington, Chaplain to the Earl of Shrewsbury, in 1783, he succeeded him at Heythrop. About 1791 he was deputed to Rome to assist Monsignor Stonor, the Agent of the Clergy, and on the death of that venerable prelate he succeeded to the Agency. In 1814, some business requiring his presence in London, he came over but never returned, dying there Aug. 24, 1814, aged 67.

ARCHER, JAMES, D.D.—He was admitted at Douay College, Feb. 5, 1769, and being ordained, left to come on the Mission, June 7, 1780. (See *Catholic Magazine*, Sept., 1834, vol. v., p. cli.)

ARMSTRONG, PETER, O.S.F. and D.D., signed the question on Usury. (MS. *Records of VV. AA.*, p. 171.)

ARNE, DR.—Dr. Arne, the greatest of English musicians, at least if we except Purcell, was a Roman Catholic. His music for *Comus* and *Artaxerxes* has always enjoyed public favour.   His ballads, containing an agreeable mixture of Italian, Scottish, and English melody, have not been surpassed and seldom equalled.   He composed for the choir of the Sardinian Ambassador two Masses, one in four and the other in three parts : the latter did not please, the former was exquisite ; it is what all church music should be—solemn and impressive, the harmony correct and simple, the melody slow and graceful. —*Histor. Mem.* ii., 334, chap. 43, and account of *Music* at the end.   See also *Cath. Gent. Mag.*, No. 18 [8] for Sept.

ARUNDELL OF WARDOUR.

Wardour Castle, *April* 11, 1820.

My dear Sir,—

I am very happy to give you any information I possess relative to my family.   The Arundells of Wardour and of Lanherne in Cornwall now united in me, have always maintained the religion of their ancestors, without a single instance to the contrary, though Dodd says the untimely end of Sir Thomas Arundell, who was beheaded unjustly in Edward VI's. time, was considered as a judgment on him for having received much Church property.   He suffered for it, and almost all his property was confiscated, and was repurchased by his son, Sir Matthew, whose son, Sir Thomas, was first Lord Arundell of Wardour.   He was succeeded by Thomas, his eldest son, as second Lord, and by Lady Blanche Somerset, fifth daughter of Edward, Earl of Worcester, had an only son, Henry, who succeeded his father as third Lord Arundell, May 19, 1643, at which time he was married, and had two sons of the age of ten and eight years (they must have been older).   His wife was Cecily, daughter of Sir H. Compton, of Brambletye in Sussex.   On coming to the title his wife and sons were prisoners and his castle in the hands of the Parliamentary troops commanded by Edmund Ludlow, to dislodge him he sacrificed his castle by springing a mine under it (vide *Mercurius Rusticus* and *Ludlow's Memoirs*, vol. I.).   He seems to have been in some employment, though not in the ministry, during the reign of Charles II.   He was employed by Clifford in the famous treaty between Louis XIV. and Charles II.   The perjured Titus Oates accused him of this plot, and with the other four Lords he was long confined to the Tower.   Many papers preparatory to his defence are in my possession.   During his imprisonment he wrote a few short poems on religious subjects, which have given him a place in Oxford's *Royal and Noble Authors*, and which do great credit to his religious feelings and some to his taste.   On March 16, 1687, by the Patent in my possession, he was appointed by King James II. Lord Privy Seal, which he held till James abdicated.   He retired afterwards to Breamore, a house on the borders of Wilts and Hants, where he died December 28, 1694, and is buried with this Wardour branch of his ancestors, at Tisbury in Wiltshire, being about 84 years of age.   His wife died March 21, 1675, aged 67, buried at Tisbury.

They left two sons, Thomas, fourth Lord Arundell, and Henry Arundell, and one daughter, Cecily, who become a nun of the order of Poor Clares at Rouen in Normandy, where she died at a very advanced age.   Henry Arundell, the second son, married Mary, daughter of Edmund Scroope, of Danby in Yorkshire, and had no children.   He died at the age of 96, August 9, 1721 ; buried at Tisbury.   Of Thomas, the fourth Lord, I know nothing except that he married Margaret, daughter of Thomas Spencer, of Upton in Warwickshire, and had three sons : Henry, sixth Lord, Thomas, and Matthew.   The fourth Lord died January 10, 1712, *aetat* 78.   Thomas Arundell, the second son ot the fourth Lord, was —— of the Embassy of the Lord Castlemaine to the Pope, *temp*. James II. and was afterwards killed at the battle of the Boyne, unmarried.   Matthew, third son, died unmarried at Rouen in Normandy. Henry, fifth Lord, married Elizabeth, daughter of Thomas Panton, Esq., by whom he had two sons, Henry and Thomas, and one daughter, Elizabeth, married to the Earl of Castlehaven. She is buried at St. Pancras, near London. Thomas, the second son, married Anne Mitchell. They had no issue, and are both buried at St. Pancras. He died April 6, 1752, *aetat.* 56 (*vid.* monument). Henry, sixth Lord, first married Elizabeth Everard, daughter of Baron Raymond Everard, of Liège, of the family of the Everards of Fethard in Ireland ; by her he had three sons, Henry, Thomas and James Everard. This lady died May 22, 1728, *aetatis* 25. He married secondly Lady Anne, daughter of the Marquis of Powis, by whom he left no issue. She died September, 1757. Of the younger sons I shall speak later. The sixth Lord died June 29, 1746, *aetatis.* 53, and is buried at Tisbury. Henry, seventh Lord Arundell, succeeded his father and was educated at the College of Louis le Grand at Paris. Married Mary, daughter and heiress of Richard Belling, or Bealing Arundell of Lanherne, in Cornwall, Esq., which united the two houses of Arundell. By her he had two sons, Henry and Thomas. Lord Arundell died September 12, 1756, *aetat.* 38. Lady Arundell died in 1768. Both are buried at Tisbury. Thomas, his second son, was educated first at St. Omers, after at Paris. He died unmarried in 1781, *aetatis* 39, and is buried at St. Omers. Henry, eighth Lord Arundell, born on March 31st, 1740, studied at the Jesuits' College at St. Omers under the name of Henry Belling, and was afterwards at the Academy of Turin in Italy. He succeeded his father at 16 years of age. He married in 1763 Mary, sole daughter and heiress of Benedict Conquest of Irnham Hall, in the County of Lincoln, by who he had only two daughters. The eldest, Maria Christina, married her cousin, James Everard Arundell (*ut infra*). She died February 14, 1805, aged 40, and is buried at Irnham. The youngest Eleanor married Charles, Lord Clifford. This Lord Arundell built Wardour House, and died Dec. 4, 1808, and is buried in the chapel at Wardour. His widow died in June, 1813, and is buried at Irnham.

I now return to the younger sons of the sixth Lord Arundell. Thomas, the second son, was at the College of S. Louis le Grand in Paris. He married Mary, the daughter of — — Porter, Esq., by whom he had no issue. He lived at Salisbury till his death on May 11, 1768, and is buried at Tisbury. His widow survived him till the year 1799, and was buried with her husband. James Everard, the third son, born in the year 1721, was also educated at Louis le Grand. He married Anne, daughter and heiress of John Wyndham, Esq., of Norrington and Ashcombe in Wilts. (a Protestant). He died March 20th, 1803, aged 82, and is buried at Tisbury, leaving two sons, James Everard and Thomas Raymond. James Everard succeeded his first cousin Henry as ninth Lord Arundell of Wardour, and whose daughter he married. He was educated at the academy at Liège, having been first at the Old Hall Green, then a small school, under the Rev. — — Willisy. Born March 4, 1763. He died July 13, 1807, aged 54. By his first wife, the Honble. Maria Christina Arundell, he had ten children, two sons and eight daughters, the fourth daughter only surviving him. (Of his second wife I shall say nothing ; she is educating her children Protestants). James Everard, tenth Lord Arundell, born November 3, 1785, studied three years at the Old Hall, and three at Stonyhurst. Henry Cavendish, second son, born November 13, 1804, was at Stonyhurst, and is now going to Ampleforth.   [ARUNDELL OF WARDOUR.]*

The co-heiresses of Sir John Arundell†—the last direct male descendant of the Arundells of Lanherne married Sir R. Belling and Sir — — Bedingfield.

Sir Richard Belling was the son of Richard Belling, Esq., of Killusky Castle, in Ireland, Secretary to confederate Catholics of Kilkenny's Supreme Council, and reputed author of the *Vindiciae Catholicorum Hiberniae* though not so (*vid.* Harris ; in fol. Edit. of Ware's *Writers on Ireland*). Sir R. Belling was Comptroller of the household to Catherine of Portugal, Queen of Charles

---

* This letter is a copy by Kirk without signature, but endorsed "Lord Arundell."
† Sir John Arundell, of Lanherne, Knt., was Master of the Horse to Catherine of Portugal, Queen of Charles II. Died October 14, 1701. Buried at St. Columbs in Cornwall. He was son of Sir J. Arundell by Eliz. Roper, second daughter of John, third Lord Teynham.

II. He died October, 1716. Buried at St. Columbs in Cornwall, leaving his
son, Richard Bellings Arundell ; his brother Charles having died young. He
took the name of Arundell, and married Ann, daughter of Joseph Sage of
Sherborne Castle, Oxfordshire, by whom he left eight daughters, of whom
Mary became, by the death of her sister, sole heiress, and married Henry, the
seventh Lord Arundell. Mr. R. B. Arundell died in ―― and is buried at
St. Columbs in Cornwall. "A worthy gentleman," (says Bshp. G[? iffard]. . .
" and the best friend I ever met with."

ASHMALL, FERDINAND.—He was the son of Thomas Ashmall, of Amerston, County Durham, Esq., born January 1, 1695. At the age of fifteen he
went to Lisbon, and May 23, 1715, took the college oath and gown, and being
ordained priest, returned to England. For about four years he lived chaplain
to Miss Mary Salvin in Old Elvet, Durham, but in consequence of bad health
retired to his father's house at Amerston, and attended the Catholics in that
neighbourhood. When Mr. Dabord removed into Lancashire, in 1745, Mr.
Ashmall succeeded him at New House near Esh, Durham, where he spent the
remainder of his days, and died February 5, 1798, aged 104. He was buried
within the Communion rails of Esh Chapel. Mr. Ashmall had two uncles,
Ferdinand and John, both educated and ordained at Rome. Ferdinand was
chaplain to the Earl of Derwentwater at Dilston for several years ; but died
in Old Elvet, Durham, April 2, 1712, where he had contributed largely to the
building of a Priest's house, and left the remainder of his property to the fund
for the support of the incumbent.   John lived many years chaplain in the
Salvin family, and died in Durham about the year 1706. (*Lisbon Register.*)

ASPINWALL, [EDWARD], S.J.—About the year 1710 he conformed to the
Established Church, and wrote an artful book against Catholics, for which he
was rewarded with a prebendal stall in Westminster Abbey. Mr. Dalton, of
Sunning Hill, a Protestant gentleman who was kindly disposed towards
Catholics knew him very well ; and told Mr. Alban Butler, that "to the end of
his life the warmest affections of his heart were for the Society."

ASTON, WALTER, LORD.—Walter, third Lord Aston of Tixall, eldest son
of Walter, second Lord Aston (who, in right of his wife, Gertrude Sadler,
succeeded to all the Sadler estates at Standon, etc.), and of Mary, second
daughter of Richard Weston, Earl of Portland. On the death of his father,
in 1678, he succeeded to his estates and title. He married first Eleonora,
youngest daughter of Sir Walter Blount, of Soddington, and by her had five
sons and two daughters ; secondly Catharine, daughter of Sir Thomas Gage,
of Firle. Lord Aston died Nov. 14, 1714, aged 81, and was buried at Standon,
the ancient seat of the Sadlers, in Herts. During the reign of James II. he was
Lord Lieutenant of the county of Stafford, and in Nov., 1688, when the Prince of
Orange landed, Lord Aston and Lord Molineux threw themselves into Chester
to preserve it for the King. Charles, his forth son, was captain of a band of
Greenwich pensioners, and was slain at the battle of the Boyne, in 1690.

ASTON, WILLIAM, S.J.—[Son of Edward Aston and Anne Bayley]. He
was born April 22, 1735. He entered his noviceship Sept. 7, 1751, and was
professed in 1769. When the College of St. Omers and of Watten was seized
by an Arret of the Parlement of Paris in the summer of 1762, about 140
scholars were conducted to Bruges and distributed into two hired houses
called *Le Gouvernement* and *L'hôtel d'argile.* Father Aston was appointed
Superior of the *Little School,* as it was called, while Father Stanley was Rector
of the other. One of the best houses in Bruges was afterwards purchased,
an additional new building was erected, and in a short time Father Aston's
little school was advanced to a great degree of neatness and elegance. On
the suppression of the Society in August, 1773, Father Aston's College was
seized by the Austrian Government of Brussels, and the Rector was conveyed
a prisoner to the College of the Flemish Jesuits, where he remained about
fifteen days, and was then taken together with Fathers Angier and Plowden to
Ghent. (MS. account of the destruction of the English Colleges at Bruges,
by Rev. C. Plowden.)

ATKINSON, MATTHEW. — Matthew Atkinson, better known among his brethren by the name of Paul of St. Francis. He was a native of Yorkshire, and entered into the order of St. Francis in the English Convent at Douay, December 27, 1673, being then seventeen years of age. In 1687 he was sent upon the English Mission, where he was noted for his zeal of souls and diligence in his pastoral functions, and brought many strayed sheep back to the fold of Christ ; till being accused by a false convert of being a Priest, he was condemned to perpetual imprisonment, and sent to Hurst Castle, where he remained a constant and pious confessor of Christ for thirty years, till his dying day, which was October 15, 1729. He departed this life aged 74, in the 56th year of his religious profession, and lies interred at St. James's, near Winchester. (*Miss. Priests*, vol. ii., p. 475.)

ATKINSON, ——, S.J.*—A native of Worcestershire. At the age of 15 he was admitted into the English College at Rome, March 19, 1703, and was placed by Fr. Mansfield, the Rector, on one of the *Free Funds*, which left him at liberty to become a Regular, even after he had taken the College Oath. After remaining here better than four years, he went to the novitiate of the Jesuits in Rome, Feb. 24, 1708. Some years after his ordination he was placed at Loretto, where and at Rome he filled the important office of Penitentiary for more than thirty years ; and made a happy end, say the *College Annals*, and much beloved by all who knew him, March 24, 1763, in the College of the Penitenziaria. [The College oath spoken of was the original form, imposed by Gregory XIII., which did not prevent entry into religious orders.—J.H.P.] (*Annals of the College at Rome*.)

ATWOOD, ——, O.S.D., *alias* PITS.—He probably belonged to the family of the Atwoods of Beverley, Co. Worcester. After studying his classics at St. Omers, he entered among the English Dominicans at Bornheim, Feb. 22, 1763, when he took his mother's name, Pits, and made his profession Feb. 4, 1664. "This Ven. Father laboured hard in the Mission for forty years, and suffered chains and imprisonment and mockeries for his religion. He was at last condemned to death, but when the cart was ready at the door of his prison to convey him to Tyburn, he received his pardon from Charles II. The remainder of his life was spent in bewailing, as a misfortune, his being deprived of the honour of martyrdom. He died in London, Aug. 12, 1712." (*Dominican Obituary*.) [Another account says that he died in 1704.—P.R.]

AUDLEY, LORD. — James Touchet, twelfth Lord Audley, eldest son of Mervin Touchet, Lord Audley, and Mary, third daughter of John, Earl of Shrewsbury, and the widow of Charles Arundell. On the death of his father, he succeeded to his title and estates. He married Elizabeth, daughter and co-heiress of —— Bord of Weston, and by her had one son, who succeeded him. He died August 12, 1700, and is buried under a black marble slab in Winchester Cathedral.

AUDLEY, LORD.—James Touchet, thirteenth Lord Audley and Earl of Castlehaven, only son of James, Lord Audley and Elizabeth Bord. He married Elizabeth, only daughter of Henry, Lord Arundell of Wardour, and had by her two sons and one daughter, Lady Elizabeth, who married Captain Philip Thicknesse. His Lordship died in Paris in November, 1740, and was succeeded by his son John, fourteenth Lord.

AUSTIN, JOHN, *alias* LAMB.—John Austin, whose true name was Lamb, was born Sept. 14, 1742. He was admitted into the English College at Rome, July 15, 1755, and being ordained priest in Sept., 1765, he left the College April 9, 1766, and came on the Mission. For several years he exercised his faculties in London ; but in consequence of some indiscretions, he left and settled at Brailes, in Warwickshire, where he took the name of Austin, and died there Sept. 28, 1809. He was a man of considerable abilities, but not without a mixture of oddities. His mother was sister to Mr. Taprel, a Priest, who for some years attended the Catholics in and about Derby. He afterwards conformed and practised Physic.

AYLMER, WILLIAM AUGUSTINE, O.S.F.—He was made Professor of Divinity, and Guardian of the Convent of the English Franciscans at Douay. He presided over Richard Colleridge's Divinity thesis Dec. 18, 1709. He conformed to the Established Church, and published *A Recantation Sermon against the errors of Popery*, preached at Oxford, Sept. 20, 1713. London, 1713.

AYLSBURY, LORD.—Dr. Ingleton says : " Father Williams, the Dominican, and afterwards Bishop of the Northern District, lived with him [*i.e.* Lord Aylsbury] in Flanders, till he was dismissed." (*Ep. Var.* viii. 339.) *Was his Lordship a Catholic and afterwards conformed ?*

AYRAY, JAMES, O.S.F.—He was Chaplain and Preacher in ordinary to his Excellency the Spanish Ambassador. He published a sermon, preached before the Queen Dowager in her Chapel at Somerset House, April 10, 1687.

BADDELEY, THOMAS.—See *Cath. Miscel*, vol. ii., p. 90.

BAKER, PACIFICUS, O.S.F.—This devout Franciscan was born and educated a Protestant. When he became a Catholic he went over to the English Franciscans at Douay, and entered among them; was several times Provincial, and had the reputation of being a good preacher. He died in 1773. " He was," says Mr. Cole (vol. xliii., p. 389), a Protestant, " my particular friend, and a very worthy, honest man. He had been long ailing, being near fourscore. He lived in Wild Street, where he had a very elegant Chapel. He was author of many books of devotion, most of which he sent me. Pray God rest his soul, and be merciful to mine on the like necessary occasion. Amen."

His principal works are : (1) *Sundays kept Holy.* (2) *The Devout Christian's Companion for Holy Days.* (3) *The Christian Advent.* (4) *A Lenten Monitor.* (5) *The Devout Communicant.*

BALL, GEORGE.—A native of Lancashire. At the age of 19 he went to Rome, and was admitted into the College December 22, 1697, by Father Postgate, the Rector. He was ordained priest, March 22, 1704, and left the College April 25. He settled in Lancashire, and died there in November, 1734.

BALL, JOHN, Priest, educated at Douay. He lived many years at Brailes, the seat of   Bishop, Esq., where his laborious exertions are still talked of with admiration, gratitude, and love. Being much persecuted by Mr. Holland, of Cleobury, an attorney, and brother to Mrs. Bishop, he quitted that Mission and became Chaplain to Sir Richard Acton, of Aldenham in Shropshire, Bart., a convert, who respected him much, and on his death, which took place at Aldenham on Jan. 6, 1781, buried him with honours in his Church at Acton-Scott. His brother, Edward Ball, also from Douay, succeeded Mr. Hinde at Paynsley, Co. Stafford, 1757, whence he removed in 1759 to Wolverhampton, and remained there for several years. When S. Omers was given to the English Clergy Mr. Ball was sent thither to teach, and died there February 16, 1789. He was born August 5, 1717. He went also by the name ot Worthington, as was often the case of Priests while the penal laws hung over their heads.

BALLYMAN, THOMAS, O.S.B.—He was professed at Lambspring Abbey. When he came on the Mission he succeeded Mr. Bradshaw at Acton-burnell, the seat of Sir Edward Smyth, Bart., where he was much respected not only by Catholics, but also by his Protestant neighbours. He was most remarkable for the evenness of his temper, which nothing could disturb. In the summer of 1795 he undertook a long journey on horseback to see his friends in Devonshire. On the road he paid a visit to the Dowager Lady Shrewsbury at Laycock Abbey, near Bath, where he was taken ill and died, August 6, much regretted by all who knew him.

BAMBER, JOHN.—He was born in 1713. On his coming on the Mission he was chaplain in the Salkeld family at Whitehall in Cumberland. When that family became extinct, Mr. B. lived as an " Itinerant Priest," as many others did in those days, and assisted the Catholics at Whitehaven, Cockermouth and Keswick. In 1745 he removed to Gilesgate in Durham, and assisted also at Staindrop, Darlington and Sunderland till 1769, when he removed to Sunderland altogether, and built a house and chapel there. He was the last priest who lived at Gilesgate. He died August 24, 1780. The Douay Diary says of him : "*Semper inter primos, valde pius, et bono ingenio praeditus.*"

BANNISTER, ROBERT.—The second son of Robert Bannister, etc. (MS. letter of Rev. Henry Rutter, Mr. Bannister's nephew.) See his character by Mr. R. Southworth in *Catholic Magazine and Review*, vol. ii., 476.

BAPTHORP, MARY.—She succeeded Mrs. Catharine Dawson, who died Feb. 10, 1697, as Superioress of the English Virgins of the Society of Mary. She died March 10, 1711. Mrs. Mary Agnes Bapthorp succeeded her.
The society was founded by Mrs. Mary Ward, who was born of noble parents. (See No. 3 of Corbinian Khamm's *Relatio de Origine, etc., Instituti Mariæ*, etc.) She began the Institution, 1609, at St. Omers. No. 21. Urban VIII., about 1630, dissolved the Community on account of some scandals alleged against it. No. 45. Clement XI. by special Bull approved the rules of this Community, but did not approve the Institute, dated June 13, 1703. *Vide* No. 88. The Community is not really religious, and is immediately subject to the jurisdiction and correction of the Ordinary (Nos. 97, 8, 9) by two Briefs of Jan. 15, 1706, and March 5, 1706. Mary Ward died Jan. 30, 1645, and is buried near York. She named Mrs. Barbara Bapthorpe to succeed her as Superioress, who was confirmed in her office by a general election. She died April 23, 1654, and was succeeded by Mrs. Mary Pointz, who died Sept. 30, 1667, who in letters found after her death, named Mrs. Catharine Dawson her successor. She died Feb. 10, 1697, and was succeeded by Mrs. Mary Bapthorpe.

BARNABY, THOMAS.—Educated at Douay. For more than thirty years he lived on the Mission in Norfolk, whence he removed to Stafford, and died there in July, 1783.

BARNARD, GERARD, D.D.—Gerard Barnard, *alias* Woodbury. He received his religious instructions from Mr. Robert Berry, a Roman Priest, but ordained in the Seminary of Monte Fiascone in 1711, and died at Winchester on March 3, 1735 (O.S.) "Being found to be a very hopeful youth," he was recommended by Bishop Giffard to Dr. Ingleton, Principal of St. Gregory's, Paris, where he was received Dec. 2, 1729 ; but was placed for some years at Picpus, which at that time served as a nursery for St. Gregory's. He was ordained Priest Dec. 19, 1739, and in the following January began his Licence, and took the Doctor's Cap March 8, 1742.* In that same year he went over to Lisbon with Mr. Jones† when that College, says Mr. Challoner,‡ "must have been lost without that seasonable supply." He was appointed Professor of Divinity, and on the death of Mr. Manley, in 1755, he was chosen President of the College, and governed it for many years with great wisdom and judgment. He resigned that office a few years before his death, which happened at Lisbon, Sept. 22, 1783. He was a worthy member of the English Chapter. (See *Catholic Magazine*, vi., 256).

BARNARD, JAMES.—After having studied at the Blue Coat School in London, he went out to South America as supercargo to a ship, where he became a Catholic, and was admitted into the Bishop's Seminary. On his return to Europe he went to Lisbon, where he studied Divinity under Mr. Preston, and being ordained priest, laboured hard on the Mission in London. In 1776 he was appointed President of the Lisbon College, and remained there six years. In 1781 or 1782 he succeeded Mr. Bolton in the spiritual charge of the school at Brook Green, and also as V. G. in the London District. (*Ita* Dr. Milner.) He died in London, Sept. 12, 1803. Mr. Barnard published :
  1. *A Catechism or Collection of some points of Christian Faith and Morality in Verse.* 1786. Both plan and execution were blamed by his brethren, and two

---

* *St. Gregory's Register.*
† Incorrect, as Mr. Edward Jones, Priest, died at Lisbon, Dec. 23, 1737.
‡ Letter dated Dec. 16, 1742.

humorous pieces in verse were written on it by Rev. Messrs. Christopher
Taylor, and Willacey. 2. *A General View of the Arguments for the Divinity of
Christ and plurality of Persons in God.* 1793. 3. *The Life of Bishop Challoner.*
4. *The Divinity of our Lord Jesus Christ demonstrated from the Scriptures
in a series of letters to Dr. Priestley.* 1790. An excellent work, which Dr.
Priestley said puzzled him more than any of his antagonists. 5. *The Apostolical
Mission.* Being a discourse at the matriculation of Messrs. Billington and
Sumner at Lisbon. (*Catholic Magazine*, vi., 407).

BARNESLEY, JOHN, *alias* PERROTT.—He was a native of Gloucestershire,
and a convert from Protestantism. See *Catholic Magazine and Review* vi.,
103. In 1670 he obtained leave to resign the Presidentship of Lisbon College
and to return to England, in consequence of his growing infirmities. At
the General Assembly of the Chapter in 1672 he was chosen Archdeacon of
North Hants and Cambridgeshire, and on the decease of Dr. Ellice, *alias*
Waring, he was chosen, Sept. 18, 1676, to succeed him as Dean. "When
the troubles and severe persecution of Catholics began on September 28, 1678,
in consequence of Oates' Plot, most of the Clergy then residing in London,"
says Dr. Giffard, Bishop, "were forced some to retire into the country, and
others to secure themselves beyond sea, Dr. Perrott the actual and acting
Superior of the clergy, chose rather to hazard all dangers and suffer all
inconveniences than quit his pastoral charge, which he continued to exercise
while no Superior of any other ecclesiastical body remained in town, keeping
a constant correspondence with the Brethren." (*Lisbon Catalogue and Chapter
Records.*)

BARR, THOMAS, O.S.B.—Born at Winchester in 1740. At the age of twelve
he went over to St. Gregory's at Douay, and remained there fifteen years.
For some years he was Chaplain to Mr. Canning at Foxcote, and then settled
at Coughton, near Alcester, seat of Sir J. Throckmorton, Bart., where he lived
till his death, 23 May, 1823, much respected and beloved by his congregation
and all who knew him. On the death of Rev. T. Ainsworth, he was chosen
Provincial of Canterbury in 1814.

BARRETT, EDWARD —Educated at Douay. He lived more than forty
years at Upholland, or Crossbrook, near Wigan in Lancashire, and died in
September, 1829, about 90 years of age.

BARRETT, GEORGE.—He was born of a good family in Warwickshire.
At the age of fourteen, he was sent to Lisbon in 1652, and took the College
oath October 10, 1655. He defended his Universal Philosophy and his
Divinity under Mr. Barnesley; and being ordained priest March 7th, 1661, he
soon after came to the Mission. In 1693, he lived with Mr. Talbot at
Longford, near Newport, Salop. He was then "an ancient Missioner, and a
very worthy person, a sincere Clergyman and lover of the public. This
testimony," says Mr. Ward, secretary to the Chapter, "is due to him from me,
and from all that knew him" (*Lisbon Diary and Chapter MS.*). He was a
member of the Chapter and Archdeacon of Hereford and Salop. Another
account says "Bishop Leyburn made him Rural Dean of Salop and Cheshire,
and under the Chapter Government he was Archdeacon of half of Herefordshire and Shropshire." He died in 1699.

BARROW, JOHN.—Was born of Catholic parents at Westby in Lancashire
on the 15th of May, 1735. He went to Rome, and was admitted into the
College February 17, 1749, but left while a student in Philosophy, June 15,
1756. On his return to England was impressed at Portsmouth, and served on
board a man-of-war for 7 years. At last escaped by swimming. When
re-taken and tried by a court-martial, he only got off by speaking no other
language than Italian ; and when told by the President that he was acquitted
and might go, he had the presence of mind to appear not to understand him,
and said to his interpreter "Che dice?" He then went to the College again,
and being ordained Priest, succeeded Mr. James Parkinson, at Claughton, the

seat of Mr. Brockholes in Lancashire, who died in 1766 of a fever taken in attending the sick of his flock. He died there February 11, 1811. Dr. Gradwell, who lived some time with him, and on his death succeeded him, gave this character of Mr. Barrow : " He was a man of a vigorous mind, and though rough, and singular in temper, was a good Missioner."

BARTLETT, BASIL.—Basil Bartlett, of Castle Morton, Co. Worcester. He married Bridget, daughter of William Fitzherbert, of Norbury, Co. Derby, by whom he had Rowland, who married Ann, daughter of John Tasborough, of Rodney Hall, Norfolk, by whom he had nine sons and four daughters, Basil, Felix, Joseph, etc.

BARTLETT, EDWARD. — Son of Rowland Bartlett, of Hill End, or Hilling, Esq., Co. Worcester, and of his wife Ann, daughter of John Tasborough, of Bodney Hall, Co. Norfolk, Esq. He was born in 1702, the lustre of his family was enhanced by his virtues, and the happy use he made of his fortune. Notwithstanding that the penal laws fell heavy on Catholics, and especially on Priests in the reign of Queen Anne, he did not hesitate to run all risks in obedience to the call he inwardly felt to enter into the Church, and went over to Douay, where advancing in piety as he proceeded in his studies, he was ordained Priest in 1726. For some time he taught the Classics ; but his principal care was to qualify his pupils properly to enforce from the pulpit the great duties of religion. In 1729 he came on the Mission, where for 23 years he was indefatigable in his pastoral duties at Mawley, the seat of Sir E. Blount, Bart. In 1752 Mr. Bartlett went over to Louvain, and became assistant and then successor to Mr. Stanley, the Confessor of the English Augustines, and for 30 years continued to edify by his example, and improve by his instructions those committed to his charge. He died January 28, 1782, at the age of 80. Mr. Bartlett was remarkably charitable to the poor, munificent where the glory of religion was concerned, and had a great hatred for whatever had the appearance of avarice. He was a worthy member of the Chapter. His brother, Felix Joseph Bartlett, became a Jesuit, and lived at Blackmore Park, the seat of ——. Horneyhold, Esq. (Obituary of Louvain Nuns).

BARTON, RICHARD.—A Priest in Lancashire, condemned to death for being a Priest. The sentence, however, was not carried into execution, and he was kept in Lancaster Castle, *Religionis causa*, from 1679 to 1684, during which time he was supported from the Common Fund. He was alive in 1701, but appears to have died in that or the following year.

BASSET, JOSHUA. — Born and educated in Lynn Regis, where his brother, John Basset, was a merchant. At the age of 16, and on Oct. 13, 1657, he was admitted a sizar in Gonville and Caius College, Cambridge. In 1664 he was junior fellow of that College, and Senior in 1673. In 1686 he was appointed the Second Master of Sidney College (on the death of Dr. Mynshull) by a *Mandamus* of James II. " He was a Roman Catholic,* and not only caused Mass to be said publicly within the walls of his College, but procured an alteration of the Statutes for the accommodation of himself and those of his communion. Upon the revocation of King James's *Mandamus* in 1688, he left the College so suddenly as to have abandoned a great part of his private property, of which it appears that he afterwards vainly endeavoured to obtain restitution ; being informed, in answer to an application which he made for the purpose to his successor, that if he did not desist he would be informed against as a Popish Priest." The Historian of Lynn (Mackerell) says this account of the injustice done to Mr. Basset "was given by the present worthy Master of Jesus College, Dr. Ashton, who remembered the time and transactions thereof." " He lived to be a very old man, and died," says Mr. Cole,† " within these few years, at London, in no very affluent circumstances as we may well imagine."

---

* *Akerman's Hist. of the Univ. of Cambridge*, vol. ii., 272. The Altar-piece of his chapel was IHS in glory, surrounded by Cherubim. It is said, in the History of Lyme, to be hanging over one of the doors in the College audit room.

† *Cole's Col.*, vol. xx., 117. MS. in the British Museum. *Additional*, 5798, etc., 5952, etc.

Mr. Basset wrote : 1. *An Essay towards a proposal for Catholic Communion.* After the Revolution the work was seized and very soon disappeared ; and the author was searched for by a warrant from a Secretary of State. Mr. Hearne, of the Bodleian, says* he was told by Dr. Grabe that Mr. Basset was the author, and that the *Observations upon it* were by Mr. Edward Stephens. 2. *A Collection of what authors say of the Church of England's Ordination.* By Mr. Basset. This work shows Mr. Basset to have been a person of extensive reading, and an able controversalist ; and to have acted in his change from a thorough conviction of mind.

BASTOR, ROBERT.—(See *Catholic Magazine* for Dec., 1832, p. 818).

BATES, JOHN, *alias* LODGE.—He was educated at Douay. I find him in 1693 living with Sir Miles Stapleton at Carlton, at which time he had been 15 or 16 years on the Mission in Yorkshire. He is described in the Chapter Records as " a sober and virtuous Priest."

BATTS, ——.—A Carthusian and Prior of his house at Newport in 1722.

BEAR, MATTHEW, D.D.—This learned divine was a native of Oxfordshire. After teaching the Classics at Douay three years, he went to the Seminary at Paris. He was ordained Priest June 7, 1721, and March 18, 1728, took the Doctor's Cap, and June 8 left the Seminary to proceed to England. After he had laboured several years on the Mission as Chaplain to the Duke of Norfolk, and given great edification, he was recommended by Bishop Stonor, the Senior V.A., to the Archbishop of Paris, Charles Gaspar de Ventemille, " as most proper to fill the important charge of head of St. Gregory's, and therein to form able men to combat the immorality and irreligion everywhere prevalent in England in consequence of the Reformation." The Archbishop confirmed the election by his letter of April 24, 1739, and Dr. Bear took possession June 28 of the same year. His infirmities, however, even then were considerable, and scarcely enabled him to attend to the office of Superior, while Mr. Hinde acted as Procurator. When Dr. Thornbury, President of Douay and Provisor of St. Gregory's, settled the accounts of the Seminary, he found that the purchase and building of a new house had exceeded the receipts by £2,810 16s. 3d. Finding himself indisposed, Dr. Bear retired to Douay in 1743, and died there Sept. 2 (N.S.), leaving the Seminary his residuary legatee. Edward, Duke of Norfolk, had a great opinion of him, and presented him with £500 when he was appointed Superior of St. Gregory's. "Dr. Bear," says Bishop Stonor, " was well versed in every department of ecclesiastical science, and was truly orthodox in faith and submissive to the decisions of the Church, both of latter and of former times, and was endowed with great prudence." He was a member of the English Chapter, and a man, adds Dr. Robt. Witham, " of learning, piety, and regular discipline." (*Register of St. Gregory's Seminary.*)

BEAUMONT, EDWARD.—Edward, son of John Beaumont, of Barrow, in the county of Derby, Esq., who having joined the Chevalier in 1715, was taken prisoner and confined for some time ; but was at length allowed to return to his seat at Barrow-upon-Trent. Edward Beaumont, the third son, was born Nov. 18 (O.S.), 1732, and after a few years passed in the Free School of Repton, in Derbyshire, was sent in June, 1745, to Douay, together with his two elder brothers, John and Robert. At this time Dr. Thornbury was President, Mr. Fr. Petre Vice-President and Procurator, and Mr. Alban Butler and Dr. Walton Professors of Divinity. In 1749 Mr. Edward came over to England at the earnest request of his mother, Joyce, daughter of John Johnson, Esq., who lived to be about 96, who was a Protestant, but a woman of most estimable character in every other respect. He returned to College the following year to continue his course of studies, and being ordained, came on the Mission in June, 1758. He arrived at Norwich Aug. 1 as Chaplain to Edward, Duke of Norfolk, living in a part of an ancient palace of

* This MS. Journal in the Bodleian, and also at the beginning of the *Essay* itself in the Bodleian, Q., 19. Th. Aug. 3, 1705.

the Dukes of Norfolk.* This appointment he probably owed to Mr. A. Butler his former director, who then lived with the Duke; and on his arrival in England wrote him two kind letters with directions how to regulate his conduct at Norwich, and in answer to some difficulties he had proposed to him. The Duke left him a legacy of £150, and his successor, in 1764, built him a new house with a handsome chapel. When the late Duke of Norfolk had conformed and come to the title, he deprived Mr. Beaumont of his house and chapel, and withdrew all support from him, so that other premises were bought and a new chapel was built. The Beaumonts of Barrow were an ancient and at one time a wealthy Catholic family. Robert, the grandfather of the Priest, married Cecilia, daughter and co-heiress of Sir Thomas Beaumont, of Grace Dieu, Co. Leicester. On the death of Sir Thomas without male issue, his estates devolved to his four daughters, and the site of the Cistercian Priory of Grace Dieu, "beautifully situated in what was formerly one of the most recluse spots in the centre of Charnwood Forest," fell to the lot of Mr. Beaumont, who soon after sold it to Sir Ambrose Phillipps. Jane, another daughter of Sir Thomas, married Charles Byerley, of Belgrave, near Leicester, whose estates also came to the Beaumonts of B[arrow] on the death of his grandson, John Beaumont Byerley, without issue. Robert died Jan. 2, 1726 (O.S.) His father, John Beaumont, was a captain in the great Rebellion under Sir Thomas Beaumont, and was afterwards made Lieutenant-Colonel. Francis was father to John, and son of Edward, a younger brother of Sir John Beaumont, Knight, and Master of the Rolls in the reign of Edward VI., and first of the family that came to reside at Barrow. Sir John Beaumont was father of Francis, Judge of the Common Pleas, whose eldest son was Sir John Beaumont, author of the poem called *Flodden Field*, created a Baronet by Charles I. The title terminated in Sir Thomas Beaumont, who had only daughters. Another son of the judge was Francis, the poet, who wrote plays conjointly with Fletcher.

BEDE, [? of St. Simon Stock, *i.e.*, Walter Joseph Travers], Provincial of the Discalced Carms., signed Usury Q[uestions]. (MS. *Records of William and Mary*, p. 171.)

BEDINGFIELD, SIR HENRY.—Sir Henry was the eldest son of Sir Henry, the first Baronet, by his wife, Margaret Paston, daughter and heir of Edward Paston, of Horton, Co. Gloucester. At the Restoration he came over with the Duke of Gloucester, whose chief favourite he was, and was soon after knighted; and on the death of his father, in 1685, he succeeded to his title and estates. "So great was his hospitality and splendid house-keeping," says *Betham* ii., 202, "that no gentleman of his rank and fortune exceeded him, and had not his religion prevented his coming into the public stations of his country, no man would have been more popular." Having no issue by his first wife, Anne, only daughter and heiress of Charles Viscount Andover, afterwards Earl of Berkshire; after her death he married Elizabeth, youngest daughter of Sir John Arundell, of Lanherne, Cornwall, Bart., by whom he had three daughters: Elizabeth, who died young at Brussels, of the small pox; Margaret, wife of Sir John Jerningham, of Cossey, and Frances, wife of Sir Francis Anderton, of Lostock; and one son, Sir Henry Arundell, who succeeded him. Sir Henry died of the gout at his seat, Oxborough Hall, Sept. 14, 1704, aged 68, and was buried at Oxborough between his two wives, at the foot of a noble monument erected by the said Sir Henry in his life-time. Sir Henry was a person of great worth and honour, and particularly eminent for his hospitality." (*Epitaph in Oxborough Church.*) Two of his sisters, Margaret and Anne, became Carmelite Nuns, at Lierre. The former was chosen Superioress of the house.

BEDINGFIELD, SIR HENRY ARUNDELL.—Sir Henry Arundell, third Baronet, was the only son of Sir Henry, the second Baronet, and his second

---

* See "A Memoir of Mr. Beaumont" in the *Catholic Magazine and Review*, for Sept., 1832, vol. ii., 566.

wife, Elizabeth Arundell, of Lanherne. He married, Aug., 1719, Elizabeth Boyle, eldest daughter of Charles, Earl of Burlington, who died Nov. 25, 1751, and by her had six sons, of whom four died young. Richard succeeded him, and Edward, born in 1730, married in A.D. 1754 Mary, daughter of Sir John Swinburne, Bart., and had by her ten children. Mary, the second, became a nun at Ghent, and was Lady Abbess when the Community came over to England and settled at Preston. Anne, the third daughter, married Thomas Waterton, of Walton, Co. York. Sir Henry died July 15, 1760. His daughter, Elizabeth, married Charles Biddulph, of Burton, Co. Sussex.

BEDINGFIELD, SIR RICHARD.—Sir Richard, fourth Baronet, was the son of Sir Henry Arundell Bedingfield, third Baronet, by his wife, Elizabeth Boyle, was born Sept. 14, 1726. He married March 30, 1761, Mary, only daughter of Anthony Browne, Viscount Montague of Cowdray, who died in child-bed Sept. 23, 1767, at Bath, when Sir Richard, inconsolable for her loss, retired from the world with his infant son to Oxborough, and died March 27, 1795. He was succeeded by his son, Sir Richard, who married June 16, 1795, Charlotte Georgina, daughter of Sir William Jernyngham, Bart.

BEDINGFIELD, CHARLES BONAVENTURE, O.S.F., was of the Protestant branch of the Bedingfields; but becoming a Catholic, he entered among the English Franciscans at Douay. He was an intimate friend of Mr. Cole, and lived for many years in his parish of Bletchley, Co. Bucks, as chaplain to Mrs. Mary Monkton, widow of Mr. Monkton, of Briggs. Being a religious man, says Mr. Cole, he forfeited his estate, which went to a Mr. Bedingfield of Suffolk, and of St. John's College, Cambridge. After the death of Mrs. Monkton, he went to live at Worlaby, in Lincolnshire, an estate of Sir John Webb; but died at Douay, June 5, 1782 aged 84, religion 57 years. "He was," says Mr. Cole, "a middle-sized, lively man, of great abstemiousness and moderation; of no great parts or literature, but what far exceeds them, of great integrity and honesty.*

BEESTON, PETER AND GEORGE.—The two brothers Beeston were born at Irnham and sent to Douay, where they finished their course of Divinity, and being ordained, Peter, the elder, came on the Mission, and was many years assistant to Mr. Richard Kendall in his school at Standon, Herts. In 1765 he went to Sedgley Park to assist Mr. Hugo Kendall, but on the death of Mr. Sutton succeeded him at Wolverhampton, where he died Nov. 26, 1767. He was a Canon of the Chapter.

His brother, George Beeston, soon after his ordination was sent to teach at St. Omers, and most gladly would have remained there, as he dreaded the responsibility attached to the pastoral charge. But when called over to the Mission by Bishop Hornyhold, he readily obeyed, and was placed in the family of the Hon. Thomas Clifford, of Tixall, Co. Stafford. Here he spent 37 years of his life, greatly loved and respected by all who knew him, and here he died, deeply regretted by his congregation and numerous friends, Aug. 15, 1797. Mr. Beeston was a gentleman of great simplicity of heart and manners, "a true Israelite," as Sir Thomas Clifford said on his tombstone, "in whom there was no guile."

BEESTON, ROBERT.—Robert Beeston. He was born at Bulby, in the parish of Irnham, Co. Lincoln, Nov. 28 (O.S.), 1743. In June, 1755, he was sent to the College at Douay, where he was ordained Priest, and came on the Mission in May, 1769. For some years he lived with Bishop Hornyhold, at Longbirch, but left Feb. 14, 1775, to be Chaplain to Roland Eyre, Esq., at Eastwell, Co. Leicester, where he resided till his death, on Oct. 24, 1832, having nearly completed his 89th year. "He had the art of pleasing the nobility and gentry of his neighbourhood, was V.G. to the Bishop of the Midland District, and a Canon of the Chapter [in London]. What a pity, he

* Mr. Cole's MS. in the British Museum. "Usher's *Free Examination* cannot, in my (Cole's) opinion, be answered in any other way than the usual one, abuse and calling the writer a Papist." V. xxiii., p. 53.

says of himself, with such advantages he was not a more worthy missionary! But he left by will a piece of land as an addition to the income of his successor, in hopes that he may make some reparation for his deficiencies." Notwithstanding this humble opinion he entertained of himself, Mr. Beeston was a very respectable and a much respected Missionary. (See *Catholic Magazine* for Dec., 1832, p. 818.)

BELLASYSE, CHARLES, D.D., Earl of Fauconberg. He was the second son of Anthony Bellasyse, Esq., and Susanna, daughter of ——— Clarvet, Esq. His father was a merchant at Leghorn, where he resided many years, and where most of his children, if not all, were born. Charles was sent to Douay College in July, 1762, and at the end of Philosophy went to Paris in Aug., 1768. He took the oath in Oct., 1771, and the Doctor's Cap in 1778, and soon after came on the Mission. He resided generally in London, where he was much respected by his brethren, and esteemed as a preacher. On the death of his elder brother, Rowland, Lord Fauconberg, he succeeded to the title, retired to Lancaster, and remained there till his death, which took place June 21, 1815.

BENYON, THOMAS.—Son of William Benyon by his wife, Mary Bradshaw. Born in Lancashire, Oct. 11, 1715. Was confirmed by Bishop Witham, and in 1732 was received into the College at Rome under the Rectorship of Father Percy Plowden. Being ordained Priest in March, 1739, he left the College in the following June, and became Confessor to the Poor Clares at Gravelines, where he died Aug. 2, 1756.

BERINGTON, CHARLES, D.D., BISHOP.—He was Vicar-Apostolic of the Midland District, and Bishop of Hiero-Cæsarea. His father, Thomas Berington, of Moat Hall, Salop, married Anne, daughter of ——— Bates, of Stock, Essex, Esq., and by her had four sons and a daughter : William, Thomas, Charles, and Philip. His daughter, Placida Berington, became a nun at Louvain. Charles, the third son, went over to Douay in Aug., 1761, and thence to St. Gregory's, at Paris, on Oct. 18, 1765. He took the Seminary oath Dec. 29, 1767 ; entered his Licence in Jan., 1774, defended his Sorbonic and Minor (*sic*) the same year, and in 1775 was ordained Priest, and took the Doctor's cap. Soon after he came on the Mission—in 1776—he was placed at Ingatestone, and remained there until he was chosen tutor to young Mr. Giffard, of Chillington, with whom he travelled for about two years through France, Italy, and Germany. On his return to England he was chosen coadjutor to Bp. Thomas Talbot, and was consecrated Bishop of Hiero-Cæsarea, at Longbirch, Aug. 1, 1786. When a Committee was chosen in 17 . . to watch over the concerns of the Catholics, and to procure the repeal of the Penal Laws, Bishop Berington, with Bishop James Talbot, and Rev. Joseph Wilks, formed the ecclesiastical portion of this Committee. (The proceedings of this Committee are detailed at large in my MS. *Collectanea Anglo-Catholica*, vols. ii. and iii., together with the interesting correspondence between Bishop Berington and Propaganda, etc.)

On the death of Bishop Talbot, in 1795, Bishop Berington succeeded to the charge of the Midland district, but did not long survive him. In his Confirmation progress through Norfolk his horse came down and his collar-bone was found to be broken ; but not till some time after the accident. He then went to Ingatestone, where his brother Thomas had succeeded him, and was long seriously ill. Indeed, he never recovered from the shock ; his constitution, otherwise very robust, suffered from that accident. Not long after, he had the misfortune to sleep, as he said, in a damp bed in Worcestershire, where he was giving Confirmation, which was followed by another severe illness ; and on Friday, June 8, 1798, he died, almost suddenly, at Longbirch, near Wolverhampton, of a fit of apoplexy. On the preceding day, the Feast of Corpus Christi, he had said Mass, as usual, and assisted at the Mass of his chaplain on the fatal day. When his death was announced in the papers, the following character was given him by a gentleman, Mr. Joseph Berington, who had known him for more than thirty years, and had many opportunities of studying his character : " He was a Prelate whose amiable virtues gave an impressive charm to the truths of Religion, a scholar of great classical taste ; a man whose judgment was profound, whose manners were peculiarly conciliating, and whose hilarity of conversation rendered him the delight of society ; " yet he, alas, even in the prime of life, lies numbered with the dead !

BERINGTON, JOHN, of Winsley, Co. Hereford.   Mr. Blount the antiquary (see Dodd) in his MS. *History of Herefordshire*, which is in the hands of Dr. Blount, of Hereford, under the Art. Winsley, anciently Windesley, says : " In Edward III.'s time a Beryton, of Stoke Lacy, married the daughter and heiress of Rowland de Windesley, and had by her this ancient seat with other lands ; but in latter times the name was changed to Berington." It appears from other accounts that the Beringtons of Stoke Lacy (who continued there for some generations after the above marriage, and after the second son of John Berington settled at Winsley), were a younger branch of the Beringtons of Moat Hall and Salop, and they were in the course of time, by the marriage with the heiress of the Sculls, or Scholles, of Corvarne, and the Gomonds, of Byford and Bishopson, divided into different branches, all of which are now extinct. At the Revolution, in 1688, John Berington, ot Winsley, was living there. He married Elizabeth Wolrych, daughter of Sir Thomas Wolrych, and Bart., of Dudmaston, Salop, and had issue : first, John Berington, born about 1674, who married Ann, daughter and heiress of Rowland Andrews, of Hereford, Esq. Secondly, Thomas, who married Elizabeth, daughter of John Russell, Esq. and Elizabeth Greenwood, and became heiress of Little Malvern (See Nash). Thirdly, Simon Berington, Priest, and author of sundry works.

John Berington, eldest son of John Berington and Anne Andrews, born about 1707, married Winifred Hornyhold, of Blackmore Park, and by her had four sons and eight daughters. He died in 1794, aged 87. First, John, the eldest son, died, S.P. Secondly, Thomas, on the death of his father and elder brother, succeeded to the estates at Winsley and in Shropshire, and married Jane Risdon, daughter of Francis Risdon, of Howfield, Essex, Esq., descended from the Risdons of Devon, and had three sons and four daughters. Thirdly, Joseph Berington, born at Winsley Jan. 10, 1743, and author of many works. He died Dec. 1, 1827, aged 84, within a few days. Fourthly, Charles Berington, who married Mary, daughter of Jay, of Wintercot, near Leominster, by whom he had many children. Fifthly, two of the daughters became nuns at Liège, and died there. (MS. account of the family by Thomas, the second son, in my hands.)

BERINGTON, JOSEPH. — Joseph* was the great nephew of Simon Berington, and son of John Berington, of Winsley and Devereux Wootten, Esq., by his wife, Winifred, daughter of John Hornyhold, of Blackmore Park, Esq., whose father, John Berington, had married Ann, daughter of Rowland Andrews, of Winsley, Co. Hereford, Esq. Joseph was born at Winsley, Jan. 16, 1743. Having learnt his first rudiments at home, he was placed for a twelvemonth with his relation, Bishop Hornyhold, at Longbirch, and when eleven years old was sent to the preparatory school at Equerchin, and thence to the College at Douay, where he was admitted Aug. 2, 1755. Here he edified all by his good conduct and the regular discharge of his spiritual duties ; and went through his studies with great eclat in a class where there were many eminent scholars. Having completed his third year of divinity, he began to teach : first, the classics, and in 1769 Philosophy, and at the same time he attended the University School, and in the following year was made Licentiate ot Divinity of the University of Douay. In 1772, having completed the course of Philosophy he came on the Mission. In 1775 Bishop Hornyhold placed him at Wolverhampton ; but at the close of 1776 he resigned this charge to live with his friend, Mr. Stapleton, of Carlton, Co. York, with whose son he afterwards

---

* Memoir of the Rev. Joseph Berington, *Cath. Miscel.* ix., 221, 297, 369.

travelled and visited the principal parts of France, etc. On his return to England Bishop T——gave him, in 1785, the charge of the Oscott Congregation, and here it was that he wrote the greater part of his works, and only quitted it in 1793 to go to Buckland, Berkshire, the seat of his friend, Sir John Throckmorton. And here it was, says the Rev. Mr. Rawbone, Vicar of Buckland, that "for the long period of thirty-four years this truly venerable man discharged his sacred functions in so even and upright a manner as to merit and secure the affections of those over whom he was in charge, and at the same time to avoid giving offence to his Protestant brethren ; to all he was equally kind, benevolent, and bountiful. Sincere, just, pious, and true, he walked through his pilgrimage on earth respected and beloved, and it may be doubted whether his loss is most regretted by those under his own charge, or by the Protestants of Buckland and its neighbourhood." Providence had blessed him with a constitution naturally strong, and by great regularity and abstemiousness he so preserved it that he never experienced any illness, till that which put an end to his life in 1827. On the evening of Nov. 27, when he had probably heard of the death of his friend, Dr. Poynter, on the 26th, a paralytic affection deprived him of the use of his limbs. As the thought of death seemed habitually present in his mind, as his letters and conversation testified, he was fully aware of his approaching dissolution, and lost no time in preparing himself for it ; and while perfectly sensible, as he continued to be till the last moment, he received all the rites of the Church. His last moments were marked with the same calmness of mind that he had always possessed in health : he said he had lived long and happily, was quite resigned to the will of God, and begged the prayers of those who attended him. He breathed his last about 5 o'clock on Friday morning, Dec. 1, "dying," says Mr. Rawbone, "as he had lived—serene, resigned, in the full possession of his mental powers, a true Christian in death as in life, and anyone who had witnessed his passage from this world could not have failed mentally to exclaim, *let me die the death of the righteous, and let my last end be like his.*"

Mr. Berington was an amiable man in society, an accomplished gentleman, a distinguished scholar, and which is of infinitely more importance, an excellent Christian and worthy clergyman, who daily exemplified in his own person those great lessons which, in a manner peculiarly his own, he every Sunday until the period of his death, preached, and forcibly pressed on his hearers, from the altar. Besides his own, the Latin, Greek, Italian, Spanish and German languages were familiar to him, and while at College he acquired a tolerable knowledge also of the Hebrew. *The Following of Christ* was his favourite spiritual book ; it always kept company with his breviary, and he seldom failed to read a chapter or two every day.

Mr. Berington was buried in the chancel of the church at Buckland, by the particular desire of his friend, Sir C. Throckmorton, who raised a mural monument to his memory, with the following characteristic epitaph on it, written by Dr. Bew, who, during an intimate acquaintance of more than forty years, was well able to appreciate his merits.

"In discharging the duties of his ministry he was assiduous, kind and charitable, at the altar devout and dignified, in the pulpit perspicuous and eloquent. His writings, religious and historical, are marked by extent of research, depth of thought, energy of expression, perspicuity and elegance of style. Sincerely attached to his faith, his undeviating virtue was the expression of his conviction ; his whole life a récommendation of his creed. He did not judge or despise his brother, but willingly formed intimate connections with many of the good and worthy of other communions. He was conciliating in his manners, moderate in supporting his own sentiments, candid in estimating the arguments of others, partial to amicable discussion, but adverse to intemperate contests. His object was truth, not victory. He was warm and steady in his friendship, calm and unmoved under unmerited obloquy. No resentment blinded him to the talents of his adversaries, no wrongs indisposed him to reconciliation. Full of days and good works, he departed this life Dec. 1, 1827, aged 85. R.I.P."

Mr. Berington's works are :—

1. *Theses ex Logica et Psychologia*. Duaci, 1771. 2. *Letters on Materialism and Hartley's Theory of the Human Mind*. Addressed to Dr. Priestley, 1776. 3. *Immaterialism Delineated, or a View of the First Principles of Things*. 1779. 4. *A Letter to Dr. Fordyce in answer to his Sermon*. 1779. 5. *The State and Behaviour of Catholics from the Reformation to the year* 1780. 6. *Reflections addressed to the Reverend John Hawkins*. 1785. 7. *The History of the Lives of Abeilhard and Heloisa from* 1079 *to* 1163. 4to. 1787. It is a general history of that period, and a particular history of those celebrated characters. 8. *The History of the reign of Henry II., and of Richard and John his sons, with the events of the period from* 1154 *to* 1216. Quarto. 1799. 9. *An Address to the Protestant Dissenters*. 1787. 10. *An Essay on the Depravity of the Nation, with a view to the Promotion of Sunday Schools*. 1789. 11. *The Rights of Dissenters from the Established Church, in relation principally to English Catholics*. 1789. 12. *The Memoirs of Gregorio Panzani*. Giving an account of his agency in England in the years 1634-5-6. These Mr. Berington published from Dodd's MS. copy, now in Oscott library. The original *Relazione* made by Panzani to Urban VIII. is in the Archives of Propaganda. Bishop Witham translated it into English while at Rome, and entitled it: "The reasons for which Urban VIII. sent Panzani to the Queen of England, and his negociation there." This MS. is at Ushaw. See the *Relazione* in Italian in *Miscel. III.*, p. 189, and in my MSS. *Records of William and Mary*, p. 489, also notes in my *Panzani's Memoirs*. 13. *An Examination of Events termed Miraculous*. As reported in letters from Italy. 1796. 14. *A Letter to the Right Rev. John Douglass, V.A., of the London District*. 1797. 15. *Gother's Prayers for Sundays and Festivals;* adapted to the use of private families or congregations. Published in 1800 by Rev. J. K. with a preface and appendix. 16. *The Faith of Catholics*; (or certain points of controversy, confirmed by scripture and attested by the Fathers of the five first centuries of the Church). 1812. Rev. J. K. revised and verified all the passages in the work; and in 1830 gave a second edition with additions. 17. *A Literary History of the Middle Ages*. Comprehending an account of the state of learning, from the close of the reign of Augustus to its revival in the fifteenth century. Quarto, 1814. 18. *The History of the Rise, the Progress and the Decline of the Papal Power*. MS. in 4 thick vols. 4to. "Though compiled," he says, "with the utmost care from authentic monuments, it is not my intention that it should ever see the light. In it are many reflections, some perhaps hazarded, that would alarm timid minds, and give offence to the well meaning, though by the more discerning and the learned, the work, I flatter myself, would be perused with pleasure and profit. It has been seen by few. Into whosoever hands it may fall after my death, my solemn instruction is, that it be not published. I write this," he adds, "after mature thought, on the 2nd of October, 1819. — Joseph Berington." The MS. at present is in my possession, but will be deposited in the Library of Oscott College. 19. *A Prayer-Book for the use of the London District*. Mr. Berington lamented a want of uniformity in our prayer-books, and proposed a plan to Dr. Poynter, "who approved of it, and threw the whole execution on him." The MS. was afterwards made over to Dr. Fletcher, who made great use of it in his *Catholic's Prayer-Book*. 20. *Metaphysica primum tradita Parisiis, dein Duaci*, a D. Jos. Berington, S.T. Licentiato. M.S. in the Chapter archives. 21. *An Exposition of the Doctrine of the Catholic Church*. MS. of 92 pages folio. Written before the passing of the Bill of 1792. In my hands. 22. *A Letter on the use of the Latin tongue in the service of the Church*. MS. He proposes that that part of the service which is read aloud should be read in English, when approved of by that tribunal where alone rests the power of enforcing or relaxing the general discipline of the Catholic Church. 23. *The case of Father Garnet further considered*. Occasioned by the defence of him by Philalethes in *Gent. Mag.*, vol. I., p. 633. 24. *Observations on Dr. Milner's unpublished Pastoral charge of March* 30, 1813. In two letters to the Editor of the *Orthodox Journal*, but refused

admission. M.S. 25. *Queries proposed to the learned members of the University,* who lately presented an Address to His Majesty, dated May 4, 1807. MS. 26. *A Letter to Rev. G. Bruning on his "Remarks on Mr. B.'s Examination of Events termed Miraculous."* M.S. 27. *A Letter to Rev. Turbervill Needham, Director of the Imperial Academy at Brussels,* in answer to two from him on his *Theses ex Logica et Psychologia.* 1772. MS. 28. *An hypothesis calculated to illustrate the mystery of the Trinity.* MS. 10 pp. 29. *Observations on the Apostolic Nicene and Constantinopolitan Creeds, and on those of St. Athanasius and Pius IV.* With an Analysis of Dr. Holden's *Analysis Fidei,* "I know not," he says in the last page, "why I did not proceed with this Analysis, which might have been useful. But it was suspended, and I never resumed it."—November 1, 1823. 30. *Extracts from the " Observations sur l'ouvrage de M. De Calonne."* Par M. Boissy D'Anglas, Deputé à l'Assemblée Nationale. MS. 31. *Letters to Mrs. Hannah More on her work, Cœlebs.* MS. 32. *A letter to Dr. Barrington, Bishop of D. on his " Charge."* MS. 33. *A Letter to a Protestant gentleman on the Doctrine of the Real Presence.* MS. 34. *Reasons for altering our Church Government.* MS. 35. *Introduction to " A Discourse proposing considerations why and how the oath of supremacy, lawfully and without scandal to any be taken.* By A. B.,* i.e.,* John Serjeant. Mr. B. conjectures. MS. of 5p. folio. 36. *A Letter to the Protestant Fabulist.* 1821. 37. *A Letter to the Right Rev. Bishop of Winchester.* 1821.

BERINGTON, SIMON.—Simon, the son of Mr. John Berington, Esq., of Winsley, Co. Hereford, by Elizabeth, daughter of Sir Thomas Wolryche, Bart., of Dudmaston, Co. Salop. Born Jan. 16 (O.S.), 1679. He studied at Douay, where he defended his Divinity under Mr. Mayes, July 22nd, 1704. For some years he was Professor of Poetry and Philosophy in the College, and in 1716 came on the Mission, and succeeded his cousin, Thomas Berington, at St. Thomas's, near Stafford, Dec., 1720. He was a member of the Chapter, and in 1748 was chosen Secretary to it, at which time he had the charge of the Clergy Library in Gray's Inn, and died at his Chambers there April 16, 1755. (See *Life of Alban Butler,* p. 43.) The many and various works which Mr. Berington wrote and published are the best proof of his great ability and acquirements. These are :

1. *A Dialogue between the Gallows and a Freethinker.* 1738. It was perused, he says, and approved of by Dr. Hawarden, Dr. Rider, Dr. Challoner, and several other learned friends, who advised him to print it. The MS. contained 400 pages. 2. *An Apology for the Catholicks.* 3. *An account of the Creation, grounded on the Scriptures, against the Hutchinsonians.* 4. *A letter to the Cosmopolite.* 5. *The origin of Masquerades.* 6. *A letter to a doctor of Sorbonne concerning the practice of innoculation.* 7. *The Memoirs of Signore Gaudenzio di Lucca.* A moral and excellent Romance. 8. *A Modest Enquiry how far Catholics are guilty of the horrid tenets laid to their charge.* By S. B. London, 1749. The language and style very much resemble Mr. Berington's. 9. *A Popish Pagan the Fiction of a Protestant Heathen.* Translated from the Dutch. London, 1743. Against Dr. Middleton. It appears to be Mr. Berington's. 10. *The Life of Abraham Woodhead,* prefixed to the third part of *Ancient Church Government,* and the preface. Mr. Simon Berington endeavoured to give Mr. Woodhead the honour of being the author of *The Whole Duty of Man.* "Certain it is," says Mr. Alban Butler, "that Dr. J. Fell, Dean of Christ Church, afterwards Bishop of Oxford, who published the other works of the author of *The Whole Duty of Man* in folio at Oxford in 1675-78, and wrote the preface, and was the only person then living who knew the true author of *The Whole Duty of Man,* gave this book, with other pieces of Mr. Woodhead's, to Hawkins, his bookbinder and bookseller, and ordered Mr. Woodhead's name to be added to the title of this as well as of other works which he gave to be bound. If Mr. Woodhead wrote that celebrated work, it was before he travelled abroad, or had any thoughts of embracing the Catholic Faith." The following works of Mr. Berington are in MS. in the Chapter archives :— 11. *The Quarrel between Venus and Hymen.* An heroic satyrical poem, in.

six cantos. 12. *The Astrologer, or the Predictions of Tycho Brahe, Junior.*
13. *A Disputation on Birds of Passage such as the Woodcock, Stork, Fieldfare,
Cuckoos, Swallow, etc.—whither they go. Whether to the Moon?* Letter to
Dr. Arne. 14. *Vis Motrix: or, Philosophical Essays on Continued Motion,
Mutual Attraction, and Gravitation.* By S.B., Gent. *Dies diem docet.*
15. *Free Thinking Deprecated.* By S. Berington. "Free thinking, which in
propriety of speech is no thinking at all." — *Dean Swift.* 16. *A true and
genuine account of the "Brazen-head,"* invented by Roger Bacon, which told
him : *Time is, time was,* and *time is past.* 17. *The Charms of Hampton Court,*
the seat of the Countess of Conisby in Herefordshire. *Paulo majora canemus.*
18. *Critical Remarks on a late poem entitled* : *"The quarrel between Venus and
Hymen.*" "The pulpits alone will never preach down the sins of the town."—
Motto. 19. *A letter of thanks from the Jews to the Cosmopolite, for his "Present"
to Protestants, Romanists, and Jews.* 20. *The doctrine and practices of the
Jesuits no just argument against the Church,* in three dialogues between Patro-
philus and Misopater, with some animadversions on a late pamphlet entitled :
"Much may be said on both sides." Extrema fuge. 90 pages in folio. 21. *An
historical and critical inquiry into the origin and nature of Masquerades.* 92
pages in folio. Probably the same as the work at No. 5. 22. *The great duties
of life,* in three parts. This was published in London in 1738.

(He also wrote and published a short encomiastic poem of 153 lines, addressed
"To His Most Excellent Majesty, James III., King of England, Scotland,
France, and Ireland, Defender of the Faith, etc.," and signed, "Simon
Berington, Priest and Present Professor of Poetry in the English College at
Douay." It is a quarto of four leaves, and was sent by me to Dr. Oliver to be
presented to Ushaw.—M.A.T.)

BERINGTON, THOMAS.—Thomas Berington, son of Thomas Berington, of
Moat Hall, Salop, Esq., and Ann, second daughter of John Berington, of
Winsley, Co. Hereford, Esq., born in 1674. He was educated and ordained at
Douay. He resided with Bishop Witham at St. Thomas's, the seat of
—— Fowler, Esq., near Stafford, and was there about seven years. For
some time he was chaplain to Mrs. Howard, at Hore Cross. In 1731 he
succeeded to Dr. Fell as agent for the clergy of the Midland District, and
paid even £53 as his composition for £1,200, which he owed them! He was
a member of the Chapter, and as Senior Capitular presided at the General
Assembly held in 1748, on the death of Mr. Day. In the second session he
was chosen Dean. At this time some of the most respectable of the Clergy
were members of the Chapter, and assisted at the General Assembly. Among
them I find Francis Petre, Mr. Maire, and Dr. Walton (afterwards Bishops in
the North), Dr. Green, Dr. Charles Howard, Mr. Manley, and Mr. Betts
(actually or soon after chosen Presidents of Douay, Lisbon, Paris and Twyford),
and Thomas Berington, Simon Berington, George Bishop, Thomas Stapylton,
and Robert Pinkard, *alias* Typper, all known to the world by their works.
Mr. Berington presided also at the General Assembly held in 1755, and was
much respected and looked up to by all his brethren, as well as by the
members of the Chapter. Some idea of his character may be formed from his
address to his assembled brethren in 1748.

After stating that the troubles of 1745 had prevented their meeting at the
usual time, and that Divine Providence had happily put an end to them, and by
the death of the late Dean (Mr. Day) had necessitated them to holding a
General Assembly for the election of a new one, he says : "Since, then, it is
by the call of Providence we now meet, and enjoy an opportunity of renewing
or creating a personal acquaintance with our brethren, we may hope the
Divine spirit of peace and love will enkindle in every breast a warmth for our
common good, and brotherly love for each fellow-member of our Society.
Many of us have formerly felt the dismal effects of dissension and animosity
for some years. But, thanks be to God, the clamorous disputes and the
harsh-sounding names of denunciations, protests, and appeals (alluding to the
conduct of Dr. Fell) are happily ceased, and no longer grate our ears nor

afflict our hearts, and the Father of Mercies and God of all comfort in the room of these has granted us perfect peace and tranquillity. Our meetings for these several years have been friendly and full of comfort, like the meetings of dear friends after a long absence ; our debates have been void of heat, and quietly carried on by calm reasoning : our elections have been made without all strife and contention ; these unbecoming passions giving way to the amiable blessing of perfect concord. *O quam bonum et jucundum est habitare fratres in unum.* May it please the Almighty to continue this inestimable gift of Heaven, this desirable blessing and great comfort of our lives : which I hope it will not be in the power of Satan to deprive us of. He may envy our happiness, and perhaps may take occasion from the business of this day to sow his seeds of division and dissension amongst us ; and if we were men wholly of a worldly spirit and governed by the wicked principles of the world, he might probably tempt us with success. For the common way of the world is, where there is any society that has places of preferment or profit to be disposed of, there will probably be more members aspiring to these places than there are places for them. And then the postponed members become discontented and piqued at the persons preferred before them, and clamorous against them, and the whole body seldom escapes the chagrin of these malcontents for want of justice done to their merits ; and then nothing is heard but complaints of maladministration and illegal practices. But all this is the way of the world, and the common practice of worldly men. But, 'tis hoped, not to be found among those who have learned Christ, and who have engaged themselves to preach Christ and His gospel to the world. The Apostles, indeed, in the time of their native weakness, before the Holy Ghost had enlightened their understandings and warmed their hearts with the flame of brotherly love, were somewhat affected with the passions and wickedness of common men. There once arose a contest among them about preferment. *Erat contentio inter eos, etc.* This instance of human frailty could not long escape the notice of their Divine Master. After a mild rebuke, He gives them to understand that this was the way of the world, directly contrary to the way He had cut out for them. Whoever appears to have any preference among you, let him do the office of waiter and servant to the rest, as I have done to you. Thus He goes before them Himself and leads them into the blessed path He had pointed out to them ; and this is no other than the blessed path of humility, meekness and brotherly love—a blessed path which directly leads to the eternal peace, love, and concord of the blessed in Heaven. The better to enforce this His heavenly doctrine, He places an infant in the midst of them, and assures them that unless they become humble as the infant before them they should not enter the Kingdom of Heaven."

Mr. Berington died in London, Dec. 20, 1755, aged 82 or 83. He published : *The Monthly Packet, or Mercury's Intelligence from the other world.*

BERINGTON, THOMAS, of Moat Hall, Co. Salop, was son of William Berington and Magdalen, daughter of John Lutley, of Bromcraft Castle, Esq. He married Anne, daughter of John Berington, of Winsley, and died in Oct., 1719, aged 79. He was buried at Pontesbury, Oct. 28.

BERINGTON, THOMAS.—Son of William Berington, and Mary Berington (More), he married Miss Bates, of Stock, Co. Essex, and on that occasion left Moat Hall, to live at Stock. By her he had three sons and one daughter. First, Thomas, a Priest, who died at Ingatestone Oct. 24, 1805. Secondly, Charles, D.D. and V.A. of the Midland District, who died at Longbirch, June 8, 1798. Thirdly, Philip, who died at Stock. Fourthly, Placida, who became a nun at Louvain, and died at Spettisbury. By the death of those without issue, the branch of Moat Hall became extinct, and the property was bequeathed by Mr. Philip to the remaining Beringtons, of Shropshire, Herefordshire and Staffordshire, the Winsley family.

BERINGTON, WILLIAM.—Son of John and Anne Berington. He married Mary, daughter of —— More, Esq. He died in 1740, aged 74, and was buried at St. Alkmunds', Salop.

BERKELEY, ROBERT.—Robert, son of Thomas Berkeley and Mary Davis, daughter of ——. Davis, Co. Monmouth. On the death of his cousin Thomas, the only son of John Berkeley, without issue, he came to the estate of Spetchley. He was great grandson of Thomas, who died in 1693. Robert married first, Anne, co-heir of Weyburn of Flixton; secondly, Catharine, daugher of Thomas Fitzherbert of Swinnerton; and thirdly, Elizabeth, daughter of Thomas Parry, Esq., of Twysog, Co. Denbighshire. Mr. Berkeley died without issue, at Spetchley, December 19, 1804, aged 91. Mr. Berkeley was much looked up to by the body of Catholics, and was perhaps the first of them that called the attention of the public to the absurdity and cruelty of the Penal Laws. He wrote: 1. *Considerations of the Oath of Supremacy.* 2. *Considerations on the Declaration against Transubstantiation;* in a letter to a friend, London, 1778. Pp. 29.

BERKELEY, THOMAS.—Of Spetchley, Esq., was the only son of Sir Robert, one of the judges of the King's Bench in the reign of Charles I. In 16— he became Catholic, to the great grief of his Father, at Brussels, and died in December, 1693, aged 63. He married Anne, daughter of William Darrell, Esq., of Scotney, in Kent, who died on September 18, 1692. She was descended from a niece of Chichley, founder of All Souls, Oxford. His grandson, Robert, founded the Hospital at Worcester.—See Nash's *Worcester* also for the Pedigrees of the Catholic families of Blount, Russells, Hornyholds, Harfords and Actons.

BERNARD, WILLIAM.—Educated and ordained at Douay. In 1692 "he had the care of the school at Silkstead, near Winchester, which he governed with great applause and public benefit." "Mr. Brown, from Douay, a Priest of very good parts, was coadjutor."* Probably this is the same school, afterwards called Twyford. Mr. Bernard died Dec. 29, 1725.

BERNARDINE, ——, O.S.F., was confessor to the nuns at Aire. He published *Three Sermons* preached at the clothing and professing of some of the Community.

BERRY, MATTHEW.—Matthew Berry. Ordained priest at Douay and came on the Mission about 1683. "He was a very active Missionary, and had a good capacity."† He resided with the eldest son of Mr. Meynell of Dalton, and assisted the Catholics in Cleveland. He died in March, 1723.

BERTIE, LORD WILLOUGHBY.—Willoughby Bertie, third Earl of Abingdon, son of James Bertie, of Stanwell (second son of James, first Earl of Abingdon), and Eleonora, daughter and heiress of Sir Henry Lee of Ditchley, by Elizabeth, daughter and co-heiress of George Willoughby, seventh Lord Willoughby of Parham. He was born November 29, 1692, and married at Florence in 1727, Anna Maria, daughter of Sir John Collins, and by her, who died December 21, 1763, he had three sons and seven daughters. 1. Lady Elizabeth, married Mr Gallini. 2. Lady Jane (married) Thomas Clifton of Lytham in 1760. 3. Bridget. 4. Anne. 5. Eleonora, wife of Lord Wenman. 6. Mary, wife of Miles Stapleton. 7. Sophia. Willoughby, third Earl, died June 10, 1760, and was succeeded by his son, Willoughby, fourth Earl. Lady Willoughby, if not her husband, must have been a Catholic, as all her daughters were, and at least three of them married Catholics. I have heard that her husband conformed.

BETTS, JOHN PHILIP.—John Philip Betts was educated at Douay. In 1732 or 3 he succeeded Mr. Fleetwood in the charge of Twyford School, near Winchester, where most of our Catholic gentry and nobility, who did not go to any of our foreign Colleges, received their early education. Among them I find the late Lord Fingall, the two Bishop Talbots (Dr. Milner says), Mr. Blount of Maple Durham and others. Alexander Pope was also an inmate of Twyford, and some of his verses may still be seen on the windows. Mr.

---

* *Chapter Records.*   † *Ibid.*

Gildon, from Lisbon, was his assistant, but died July 26, 1736. The alarms of 1745 are thought to have caused Mr. Betts to close his establishment, which seems to have been declining from the time of Mr. Fleetwood's quitting it ; who soon after, my memoirs say, became a Jesuit (after living some time at Paynsley, Lord Langdale's seat in Staffordshire) and died at Liège on February 14, 1737. It was then, Bishop Stonor says, difficult to supply Mr. Fleetwood's place, and Mr. Betts was obliged to apply to the Dean and Chapter, who advanced him £200, for which he gave a bill of sale of all his household goods and chattels, dated February 15, 1734, to Mr. John Shepherd, Treasurer of the Chapter. The house, too, was mortgaged to Mr. Holman of Warkworth, who had property near Winchester. On his quitting Twyford, Mr. Betts retired to Gray's Inn, London, where he had the care of the Clergy Library. In 1758 Mr. Betts "found in an old neglected box the original instrument constituting the Chapter, and produced it at the Consult held May 11. So that it appears," says Dr. (Bishop) Walton, " there are two originals, one at Rome, found there by Mr. Holt, who sent a copy of it to England."* Mr. Betts died at Gray's Inn, March 28, 1770. He was a member of the Chapter and had the title of Archdeacon of London and Middlesex, and was in high estimation among the clergy and laity. He translated a devotional work of Fr. Morell, O.S.B. I know not the title. It is said that Twyford School, 2½ miles from Winchester, was begun in the time of James II. In 1692, a Mr. William Bernard (as above) had the care of a school at Silkstead near Winchester. Is this the same as Twyford ? Mr. William Sheldon, of Gray's Inn, told me Mr. Betts "was a quaint, queer old chap, and that he sometimes plagued him with questions."

BEW, JOHN, D.D.—John Bew, D.D., was born in London, and was sent young to Sedgley Park School. In June, 1769, he went to Douay, and after a year's Philosophy went to St. Gregory's in Paris,* and took the Seminary oath in 1786. When Dr. Howard became wholly unfit to conduct the affairs of the Seminary, and retired in 1782, Mr. Bew acted as Procurator, and on the departure of Dr. John Rigby in 1784, he was the only student left in the house. The joint opinion of Bishop Talbot, the Archbishop of Paris, and of Mr. Gibson, President of Douay and Provisor of the Seminary at that time, was that the most expeditious method of retrieving the disordered affairs of the house was to interrupt the usual course of studies for a time, and commit the management of the vacancies to Mr. Bew, and to receive ecclesiastics as boarders. "But though wise in his choice, nor received any without good recommendations, he found these to be mere ceremonies, and that persons whom he received, so far from answering his intentions, gave him much trouble, and their conduct was so improper, that after fifteen months he dismissed them all and lived quite alone for some time." In 1786 Dr. Bew was formally appointed Superior by the Archbishop. In August, 1786, President Gibson went over to Paris, as Provisor of the Seminary, and found the debts of the House were nearly extinguished, when Dr. B. was enabled again to receive students, and resume again the usual system of studies. But the Revolution dissipated all his hopes and flattering expectations. On his arrival in England he went to live with John Giffard, Esq., at Narquis in Flintshire, till Bishop T. Talbot determined in 1794 to open a seminary at Oscott, when he was appointed the first President. He drew up the plan of studies, which was read at the General Meeting of the Clergy of the M.D. and approved by them. In 18— he resigned the Presidentship and accepted of the Mission of Brighton. On the death of Bishop Douglas, he succeeded Bishop Poynter as President of St. Edmund's College, but shortly after ill health obliged him to relinquish the situation, and to retire to Havant, where he died October 25, 1829. Dr. Bew's abilities were very considerable. Bishop Berington made him his V.G.; and he was much esteemed and looked up to by his brethren who had the happiness of his acquaintance.

---

* Chapter Register.   † Register of St. Gregory's Seminary.

BIDDULPH, JOHN, of Burton, Esq., died in London in 1835. His charities were great.

BIDDULPH, RICHARD, of Biddulph Hall, Co. Staffordshire, Esq. His daughter, Elizabeth, was second wife of Charles, fifth Lord Dormer.

BILLINGE, CHARLES, S.J. — He lived several years in the family of Mr. Whitgreave, at Moseley, till love and music led him astray and caused him to conform first, and then to marry. He preached his recantation sermon in Lichfield, but does not seem to have been much respected in the Church, as he never got any preferment in the Church, except that he officiated occasionally as a curate in the parish of Wan——. He had a numerous family, was always wretchedly poor, and is said to have made a miserable death. A collection was made in Wolverhampton, where he lived, to carry him to the grave.

"My townsman, Billinge," says Dr. Milner, "finding himself summoned away, sunk into despair, starting continually, and exclaiming: 'I am a lost man! I dream of nothing but hell-fire!'"—*Appendix to an address to the Bishop of St. David's.*

BILLINGE, THOMAS, "a worthy brother labourer," says Mr. Thos. Berington, "who, having served many years on the Mission, went to end his days at Rome, and died there on Jan. 9, 1740."

BING, EDWARD, O.P.—In his younger days he held a commission under Cromwell, and after the Restoration, also under Charles II. After the death of his wife he became a Catholic through the instructions of Mr. Wright, a Priest, and soon after going over to Bornheim, he received the habit of St. Dominic from Father Howard, afterwards Cardinal, Feb. 22, 1662. In 1672 he was made chaplain to the English troops, sent to Holland under the Duke of Monmouth. He was afterwards many years on the Mission, and was made "Preacher General," a title in the Order of Dominicans. He was also Provincial. He died at Bornheim Sept. 25, 1701, in the 82nd year of his age and the 38th of his profession. (*Annales Prædicatorum*, and a *MS. Obituary O.S.D.*)

BISHOP, ELIZABETH.—Elizabeth, daughter of —— Bishop of Brailes, Esq. Having formed the resolution to quit the world and consecrate herself to God in some convent, she left England in Sept., 1707, in the company of Winifred Elliot and Elizabeth Hilliard, both actuated by the same spirit, and going abroad for the same purpose. To their care were entrusted Ann Scandrele and Catharine Jeffs, not yet 16 years of age, who were in search of Catholic education abroad, which the penal laws deprived them of in their native land. The former of these two was the daughter of a clergyman of the Church of England who had lately embraced the Catholic faith. On their arrival at Ostend they were soon discovered by a Scotch gentleman named Douglass, who though honourable by name. and by his commission, yet dishonoured both by his misconduct. For being prisoner in France on his parole of honour, he broke that parole, and repaired to Ostend in order to pass over to England. In his conversation also with these young ladies he gave himself such liberties that he was deservedly expelled their company.

Piqued at their reserve and resolution no more to see him, in revenge he accused them to the Mayor of Ostend as guilty of High Treason against their country for going to France without leave, by the 3rd of William and Mary;* and so far succeeded that on Sept. 23 the ladies were placed under a guard and forbidden to quit the place. The affair was carried to the Court of Brussels, where the Pastor and Dean of Ostend, Mons. Willemans, powerfully pleaded the cause of oppressed innocence, but in vain. For Douglass repaired to the Court of England, and by such arts as the spirit of revenge inspires, obtained an order for their being sent, well-guarded, to England. What was the wish

---

* In point of Law, indeed, these ladies were guilty of High Treason, as going to France without leave was made High Treason by the 3rd of William and Mary.

or intention of the Queen or her Ministry to do with these ladies, for thus abandoning their own country in quest of another, where they might profess their religion and have a Catholic education, (for this was treason, by the 3rd of William and Mary), does not appear. But Divine Providence disposed of them otherwise. They used the liberty allowed them of frequenting the Parish Church, and in the midst of their difficulties they were never dismayed, and placing their trust in God, they prepared themselves for greater by frequenting the house of prayer, and receiving the Blessed Eucharist, which they did regularly every week, and on the very day they embarked, to the great edification of the faithful. At length, on Dec. 8, they were ordered on board in the evening, notwithstanding the violence of the tempest and of the tide. In less than an hour the vessel was wrecked on the western pier, and soon after was dashed to pieces. All assistance proved ineffectual, and of 63 only 13 were saved. Miss Bishop and her pious companions were dashed against the piles, and at last washed on shore, when it was found that both their legs and arms were broken, and their bodies miserably bruised and lacerated. On the 10th M. Willemans and a procession of thirty virgins conveyed their mortal remains to the Parish Church, in the midst of an immense concourse of the inhabitants ; they were buried, says M. W———, in one and the same grave ; but their pure souls were gone to their spouse— martyrs of His Faith, and conquerors of impiety. (See MS. *Records Miscel.*)

BISHOP, GEORGE.—George, son of —— Bishop, of Brailes, Esq., and nephew of Rev. Henry Harnage. Having finished his Logic at Douay, he went to St. Gregory's at Paris with Mr. M. Bear, in Sept., 1717, where both took the Seminary oath the following Jan., and together entered their Licence. For some time he resided at Brailes, and after that at Irnham, in 1742-4. On the death of Mr. Ch. Williams, in 1750, he succeeded him at Harvington in Worcestershire, but left it again in the beginning of 1752 and retired to Brailes. He died at Marnhull, in Dorsetshire, Aug. 16, 1768. Mr. Bishop was much respected by his brethren, was General Vicar to Bishop Stonor in Oxfordshire, etc., and as a member of the Chapter was Archdeacon of Hereford and Salop.*

His works are : 1. *Moral Philosophy :* in which a true idea is given of *Summum Bonum* and of all the virtues, theological and moral, which are to lead us to it ; as also of their opposite vices. The moral philosophy of the ancient heathens is shown to be insufficient and not of perfection enough to lead Christians to Heaven. The work consists of 26 chapters. 2. Lambert's *Manière d'instruire les pauvres de la Campagne.* Translated into English. The MS. was at Longbirch in 1800, and probably is now at Wolverhampton in Dr. Walsh's possession. The MS. of his *Moral Philosophy* was in the hands of Rev. Robert Beeston, at Eastwell, in 1815. I never heard that either work was ever published, though both have great merit. 3. *Father Mannock's Poor Man's Catechism.* Published by Mr. Bishop, with a preface, in 1752. He is thought to have prepared for publication *The Poor Man's Controversy*, of the same author.

BISHOP, HENRY, O.S.F.—Henry was the nephew to George Bishop. He went to Douay College with his brother Francis in 1738, and when he left the College entered cadet in the Irish Brigade. At the battle of Fontenoy a bullet struck against and shattered to pieces a pebble in his waistcoat pocket, which he had providentially picked up as he marched to the field of battle. The circumstance, and as he said "his miraculous preservation" caused serious reflections, the result of which was that he quitted the army and entered among the English Franciscans at Douay. His principal residence on the Mission was Baddesley Green, where he was much respected and beloved. In his old age he lived principally at Wootton [Wawen], near Henley, the seat of Peter Holford, Esq., and died June 19, 1811.

BIX, ANGEL, O.S.F.—*A Sermon on the Passion*, preached before the Queen Dowager at Somerset House, April 13, 1688.

---

* *St. Gregory's Register*

BLACKBURNE, EDWARD, educated at the English College, Rome. He was a native of Lancashire, and on his return exercised his missionary faculties in his own county, and was Rural Dean of Amunderness, one of the Hundreds of the county including the Filde, Preston, Garstang, etc. "He told me," says Mr. Christopher Toottell, "that in a private familiar conversation at Rome with Dr. Plunket about the Jesuits' hardness and unkindness to the Secular Clergy, the Dr. said: "*Revera Jesuitæ sunt nobis Amici leves, inimici graves.*" (*Ushaw Collection*, p. 369.)

BLACKBURNE, JOHN, probably nephew of Edward Blackburne, was admitted into the English College at Rome Oct. 4, 1674, by Father Charles Anderton, the Rector, being then in his 20th year. He was ordained Priest at St. John Lateran, April 1, 1679. After continuing his studies till 1682 he left the College April 21, and came on the Mission. He lived at Claughton, and died there in Dec., 1727 or the beginning of 1728.

BLAKE, JAMES, S.J.—He published: *A Sermon on the Blessed Sacrament*, preached in the Chapel of the Spanish Ambassador on Corpus Christi, June 3, 1686.

BLOODWORTH, THOMAS.—Born at Kimbolton, and having passed two years at Sedgley Park, he went over to Valladolid in 1772, when he was ordained Priest, and for some time taught the classics there. In 1783 or 84 he came on the Mission, and succeeded Mr. Manning in the wide Mission of Derby, where he had to attend not fewer than four or five different congregations, which, though small, were very distant one from the other : to wit, at Derby, West Hallam, Weston, Norbury, and occasionally Ashbourne and Barrow. He died at West Hallam January 26, 1815. Mr. Bloodworth had a cultivated mind, and was much respected in and about Derby, both by Catholics and Protestants.

BLOUNT, ——, of Orleton, was descended from Thomas Blount the Antiquary (on whom see Dodd). He died without issue, and the heir was nephew or collateral branch about the time of the Revolution. His grandson Thomas married Elizabeth, daughter of John Berington of Winsley, but left no issue, but was succeeded by his brother, whose son William was educated at Douay and Paris, studied Physic, and having taken the degree of M.D. at Edinburgh, settled at Hereford, and was a physician of eminence there. He married —— Lambe, daughter of Lacon Lambe of Henwood, Co. Hereford, Esq., and Elizabeth Berington of Winsley, and had many children by her. Is still living at Hereford. Mr. Blount the Antiquary wrote a history of Herefordshire, part of which is now in the hands of Dr. Blount.

BLOUNT, CHARLES.— Charles was third son of Sir Edward Blount of Soddington, Bart., by his wife Apollonia, daughter of Sir Robert Throckmorton, Bart. He studied at Douay, and for some time taught Poetry and Philosophy. When he returned to England, he lived chiefly with his own friends, and after the death of his elder brother, Sir Edward, with his widow, Lady Blount at Snitterfield. At her death, he retired to Warwick, and died there January 19, 1810.

BLOUNT, EDWARD.—Edward Blount of Blagdon was the eighth and youngest son of Sir George Blount of Soddington, Co. Worcester, Bart., and of Mary Kirkham, daughter and heiress of Richard Kirkham, of Blackdown or Blagdon, Co. Devon, who was the son and heir of Sir William Kirkham, Knight. His eldest brother, Sir Walter Kirkham Blount, died without issue in 1717, when the title devolved on his nephew, Sir Edward, son of George, the first brother. Five of the other brothers died young, and thus Mr. Edward Blount became possessed of the maternal estate at Blagdon ; it lies on the sea shore, nearly in the centre of Torbay. The mansion was situated at the foot of the hill, which obstructed all prospect of the sea, but on the top of it stood a summer house that commanded the whole expanse of the Bay. About the year 1700 he married Anne, eldest daughter of Sir John Guise of Rendcomb,

Co. Gloucester, Bart., and of Elizabeth Howe, whose mother was daughter and co-heiress of Emmanuel Scroop, Earl of Sunderland. Anne G. was a lady of uncommon talents and acquirements, and brought her husband four daughters : Elizabeth, Mary, Anne, and Henrietta. The odium which fell upon Catholics in consequence of the Rebellion of 1715, in which some of them in the north were concerned, and the inconveniences and persecutions they suffered from the strict inforcement of the penal laws, induced Mr. Blount in 1717 or 6 to quit the delightful shores of Torbay, and remove with his family to Bruges, but we find him again settled in Blagdon in 1721. In 1725 his eldest daughter Elizabeth was married to Honble. Hugh Clifford, afterwards third Lord Clifford of Chudleigh. Mr. Blount died in London in July, 1727. Mary, his second daughter, was married to Mr. Edward Howard, Nov. 17, 1727, who took her into the South of France, till upon the death of his eldest brother Thomas, eighth Duke of Norfolk, in December, 1732, without issue, he succeeded to that high dignity. She graced that high station by the beauty and dignity of her person, and the splendour of her wit and talents. She died in 1773, but the Duke survived her and died in 1777 at the advanced age of 92. Mrs. Blount afterwards crossed the seas with her two unmarried daughters and fixed her residence at Antwerp, where her daughter Anne took the veil in a convent of Ursulines, and Henrietta married Peter Proli, a merchant of Antwerp. The Countess of Pomfret saw her there in Aug. 1741, and gives a very interesting and curious account of her sentiments and mode of life. (See the correspondence between the Countesses of Hertford and Pomfret, iii., 348). Anne, the third daughter, took the veil of the Ursulines. Though a foreigner, she was soon elected Superioress of the house, which at the time of her admission was on the verge of ruin, but by her talents and exertions, she re-established its reputation and repaired its broken fortunes, so that it became one of the most celebrated convents for education in the Low Countries. Her superintendence was thought so necessary for the welfare of the house, that application was made to the Pope to dispense with the rule that forbad anyone to govern the house longer than three years, and she remained Superioress till her death in 1779. The Cardinal Archbishop of Mechlin came to visit her in her last sickness and administered her spiritual consolation. She possessed much wit and cheerfulness, and her conversation was lively and amusing. Henrietta, the fourth daughter, after the death of her husband, Peter Proli, of Antwerp, married Mr. Philip Howard of Buckenham in Norfolk, younger brother of Edward, Duke of Norfolk, in 1739, and she bore him one son, Edward, who died much lamented in 1767, and one daughter, Anne, born in 1742, who in 1762 married Robert Edward, Lord Petre. Mr. Philip Howard died in Feb., 1750, but his widow survived him till 1781. A good portrait of Mr. Edward Blount is at Thorndon.—(Sir Thos. Constable's account, who adds that there were living, at the beginning of this century, more than 70 descendants of Mr. Edward Blount by his two daughters, Lady Clifford and Mrs. Howard.)

BLOUNT, SIR EDWARD.—Fourth Baronet, only surviving son of George Blount, second son of Sir George Blount and of Constantia his wife, daughter of Sir George Cary, of Tor Abbey, Knight. He was born at Blackdown. On the death of his uncle, Sir Walter K. Blount, Bart., in 1717, he, then at Douay College, succeeded to his dignity and estate. He married Apollonia, daughter of Sir Robert Throckmorton, who died at Mawley, Jan. 28, 1749, and was buried in the family vault at Mamble. Sir Edward died Feb. 16, 1758.

BLOUNT, SIR EDWARD.—Fifth Baronet, the eldest son of Sir Edward, fourth Baronet, by his wife Apollonia Throckmorton. He succeeded his father in 1758. In 1752 he married Frances, daughter and heiress of William Molineux, of Mosborough, Lancashire, by whom he had one son, Edward, who died young, and Sir Edward dying at Bath, Oct. 19, 1765, the title and estate devolved on his brother Walter. His sister Mary became a nun and died at Paris, Oct. 21, 1758.

BLOUNT, GEORGE, second son of Sir George Blount, Bart. He married, first, Mary, daughter of Henry, Earl of Thomond, and relict of Charles, Viscount Cullen, and after her death, Constantia, daughter of Sir George Cary, of Tor Abbey, Knight, by whom he had Edward, who succeeded his uncle, Sir Walter Kirkham Blount, and Constantia, Mary, Ann, and Elizabeth. The two latter were nuns at Cambray, Ann died there Mar. 15, 1769. (Nash's *Worcestershire* and Betham). Mr. George Blount wrote a Treatise on *The right use of Moral Philosophy according to the Doctrines of Christianity*, in three books, dedicated to his brother.

BLOUNT, SIR WALTER KIRKHAM.—Third Baronet, was eldest son of Sir George Blount, of Soddington, Bart., and Mary, daughter and heiress of Richard Kirkham, of Blagdon, son and heir of Sir W. Kirkham, Knt. He married, first, Alice, daughter of Sir Thomas Strickland, of Thornton Brigg, Co. York, Knight, (says Betham); and secondly, Mary, daughter of Sir Caesar Cranmer, Knight, of Astwood, Co. Bucks. He died at Ghent, May 12, 1717, without issue, and was succeeded in the title and estates by his nephew, Sir Edward Blount, Bart. His grandfather, Sir Walter, the first Baronet, was a great sufferer for Charles I., for whom he was imprisoned first at Oxford and then in the Tower of London. His brothers and four sons were also in the same service. I find the following works: *The Holy Ideot's Contemplations on Divine Love rendered into English.**

BLOUNT, SIR WALTER.—Sixth Baronet. He studied at Douay, and afterwards Physic with a view to the practice of Medicine, but his brother dying in 1765 he succeeded to his estates and title. In 1766 he married Mary, the eldest daughter and co-heiress of James, Lord Aston of Tixall, Co. Stafford, and Baron of Forfar in Scotland, by whom he had three sons: Walter, who succeeded his father and married, Nov. 25, 1792, Anne, youngest daughter of Thomas Riddell, of Swinburne Castle, Northumberland; Edward, who married Frances, daughter of Francis Wright; and George, who married Courtney, daughter of —— Chichester, of Arlington, Co. Devon. Sir Walter died at Lille in Flanders, Oct. 5, 1785. His lady was burnt to death and died on Jan. 20, 1805. "She used to say with honest pride that the Blounts had held their Worcestershire estates in lineal descent from the Conquest, and had in no instance been known to abandon their Religion or their King."

BLOUNT, WALTER.—Fifth son of James Blount, of Cleobury Forge, and Isabella Turner, of Pembridge; grandson of George Blount and Elizabeth Bowyer; great grandson of John Blount, and great great grandson of Walter Blount, of Soddington, created a Baronet for his loyalty by Charles I. in 1642. From Douay he went to S. Gregory's at Paris, but was obliged to quit it at the Revolution. He went to Old Hall, and being ordained he came to Wolverhampton in 18—.

BLUNDELL, HENRY.—Of Ince, son, I think, of following. He married Elizabeth, third daughter of Sir George Mostyn, fourth Bart., and his wife, Teresa Townley (who died Mar., 1767); by whom he had Charles Blundell and two daughters, one married to Stephen Tempest, of Broughton, Esq., and the other to Thomas Stonor, Esq. Mr. Blundell died Aug. 28, 1810, aged 86. His son died unmarried 1838 and left Bishops Bramston and Walsh his residuary legatees—to the amount of £——, which all centred in Dr. Walsh, as Dr. Bramston died before Mr. Blundell.

BLUNDELL, ROBERT.—Of Ince, Lancashire. He married Catharine, youngest daughter of Sir Rowland Stanley, of Hooton, who died at Hooton in 1737.

BLYTHE, [FRANCIS].—A Discalced Carmelite. His parents were Protestants, and he was educated in their principles. He occasionally, however, felt

---

* By W. K. B., of Soddington, An. Dom. 1669, dedicated to his sister, Mrs. Anne Blount; secondly, *The Office of the Holy Week*, translated out of the French, 1670, dedicated to his mother, Mary Blount, by W[alter] Kirkham Blount.

dissatisfied with them and proposed his scruples to his parson. On one occasion, observing the manner in which he administered baptism, he took the liberty of expostulating with him, and expressed his apprehension that the child had not been duly baptised. To which the clergyman answered that *he had better become a Papist at once.* From this time Mr. Blythe redoubled his enquiries, and these ended in his becoming a Catholic. Soon after he entered among the English Carmelites, who had a house at Tongres, and became a noted preacher. He was also Professor of Divinity there. He was Provincial of his Order during the time that Bishop Stonor lodged complaints at Rome against Father Gordon, a Carmelite who lived at Longford, near Newport Salop, the seat of ——— Talbot, Esq., which with some other complaints against Father Hall, O.S.F., led to the Brief of Benedict XIV., *Apostolicum Ministerium*, entitled also the *Regulae Missionis.* Father Blythe wrote the following works : 1. *The Streams of Eternity.* 2. *Sermons for the whole year.* 3 vols., *credo.* 3. *Explanation of the respect paid to the Holy Cross.* 4. *Sermon on the Passion of our Lord.* 5. *Eternal misery the necessary consequence of infinite mercy abused.* 6. *A farewell Sermon.* 7. *Caution against prejudices in matters of Devotion.* "In which," observed Dr. Milner (Aug. 28, 1816), "he shews himself to have the greatest."

BODENHAM, CHARLES.—Of Rotherwas, Co. Hereford. The family of Bodenham is very ancient and was originally from a place of the same name in Herefordshire. The elder branch ended in a daughter many years ago, when the younger branch was settled at Dunchurch, not far from Hereford, and much increased the property by marrying a daughter and heiress of Walter de la Barr, by whom they became possessed of Rotherwas, their present residence. At or about the time of the Revolution Thomas Bodenham married a daughter of Guldeford of Kent. His son Charles married : 1. ——— Stonor, of Stonor, by whom he had one son, Charles, and a daughter, a nun, at Brussels ; 2. ———, a daughter of Mr. Huddleston, of Sawston, Esq., who brought him two daughters. He built a large handsome [house] at Rotherwas. He was succeeded by his son Charles, who married a Miss Pendrel [of Boscobel], and by her had one son, named Charles, who was educated at the English Benedictines at Douay, and married Bridget, d. of Thomas Hornyhold, of Blackmore Park, by whom he had one son, called Charles, who married Elizabeth, daughter of Thomas Weld, of Lulworth Castle, by whom he has one son, De la Barr Bodenham, and a daughter, Elizabeth.

BOLTON, JOSEPH.—Born in the neighbourhood of Preston and educated at Douay. On his return to England he was placed in London, and for many years lived with Bishop Chaloner as his chaplain, and after his death was V.G. to his successor, Bishop Talbot. When the act of 1778, for the repeal of of a few of the Penal Laws, was before the House of Commons, and being asked by one of the members if the number of Catholics increased, he candidly answered, "*I fear not*" ; his answer caused much laughter. At the time of the riots, in 1780, he shared in the anxieties, difficulties, and dangers of his Ven. Bishop, and tho' he escaped unhurt, yet his health was materially impaired in consequence of them. He was in so precarious a state in the summer of 1783 that he was obliged to leave London, and accompanied Mr. Wilkinson to St. Omers, but he derived no benefit from his journey, and on the 16th of Dec. following died in London, sincerely regretted by all who knew him and were acquainted with his many virtues. He was member of the Chapter, and was Agent for Sedgley Park, and materially served that and its sister establishment at Brook Green, Hammersmith.

He wrote "*A Sentimental Letter from a Gentleman to a Lady*" ; *i.e.* to Mrs. Bayley, of Brook Green, whose school Mr. Bolton attended.

BOOTH, CHARLES, S.J.—Born Sept. 18, 1707. On the 7th of Sept., 1724, he entered his Noviciate, and was professed Feb. 2, 1742. In 1761 or 2 he succeeded Father Elliot in the administration of the Roman College, but having imprudently invited Prince Charles to the College after the death of his father, in 1765, and having erected a throne for him in the hall of Saint George, and acknowledged him for King of Great Britain, France and Ireland, and having sung or said the Te Deum on the occasion, he was expelled the College by an order of Benedict XIV.'s Secretary of State. The Superiors of the other British Houses, Secular and Regular, it is said, were guilty of the like indiscretion, to say no more of it, and were in like manner obliged to leave their houses. Mr. Booth died at Wardour Castle, Mar. 11, 1797.

His brother, Ralph Booth, was also a Jesuit. He was born April 21, 1721, entered his novitiate Sept. 7, 1747, and was professed Feb. 2, 1755. He died Nov. 19, 1780.

BOOTH, JAMES.—"Succeeded Mr. N. Piggott in eminence and is acknowledged to be the father of the modern practice of conveyancing. He was not author of any work, but his written opinions were given at great length and are very elaborate. They are held in great esteem and always mentioned at the Bar and from the Bench with great respect. The copies [of the opinions] are numerous and, in a work, entitled *Printed Copies of opinions of Eminent Counsel*, several of them found their way to the press." Butler *Memoirs*, iv. 460.

Mr. Booth's opinions in the MS. Cases on the Popery Laws, at Ushaw, are dated from 1738 to 1764. He wrote two papers on the claim made by Father Grey and the Jesuits on the personal estate of the Duke of Shrewsbury in 1743. (See Butler's *Memoirs*).

QUERY.—Are not James and Nathaniel one and the same person? Mr. Butler is often incorrect in names and dates. In his 98th chap., on Lawyers, he never mentions *Nathaniel*, which shews he confounded him with *James*.

BOOTH, JOHN.—Clergyman. He lived with Dr. Witham (Q. Bp.?), of Preston upon Skern, near Stockton, in the Bishoprick of Durham, and for several years assisted the Catholics in that vicinity as occasion required. He died Oct. 1, 1722.

BOOTH, NATHANIEL.—An eminent Catholic Counsel of Gray's Inn. He wrote :

A Military Discourse : whether it be better for England to give an invader present battle or to temporize and defer the same. By N. Booth, &c. London, 1734. It was dedicated to the Duke of Argyle.

BORDLEY, SIMON GEORGE.—Born at Thurnham, near Lancaster, Oct. 28, 1709. For some time was a student in Oxford, it is said, but becoming a Catholic he went over to Douay, 1728 [*sic*]. He began Philosophy with Mr. Alban Butler and displayed considerable abilities in every department of his studies. Being ordained Priest he left the College Sept. 13, 1735, after saying Mass at Our Lady's Altar that morning. Aughton, near Ormskirk, seems to have been the first seat of his labours, when his annual income, he says, was only £5 ! Here, and in other places where he lived as a Missionary, he accommodated the language of his instructions and his manners to the poor in the midst of whom he lived, and by that means was enabled to do much good. At Ince Blundell he was enabled by his savings from a scanty income and by the charity of others, particularly of Edward, Duke of Norfolk, to build a school, where he had frequently not less than 70 or 80 scholars. One of his principal objects in adding this to the labours of a large and poor congregation was to rear youth for the Priesthood, and many Missionaries were indebted to him for the education they received afterwards at Douay, Lisbon, and Valladolid. In this manner did he employ his time and money during a long life, in the course of which, he says, "the moneys got or saved by him amounted to £5,170 18 0." Towards the close of his life he became almost blind, and died Nov. 3, 1799. Mr. Bordley, with some oddities, was a very zealous and laborious Missionary, and a learned man. In his old age he published :

1. *Quintilianus Britannicus.* 2. *Cadmus Britannicus*, or *the Art of writing improved;* containing : i. A Shorthand ; ii. A Swifter Shorthand ; iii. A Shorthand for Music ; iv. An Universal Character—all which four schemes or systems are warranted to be *Originals*, and not one single character borrowed or taken out of any former author. This very curious and ingenious work he

dedicated to Sir Joseph Banks, President, and to the Council and Fellows of the Royal Society, in the hope that they would recommend it to Foreign Societies and Academies for the benefit of mankind, otherwise, he adds, "the Universal Character should never have been communicated to any private person, much less to the public and should have died with its author."*

BOSTOCK, GEORGE, *alias* WEST.—Son of Thomas and Ann Bostock, of Denbighshire. Born in 1664, was received into the College at Rome by Father William Morgan, the Rector, by order of Cardinal Howard, the Protector. He was ordained Priest in S. John Lateran's, June 12, 1688, and departed for the Mission July 1, 1690. He lived in the north of Staffordshire or Derbyshire, and died Sept. 17, 1728.

BOSTOCK, GEORGE, *alias* BARON. Son of Roger and Alicia Bostock. At the age of 23 he was received into the English College at Rome, Oct. 18, 1695, and having completed his Philosophical and Theological course of studies was ordained Priest June 5, 1700, and on the 12th of April following he left the College for England. He was placed at Hathersege in the High Peak of Derbyshire soon after his arrival and not later than Lady Day, 1702, and died there Dec. 28, 1727. He was long disabled before his death and had Mr. William Brown for his coadjutor from Midsummer, 1725.

BOSVILE, JOHN.—Educated at Douay, served the Mission many years at Llanarth, in Monmouthshire, and died there Mar. 2, 1779. He probably [succeeded] Mr. Owens at L. or Mr. Davies in 1760 or 1761.

BOWER, ARCHIBALD, S.J. (APOSTATE). — See Chalmer's *Biographical Dictionary.*

BOWER, WILLIAM.—Was an Alumnus of Douay College and came on the Mission in 1767. He was one of the Chaplains to the Ambassador of Sardinia and was very assiduous in assisting the poor. He died in London June 17, 1773.

BOWES, ROBERT, *alias* LANE.—Of the Diocese of Chichester and born at or near Arundel in Aug., 1673. He took the College Oath April 5, 1695, and having finished his Theological course was ordained Priest at Tournay, and left Douay in company of Hugo Tootle (better known by the name of Charles Dodd) in May, 1698. Hathrop, in Gloucestershire, the seat of Sir J. Webb, was the place of his residence. In 1716 he was urged to go to the nuns at Brussels as their Director, but he excused himself and remained there till a short time before his death, which took place at Bath Dec. 15, 1735. (*Douay Diary.*)

Mr. Robert Bowes, *alias* Lane, published "*Practical Reflections for every day in the year.*" The work has been ascribed to Mr. Darell, S.J., and even to Mr. Gother (in an Irish Edition); but Mr. Darell, of Calehill, being asked by Dr. Poynter at my request, May 6, 1821, whether he knew of any tradition in his family of its being the work of Father Darell, answered that "he knew of none." On the other hand, the late Mr. Eyre, of Ushaw Col., in a letter to his brother of Jan. 17, 1735, says: "Mr. Bowes was author of the *Practical Reflections.*" The late Mr. John Lee, of Hammersmith, and Dean of the Chapter, declared to me in 1815, and to Reverend Joseph Hodgson frequently, that his original MS. was at Hathrop when he lived there. It may be added that Mr. Crathorn, author of the *Practical Catechism,* who was no friend to the Jesuits and had been accused of Jansenism, gave the fifth edition of the *Practical Catechism,* which he would hardly have done had he thought it was the work of a *Jesuit,* nor have spoken so favourably of it as he does in his Preface. Mr. Crathorn was contemporary with Mr. Bowes at Douay.

---

* For a fuller account of the man and his important work, see *Memoir of Simon Bordley, author of Cadmus Britannicus, 1787, the first Script System of Shorthand,* by John Westby-Gibson, LL.D., London, 1890.

BOWES, STANISLAUS.—Son of Stephen Bowes and Mary Stokes his wife, was a native of Sussex. At the age of 27 was received into the College at Rome by Father Postgate Mar. 12, 1707. He was ordained Jan. 27, 1709. On the 1st of Sept., 1710, his devotion led him to take a pilgrimage to Loretto, whence he returned on the 15th, as it was thought, in perfect health; but 10 days afterwards a fever came on, and on the 11th of Oct., 1710, he made a happy end, having first received, in a most edifying manner, all the rites of the Church. He was a pattern of piety to all and was much lamented by his Superiors and fellow Collegians. (*Diary of Roman College*.)

BOWES, STEPHEN.—Also of the Diocese of Chichester and probably brother of Robert and Stanislaus, was at Douay School and took the oath in April, 1696. For some time he taught the Classics *cum applausu*, says the Diary, and being ordained came on the Mission Mar., 1703. He was Chaplain in the family of the Fowlers (of S. Thomas?) and in 1712 in that of Lady Sussex. He died suddenly in 1713.

BRACEY, EDMUND, S.J.—Was born in April, 1709. He entered the novice-ship of Jesuits Sept. 7, 1730, and made his profession Feb. 2, 1748. He lived many years at Beoly, which had been in the family of the Sheldons of Weston upwards of 200 years, but was sold by Ralph Sheldon, Esq., to pay his own and father's debts. The Sheldons had been zealous Catholics and afforded great support to Religion at and about Beoly, which, of course, suffered much when it was sold to a Protestant. Mr. Bracey died July 28, 1782.

BRADSHAW, ANSELM, O.S.B.—A relation, if not a brother, of Mr. John Bradshaw, he succeeded Mr. Elliot at Actonburnell and was much admired as a preacher and a zealous Missionary. He died at Actonburnell June 20, 1799.

BRADSHAW, BASIL, O.S.B.—Died April 12, 1770.

BRADSHAW, BERNARD, O.S.B.—Died August 19, 1774.

BRADSHAW, JOHN.—Eldest son of Robert Bradshaw and his wife, Ann Jackson, both Catholics, He was a native of Lancashire and studied at Rome where he was admitted into the College Feb. 26, 1755, and being ordained Priest Dec. 20. 1766, left the College April 18, 1767, for the Mission. He was placed at Ugthorpe, near Whitby, in Yorkshire, and remained there till his death, which happened April 30, 1790.—*Diary of Roman College.*

BRAILSFORD, PETER.—Priest, died at Wolverhampton Dec. 2, 1734.

BRAND, JOHN, *alias* STAVELEY.—He left Douay Mar. 23, 1707, with the character of a "very virtuous and good man, of an indifferent capacity, but by extraordinary diligence had made good use of his time." He died at Stenley (perhaps Hanley) a seat of the Horneyholds, near Worcester, in 1750.
A Dr. John Brand, probably the same with the above-named, lived with Sir Edward Simeons at Aston, near Stone, from 1721 to 1739 or 1740.

BREWER, JOHN, S.J.—Born Dec. 29, 1732. He entered his noviceship Sept. 7, 1752, and made his profession Feb. 2, 1770. He had the care of the Catholics at and about Shepton Mallet, [a little town famous for its woollen manufactory], in Somersetshire, and died Sept. 2, 1797.

BREWER, JOHN, O.S.B.—He was a native of Lancashire. He entered among the English Benedictines at Dieuleward in Lorraine, and being found to be blessed with extraordinary abilities, he was sent to their house at Paris to pursue his studies at the Sorbonne, where "tho' a religious and a foreigner," says Mr. John Eyre, then in the same licence with him, "he gained the first place of merit in the Licence of 1774—a thing almost unexampled." For some time he was Confessor to the Benedictine Dames at Paris. In the year of the Riots he resided at Bath, and with some difficulty escaped from the fury of the mob, who demolished his chapel and, had they laid their barbarous hands on his person, might also have demolished him. He then went into Lancashire where he was placed by his Superiors at Woolton, near Liverpool. Here he lived, highly respected and beloved by all who knew him, till his death, which happened on the 18th of April, 80 years old.

Dr. Brewer was a most able Divine, a good linguist, a most zealous pastor, and a warm friend. In 17— he was chosen President of the English Congregation of Benedictines, and was continued in his office, or, rather, was re-elected at every Chapter. (See *Catholic Miscel.* vol. i., p. 240.)

BREWER, THOMAS, S.J.—Born June 19, 1743; entered his noviceship Sept. 7, 1761. After living some years in Lancashire he was charged with the Congregation at Bristol—"about 1780 he came from a seat of Mr. Blundell's, of Ince to Bristol"—and died there April 16, 1787. I find him described as "a jolly worthy Jesuit."

BREWSTER, [WILLIAM], S.J.—Resided in Norwich many years. He died in 1758 of a typhus fever, "which was then more prevalent and more fatal," says Mr. Beaumont in 1815, "than I have ever known it before or since."

Mr. Brewster was succeeded by Mr. Redford who wrote a controversial work, entitled, *An Important Inquiry.*

BRIAN, [JOHN].—"In 1694," says Mr. Christ. Tootell, "Mr. Brian, Chaplain at the Cross-Keys in Holywell town, gave me an account on June 22 of the said year, that after he had procured a lease of Holywell Chapel, and had possession given him by the landlord, the Jesuits' agents demanded the key of Mr. Brian : but he refused to deliver it. Whereupon they broke open the door and delivered possession thereof to the Jesuits. For redress of this wrong done to Mr. Brian, he had recourse to the Landlord, who fairly owned that his lease was good and duly executed, but withall declared that in regard it was the Queen's pleasure, that the Jesuits should have the chapel for their use, he was not willing to incur her displeasure by opposing their proceedings " (*Ushaw Collection*, I. 369.) (See also " Bryan.")

BRIDGWOOD, THOMAS, *alias* STYCKE.—Which seems to have been his true name. He attended the Catholics at and about Rushton Grange and Oulton, near Stone, and for some years lived at Bellamore, a seat of the Astons of Tixall, at which time he occasionally assisted the Catholics at and about Horecross and Pipe Hall. He died in 1732.

BRITTAIN, LEWIS, O.S.D.—Born in 1744. He was educated at and became a Dominican at Bornheim, and was afterwards Regent of that house. "While there," he says in his letter to me of July 15, 1817, " almost fifty years ago, I was directed to transcribe and collect from our Archives the lives of all our Fathers anywise conspicuous, for a Flemish Dominican, who was about to publish a history in Latin of the Dominicans of the Netherlands. But this history was never published, and my collection has, I fear, perished during the late French invasions. I well remember seeing the *original* letters to and from Cardinal Howard, how the Duke of Norfolk, his father, wrote to the Pope to stop his religious profession, and the Pope's answer was : 'that if his vocation was from God, it exceeded his power to stop it ; but that he would order (as he did) his novice master to give him a very rigorous trial.'"

Father Brittain was much respected and beloved, especially among his brethren ; and for many years had the spiritual care of the Dominicanesses after they were obliged, during the French invasion, to leave Brussels, and settled at Hartpury Court, near Gloucester. Here Mr. Brittain died May 3, 1827, in his 83rd year, and the 60th of his religious profession. He published : 1. *The Principles of the Christian Religion, and Catholic Faith investigated.* 2. *Rudiments of English Grammar,* written while he was Regent of the English College at Bornheim.

BROCKHOLES, ROGER.—Son of Thomas Brockholes of Claughton in Lancashire, Esq., and Mary, daughter and sole heiress of John Holden of Chorley, Co. Lancaster. He was sent young to Douay College, and having completed his third year of divinity, he went to finish his course at Lisbon, where he was admitted June 15, 1683. After he was ordained Priest, he taught the Classics for three years, and was appointed to teach philosophy on April 3rd, 1687, and divinity in 1690. Soon after he came on the mission, he was admitted into the Chapter, and was made Archdeacon, October 10, 1698. " He was a laborious and zealous Missionary, and died, with great sentiments of piety, at York in 1700." (*Register of Lisbon College and Chapter Records*).

BROCKHOLES, ROGER.—Nephew of the former, and son of John Brock-holes, Esq., and Ann Barcroft his wife, At the age of 21 he was admitted into the College at Rome Oct. 17, 1703, by Father Mansfield, when he began logic. Having finished his course of studies he was ordained priest June 2, 1708, and left the College to go to Paris, April 25, 1710. On the death of Mr. Richard Taylor, *alias* Sherburne, he succeeded him at Claughton Hall, the seat of his family, and there died Dec. 30, 1742. This family has always remained Catholic, and a Priest has always resided at Claughton. Mr. James Parkinson, born at Claughton and educated at Douay, succeeded Mr. Brockholes, and served the Congregation 22 years, and died of a fever, which he caught in attending his flock, January 26, 1766. (*Diary of the Roman College*).

His brother, Thomas Brockholes, was also a Priest from Douay, and died at Burgh, near Chorley, Co. Lancaster, Nov. 10, 1738.

BROCKHOLES, THOMAS.—Nephew of the last-named Roger and Thomas. Studied at Douay, and was ordained Priest in December, 1706. Soon after he was made General Prefect and then procurator of the College, and continued in the latter situation for some years. On May 18, 1727, he came to Wolver-hampton, and in 1730 succeeded Mr. (afterwards Bishop) Dicconson at Chillington, where he was much respected by his patron, Peter Giffard, Esq., and among his brethren, and proved himself to be a laborious and zealous Missionary. He was a member of the Chapter, and in 1754, was chosen Archdeacon of Staffordshire, Cheshire and Derbyshire. He was also G.V. to Bishop Stonor. He died Jan. 16, 1758, and was buried at Brewood.

BROMWICH, ANDREW.—Was born of a respectable family at Oscott. Was accused of being a Priest, and convicted, but though condemned was not executed. On his release from prison, returned to Oscott and died there Oct. 15, 1702, and was buried in his own vault, Oct. 23, at Handsworth, his parish Church ; [as was also Gilbert Swift his executor, and his uncle, Francis Fitter]. He is much recommended in the Records of the Chapter "for his prudence and diligence." (See *Cath. Mag.* vi., 154).

BROWNE, SIR CHARLES.—Second Bart., son of Sir Henry Browne and Frances Somerset. He married Mary, eldest daughter of George Pitt, of Strathfieldsay, Hants, grandfather of Lord Rivers. Sir Charles died in Dec., 1751, aged 88. He had two brothers, Peter and Francis, and three daughters, Mary, Catharine, and Frances, who married Francis Anderton, of Lostock, Co. Lancaster.

BROWNE, SIR GEORGE.—Third Bart., only son of Sir Charles and Mary Pitt. Succeeded his father in 1751. In 1725 he married Lady Barbara Lee, daughter and co-heiress of Edward Henry, first Earl of Lichfield by Charlotte Fitzroy, daughter of Henry Fitzroy, first Duke of Grafton, son of Charles II., by Barbara, Duchess of Cleveland. By his wife he had only one daughter, Barbara, married to Sir Edward Mostyn, fifth Bart., and after the death of Lady Barbara Lee Sir George remained a widower several years, and then married Mrs. Holman, of Warkworth, who had been a widow for three or four years, and died in child-bed, but seven years after her marriage. He then married for his third wife Frances Sheldon, the widow of Henry Fermor, of Tusmore. Sir George died in June, 1754, aged 60, without male issue, when the baronetage became extinct. By his will Sir George devised his estates, after the death of his lady, to Charles Browne Mostyn, the second son of his daughter Barbara, by her husband, Sir Edward Mostyn, the fifth Bart., who then took the name and arms of Browne. Sir George was lineally descended from Sir Henry, third son of Sir Anthony Browne, Kt., first Viscount Montague (grandson of John Neville), Marquis of Montague by his third wife, Magdalen, daughter of William Lord Dacres, of Gillesland. The family of Browne have constantly resided on their estate at Kiddington. In the house are preserved many valuable and capital portraits of the family of Browne and their honourable intermarriages), by Cornelius Jansen and other eminent masters in the reigns of Mary, Elizabeth, and Charles I. Sir George was a very popular man in Oxfordshire, a decided Jacobite, as were also the family into which he married.

BROWN, SIR HENRY, BART.—Created July 1, 1659. He succeeded his father, Sir Peter Brown, Kt., who was slain at the battle of Naseby fighting for Charles I., June 14, 1645, at the age of 30. He married Frances, third daughter and co-heir of Sir Charles Somerset, of Troy, Co. Monmouth, Kt. of the Bath, and sixth son of Edward, fourth Earl of Worcester, and of his wife, Elizabeth, daughter of Sir William Powell, of Lampylt, Monmouthshire, by whom he had three sons and three daughters. His daughter, Elizabeth, married Francis Anderton, of Lostock. Sir Henry died in 1689, aged 50. He built, or rebuilt, in 1673, the present mansion of Kiddington on the foundations of the old one. (Betham's and Warton's *Hist. of Kiddington.*)

BROWNE, JAMES, was educated at Douay. He resided nearly fifty years at Buckenham House, Co. Norfolk, the seat of the Hon. Philip Howard, and died there Oct. 26th, 1778. He was chosen a member of the Chapter Oct. 12, 1748.

BROWNE, LEVINUS, S.J.—Son of Richard and Mary Browne. He was a native of Norfolk, and was admitted into the College at Rome, Oct. 18, 1691, by order of Cardinal Howard, the Protector, and under the Rectorship of Father Lucas, S.J. He was then in his twentieth year, and after going through his course of Philosophy and Divinity, he was ordained Priest June 16, 1696, and on April 21, 1698, left the College to go on the Mission, with this character from his Superiors : *ingenio et pietate insignis.* I do not, however, find that he did enter the Mission or remained on it as a secular Priest, for a few months after his departure from the College, in which he had been educated and lived six and a half years, and had taken the oath of Alexander VII., by which he bound himself to go on the Mission, and not to enter into any religious Order, he obtained a dispensation from the latter part of the oath, and became a Jesuit at Watten. I find him afterwards Rector of the College at Rome in March, 1724, and till the autumn of 1730. (*Diary of Roman College.*)

One Mudton, *alias* Browne, S.J., translated Bossuet's *Variations of the Protestant Churches.* Another was Chaplain to Mr. Caryll, of Lady-Holt, in Sussex, Esq. It was at the request of Father Browne that Mr. Pope gave a translation of a celebrated hymn of St. Francis Xavier, beginning with the lines :

"O God ! I love thee, not to gain
The joys of thy eternal reign."

I am unable to say whether the above be the same or different persons.*

Mr. Butler, in vol. iv., 429 of his *Hist. Mem.*, mentions the above translation of Pope on the authority of Mr. Wheble, a distinguished preacher, S.J., who had it from Mr. Pigott of the same Society.

From the year 1579, when the administration of the College at Rome was taken from the Clergy and entrusted to the Jesuits, the Clergy had frequently reason to complain that their College was rather a nursery for the Society than a seminary for secular Priests, agreeably to its original institution. I find in the *Annals of the College*, which were always written *by the Father Rector* for the time being, that the number of students who became Jesuits and who are *named* in the Annals, is 242 ! Of these 14 are said to have made their vows in *articulo mortis.* Between 1579, when in April the Jesuits received the

---

* They are the same, and are generally identified in the Father Levinus Browne, S.J.—E.B.

administration of the College, and 1679, no fewer than 216 became Jesuits ; and of these, 59 during the 12 years that Father Parsons was Rector the second time, that is about five per annum. During his second Rectorship not more than 156 were admitted into the College, and of this number at least 43 returned *re infecta,* or died in the College, &c., so that more than half of the whole number of Priests became Jesuits ; that is, 59 became Jesuits and 54 secular Priests, but six of them, it is observed, were admitted only in *articulo mortis.* From 1578 to 1773, the number admitted into the College was 1,465.* Of these 242 became Jesuits as stated above, and not more than 691 became members of the Secular Clergy in the space of 195 years ; the rest either returned *re infecta,* died in the College, or became Benedictines, Franciscans, &c.

BROWNE, PETER.—Educated at Douay, and for many years was senior Chaplain to the Sardinian Embassy, at Lincoln's Inn Field Chapel. In 1770 he succeeded Dr. Walton (Bishop) as agent for the Clergy of the Middle District, of which he was also a G.V. He received the Rev. George Chamberlayne into the Church, and was much respected by all his brethren. In 1789, he succeeded Mr. Shepherd as Dean of the Chapter, but did not enjoy the dignity long. He died rather suddenly, May 31, 1794. Though much esteemed as a Clergyman, in his old age, at least, he proved himself to be a bad accountant, and little conversant with business : as his broker contrived to embezzle upwards of £3,000 in the 3 per cents which belonged to two Missions in the Middle District. The money was afterwards repaid from his own purse by Bishop Thomas Talbot, who having transmitted the money to Mr. Browne, that he might invest it in the funds, kindly deemed himself, in some measure, answerable for it.

BROMHEAD, ROLAND.—Born at Stannington, near Sheffield, Aug. 27, 1751. He was sent when young to Sedgley Park, and after a stay of two or three years there, was sent to Rome in 1765, and was received in the College Oct. 7, Fr. Booth being the Rector. He was ordained Priest in 1775, and on his arrival in England, resided for some time at Sheffield, and then settled finally at Manchester. (See the Memoir of his life in *Catholic Magazine,* vol. ii., p. 522).

BRUDENELL, ROBERT.—Earl of Cardigan, son of Thomas, first Earl. He succeeded his father in 1664, and married, first, Mary, daughter of Henry Constable, Visc. Dunbar, by whom he had one daughter Mary, married to the Earl of Kinnoul, in Scotland ; secondly, Anne, daughter of Thomas Visc. Savage, by whom he had three sons, who all died young, and three daughters. He died in July, 1703, aged near 100, and was succeeded by his grandson.

BRYAN, JOHN, *alias* PRICE. — Born at St. Asaph's. He studied first at Douay, and when he was 22 years old, he was admitted into the English College at Rome on Sept. 29, 1669. On April 16, 1672, he was ordained Priest, and on April 21, 1676, he left the College. He resided at Holywell many years, but being very infirm was not able for much service. He was alive at Holywell in 1692, and had been 16 years on the Mission, and is described as "a faithful clergyman" in the Chapter Records. (See MS. *Records of Jansenism* p. 133, where will be found the account given by Mr. Tootell.) (See "Brian," above.—P.R.)

Mr. Roderick, *als.* Thos. Roberts, S.J., lived at the Star in Holywell at the same time. He was a native of Carnarvonshire.

---

* In the "original institution" of the English College there was nothing to exclude the reception of a student who might eventually elect to join a religious order (see the "Bull of Foundation" in Tierney's *Dodd,* iii. Ap., p. 337), and this liberty was upheld by a decision of the Holy Office, December 10, 1608. It was in consequence of this decision that the excessive number of youths were admitted, whose vocations turned out to be for the Jesuits. This brought about the "Oath of the Mission," imposed April 27, 1624, which made this abuse impossible in future. I am unable to check Kirk's figures, though some of them seem to need revision. —J.H.P.

BULLEN, ROBERT.—Second son of Robert Bullen, and his wife Helen Cockshed, Catholics. He was born in Lancashire July 31, 1740. Went to Rome, and was admitted into the College, Feb. 26, 1755. He was ordained Dec. 22, 1764, and left Rome, Apr. 25, 1765. His missionary labours were principally in Yorkshire at ——— , where he died Oct. 9, 1792.

BULSTRODE, SIR RICHARD, KNIGHT. — He followed the fortunes of James II. and died at St. Germains. Oct. 3, 1711, N.S., *aetatis* 102. (See his life in *The Lives of Illustrious Men*, pp. 553-557).

BURGESS, AMBROSE, O.S.D.—He was a native of Bristol, and became a Dominican. In 1718 he was chosen Rector of the College of St. Thomas of Aquin in Louvain, which he governed with great prudence and ability till 1730, when he was chosen Provincial of the English Province. He died at Brussels, April 27, 1747, aged 67. Mr. Burgess was much looked up to by his brethren, and has left as a monument of his abilities and researches : 1. *The Annals of the Church*. In 5 vols., 8vo. 2. *An Introduction to the Catholic Faith*. Published in 1709. (*Synopsis fundationis Collegii S. Thomæ Aquin. FF. Præd. Angl. Lovanii.*)

BUSBY, ANNA.—When young she went over to the English Augustines at Bruges, and after staying three years with them, was desirous to receive the veil, and remain with them for life. In this, however, she was opposed by her parents, who under the pretext that she was too young and tender for so severe a rule, ordered her back to England. She obeyed, but with great reluctance, and remained at home twelve months, during which time means were used to estrange her mind from a religious life, and even to settle her in the world. But she was proof against them all, and often entreated her parents to allow her to return. Finding at last that entreaties were of no avail, with the help of her brother she quitted her father's house and proceeded to Brussels, where she entered among the English Dominicanesses. This was then an infant establishment, under the direction, I believe, of one of the Howards, and was greatly in want of subjects, while the Augustines at Bruges appear to have been so numerous as to be straitened for room, having no fewer than 40 religious at this time in the house. Here she soon became a bright pattern of all virtues, and was in such estimation with the rest of the community that she was chosen Superioress of the house. While she filled this station, her eldest sister, Teresa, went over to see her, and was so affected by the edifying example of the Rev. Mother and the Community that she also took the veil, and after some years made a happy end in the arms of her younger sister. Mrs. Busby kept her jubily in 1715 on June 5, when, as the Confessor of the house, Dr. Raymond Greene attests, in " an address to her in verse on her jubily," the zeal and ardour of her noviceship remained still unabated. (*Dominican Obituary.*)

BUSBY, JOHN.—Born Feb. 23, 1714, of a good family in the diocese of Peterborough, but relinquished a large fortune for the sake of his religion, and going over to Douay, became a Priest. Soon after he came on the Mission he settled at Grantham, in Lincolnshire, where he was much respected as a zealous Missionary and a gentleman. He was many years V.G. to the Bishop of the Midland District, and died at Barrowly, near Grantham, April 3rd, 1794.

BUTLER, ALBAN.—Educated at Douay, where he was successively Professor of Philosophy and Divinity. He came on the Mission in 1749, and was sent by Bishop Stonor to Paynsley, the seat of Lord Langdale, near Draycott, Staffordshire, where I find him in 1751, when he was succeeded by Mr. George Hardwicke. (See his *Life*, by C. Butler, Esq.)

BUTLER, PHILIP.—Was educated at Douay, and when he came on the Mission was placed at Blackbrook, near St. Helen's, Lancashire, where he built the chapel and was much respected by all who knew him. He was the personal friend of his Bishop, Francis Petre. He died at Blackbrook, Dec. 9, 1777, and was succeeded by Mr. John Orrell.

BUTLER, RICHARD.—Of Rawcliffe, Lancashire. He was taken prisoner at Preston, and on his trial, June 4, 1716, it appeared that he joined the Prince's army at Kirby, and marched with them to Lancaster, Garstang, and Preston, where he was seen in the company of the Earl of Derwentwater, Lord Widdrington, and among the volunteers in the Churchyard, at the latter place. The jury, without quitting their seats, brought him in "Guilty." He died in Newgate. His estates, which were forfeited to the Crown, were valued by the *Commissioners of Enquiry*, in 1716 at £958 12s. 7½ per annum.

BUTLER, THOMAS.—He was educated at Douay, and having finished his studies and received Holy Orders, he left the College June 25, 1761, and came on the Mission. The good Mrs. Fenwick, having built a chapel on her estate at Hornby, near Lancaster, Mr. Butler was appointed to the place, and lived there many years, much respected in his neighbourhood. He died there Oct. 8, 1795.

BUXTON, GEORGE, *alias* THOMPSON, *alias* HANMER. — Born in Northamptonshire, March 22, 1687, or 6. His parents were Protestants, and he was brought up in their principles; but going to Rome he became a Catholic at the *Convertiti*, a house where converts are received and instructed. On May 23, 1710, he was received by order of Cardinal Caprara, the Protector, into the English College, by Father Powell, the Rector, and was ordained Priest April 15, 1713. On April 27, 1715, he went to Paris to finish his course of Divinity there. On his return to England he lived at Bettisfield, or Batchfield, on an estate belonging to John Fowler, Esq., of St. Thomas' Priory, near Stafford, between Ellesmere and Whitchurch, where the three counties of Salop, Flint, and Chester, and the three ecclesiastical districts meet. Here he resided about 7 years, and gave his assistance to the Catholics in that neighbourhood. In 1722 he was induced to accompany to Paris Mrs. Betham, sister, and Miss Betham, niece of his patron, Mr. Fowler. While there he took the name of Hanmer, and resided in the Seminary of St. Gregory, and superintended the education of the young lady, who was afterwards married to Lord Fauconberg. In the beginning of Feb., 1730, Mrs. Betham died suddenly; and being now at liberty he set off for Rome on horse-back the 14th of the same month, with the intention of becoming a Carthusian, provided he could obtain a dispensation from the oath he had taken at College to serve the Mission. In this he was opposed by Bishop Stonor, who claimed him and wanted his services on the Mission. He therefore resolved to return again to the English Mission, and as Dr. Ingleton, the Superior of St. Gregory's, says: "effected his journey to Paris in 25 days on the same blind horse that carried him to Rome." He adds that "he was full of zeal and fervour; a zealous good Priest." About this time he took the name of Thompson, "your old acquaintance," says Mr. Thomas Berington, Dean of the Chapter, to Mr. Brockholes, of Chillington, "Mr. Buxton, *alias* Thompson, *alias* Hanmer, is a man of single heart, though of a triple name." This was in 1748, not long after the attempt of Prince Charles in 1745, when it was found necessary for Priests frequently to change their name. He was then living in Essex, as chaplain to a Mrs. Elliot. Business of some kind called him again to Paris, and on his return to England, in 1759, he died at Boulogne, Feb. 12. In 1743 he was chosen a member of the Chapter, and treasurer in 1756; but shortly after resigned that office, probably on his leaving England to go to Paris. (*Diary of Roman College*, and *Register of Paris Seminary* and other MSS.)

BYARLEY, CHARLES.—Of Belgrave, eldest son of Charles Byarley and of Mary, daughter and heiress of Samuel Cutler, of Ipswich. He married Jane, daughter and co-heiress of Sir Thomas Beaumont, of Grace-Dieu, Bart. He died in 1738, aged 74, leaving one son, John Beaumont Byarley, who married Elizabeth, daughter of Thomas Berkeley, of Spetchley, and died May 28, 1742, aged 56. He left one son, John Beaumont Byarley, who married Esther, youngest daughter of Thomas Boothby, of Tooley Park, who died Nov. 8, 1760, without issue, when the estate at Belgrave came to the Beaumonts, of Barrow-upon-Trent, near Derby. (See Art. *Beaumont, Edward, Priest.*)

BYFLET, WILLIAM.—His true name was Gildon. He was a member of
the Chapter, and on Feb. 17, 1672/3, was chosen treasurer of it, which office he
retained for many years. He died in 1703.

BYON, ———.—He studied at Douay, and lived many years in the north of
England, where, says Bishop Leyburn, he was a " most excellent and useful
labourer." When Mr. Digby, who had been General Prefect at Douay for
some years, and under whom, as it seems, the discipline of the house was a
little relaxed, was removed and went as Confessor at Dunkirk, May 27, 1693.
Bishops Leyburn, Giffard, and Smith recommended Mr. Byon to the President,
Dr. Paston, as a fit person to succeed Mr. Digby.* He accordingly was
appointed, and his success fully justified the recommendation of the Bishop.
(See their letter to Dr. Paston in *Records of Douay College*, p. 52.)

CARDWELL, JOHN.—Son of Thomas and Helen Cardwell, a native of
Lancashire. He went to Rome when twenty years old, and was received in
the College by Father Postgate, Oct. 18, 1695. He was ordained March 26,
1701, and on May 17 of the following year left the College for Paris, where he
stayed some time in the Seminary of St. Gregory's, for the purpose of resuming
his studies. He then came on the Mission. He died Sept. 17, 1728. (*Diary
of Roman College.*)

CARNABY, ROBERT, *alias* LUKE GARDENER, D.D.—Having finished his
course of Philosophy at Douay, he went to the Seminary at Paris on Sept. 4,
1704. He was ordained Priest Dec. 23, 1713, together with Dr. Fell, and on
Jan. 1 both entered their License together. At this time he was Procurator of
the Seminary, and in the Lent of 1715 took the Doctor's cap, and soon after
set off for Rouen on his way to England. In August, 1717, I find him Chaplain
to Lady Mary Ratcliffe in Old Elvet, Durham, and continued with her till her
death, March 3, 1724. After this he resided some years in York till about 1730
or 36, but he returned to Durham, or rather settled at Esh, to be nearer to
Nafferton, Redheugh, and Norhamshire, Lady Mary's estates, which were
entrusted to him by her executor, Cuthbert Constable, Esq.

In 1736 he was head superior and V.G. of Yorkshire to Bishop Williams,
O.S.D., who in that year "thought of a Coadjutor, and declared for Dr.
Carnaby," as Bishop Dicconson says. Having caught a contagious flux by
attending some of his flock, he lingered several months with some hopes, at
intervals, of recovering. These hopes, however, did not possess his own
mind. In one of these states of apparent convalescence he paid a visit to a Mrs.
Taylor, Stobbilie, who observing that he wore a new suit of clothes, gave him
joy, and hoped he would live to wear them out. " Madam," said he, " I
have just got a new suit of clothes to die in ; " and in fact he never visited her
again. His house, which was thatched with straw, was set on fire by a cat
removing from a clothes-horse some linen that was drying in front of the fire,
and again at the time of Mr. Debord, who succeeded him, by firing his gun
out of his window. Dr. Carnaby died at Newhouse, Esh, Oct. 2, 1740. He
was a member of the Chapter, and on May 25, 1717, was chosen Archdeacon.
He was much looked up to and much respected by his brethren. On the
death of Bishop Williams, he, as General Vicar, conveyed the intelligence to
Rome in a letter which see in *Records of VV.*, *AA*. (*St. Gregory's Register.*)

CARPENTER, RICHARD.—He conformed to the Church of England,
and was employed in it, as a Clergyman, for some years. At last he saw his
error, returned to his duty, and did what he could to repair the scandal he had
given.

CARPUE, MRS. FRANCES.—A pious lady, who, lamenting to see so many
young girls running about the streets without education and religious instruction, thought of opening a house for them at Hammersmith, in 1760, where,
as in the Ark, they might be saved from the deluge of vice. Here she took
great pains to instruct and form them to piety, and gave the charge of it to

---

* If I recollect right, Mr. Digby was rather blamed for his severity than for any neglect.

Mrs. Bayley, who was possessed of a masculine mind, and managed her Ark so as to give great satisfaction. It could not, however, be expected but that some, after all, would turn out ill, and being discouraged by the misconduct of some on whom she had bestowed the greatest endeavours, and by the opposition she met with from others in her charitable undertaking, she retired to a convent abroad, in order to attend to her own sanctification. On this occasion the Venerable Bishop Challoner, who had been her principal adviser and assistant in her pious undertaking, wrote the following letters :—

" Madam, I cannot think it is the holy will of our great Master that you should withdraw yourself from this field, where with His blessing you have during so many years reaped notable fruit in rescuing a number of souls from the jaws of Satan ; and though some of them may have afterwards fallen, we have had at least the comfort that by your means a multitude of mortal sins have been prevented, and seeds have been sown that may produce great fruit another day. Wherefore, as I know not any place or calling in the world wherein you can either do more service to God and your neighbour, or labour more effectually for the salvation of your own soul, than that in which His Divine Providence has placed you, I beg of you, for His sake, to return amongst us.—I remain, Madam, your devoted servant in Christ Jesus, Richard Challoner. July 7, 1775."

On the 28th of the same month he wrote again to her : " Dear Madam— The grace, mercy, and peace of God be always with you. We have told you what our thoughts are in relation to His Divine Will concerning you. We can find no reason for altering our mind. Follow, then, the will and call of God without waiting for a commandment from your devoted servant in Christ, Richard Challoner. July 28, 1775."

Soon after the receipt of this second letter she returned and continued her support of her charitable establishment till her death, which took place ———. (Barnard's *Life of Bishop Challoner*, p. 95, etc.)

CARROLL, JOHN, S.J., Archbishop of Baltimore, in North America. He was born of a respectable family on Jan. 8, 1736, entered his noviceship Sept. 7, 1753, and was professed Feb. 2, 1771. When the late Robert, Lord Petre, went on his travels, Mr. Carroll accompanied him as his tutor through France and Italy, and soon after his return was made the first Bishop in North America, and resided at Baltimore. When the number of Catholics was so much increased in America as to require additional Bishops, Dr. Carroll was made Archbishop, and governed his See with great prudence and wisdom, and gained the esteem of all around him. He died at Baltimore, Dec. 23, 1815. (For more and correct particulars see the memoir of him in Mr. Butler's *Historical Memoirs*, iv., 403.)

CARTER, JOHN (I.), a native of Lancashire. He studied at Lisbon, and lived many years highly respected at New House, near Preston. He died Oct. 18, 1789, and was succeeded by his nephew, Mr. James Maudesley, who died Feb. 4, 1814.

CARTER, JOHN (II.), nephew of the former, was born at Standish, in Lancashire, in 1748. In 1762 he was admitted into Douay College, where he distinguished himself particularly as Classical student and teacher. He defended Philosophy under Mr. Joseph Berington. He came on the Mission at the end of 1776 or Feb., 1777, and was placed at Wolverhampton with Mr. Joseph Berington, where he remained till his death, which occurred March 31, 1803. Mr. Carter was gifted with a fine imagination and a good memory, was an eloquent and powerful preacher, and was highly respected by Protestants as well as Catholics. Nor is it too much to say of him that no one laboured more and with better success than he did to remove from the minds of his Protestant brethren the many prejudices which they entertained of Catholics and the Catholic Religion. He was buried in Bushbury church-yard, where a stone was erected to his memory by his friend, Mrs. Green, of Wolverhampton, with a long inscription commemorative of his great abilities and good qualities.

CARYLL, [JOHN].—He followed the fortunes of King James, and resided at his court at St. Germains, where he published a new version of the Psalms in 1700, in which he took Bellarmine for his guide, and is said by Dr. Geddes (*Prospectus of a new translation of the Bible*, p. 110) to have often expressed the meaning of the Vulgate much better than the Douay translators. One of his descendants was the principal person about the late Charles Stuart in 1773, and some years after, when he left his attendance, and came over to England, and died.

CATROW, CHARLES.—He was educated at Douay, and for twenty-six years was Confessor to the Austin nuns at Louvain; and was indefatigable also in promoting their temporal interests. When the Community was obliged to leave Louvain, Mr. Catrow conducted them by sea and land, and safely landed in England forty-eight or fifty persons. They then settled at Spettisbury, in Dorsetshire, and Mr. Catrow continued with them till his death, which occurred Mar. 12, 1804, aged 51, Confessor to this monastery 26 years. He never omitted any occasion of exercising his zeal and charity, and died universally regretted by all ranks of persons. Mr. Ralph Southworth, who had long been his assistant, and at his death succeeded him in the spiritual charge of the Community at Spettisbury House, wrote the following lines to his memory:

> " To thee the Virgin wandering in her grove,
> Sacred to solitude and heaven-born love,
> With mournful looks shall view the azure sky,
> The tender tear still trembling in her eye;
> And as she sighs, a vow to heaven shall send,
> ' Peace to my Guide, my Father and my Friend.' "

CHADWICK, JOHN.—(Of the Chadwicks of Preston). Was born near Preston. He studied at Douay, and for some time was Professor of Poetry, 1753, and of Rhetorick, 1754. He came over about 1758; and lived at Weldbank, near Chorley, where he built a house and the old chapel, and was much respected in his neighbourhood and wherever he was known. On 27 Nov., 1770, he was chosen a member of the Chapter, and in 1780 Bishop Matthew Gibson made him a Special Vicar, agreeably to the brief of Benedict XIV. The instrument was dated Sept. 18, and by it he was authorized to act after the Bishop's death as Vicar General of the Northern District till a successor should be appointed. Mr. Chadwick died at Weldbank Oct. 17, 1802. Mr. Thompson succeeded him and built a new and handsome chapel (Mr. Chadwick's being found much too small for his numerous congregation) and in 1833 he added two side aisles, so as to give it the appearance of a large church or cathedral.

CHALLONER, RICHARD, son of Richard Challoner, of [Lewes], Sussex. He arrived at Douay, June 29, 1705, being recommended by Mr. Gother and Lady Anastasia Holman, and was placed on one of Bishop Leyburne's funds. V.G. of Bp. Petre in Nov. (17)56. See his *Life* by Mr. Barnard, and that by Dr. Milner.

CHAMBERLAIN, JOHN, S.J., son of Thomas Chamberlain and his wife Mary Johnson, both Catholics. He was born August 14, 1727, N.S., *in oppido Rhigoduno*,* say the Annals, in Lancashire, and in 1742 was sent to Rome, where, he being not yet fifteen years old and too young, by the original rules, to be admitted into the College, Benedict XIV. granted an indult in his favour, and he was admitted July 20 by Father Henry Sheldon. After living on the College funds for three years, in 1747 he was placed on one of the free funds on which, when ordained, he would be bound to serve the mission, but not as a secular Clergyman if he proposed becoming a religious. He was ordained Priest Dec. 8, 1751. In the following year he left the College, Aug. 23, to go to Watten, where he entered his novitiate on the 3rd of November, and was

---

* By *Rigodunum* may be meant Manchester, Wigan, or Ribchester.—P.R

professed Feb. 2, 1764. *Non constat* where he lived, but he died Jan. 17, 1796.
(Foley, vii., 126, says he lived at Watten, and at Bar Convent, York, from
1770.—P.R.)

CHAMBERLAYNE, GEORGE.—See a Memoir of him in *Catholic Magazine*,
vol. iv., p. 17.

CHAMPION, JOHN, S.J., was born Jan. 18, 1695. He entered his novitiate
on Sept. 7, 1713, and was professed Feb. 2, 1731. He lived more than 40 years
at Sawston, the seat of ―― Huddleston, Esq. "He was a worthy Jesuit,"
says Mr. Cole, vol. xxiii., p. 21 ;* "and a very learned, modest and sweet-
tempered man, *in quo non est dolus* ; tho' he is of what is vulgarly called the
cunning order, yet I dare say he only deceives in not appearing by his humility
what he really is." Father Bedingfield, O.S.F., in a letter to the same Mr.
Cole, also says that he was "one of no guile, of a meek, quiet, peaceable and
inoffensive disposition ; near such neighbours how happy must be one's
situation." (Cole's MSS. vol. xxiii., p. 30). "Mr. Champion was a good
scholar, but a man of few words, even with his most intimate friends." He
died at Sawston, July 21, 1776, aged 82, and was buried there.

CHAPLAIN, ANSELM, O.S.B., probably brother of James, died at Liverpool
Dec. 30, 1784.

CHAPLAIN, JAMES MAURUS, O.S.B., was a native of Norwich. When
young he went over to Lambspring, where he entered among the Benedictines
of the English Congregation at that place. When ordained Priest he came
over to England, and for several years had the care of the Catholics in or
about Whitehaven. He returned to Lambspring in　　　When the late King
of Prussia seized on the Abbey with all its appurtenances, revenues, &c., and
allowed the members of the house in return the option of removing to England
or accepting a small pension on condition of remaining in his dominions,
Father Chaplain chose to remain, and died there on April 22, 1808.

CHAPMAN, FRANCIS, O.S.F., son of Richard Chapman, and Catharine
Haynes, his wife. He was born at Henley in Arden, Warwickshire, June 1,
1704. Having studied his Classics in England (at Edgbaston or Rowneywood,
near Henley ?), he went to Rome, and was admitted into the College June 27,
1721. He took the oath of Alexander VII., in 1722, and received minor orders ;
but feeling an inclination to religion, he obtained a dispensation from that part
of his oath by which he had engaged not to become a Religious unless leave
should be granted him. He left the College Nov. 25, 1726, and came to Douay
where he made his profession amongst the English Franciscans May 2, 1728.
When ordained he came on the Mission. In 1736 he accompanied Bishop
Pritchard, himself a Franciscan, and Bishop of the Western District, to Rome,
after which time I find no other trace of him. Obiit Dec. 14, 1794. (*Annals
and Diary of Roman College.*)

CHAPMAN, ROMANUS, O.S.F., died in London, Dec. 4, 1794.

CHARLETON, EDWARD, son of Mr. Charleton, of the Bower, in Northumberland. He studied Physic, and took his degree of M.D. Having married a
Catholic lady he returned to the faith of his ancestors. He joined the army
of the Chevalier in 1715, and was taken prisoner at Preston. (*History of the
Rebellion.*)

CHARNOCK, ROBERT, Papist fellow of Magdalen College. Concerned in
the Conspiracy of 1696. (*State Trials.*)

CHESTER, JAMES, [*vere*] LOLLI, studied at Douay. Of an unsettled
disposition, as appears from his living at Mawley, Longbirch, Paynesley,
Heythrop, seat of Sir John Webb, and other places, and never settling in any.
And lastly, he quitted his profession and probably conformed. For he practised

---

* Now British Museum Additional MSS. 5,824.—P.R.

Physic, and had the title of M.D. At last he got into the King's Bench, "and after many variations," says Dr. (afterwards Bishop), Walton, in his Obituary of the Clergy, " died penitent there, April 13, 1779."

While Mr. Chester lived at Longbirch with Bishop Hornyhold, and Mr. Grannan at Paynsley, the latter called Mr. Chester a puppy. The Bishop took him up and said Mr. Chester was a gentleman. "Then my Lord," said Grannan, "he's a gentleman puppy."

CHORLEY, CHARLES, was the son of Richard, a young gentleman of good parts, and partner with his father in 1715, and like him was found guilty at Liverpool, but died in prison.

CHORLEY, RICHARD, of Chorley, Co. Lancaster. He was a man of singular piety and abilities, but happening to join the Chevalier, he was taken at Preston in 1715, and was ordered up to London with Mr. Collingwood to take his trial. But falling sick at Wigan, he was tried at Liverpool and executed at Preston, Feb. 9, 1715, or 6. His estates were forfeited to the Crown : they were valued by the Commissioners of Enquiry at £394 4s. 8½d. per ann., and £123 7s. 10d. of personalty.

CHURCHER, JOHN.—He studied at Valladolid, and on his return to England resided in the family of Sir Henry Tichborne, Bart., in Hampshire. " He laboured hard for about 45 years in his Mission, and took great pains in instructing his flock." He was very old in 1692, and past labour, being troubled with a cancer in his breast. (*Chapter Records.*)

CHURCHILL, THOMAS.—He was a member of the Chapter, and chosen Archdeacon of Sussex May 15, 1683. He sat as Secretary in the General Association in 1684, 1687, 1694, and 1703. He died in 1705. When Bishop Leyburne came over and made his Ecclesiastical arrangements, he made Mr. Churchill Dean of Sussex and Surrey. (See *Catholicon*, no. 23, vol. iv., p. 198.)

CLAVERING, ANN, was Abbess of the English Benedictine Dames at Pontoise. She withdrew from the world at an age when others often covet it, and chose the retirement of a cloister. Constant to her engagements, she was an exact observer of religious discipline. When raised to the government of the Community, she was the foremost in every regular observance. She ruled rather by example than by precept ; and when circumstances made it necessary for the family to separate, she retired to the ancient monastery of her Order at Dunkirk, where she lived in the practice of holy obedience, meekness and humility : an example to all who knew her. Her death, like her life, was peaceful and calm. She died on Nov. 8, 1795, at Hammersmith, in the house of the English Benedictine Dames, late of Dunkirk, in the 65th year of her age. When the Community of Pontoise was dissolved some years before the Revolution, the Religious united with other Communities. (*Obituary*). " She was a lady," says Bishop Hornyhold, "endowed with all virtues, but most remarked for her charity to the poor and Christian fortitude under diverse afflictions."

CLAVERING, NICHOLAS, of the Claverings of Callaly Castle, studied at Douay, and in 1768 succeeded Bishop Maire as the incumbent of Old Elvet, in Durham, and as the Agent of the Clergy of the Bishopric of Northumberland. Both situations he held till Oct. 23 or 25, 1786, when he repaired to his brother's seat of Callaly Castle, and was succeeded by Mr. Lodge. He died at Hammersmith Oct. 18, 1805. He was Archdeacon Oct. 16, 1770, in the Chapter, and G.V. to Bishop Petre in the Northern District.

CLAVERING, RALPH, son of Thomas and Mary Clavering, was born in Northumberland, and probably at Callaly Castle. After passing five years with the English Benedictines at Douay, he proceeded to Rome, and on the recommendation of Father Hitchcock, President of the Benedictines, and of Mr. Clare, Procurator of the Seminary at Paris, he was received into the

College May 11, 1683, by order of Cardinal Howard, the Protector, Father William Morgan being the Rector. On April 13, 1686, he was ordained Priest at St. John Lateran's, and in 1688 went into France, whence he came on the Mission, but where he resided or when he died I have not been able to discover.

CLAVERING, WILLIAM AND JOHN, of Callaly, Northumberland; brothers, were taken prisoners at Preston in 1715.

CLAYTON, RALPH, studied at Douay. When on the mission he lived sometimes with Mr. John Russell, of Little Malvern, and sometimes with Mr. Bartlett, of Hill End in Worcestershire and assisted the poor Catholics in the neighbourhood of these gentlemen. He was in great estimation among his brethren, was a member of the Chapter, and on July 10, 1710, was chosen Archdeacon. He died in London Mar. 23, 1742. O.S.

CLAYTON, THOMAS.—He was a Missionary for some years, Jan. 7, 1725, at Redlingfield, in Suffolk, and then in Norfolk, where he died July 6, 1746.

CLIFFORD, ARTHUR.—Works published by Arthur Clifford, Esq. :— *State Papers and Letters of Sir Ralph Sadler;* 2 vols. 4to, 1809. *Tixall Poetry,* with Notes and Illustrations; 1 vol. 4to, 1813. *Tixall Letters,* from correspondence of the Aston family and their friends during the 17th Century; 2 vols. 12mo, 1815. *History of the Parish of Tixall;* 1 vol. 4to, 1817. *Collectanea Cliffordiana;* 1 vol. 8vo, 1817. (Galignani) *Guide of Paris;* 1 vol. 12mo. (Do.) *Guide of France;* 1 vol. 12mo. (Do.) *Guide of Italy;* 1 vol. 12mo. (Do.) *Guide of Switzerland;* 1 vol. 12mo. *Antiquities and Anecdotes of the City of Paris, from the earliest record of History down to the present time* (Not yet published I believe); (Galignani) I have heard Arthur was once the editor. [The last phrase is in Kirk's handwriting, the rest of the paper is a note addressed to Kirk, presumably by Arthur Clifford himself. See below: Clifford, Thomas.—P.R.]

CLIFFORD, CHARLES, seventh Lord Clifford of Chudleigh, second son of Hugh, fifth Lord Clifford, and of Lady Anne Lee, was born Nov. 28, 1759. On the death of his elder brother without male issue, he succeeded to his estates and title, in 1793. He married, in 1786, Mary Eleanor, youngest daughter of Henry, eighth Lord Arundell.

CLIFFORD, ELIZA, was daughter of ——— Thimelby, of Irnham, Esq. She married Henry Clifford, of Brackenburgh, Esq., and by him was mother of nine children, of whom the Reverend William Clifford was the youngest She is said to have been "a remarkably fine and well-informed woman." On the death of her husband she entered among the English Austin nuns at Louvain, at the age of 50, and made her profession Oct. 11, 1615. "She had been a convert, and had suffered much for conscience-sake." She died Sept. 3, 1642. She used facetiously in the convent to call Reverend William Clifford "our son," an expression which often caused a smile among the nuns. (*Louvain Records.*)

CLIFFORD, HENRY, brother of Sir Thomas Clifford, was born Mar. 2, 1768. He studied at Liège with his brother, and on his return to England applied himself to the Law, and soon after the passing of the Catholic Bill of 1792, was called to the Bar and became an eminent Counsel. [He died in 1813. —*Gillow.*]

CLIFFORD, HUGH, third Lord Clifford of Chudleigh, second surviving son of Sir Thomas Clifford and his wife Elizabeth, daughter and co-heiress of William Martin of Lindridge. His father was created Lord High Treasurer of England. On the death of his elder brother, George, the second Lord Clifford, who died unmarried in 1690, Hugh succeeded to the title and estates. He married Anne [Edmondson calls her Elizabeth], daughter and co-heiress of Sir Thomas Preston, of Furness, by whom he had nine sons and six daughters . Thomas, married Charlotte Livingston, Countess of Newburgh in Scotland ; Elizabeth, married William Constable, Lord Viscount Dunbar, and secondly, Charles, Viscount Fairfax; Amy, married Cuthbert [Edmondson calls him William] Constable, of Burton-Constable; Anne, married George Cary, of Tor Abbey; Catharine, Mary, and Preston took the veil at Ghent. Hugh, Lord Clifford, departed this life Oct. 12, 1730, and his Lady in July, 1734.

CLIFFORD, HUGH, fourth Lord Clifford of Chudleigh, was the seventh but eldest surviving son of Hugh, third Lord, and Anne Preston, of Furness Abbey, was born in 1700, and succeeded his father in 1730. He married Elizabeth, daughter of Edward Blount, of Blagdon, and sister to Mary, Duchess of Norfolk, and to Henrietta, lady of Honble, Philip Howard, brother of the said Edward, ninth Duke of Norfolk. By this lady he had four sons and two daughters; Thomas, his fourth son, married Barbara, youngest daughter and co-heiress of James, Lord Aston, and Mary, his second daughter, Sir Edward Smythe, of Acton-Burnell. His Lordship died Mar. 25, 1732.

CLIFFORD, HUGH, fifth Lord Clifford of Chudleigh, eldest son of Hugh, fourth Lord, and Elizabeth Blount, was born Sept. 29, 1726, and succeeded his father in 1732. On Dec. 17, 1749, he married Lady Anne Lee, daughter of George Henry, Earl of Lichfield, and by her had issue four sons and four daughters [at least]. He died Sept. 1, 1783.

CLIFFORD, HUGH EDWARD HENRY, sixth Lord Clifford of Chudleigh, eldest son of Hugh, fifth Lord, and Lady Anne Lee, was born July 2, 1756. He married May 2, 1780, Apollonia, youngest daughter and co-heiress of Marmaduke, Lord Langdale. He died at Munich, Jan. 15, 1793. He was educated at Douay under the name of Hugh Preston.

CLIFFORD, THOMAS.—The Honble. Thomas Clifford, fourth son of Hugh, fourth Lord Clifford, by his wife Elizabeth Blount, of Blagdon, was born Aug. 22, 1732. In his youth he was a mousquetaire in the service of Louis XV. On Feb. 2, 1761, or 2, he married Barbara, youngest daughter of, and co-heiress of, James, fifth Lord Aston (who died Aug. 2, 1786), by whom he became possessed of the Tixall estate. He built the present house at Tixall, and greatly improved and beautified the environs, in which he was assisted by Lancelot Brown,* who attained such celebrity for his skill and taste in laying out grounds. He died June 16. or May 16, 1787, leaving seven sons and five daughters. "His life was a pattern of every social and moral virtue, and his death of heroic patience and resignation. His Lady lived happy with him, and deserved to have it said of her that she was "a faithful, patient, compliant wife; a tender and affectionate mother; an indulgent, careful mistress, giving good example to her children and family by her piety, mildness, and good nature, humane character, benevolent and compassionate to the poor. She was a pattern for all wives and mothers, and leaving a numerous family of 12 children, she died, after a miscarriage, Aug. 2, 1786, aged 39." (Hist. of the Parish of Tixall, p. 272.) Mr. Clifford's eldest son, Thomas, born Dec., 1672, was created a Bart. Dec. 27, 1814, and died at Ghent Feb. 25, 1823; Henry was called to the Bar, and was a powerful pleader; Walter became a Jesuit, and died at Palermo July 23, 1806; Mary, the eldest daughter, became a nun at Liège, and is still living at New Hall, Essex. Arthur published many works as per catalogue by himself. Constantia married Mr. Weld (afterwards Cardinal), by whom she had one daughter, married to Lord Clifford.

CLIFFORD, WALTER, S.J., brother to Sir Thomas and Henry Clifford, was born March 13, 1773. After staying some time at Sedgley Park he went over to Liège, and when the French invaders caused the Gentlemen of the Academy to leave, he accompanied them to England and to Stonyhurst, where he was ordained Priest. In consequence of bad health he went over to Palermo, and died there, July 23, 1806.

---

* " Brown, Lancelot (1715-1783), landscape gardener and architect, known as 'Capability Brown,' was a pioneer of the modern or English style of landscape gardening, which superseded the geometric style."—Dict. Nat. Biog., vii., 22.

CLIFFORD, WILLIAM, was son of Henry Clifford, of Brackenburgh, Esq., and of his wife, Elizabeth Thimelby, of Irnham, Co. Lincoln. He was lineally descended from the ancient and noble family of the Cliffords, who were first created Barons and afterwards Earls of Cumberland. By the right of sucession the barony fell to him, his father coming out of the family before the Earldom was conferred on it, and he might justly have assumed the title of Lord Clifford; but so great was his humility that nothing displeased him more than to hear this mentioned; and when any took the liberty to speak of his noble extraction, he presently checked that discourse, saying that he valued the character of Priest above all the titles of worldly honour, and therefore deserved not to be taken notice of on any other account.

The English Seminary at Lisbon having been lately founded, and standing in need of able and discreet Superiors to undertake the government of it, the Bishop of Chalcedon made choice of Mr. Clifford for President, and the event showed he was not mistaken in the judgment he had formed of him.

For whosoever has been acquainted with the history of that College cannot but be convinced that the preserving of it was owing to the prudence, patience and piety of Mr. Clifford. He had incredible difficulties to struggle with, both from the strange humours of the founder and the extreme poverty the house laboured under; but Mr. Clifford, supporting those, and by his wise conduct and management as to the other, so far overcame all, that he left the College in a flourishing condition.

His next employment was the government of Tournay College, in Paris, which the Cardinal Richelieu granted to the Bishop of Chalcedon for the education of the English Clergy. Whilst Mr. Clifford was Superior of this house, the late Bishop Leyburn and the much esteemed Dr. Gage, who was Dr. of Sorbonne, and died President of the English College at Douay, resided there. After some years spent in the above-mentioned employments he retired to the *Hôpital des Incurables*, where he divided his time betwixt his own private devotions and his charitable assistance of the poor infirm persons of the said hospital, whom he often served with his own hands, and edified with his pious discourses. But the charity he showed them did not make him forget the poor of his own country. For during his retreat in that hospital he composed two excellent books for their sakes, the one called *Christian Rules*, the other, *The Poor Man's Manual of Devotion*; which, such was his humility, he judged only fit for the poor and persons of a mean capacity, and therefore styled it accordingly.

Though Mr. Clifford had, as he thought, sequestered himself from the world by lying hid in his retreat, yet the sweet odour of his most virtuous life broke forth abroad and drew many to partake of his advice and profit by his example. Amongst others, the Abbot Montagu, after the death of the Queen Mother of England, retired to the hospital where Mr. Clifford then lived, and when this humble Priest saluted the Abbot at his first entrance with these words: "My Lord, you are come to help me to die," the Abbot replied: "No, Mr. Clifford, I am come to learn of you how to live." And indeed the chief motive he had in choosing this retirement was the great opinion he had of Mr. Clifford's virtue and hopes of profiting by his example. The usual conduct of God's Providence towards his best servants and most beloved friends is to exercise their patience with long and painful infirmities. This trial was not wanting to Mr. Clifford, and he bore all the incommodities of a long sickness not only with patience but also with such a cheerfulness and sweetness as extremely edified all who came near him. Abbot Montagu frequently visited him in his sickness, and when he found him drawing near his end, he urged him, by many obliging expressions, to signify what he should do for him. The holy man for some time remained silent. But the good Abbot pressing again the same question, Mr. Clifford answered him in these words: "My Lord, the only thing I desire of your Lordship is that you will procure a hive for St. Peter's Bees;" meaning thereby, as he afterwards explained himself, a house in Paris for the English Clergy. The Abbot promised to comply with his request. And though the small remainder of his life after Mr. Clifford's

decease, or other engagements of charity, did not permit him to execute this
promise, yet God Almighty, who does the will of those that love and serve
Him, did by other means effect what the pious Mr. Clifford so much desired.
And indeed, whosoever has heard of the strange and altogether unforseen methods
by which Providence effected the establishment of the Seminary the English
Clergy procured in Paris not long after Mr. Clifford's death, will easily believe
that he obtained by his prayers in Heaven what he so earnestly begged for
whilst he was upon earth.   We may also piously suppose that the continuance
of his powerful prayers obtains those blessings God has been pleased to bestow
on that house in the many (considering the smallness of their number), very
able and learned Clergymen it has raised to the dignity of the Doctors of
Sorbonne.   For of the said house was Bishop Giffard and Bishop Witham, as
also Dr. Belton, whose eminent learning and piety moved the late King James
to make choice of him for preceptor to his son ; and the great success of the
Doctor's labours in that important charge has convinced the world his Majesty
could not have made a better choice.   Of the same house also was Dr.
Meynell, whose solid learning and most exemplary piety drew the veneration
of all that had the happiness to be acquainted with him.   Dr. Thomas Witham,
sufficiently known for his great talent of preaching and directing of souls, is
another member, and President of that house.   Dr. Ingleton, chosen by the
late King for sub-preceptor of his son, is also of the same society.

To these Drs. of Sorbonne who were members of the Seminary at Paris may
be added : Dr. Rider, Dr. Barker, Dr. Hall, Bishops Strickland and Stonor
and Berington ; Drs. Fall, Carnaby, Heydon, Bear, Holden, Hunt, Bernard,
Christopher Stonor, Howard, Strickland (James and Joseph), Perry, Witting-
ham, Howard, Wright, Bellasyse, Thomas Rigby, and Bew.

All this is here mentioned to set forth the merits of Mr. Clifford, whose
powerful prayers, as we piously believe, gave a beginning, and continue to
draw down those blessings on that house.   In fine, the end of this holy man
was suitable to his life, most pious and Christian, and as he lived amongst them,
leaving it expressly in his will that his body should be interred in the churchyard belonging to the hospital, the common burying ground of such poor as
died there.   Mr. Clifford died April 30, 1670.   His works are : 1. *The Poor
Man's Manual of Devotion*, often reprinted. 2. *Christian Rules, proposed to
the virtuous soul aspiring to holy perfection*. 3. *Observations upon all the
Kings' reigns since the Conquest*. MS. 4. *Collections, concerning the chief
points of controversy*. MS. (From *Life* prefixed to the *Manual*, see also
Catholic Magazine, v. 481).

CLIFTON, BERNARDINE, O.S.F.—He taught Divinity in his Convent at
Douay, and was the Guardian in 1727.

CLIFTON, SIR THOMAS, of Lytham, Co. Lancaster.   His daughter Mary
married Thomas, sixth Lord Petre, in 168—.   George Clifton, his son, forfeited
personalty in 1715 to the amount of £302 18s.

Thomas Clifton, of Lytham, married Margaret, eldest daughter of Richard,
fifth Viscount Molyneux, who, on his death, married William Anderton, of
Euston Hall, and died Feb. 3, 1752.

Thomas Clifton, of Lytham, married in 1760, Jane, second daughter of
Willoughby Bertie, third Earl of Abingdon.

CLIFTON [FRANCIS, SENIOR], S.J.—He was brother to Sir Gervase Clifton.
He lived at Swinnerton in 1750.   Hence he went to Lincoln, where he
succeeded Mr. Meredith.   He was a worthy pastor, and in his manners a
gentleman.   He was followed by Mr. Platt, who was much esteemed by all
who knew him.   Mr. Platt's successor was Father Gillibrand, " a religious
man, but was thought rather enthusiastic."

CLIFTON, ———, another brother of Sir Gervase Clifton.   He was a gallant
officer and an accomplished gentleman.   At the battle of Preston, in 1715, he
received a shot in his knee, and died some hours after.

CLINTON, ALEXANDER, S.J., was born March 23, 1730. He entered his noviciate Sept. 7, 1749, and was professed in 1767. He lived many years at Lulworth Castle, but left some time before his death, Mr. Weld saying he wished them to continue friends, which could only be done by his leaving. He died in London, June 5th, 1800. Mr. Clinton was much esteemed as a spiritual director of conscience, and was the author of the following works :

1. *The Morality of St. Austin* (2 vols.). 2. *Character of real devotion.* 3. *A Spiritual Guide, or chief means which lead to perfection.* 4. *The advantages and necessity of frequent Communion.*

CLOUGH, ANTHONY, of a good family at Mintown, near Bishop's Castle, Co. Salop, was born April 15, 1729 (O.S.). His father was Counsellor, and he was sent early in life to Douay College [and was there in 1741]. He was distinguished by his talents, application and good conduct. Having taught Poetry for two years, he left the College Oct. 2, 1755, and soon after his arrival was placed at Norwich, where he succeeded Mr. Alban Butler. But after staying there about fifteen months, on the death of Mr. Brockholes, in 1758, he removed to Chillington, the seat of Thomas Giffard, Esq., and was the respected and beloved pastor of that Congregation for thirty-three years, till the year 1791. He was, however, obliged to leave Chillington House on the marriage of Mr. Giffard's son to Miss Courtney, daughter of Lord C———, of Powderham, Co. Devon, who was a Protestant. He resided in the neighbourhood [at Gunston], still retaining the charge of the Congregation, and said prayers at Black Ladies, where the old chapel had been fitted up for the Congregation. As Mr. Clough had always been much attached to the Giffard family and to his Congregation, his removal caused him great regret and affected his health, so that he lost his usual spirits and gaiety of conversation. When therefore the late Earl of Shrewsbury offered his chaplaincy at Heythrop, in 1791, he readily accepted it, but more readily accepted that of Oscott, in May, 1793, when Mr. Joseph Berington quitted it, in whose favour he had resigned it in 1785. But as his health was now much broken, he did not long survive the change, and died Sept. 7, 1793, much lamented by all who knew him [and was succeeded by Dr. Bew]. He was buried at Brewood.

Mr. Clough had three sisters, who all became nuns, one at Liège, and two at Lierre. [Ursula Clough, Austin Nun at Bruges ; died there April 26, 1789, aged 89. Religious 60 years.] His elder brother, Richard, born Nov. 28, 1728, who became a Jesuit on Sept. 7th, 1744, and made his profession Feb. 2, 1762. He was Missionary at Worcester, and died there.

Mr. Clough was a member of the Chapter, and G.V. in the Midland District. He was nearly related to the Hornyholds, of Blackmore Park, Co. Worcester, and to the Beringtons, of Winsley, Co. Hereford. [In 1775 attended at Salop (£12 12s. paid him). In 1781 at Longbirch half-a-year ; probably before Mr. Hare became member of the Chapter in 1771. Bp. T. T(albot) named him second in his list for coadjutor and V.G.]

COATES [OR COTES], JOHN, was born at Alnwick, April 15, 1700. He was sent to Douay, and took the College oath Dec. 27, 1720. Here he distinguished himself by his talents, his piety, and particularly by his humility, and was generally at the head of his schools. (*"Qui in litteris humanioribus primus aut inter primos semper fuit ; optimo præditus ingenio, et pietatis et humilitatis signa hactenus præbuit."*—Rom. Col., iii., 29.) In August, 1730, he came on the Mission, and lived seven years at Hardwick, and in 1737 removed to Nether Witton. In 1773 he retired to Witton, Shields. The chapel at South Shields appears to have been first erected by him on Aug. 18, 1783. He died July 8, 1794, in Northumberland. He was chosen Canon Oct. 12, 1748, and Archdeacon of the Chapter Oct 12, 1762.

He published *A Catechism.*

CODRINGTON, ANTHONY, O.S.F., taught Divinity in the house of the English Franciscans at Douay, in 1727, while Father Clifton was Guardian.

CODRINGTON, BONAVENTURA, D.D.—He was from Douay. He returned on the Mission about 1677. In 1692 he "had been on the Mission," says Mr.

Ward, Secretary to the Chapter, "fourteen years or upwards, most of which time he spent in Hampshire. He was a very faithful labourer, exceeding zealous and diligent, and resided mostly with Mr. Barlow, of Compton, near Winchester." He died Jan. 3, 1727 (O.S.).—*Chapter Collection* i., p. 324.

CODRINGTON, THOMAS, was educated at Douay College, where he was ordained Priest, and became an eminent professor of Humanity. Being after-wards invited to Rome by Cardinal Howard, he was for some time his Chaplain and Secretary. About the beginning of July, 1684, he left Rome in company of Sir John Yate, Bart., and taking Douay in his way, left that place Aug. 1, the same year. King James II. made him one of his chaplains, preachers, &c. At the Revolution he shared his royal master's fate, followed him to St. Germains, and continued his chaplain till his death, which happened about 1691.

While Mr. Codrington was at Rome he seems to have enrolled himself among the members of the German *Institute of Secular Priests living in common*, or in community, and on his return to England in the spring of 1684, he and his companion, Mr. John Morgan, were appointed by Hofer, the President, and Appelius, the Procurator-General at Rome, their Procurators for the special purpose of "introducing, promoting, and spreading" the Institute in England. *The Institute* was founded in Bavaria by one Bartholo-mew Holtzhauser, and at the instance of several of the German princes, Ecclesiastical and Secular, its Constitutions were approved by Innocent XI., in 1680. It met with a warm approver and supporter in the person of Cardinal Howard, at that time the Protector of England, as was his title, and at the head of the English Mission. The primary object of the Institute was to induce two or more parish Priests to live in common and in the same house, with the exclusion of all female attendance, and in subjection without any exemptions of Regulars, to the Ordinary of the Diocese. Mr. Codrington was the bearer of a letter from Cardinal Howard, addressed to the Secular Clergy of England, in which he exhorted them to become members of the Institute. Appelius also wrote by him to Dr. Perrot, the Dean of the Chapter, to the same effect, and delivered to him a *Brevis Informatio*, in which he described at length the manner in which the English Clergy in their present circum-stances might become members of the Institute, and conform themselves to its constitutions.

In 1697 these were published in England with this title : *Constitutiones Clericorum Saecularium in communi viventium a SS.D.N. Innoc. XI. stabilitæ usui Cleri Saecularis Anglicani pro temporum circumstantiis accommodatæ et a RR.DD. Episcopis approbatæ.*

From the preface it appears that in the two preceding years especially, several of the English Clergy became members of the Institute ; among them I find in the London District the respectable names of Andrew Giffard and Dr. Jones, the first the brother, and both Grand Vicars of Bishop Giffard, Mr. Parsons, and Mr. Pygott. In the Midland District, or rather, in the Stafford-shire District, which comprised Staffordshire, Shropshire, Derby and Worcestershire, *The Institute* was embraced by Daniel and Francis Fitter, Andrew Bromwich, Fr. Richardson, Ralph Clayton, Robert Woodroffe, Edward Coyney, John Millar, and Robert Fitzherbert. They also endeavoured to introduce *The Institute* into all our Colleges subject to the jurisdiction of the Cardinal Protector, and to make that introduction even obligatory on their Superiors by a decree for which they assigned many reasons. On this subject Mr. Codrington wrote from Rome to Dr. Smith, the then President of Douay College, but I do not find that such Decree was ever obtained from Rome.

Considerable opposition, however, was made to it, especially by the Chapter. "It may be wondered," says Mr. Ward, "what should move or rather transport some few of our brethren to invent a particular body or Society of Clergymen, called *in communi viventium*, in imitation, though but in very few things, of the *German Institute*, wholly impracticable here, and unsuitable to our circumstances, having in Bishop Smith's golden treatise, *Monita Utilia pro Missionariis in Anglia* and the Appendix all that is proper for our state and condition in England." (Ward, *MS. History of the Chapter.* Mr. Ward was the Secretary of the Chapter.)

The publication of the above-mentioned *Constitutions* drew from the pen of John Serjeant, the far-famed controvertist, and in the name of the Chapter, of which he was a distinguished member, *A letter to our worthy Brethren of the New Institute.* It is written with temper, but with great earnestness. The principal objections in this letter are—that the Constitutions have avowedly been altered, and could not therefore be said to be approved by the Pope ; that even thus altered, they were, in the two principal points of the *Institute*, unsuitable to our state of life, and impracticable in England, where the Clergy are necessarily dispersed, and where no house is without a wife or house-keeper, or maid servant, or daughter of the family ; that their title, *Clergy living in common*, and the principal object of their vow, is a chimera, and being impracticable, is at best but a mere possibility, not likely to take place, and consequently not a proper subject of a vow ; that their promise of obedience enjoined by the rules approved by Innocent XI. being made to the Ordinary, it may at least at some future time be eluded, on the plea that the Bishops in England are not Ordinaries but only Vicars-Apostolic, and on the same the common exemptions of Regulars may be applied for and obtained, especially as "they had also given out that they intended to get a General or Chief Superior at the Roman Court ;" that such appointment and application "are contrary to the ancient laws of England made in Roman Catholic times, and may in any unfavourable or angry juncture be improved by our enemies to bring a persecution upon all Catholics ;" "that they have a distinct immediate Superior or national President, distinct Diocesan Presidents, we know not how many distinct Consultors, distinct Diocesan Stewards, a distinct interest, a distinct purse, and as we hear, are about to have a distinct new General at Rome." By thus "forming themselves into a distinct party, they have broken the union of the clergy, and sowed the seeds of perpetual dissention between the *separating party* and the *Standing Body*." That *The Institute* "in many regards prejudices the *Common Good*, and tramples under foot many *weighty pre-obligations* ; and finally, that notwithstanding the alleged appro-bation of the Constitutions by the Bishops, they had good reason to believe that the Bishops of England had no more approved of them than His Holiness had ; that Bishop Ellis, then in Rome, had not so much as seen them, much less approved them ; that Bishop Smith had made such orders for his District as quite spoilt any pretence of the necessity of such Institute amongst those who are under him, nor had they heard of so much as one of them, or any person in all the north of England, who had thought fit to join with them ; that Bishop Leyburn had prudently suspended his judgment till he saw how the English Institute will fudge with the German one ; that some in Bishop Giffard's district had been severely reprimanded for their hot zeal in promoting it, as they had reason to think by his order ; nor did it suit well with his prudence to be *singular* in this business from the rest of his colleagues, however he might incline to the *pious* part of it ; nor can any man think the known prudence and goodness of the Bishops will abet and approve the breach of an oath in those of *The Institute* who are Capitulars, and as such had previously taken an oath to promote the temporal interest of the common body, with which the other to promote that of *The Institute* was inconsistent, or patronise a Society whose first foundation was perjury." This letter seems to have given the death-blow to *The Institute*, and Bishop Giffard when removed to the London District in 1703, "for very good reasons," says Mr. Brockholes, "thought proper to abolish [*The Institute*]."

We have of him two Sermons, one at St. James's, the other at Somerset House. (See *Catholic Magazine* ; *Chapter Collection* ii., 141 ; *Records of the Institute.*)

COLLINGRIDGE [PETER BERNARDINE, D.D.], O.S.F., Vicar-Apostolic of the Western District after the death of Bishop Sharrock. Before he was raised to the prelacy he had been at the head of Baddesley School, and afterwards Chaplain at St. George's in Southwark, and in both situations was much esteemed and respected, as he was afterwards, as Bishop. He died at Cannington, March 4, 1829.

COLLINGWOOD, GEORGE (I.), of Eslingdon, Northumberland, where he had a valuable estate of £1,200 a year. He joined the Chevalier in 1715, and was taken prisoner at Preston. Being ordered up to London to take his trial, he was seized with gout at Wigan, and was sent to Liverpool, where he was found guilty of rebellion and high treason, and was executed Feb. 25, 1716. " Mr. Collingwood," says Mr. Patten, "was a very pious gentleman, and was much beloved in his own county." He married Catharine, daughter of Lord Montague, and after the death of her husband she retired to Longbirch, near to Wolverhampton, and lived there with Mrs. Giffard, the widow of the last of the Chillington branch of the Giffards, and Bishop Hornyhold, and died there much respected, Dec. 28, in 1776, aged 91. Her daughter married Sir Robert Throckmorton, by whom she had a daughter, Barbara, who married Thomas Giffard, of Chillington, Esq., and Mr. —— Throckmorton, the father of John, George, Charles, Francis, and William Throckmorton ; of whom the three first came to the title and estates of their grandfather, Sir Robert, by their father dying during his life. (MS. Records Miscel.; Hist. of the Rebellion.)

COLLINGWOOD, GEORGE (II.), was son of Thomas and Ann Collingwood, respectable Catholics in the Bishopric of Durham. In 1694 he went to Rome, where he was admitted into the College by order of Cardinal Howard, the Protector, Feb. 21, being then in his 18th year. He was ordained Priest June 15, 1698, by a dispensation from the Pope, not being of the proper age, and left the College on March 19, 1700. After remaining a short time at the Seminary in Paris he came on the Mission, and was much respected and beloved by those who best knew him. He was admitted member of the Chapter Oct. 13, 1714, and died May 31, 1734. (Annals of the English College in Rome.)

COLLINGWOOD, ROBERT, S.J., lived many years at Boscobel, in Shropshire, and was " the Superior of the College of St. Chad," and much respected in his neighbourhood. The Relics of St. Chad, which had been removed from the Cathedral of Lichfield when Protestantism became the established religion of England, came, after passing through various hands, at last into the possession of Father Collingwood. (See account of their removal in Catholic Magazine iii., 298). Mr. Collingwood was alive in November, 1735. The tradition of the country is that he was buried in the Chapel of Black Ladies, distant from Boscobel about a mile.

[In Dr. Kirk's drafts we find the following details as to certain money transactions : " I find his account of monies owing to Stafford district, £600 from ye College at Liège, lent by order of Mr. Rob. Hill, then Provincial. Mr. Ric. Plowden, then Rector, gave a note for it Sept. 10, 1723. Owing from St. Omer's £300, borrowed by Mr. Coxon, then Procurator ; his note dated April, 9, 1720. Do. from Mr. John Gifford, merchant in London, Jan., 1734-5. Mr. C[ollingwood] consented to a reduction of interest to 4%."—P.R.]

COLSTON, WILLIAM, was born in London, and studied at Lisbon, where he was ordained Priest Nov. 13, 1678. In Sept., 1680, he came on the Mission, and was several years Agent for his College in London, and at his death bequeathed £25 per annum for the education of a student at Lisbon. He was chosen a member of the Chapter June 2, 1690, and died Dec. 4, 1695.

CONQUEST, BENEDICT, of Irnham, had a daughter who married Lord Arundell of Wardour. He died in 1753.

CONSTABLE, CUTHBERT (olim CUTHBERT TUNSTALL).—By the death of his two brothers the estate at Wycliff came to him, and to him Lord Dunbar had also bequeathed in tail Burton Constable. He took the name of Constable, and married first, Amy, fifth daughter of Hugh, second Lord Clifford, by Anne his wife, daughter of Sir Thomas Preston, Bart., and by her had William,

Cicely and Winifred. On the death of his uncle he settled at Burton Constable. Here he collected an extensive and well-chosen library of books and MSS. Among the latter is a volume of letters from Mr. Nicholson, formerly of University College, Oxford, to Mr. Cuthbert Constable. From these it appears that Mr. Abraham Woodhead's executor was Obadiah Walker, who left Mr. Woodhead's MSS. to Mr. Dean, of University, Mr. Nicholson, and Mr. Perkins ; that Mr. Dean hired Wilde House, near London, which being burnt down at the Revolution, some of the MSS. were also burnt or lost ; the rest were conveyed to Lisbon by Mr. Nicholson, that a warrant had been issued by James II. for the publication of his papers at Oxford by Mr. Walker ; that Mr. Constable applied to Mr. Nicholson for the MSS. with a promise that he would publish them. Mr. Nicholson consented and sent them over in January, 1728, and with them a sketch of Mr. Woodhead's life, "which may be depended upon," says Mr. Constable, "as to the facts, but being too bombastic, but very little can be taken from it." On this Mr. Constable applied to Mr. Hearne, Librarian of the Bodleian, and so well known for his antiquarian researches. A volume of his letters to Mr. Constable is at Burton Constable, but they contain little information on Mr. Woodhead. In a letter of Aug. 17, 1730, he says : " I always looked upon Mr. Abraham Woodhead to be one of the greatest men that ever the nation produced ;" and April 8, 1734, "I am sorry the life of that holy and learned man Mr. Abraham Woodhead, is at a stand for want of materials." Agreeably to the engagement entered into with Mr. Nicholson, Mr. Constable (before he came to the estate he studied Physic, and took his degree at Montpellier), published the third part of Mr. Woodhead's *Church Government* in 1736, and prefixed it to the life of him, taken principally from that of Mr. Nicholson, with such additions as he was able to collect elsewhere.

In 1732 Mr. Constable had Mr. Abraham Woodhead's grave opened, and after digging about a foot from the surface of the earth, a small but firm cemented arch was found, just sufficient to encompass the coffin, which being laid open the coffin was found to be decayed, and the bones, bare of flesh, were carefully gathered together and preserved decently until a new coffin was brought, in which they were deposited, and a handsome marble monument was erected to his memory by the pious care of Mr. Constable, and to that of a young lady of great merit, flanked and covered with white marble, on which was inscribed a Latin epitaph (see *Records Miscel. James II.*) collected from his character as found in the Register of University College, Oxford, and such other monuments as his very humble and retired life would permit ; " but not so perfectly," says Mr. Constable, "as we might wish, and far short of his great piety, virtue, and merit." The Epitaph designed for Mr. Woodhead when his body was to have been removed to the Chapel of University College is preserved in P. le Neve's Collection of Monuments. Mr. Woodhead's MSS.* are still at Burton Constable in the Room of MSS. over the kitchen and adjoining the great library, and also a volume of his letters to Dr. Wilby, a Catholic Physician at Oxford. The second and fourth parts of *Church Government* are also there in MS., with the approbation annexed of Father Gage, Dr. of Sorbonne, dated Aug. 1 and Sept. 19, 1662. Mr. Constable died March 27, 1746. He was one of those gentlemen who patronised Dodd, and contributed to the publication of his history. (See Dodd's letters to him among the *Records Miscel.*)

" Mr. Constable," says Mr. Nicholson, " was well versed in languages, ancient and modern, knowledge of books, and antiquity, and has held correspondence with the most eminent persons for learning in the kingdom, both Catholic and Protestant, particularly with the learned antiquary, the late Mr. Hearne." By his wife (who died July 25, 1721, in the twenty-sixth year of her age), he had issue William, Cecily, and Winifred ; Winifred died unmarried. Cecily married Edward Sheldon, and had two sons, Edward and Francis, to

---

* At the end of the Life Mr. Constable has given a much more complete catalogue of his works than is found in Dodd.

whom by his will William Constable gave both his estates of Burton Constable and Wycliff, and failing their issue, to Sir Thomas Clifford, his relative of his mother's lineage. Mr. Constable married second, Elizabeth Heneage, and by her had Marmaduke, who took the family name of Tunstall, and by his father's will the estate of Wycliff. "Mr. Nicholson," says Dr. Seth Ward, *alias* Dr. Ward, Bishop of Salisbury, "said of Mr. Abraham Woodhead's *Dr. Stillingfleet's principles considered*, it contained more reason than all the huge volumes written by Stillingfleet did."

MSS. AT BURTON CONSTABLE.—A thick volume of original letters from 1567 to 1625 to and from great men. Abraham Woodhead's *Ancient Church Government*, parts 2, 3, and 4 (parts 1, 2, and 3 printed). Original letters from Mr. Hearne and Mr. Nicholson. *An historical discourse on the Eucharist*, in four parts of 1,283 pages. *A translation of the Bible*, pp. 1,123, the beginning and end wanting. *Father Parson's Author of the Book of Titles*. *A folio translation in verse of all the Psalms*. *The Itinerant Missioner*, Tom. 6th and last. Curious and Controversial. *Mr. Knaresborough's Sufferings of Catholics who suffered under Elizabeth:* 1573. Thos. Woodhouse to William Southworth in 1654, with general histories of this reign ; in five volumes. Both Dodd and Bishop Challoner perused these MSS. of Mr. Knaresborough, and Dodd added some marginal notes. *A Journal of my travels since the Revolution*, and an account of the war in Ireland ; MS. by Mr. Stevens, a Catholic and continuator of Dugdale's Monasticon. A volume of *Mr. Woodhead's Letters* to Dr. Wilby, with Abraham Woodhead's life, and list of his books. Many other MSS. and pedigrees of most of the families in Yorkshire.

CONSTABLE, JOHN, S.J.—He lived many years in the Fitzherbert family, at Swinnerton, where he wrote the greater part, if not all the following learned works, which he published : 1st, in the year 1723 ; Père le Courayer published at Nancy, but with the date of Brussels, his *Dissertation sur la validité des ordinations Anglais* and *Sur la succession des Evêques de l'Eglise Anglicane*, in two volumes. Father Constable answered this work. When he had written the first part of his answer he sent it to Father Coxon, the Provincial, [? Procurator] of the Jesuits for his perusal, and the approbation of the Revisors. In his letter he lamented much the want of books in his retired situation, and suggests that if some careful persons could get admission to the Lambeth Register and the Cotton MSS., many important observations might be made. Before he published his answer a correspondence took place between him and Père le Courayer. Mr. Constable applied to the Père to obtain from England permission for a person to accept of the challenge that had been given to answer his work. In his answer Courayer expresses his surprise and astonishment that he should apply for the mediation of a stranger for such a purpose, and that in England, where everyone, he says, has such liberty to write what he pleases as for or against Religion ; yet professes his readiness to do his best to obtain his request ; at the same time advises him, as he has already waited three years, to wait three months longer, when he should publish an answer to all that had been written against his *Dissertation*. To this Mr. Constable very properly answered that Arians, Socinians, &c., have a liberty which Catholics have not in England, of writing their sentiments on Religion ; that lately a Catholic Printer was prosecuted for publishing a book taken chiefly from Protestant authors (Manning's *England's Conversion and Reformation compared*) ; that he wanted no other connivance and impunity honourably assured than what Courayer himself enjoyed in France after he had owned his work ; that if he had waited three years, it was because he had only seen the *Dissertation* about a year and a half ago ; that the answer only waited for the above honourable assurance, which he might with his credit so easily obtain, and the English could not refuse after adopting his challenge, and finally, no one, in his opinion, in England, will answer it so fairly and well as himself. When further pressed by Mr. Constable to obtain this honourable assurance of impunity, he pretended to have discovered, even from the beginning, that the whole was but a snare laid for his sincerity, and therefore refused to apply for it, as being in itself ridiculous and unnecessary, and might be abused. Mr. Constable reminded him that so far from suspecting a snare, he had in his first letter said that he was edified at the motive which induced him to write, and even promised to see what could be done to obtain his request when his second work should appear, which he would hardly have done had it been ridiculous. And to prevent any apprehension of the desired assurance being abused, he solemnly engaged that persons of eminent credit should be securities to the French Embassador or any other he should name, that the desired favour should be used with the moderation mentioned in his last letter. Finally Mr. Constable requests in a note that he will barely insert in *The Evening Post* that " Mr. B. may depend," &c. Courayer persisted in his refusal, and here the correspondence closed. Mr. Constable, however, published his answer to Courayer's *Dissertation* with this title : [*Remarks upon F. le Courayer's Book in defence of the English Ordinations*]. Of his performance I find the following general character given in a letter to an eminent Divine to whom Mr. Coxon had submitted the MS. : " As the subject of this book is of great consequence, so is the performance most excellent. I do not know that anything has appeared these fifty years in this kingdom of greater advantage to the Church and credit to us." 2. In 1726 Courayer published *Défense de la Dissertation sur la validité*, &c., in four vols. Mr. Constable answered it in *The Stratagem discovered, or an Essay or an apology for F. le Courayer's late work in four vols. entitled : "Defence of the Dissertation, etc. ;"* wherein strong instances are produced to show that he writes *Booty*,* and is only a *sham defender* of those ordinations, while he very much confirms the judgment of their invalidity, and at the same time all that might seem seriously urged by him in their defence is fairly answered by Clerophilus Alethes, Dec. 30, 1727. 3. *The Convocation Controvertist* advised against pursuing wrong methods in his endeavours to reduce Dissenters and convince Catholics, in which is annexed a letter in the name of the Church of England to Dr. Trapp upon his strange libel entitled *Popery Stated*, by Clerophilus Alethes. *Qui consilium dat, fidem non eventum, praestare debet*, printed An. 1729. The MS. is at Aston. 4. *De Styli ratione accurata*. In English, under the name of Eudoxius. 5. *Epistolae Eudoxianæ, Eruditionis variae argumentis miscellaneae.* They are written with great elegance, and contain his judgment of the writings of Bongarsius, Postellus, Lord Bacon, Lipsius, &c. 6. *De Novi Testamenti auctoritate.* 7. *The Doctrine of Antiquity concerning the most blessed Eucharist*, by Clerophilus Alethes, printed in 1736, but sent with a letter to Mr. N. N., for whom it was first written, Oct. 15, 1714. 8. *A specimen of amendments candidly proposed to the compiler of a work which he calls "The Church History of England,"* etc., by Clerophilus Alethes, 1741. In 1742 Dodd published his *Apology for the Church History of England, being a reply to a quarrelsome libel intitled "A specimen of amendments, etc."* 9. *Advice to the Author of the Church History of England, in answer to it and to his Apology.* MS. of 241 pages dated Jan. 3, 1742-3. Mr. C. Plowden in a letter to William Talbot, of Castle Talbot, Esq., dated April 5, 1804, in my possession says the MS. was then in his hands. 10. *Controversial Notes.* MS. in my possession.

CONSTABLE, MARMADUKE CUTHBERT [OR TUNSTALL], of Wycliffe, was son of Cuthbert Tunstall Constable by his second wife, Elizabeth, daughter of George Heneage, of Hainton, by his wife Elizabeth, daughter of Sir H. Hunloke, Bart. He was educated at Douay College, and on the death of his father succeeded to the Wycliff Estate. He married a Miss Markham, of Hoxly, Lincolnshire, " whose constant and affectionate attention to him," says Dr. Pegge, " together with a taste like his own for retired life, rendered them perfectly happy in each other. Had it not been for their predilection for retirement, their suavity of manners and cheerful, polite conversation would have been a great acquisition to society. He was selected F.S.A. in 1764 and F.R.S. in 1777, and was honoured with the correspondence of many distinguished literary characters, at home and abroad. His morals were the

---

* *To play Booty* is to join other confederates in order to victimise some third party—the confidence trick. (See Murrray's *Oxford Dictionary* under *Booty*).

morals enforced by our common Lord and Saviour in the Sermon on the Mount. He was a friend to merit in distress, however distant the object, and it is hard to say whether his domestics, his tenants, or the poor will most lament his death. In a word this excellent man believed what he professed, and acted upon principle, and though his mode of faith was in many articles different from mine, may my soul be with his." Such was the character given of Mr. Tunstall after his death, which happened at Wycliff Hall, on Monday, Oct. 11, 1790, by Rev. Dr. Pegge, a Clergyman of the Church of England. (*Literary Anecdotes of eighteenth century, viii.*, 473.)

Mr. Tunstall formed a noble library, and had a large collection of fine and valuable prints, both of which did equal honour to his good taste. And such was the pleasure he took in the study of Natural History and Antiquities that few private gentlemen possessed a museum containing so large a collection, especially of the feathered race, or such a cabinet of antiques. After his death his estates devolved upon his nephew, Francis Sheldon, Esq., who, succeeding also to the estates of Burton Constable, took the name of Constable, and removed the museum and part of the library to Burton Constable, when the remainder was sold to Mr. Todd, bookseller, in York.

"Mr. Constable," says Mr. Watson, Rector of Middleton Tyas, in Yorkshire, "was not a friend to establishments in religion, but a warm advocate for a general toleration. He spoke with abhorrence of religion being taken up as the luxury of a party." Mr. Tunstall's widow was well known for her charitable assistance to the needy and distressed, for her large contributions to the suffering French Clergy and their English establishment when driven from their native land in 1794, and for her foundation of the Monastery of the Visitation Nuns, in 1804, at Shepton Mallet, where she lived in seclusion, reserving for herself from a large fortune a jointure above sufficiency for her life. There she died, ——, or at Spettisbury? Mr. Tunstall had four aunts, nuns at St. Monica's, Louvain, daughters of Francis Tunstall, Esq., who died at Wycliff in 1713, aged 61. Ann died March 14, 1758, aged 80, Jubilarian ten years; Mary, who died Aug. 18, 1770, aged 88, Jubilarian 18 years; Cecilia, who died June 30, 1775, aged 88, Jubilarian 21 years. His uncle, Marmaduke, son of the above Francis, died without issue in 1760, in the 90th year of his age.

CONSTABLE MAXWELL, MARMADUKE, of Terregles and Everingham. Died at Abbeville June 29, 1819, aged 58.

CONSTABLE, ROBERT, S.J., son of John Constable and Ann Otterbourn, born Oct. 7, 1705 (O.S.), in Yorkshire. He studied his Classics at St. Omers, and thence proceeded to Rome, where he was admitted into the College by Cardinal Gualterio, and was placed by the Rector, Father Eberson, on one of the Free Funds. He was ordained Sept. 18, 1728, by Benedict XIII., and July 19, 1729, went to Watten, and became a Jesuit. (*Annals of the Roman College.*)

CONSTABLE, ROBERT, third Viscount Dunbar, son of John, second Viscount. He succeeded his father about 1665.

CONSTABLE, SIR THOMAS, BART., was eldest son of Hon. Thomas Clifford and Barbara Aston, of Tixall. He was born Dec. 4, 1762, and when young was sent to the Academy at Liège, which the English ex-Jesuits had opened there after their expulsion from Bruges. Soon after the death of his father he married Miss —. Chichester, of Arlington, Co. Devon, and by her had one son and two daughters. In 1815 he was created a Baronet by George IV., at the request, as it is said, of Louis XVIII., and on the death of the late Mr. Constable without male issue, he came into possession of Burton Constable, which had been entailed upon him by William Constable, Esq., whose mother was a Miss Clifford, daughter of Lord Clifford of Chudleigh. He then took the name of Constable, but did not live long to enjoy this great addition to his property. He died at Ghent, February 25, 1823. Sir Thomas was a most respectable and zealous Catholic, and was much looked up to and beloved by

all who knew him for his affability, generosity, zeal of religion, and charities
to the poor, who always found a friend and protector in him.   He has left us
Meditations for every day in Lent, taken principally from the *Evangile Médité*.

CONSTABLE, WILLIAM, fourth Viscount Dunbar, son of John, third
Viscount.   He died without issue, when the title became extinct.   His sister,
Cecily, married Francis Tunstall of Scargill Castle, whose son Cuthbert took
the name of Constable, and died in 1745, leaving William an only son.

CONSTABLE, WILLIAM LORD.—William Constable, Lord Viscount Dunbar
of Scotland, married Elizabeth, eldest daughter of Hugh, third Lord Clifford,
and Anne Preston, who after his death married, in 1729, Charles Fairfax,
of Gilling, only son of Thomas Lord Viscount Fairfax.   Lord Dunbar died in
1718.   His daughter Cecily married Francis Tunstall, of Wycliff, who was
the generous and distinguished friend of Bishop Smith, and at the Revolution
dared to receive him into his house, and had the charity to make the Bishop
consider his house as his home.   He died in 1713, leaving three sons, Marmaduke, Cuthbert, and Matthias.

CONSTABLE, WILLIAM, second son of Sir Carnaby Haggerston, Bart., and
his wife Elizabeth, daughter, and after the decease of her brother William,
who died without issue in 1763, heiress of Peter Middleton, of Middleton, Esq.
He took the name of Constable, and married Lady Winifred Maxwell, daughter
of the Earl of Nithisdale.   Their second son, William, took the name of
Middleton, and is the present owner of Stubham and Stockheld.

CONSTABLE, WILLIAM, was son of Cuthbert by his first wife, Amy Clifford.
He succeeded his father in the Burton Constable establishment in 1749, and his
half-brother, Marmaduke, in that of Wycliff, and thus both estates were
united.   Though the son of most virtuous parents he followed not their good
example, but associated himself with freethinkers and libertines.   Rousseau
was his guest for some time, and he imbibed many of his principles, &c.
When his end drew near, and Dr. Howard, *alias* Formby, who was the Priest
of the Congregation, offered him his assistance, he said : " For my part I
believe nothing ;" or words to that effect, and expired soon after.   By his
death without issue the estates of Burton Constable came by his will to his
nephew, Edward Sheldon.

COOMBES, WILLIAM, studied at Douay, where he distinguished himself by
his talents and application, particularly in his classical studies and his knowledge of Greek.   He resided in the Western district and at Bath, where he
was General Vicar to the Bishop, and where he was greatly respected by
Clergy and Laity.   He died at Bath, April 18, 1822.

CONYERS, JOHN, S.J., was son of James and Elizabeth Conyers.   At the
age of seventeen he was sent to Rome, and by order of Cardinal Howard was
received into the College by Father Postgate, the Rector, Oct. 24, 1693, when
he began Philosophy.   On the seventh of the following May he left the College
and entered the Noviciate of St. Andrew on the Quirinal, and became a Jesuit.
(*Annals of the English College at Rome.*)

CORDELL, CHARLES, was educated at Douay. [Began Philosophy at
Douay in 1739.]   He left Douay June 10, 1748 (*Douay Diary* iii., 284), and by
the end of that month was acting as Chaplain in Arundel Castle, where he
remained at least until April, 1755.   The last entry made by him in the Register
is dated March 30, 1755.   On his arrival in England he assisted the Catholics
at Roundhay, in Yorkshire, and in the Isle of Man and at Newcastle.   When Mr.
Thomas Gibson, uncle to Bishop Gibson, died at Newcastle-on-Tyne in 1764,
and Mr. Jones quitted after two years' residence, Mr. Cordell succeeded him
at the Clergy Chapel in Newgate Street, and continued there until his death,
Jan. 27, 1790 [Jan. 26, 1791].   Mr. Cordell was a learned and zealous Priest,
and was particularly admired for his method of preaching, which was easy,
pleasing, and instructive.   In 1778, when Mr. Wilkinson wished to resign the
government of St. Omers College, and Mr. Arthur Storey refused to accept of

it, the situation was offered to Mr. Cordell, but he declined the honour. In politics Mr. Cordell was attached to the exiled family, and was called a Jacobite. On the supression of the Society of the Jesuits he deemed it his duty to step forward in defence of the conduct of Clement XIV. against the attack made upon him in the Newcastle papers by Mr. Warrilow, of the Jesuits' Chapel there, who asserted that the Pope had assigned no reasons for the suppression. In this and some other skirmishes with the same gentleman, Mr. Cordell is acknowledged, says Mr. James Worswick, of Newcastle, to have shewn his superiority as a writer. Mr. Cordell was a Correspondent Member of the R.S.S.A. in 1786.

Mr. Cordell published : 1. *The Divine Office*, being a translation of the *Roman Missal*, in four vols., 8vo. Published by [?] Magres. 2. *Ganganelli's Letters*. A translation from the French of Carracciolo. 3. *The Travels of Reason*, of Dr. Gillow Fronsletin. 4. *Bergier's Deism self-refuted*. Translated from the French answer to Rousseau's *Emile*. 5. *Fleury's Manners of the Israelites and Christians*. Translated. 6. *A letter to the author of a book called "A candid and impartial Sketch of the Life and Government of Pope Clement XIV."* 1785. This sketch consists of letters written from Rome by Mr. John Thorp, an ex-Jesuit, and is a collection of what was said of Ganganelli in Rome by his enemies, and the friends of the extinct Society. The writer pursues him from "the village to the throne, through every convent in which he lived." The letters were sent by Mr. Thorp to Mr. Charles Plowden, who was then tutor to Mr. Weld's sons at Lulworth Castle, and who is supposed to have published them. I was the bearer of one packet directed to Mr. Plowden, and I know of two others sent by students who left the College *re infecta*. "The contents," says Mr. Cordell, "tend to render the late head of the Church odious and contemptible in the eyes of the Christian world. It is in vain to deny that this is your design. . . . It is evident that as things now stand, you cannot thereby benefit the late Society, and it is equally plain that you afford subject of scandal to the children of the Church, and of triumph to her enemies. . . . Admitting then, for a moment, Clement XIV. to have been *as bad a man* as you seem to suppose, is it for you, Sir, to propagate his infamy?" This work was deemed so scandalous, said Dr. Milner to me and others at Oscott, that Mr. Weld insisted on the suppression of it. Accordingly it was suppressed, and from 1785, when I saw it in Coghlan's shop, though with the date of Ireland, I have never been able to find it, and know of no one who has ever seen it. In 1783 or 4 Messrs. Plowden and Thorp called on me in the College, and in a long conversation I heard from them several anecdotes respecting Ganganelli, which greatly scandalised me. Whence I have no doubt of the writer and publisher.

CORNE, JAMES, nephew of Mr. Charles Corne, was born at Betley. He studied at Douay, where he distinguished himself by his talents, application and regularity. He was for some time spiritual director at Sedgley Park, and in 1783 was placed at Shrewsbury. He was a gentleman of deep and general literature, and also of the most edifying piety, in the sentiments of which he prepared himself for a long time for his dissolution, which took place at Shrewsbury, Dec. 4, 1817. (*Catholicon*, vol. v., no. 30, p. 250.)

CORNE, JOHN, brother of the above, studied at Douay. He lived at Cobridge, in the Potteries, where he built a Chapel, and another at Stafford, "whither he was removed in 1784," said Mr. G. Beeston, "on his failing in business in the Potteries." From Stafford he went to Linley in 1804, and in 1806 to Harvington, where he died, Aug. 4, 1817. Bishop Milner said James Corne was all soul, John all body. James was desirous of solid knowledge, John of gossip.

CORNETHWAITE, RICHARD.—Studied at Douay, when he came on the Mission, was for a short time at Sedgley Park. He succeeded Bishop Thomas Talbot, at Brockington, near Havant, in 1778, if not sooner. After the death of Mr. Munford he was made Procurator of St. Omers, and was of great

service to the College in that capacity. At the beginning of the French
Revolution attempts were made by the Jacobins to involve him in plots against
the Convention,* when he deemed it prudent to withdraw, and come over to
England. He then settled at Harvington, in Worcestershire, and died there
Sept. 11, 1803.

CORNFORTH, THOMAS.—Was educated at Douay. Lived some time with
——Scroop, of Danby, Esq., and died at Shaftesbury, Aug. 5, 1749. He had
the character of being " an honest, worthy, and zealous labourer." He was a
member of the Chapter, and July 14, 1739, was chosen Archdeacon. " He was
an author," says Mr. Thomas Berington, the Dean of the Chapter, " and that
in folio too, but his whole piece consists of one sheet of paper to be hung in a
frame." I have not discovered the title or subject of his work. (See Berington's Letter, Sept. 27, 1745.)

CORNWALL, JOHN MAILS, was educated at Douay, and was afterwards
many years Confessor to the Benedictine Dames at Dunkirk, where he died
January 6th, 1756.

COWBAN, JOHN, was born in the Fylde, and educated at Douay. He was
missionary some time [at Exeter], and Cottam, near Preston, and afterwards
many years at Crathorne, in Cleveland. Having laboured more than forty
years on the mission, he died at Crathorne, Oct. 6, 1777.

COYNEY, EDWARD, son of Mark Coyney, and brother of John Coyney,
Esq., who succeeded to the Weston Coyney Estates after the death of
Wm. Gower, who was killed in a duel Feb., 1725 (O.S.), and who was son to
Wm. Gower, Esq., who married Helen Coyney, sole heiress of John Coyney,
Esq., of Weston Coyney, near Cheadle, Staffordshire. Edward was sent to
Douay, and when he came on the Mission lived sometime with his aunt, Mrs.
Antony Hill, at Offley Park, then at Bramshall, near Uttoxeter, and lastly at
Weston Coyney and at Paynsley, the seat of Lord Langdale, where it is thought
he died, and was buried at Draycott. Mr. Coyney was highly respected by
his brethren, and was entrusted by them with the management of their property
after the death of Mr. Francis Fitter and Mr. Pegg. " As the times in which
he lived were troublesome," says his niece, Mrs. Newton, and aunt to Mrs.
Coyney, " he was obliged to disguise himself as a bagpipe player or a pedlar in
order to gain admittance into Catholic families." Mr. Coyney died Sept. 27,
1722.

CRATHORNE, ——, the last Abbot of Sismer, a monastery in the Diocese
of Lubeck and Duchy of Holstein. It was made over to the English
Benedictines on certain conditions, May 18, 1628, and was confirmed by the
Emperor Frederick II., April 22, 1629. Another Monastery, called Rintilin,
in the diocese of Minden, was made over to them by the Brussels Congregation on Aug. 29, 1629. Also about the same time they obtained the Abbey of
Dobran, in the dukedom of Mecklenburg ; Scharnabeck, in Luneberg ; Weine,
in Brunswick ; and Lamspring, in Hildesheim. But revolutionary rapacity and
infidelity have unfortunately deprived them of all.

CRATHORNE, FRANCIS.—After staying some time at Sedgley Park, he
went to Valladolid, and was ordained Priest there. On his return to England
he was placed at Garswood, in Lancashire. He had a good knowledge of
Physic and practised it very successfully, chiefly amongst the poor in his
neighbourhood. Being invited by Mr. Gerrard to accompany him and others
on a fishing party at Southport, the boat was unfortunately upset, and Mr. Gerrard
with Mr. Crathorne and two or three others were all drowned, May 23, 1822.

CRATHORNE, WILLIAM, *alias* AUGUSTIN SHEPHERD, probably of the
Crathornes of Ness, Co. York, studied at Douay, where he was ordained, and
for some years was " Confessarius, Proner,† and Prefect of Studies." On account

---

* Some malicious person forged a letter, and signed Mr. Cornethwaite's name to it, and
dropped it on the ramparts, where it was found, and was pronounced to be treasonable, and conspiring against the Convention !   † "Proner," *i.e.*, Prefect of *Prônes* or Sermons.

of his infirmities he left the College in Sept., 1707. Hammersmith was the theatre of his missionary labours, where he had also the charge of the nunnery. He lived with Bishop Giffard, who commissioned him to collect all the published and unpublished spiritual works of Mr. Gother, which were published in 1718, if not sooner, by Meighan, in sixteen vols. The translation of the Missal Mr. Crathorne did not deem the production of Mr. Gother, and would not allow Mr. Meighan to publish it as his. This roused the zeal of the Rev. Mr. Vane, the Agent of Lisbon College, who, in a letter to Mr. Crathorne, says : " July 13, 1718.—After Mr. Gother's decease the Superior of Lisbon College sent over to me a manuscript of his, writ in his own hand, in order to have it printed for the good of that family and others. This book I brought to Bishop Giffard, who ordered it to be examined and read, which was done, and approved of as a most excellent piece. The book of Epistles and Gospels is in Bishop Giffard's own custody, whose hand, as he told me yesterday, is so well known to him, that it is inimitable, as well as the author " (*Chap. Coll.*, vol. i., p. 597). This letter satisfied Mr. Crathorne that the work was Mr. Gother's, and the Missal was published in two vols. Mr. Crathorne was a member of the Chapter, and died at Hammersmith, March 11, 1739 (O.S.). He was a zealous and indefatigible Missionary, and " was seldom without his pen in his hand." His works are numerous, of which I find the following list, but some of them were published after his death. (In the list that I allude to, it is not said that they are the works of Mr. Crathorne ; but some of them certainly were his, and hence I conclude they were all his.)

1. *The Life of St. Francis of Sales*, by Marsolier, translated from the French. 2. *The Life of our Lord Jesus Christ*, translated also from the French. 3. *Fleury's Historical Catechism*, do., do. 4. *Lessons for Lent, or Instructions on the Sacraments of Penance and the Blessed Eucharist.* 5. *A Practical Catechism on the Sundays, Feasts and Fasts of the whole year,* 1749. 6. *Daily Companion, or Morning Prayers,* &c. 7. *Account of a Miracle.* Stitched, 1s. 8. *Catholic Reasons for not becoming a Protestant.* 4d. 9. *Abstract of Christianity.* 10. *Practical Reflections.*

CREIGHTON, HENRY, O.P., born in London of Catholic parents, Aug. 25, 1750. Was received into the College at Rome by Father Hothersall, the Rector, Jan. 16, 1767. After remaining there three years and a half he went to Viterbo to enter among the Dominicans, Aug. 23, 1770.

CROSS, BERNARD, S.J., was born April 8, 1715. He entered his noviceship May 8, 1737, and was professed Aug. 15, 1755. He was missionary at Worcester, and died there, much respected, April 22, 1785.

CROSS, NICHOLAS, O.S.F., was Chaplain-in-Ordinary to the Queen, and has left us *A Sermon*, preached before her at Windsor, April 21, 1686 : *On the Joys of Heaven.* Ps. 83, v. 5.

CROSS, THOMAS, S.J., was born Nov. 7, 1739; entered his noviceship Sept. 7, 1758 ; was professed, and made his three vows. He lived many years at Spinkhill, in Derbyshire, was highly respected and beloved by his congregation and aquaintances. Towards the close of his life he retired to Holbech, where part of the Spinkhill Congregation lived, and died there, Oct. 18, 1813.

CUERDON, THOMAS, S.J., was born June 25, 1718, entered his noviceship Sept. 7, 1737, and was professed Feb. 2, 1755. He succeeded Fr. Hunter at Westby, near Lytham in the Fylde, and died March 31, 1793.

DALTON, JOHN [HOGHTON], of Thurnham, Co. Lancaster, where he possessed a good estate. He was tried at the Marshalsea, May 30, 1716, for being a party in the rebellion of 1715, and was found guilty. In his defence his counsel stated that he was forced into the rebellion, and one witness swore that the Earl of Derwentwater and others came to his house on Tuesday, Nov. 8, and there lived at discretion and called for and took whatever the house afforded, that when persuaded by them he refused to go, said he had no inclination, but they threatened him with death and took away his arms. The clergyman of his parish in particular deposed that, hearing Mr. Dalton read a letter in which it said that many were expected to rise both in Scotland and England, he said he hoped he would not meddle in the matter; to which Mr. Dalton answered that he had neither intention nor inclination to do it, that he lived very happily and would not endanger himself. He added that, though he had frequently discoursed with the prisoner, he never heard him express himself against the government, and gave him the character of a very peaceable Roman Catholic, as several others did. One in particular deposed that, when he heard of the rebellion in Northumberland, he said to the prisoner: "Perhaps they will come into Lancashire and then they will be about your house," that the prisoner answered he would have nothing to do with them. This and other witnesses said that Mr. Dalton was the most peaceable of all the Roman Catholics, and never at the time of elections meddled in the least as some did. One of the members for the County justified this, declaring that when he once asked his interest he told him he would meddle on no side. The jury went out and after a very considerable stay brought him in *Guilty*. Before sentence was passed he said he begged the King's pardon, and desired the Court to intercede with him for mercy. The Commissioners valued his estates at £1,588 12 6 per annum, which became forfeited as well as £385 15 6 of personalty. John Dalton married Frances, second daughter of Sir Pyers Mostyn, second Bart. of Talacre, and Frances Selby, his wife.

DALTON, MARMADUKE, *alias* JOSEPH BOOTH. His mother was daughter of the old Lord D'Arcy, "who used to say he had lived to see many scores out of his loins, and yet not one idolator amongst them." He was sent to study at Cambridge, but after his father's death he became a Catholic, with the assistance of Mr. Richard Franks, at that time General Vicar under the Dean and Chapter of all the northern counties, including Nottingham, Rutland and Lincolnshire. This so offended his mother that she would scarcely look on him after, and though extremely rich, left him little or nothing at her death. His father, however, had settled on him an annuity of £40; sufficient in those days to support him. After he became a Catholic he went over to Douay, but being sent away in the latter part of Dr. Leyburn's presidentship, "not for any fault, but what was common to the best of the house," to whom his government was obnoxious, he received dimissorials from the Dean and Chapter, and being ordained Priest in Ireland, about 1670, received his faculties from them and resided near Wycliff in Yorkshire. In his person he was somewhat contemptible, but was far from being so in wisdom and virtues. He was a "very temperate, discreet and true-hearted brother; had an excellent pen, and was most zealous for the good of the Dean and Chapter, and after the death of Mr. Meynell managed the concerns of Douay College in Yorkshire." As in life, so at his death, he proved himself a true friend to the poor Catholics about Crathorne, in Cleveland, and Wycliff. "He died," says Bishop Smith to Mr. Barlow his G.V. in Lancashire, "April 5, 1695, at Burniston, at an ale-house upon the road, being taken ill on his way from Fountains to Wycliff; in him we have lost a zealous brother."

DANIEL, EDWARD, *alias* BARRET. He was related to the Tootells in Lancashire. He studied at Douay and exercised his missionary faculties at Scorton, near Garstang. As he was rather too active in 1745, he was obliged to leave his mission and go abroad. On his return to England, he was placed at Hornby or Robert Hall, near Lancaster. He afterwards removed to Scarbro', and died at York, May 1, 1765.

DANIEL, EDWARD, brother to the President, also from Douay, lived in Lancashire, and died there, April 13, 1819. He wrote:
The Divine Economy of the Church of Christ. An original work and betrays an eccentricity of character in the author.

DANIEL, JOHN, born in Lancashire on Nov. 16, 1755. On Jan. 25, 1768, he was admitted into the College at Rome by order of Cardinal Lante, the Protector, then under Father Hothersall, the last Jesuit Rector. On the dismissal of the English and the introduction of Italian Superiors into the College, Mr. Daniel obtained leave, Jan. 28, 1774 [from Card. Corsini, the Protector], to go to Douay, where he completed his studies and, being ordained Priest, had the care of a congregation, first in Northumberland, and then settled at Stockton-upon-Tees, where he died, Feb. 17, 1802.

DANIEL, JOHN, a native of Lancashire, was sent to Douay, where he distinguished himself by his talents, regularity, and piety. For several years he taught Philosophy, and Divinity from 1778 to the period of the French Revolution. On the retirement of Mr. Kitchen from the Presidentship, he succeeded him in 1792, and with his Seniors, Professors and Students was conveyed prisoner, first to Arras and then to Dourlens, where he continued till Nov. 27, 1794.* They were then removed to the Irish College in Douay, and in February of the following year were allowed to return to England. Mr. Daniel, however, deemed it necessary for him soon after to go to Paris to watch over the concerns of his College, and prevent, if possible, the entire loss of the property belonging to it. He resided in the Seminary of St. Gregory, and spared no pains to recover the property of his College and that of the other British establishments. He died at Paris, Oct. 3, 1823.

He wrote : *The Ecclesiastical History of the Britons and Saxons.* 8vo.

DANIEL, RICHARD, son of Edward Daniel and Grace Carter, was a native of Lancashire. At the age of 17 was admitted into the College at Rome by Father Postgate, Nov. 19, 1704 [when he began Logic]. He was ordained Priest at St. John Lateran's, April 19, 1710, and left the College, April 13, 1712, to go to Antwerp, where he was made Confessor to the English nuns in that city. He died Feb. 20, 1753.

DANIEL, THOMAS, born in Lancashire Mar. 20, 1714, (O.S.), was educated at Douay and returned to England Aug. 5, 1740, when he was placed at York, Aug. 5, and where he succeeded Mr. Bryan Tunstall as agent for the Brethren of Yorkshire. He also assisted the Catholics at Linton-upon-Ouse, and was G.V. to Bishop Francis Petre. In 1745 [July 11, 1743] he was chosen a member of the Chapter. [He lived in Blake Street, York, in 1768.]. He died at York, Aug. 25, 1770.

His brother, William, *alias* Foster [Mr. Foster was their uncle], was also educated at Douay. He lived some time with Sir William Vavasour at Hazlewood, in Yorkshire, and afterwards at Euxton Hall, in Lancashire, where he died, July 25, 1777.

Another William Daniel, educated at Douay, was Confessor to the Blue Nuns at Paris, and died there Feb. 9, 1761.

DARBYSHIRE, DOMINIC, O.P. After teaching the classics at Bornheim he was chosen to fill the different offices in his province, which he did with great credit to himself and advantage to his Brethren. He was at last chosen Prior of Bornheim, and died there in 1757, in the 68th year of his age, 46th of Religion, and 44th of his Priesthood.

DAVIES, CHARLES *or* SAMUEL, son of Thomas and Blanche Davies, was born in Montgomeryshire. At the age of 20 he was admitted into the English College at Rome, then in the administration of Father Robert Mansfield, Oct. 8, 1699. He was ordained Priest Mar. 22, 1704, and left the College April 15, 1706, to go to Paris. His Missionary labours were at Llanarth, where he lived in the family of —— Jones, Esq., for 54 years, much respected and beloved, and died there Mar. 20, 1761, aged 84.

DAVIES, JAMES, was elder brother to Charles and was educated with him and ordained at Rome, Oct. 10, 1694, where he was admitted [by order of Cardinal Howard] with him Oct. 25, 1690, aged 23. He came on the Mission in 1696 [Mar. 10]. Probably the same with John Davies, who died in London in 1753, and, if so, must have been 86 years old when he died.

---

* See Mr. Hodgson's Narrative of the seizure of Douay College in the *Catholic Magazine*, I., p. 14 and *sqq.*, &c. Observations on Mr. Daniel's Claims, p. 107.

DAVIES, ROWLAND, in his youth was a pupil of Handel, and made such progress under him that it is said he presided at the organ in Westminster Abbey at the coronation of George III.   Some time after that event he became a Catholic and, going over to Douay, was ordained Priest, and taught the Classics and Philosophy, and on his coming on the Missions had the care of the Catholics at and about Clints in Yorkshire.   For some time he served at Warwick Street, in London, and at last settled at Bosworth, in the family of Francis Fortescue Turvile, Esq., where, as he had been in every other situation, he was much loved and respected, and where he died Mar. 16, 1797. He set to music many Masses, a *Te Deum*, a *Magnificat*, Responsories for the Dead, &c.

DAVIES, ——, *alias* POLLET.

DAY, THOMAS, was a native of Wales.   At Douay he displayed considerable talents, and taught Rhetoric. [He was adverse to Dr. P——'s reform].   He lived chiefly in London after he came on the Mission, and was in high estimation among his Brethren.   He was chosen a member of the Chapter [on Mar. 10, 1711, (O.S.), made Treasurer], and in 1712 Archdeacon, and in the second session of the General Assembly of the Chapter he was chosen Dean [July 12, 1732], on the death of Thomas Berington, and presided in that Assembly, and also in those of 1736, 1739 and 1743.   He died in London, July 8, 1748, aged 83.

DEAN, THOMAS, *alias* PLOWDEN, S.J., [son of John Dean and Frances Plowden] was born at Cadiz.   His father was a native of Ireland and by the rules of the College at Rome he was not admissible, as it was founded solely for English, but by special licence, obtained from Clement XI, he was admitted in his 14th year by Father Postgate, Dec. 14, 1706.   After remaining in the College, *on the College Funds*, three years, he repaired to the Noviceship at Monte Cavallo, Dec. 20, 1709, and became a Jesuit.

DEBORD, JOHN, *alias* DAWSON [? DAVISON], was born Jan. 24, 1715.   He took the College oath May 25, 1734.   *Semper primus aut inter primos in litteris humanioribus*, says the *Douay Diary*.   He was a native of Darton [?Durham].   On his return from Douay he settled at New-house, Esh, near Darton, Dec. 10, 1740, but quitted it Aug. 11, 1744, to retire to Salwick, near Preston, where he died Sept. 29, 1775.   Mr. Debord was "a good Greek and Hebrew Scholler, and a solid Divine, yet modest and never boastful." [In Dr. Kirk's draft he is called Dabord, *alias* Davison. P.R.]

DICCONSON, EDWARD, BISHOP, was son of Hugh Dicconson, of Wrighting-ton, Esq., and his wife Agnes, daughter of Roger Kirkby, of Kirkby.   He studied at Douay.   On [Aug. 4] 1691, at the end of Philosophy, he came over to England, but soon returned to resume his studies.   Soon after he was ordained Priest, he was made Procurator,* and on the departure of one of the Rigbys he succeeded him as Professor of Divinity.   At the time of the troubles at Douay, when a charge of Jansenism was brought against the College, and Delcourt, the accuser, was appointed the Visitor, with another, Mr. Dicconson was very active in procuring his removal and in obtaining others more impartial.   These cleared the College entirely from the odious imputation.   Dr. Paston made him Vice-President, and on his death Mr. Dicconson announced to Propaganda his unqualified acceptance of the Bull *Unigenitus*.   Mr. Dicconson continued in the same office under Dr. Robert Witham and also taught Divinity, but resigned both situations July 13, 1720, and came on the Mission.   He lived some years in the family of Peter Giffard, Esq., at Chillington, and became Bishop Stoner's principal adviser as G.V. While here, as at Douay, he assisted Dodd in his work.   In 173—, he was sent to Rome to assist Mr. Mayes, the Clergy agent there, and for the particular purpose of reducing the English Franciscans to the observance of the Decree of Innocent XII., respecting Regulars when they came on the

---

* ["Bp. D——n resigns Procuratorship to Mr. Green in Sept., 1708."]. Note in Dr. Kirk's draft.

Mission. In this he succeeded, but failed in another object of his journey, which was to procure the removal of the Jesuits from the administration of the College and to get it *restored* to the Clergy for whose benefit it was first founded, and to whose administration it was given by Gregory XIII. On the death of Bishop Williams, and while he was at Rome, he was appointed to succeed him in the Northern District, and was consecrated at Ghent by the Bishop of that place, on Passion Sunday, Mar. 19, 1741,* with the title *Episcopus Mallensis.* He chose for his residence a place belonging to his family, near Wrightington, called Finch Mill, whence the *Padri* styled him the *Auditor di Ruota.* Bishop Dicconson was very instrumental, together with Bishop Stonor and Bishop Petre, in procuring the Brief of Benedict XIV, *Apostolicum Ministerium,* which settled the rules of the Mission on a more firm footing than they had hitherto been. In 1750 he obtained of Benedict XIV. for his Coadjutor Mr. Francis Petre, of the family of Fitlers, and died at Finch Mill, April 24, 1752. In 1744 Bishop Challoner "begged to be informed of his sentiments concerning a proposal of an oath of allegiance, as he understood it was likely to be revived again before it was long." [This probably was in view of the approaching rebellion]. Bishop Dicconson left behind him *A Detailed Account of his Agency at Rome,* in 4 vols., MS., full of curious matter.

DICCONSON, ROGER, of Wrightington. His estates became forfeited to the Crown in 1715. They were valued by the Commissioners at £641 16 10 per annum.

DICCONSON, WILLIAM, Gent., was son of Hugh Dicconson, and Agnes, daughter of Roger Kirkby, of Kirkby, and elder brother of Bishop Dicconson. He followed the fortune of the exiled family to St. Germains, and there held the situation of Under-Governor to the young Prince, and of Treasurer to the Queen, and afterwards accompanied the Chevalier to Rome. He died at St. Germains-en-Laye, in 1743 [so says Fr. H. Lawson in his pedigrees]. His nephew, Edward Dicconson, of Wrightington, Esq., married Mary, second daughter of George Blount, Esq. She died Oct. 17, 1746.

DIGBY [?JOSEPH], "of noble descent and virtue," say my memoirs. He was educated at Douay, and when ordained was made General Prefect. He was afterwards appointed to the situation of Confessor to the Poor Clares of Dunkirk, and was a true father to them, and an example to the world of humility and charity, in the exercise of which he died in the 46th year of his age, in 1708. Mr. Cave succeeded him.

DIGGS, JOHN DUDLEY, *alias* HALL, was son of William and Elizabeth Diggs. He was born in Maryland, and studied his Classics at St. Omers. In 1712, being then twenty-three years old, he was received in the College at Rome by Father Plowden, the Rector, Oct. 17. He was ordained Priest April 20, 1715, and on Nov. 4, 1719, left the College for England, when he was placed at Ingatestone, where he lived nearly fifty years, and died in May, 1771.

DINMORE, ——. He appears to have studied and to have been ordained at Valladolid. He came on the Mission about the year 1680, and lived with Sir Solomon Swale, Bart., at Stanley, and in 1693 had been there about fourteen years. I do not find where he died or any other particulars of him, except, say the *Chapter Records,* "that he was a sober and prudent man."

DOBSON, THOMAS.—"Feb. 25, *Rev. T. Dobson,* Virginia Street, London. The circumstances which led to the imprisonment, and ultimately caused the death of this lamented Missionary, are surrounded by a melancholy interest, afford some insight into the hardships frequently attending suits in Chancery, and hold out a strong lesson of caution against clergymen consenting to act as executors or trustees." [Here follows a long account of how Mr. Dobson, as executor and trustee, after the lapse of many years, became, technically, a defaulter under the Chancery Laws and had a writ issued against him. He

---

* See Letter of Mgr. Tempi, Mar. 21 [1741], col. v. —, p. —.

was arrested in his vestry immediately after Mass and was thrown into the Fleet prison. "From the moment he entered the prison gates to the hour of his death, he never held up his head : he confined himself to his chamber, his appetite left him, his spirits entirely failed, and sleep became a stranger to his pillow. Kind friends liberally administered to his wants and his comforts, and strove to arouse him to exertion ; but all was in vain. In two months he had wasted to a skeleton, and was as feeble as a child ; in less than three months he was a corpse. He continued to the last reciting the divine office, but this was the only exertion of which he seemed capable. Before he was considered to be in danger, Master Brougham had reported favourably on his case to the Lord Chancellor, as one of great hardship, and hopes were held out of his speedy liberation, his brief reply was, ' I shall never go out alive !' At his own desire, the last Sacraments were administered to him on Feb. 17, on the 24th he became insensible, on the 25th he died. On the following Monday a solemn dirge was celebrated for his repose at Virginia Street chapel, which was attended by many of his brother clergymen and by a numerous congregation, and on the same day he was buried as he had directed, at St. George's in the East, in the same grave with his predecessors, the Rev. Mr. Coen and the late Rev. Mr. Daniel. A crowd, consisting of some thousands, followed him to his grave. Out of respect to his memory several of the shops were closed, and the many sobs that were heard and tears that were shed, proclaimed how deep was the impression that in him the poor had lost a kind friend, society a cherished ornament, and religion a pious and zealous pastor. R.I.P." (*Catholic Magazine and Review*, vol. vi., April, 1835, p. cxxvi.)

DODD, CHARLES, whose true name was Hugh Tootell. (See Memoir of him in *Catholicon*, vol. iv., p. 120.)

DORAN, JAMES [Apostate Priest].—The account given of him by Dr. Milner is the following : " He was an Irish Priest, who, after behaving scandalously in Ireland, went over to Cadiz, where he succeeded in obtaining a recommendation from a merchant to Bishop Challoner, who on the strength of it, employed him in the London District. There he gave no better example than he had in Ireland, and as no amendment appeared after repeated admonitions, Bishop Talbot suspended him. Against this Mr. Doran appealed to Rome, but not succeeding there, he threw off all restraint, and clandestinely married, in St. James' Church, the rich widow of a city merchant, who, after being kept by him, had been married to him at Winchester. With this woman Mr. Doran went down to her seat at Binfield, near Newbury, in quality of a chaplain, but was found to live with her as her husband. On her death-bed she entered seriously into herself through the means of good Mr. Lindow. Although she left to Mr. Doran all she had received from Mr. Duncastle except £1,000, he was dissatisfied, and after destroying the will, embezzled the whole. He married again, after he had been rejected by the sister of a noble Lord [?Abingdon], and in the end, shot himself with a pistol." Such is literally the account given me by Dr. Milner, and which he dictated to me at Wolverhampton.

DORMER, CHARLES, S.J., sixth Lord, was eldest son of Charles, fifth Lord Dormer, and Catharine, daughter of Edmund Fettyplace, Esq., of Suncombe, Oxon. He became a Jesuit, and on the death of his father, in 1728, succeeded to the title and Dormer estates ; the latter, however, he resigned to his second brother, reserving only a small annuity to himself. After his ordination he came on the Mission, and lived many years as chaplain of Mr. Massey, of Puddington, Cheshire, who succeeded to the title of Stanley, and took the name. In 1745 he was arrested as a Priest, and on suspicion of favouring Prince Charles and his army, which was then in the country retreating into Scotland. He is said to have liberated himself on that occasion by claiming his peerage. He died in Essex, March 7, 1761. Three of his half-brothers also became Jesuits. He was succeeded in his title by his second brother, who lived to be ninety-three years of age, and died Oct. 7, 1785.

DORMER, JOHN, S.J.—He was a preacher at the Court of St. James's, or whom we have: 1. *Sermons*, preached there and at Somerset House. 2. *Usury explained ;* or *Conscience quieted in the case of putting out Money at interest,* by Philopenes, London, 1696, and again in 1699. It was published in No. 21 of the *Pamphleteer,* 1817. This was written ostensibly against Thoranlier, a Doctor of Sorbonne, who had published, in 1672, *L'Usure expliquée et condamnée par les Ecritures Saintes,* under the name of Du Tertre ; but in fact it seems against Bishop Smith's treatise on the subject. "I should not," he says, "have concerned myself in answer to Monsr. Du Tertre's book, long since printed, as I question not, but already answered by some of his own nation, had not *his genius* passed the seas, and appeared with no other weapons than his, to the terror of timorous souls and perplexing of consciences." It was published again in 1699 with this title : *A vindication of the practice of England in putting out money at use.* In 1701 it was translated into Latin by Dr. Hawarden, S.T.D., and Vice-President of Douay : *summa fide, ut qui nostram minus intelligunt linguam, de ejus opinione, et scriptis judicium ferre possint.* It was then sent to Rome to be examined by the Holy Office, and was condemned ; and this among other things was the cause of the persecution which raged against him. 3. *A short justification touching the Oath of Allegiance, by way of Dialogue,* 1681. By J. D. (probably Father Dormer), in 12mo or 8vo pages, 4s. It is written against the oath. (See *Catholic Miscellany* for 1826, p. 254. *Oliver,* p. 67.—P.R.)

DORMER, ROBERT, S.J. Son of John, seventh Lord Dormer, was born Feb. 26, 1726, entered his Noviceship Sept. 7, 1743, and was professed Feb. 2, 1761. He lived at Wappenbury, near Coventry, and died there May 23 [May 4], 1792.

DOUGLASS, JOHN, V.A., D.D., Bishop of Centuria. He defended Universal Divinity *cum laude,* in 1768. Ten months after, in compliance with the wish of the President, he went to Valladolid, where he taught [Humanity and] Philosophy till 1773, when he returned on account of his health On the death of Bishop James Talbot, Bishop Matthew Gibson recommended him to succeed, and in his letter said : "Eboraci 17 annos vigilantissimi et obedientissimi Pastoris munia explevit." See *Catholic Magazine,* new series, 124.

DOWNS, RICHARD, *alias* HASKETT, son of Stephen and Christina Downs, was born in London, Sept. 20, 1694, and was admitted into the College at Rome, then under Father R. Plowden, Oct. 16, 1714 ; after having studied his Classics in London first, then at Douay for a short time, lastly at St. Omers. He was ordained Priest April 8, 1719, and on the following April [25, 1720] departed for England. His first place of Mission was Eastwell in Leicester-shire. At Midsummer, 1726, he succeeded Mr. Brown at Hathersage, in Derbyshire, and remained there some years [till April 15, 1730], when he removed to London and died there Aug. 22, 1774, aged 80.

DOYLY, JAMES, educated at Douay. After he had studied four years in the Seminary, of St. Nicholas, he was admitted into the English Seminary at Paris, partly at the expense of the Queen, and partly at that of the Seminary. In July, 1706, he was appointed Governor to the Duke of Norfolk and his brothers; from which time I found no other account, except he be the same with *William* Doyly [? Doyle], who died at Cowley Hill.

DRYDEN, SIR ERASMUS HENRY, BART., O.P., was third son of John Dryden, poet-laureate, by Elizabeth, eldest daughter of Henry Howard, Earl of Berkshire. Having studied his Philosophy at Douay, he was sent, at the age of 22, to Rome, and was received in the English College by Father Anthony Lucas, by order of Cardinal Howard, the Protector, Oct. 25, 1690, but left again Mar. 1, 1691, to go to Florence, where he entered among the Dominicans. He was in Rome with his brother Charles, in 1697, when he probably resided in the Convent of SS. John and Paul, on the Cœlian Hill, which Cardinal Howard had obtained for the English Dominicans. When he returned to England, he laboured on the Mission in Northamptonshire, his native county ; and on the death of his cousin, Sir John Dryden, Bart., without issue, he succeeded to the title. He died Dec. 3, 1710, and was buried at Canons Ashby, the family seat. At his death the title devolved on Sir Erasmus Dryden, his uncle, second son of Erasmus Dryden, of Tichmarsh. Sir Erasmus Henry Dryden, of whom we have been speaking, inherited the poetic vein of his father, whence he is styled in the Dominican Obituary, *Haud degener filius Poetae Dryden*, though I do not find that any specimen remains. He had two elder brothers, Charles and John. Charles was brought up at Trinity College, Cambridge, and had a genius for poetry, as appears by a copy of his verses, printed before the Earl of Roscommon's *Essay on Translated Verse*. After the Revolution he was made Usher of the Palace to Clement XI., and on his return was unfortunately drowned in swimming across the Thames, in 1704, at Datchet ferry, near Windsor. He wrote several pieces and translated the 6th [? 7th] Satire of Juvenal. John, the second son, went also to Rome and was entertained by the same Clement XI. as Gentleman of his bed-chamber. He likewise turned his thoughts to poetry ; translated the 14th Satire of Juvenal, and was author of a comedy entitled : *The Husband his own Cuckold*, printed in London, 1696. He died at Rome, of a pleurisy, not many months after his father, and was honourably interred there by the Pope's command. (*English Baronetage ;* Epitaph in Nichols' *Leicestershire*, ii., 692 ; *Annales Col. Angl. de Urbe. ;* Chalmer's *Biog. Dict.*)

DUNN, FRANCIS, from Douay, lived at Mr. Piggot's, at Whitton [near London], and died Feb. 19 [20], 1757.

DUNN, JOHN, born Jan. 27, 1718, in Lancashire, educated at Douay [began Philosophy Oct. 1, 1737], where he afterwards taught Philosophy first, and then Divinity, and while a student Dr. R. Witham, the President, gave this character of him ; " Dioceseos Cestrensis inter primos in sua classe, pius, prudens, et optimae spei adolescens." When he came on the Mission he lived at Croxdale, near Durham, then at Burton Constable, and last in London, where he succeeded Mr. Betts in the charge of the Clergy library, then left in Gray's Inn. He was "a most worthy man," says Mr. William Sheldon, of Gray's Inn, was a chapter-man and treasurer to the Chapter [and died Archdeacon]. He died suddenly immediately after saying Mass in Lincoln's Inn Fields Chapel, Jan. 14, 1778.

DUNN, JOSEPH, *vere* EARPE, S.J., brother to the Doctor, born Mar. 19, 1746, noviceship Sept, 7, 1764. Was the father of the Preston Congregation, where he built a large chapel, and was much respected and beloved.

DUNN, PETER, Priest, died Jan. 1723-4.

DUNN, WILLIAM, *vere* * EARPE, D.D., was born at Brough or Lartington in Yorkshire. Having completed his second year of Divinity at Douay he went to Paris, Oct. 13, 1772, entered his license Jan. 1, 1780, and was ordained the same year. He took the Cap in 1782, came on the Mission in [June] 1782, with Dr. Thomas Rigby. He was an excellent Missioner and the father of the Congregation at Blackburn, where he built the first chapel and, some years after, doubled its dimensions, and yet, at the period of his death, the chapel was not able to hold the Congregation. He was in great esteem there both with Catholics and Protestants. On Oct. 27, [1805], being Sunday, an *angina pectoris* struck him while saying the *Creed*, but he continued till the Post-Communion, when he was carried into the vestry, and expired while the persons around him took off his vestments.

DUVALL, EDWARD, was educated at Lisbon. When he came on the Mission he was placed in the family of Mr. Manby, in Essex, where he lived upwards of 50 years, and died there Dec. 25, 1778.

ECCLESTON, JAMES, *alias* GORSUCH, from Douay, was G.V. in Lancashire, and died there Jan. 19, 1738 (O.S.). He was also Archdeacon in the Chapter [Nov. 23, 1737].

---

* *St. Gregory's Register.*

ECCLESTON, THOMAS [*alias* HOLLAND AND GORSUCH], S.J., was son of
Henry Eccleston, Esq., of Eccleston, in Lancashire. It is said that he went
over to Ireland with James, and was wounded in a duel.* In his 18th
year he was admitted as a convictor into the College at Rome by Father
Christopher Anderton, Oct. 6, 1677. When he left [Oct. 3, 1679] he went into
France; but in 1697 returned to Rome, and entered into his Noviceship at St.
Andrew's, on the Quirinal Hill. He was seized in fee simple of property in
Eccleston of the yearly value of £352, which by becoming a Jesuit, he would
only hold for the use and benefit of the Society, and by the operation of law
was found to be given to Popish or Superstitious uses. This was discovered
by Richard Hitchmough Clerk, as certified by four of the Commissioners in
1723. A Thomas Eccleston was Dean of the Derby Hundred in Lancashire,
where he lived, and in 1694 gave £50 to the Common Fund. I am unable to
say whether they be the same; but he may have been Rural Dean before he
became a Jesuit. Mr. Eccleston wrote: *The Way to Happiness.* 8vo, 1726.
(*Annals of the College at Rome.*)

ECCLESTON, THOMAS, Esq., of Eccleston Hall, Lancashire, died there
May 23, 1789, aged 77.

ECCLESTON, THOMAS RALPH, *alias* SCARISBRICK, of Scarisbrick, died
there Nov. 1, 1809, aged 57. His son took the name of Scarisbrick.

EDEN, JAMES, *alias* CLARE, *ex*-S.J., was born in the Bishopric of Durham.
Having studied his Latin and Greek Classics in England, he went to Lisbon in
1683. In his first year of Divinity he took the College oath, and gown in Sept.,
1686, but was afterwards expelled for his misconduct. He then went into
Flanders, says the Lisbon *Register*, and was entertained at Watten by the English
Jesuits, and thence was sent to Rome, where he was admitted into the College
by Father Lucas, the Rector, Jan. 10, 1689, and in March, 1690, was ordained
Priest. He had taken the oath of Alexander VII., at Lisbon, but a dispensation was obtained, and "he entered the Society but was afterwards ejected,"
say the *Annals*, covering the reasons with an *Et cetera.*

EDISFORD, JAMES [?WILLIAM], son of William and Ann Edisford, was
a native of Yorkshire, and at the age of 18 went to Rome, and was admitted
into the College Oct. 18, 1691, under Father Lucas, by order of Cardinal
Howard. He was ordained March 2, 1697, and left for the Mission April 21
the same year. Mr. Roger Mitford left a fund for a Priest in the parish of
Rothbury, which was fixed at Thrapton,† in Northumberland. Mr. Edisford
was the first incumbent. He died in the early part of the eighteenth century,
and was succeeded by Mr. James Mitford, nephew of the founder.

EDMONDSON, HENRY, born at Broughton, in Lancashire, was son of
Richard Edmondson, by his wife, Helena Beesley. "He was taught by his
parents," says the *Obituary Letter*, "to fear God from his infancy; and being
sent to Douay College, was careful to join piety with his studies. Being ordained
Priest, he was sent on the Mission; but after labouring with great fruit for
some years in Lancashire, &c., was obliged by ill-health to retire to Flanders,
where he was made Confessor to the English Benedictine Dames of Dunkirk,
by Delvaulx, Bishop of Ypres, July 6th, 1756. Mr. Edmundson was always the
first to practise what he preached to others, and made himself all to all, that
he might gain all to Christ. He died Oct. 12, 1785, in the 65th year of his age,
having first received all the rites of the Church."

EDMONDSON, HUGH, probably uncle to Henry, was educated at Douay
and was a Missioner in Lancashire, where he died Sept. 19, 1755.

* Kirk's draft adds: "After this [the duel], I suppose, left the estate to Mr. Thos. Ben[edict]
Scarisbrick, of Scarisbrick, and went to Rome, aged 18,—was Priest at Eccleston—?before or
when S.J."
† Dr. Kirk's draft adds of Edisford: "Supposed from Italian books left by him to that
place, to have been educated at Rome," and gives his Christain name as William.

ELLIOT, AMBROSE, O.S.B.—He was a brother of Nathaniel, and lived many years in the family of Sir Edward Smythe, Bart., at Acton-Burnell, where he was much respected and beloved. He died June 16th, 1773. Another brother was an eminent oculist, and lived near Bridgenorth.

ELLIOT, NATHANIEL [*alias* SHELDON], S.J., was born of good family in May, 1705. He entered his Novitiate Sept. 7, 1723, and was professed Feb. 2, 1741. He was Rector of the English College* at Rome from 1750 to 1762, and was much beloved there. While Provincial in England he lived in the family of Mr. Nevill, at Holt. When Mr. Charles Nevill, the elder brother, became a Jesuit, and gave up his estate to Cosmas Nevill, Esq., Lord Lichfield, who was his uncle and guardian, insisted on a settlement being made for him out of the estate he had relinquished, and was surprised to hear the Father Provincial ask no more for him than £50 per annum. "I thought," said his Lordship, "you Jesuits grasped at everything you could get, and am much suprised that you ask so little." Father Elliot died Oct. 10, 1780.

ELLIOT, —— (MRS.), of Portarlington, in Cornwall. She was maid of honour to Queen Caroline, and much in her favour. On becoming a Catholic she retired to the nuns at Hammersmith, and built what is called the Gallery, where she lived in retirement, and the exact performance of all the duties of a Christian. It is said she was present at the Conference held before the Queen between Dr. Howard and Dr. Clarke. *Ita* Dr. Milner.

ELSTON, JOHN, *alias* PHILIPS, was son of Richard and Ann Elston. At the age of 19 he was admitted into the Roman College by Father Postgate, Dec. 22, 1697. He was ordained March 3, 1703, and left the College the following April [25], in the company of Mr. Gerard, and passed by Douay in September. I do not find where he lived, but he died Feb. 6, 1737 (O.S.).

ENGLEFIELD, SIR CHARLES, fifth Bart., of Wootton Basset, Wilts, was son of Sir Thomas Englefield, Bart., and Mary, daughter of George Huntley, of Gloucestershire. He succeeded his father in title and estate, and married Susan, natural daughter of John, Lord Culpepper, and owned by him, as one of his children, by whom he had a son, Thomas, and a daughter, Charlotte, but both dying young, he was succeeded by his cousin, Sir Henry Englefield. Sir Charles died in April, 1728. (*Betham*, p. 145.)

ENGLEFIELD, [CHARLES *or* FRANCIS FELIX], O.S.F., was son of Henry Englefield, of White Knights, Berks, and Catharine Day, daughter of Benjamin Poole, of London, remarried to Edward Webb, Esq. The said Henry was descended from a younger branch of that family, and succeeded to the title on the death of his cousin, Sir Charles Englefield, *sine prole*, in 1728. Father Englefield was sent to Rome to procure the repeal of the *Regulae Missionis* established by Benedict XIV., but failed in his endeavours. He was also said to be disappointed in his expectations of a mitre, before which he was represented in a caricature to be in the act of praying.

ENGLEFIELD, SIR HENRY, sixth Baronet, was eldest son of Henry Englefield, of White Knights, near Reading, and grandson of Anthony Engle-field, who died in 1711, and who, by Alice his wife, daughter of Thomas Stokes, of London, had ten sons and seven daughters. The ten sons died all unmarried except Henry, the fourth son, who succeeded to his father's estate, and was father of Sir Henry, who, in 1742, married Mary, daughter of Thomas Berkeley, of Spetchley, Co. Worcester. On her death he married, in 1751, Catharine, daughter of Sir Charles Bucke, of Hanby [Hambeck] Grange, Co. Lincoln, Bart., by whom he had five children, Sir Henry Charles, his eldest son succeeded him. Sir Henry died May 25, 1780.

ENGLEFIELD, SIR HENRY CHARLES, seventh Baronet, was a distinguished Member of the Antiquarian Society. (Was he not of the Royal

---

* Dr. Kirk's draft says that Father Elliot was "appointed Rector of R. Coll., or Liège, rather, in 1748," and that he was "Rector of Rom. Coll. end of 1755 or beginning of 1756 till 1761, if not 1762."

Society?) He wrote: 1. An excellent *Treatise on the Parabola*.   2. *A Walk through Southampton*.   3. *A Translation of [Terence's "Andria," in English Metre]*.   Sir Henry died and the title became extinct.

ENGLEFIELD, MARTHA, O.S.F.   She became a nun at Princenhoff, Bruges, and died April 4, 1793, aged 82, in the 65th year of her religious profession.

ENGLEFIELD, MARY WINIFRED, O.S.B.   Having received a pious education from her parents, and learnt to despise the world, she resolved to quit it, and retired to the English Benedictine Dames at Dunkirk, where, after practising for thirty years the virtue of obedience, she was at last chosen Abbess, and governed the house with great prudence and virtue for twelve years.   During an illness of six months she bore with heroic patience and fortitude a complication of disorders which at last ended in a dropsy, and never ceased daily to recommend her soul into the hands of her Creator.   She expired, in the midst of the prayers and tears of her spiritual children, on Feb. 12, 1777, in the 60th year of her age, the 42nd of her religious profession, and 12th of her Abbatial dignity.   (*Obituary Letter.*)

ERRINGTON, THOMAS, of Beaufront in Northumberland.   He was Captain of Lord Widdrington's troup in 1715.   He was of an ancient family and endowed with good natural abilities.   He had formerly been in the French service, where he had the reputation of being a good soldier.   He lay under many obligations to the Earl of Derwentwater, and this circumstance is supposed to have drawn him into the rebellion.   He was taken prisoner at Preston.   At his trial, May 31, 1716, in the Court of Exchequer, he humbly submitted to the King's mercy and appealed to the King's evidence.   The Rev. Mr. Patten, the author of the *History of the Rebellion*, to do him justice in respect to his being under such obligations to the Earl of Derwentwater, says that he could not resist going with him.   He possessed an estate of £328 per annum.   [Dr. Hooke.]

ERRINGTON, WILLIAM (I.), a native of Yorkshire, was admitted into the College at Lisbon, July 15. 1684.   He dedicated his thesis of Universal Philosophy to Queen Catharine, and having received Priestly Orders, he returned to England in 1695.   He lived many years as chaplain in the family of Bryan Salvin, of Croxdale, Esq.   He died Feb. 12, 1732. (O.S.), and left his effects for the religious benefit of the Catholics in the neighbourhood of Croxdale.   [*Lisbon Register, Miscell.*, p. 1085.]

ERRINGTON, WILLIAM (II.), went over to Douay in 1737 or 8, and being ordained Priest came on the Mission and lived many years with Bishop Challoner, who had a high opinion of him, both as an active and zealous Missionary and as a man of business.   He accordingly employed him to establish a school for Catholics in the middle walks of life.   He therefore appointed Mr. John Hurst to open a school at Betley, near Newcastle-under-Lyne, in Staffordshire and on the border of Cheshire, in 1762.   This was, at Lady-Day 1763, removed to Sedgley Park, where it continues to flourish, and has been the principal nursery ever since for our Foreign and Domestic Colleges.   Mr. Errington was Archdeacon in the Chapter, and also its treasurer.   [He was chosen Canon Sept. 25, 1754.]   He died in London Sept. 28, 1768, aged 52, much regretted by all who knew him.

EUSTACE, JOHN CHETWODE.   He received the first elements of education at Sedgley Park.   About the year 1773 he was sent to Douay, and remained some years with the English Benedictines, but never became a member of that Religious Congregation.   For some time he taught Rhetoric at Maynooth, and afterwards assisted Dr. Collins in his establishment at Southall Park.   When Mr. Chamberlayne retired from the Mission, Mr. Eustace succeeded him at Cossey Hall, the seat of Sir William Jerningham.   He was appointed tutor to George Petre, Esq., and accompanied him to Cambridge.   He afterwards travelled for some time on the Continent, in 1802, and in a second tour he was taken ill and died at Naples, Sept. or Oct., 1815, aged 52.   " The last days of his life," says the *Diario di Roma*, "which were days of trouble and of suffering, have shewn with what Christian resignation he had learnt to suffer, and how well he was prepared, as became a good ecclesiastic, to undergo the common lot of mankind which, however, his name and his works will never experience."

His works are: 1. *A Classical tour through Italy.* 2. *An Answer to the Charge of the Bishop of Lincoln.* 3. *A Letter from Paris*, with critical observations on the state of society and the moral character of the French people. 4. *A Political Catechism*, adapted to the present moment, 1810. 8vo, pp. 44. 5. *The Proofs of Christianity*, 1814. 12mo, pp. 48. The chief arguments are here arranged and examined under 12 heads. See Butler's *Historical Memoirs* (second Edition), iv., 448.

EYRE, ADAM, of Bradway,* third son of Rowland Eyre, of Hassop, Esq., by his wife Gertrude, daughter of Humphrey Stafford, of Eyam, Esq., married Elizabeth, daughter of Thomas Burley, of Woodhouse by Dronfield. He died in 1684, and was buried at Norton. He must have been father or grandfather of this Vincent Eyre.

EYRE, EDWARD, after he was ordained at Douay was sent to St. Omers to teach the Classics, and where I find him in April, 1778. About 1781, when Bishop Talbot removed from G. Haywood to Longbirch, Mr. Eyre came to live with him till his death in 1795. He then removed to Hathersedge, in Derbyshire, where he died Nov. 15, 1834, at a very advanced age. Mr. Eyre was a true Israelite in whom there was no guile, nor was he void of talent.

EYRE, FRANCIS, of Warkworth, was fourth son of Thomas Eyre, of Hassop and Eastwell, and of Mary Holman, and uncle of Thomas named . . . . and brother of Rowland. By the death of his elder brothers, Edward and John, before his father, the property of his mother became vested in Francis. He married, for his first wife, the daughter of Mr. Radcliffe and the Countess of Newburgh before she became Lady Mary Eyre. By his lady, who died Aug. 28, 1798, he had three sons—Francis, James and Charles—and one daughter, who married Arthur Onslow, of the Middle Temple, and serjeant-at-law. His eldest son, Francis, on the death of Lord Newburgh, in 1814, in right of his grandmother Charlotte, who was a princess in her own right, succeeded to the title of Earl of Newburgh. Mr. Eyre, an able and "most amiable worthy man," died Oct. 7, 1804, aged 72. After the death of his first wife he married a Miss Hernon, still living in London. Mr. Eyre wrote the following works :—

1. *A few Remarks on the History of the Decline and Fall of the Roman Empire, relative chiefly to the two last chapters.* London, 1778. 8vo, p. 154. 2. *A Short Appeal to the Public by the Gentleman who is particularly addressed in the postscript of the Vindication of some Passages in the 15th and 16th chapters of the Decline, etc.* London, 1799, p. 41, 8vo. 3. *A short essay on the Christian Religion, etc. The whole proposed as a Preservative against the pernicious Doctrines which have overwhelmed France with misery and desolation. By a Sincere Friend of Mankind.* London, 1795, pp. 140, 8vo. 4. *A Letter to the Rev. Ralph Churton, etc., from Francis Eyre, of Warkworth, Esq.* London, 1795, 8vo, pp. 104. This letter was occasioned by a sermon of Mr. Churton, Rector of Middleton-Cheney, to which parish that of Warkworth adjoins, addressed to his parishioners on his first coming among them, called "A Defence of the Church of England." This letter was answered by Mr. Churton when Mr. Eyre published 5. *A reply to the Rev. R. Churton, etc.* London, 1798, 8vo, pp. 494, which brought forth a short "Postscript" from Mr. Churton, and here the controversy ended. See Nichols' *Leicestershire*, iv., 398, and *Gentleman's Magazine*, vol. vi. and p. 694.

EYRE, HENRY, of Gray's Inn, was eldest son of Thomas Eyre, of Hassop and Eastwell, by his second wife, Mary, third daughter of Sir Henry Beding-

---

* Pedigree of Eyre of Hassop in Nichols' *Leicestershire*, iv., 398.

field, Bart. He was an eminent Counsellor-at-law, and was seated at Bures
Hall, in Hale, which, with the Manor of Necton, in Norfolk, had been
purchased by the Eyres. He also possessed a moiety of Eastwell, by settlement on his father's second marriage. Mr. H. Eyre had five brothers, of
whom Thomas and William were Priests, and Francis and James physicians.
At his death, in 1728, he left Bures Hall to his younger brother, John, who is
said by Mr. Nichols, on the authority of Blomefield, vol. iii., pp. 367, 394, to
have been possessed of £4,000 per annum, and at his death in 1739, without
issue, he left Dr. Eyre his successor at Bures Hall. Mr. Henry Eyre's only
daughter, Elizabeth married, in 1741, Clotworthy Skeffington, Viscount
Massareene, created Earl in 1756, and died in Dublin at the advanced age of
89, May, 20, 1805. Their eldest son was a prisoner. See *Gentleman's
Magazine*, vol. 75, p. 290.

EYRE, JOHN, brother to Thomas Eyre [No. IV.]. After staying one year at
Douay he went to St. Gregory's, at Paris, in 1766, was ordained June 13, 1771,
and entered his Licence Jan. 1, 1774. In his second year, in consequence of a
putrid fever, his health was so much impaired that he returned to England in
1775. He lived for some time with Henry Howard, Esq., at Cromsall, near
Manchester, and then at Heath Hall, near Wakefield, and, at last, in
consequence of continued bad health, he retired to "The Farm," near
Sheffield, and died Feb. 19, 1790.

EYRE, ROLAND, of Hassop and Eastwell, was the only surviving son of
Thomas Eyre by his wife Katharine, daughter of Sir Philip Kemp, of Slindon,
Knight. His family pedigree says that his grandfather, Rowland Eyre, the
original purchaser of the estate, "was a Colonel of Horse for Charles I., that
he raised a regiment of horse and a regiment of dragoons, at his own charge,
for the King's service, and that he paid £21,000 for his composition with the
Parliament." (Nichols' *Leicestershire*, ii., 171.) Mr. Roland Eyre married
Lady Elizabeth Plunket, daughter of Luke, Earl of Fingall, by whom he had
four sons and two daughters. Catharine married Sir William Stanley, of
Hooton, Co. Chester, and Margaret, Thomas Thornton [of Netherwitton
probably.] Mr. Eyre died after 1718. (Pedigree in Nichols' *Leicestershire*, iv.,
p. 398)

EYRE, ROWLAND, [eldest] son of [Thomas Eyre and Mary Holman]. He
married Honble. Mary Widdrington, heiress of Lord Widdrington of Stella.
On the death of her sisters, Alethea and Anne (who both died at Eastwell and
were buried there) he purchased, in 1751, that part of the Eastwell estate which
was devised by his [great] grandfather to the children of his second wife, Mary
Bedingfield. This purchase seems rather to have (been) made by his son
Thomas.

EYRE [THOMAS] (I.), S.J., was Confessor to the Court at St. Germains.
While there he kept up a correspondence with Dr. James Barker, *alias* Rigby,
Professor of Divinity at Douay. In one of his letters in answer to one from
Dr. Rigby, written on the eve of the siege of Douay, and of the visitation of
the College by Dr. Delcourt, &c., and written to give his own explanation of
the five propositions of Jansenism, he "approved of his submission, but
advised him in a threatening way to have a care of joining with his own body,
the Clergy, for that it was in a pitiful way." *Ita* Bishop Dicconson in MS.
Memorandum at Ushaw, who adds that the King left the Jesuits.
Father Eyre wrote (*credo*): *The Life of James II*.

EYRE, THOMAS (II.), of Hassop, Eastwell, and Stella, son of Rowland Eyre,
and nephew of Francis, was born Sept. 29, 1743 (O.S.). He married July 23, 1776,
[at St. George's, Hanover Square], Lady Mary Bellasyse, daughter of Thomas,
Earl Fauconberg. "Mr. Eyre," says Mr. Robert Beeston, his Chaplain, "was
a learned man, and a great supporter of the Catholic Religion." He was
many years afflicted with violent fits of the gout, and was a most patient
sufferer under them, and at last died of it at Nice, whither he was gone for
the benefit of his health, March 26, 1772, without issue. His Lady survived

him, and continued abroad till her death, which happened at Pisa, Jan. 27,
1804. Mr. Thomas Eyre made four foundations to support four Catholic
Chapels with their incumbents, at Stella, Hassop, and Hathersage, in Derbyshire, and Eastwell, in Leicestershire. He also established a library, well
furnished with valuable books, for the use of the Priests at Hassop and
Hathersage, together with £5 per annum to keep up the library. It is kept
at Hassop. His Lady's father, Earl Fauconberg, married Catharine Betham,
co-heiress to Mr. William Fowler, of St. Thomas' Priory, near Stafford. He
conformed, and embezzled money left by Mr. Daniel Fitter in the hands of Mr.
Fowler, whose Chaplain he had been, for religious purposes, on the plea of
being left for "superstitious purposes." ["On the death of Mr. Eyre, without
issue, the estate of Eastwell, containing about 1,400 acres, was purchased by
the guardians of the Duke of Rutland, who was then a minor."—From Dr.
Kirk's draft.—P.R.]

EYRE, THOMAS (III.), of Hassop and Eastwell, eldest son of Rowland Eyre,
and his wife, Lady Elizabeth Plunket. He married Mary, daughter of — Holman,
of Warkworth, and Lady Anastasia Stafford, by which marriage and the will
of her brother the Holman property became vested in his two surviving sons,
Rowland and Francis. This appears to be the same who married for his
second wife Mary, third daughter of Sir H. Bedingfield, Bart., of whom below,
mother of Henry Eyre, of Gray's Inn.

EYRE, THOMAS (IV.) [PRESIDENT OF USHAW].—He was the fourth son of
Nathaniel Eyre, Esq., and his wife, Jane Broomhead, and was born at Glossop,
in Derbyshire. In 1758 he accompanied his brothers Edward and John to
Douay, where they arrived June 24. In that seminary of piety and learning he
gave great satisfaction by his application and religious deportment; and
being ordained Priest, was employed in teaching the Classics. When Thomas
Eyre, of Hassop, Esq., became possessed of the Stella estate, in 1775, in the
parish of Ryton and county of Durham, he invited his kinsman, Mr. Thomas
Eyre, to come over from Douay. The invitation was accepted by him, and
here he resumed his apostolical labours, Oct. 21 [Oct. 11], 1775. He succeeded
in the charge of that large flock Fr. John Turner, S.J. A large field was here
opened to his zeal, as the congregation was numerous, and he endeavoured to
comply on his part with the important duties of his calling. Preaching being
one of those duties, when he first entered on the Mission he composed and
wrote out about sixty formal discourses ; so that in 1780 he was enabled to
preach every Sunday extempore with great facility and with greater advantage
to his hearers than reading his sermons. He delighted in reading Massillon,
and preferred his sermons to all others. Among the preachers of his own
acquaintance, he admired most Dr. Green, the President of Douay College,
and often lamented he had not imitated him by writing down the substance of
these excellent discourses, which he frequently heard at College. But though
he preached extempore, "he generally wrote down the plan of every sermon,
and what he wished chiefly to inculcate ; so that he altered the following year
what he thought deficient in the preceding. Every year he preached one
sermon at least upon each Sacrament, except Holy Orders." Thus did he
provide for the spiritual wants of his own flock ; and for the benefit of the
Catholic body at large he published *Instructions for Confirmation*, and republished Gobinet's *Instructions of Youth*, and in a little more than a twelvemonth disposed of 4,000 copies of that valuable work. He also gave an
edition of Gother's spiritual works. In 1784 "it was a great satisfaction to
him that Bishop Matthew Gibson was pleased to take up his residence at
Stella, as it gave him a daily opportunity of improvement by discoursing, as
occasion offered, upon every topic of Divinity." [About this time he and
Bishop Gibson had it in contemplation to give a new edition of Bishop
Challoner's Bible, which was become extremely scarce. "Upon a close and
attentive perusal of that edition we find," says Mr. Eyre, "much room is left
for improvement, not only as to the mere errata of the Press, but as to
grammatical inaccuracies, even deviations from the sense of the Vulgate."

These, however, were not pretended to be material.   At the desire and request of Bishop T. Talbot, the undertaking was dropped.]

About the year 1791 he formed the idea of writing a more detailed life of Mr. Gother, and of continuing Dodd's *Church History of England*, and in that year began to circulate queries and collect materials for these purposes.   But the destruction of our foreign establishments called him into a more active life, and prevented his proceeding in a work which in his hands would have been so ably executed.   On Oct. 22, 1792, he removed from Stella to Wooller, and thence to Tudhoe, where he presided over and taught the students from Douay that belonged to, or chose to continue their studies in the Northern District.   When this place was found to be too confined and the noble College at Ushaw was ready for the reception of Students, on July 19, the Feast of St. Vincent of Paul, the founder of the Fathers of the Mission, and in the year [1808, July 19], Mr. Eyre removed thither with his professors, seniors, and students, and there established that admirable system of studies, discipline, and religious duties which he had imported from Douay, and under which that College continues to flourish.   Mr. Eyre died May 8, 1810, much lamented in death as he had been respected and beloved in life by all those under his care and that had the happiness of his acquaintance.

EYRE, VINCENT, of Dronfield Woodhouse.   He received his education from the Jesuits at St. Omers, and ever after retained a great regard and veneration for that body of Clergy, and was occasionally consulted by them in their affairs.   He married, Nov. 1, 1703, Ann Bostock, daughter of Nathaniel Bostock, of Wrixall, in Staffordshire, the form of whose person was such as to entitle her to be called "the pretty Miss Bostock."*   Mr. Eyre early took a fancy to the study of genealogies, and employed therein great part of his time, whereby he became well acquainted with the connections of all the principal families in the kingdom.   He wrote a great number of pedigrees, and from his writings it appears that he entered fully into the pedigrees and connections of most of the crowned heads in Europe.   He had an extensive personal acquaintance with families, and was intimate with the Dukes of Norfolk and Devonshire.   It was at the house of the former, at Worksop Manor, that he met with an accident that was doomed to shorten his days.   He was a great smoker of tobacoo, and one day, in endeavouring to lay his pipe on a shelf, which was out of his reach, he got a fall, and hurt his thigh so much as to be confined to his bed for a considerable time ; and though he lived several years afterwards, he felt the consequences of his fall to the last.   (MS. of Vin. Eyre, Jun., at Ushaw).   Mrs. Eyre died Dec. 10, 1746, and he [then married Ann Broomhead, *credo*].

EYRE, VINCENT (II.), son of [Nathaniel Eyre and of Jane Broomhead], was born at Glossop, in Derbyshire.   In 1755 he and his brother Edward were sent to the school opened by Mr Bordley, at Ince, near Liverpool, but returned to Glossop the year following.   In 1758 his father took him and his three brothers, Edward, John, and Thomas, abroad, and placed them at the school opened by Mr. (Bishop) Talbot, at Esquerchin, previous to their admission to Douay College, where he and Edward were admitted in 1760, and John and Thomas in 1761.   Here he remained four years, and returned to Glossop Sept., 1764.   Being destined for the Law, he studied three years in the office of Mr. Tomkinson, in Manchester, and then went to London, where he attended the chambers of Mr. Maire and of Mr. Booth, two eminent Catholic Conveyancers.   Soon after his return from Ireland, where he had been with Mr. MacMahon to settle his affairs, he became assistant to Mr. George Wilmot, of Lincoln's Inn, especially in the Norfolk affairs, and at his death, being appointed one of his executors, intended to be, which he was, the most active of them, with a legacy of £300, and his Chambers at prime cost, which in 1779 produced him about £1,000 more ; he succeeded to a considerable part

---

* Kirk at this point confuses the issue of this Vincent with that of his son, Nathaniel ; but the genealogy is correctly stated under Eyre, Thomas, President of Ushaw.

of his business. Mr. Wilmot died June 4, 1776, and was, as Mr. Eyre says, "a very regular Christian, and always very moderate and scrupulous about his charges to his clients." As he had few, or rather, no relations he knew of, and had acquired all he had in business, after a few legacies he left the residue of his property to such charitable purposes as his executors should think fit, thinking thus to make some kind of a return to the kind hand of Providence. In April, 1774, Mr. Eyre married Miss Parker of, or at Prescott, Lancashire, and was entrusted by the Duke of Norfolk with the care of his great and valuable estates at and about Sheffield and at Worksop, in which charge he continued till his death, much to the satisfaction of his Grace, and of his numerous tenantry. He died . . . . and left four sons and three daughters, one of whom married Mr. Scully, the author of the *Statement of the Penal Laws against Catholics in Ireland*. Mr. Eyre's three brothers became Priests ; John died at Sheffield, Feb. 19, 1790 ; Thomas, President of Ushaw, May 8, 1810 ; and Edward at Hathersage, in Derbyshire, Nov. 15, 1834, aged 89.

EYSTON, BASIL, O.S.B., died at Douay April 29, 1785.

EYSTON, BERNARD FRANCIS [A S. FRANCISCO, D.D.], O.S.F., died at Douay in 1709. Published *The Christian's Duty Compared, by Brother Bernard Francis, Student in Divinity*. Aire. 1684.

EYSTON, CHARLES, eldest son of George Eyston, ot East Hendred, Esq., was born in 1667. He was, as his epitaph says truly, "antiquitatum ecclesiasticarum studiosus, fide et charitate conspicuus ac religione devotus." He lived on terms of great friendship with the celebrated antiquary Thomas Hearne, of the Bodleian, who in a MS. notebook, his diary in the Bodleian, speaks of him thus. "On Sunday morning died Charles Eyston, of East Hendred, Berks, Esq., a gentleman of eminent virtues and my very great friend and acquaintance. He was a Roman Catholic and so charitable to the poor that he was lamented by all who knew him, insomuch that on Saturday last, being the day before his death, I heard a woman of Hendred say that she would rather all the people in Hendred, except her own husband, should die rather than this gentleman. He was a man of sweet temper, and was an excellent scholar, but so modest, that he did not care to have it at any time mentioned, &c." Mr. Eyston died Nov. 5, 1721, aged 54.

His works are : 1. *A little Monument to the once famous Abbey and Borough of Glastonbury, or a short Specimen of the History of that ancient Monastery and Town. With a description of the remaining ruins of Glastonbury collected out of our best Antiquaries and Historians*. Finished April 28, 1716. MS. at Hendred in 4to, pp. 119. It was published in a volume of Hearne's works. 2. *A poor little Monument to all the old pious, dissolved Foundations of England, or, a short History of Abbeys, Monasteries, Colleges, Hospitals, Chantries, etc.* In Two Parts. Part I. "finished Sept. 4, 1719." In the second he says, p. 12 Preface, he intended to describe the habits of all Religious, with a plate of them, and to give an account of the founders, of their first coming to England and settling ; of canonised Saints, Bishops, Writers and Houses each Order had, together with a history of English Colleges, etc., abroad. MS. at Hendred of 433 pages in folio. 3. *First Part of the Prevarication of the Holy Church-Libertys*. Copied by W. Eyston, in 1706, from a MS. originally in Sir William [? Henry] Spelman's library, and written, it is said, by a lawyer in the reign of Charles I. It came into the hands of Charles Eyston, Esq., from Mr. Francis Young, O.S.F., living with Henry Englefield, of White Knights, Esq., who received it from Mr. A. Hill, O.S.F., who lived with Sir Henry Tichborne, of Tichborne, who had it from the Right Reverend Bishop Ellis, who was living in 1719. See his account of Authors* used in No. II. Also some articles of Mr. Eyston in Dr. Richard Warner's *History of Glastonbury*, to whom Mr. Eyston, of Hendred, lent some of Mr. Hearne's letters.

---

* [The original MS. is now in the Archives of the Bishop of Clifton.—J. H. P.]

EYSTON, GEORGE, of East Hendred.   He married Anne, third daughter of Robert Dormer, of Peterley, Bucks, Esq.

EYSTON, JOHN, died Dec. 13, 1795.

EYSTON, JOSEPH CHARLES, O.P., *previously* O.S.F.   "He was of an ancient and noble family in England, where he received the first documents of piety.   As soon as his age permitted, he desired to be received amongst the English Franciscans at Douay, under whose care and conduct he finished his studies.   There he was called to the Mission, where for some time [three years] he laboured in gaining souls to God ; but, thirsting with a devout desire of visiting the Holy Land, he asked and obtained leave to go.   Great were the labours and pains he underwent in the journey and during his sojourn there.   In submission to his Superior's commands he went to Canada, where for some time he resided, exercising the functions of Superior.   At length, having spent above thirty years in the Seraphical Order, partly on the English Mission, partly in travels to Jerusalem, Constantinople, Egypt [was two years a missionary in Egypt], in a word, in visiting Europe, Asia, Africa and America ; returning to Rome, out of a singular devotion to our Blessed Lady and the Rosary, he petitioned to be admitted into the order of Dominicans, being above sixty years of age.   By the consent of both Generals, and the approbation of Pope Benedict XIII., he was admitted into that sacred institution.   No sooner was his solemn profession made at Bornheim but his merits in diligently frequenting the Divine Office and performing humble works, raised him to the dignity of Sub-Prior, in which employ his prudent administration and affable conversation acquired him the goodwill of all he conversed with.   In the end he peaceably finished his days, worn out by age, labour, and long sicknesses (in the 97th year of his age, the 62nd of his Priesthood, and the 63rd from his first profession), in the Convent of Bornheim, April 27, 1758, amidst the prayers and sighs of his Brethren, and assisted by the last Sacraments of the Church."   (*Dominican Obituary.*)

Another account only says "he was upwards of 90 years old ;" if so, he may have been younger brother to Charles Eyston, Esq., who was born in 1667, and was the eldest son, and Joseph in 1668 or 9.

FAIRFAX, CHARLES GREGORY, of Gilling, Co. York, and Viscount Fairfax, of Emile, in Co. Tipperary, Ireland, was educated at Lambspring. Collins says he was eldest son of William, Viscount Fairfax.   He married a daughter of Lord Clifford, and secondly, Mary Fairfax, he the great-grandson and she the great-great-granddaughter of the first Viscount Fairfax.   By her he had four sons and five daughters.   His daughters Anne and Elizabeth are said in the Peerage to be the only children that survived him ; yet Dr. Rooke [? Rooker], writing from Ampleforth, says Anne alone survived him, and died May 2, 1793.*   She built a house at Ampleforth, at a short distance from Gilling, for her Chaplain, Mr. Bolton, O.S.B., and this was the beginning of the present establishment belonging to the Benedictine Monks of Dieulevart, who settled here and added greatly to the house built by Anne Fairfax.

FAIRFAX, THOMAS [*alias* BECKETT], S.J.—Mr. Sylvester Jenks, who wrote the *Review of the Book of Jansenius*, in his letters to Father Fairfax, copies of which are at Ushaw, gives Mr. Fairfax the praise of being "one of the chief Anti-Jansenists in this country, or the next to it."   Indeed, Mr. Andrew Giffard asserts that Father Fairfax "was the first to begin printing and publishing those books of controversy concerning Jansenism, which was the first origin of the liberty which others took afterwards."   I have no doubt he thought it was necessary to sound the alarm, and guard the Catholics of this country against the infection of that heresy.   Yet at the very time "it is most certain that no people were more averse to Jansenism than the English Clergy.   It was never mentioned nor spoke of before those unhappy controversies."   We know nothing at all of the matter, so that I may assuredly

---

* [Honble. Anne Fairfax, of Gilling Castle, who, neither in life nor in death, was unmindful of the poor, died May 2, 1793.]   Part of her epitaph from Dr. Kirk's draft.

affirm that there were not so many as five Priests in all England who so much as knew the five propositions : perhaps not so much as one of them ; so little concern we had in this business. (Mr. A. Giffard to Mr. Dicconson, May, 1710, at Ushaw.)

The same is asserted by Bishop Smith (who as well as Mr. A. Giffard, had taught Divinity at Douay many years) in his letter of Feb. 23, 1707, to Cardinal Caprara (Dodd iii., 520): *Unum addo me meosque clericos et collegas, adeo esse pacis et tranquillitatis amantes ut sublimiores illas de Gratiae auxiliis controversias semper prætermiserimus; scholarum concertationibus aptiores rati, quam Fidelium moribus informandis."*

In 1709, in consequence of accusations of Jansenism brought against the Clergy, the Bishops were requested to declare if they had any person or persons, either of the secular or regular Clergy, in any parts subject to their jurisdiction, who might justly be accused or suspected as favourers of the erroneous doctrine of Jansenius, or in their conscience did think there was any such person in England. They all answered in these express words: *I declare I neither know anyone, secular or regular, guilty of holding the errors of Jansenism, nor do I suspect any of them of holding the said errors ; but on the contrary, in my conscience, I do verily believe that there is no such person or persons amongst us.* And when the Superiors of the Regulars were asked by Bishop Giffard: "If they knew any person of the Clergy who might be accused of holding the erroneous doctrine of Jansenism," they answered : "They knew none." (Dodd, iii., 525.) "This being the state of things, when Father Fairfax sounded the alarm, and such the unhappy consequences which followed from it, as the charges brought against the Bishops and Clergy, and Douay College, &c., it may be concluded that his zeal was not always according to knowledge ; though I am far from thinking that anything but what was right was intended by Father Fairfax and some others who afterwards joined in the same cry of Jansenism against the Clergy of England."

1. Mr. Jenks says that Father Fairfax translated *The Case of Conscience,* and published it. Perhaps also 2. *The Secret Policy of the Jesuits, and the present State of the Sorbonne, with a Short History of Jansenism in Holland.* 2nd edition in 1702, in 24mo.

FALKNER, THOMAS, S.J., was a native of Lancashire, and born Oct. 6 1707. On May 5, 1732, he entered his novitiate, and was professed in 1749. In his youth, after a grammar-school education, he studied medicine and surgery. The South Sea Company being at that time in possession of what was called the Assiento contract for supplying Spanish Settlements with slaves, Mr. Falkner went out as surgeon on board a slave-ship which sailed to the coast of Africa, and thence to Buenos Ayres. There he was detained by sickness, and became a Catholic ; and after a due probation, entered into the Order of Jesuits. Some time after, he entered on his Missionary labours, and in these and in the extensive practice of medicine, at the same time civilizing the Indians, preaching to them the truths of the gospel, and associating with them in peace and war, he passed nearly forty years. But when the Jesuits were suppressed in Spain in 1767, the same hard fate expelled them from South America. Mr. Falkner then came to England, and after some time spent with his friends in Lancashire and other places, he at last settled as chaplain at Winsley, in the family of —— Berington, Esq., in Herefordshire. He afterwards removed to Plowden Hall, in Shropshire, where he died Jan. 30, 1784, aged 77. " Mr. Falkner was a man," says Mr. [Joseph] Berington, who knew him well, " of a vigorous mind, well exercised in various points of science, and had he been allowed to tell his story in his own way, stored as his mind was of anecdotes and incidents, on which he delighted to dwell, we should have had from him an amusing and interesting performance. But his papers were put into the hands of the late Mr. Robert Berkeley, of Spetchley, Esq., who extracted from them the whole spirit of the original. He made them what they are." Mr. Berkeley wrote the preface. The title is : *A Description of Patagonia and the adjoining parts of South America : containing an account of the soil, produce, and the religion, government, etc., of the Indian Inhabitants, and some particulars relating to the Falkland Islands.* By T. Falkner. Illustrated by a new Map of some of the Southern parts of America. Hereford. 1774.

FARMER [?FERMOR].—" A Priest who was condemned," says the *Chapter Obituary*, " for his priestly functions, in 168—, and died in Stafford Jail."

FAUCONBERG.—ROWLAND BELLASYSE, sixth Viscount Fauconberg, was eldest son of Rowland Bellasyse, brother of Thomas, third Viscount, and third Earl Fauconberg. On the death of Henry, fifth Viscount and third Earl Fauconberg, March 23, 1802, he succeeded to the Barony and Viscounty, but not to the Earldom or the estate. He lived privately at Lancaster upon a small fortune, and on his death . . . was succeeded by his brother, Charles Bellasyse, Dr. of Sorbonne, who died at Lancaster, June 21, 1815.

FAUCONBERG.—THOMAS BELLASYSE, third Viscount Fauconberg, was the eldest son of Sir Rowland Bellasyse, Knt. (who died at Sutton in 1699), and Anne, daughter of Humphrey Davenport, of Sutton. On the death of his uncle Thomas, that title became extinct, and he succeeded to the title of Viscount Fauconberg. He married Bridget, daughter of Sir John Gage, of Firle, and co-heiress to her mother, who was daughter and co-heiress of Thomas Middlemore, of Edgbaston, and by her, who died Nov. 18, 1732, he has issue four sons and three daughters. Viscount Fauconberg died at Brussels, Nov. 26, 1718, and was buried at Cockswold, Co. York.

FAUCONBERG. — THOMAS BELLASYSE, fourth Viscount Fauconberg, eldest son of Thomas, third Viscount, and Bridget Gage, was born April 27, 1699. On Aug. 5, 1726, he married Catharine, daughter and heiress of John Betham, of Rowington, Co. Warwick, and co-heir to William Fowler, of St. Thomas's Priory near Stafford, and by her, who died May 30, 1760, he had issue three sons (of whom only Henry, the third son, survived him) and four daughters (1) Catharine; (2) Barbara, wife of George Barnewell; (3) Mary, wife of Thomas Eyre, of Hassop; and (4) Anne, wife of Francis Talbot. By his will, made in 1712, Mr. Fowler had devised his whole landed property (subject to two small annuities to his sister, Dorothy Grove, and her son Thomas) to his niece, Catharine Betham, on condition that she and her husband took the name of Fowler. Lord Fauconberg, therefore, on his marriage took the name of Fowler and came into possession of all the Fowler estates, which at that time yielded more than £2,000 per annum. But in the following year another will of Mr. Fowler was discovered, made in 1715, by which he revoked the one of 1712. This discovery was followed by a long suit in Chancery and an appeal to the House of Lords, when it was determined, in 1733, that the estates of the late Mr. Fowler were vested in the representatives of his sisters, Mary and Dorothy, and that Lord Fauconberg should render one half of the estate to Mr. Fitzgerald, an Irish Barrister, who had married Rebecca, only daughter of the above-named Thomas Grove; but should not be liable to refund any part of the income he had received. Upon this, his Lordship losing all relish for what remained to him of the property, soon after sold the Priory of St. Thomas to Sarah, Duchess of Marlborough. This disappointment seems to have greatly affected both the religion and principles of his Lordship, for soon after he conformed to the Established Church and then added robbery to his apostacy, by refusing to pay any longer the interest or principal of money left in the hands of Mr. Fowler by his chaplain, Mr. Daniel Fitter, on the plea of its being left for superstitious purposes. In 1756, his Lordship was created Earl of Fauconberg and of the Privy Council. Dr. Milner told me, July 16, that he returned to the Catholic Church before his death, which took place at his seat at Newburgh, Feb. 4, 1774.

FELL, CHARLES, *vere* UMFREVILLE, D.D., was born in England but of French extraction. After having been educated from a child at Mons. Duvieux's Communauté, and having studied his Philosophy and two years' Divinity, he went to the Seminary of St. Gregory in Sept., 1706, a friend allowing 300 livres per annum. But in Sept., 1707, he went to Douay to learn English and perfect himself in School Divinity. In Aug., 1709, he returned to Paris and in March took the Seminary oath, and was ordained Dec. 23, 1713, with Dr. Carnaby. On Jan. 1, 1714, he entered his license, and took the Doctor's Cap in April, 1716. [For some time he was Procurator of St. Gregory's.] When he came on the Mission he resided principally in London, where his time was spent in his missionary duties and in writing the lives of the Saints. The publishing of these was found to exceed his means, and this, together with a confined sale, involved him in great difficulties, so that when he was called on to give a statement of his accounts of the Clergy property, for which he was adminstrator in London, he was found to owe £1,272, for which he was not able to pay more than 10d. in the pound in 1731. In 1732, Doctor Fell was the cause of much contention and afterwards of some publications on account of his being irregularly chosen a member of the Chapter. The case was submitted to the General Assembly in 1739, and decided against him. This not satisfying the Doctor, it was referred to Bishop Petre, of London. "The worthy arbitrator," says Mr. Thomas Berington, "after mature consideration, and after hearing both sides, and taking the best advice, and having begged the light of the Holy Ghost, decided in favour of the Chapter against the Doctor." ["Which decision he sent to Dr. Ryder, Feb. 10, 1736, (O.S.)" (Mr. Thos. Berington's account of it in my hand.)] In 1755, Doctor Fell was appointed Superior of St. Gregory's by the Archbishop of Paris, though he was only the second in the list named by Bishop Stonor; but on account of his age and infirmities, he declined to accept the intended honour. He died in Gray's Inn, Oct. 22, 1763, and in the 77th of his age.

He wrote: 1. *The Lives of the Saints*. In 4 vols, 4to. Dr. Robert Witham, of Douay, wrote Observations on them and denounced them at Rome. These Observations in MS. were in the library of the English College at Rome. His principal complaint was, that he had taken them principally from Baillet and had recorded few miracles. 2. *A Letter from a Catholic Gentleman to his Protestant Friend*. By C. V., *Christian Catholic*, Nov. 19, 1745. Folio of six pages "bound up in the large thick vol. of MS. cases sent to me by Dr. Lingard, p. 1,443." (*St. Gregory's Register*).

FENNEL, EDMUND, was made Confessor to the nuns at Pontoise, on Sept. [15], 1699, and lived in that capacity many years [? to 1719]. He supplied Dodd with his account of these nuns through Dr. Ingleton, of St. Gregory's Seminary. Mr. Fennel's predecessor was Mr. Lawrence Breers, who succeeded [for near two years] Mr. Edmund Kelly, a Doctor of Sorbonne, who was called away, about 1697, to be Theologian to the late Elector of Treves, and at the Elector's death was made Bishop of Clonfert, in Ireland, his native country.

FENTHAM, HENRY, *alias* GIFFARD, S.J., was born in Notts. Having finished his Classics at St. Omers, he proceeded to Rome and was admitted into the College, as a Convictor, by Cardinal Lante, then under the administration of Father Matthew Elliot. After he had finished his Philosophy, he left the College, June 5, 1758, and became a Jesuit at Watten.

FENWICK, ANN, daughter and heiress of Thomas Benison, of Hornby, Esq., married John Fenwick, of Burrow Hall, Co. Lanc., Esq., in 1752, who died in 1757. He was a Protestant, but she a Catholic.

FENWICK [EDWARD DOMINIC, O.P.], was Bishop of Cincinnati, in the Ohio Mission. The State of Ohio is situated in North America, between the 38th and 42nd degrees of N. Lat. The population, in 1800, was computed at 45,000 souls; it has since increased to the number of 600,000. That country is chiefly indebted for the propagation of the true faith to the labours of the Right Rev. Dr. Edward Fenwick, a descendant of the ancient family of the Fenwicks, originally of Fenwick Tower, in the county of Northumberland. He was born in Maryland in 1768. At the age of sixteen he entered the Dominican College of Bornheim, in Flanders, and was there ordained and professed. In the year 1804 he returned to his native country. Two years after, the late Dr. Carroll, Archbishop of Baltimore, sent him to Kentucky, where he found but one Priest, Mr. Badin. He there exercised Missionary duties, and devoted the whole of his patrimony towards establishing a convent of his Order, in which eleven Priests have already been educated for the American Mission. In 1810 he extended his labours into the forests of Ohio, where no Catholic Priest had before penetrated ; but he found there three Catholic families only, of German extraction. Ten years had elapsed since they had seen a Priest. They welcomed him as an angel sent from heaven into their wilderness to administer to them the consolations of religion. A parcel of land was bought and cleared, a wooden chapel was erected, and a house built in the rude style of the country, for the reception of a Priest. Four years ago, Pope Pius VII., to encourage the progress of religion, erected the See of Cincinnati. This town, situated on the Ohio river, contains at present about 20,000 souls, of which 1,000 are Catholics. The Rev. Edward Fenwick was appointed to fill the new See. Never, perhaps, were the resources of a Prelate less proportioned to his wants. Aided by the contributions of his former parishioners in Kentucky, he was enabled to proceed to Cincinnati. On his arrival there, obstacles presented themselves on all sides. He was compelled to purchase the very ground for the site of his Cathedral on credit. This small chapel is not yet paid for. The Prelate had still no seminary, when providentially a suitable building, with fifty-six acres of land, situated within half-a-mile of the Episcopal town, was offered for sale. 7,000 dollars, payable in seven yearly instalments, was the sum demanded. The opportunity of making a cheap purchase, and the promotion of the greater glory of God, were objects not to be neglected : the land was accordingly purchased. The debt remains unpaid, and a failure in complying with the conditions of the contract must prove detrimental to the interests of religion. No substantial contributions can be expected from the humble means of the Christians of Ohio ; the offerings of the faithful are indeed so scanty from real penury, not from want of good will, as scarcely to afford their pastor a subsistence, after having made the utmost effort in raising chapels, and meeting the usual expenses of the sacred altars. There are in the new dioceses many Indians. Some of their tribes traverse the Lake Erie in order to have access to a Priest who understands their language, at Malden. They have recently addressed petitions to the President of the United States to obtain Catholic Missionaries. That of Magate Pinesinidjigo, Chief of the Otawas, is here subjoined :

" Father,—At this present time I desire of thee to listen to me, and to all my children. From this distant country they extend their arms to grasp thee by the hand. We, the Chiefs, the fathers of families, and other Otawas residing at l'Arbre Crochu, pray earnestly and supplicate thee, our respectable Father, to procure for us a Magate Ogs 8 a (sic, a black robe); that is to say, a Missionary like those who instruct the Indians in the neighbourhood of Montreal. Father, be charitable towards thy children, listen to them : we desire to be instructed in the same principles of religion as our ancestors professed, when the Mission of St. Ignatius existed. We address thee, the first and principal Chief of the United States ; we pray thee to assist us to build a House of Prayer. We will give land to cultivate to the Minister of the Great Spirit, whom thou wilt send to instruct us and our poor children. We do please ourselves to please him, and to follow his good advice. We shall find ourselves happy if thou wilt send to us a man of God of the Catholic Religion, of the same kind as those who instructed our fathers. Such is the desire of thy devoted children ; they have the confidence that thou, who art their father, wilt have the goodness to listen to them. This is all that thy children demand of thee at present. All thy children, father, present thee their hand, and grasp thine with all the affection of their heart. (Signed) MAGATE PINESINIDJIGO " (Blackbird). Many other marks follow (Signatures).

Dr. Fenwick is very grateful, and hereby returns his warmest thanks for the liberal succours which he obtained in England and other countries during

his last visit to Europe. His benefactors will have the cordial satisfaction of
feeling that they have lent their aid through the purest motives of charity ;
that their contributions and names will be connected with the rising religion
of the most destitute diocese in Christendom ; that their memories will be
cherished and handed down to posterity by the reclaimed settlers and
Christianised savages of Ohio. But much remains to be done before religion
can be said to be firmly established in that new country, and a large field is
here open to the charities of the religious Europeans. Englishmen annually
vote thousands of pounds to the furtherance of their foreign missions, and to
the dissemination of the Bible. Now can any claims be more urgent upon the
generosity of Christians than the distressed circumstances of the Ohio
Mission ? The Bishop of Cincinnati and the Catholic population of Ohio
humbly present this short statement of their condition, and address with
confidence this appeal to the friends of humanity and religion. In confirmation of the above statement, the public are referred to the following (end of
newspaper cutting) :

" Reverend Sir,—Being informed that the late Mrs. Mercer had made a
legacy to the R.R. Bishop of Bardstown, I deemed it my duty, as agent of
that mission, to call on the R.R. Dr. Milner for information. He referred me
to you and to the Rev. Mr. Jink [Jenks]. I have long delayed to trouble your
reverence in this case, because a friend in Staffordshire promised his interfer-
ance, for which I am under obligation to him. But as I have lately heard
nothing of his progress in that affair, and my further stay in England will be
short, the term for payment having elapsed ; as I do suppose that the legacies
left to the Midland Mission Fund and to the Sunday School of Hathersage must
or may by this time have been paid, I take the liberty to trouble you with this
letter in order to be made acquainted with your mode of proceeding, with your
success, or any difficulty which may be in the way either from the executor of
the will or from the heirs. I applied to Doctors' Commons to know the nature,
extent, and expression of the legacy ; but the will has not been entered into
the Commons, and I have been directed to apply to the Bishop's Court at
Lichfield. This I have neglected to do, because I depended on the exertions
of my friend in Staffordshire. Allow me, my dear Sir, to request you now to
favour me with an answer, as soon as you can make it convenient, and with a
copy of the will above mentioned, if it is in your possession or accessible to
you. In union to your good prayers and SS., I remain, very respectfully,
Reverend Sir, Your obedient, humble servant, STEPHEN T. BADIN, V.G. of
Kentucky and Ohio.—Nov. [? 2], 1825. Paternoster Row, London."

" P.S.—I must not close this without informing your Reverence that I
advised Bishop Flagel to send a power of attorney to Rev. Mr. Weld and Mr.
Sidney, of Star and Garter Yard, Ratcliff Highway, London, to act jointly or
separately."

FESBY, or FACEBY, THOMAS. He studied at Douay, and on his return
lived with Mr. Meynell, of North Dalton. In 1693 he had been more than
thirty years on the Mission. " He was a gentleman of great sobriety and
regularity," say the *Chapter Records*, "but withal of great singularity, and of
great inflexibility in it."

FIRBY, THOMAS, eldest son of Thomas Firby by his wife Dorothy
Lumsden, was born in Yorkshire, Mar. 25, 1740. He studied at Rome
[admitted July 15, 1754], and was ordained Dec. 17, 1763. On the following
May [1], he left the College and came on the Mission. He lived many years
as Confessor to the nuns at Scorton Hall, and died there, June 11, 1823, in
his 84th year.

FIRTH, or FRITH, RICHARD (of St. Silvanus), was Vicar-Provincial of the
English Discalced Carmelites. He died at Tongres, Aug. 17, 1792, aged 76,*
[religious 50].

---

* Zimmerman *Carmel in England*, p. 379, says he was born Jan. 7, 1719.

7

FISHER, *alias* FITTER, DANIEL, son of Francis Fisher, Esq., in the County of Lancaster, by his wife Susanna Hudson. Daniel was born in London June 4, 1645, and in [Feb.] 1662 went over to Lisbon in the company of Mr. Russell, Bishop of Portalegro. At that time he was a member of the Church of England ; but becoming acquainted with the superiors of the College, and particularly with Dr. Godden, who had himself been educated a Protestant, he became a Catholic and was admitted into the College. Here his application was great and his success corresponded with it. His thesis in Logic he dedicated to Lady Ann Ratcliff, and his Universal Philosophy to Bishop Russell, Mar. 31, 1667, on both of which occasions he was greatly applauded. On May 1, 1670, he was made Professor of Philosophy, and in April, 1675, was sent on the Mission. Of his labours here I find no mention, but he died in London in 1685-6. (*Chapter Obituary ; Lisbon Register*, p. 1062.)

FISHER, JOHN, O.S.B., died [a Jubilarian] Jan. 27, 1793, aged 84, at Dieuleward.

FITTER [? *vere* FISHER], DANIEL (*Lisbon Catalogue* or *Diary*, p. 1046), was younger brother of Francis Fitter. Having studied the rudiments of the Latin tongue in England, he was sent by his uncle, Mr. Harfield Pretty, a Priest, to join his elder brother Francis at Lisbon, where, at the age of nineteen, he was admitted into the College, Nov. 24, 1647. On Dec. 12, 1651, he took the College oath, was made sub-deacon on the 18th, deacon on the 21st, Priest on the 24th, and on the 25th said his first Mass. He defended Universal Philosophy under Dr. Godden Feb. 3, 1653, with great applause, and in the same year a treatise of Divinity, on June 29, under Dr. Clayton, the President. Having suffered much, as it was thought, from the stone, by the advice of the physicians he left the College to go into France in 1654. "After sailing twenty-six days, says the Diary, "the ship was attacked by a privateer of Ostend, and in the engagement the powder magazine exploded, the vessel was shattered to pieces and the boat was carried to a considerable distance. Mr. Fitter was blown up into the air, but providentially fell into the boat, where he was found by a Spanish soldier, dreadfully burnt, bruised, and half dead. It was, indeed, reported at Lisbon that he was dead, and prayers were said for the repose of his soul, yet he escaped with his life ; but three of his ribs were broken, and one of his legs. On his arrival at Ostend he was most kindly treated by the owner of the privateer, as he had been before by the captain, especially when it was discovered that he was a Priest." From Ostend he gave an account of his misfortune and providential escape to the President of Lisbon College, and as soon as he was sufficiently recovered, he passed over to England and was placed in the family of William Fowler, Esq., of St. Thomas's Priory, near Stafford, where he was in high estimation, and also with his brethren. He was, however, one of those who, about the time of Oates' plot, approved of the Oath of Supremacy, and wrote in defence of it, explaining the word *Spiritual* agreeably to the sense given to it in the *Injunctions* of Queen Elizabeth, and by the generality of Protestant Divines. [" 'Tis said also that Cressy, Fr. John Winter, Mr. Hutchinson, *als.* Barry, and Dr. Short espoused the lawfulness of the Oath.—Dodd's MSS., see *Panzani*, p. 325."] The explanation, however, was not deemed satisfactory by Catholics in general, and his former Professor, Dr. Godden, wrote a treatise against the Oath. In the General Assembly of the Chapter, in 1687 (*Minutes of the Chapter*), he was chosen V.G. of Staffordshire, Derbyshire, Cheshire, Salop, "upon condition that he signed the declaration made by our Brethren in Paris against the Oath of Supremacy " ; Mr. Fitter was also at the head of those in the Midland District who enrolled themselves Members of the Institute, *Clericorum Secularium in communi viventium*, and on the dissolution of that assembly by Bishop Giffard, was the founder of what is called the *Common Purse*, of which he continued to be the administrator and trustee during his life. He also left a fund for a Priest, " who was to have no servant, nor depend upon any family, but was to reside in the County of Stafford, and was to assist any poor body in the county, and within four or five miles of it, who might want help, either by reason of their own ghostly father being absent, or by reason of the want of one in those parts where such poor may live." During the reign of James II., he opened a school in Stafford for the benefit of poor Catholics in that town and neighbourhood. It was suppressed at the Revolution; but Mr. Fitter continued to live peaceably at St. Thomas's till Feb. 6, 1700, on which day he died, aged 72. He was much respected and beloved by all in the neighbourhood, and particularly in the family of the Fowlers, to whom he had been of great service in some family concerns; and especially in the charge he undertook of Gertrude Fowler, who by some accident or other was almost an idiot.

FITTER, *alias* FISHER, FRANCIS (*Lisbon Catalogue*, p. 1031), was son of William Fitter and uncle of Andrew Bromwich. He was born of respectable parents in the neighbourhood of Wolverhampton, where he studied his first rudiments of Latin. At the age of eighteen he went over to Lisbon, where he was admitted into the College, Dec. 7, 1640, and on July 25 in the following year he took the College oath. Having finished the usual course of studies, he was ordained Priest on July 30, 1645, and on April 7, 1647, he left the College to proceed through Holland to England. Staffordshire and Shropshire were the theatres of his Apostolic labours, and on the death of Andrew Bromwich he succeeded him at Oscott. On the death of his younger brother, Daniel Fitter, he succeeded him in the administration of the Clergy funds, and was a great benefactor to them. He was a most laborious and zealous Missionary, and tho' naturally of a weak constitution, yet he so managed it that he lived to the age of 89, and died in 1711, universally regretted in death, as he had been beloved and respected in life. [Resided at Dulton in 1692.] Mr. Francis Fitter was a member of the Chapter, and in 1667 was chosen Archdeacon of Cheshire, Derbyshire and Staffordshire. In this capacity he assisted at the General Assembly of the Chapter in 1667 (*Chapter Records*). This was the second that was held after the death of Dr. Smith, the Bishop of Chalcedon [in 1655]. The first was in 1657, when it was resolved that they should be held every three years. But no extra business occurring at the time to warrant the trouble and expense of such meeting from all parts of the kingdom, and the plague appearing in 1660, it was put off till 1667, when it was called by Dr. Ellice, the Dean of the Chapter. At that time there was a prospect of opening a house in Paris to enable the Clergy to take degrees there, and Abbot Montagu, the Lord Almoner to the Queen Dowager, had proposed to the Dean to send an Agent to Rome for the purpose of obtaining a Bishop. On these accounts it was deemed proper to call a General Meeting of the Chapter. The Assembly consisted of Dr. Ellice, the Dean, who presided, three Vicar-Generals, eighteen Archdeacons, and nine Canons, but seven appointed their deputies. The Assembly was held in London and opened on May 6 with a Mass of the Holy Ghost solemnly said by the Dean, at which all were present. The names of all were read, who then proceeded to make the profession of Faith of Pius IV. After some vacancies had been filled, the Confirmation of the Chapter by the late Bishop of Chalcedon was read, and was ordered to be read at the beginning of any future Assembly of the Chapter. In the second Session, held May 7, the Acts of the Assembly of 1657, in one of which they disclaimed the Pope's power to depose Princes, was read and approved. A Committee was appointed to draw up Rules for the Dean, the Vicar-General and Archdeacons. The distress of Lisbon College was explained by the Dean; and Mr. Singleton stated that Mr. Carr had given £600 to the establishment at Paris, Abbot Montagu and Mr. Clifford had promised as much, Lady Abbess £200 and part of their house, Mr. Thomas White £50 per annum out of the Arras money, and £100 per annum was expected from the Town House formerly given to Arras College, for which they received the thanks of the Assembly in a letter, in which they signified to them that "the end and intent of the establishment must be for the Clergy's good in general, and to raise and season Missionaries; some by instructing them in clerical and pastoral duties, others by taking degrees; others in other kinds of studies as shall be thought fit by the Superior of the Secular Clergy in England, on whom the donations must be settled, and by whom the Superior of the house must be appointed." Mr. Thomas Carr was then nominated the first Superior. In the third Session, Dr. Godden brought up the state of Lisbon College, and as Bishop Russell, then present, declared that £200 was necessary to supply their present necessities, and that he would supply the same, that sum was partly raised by contributions from the Bishops assembled and partly from the Clergy rents. The Rules for the Dean, etc., were read and approved. Rural Deans were proposed by the Vicars-General and Archdeacons, and accepted by the Dean and Chapter, who gave them letters patent. It was then resolved that "all Brethren thro' England be forbidden to censure or intermeddle with any actions of his Majesty, or his affairs of State, but humbly to obey and to expect God's and their pleasure, and that it be recommended to all our Brethren to pray daily for His Majesty, the two queens and the Royal Family." In the fourth Session, held May 9, it was resolved "to petition for a Bishop, when the time shall be judged fit by the Dean and ten other members of the Chapter," and in the meanwhile a letter was to be written to Mr. Lesley, at Rome, expressing the great desire they had of a Superior from His Holiness, but that to receive an Apostolic Vicar is displeasing to the State and against the ancient laws of the kingdom. Resolved to move for an absolute Ordinary, but if that cannot be had, for a Bishop on the same tenor as the Bishop of Chalcedon was; that each member propose three for that dignity and that the five who have the majority of votes be proposed at Rome. These were found to be Dr. Godden, Dr. Ellice, Mr. John Leyburne, Dr. Gage, and Mr. Manley. It was then ordered that the *Pax* be given in the Mass throughout England and Wales, and that the Brethren be very cautious in marrying Protestants with Catholics. In the fifth and last Session, held May 11, it was ordered, besides other things, "that every Priest be admonished and strictly commanded by the Dean and Chapter not to maintain any opinion, whether speculative or practical, against the common doctrine and common practice of the Church, as also to avoid in practice all extravagant cases." The Acts of the Assembly were then read and subscribed by all the persons present. From infirmity, or other cause, Mr. Fitter named his deputy to the General Assemblies of 1672 and 1676.

FITZHERBERT, ROBERT (*Lisbon Catalogue* and *Chapter Records*), was son of Francis Fitzherbert, of Tissington, Esq., Co. Derby. He studied the rudiments of Latin in England, and at the age of eighteen he was sent to Lisbon and admitted into the College, Aug. 15, 1647. Having been ordained Priest he was sent on the Mission in 1652, and lived with ―――― Draycott, of Paynsley, Esq., in the north of Staffordshire. He was a member of the Chapter, and on the resignation of Mr. Francis Fitter he was chosen Archdeacon of Staffordshire, Derbyshire and Cheshire, Aug. 5, 1682. In this capacity he assisted at the General Assembly in 1684. This Assembly consisted of Dr. Perrot, the Dean, who presided, and of three Vicars General, sixteen Archdeacons and eight [nine] Canons. They met at a house in Wild Garden on June 3. This house belonged to the Chapter and had been found so convenient for the security of Priests and chapel furniture, during Oates' plot, that they were at the expense of £50 in repairing it in 1683. After the Dean had said Mass of the Holy Ghost and all had made the Profession of Faith of Pius IV., "he proposed to them the chief business which had occasioned their meeting, *viz.*, that of *procuring a Bishop*. It was then unanimously resolved and ordered that everyone should write down five names of such persons as they thought most proper for that great dignity, and those five that had most votes should be presented to his Holiness. When these were opened, Dr. Godden, Dr. Perrot, Dr. Betham, Dr. Giffard, Mr. John Leyburn, and Dr. Smith, were found to have the most universal concurrence of the votes. As the last two had equal votes the Assembly resolved to present six instead of five to his Holiness." They had previously resolved to communicate the design of the General Meeting to government, and to ask permission to hold it. In the first Session a letter was read from Mr. Franks, the Archdeacon of Yorkshire, in which he informed the Assembly that "the practice of abstaining from eggs on Fridays, in the parts north of the Trent, was in a great measure laid by, that those few that observed it did it chiefly in compliance with the decree of the General Assembly of 1676; that from this variety of practice happened often very scandalous disputes, in fine, that most of the gentry desired conformity to the rest of England, especially since of late years, that plenty of fish, that had made their abstaining from eggs more easy, had much failed." On the proposal of Mr. Franks, "it was agreed and resolved by much the major part that the northern Catholics, on the other side of Trent, may take the same liberty as to eating eggs on Fridays, which is practised in other parts of England; and that this decree also extended to those on the other side of Ribble." In the second Session, held June 4, after filling up some vacancies, "a Committee was appointed to consider of such things as may be expedient for a reformation of manners, in all particulars relating to a Missionary Apostolic." In the third, held June 5, Dr. Betham informed the Assembly that he had procured an establishment for his Community of St. Gregory under the broad seal of the King of France, and that the Archbishop of Paris had been extremely obliging and assisting therein, and in settling the establishment. It was then resolved that a letter of thanks be written to the Archbishop in the name of the Assembly. "It was also resolved, besides other things, by the unanimous judgment of the Assembly, that 'tis unlawful for Catholics, who are first married by a Priest, to be again married by a [the] Parson, or to take a certificate from him, that they were married by him, and that this decree should be communicated to all the country Brethren." In Session four, held June 9, the rules of reformation were brought up by the Committee and read, and being approved by the Assembly, "they were ordered to be inserted in the Acts of the Assembly and communicated to the Brethren" (See *Records Miscellanea*). In the same Session, which was the last, "the question concerning the Bishop's title being moved, it was unanimously agreed that they should move for *an Ordinary*." The Acts of the Assembly were then read over by the Secretary, Dr. Giffard, and were signed. (Dr. Giffard's *Minutes*, in the *Chapter Archives*.)

NOTE.—In the year preceding (1683), the Dean and Chapter wrote a letter to Cardinal Howard, "to acquaint him with their ardent desire of a Bishop, and to desire his Eminence's judgment and direction, whether it might be proper at that time to move in order to the obtaining of one."

In the following August, of 1684, the names of the "six gentlemen proposed for Bishops in the Assembly, were sent to Rome in a letter to Cardinal Howard, and at the same time, as the Dean and Chapter were given to understand that the Cardinal would not be unwilling to accept of the Character, they expressed their desire of having his Eminence for Bishop; and since his circumstances might not permit him to reside in England, they requested he would make choice of one of the six nominees to be his Suffragan or Coadjutor in England. In the same, they requested that the Bishop might be *an Ordinary*. To this letter an answer was received in April, 1685, in which his Eminence tells them that *an Ordinary* in the manner they desired was not likely to be procured. Soon after, Bishop Leyburn arrived with the title of *Vicar-Apostolic*. Mr. Fitzherbert, like his friend and fellow collegian, Mr. Daniel Fitter, enrolled himself a member of the Institute or Society *Clericorum Secularium in communi viventium*. He was made Rural Dean of Staffordshire by Bishop Leyburn, and died in 1701.

FITZHERBERT, THOMAS, of Swinnerton, Esq., in 1778, married the widow of Edward Weld, of Lulworth Castle. His Lady, so well known and so highly respected in the fashionable world, was the daughter of Walter Smythe, of Brambridge, Hants, Esq., brother of Sir Edward Smythe, of Acton Burnell, Bart. Her first husband left her a young widow, without any family. By her second husband, Mr. Fitzherbert, she had an only son, who lived but a few months. "Mr. Fitzherbert was an astonishing pedestrian, and being inclined to corpulence, he endeavoured to counteract that tendency by the most extraordinary bodily exertions, by which he was supposed to have impaired his constitution. During the riots in London in 1780, his curiosity led him, on one occasion, to mix with the mob; and at the close of the day, being much fatigued and over-heated, he had the imprudence to throw himself into a cold bath, the consequences of which proved fatal. Symptoms of consumption and of a rapid decline appearing soon after, he went with his Lady to the South of France, and died at Nice in 1781, and was buried in the Church of the Dominicans in that city, with this epitaph:

NOBILI VIRO
THOMAE FITZHERBERTO ANGLO
MARIA SMYTHE CONJUGI B.M.
JOANNES FRATRI OPT.
MOERENTES P.P.
III. ID. MAIJ MDCCLXXXI.

"By the untimely death of her husband, without issue, the Swinnerton Estates devolved on his brother, Basil Fitzherbert, who married a daughter of Mrs. Windsor Heneage. The Fitzherberts of Tissington, in Derbyshire, are descended from a second son of John Fitzherbert, of Norbury; the Fitzherberts of Swinnerton, from the eldest, in the reign of Henry III. This branch of the family has been raised to the peerage in the person of Alleyne Fitzherbert, Lord St. Helen's."

Mrs. Fitzherbert's long and intimate and mysterious connection, after the death of her husband, with George IV., while Prince of Wales, rendered her the topic of general conversation, more than perhaps any other female of her time; but by her friends and relations, and by all those who have ever enjoyed the honour of her acquaintance, she has always been regarded with the most unqualified sentiments of approbation and esteem.

FLANN, OR HANNE [CHARLES], S.J.—He lived many years at Haggerston Castle, till, being incapable of the duty of the place through his age and infirmities, Mr. Tidyman, from Valladolid, was invited to assist him in 1790, and on his death succeeded him.

FLEETWOOD, SIR JOHN, fifth Baronet. He married Philippa, daughter of William Berington, of Salop, niece to his brother, ——, and died in 1741. She died June 4th, 1716, aged 70, by whom he had Sir Thomas, sixth Bart., who succeeded his father, and died a bachelor, Jan., 1781 [1780]. This Sir Thomas, seventh Bart., married Mary Bostock, a branch of the ancient Bostocks, of Bostock, in Cheshire, and died at Bath, December 3, 1802, aged 61. His widow married the Count de Fronte, Sardinian Embassador.* and after his death, Thomas Wright, of Kelvedon, Co. Essex.

FLEETWOOD, SIR RICHARD, third Baronet, was eldest son of St. Thomas. He married Anne, daughter of Sir Edward Golding, of Colston Bassett, Notts, by whom he had three sons; Thomas, who died before his father, Rowland, and Edward, who both died unmarried, and five daughters. (*Betham*, p. 120.)

FLEETWOOD, SIR THOMAS, of Calwich, Co. Stafford, second Baronet. He was son of Richard, the first Baronet, and Anne, daughter of Sir John Peskell, of Horsley, Co. Stafford. He succeeded his father in his title and estate, and married Gertrude, daughter of Rowland Eyre, of Hassop, Co. Derby, by whom he had four sons: Sir Richard; Thomas; Rowland, of Prestwood, in Ellaston Parish, who died *sine prole*; and William, and one daughter, Anne. (*Betham.*)

FLEETWOOD, SIR THOMAS, the fourth Baronet, was son of Thomas, the second son of Sir Thomas Fleetwood, of Calwich, by Elizabeth, daughter of —— Coyney, Co. Stafford, his first wife. He [the fourth Baronet] married Magdalen, daughter of Thomas Berington, of Moat Hall, Salop, and on the death of his uncle, Sir Richard, without male issue, the title devolved on him. In the life-time of his father, or at his death, Calwich ceased to be the property

---

* In a letter dated Winsley, Aug. 5, 1820, Mr. Thomas Berington says: "Envoy from the Court of Turin to England."

of the family of the Fleetwoods, and Sir Thomas and his successors were seated at Morton Hall, Cheshire, which was afterwards sold to Mr. Cholmondely, of Vale Royal. Sir Thomas died [without issue, in Dec., 1739], at New Church, Cheshire. His father by a second wife had two sons ; William, who died a bachelor, and Sir John, who succeeded his half-brother, Sir Thomas.

FLEETWOOD, THOMAS, of Gerard's Bromley, married Frances, the only sister of Charles, sixth Lord Gerard, by whom he acquired the estates of that nobleman, at Gerard's Bromley, and Dutton Hall, in Cheshire, which had been settled on her to the exclusion (except an annuity of £60) of her brother, Philip, the seventh Lord Gerard, who was disinherited. He died July 15th, 1720, at Gerard's Bromley, and his wife at Liège, Feb. 3, 1736, *aet.* 74. By her he had one son, Charles Gerard Fleetwood, who squandered away the ample estates of his father by gaming. That of Bromley was won at play by Hugo Meynell, and that of Dutton Hall was sold about the middle of last century to Mr. Lant, and is now the property by purchase of the Brookes, of Mere, Cheshire. This graceless son afterwards took to the stage, and at the time of his death was, it is said, Manager of one of the London Playhouses.

FLEETWOOD [WALTER], S.J.—As Mr. Thomas Berington, Dean of the Chapter, calls him *Cousin*, I conclude he was of the family of Calwich, in Staffordshire, as Mr. Berington's sister, Magdalen Berington, married Sir Thomas Fleetwood, Bart., who died Dec., 1739. Mr. Fleetwood was educated at Rome ;* was Master of Twyford School till 1732 or 3, when he was succeeded by Mr. Betts. He then retired to Paynsley, in the north of Staffordshire, the seat of Lord Langdale, and a few miles from Calwich. How long he stayed there I cannot find ; but my memoirs add that he became a Jesuit, and probably carried with him to the Society the interest he had with the scholars of Twyford and their parents, which caused the school to decline, and made it difficult, says Bishop Stonor, to supply his place. Mr. Berington says : " Cousin Fleetwood died at Liège Feb. 14, 1737† (N.S.)."

FLETCHER, SIR HENRY, of Hutton, Cumberland, Baronet, was son of Sir George Fletcher, by his wife Alice, daughter of Hugh, Viscount Colerain, " a gentleman," says Betham, " of great hopes and expectations." He was educated a Protestant but became a Catholic, and settled his estate of about £1,500 per annum on a distant relation, Thomas Fletcher, of Moresby, Esq., reserving only a small competency for life. He then retired to Douay, and fitted up an apartment for himself adjoining the English Franciscans, whose elegant church he built. He died May 19, 1712, in the 54th year of his age, and was buried in the north side of the Choir, before the high altar. By a codicil in his will Sir Henry left legacies to the amount of £850, which the Commissioners of Enquiry, in 1716, declared to be for superstitious uses. They were accordingly seized, as also "a large altar," with other plate of Sir Henry Fletcher's, which sold for £960 ; of the latter sum, £225 was paid to the Discoverer.

FOURNIER [BERNARD], a French Priest, who came over to England and conformed to the Established Church. This slip procured him some friends and the protection of Bishop Hoadley, of Winchester, who seems to have had a good opinion of him, and to have admitted him to his palace, or to have corresponded with him. Having by some means procured a piece of blank paper on which the Bishop had written his name, he repaid the kindness of his patron by forging a draft on him for £8,800. " This," says my manuscript, " was proved in Court, but not what became of him in consequence."

---

* From the draft we glean the following : Ordained at Valladolid ; born Mar. 9, 1699 ; entered noviceship June 20, 1735 ; had the care and direction of Winchester (Twyford) School in 1733, with more than one hundred Pensioners. A Mr. Fleetwood, relation of Sir Thomas F[leetwood] was at Paynsley ; *said* to have left £1,000 to that Mission. Mr. Blount, father to Mr. Michael Blount, was there under him about 1730. Mr. Joseph Gildon, from Douay College, who succeeded him, died at T[wyford], July 26, 1736.

† Foley, vii., 262, gives the date of his death as July 10, 1774.

FOWLER, WALTER, of St. Thomas's Priory, near Stafford, was son of Walter Fowler, by his wife Constantia, youngest daughter of Walter, first Lord Aston, of Tixall. He succeeded to his father's property in 1681, and married Maria, daughter of Walter Heveningham, of Aston Hall, Esq. His sister Mary married John Betham, of Rowington, Co. Warwick, Esq., and his sister Dorothy, Thomas Grove, Esq. In 1712 Mr. Fowler made his will, and having settled an annuity of £300 on his daughter Dorothy, and after her death another of £200 on her son Thomas, he devised his whole landed estate to his neice, Catherine Betham, only daughter of his sister Mary, on condition that she and her husband, if she married, should bear the name of Fowler. However, in 1715 he executed another will, by which he revoked the settlement of 1712, and left his estates equally to his two sisters. This alteration seems to have arisen from some conscientious difficulties suggested by the marked partiality shown to the eldest, when both, as being equally related to him, had equal claims. Mr. Fowler died in 1716, and left behind him the best of characters for his piety, hospitality, and charities to the poor. Mr. Thomas Berington, afterwards Dean of the Chapter, and Simon Berington, lived with Mr. Fowler as his Chaplains, and Bishop Witham also resided at St. Thomas' till he left the Midland to go to the Northern District. Mr. Simon Berington wrote : [*The Memoirs of Signor*] *Gaudenzio de Lucca*, in which a new Utopia is described in elegant language and with great fertility of imagination. (*Description of Tixall Parish*, by Sir Thomas and Arthur Clifford, p. 38. *Ibid*, p. 40.)

FOXE, JAMES OR JOHN, S.J., was born in April, 1730, and entered his novitiate Sept. 7, 1747. Being ordained Priest he came on the Mission, and for several years lived at Gerard's Bromley,* in Staffordshire. When this estate (which came into the Fleetwood family by the marriage of Frances Gerard, sister of Charles, Lord Gerard, to Thomas Fleetwood, Esq.), was lost by the gambling of his son, Charles Gerard Fleetwood, Mr. Foxe was obliged to leave, and retired to Aston, near Stone. His stay here was not long, and Aston was exchanged for Southworth Hall, near Warrington, where he died May 29, 1795.

FRANKS, RICHARD, was born in 1630 of Protestant parents, but becoming a Catholic, he was sent to Valladolid. Being ordained Priest, he came on the Mission about the year 1656, and was placed in Yorkshire, where he lived with Mr. Beckwith, at Marton in Holderness, but paid for his board, and assisted the Catholics in that neighbourhood. In February, 1674 or 5 (O.S.), he was chosen Archdeacon of Yorkshire, in which office he succeeded Mr. George Hodgson, and as such sat in the General Assemblies of 1676, 1684, and 1687. On December [12th], 1692, on the death of Mr. Peter Giffard, he was chosen to succeed him as V.G. of Northumberland, Cumberland, Westmorland, Lancashire, Yorkshire, and Bishopric, and in that capacity deputed Mr. Ward to vote for him in the General Assembly of 1694. I find the following names of Priests in his Archdeaconry : Messrs. May, Metcalf, Gilpin Vinter, Robert Ward, Fesby, John Marsh, M. Dalton, Fathers Hodgson, Cornsforth, Berry, Christopher Witham, Parkinson, Hildreth, Calvert, Stephenson, Smithson, William Pearson, Hardcastle, Dinmore, Shropham, Simson, and Lodge. Mr. Franks died in 1696 or 7. He was " a learned and very virtuous person, a true Clergyman. and sincerely affected to the Chapter, in defence of whose authority," says Mr. Ward, the Secretary, " he wrote a very learned treatise." (*Chapter Records.*)

FROST, PETER, O.S.F.—He lived many years in the family of Peter Holford, of Wootton, Esq., beloved and respected, and died suddenly while saying night prayers for the family, Oct. 3rd, 1785.

FRYER, WILLIAM.—In the year 1760 he was sent to Douay College, together with his brother, Charles, where they arrived May 12. When

---

* The draft says : " Lived at Bromley in 1761-5."

Valladolid was restored to the Clergy, Mr. William Fryer was one of those first sent to it. Having completed his studies, he was sent to Lisbon "to Gibsonize that College," to use the expression of Mr. William Coombes in a letter [to Mr. Eyre] of Dec. 21, 1783, and succeeded Mr. Bernard [Doctor of Rubrick], in the Presidentship, which office he filled to the entire satisfaction of the students, and died there, Aug. 15, 1805. (See *Cath. Mag.* vi., 408.)

FULLER, JOHN, was educated at Douay, and served many years at Moorfields. He was indicted and arraigned for his priestly character on the information of Payne, the carpenter. He retired to Douay some years before his death, and died there Feb. 22, 1792.

FULLER, WILLIAM, Gentleman, was born Sept. 20, 1670, and was related on his mother's side to the Marquis of Powis, in whose family he was placed, under the spiritual direction of Father Lewis Sabran, his Lordship's chaplain. When the Marchioness was made governess to the Prince of Wales, Fuller acted as her page, and here observed, he says, what he published to the world respecting Mrs. Gray's lying-in at the Marchioness's, and accompanied Mrs. Gray to Dover. On his return he was made page to Lady Melfort, and was instructed by Father Maxwell, S.J., tutor to Lord Forth, Lord Melfort's eldest son. At the Revolution he accompanied the Queen to France and St. Germains with Lady Melfort, and was afterwards employed several times in carrying letters from St. Germains to King James while in Ireland, and to his friends in England and Scotland. One time, he says, he brought over forty-seven letters, all of the Queen's, King of France's, and Mons. Lovay's own letters, and a commission for my Lord Dundee, and bills of exchange for £35,000 to be remitted to Scotland. In his twelfth journey to England, with letters in his buttons, [pipes of keys, linings of his boots], he was apprehended by his former guardians, Mr. Harflets? and Major Kitchen, and was taken to Lord Shrewsbury's and examined, when he was sent to Dr. Tennison, Dean of St. Paul's, and by him convinced of the necessity of turning, in order to his salvation from the superstitions of the Church of Rome to the solid faith and principles of and held by the Church of England. After this he was urged to confess what he knew of King James, &c. He was taken to the King at Kensington, where he cut off his buttons, and delivered up the letters he had about him. He was afterwards employed by King William in going to St. Germains, where he acted the hypocrite so well, going to Mass as usual, &c., to Confession to Father Sabran, but did not receive the Sacrament. He returned to England with letters from the Queen and others, which, as well as the answers, he always received open, and consigned them first to King William, and Lord Shrewsbury, and Sydney, which they read and copied, and then Fuller delivered them as they were directed. He was now become a spy of the Court of England, and acknowledges that his life is become much more debauched than formerly. He there became acquainted and lived with Dr. Oates, John Saville, and John Tutchin, whom he looked on as saints, and who tutored him, that he who would serve the nation must do as he had done : fear nobody, but strike at all that stood in his way. In the beginning of 1702 he was committed to the Fleet prison by a warrant from the Lords spiritual and temporal for having written and published two books, twenty-six Depositions, &c., proving the management of the supposititious birth of the pretended Prince of Wales, and *Original letters of the late King James to his greatest friends in England.* He says Sir John Saville, John Tutchin, and the rest which he became acquainted with at Dr. Oates " writ all the scandalous matter, though he put his name to it," and that he was made a tool, to set their own engine at work. For these he was tried at Guildhall before Lord Chief Justice Hall and found guilty of writing them, and of a libel. [He was censured by the votes of both Houses of Parliament, and by their vote ordered to be prosecuted.] His sentence was " that he go to all the Courts in West-minster with a paper pinned on his hat expressing his name ; that he should stand three times in the pillory, two hours at a time, at Charing Cross, Temple Bar, and before the Royal Exchange ; that he should be sent to Bridewell the

Friday after and there be whipt, and afterwards kept to hard labour until the second day of the next term, and to be fined 1,000 marks." He acknowledges that Dr. Oates was one of his prompters. (*Ibid*, pp. 131-2.) " As to what I writ and published concerning the [pretended] Prince of Wales and of one Mrs. Mary Gray, I must own that all my assertions did not amount to any proof of the matter ; but it is no secret, nor would I have it to be so, that the affair was much improved by Mr. Richard Baldwin, John Daunton, and other booksellers, who were zealous for the cause, and as fond of the gain they reaped thereby. I had a great many encouragers in the matter, and was persuaded thereby to get an opportunity to regain my reputation, which being seconded with the advantage of new friends and daily benefactors (of which I stood in great need), I was led unhappily on from one thing to another, which brings to my mind :

> " Rebels, like witches, having signed the Rolls,
> Must serve their masters, tho' they damn their souls."

He seems to have been a vain, extravagant, weak, and even wicked man, who became the tool of designing men much more wicked than himself. (*Life of W. Fuller impartially written by himself, in ye Queen's Bench.* London, 1703.)

GABB, THOMAS. At the age of twenty-one he went to Douai College, in Sept., 1763, and was ordained Deacon in 1772. The same year he left the College in consequence of bad health, and lived with his father in London, but continued his studies under the direction of Bishop James Talbot. Being ordained Priest in the Advent of 1772, by direction of Bishop Challoner, he was immediately sent to Old Hall to assist Mr. Willacy, who had lost his voice in a severe illness, but in Aug., 1773, he was removed to Lord Dillon's at Braywick, in Berkshire. In 1777, he was placed at East Hendred, where he remained ten years, till the death of Mrs. Eyston. In 1788 he was appointed one of the chaplains to the Sardinian Ambassador, and when St. Patrick's Chapel was opened in Sutton Street, in 1792, Bishop Douglass gave him the charge of it. In this laborious mission he continued about four and a half years, when, his health being greatly impaired, he was obliged to resign his charge, and retired to the Isle of Wight, where he soon recovered his health and superintended the building of the chapel at West Cowes (erected on the plan he had given) by Mrs. Heneage at the expense of £3,000. But another person was employed to procure materials, &c., "while more than a third of the expense, he said, he could have saved had he directed all." For more than three years Mr. Gabb had the care of the Congregation at Portsea, and in 1803, at the request of the late Duke of Norfolk, with whom he had been fellow-collegian at Douai, he was placed at Worksop Manor, "where, he says, most of his leisure time was filled up by the agreeable study of Architecture, for which, he said, he had more taste than for any other study." Here he died April 16, 1817, in the 76th year of his age.

He was author of : *Finis Pyramidis*.

GAGE, BASILIA, maid of honour to Mary d'Este, the wife of King James II., was one of the daughters of Sir Edward Gage, Bart., of Hengrave, Suffolk, by his fourth wife, Lady Elizabeth Fielding, daughter of George, Earl of Desmond, and sister of Basil, Earl of Denbigh and Desmond. Her father appointed her executrix of his will, which she proved in the month of January, 1707.

GAGE, SIR EDWARD, [first Baronet of Hengrave] Suffork, Bart., was third son of Sir John Gage, of Firle, Sussex, Bart., by his wife, Penelope, daughter and coheiress of Thomas, Lord D'Arcy, of Chirk and Earl Rivers. The title of Bart. was granted by Charles II. to Colonel Gage as a recompense for the services of his father, Sir Henry Gage, Knight, who had been Governor of Oxford for Charles I., and lost his life in his cause at Cullumbridge, near Abingdon. As the Colonel had no issue he procured the patent to be settled on Edward, his kinsman, who, being made heir to his mother's inheritance of Hengrave, became seated there, was knighted, and at last, July 15, 1662, was

created Baronet. This Sir Edward had five wives : first, Mary, daughter of
Sir William Hervey, of Ickworth, Suffolk, Knt.; second, Frances, second
daughter of Walter, Lord Aston, of Tixall, by whom he had one son, Francis,
who had Packington Hall, near Lichfield, in right of his mother, who died in
child-bed of him ; third, Anne, daughter of ———— Watkins ; fourth, Elizabeth
Fielding, daughter of George, Earl of Desmond ; fifth, Bridget Fielding, of the
same family, relict of ———— Slaughter, Esq. Sir Edward died Jan. 31, 1707, in
the 8oth [9oth] year of his age [and was succeeded in the baronetage by William,
his eldest son]. The draft adds [he had issue by his four first wives] (*Betham,*
ii., p. 318).

[It may be well to complete the list of the Baronets of this family, they were :
2. Sir William, eldest son of above, died Feb. 8, 1727. 3. Sir Thomas, grandson of last, died unmarried, 1741. 4. Sir William, brother of last, died 1767.
5. Sir Thomas Rookwood, *see below.* 6. Sir Thomas, son of last, died 1798.
7. Sir Thomas, son of last, died 1820. 8. Sir Thomas, son of last ; he assumed
the additional name of Rookwood, and died in 1866. 9. Sir Edward, died
sine prole, 1872.]

GAGE, SIR HENRY, Knt. of Haling House in Surrey, descended from
Robert, younger son of Sir John Gage, K.G., of Firle, in the County of Sussex,
commanded the English regiment in Flanders, and with permission offered his
services to King Charles I., during that monarch's residence in Oxford.
Clarendon has drawn the following character of this distinguished personage.
" He was in truth a very extraordinary man, of a large and graceful person,
of an honorable extraction, his grandfather having been Knight of the Garter ;
besides his great experience and abilities as a soldier, which were very
eminent, he had very great parts of breeding, being a very good scholar, in
the polite parts of learning, a great master in the Spanish and Italian tongues,
besides the French and the Dutch, which he spoke in great perfection, having
scarce been in England in twenty years before. He was likewise very
conversant in courts, having for many years been much esteemed in that of
the Arch-Duke and Duchess Albert and Isabella, at Brussells, which was a
great and very regular court at that time, so that he deserved to be looked
upon as a wise and accomplished person. Of this gentleman the Lords of the
Council had a singular esteem and consulted frequently with him, whilst they
looked to be besieged, and thought Oxford to be the more secure for his being
in it ; which rendered him so ungrateful to the Governor, Sir Arthur Aston,
that he crossed him in anything he proposed, and hated him perfectly, as they
were of natures and manners as different as men can be." (*History of the
Rebellion,* folio edition, ii., 407.) Sir Henry Gage twice relieved the garrison
at Basing House, the seat of John, Marquis of Winchester, and he also assisted
with equal success in the relief of the Castle of Banbury and Donnington.
Sir Arthur Aston, being subsequently removed from his situation as Governor
at Oxford, the King gave this important trust to Sir Henry Gage. Clarendon
says : this appointment was given " to the most general satisfaction of all
men." The same noble author, to complete the character of Sir Henry Gage
by showing that he was as faithful to God as he was loyal to his King, closes
this history of him with the following remarkable passage. " Sir Arthur Aston
was so much displeased with his successor that he besought the King to confer
that charge upon any other person. And when he found that his Majesty
would not change his purpose, he sent to some Lords to come to him, who he
thought were most zealous in religion, and desired them to tell the King from
him, ' that, tho' he was himself a Roman Catholic, he had been very careful
to give no scandal to his Majesty's Protestant subjects, and could not but
inform him that Gage was the most Jesuited Papist alive, and that he had a
Jesuit who lived with him, and that he was present at all the sermons among
the Catholics ; which, he believed, would be very much to his Majesty's
disservice.' So much his passion and animosity overruled his conscience.
The King liked the choice he had made, and only advised the new Governor,
by one of his friends, ' to have so much discretion in his carriage that there

might be no notice taken of the exercise of his religion'; to which animadversion he answered, 'that he never had dissembled his religion nor never
would ; but that he had been so wary in the exercise of it, that he knew there
could be no witness produced who had ever seen him at Mass in Oxford, tho'
he heard Mass every day ; and that he had never been but once at a sermon,
which was at the lodging of Sir Arthur Aston's daughter, to which he had been
invited with great importunity, and believed now that it was to entrap him.'
But the poor gentleman enjoyed this office very little time, for within a month,
or thereabouts, making an attempt to break down Culham Bridge, near
Abingdon, where he had intended to erect a royal fort that should have kept
that garrison from that side of the country, he was shot through the heart with
a musket bullet. Prince Rupert was present at the action, having approved
and been much pleased with the design, which was never pursued after his
death ; and in truth the King sustained a wonderful loss in his death, he being
a man of great wisdom and temper, and one among the very few soldiers who
made himself to be universally loved and esteemed." Sir Henry Gage's death
took place Jan. 11, 1644. He was interred in Christ Church Cathedral,
Oxford, at the public expense, being attended to his grave by all the court,
the army, and members of the University. A monument was erected in the
same church at the public charge, bearing the following inscription to his
memory.

P. M. S.

Hic Situs est Militum Chiliarcha
Henricus Gage, Eques Auratus, filius ac
Haeres Johannis Gage de Haling in Agro
Surriensi Armigeri, pronepos Johannis Gage,
Honoratissimi Ordinis Periscelidis Equitis.

In Belgio meruit supra Annos XX in omni proelio et obsidione Berghæ ad
Zomam, Bredæ, ac praecipue S. Audomari. Ex Belgio ad M. Britt. Regem
missus attulit armorum, VII.M. Missus cum imperio, Bostalii Ædes expugnavit. Mox Basingianis praesidiariis commeatu interclusis, strenue (re jam
desperata) suppetias tulit. Castrum Bamburiense cum Northamptoniæ comite
liberavit. Hinc Equestri dignitate ornatus Hostes denuo Basinga fugavit.
Iamque Gubernator Oxon. creatus, cum ad Culhami pontem in hostes jam tertio
milites audacter duceret, plumbea trajectus glande occubuit die XI. Jan., 1644,
Aet 47. Funus Solemni luctu prosecuti Principes, proceres, milites, Academici,
Cives, omnes Dolorem testati ex desiderio Viri Ingenio, Linguarum peritia,
Gloria Militari, pietate, fide et amore in principem et patriam eminentissimi.

Hanc Memoriæ Epitomen posuit illi
Pietas mœrens lugensque fratris, Georgii Gage.

Particulars of his life are contained in a scarce tract intituled, *Alter
Britanniæ Heros ; or, the Life of the most remarkable Knight, Sir Henry Gage,
late Governor of Oxford, epitomised.* Printed by Leonard Lichfield, 1645. He
was born in London, in 1597. His father, John Gage, of Haling, suffered much
for the Catholic cause. Sir Henry Gage married Mary, daughter of John
Daniel, of Daresbury, in the County of Chester, Esq., and had a numerous
issue—his eldest son, Henry Walgrave Gage, was warmly attached to the
cause of King James II., and a slight memoir is given of this personage.
[This memoir was sent to Kirk by Mr. John Gage with a covering note dated
Lincoln's Inn, Jan. 23, 1827.—P.R.]

GAGE, HENRY WALGRAVE, eldest son of Sir Henry Gage, the loyal
Governor of Oxford, was Colonel of the English regiment in Flanders, which
his father had commanded before him. He was high in the confidence of
King James II., and attended his Majesty to St. Germains. On his quitting
England he married Jane Vandenkerchove, daughter of John, Seigneur de
Vaux and Champagne, by his wife Jacqueline de la Deuse, and acquired the
Seignory of La Woestyne. He died at Tournay in 1702, leaving a son, Henry
Gage, who, by his wife, Angélique de Brune, had issue Emmanuel, Comte de
Gage, created a Count of the Roman Empire by Charles VI. Mary Gage

the only child of Count Gage by his wife, Mary de Spangen,* married Baron Hoogvorst, who was Mayor of Brussels at the period of the battle of Waterloo.

GAGE, SIR JOHN, of Firle, fourth Bart, was second son of Sir Thomas, second Bart., and Mary, eldest daughter and co-heiress of John Chamberlaine, of Sherburn, Oxon. His eldest brother, Thomas, the third baronet, dying unmarried at Rome, in 1660, he succeeded to his dignity and estates. He married first, Mary, daughter of Thomas Middlemore, of Edgbaston, Co. Warwickshire ; and second, Mary, daughter of Sir William Stanley, of Hooton, Bart. By the first he had three sons and seven daughters, of whom only two daughters survived him : Mary, wife of Sir John Shelley, Bart., and Bridget, wife of Thomas, Viscount Fauconberg ; and by the second, Mary, wife of Henry, Lord Teynham, and three sons, John, Thomas, and William. Sir John died May 22nd, 1699, in the 58th year of his age, and was succeeded by his eldest son, Sir John, fifth baronet, who only survived him a few months, dying in Jan., 1700.

GAGE, JOHN, S.J.—He was younger son of John Gage, Esq., of Coldham Hall, Suffolk, by Elizabeth his wife, daughter and heiress of Thomas Rookwood, Esq., and the brother of Sir Thomas Rookwood Gage fifth baronet, of Hengrave. Mr. Gage was born July 28, 1720, and received his early education at St. Omers. On September 7, 1740, he entered his noviceship, and made his profession in 1756. He founded the Catholic Chapel in Bury St. Edmunds, and for many years exercised his missionary functions there, respected and beloved by all classes of persons. His manners were remarkably plain and unaffected. He died in his 70th year, October 31, 1790, and was interred with his maternal ancestors, at Stanningfield, Suffolk.

GAGE, JOSEPH, (I.), fourth and youngest son of Sir Thomas Gage, second baronet, of Firle, and Mary Chamberlaine, of Sherborne, Oxon. He had his mother's inheritance of Sherborne Castle, and her sister Elizabeth dying without issue, he inherited the remainder of what she died possessed of. By this means the Castle of Sherborne became the family seat till sold in 1716 to Thomas, Earl of Macclesfield. He also acquired a great estate by marriage of Elizabeth, daughter of George Penruddock, of Hants, and was at length heir to her brother, who died childless. By her he had two daughters : Elizabeth, wife of John Weston, of Sutton, and Ann, wife of Richard Arundell Bealing, of Lanherne, and two sons, Thomas, created Viscount Gage, and Joseph.

GAGE, JOSEPH (II.), second son of Joseph Gage (I.). He acquired an immense fortune by the Mississippi scheme in France in 1719 ; but, by the bursting of that bubble he was nearly ruined and retired to Spain. But being of an active and enterprising genius, he obtained a grant for the working and draining of the gold mines of Old Spain, and fishing for all the wrecks on the coasts of Spain or the Indies, and in 1741 was presented by His Catholic Majesty with a silver mine of great value, and was made a Grandee of the Third Class. He was afterwards made General of the Spanish armies in Sicily, and in 1743 a Grandee of the First Class, and Commander-in-Chief of the army in Lombardy. The King of Naples also presented him with the Order of San Gennaro, and with an annual pension of 4,000 ducats. He married Lady Lucy Herbert, fourth daughter of William, first Marquis of Powis.

Thomas, his eldest son, was created Viscount Gage, of Castle Island, and Baron Gage, of Castlebar. Before this he had conformed to the Established Church ; but returned, says Dr. Milner, to the Catholic Church before his death.

---

* Collected from the family papers of Gaspar, Baron Draeck, of Ghent, whose mother Maria Lucy was sister to Emmanuel, Count Gage ; and from the information of Mons. Kerner Beerenbroek, of the city of Amsterdam, descended by females from Sir Henry Gage.

GAGE, PENELOPE, fourth daughter of Sir William Gage, Bart., of Hengrave, by Charlotte, daughter of Sir Thomas Bond, Bart., was an Austin Nun of the English Convent in Bruges. Mrs. Moon, the present Abbess, in a letter addressed to Mr. John Gage, of Lincoln's Inn, says : " Mrs. Penelope Gage, called in religion Sister Stanislaus, made her religious profession at the Convent at Bruges, July 12, 1711, and piously departed this life Oct. 27, 1773 [1772], in the 80th year of her age. She had been Superioress a great many years, was remarkable for regular observance of all her duties, for her mildness and humility."

GAGE, SIR THOMAS, of Firle, Bart., second son of Sir John Gage, fourth Baronet, and Mary Stanley. On the death of his elder brother, Sir John, fifth Baronet, the title and estates devolved on him, but in his 27th year he resigned them to his brother William, dying during his travels in France in Oct., 1713. This Sir William [seventh Baronet], who was born in 1695, conformed to the Established Church, and was elected Member for Seaford [in Sussex, in 1772], which place he represented till his death, which took place April 23, 1744. The Baronetage then devolved on his cousin Thomas, son of Joseph, fourth son of Sir Thomas, second Baronet [who, having conformed, had been created Viscount Gage in 1720]. Lord Gage returned to the Catholic Church before death. [Ita Mr. Milner, July 16, 18—.]

GAGE, SIR THOMAS ROOKWOOD, of Coldham Hall and Hengrave, fifth Baronet, was eldest son of John, second son of Sir William Gage, Bart., by his wife Elizabeth, daughter of Thomas Rookwood, of Coldham Hall. On the death of his father she became sole heiress of all the estates. On the death of his cousin, Sir William, without issue, Sir Thomas Rookwood Gage succeeded to the title and estates of Hengrave and Coldham. In 1747 he married Lucy, daughter of William Knight, of Kingerby, Lincolnshire, by whom he had one son, Thomas, and three daughters : Lucy, wife of George Maxwell ; Elizabeth, wife of Henry Darell, of Cale Hill, Kent, and Mary. Sir Thomas died in 1795, and was succeeded by his only son, Sir Thomas Gage, who married Charlotte, daughter of Thomas Fitzherbert, of Swinnerton, Co. Stafford, by whom he had four sons : Thomas, who succeeded to the title, and born in 1781 ; Robert, who took the name of Rookwood ; William, and John, of Lincoln's Inn. Sir Thomas, Bart., died in Nov., 1798.

GALLOWAY, EDWARD, S.J., was born of a respectable family, June 22nd, 1706. He entered his noviceship Sept. 7, 1724, and was professed in 1742. For some years he exercised his missionary functions in Norwich, and probably died there. Enquire of Edward Huddleston, Esq., to whom I have heard he bequeathed some considerable property.

GANDY, JAMES.—He was educated at Douay, and was missionary many years at Kendal, in Westmorland. He was much respected, was a member of the Chapter [chosen Canon July 11, 1743], and died at Kendal, Sept. 4, 1761.

GASCOIGNE, SIR EDWARD, BART.—He travelled into Italy in 1725. He returned to England by Munich, Lorain, and Flanders. "At Milan he bought a suite complete des Medailles Impériales d'argent, enrichi d'environ 100 d'or and odd to his Consular and got some pictures." (Var. ix., 40.)

GASCOIGNE, RICHARD.—He was a native of Ireland, and seems to have been very active in the rebellion of 1715. After a long and full hearing he was found guilty, and received sentence of death, May 17, 1716. From this time to the day of his execution, May 25, he gave himself up wholly to prayer and meditation, in which he was assisted by a Priest, recommended to him by a friend ; for which, in a letter to him, he says he could not sufficiently express his gratitude. While his friends were interesting themselves in this behalf with Government, he entertained little hopes of their success, and lost no time in preparing himself for another world ; in entreating them rather to join with him in prayers for the forgiveness of his many and grievous sins. The letters he wrote to his mother and to a Catholic of eminence the day before his execution shew his submission and his resignation in his awful situation. When the Sheriff's officers came to demand him he received the message with such a composed countenance as shewed he was not unprepared for death ; and when his fetters were knocked off he took them up and kissed them, as he afterwards did the gallows. During his passage from Newgate to Tyburn he sat with his hat off and with his eyes fixed on Drexelius *On Eternity.* He told the spectators " he was not ashamed of suffering the ignominious and terrible death he was to undergo, since he trusted he should thereby make his peace with an incensed Deity, whom he had many ways heinously offended, and as for his religion, he died in the faith of the Roman Catholics, and desired the prayers of all good Christians for the welfare of his immortal soul." He then cleared the Duchess of Ormond, Lord Landsdowne, and Sir William Wyndham from the imputations thrown out against them at his trial. And having given to the Sheriff a paper he betook himself to prayer alone, refusing the assistance of the Ordinary. He was observed to strike his breast three times after the cart was drawn away and he was left hanging. (*Faithful Register* [*of the late Rebellion.*])

GAWEN, THOMAS, was of New College, Oxford, Prebendary of Winchester and Rector of Exton, Hants. He afterwards became a Catholic. He translated into Latin *The Rebellious Scot,* of Cleveland. It is a keen satire on the Scotch Covenanters, of which this is a good specimen. " Had Cain been Scot, God would have changed his doom ; not forced him to wander, but confined him at home." (Nichols' *Leicestershire*, iii., 916.)

GEDDES, ALEXANDER.—(In Butler's *Memoirs*, iv., 417, and his life by Mr. Mason Goad.)

GENNINGS, MICHAEL, studied at Douay, where, after his ordination, he was made Professor of Divinity. He was Missionary at Harvington, in Worcestershire, where he is supposed to have died.

GERARD, CARYLLEY, son of Thomas Gerard, and his wife, Mary Wright. He was born in Lancashire, Nov. 18, 1695 (O.S.) He studied first at St. Omers and then at Rome, where he was admitted in the College Oct. 21, 1717. He was ordained Priest Dec. 21, 1720. He defended *Universal Divinity* with great applause in the Roman College, where the English Students attended the Public Schools. He left Rome Sept. 20, 1723, and was appointed Confessor to the Austin Nuns at Bruges.

GERARD, CHARLES, sixth Lord Gerard, of Gerard's Bromley, Co. Stafford, was son of Richard Gerard, and great-grandson of Thomas, created Baron Gerard of Bromley in 1603. On the death of Digby, fifth Lord, without male issue, Nov. 8, 1694, the title devolved on his cousin Charles, sixth Lord Gerard, who became possessed also of the bulk of the estates in Staffordshire, Salop, and Cheshire, in virtue of a settlement made by Charles, fourth Lord Gerard, in 1660. " After a variety of legal forms this Charles, sixth Lord Gerard, settled his estates for want of heirs of his body on his sister Frances, and confirmed the same by his will dated the 14th March, 1706, reserving to his brother Philip Gerard, who succeeded to the title and was the seventh Lord Gerard, only an annuity of £60 for life for the support of that dignity." (Blore's *Staffordshire Collections* and Ormerod's *History of Cheshire*, p. 482. This Lord died April 12, 1707 (O.S.), aged 48. He married Mary, daughter of Sir John Webb, who survived him many years, and died at Joppa in 1731, on her return from the Holy Land. From the Report presented by the Commissioners to the House of Commons in 1718, it appears that the annual income of the Cheshire and Staffordshire estates amounted to no less than £4,644 12s. 4d., out of which Lady Gerard received £2,000 per annum, a noble jointure in those days, which enabled her to bestow largely on those who were the objects of her charity.

GERARD, FRANCES.—She was daughter of Digby, the fourth Lord Gerard, and sister of Charles, the fifth Lord Gerard, of Gerard's Bromley.

On the death of her brother she inherited his estates, and married Thomas Fleetwood, Esq., by whom she had one son, Charles Gerard Fleetwood, who squandered away the large estates of his father by his gaming and extravagance, and was at last driven to the dire necessity of seeking a livelihood on the stage. After the death of her husband Mrs. Fleetwood retired to Liège, and there died in 1736, in the 74th year of her age, five years after the death of her sister-in-law, Lady Mary Gerard, at Joppa.

GERARD, MARY.—She was the daughter of Sir John Webb, of Hethrop, Co. (? Gloucester), and was married to Charles, the fifth Lord Gerard, of Gerard's Bromley. On his death, April 12, 1707, she entered upon her jointure of £2,000 per annum, which enabled her to bestow largely on those who were the objects of her charity. In her old age she visited the Holy Land, and on her return died at Joppa, in 1731.

GERARD, SIR THOMAS, eighth Baronet. On the death of his elder brother, Sir William, the seventh Baronet, who died unmarried, he succeeded to the title. He married a daughter of —— Tasborough, by whom he had two daughters. Clare, the younger, died April 5th, 1798, and gave three-quarters of her ample fortune to the poor. Sir Thomas died at Liège,* June 25, 1781, and his Lady, Aug. 20, 1783. He was succeeded by Sir Francis Gerard, who died Sept. 14, 1791, when the estate devolved to Sir William Gerard [the present Bart. (1801)].

GERARD, SIR WILLIAM, of Bryn, Lancashire, the fifth Baronet, was son of Sir William Gerard, fourth Baronet, by his first wife, Anne, daughter of Sir John Preston, of Furness, Lancashire.† He married Mary, second daughter of John Cansfield, of Cansfield, and Elizabeth, his wife. She, by the death of her eldest sister, Ann, wife and relict of Richard Sherburne, of Stonyhurst, became sole heiress of her father's estate, as also of her mother's, who was the daughter of James Anderton, of Birchley.

GERARD, SIR WILLIAM, sixth Baronet, was son of [Sir William, fifth Baronet], and Mary his wife. He succeeded to his father's estates. He married Elizabeth, fourth daughter of Thomas Clifton, of Lytham, by whom he had three sons : Sir William, his successor, Thomas, and Robert ; and one daughter, Mary.

GIBBONS, TOBIAS, was son of Walter Gibbons by his wife, Cecilia Macdaniel. They were natives of Ireland and both Catholics. Tobias, however, was born at Tangiers, in Africa. He was admitted into the English College at Lisbon, and when he had completed the usual course of studies, was ordained Priest. When the King of Portugal determined to send Don Lewis de Cunha extraordinary Ambassador to William III. in 1696, Mr. Gibbons accompanied him through Spain, France, and Holland, and on their arrival in London he was appointed head chaplain, to the great satisfaction of Bishop Leyburn and the comfort of the Catholics, who thus obtained at last a chaplain under the protection of the Ambassador, where they partook without any molestation of the benefits of religion. When de Cunha was recalled in 1718, and sent to Madrid, Mr. Gibbons returned to Lisbon and became a guest in the College, where he died Sept. 4, 1737. (*Lisbon Catalogue.*)

GIBSON, GEORGE, was the third son of Jasper Gibson, of Stonecroft and [Margaret] Leadbitter, and elder brother of the Bishops. He was educated at Douay, and was General Prefect there for some years. When he came on the Mission his labours were at Hexham, in Northumberland, and for many years assisted the Catholics at and about Nafferton. He had the character of being a "zealous and pious missionary." He died at Hexham, Dec. 3, 1778. [He had served at Congleton from Oct., 1752, General Prefect from 1751 to 1756.]

---

* *The Directory* says he died Aug. 26, 1792.
† Sir Thomas Preston, of Furness, married Mary, eldest daughter of Caryl, Lord Molineux.

GIBSON, GEORGE, of Stonecroft, in Northumberland, Esq., where he was well beloved in his neighbourhood. He joined Prince Charles in 1715, and was taken prisoner at Preston. At his trial, which came on June 15, 1716, he pleaded like many others that he had been forced by the rebels to join them, that he had once made his escape but was brought back by them. This, however, not being proved to the satisfaction of the Jury, he was found guilty and condemned, but died in Newgate. [His estate in the Parish of Newbrook, Northumberland, was valued at £227 per annum.]

GIBSON, MATTHEW, Bishop [of Comana], nephew of Thomas, and fourth son of Jasper Gibson, of Stonecroft, gentleman, by his wife, [Margaret], daughter of [Nicholas] Leadbitter, of Warden, gentleman. According to his own account in Mr. Eyre's papers, he was born March 25, 1734 (O.S.), but according to the Hexham Register, was baptised March 23. This latter date *may* be according to the *New* Style. In Sept., 1747, he was sent to Douay, and in 1753 defended Universal Philosophy. He then taught one of the schools of Humanity, and after he had finished his theological course, and was ordained Priest, he was made Professor of Philosophy, which he taught for four years, and then Divinity for six. In July, 1768, he returned to England, and received his missionary faculties from Bishop Maire, *Episcopus Cinensis*, Aug. 9, 1768. On March 6, 1776, he was appointed V.G. in the Northern District, by his [Maire's] successor, Bishop Walton, and also his Special Vicar in 1777. For some years he lived at Headlam; but on the death of Mrs. Mary Maire, of Headlam, April 2, 1784, he removed to Stella Hall, "where he revised in the same year," says Mr. Thomas Eyre, "and much improved the *London* or *Little Catechism* in many places by substituting *correct* answers in lieu of some that were found, upon serious examination, to be very *inaccurate.*" In this he was assisted by others, and especially by Mr. Thomas Eyre, with whom he then lived, and who did not fear to pronounce it to be, after those improvements, "by far the most perfect in the English tongue, in every sense and in every respect." As many Catechisms were daily issuing from the press, "without either inspection or approbation, and not without glaring, inexcusable inaccuracies," it was the wish of Bishop Gibson to have a standard Catechism, and for that purpose he applied for and obtained the approbation of the other Bishops to the one he published in 1784.

On the death of Bishop Walton, in 1780, Mr. Gibson was chosen to succeed him, with the title of *Episcopus Comanensis*. His bulls were dated June 17, 1780, but by the blunder of the Secretary he was stiled *Pomanensis*. He was consecrated by Bishop James Talbot in London, Sept. 3, 1780; the venerable Bishop Challoner, then closing his 89th year, assisted on the occasion [and P. Brown Capellæ-Archicapellanus. Faculties dated June 25, 1780]. He was also member of the Chapter, was chosen Archdeacon of Kent and Surrey. He died of gout after about ten days' illness at Stella Hall, May 17, 1790. Bishop Gibson was allowed by everyone to be a very able Divine and most zealous pastor. He published:

1. *The Little Catechism*, in 1784. 2. *A Pastoral against the Oath proposed to Catholics*, in 1789. This dated Jan. 15, 1790. "This Pastoral," says Rev. Edward Kitchen, "is a masterpiece. I scarcely recollect to have seen reason, learning and piety in closer combination; nor is there any danger of its giving umbrage to Church or State. Should it ever reach the Minister's or Monarch's hands, it is impossible they should not inwardly thank the author." The oath was afterwards changed and made acceptable and unobjectionable to the Catholic body.

GIBSON, RICHARD, was the sixth son of Jasper Gibson. Like his brothers, he studied at Douay, and when ordained came over to England, and for some time assisted at Standon School, in Herts. In 1784, if not sooner, he removed to Mawley, the seat of Sir Walter Blount, Bart., where he lived till the time of his death, much respected and beloved by the family and his congregation, notwithstanding his constitutional roughness and apparent harshness. He died Sept. 13, 1801. Mr. Gibson was a gentleman of great

fortitude, as appeared when he had to undergo a severe operation for the
purpose of extracting a large splinter on which he had fallen in getting over a
hedge. When desired by his surgeon, Mr. Russell, to suffer himself to be tied
down on the table on which he lay, he refused and went through the operation
without uttering a groan or a sigh, to the great astonishment of Mr. Russell
and his assistants.

GIBSON, THOMAS, was son of George Gibson, of Stonecroft, gentleman.
He studied at Douay, and on his return was placed at Newcastle, where he
lived many years, much esteemed and respected. He was a member of the
Chapter, and on March 17, 1735, was chosen Archdeacon of Yorkshire. [He
received faculties from Mr. Maire, V.G., Nov. 18, 1748]. He died Jan. 20,
1765, aged near 80.

GIBSON, WILLIAM, Bishop [of Acanthos], was fifth son of Jasper Gibson,
of Stonecroft, gentleman. He studied at Douay, and being ordained, came on
the Mission in 1765, and received (July 28) his faculties from Bishop Maire.
He lived many years in the family of Silvertop, of Minster-Acres. When
Mr. Blount resigned the Presidentship of Douay College, Mr. Gibson succeeded
him in that honourable station, May 31, 1781, which he held till 1790, when he
resigned it on June 12 on his being chosen to succeed his brother Matthew
as Vicar Apostolic of the Northern District, with the title of *Episcopus Acan-
thensis*. On the seizure of Douay College by the French authorites and the
arrival of the inmates in England, he projected and completed the building of
Ushaw College, in which he displayed great skill and indefatigable exertions,
by which his name will be lauded with their unceasing benedictions. He had
the happiness to see his new College filled with students and flourish and send
out many able and zealous Missionaries for the Northern District. He died at
Durham, which had always been his episcopal residence, June 2, 1821. His
works are : 1. *A French Grammar*, for the use of Douay College. 2. *Truth of
the Catholic Religion, translated from the French of M. de Mahis*, 1799.

GIFFARD, ANDREW *alias* JONATHAN COLE, son of Andrew Giffard, Esq.,
a branch of the Giffards of Chillington, and of Catharine, daughter of Sir
Walter Leveson, of Wolverhampton, Kt. He was sent to Douay with his
brothers, Augustin and Bonaventure (Bishop), and having finished his course
of studies with great applause was successively made Professor of Philosophy
and Divinity. On coming to England, he exercised his missionary faculties
for some years in Staffordshire, where he was G.V. to his elder brother,
Bishop Giffard. He was a member of the Institute and also of the Chapter ;
and at the General Assembly held in 1684 he was [June 4] chosen V.G. of
Stafford, Cheshire, Derby, and Shropshire, " but humbly desired to be excused
from accepting that charge." [*Dr. Giffard's Minutes.*] " In 1686 the Clergy
took a large house (Fishmonger's Hall) in Lime Street, London, and at their
and their friends' great cost and charges fitted a very good room for a fair
chapel ('by Mr. Gother's contrivance and management,' says Mr. Tootell)."
" And then I," says Mr. Andrew Giffard, " living in Staffordshire,* was commanded by Bishop Leyburn to repair to London and to take care of the said
chapel with another good Priest, Mr. James Dimmock." (Mr. Christopher
Tootell says he was the third). " We had not been there a month but we
were defamed as Blackloists and Jansenists, and this bad reputation was
spread over all London, and was the general discourse of all people and at
last had its intended effect ; for in less than six months time we were turned
out of house and chapel, and no recompense made for all our charges, and one
Father Kanes [Keynes], a Jesuit was introduced with other companions.
This I mention to show what sort of batteries those gentlemen use against a
place which they intend to assault. They take away the good names of the
owners, and so by right or wrong get them turned out, and then the world
judges it well done because the owners, by these previous calumnies being
generally judged men of bad principles, are thought unfit to hold it. No

---

* *Ushaw Collections* i., 303, Original of Mr. Giffard.

person could be more innocent than myself as to both these accusations. As to Jansenism, I was so far averse to it that I always taught the opposite opinions, and generally stuck to the doctrines of the Society both in morality and speculation ; and this the Jesuits themselves know and own to be true. Yet when a fit occasion offered and a good station was to be gained, I was presently rendered a rank Jansenist. I told this passage concerning the house in Lime Street to Father Wakeman and Father Medcalf, two principal Jesuits here. Father Wakeman, who knew me very well, seemed much to admire that such a report should be laid upon me, for that he owned that I was always a man of sound principles and had taught their doctrine both in Philosophy and Divinity, and had nothing to say but only: " Did we do this?" A pretty question to fool the world with. Who is ignorant that they have 10,000 mouths besides their own to open against any person whom interest or passion persuade them to persecute. As to Blackloism, no person in the world can have a greater aversion against his books and doctrine than myself, and I am certain that in my whole life I have not spent one half-hour in reading that author. All that is here written concerning the chapel in Lime Street is certain truth, notoriously known to be so by all who were concerned in that affair* and by many thousands more, and I here relate it to show that these gentlemen are uniform in their methods and always the same. What they have done they will do again, when interest and time serve, and therefore, no manner of regard ought to be had to their alarms of Jansenism,† because as it is seen in this example, they fix that character, not where it is most deserved but where it is most convenient."

" About a year and a half," continues Mr. A. Giffard, " after departure from Lime Street House, I was made fellow of Magdalen College, where I stayed until we were turned out by the return of the Protestant Fellowes into their college again. I compared these two passages together, my being turned out of Lime Street House by the Jesuits, and out of Magdalen College by the Protestant Parsons, and I must needs do justice to the truth and to those of Magdalen College, that I was dismissed that place with much more civility and much less reproach than what I found at my dismissal from Lime House, where besides the loss of our money spent in the fitting up of the house and chapel, we were sent away loaded with ignominy : *Pudet haec dici posse et vere dici.*" (*Ibid*, p. 304.)

When Bishop Ellis, who retired from England at the Revolution, and was afterwards chosen Bishop of Segni, resigned his Vicariate, Mr. Andrew Giffard was chosen to succeed him as Vicar Apostolic of the Western District, with the title of Bishop of Centuria. This happened in 1706. But though requested and urged strongly by his brother and his friends to accept of the dignity, nothing could induce him to take upon himself the burden and duties of that office. His health was then very indifferent, and this he pleaded as a sufficient ground for declining the honour. At this time he was the zealous agent for Douay College, and never was such an agent more wanted to repel the charges brought against the College and the Bishops and Clergy of England of Jansenism. In this he was indefatigable, as his numerous papers (which are still preserved in the Chapter and Ushaw Collections) abundantly show. Mr. Giffard died in Sept., 1714, and was buried in St. Pancras Church-yard, where a marble slab, with an epitaph, was placed over his grave and that of Bishop Giffard, who was buried by his side in 1733, O.S.

Mr. Giffard wrote :—Remarks on *The Jesuits new Gospel.* " It was a silly book," he says, " full of faults, and was disliked and complained of by the whole Clergy. By whom written," he adds, " I know not." In a letter to Dr. Paston [Aug. 3, 1710], he says that neither Bishop Leyburn nor himself ever did or would marry Protestants and Catholics, because it was concurring to

---

* Bishop Giffard told Mr. J. Shepherd, May 29, 1725, that "what is said of the three being turned out of the Lime Street Chapel is true."—*Ushaw Collection* i., 370. J.K.

† This was written in 1710, when the clergy of Douay College were maliciously accused of Jansenism.

profane a Sacrament.   He owns the contrary practice was common, upon the strength of some Popes allowing it, though the children were certainly to be brought up Protestants.   [*Dodd's Papers at Oscott.*]   Bishop Giffard procured many considerable benefactions for the good of religion and benefit of the Clergy, and at his death left about £3,000 for the same ends.

[Dr. Kirk's drafts contain the following detached items of information about Andrew Giffard :—" About one-and-a-half years after he left Limehouse Chapel he was made Fellow of Magdalen Coll., and appointed Vice.-Pres., and Pres. of Douay."   "Lived constantly at Mr. Thimelby's, in Red Lion Square, in 1709. . . ."   "See his Epitaph in *C. G. Mag.* ii., 43.   He became a member of the Institute, and was the founder of the London Clergy Fund, as Mr. D. Fitter was that of Staffordshire and three adjoining counties."]

GIFFARD, BONAVENTURE, Bishop, the son of Andrew Giffard, a branch of the Giffards of Chillington, Staffordshire, was born at Wolverhampton, about the middle of the 17th century [1642].   When young he was sent to the English College at Douay, where he completed his studies.   Quitting Douay, he went to Paris the 23rd of October, 1667, and resuming his studies, after spending ten years in that University, he was at length created Doctor of Divinity. Being thus qualified, he could not fail being taken notice of by James II. when he ascended the throne, who, having himself experienced some effects of his zeal by the private admonitions he had given his Majesty for the good of his soul, made choice of him to be one of his chaplains and preachers ; and when it was afterwards thought proper to establish an ecclesiastical hierarchy in England for the benefit of the missioners, as well as the whole body of English Catholics, he was raised to the episcopal dignity and consecrated the 22nd of April, 1687, with the title of *Episcopus Madurensis.*   About the same time also were consecrated Drs. John Leyburn, Bishop of Adrumetum, V.A., of the Midland District ;   Philip Ellis, Bishop of Aureliopolis, V.A. of the Western District ; and James Smith, Bishop of Callipolis, V.A. of the Northern District.

When the remarkable contest afterwards took place between the King and the seniors of Magdalen College, Oxford, concerning the visitorial power, and the pretensions of the latter were not allowed by the ecclesiastical commissioners, Bishop Giffard by the royal Mandamus, was appointed President, and on the 31st of March, 1688, invested by proxy in the place of Samuel Parker, Bishop of Oxford, lately deceased, but ousted again on the 25th of October following, by order of the King and Council, to make room for Mr. John Gough, formerly elected by the seniors.   The Revolution happening shortly after, Bishop Giffard concealed himself for a while, but was at length seized and committed prisoner to Newgate, where he remained about twelve months ; and being at length discharged, he dwelt privately in London under the connivance of Government, who, being fully satisfied with the inoffensiveness of his behaviour, gave him little or no disturbance.   On March 12, 1733, O.S., he departed this life at Hammersmith, leaving behind him the character of a truly pious Christian primitive prelate.   If any trait in his amiable character was more conspicuous than the rest, it was his *extensive charity towards the poor.*   The words of St. Paul—*Nihil habentes, omnia possidentes*—were truly applicable to him.   Under the most indigent circumstances he could command vast sums, which passed like continual streams through his hands to the support of innumerable distressed objects, who were entirely ignorant from what source they flowed.   He made it his chief study to find out such as had abilities and inclination to co-operate with him, and happy were the poor in having so powerful an intercessor, for he seldom pleaded their cause in vain. The pains he took to discover such as were real objects of charity was such, that he penetrated garrets and cellars to make himself acquainted with their wants, but more especially with the necessities of such decayed families as in those troublesome times were reduced to a state of poverty, and, being unaccustomed to labour, had no other way of obtaining relief but through one who seemed ordained by divine providence for that purpose, who possessed the prudence to conceal their circumstances.

GIFFARD, JOHN (I.), of Black Ladies, married Catharine, daughter of —— Langton, of Kent, Esq., and by her had three sons, Peter, John, and Walter, and two daughters, Mary, who married John Parry, of Twissog, Co. Denbigh ; and Catherine, who married —— More, Esq. John Giffard died Jan. 21, 1709, O.S.

GIFFARD, JOHN (II.), the second son of Peter Giffard [II.], married the heiress of Narquis, Co. Flint, by whom he had two daughters. His mother-in-law was a bitter Protestant, and caused him much trouble. She placed his eldest daughter in the hands of the Lord Chancellor, and would have done the same with the younger, had not Mr. Giffard taken her over to Paris and placed her in one of the English nunneries. This obliged him to reside abroad several years, in France and Italy. On the death of his mother-in-law he returned to England, lived comfortably with his lady at Narquis, and had Dr. Bew for his Chaplain. Mr. John Giffard died at Narquis, April 15, 1797.

GIFFARD, MARTIN, *alias* BISHOP, lived in Cornwall [1681 to 1686] and assisted the scattered Catholics in that county. He was a member of the Chapter, and July 13, 1694, was chosen Archdeacon of Cornwall, Devon, and Dorsetshire, and as such sent two deputies to the General Assembly held in 1703. He died in 1715.

GIFFARD, PETER (I.), son of Thomas Giffard,* of Chillington (or of Wolver-hampton), Esq. At the age of 18 he was sent to Lisbon and was admitted into the College, Nov. 24, 1647, where he afterwards taught the Classics, and in Oct., 1652, was made Procurator of the College. He was ordained July 1, 1653, and on account of the pecuniary difficulties of the College went to prosecute his studies in France, but returned to Lisbon Dec. 2, 1655. On the 7th of Sept., 1661, he left the College for England and was placed at Townley, in Lancashire, where he lived many years,† much beloved by his congregation and highly respected by his brethren, who recommended him in 1668 as a proper person to be President of Douay, and in 1670 to be President of Lisbon, on the resignation of Dr. Barnsley (Perrott), neither of which offices could he be prevailed on to accept. He was a member of the Chapter, and May 29, 1682, was chosen V.G. of Northumberland, Cumberland, Westmoreland, Lancashire, Yorkshire, and Bishopric, and in this capacity he assisted at the General Assemblies in 1684 and 1687. This latter Assembly consisted of 28 members, viz., Dr. Perrot, the Dean, who presided, four Vicars-General, thirteen Arch-deacons, and ten Canons ; but six sent their deputies. It opened on the 18th of April, but, as Bishop Leyburn had declared on his arrival in England that he came "with the powers of an Ordinary and that he should govern according to the authority of an Ordinary," the Assembly resolved that "their jurisdiction must be esteemed to have ceased during the exercise of the said authority." Little therefore remained to be done besides filling up some vacancies, places, and settling some private concerns of the Chapter. Some of the Assembly were deputed to "wait on his Majesty (James II.) to express the humble duty of the Secular Clergy, and to say further what in prudence they shall judge most proper upon the occasion." Others were chosen to wait on the Nuncio, and others, in fine, on Bishop Leyburn, "to pay to them the respects of the Secular Clergy assembled in the present Chapter." It was also unanimously resolved in the 3rd Session that "they should endeavour to set up Chapels for the increase and propagation of the Faith ; to keep peace and conserve charity with the Regulars ; and to promote the good of the Clergy by sending persons to their Colleges at Rome, St. Alban's at Valladolid, and St. George's at Madrid." The Assembly closed with the 4th Session, on the 22nd of April. Mr. Giffard died some time before 1692. (*Lisbon Catalogue and Chapter Records*).

GIFFARD, PETER (II.), was eldest son of John Giffard, of Black Ladies and Catharine Langton. By the death of his cousin, Thomas Giffard, of

---

* The draft says : "Reg. of Lisbon calls him *Salopiensis.*"
† The draft says : "In 1682 lived at Townley, in Lancashire."

Chillington, without issue in 1718, Peter Giffard succeeded to his estates.   He
married : 1st, [Winifred] daughter of [Robert] Howard, of Hore Cross, Esq. ;
2ndly, Barbara [8th and] youngest daughter of Sir Robert Throckmorton,
Bart., and of Mary, 2nd daughter of Sir Charles Yate, of Buckland, Bart. ;
3rdly, Elizabeth [? Helen], daughter of [Robert] Roberts, of Narquis, Co. Flint.
   Mr. Giffard was one of the principal contributors to the printing of *Dodd's
Church History*, as his chaplain, Mr. Dicconson, afterwards Bishop, was one of
his greatest assistants in the compilation of it.   He had studied at Douay, was
a great friend to his Alma Mater and to the Clergy.   He defended Universal
Philosophy in 1714 under Dr. Challoner, and when he caused to be printed, at his
own expense, Mr. Gother's *Sincere Christian's Guide*, Dr. Challoner wrote the
preface.   Mr. Giffard died July 5, 1746, much respected by all who knew him.
The poor, in particular, lost a great friend and benefactor by his death.
   [Besides this notice of Peter Giffard, Kirk has retained among his notes
another less complete description of the same man, perhaps written sooner.
It ends as follows :—Mr. Giffard was a zealous Catholic and a staunch friend
to the Clergy.   He built a new wing to his house and greatly improved his
estate, and was generally known by the name of Peter the Great, of
Chillington.]

   GIFFARD, THOMAS (I.), of Chillington, married Mary, daughter of John
Thimelby, of Irnham, Co. Lincoln. He died *sine prole* in Oct., 1718. Mrs.
Giffard survived him and retired to Longbirch with her chaplain, Mr. John
Johnson, where she lived to the great age of 95, in the practice of all Christian
virtues, particularly in charity to the poor and distressed.   " She was a lady,"
says Bishop Hornyhold, who succeeded Mr. Johnson as her chaplain, "of great
piety, strictness of morals, and regularity of life ; and has left an example
worthy of imitation of the most extensive charity to the poor and distressed
and of singular liberality towards relations and friends."*   She died Feb. 13,
1753.
   GIFFARD, THOMAS (II.), eldest son of Peter Giffard.   He married, first,
Barbara, 2nd daughter of Robert James, 8th Lord Petre, by whom he had one
daughter, Mary Catherine, married to Mr. (after Sir John) Throckmorton ;
secondly, Barbara, daughter of Sir Robert Throckmorton, Bart., by whom he
had Thomas Giffard, who succeeded to his father's estates ; and thirdly,
Frances, daughter of Thomas Stonor, by whom he had John Giffard.   Mr.
Giffard died Jan. 7, 1776.   Catholics owe a deep debt of gratitude to the
Chillington family, not only for the support of a priest in the house and thus
affording to a numerous tenantry and congregation the means of practising
their religious duties, but also by being the faithful trustees of Clergy property
in difficult times.   It was also through the influence of Mr. Giffard that Lord
Dudley was prevailed upon to let his house—Sedgley Park—to Mr. Errington
for the purpose of assuring his school there in 1763, which has been the nurse
of so many zealous missionaries and other valuable members of the Catholic
body.   Mr. Giffard also engaged to be guarantee to Lord Dudley for the rent
of the premises.

   GILDON, JOHN, D.D., was son of Richard and Frances Gildon his wife, of
a good family at Dorchester, from Caen in Normandy.   Having completed his
classical, philosophical, and theological course, and also taught two courses of
philosophy at Douay, he was dismissed by Dr. Leyburne, the President, on the
pretence that in the disputes which he had with the English Chapter he had
been too favourable to the latter.   He was then 24 years of age, but had not
received even the minor orders, and being sent to Lisbon he took the College
oath in 1661 ; in the same year was ordained Priest and sent upon the Mission.
In January, 1675 O.S., he was chosen a member of the Chapter, and was held
in great estimation among his brethren, and is placed by Dodd among the
Flores Cleri Anglicani.   He died in 1700.   (*Lisbon Catalogue, in Miscell. vi.*).

---

* The draft adds : " Epitaph in Brewood Church."

GILDON, JOSEPH, went over to Lisbon in May, 1693, and took the College oath and gown Dec. 31, 1701. After he was ordained Priest, he was appointed to teach Philosophy, but his health not permitting him long to continue to hold that engagement, he departed for England Aug. 6, 1707. When Mr. Fleetwood, who had the charge of the Catholic School at Twyford, near Winchester, where Pope passed some part of his youth, resigned the charge and afterwards became a Jesuit, Mr. Gildon was appointed his successor, and conducted that establishment much to his credit and to the benefit of his pupils. His death is thus recorded by Mr. T. Berington, Dean of the Chapter : " We have lately had a great loss in good Mr. Gildon, Master of the School at Twyford, who dyed on the 26 of July, 1736." (*Lisbon Catalogue, Miscell. vi. 1094.*).

GILDON, WILLIAM, *alias* BYFLEET, died in Dorsetshire, Oct. 19, 1743.

GILLOW, JOHN, D.D., President of Ushaw, was born at Lancaster. He was educated at Douay, was prefect of studies and taught Philosophy from 1782, Divinity from 1786, and after his ordination taught Philosophy and Divinity for some years. When he car·e on the Mission he was placed at York, where he built a new chapel which, in its day, was much admired for its neatness and tasteful execution. On the death of Mr. Thomas Eyre, President of Ushaw, in 1810, Mr. Gillow was appointed his successor, and governed that house greatly to the satisfaction of Bishop Gillow and of the Clergy in general, as well as of its inmates in particular, till the day of his death, Feb. 6, 1828.

GILLOW, THOMAS, born at Great Singleton, in Lancashire. He studied at Douay, and while a student in Philosophy was fortunate enough to escape when the French seized the College and conveyed its inmates to Dourlens. He stayed at Old Hall till Crook Hall was prepared for the reception of the students that belonged to the Northern District. Here he finished his divinity, and was ordained Priest, and for some years lived with John Clavering, of Callaly, Esq. In 1817 he stood so high in public estimation and in that of the Vicars Apostolic, that he was recommended as a proper person to fill the important station of Bishop of the West Indies, and was actually appointed ; but on account of his health declined accepting that dignity. He was then placed at North Shields, where he has built a large and beautiful Chapel, and is acting the part of a zealous pastor, not only in his great attention to his own flock, but also in the conversion of many, that he has happily brought into the Catholic fold. Mr. Gillow, who is still living, published in 1807 *Catholic Principles of Allegiance Asserted*, 8vo.* [He died 19 March, 1857.]

GILPIN, THOMAS, *alias* SEVERISON.—He was educated at Douay, and after he came on the Mission lived most of his lifetime with Mr. Henry Constable and his sister at Garton, in Holderness. It is noticed in the Records of the Chapter that "he was a very virtuous and learned Priest." This was the character given of him by Archdeacon Franks in 1692, at which time he had been 13 or 14 years on the Mission.

GIRLINGTON, JOHN, was educated at Lisbon, and came on the Mission about 1685. In 1697 he lived at Mr. Witham's, at Sladwish, and in 1705, and for some years after, at Dilston, the seat of the Earl of Derwentwater. He afterwards retired to Sunderland, where he died Aug. 13, 1729. He was succeeded by Mr. N. Berry, who died there between 1730 and 1740.

GLOVER, EDWARD BENEDICT, O.S.B.—He was born at or near St. Helen's, in Lancashire, and entered young, together with his brother Vincent, among the English Benedictines. His brother [Thomas] became a Jesuit. When Edward had finished his theological course at Ampleforth, he was placed with Rev. Thomas [Wilfrid] Fisher, at St. Mary's Chapel, in Edmund Street, Liverpool, on the death of Rev. Mr. Tarlton ; but the labours of this Mission being too great for his delicate health, he was removed to Little Crosby, where he remained till his death, which happened May 14, 1834, in the 47th year of his

---

* The draft adds that he was schoolfellow of Messrs. Thompson and Tho. Penshurst.

age. Mr. Glover's talents were of no common order: his turn of mind, his
learning and piety were calculated to effect much good, had the Disposer of all
things given to him length of days.   Of this the various papers in the *Catholic
Magazine*, written by him, signed with a little cross, are proofs.   He retained
his calm and equanimity to the last, and was buried in Seel Street Chapel,
Liverpool, deeply regretted in death, as he had been respected and beloved in
life.

GOOD, THOMAS.—He studied and was ordained at Lisbon.   He lived many
years at Mr. Lacon's, in Linley, in Shropshire, and died Dec. 3, 1732.   He left
a legacy to his Alma Mater and £200 to the Common Purse of Staffordshire,
and was much esteemed while living among his brethren.   The draft adds :
["In 1695, went to Mr. Lacon's . . . was esteemed 'a very capable and
well-tempered person.'"]

GORDON, [JAMES], a Carmelite.—He succeeded Mr. Griffith at Longford
the seat of —— Talbot, Esq., in Shropshire.   But his stay here was not long,
from 1732 to about 1742, in consequence of some irregularities laid to his charge,
for which he was removed by Bishop Stonor.   This gave rise to a dispute with
him and his Regular Superiors, which was carried to Rome, and was one of
the causes that drew from Benedict XIV. the *Regulæ Missionis*.   [His name in
religion was James Mary of St. Margaret. Zimmerman, *Carmel in England*,
p. 372.   P.R.]

GORSUCH, JAMES, *alias* ECCLESTON.—He was a member of the Chapter,
and on November 23, 1737, was chosen Archdeacon.   He was educated at
Douay, and died in Lancashire, Jan. 19, 1738, O.S.

GRADWELL, CHRISTOPHER.—Born at or near Preston ; was educated at
Douay.   On his return to England he was placed at Sheffield, and was pastor
of the Catholic Congregation there for 22 years, and died there, Sept. 25 or 27,
1758.   He was succeeded by Mr. Lodge.   Mr. Gradwell was a relation of the
Orrells of Blackbrook.   He was a member of the Chapter.   The character
given of him by Rev. Thomas Eyre, who received his first instruction in
Catechism from him, and always spoke of him with respect and affection, and
by others, was, that "he was a plain, sensible and pious man, a good scholar,
and was much beloved by all people."

GRADWELL, ROBERT [Bishop of Lydda], the younger of twins, was born
at Clifton, near Preston, Jan. 26, 1777.[*]   He went to Douay in 1791, where he
arrived Sept. 30.   On Oct. 12, 1793, he was imprisoned with the rest of the
Students, and was taken to Dourlens, and returned with them and the St.
Omerians to England and landed at Dover, March 2, 1795.   He then proceeded
to Crook Hall, where he finished his studies and was ordained Priest Dec. 4,
1802.   For seven years he taught Poetry and Rhetorick, and on July 22, 1809,
was placed at Claughton as assistant to Mr. Barrow, and in 1811 succeeded
him.   He was the last of the Douay Students who took to the Church.   In 1817
he was chosen by the Bishops to go to Rome as Rector of the English College,
and left England in September.   He died March 5, 1833. (See Dr. Griffith's
Funeral Discourse).

GRAHAM, ROBERT, *alias* FRÈRE ALEXIS.—At la Trappe. (See Mr.
Butler and *Relation de la mort de quelques Religieux de la Trappe*).

GREEN, FRANCIS, a secular Priest, confessor to the Benedictine Dames of
Ghent for many years.   When incapable by age and infirmities of performing
his duties Mr. Richard Daniel was elected to assist him, and on his death
succeeded him ; the Benedictine Dames of Ghent, now of Caverswall Castle,
having been always under the jurisdiction of the Bishop in whose diocese they
live.

GREEN, JAMES, *alias* KING.—In 1738 or 7 he went to Douay, where he
distinguished himself in all his studies.   For some time he taught Rhetoric, and

---

[*] The draft adds [schooled there] ? *i.e.*, Preston.

afterwards Divinity, in which latter employment he was succeeded, in 1758, by Dr. James Talbot afterwards Bishop of London. When he came on the Mission, for some years had the care of the Catholic Congregation at Welshpool, in Shropshire, and then at Kiddington. Being allowed by Bishop Challoner to retire from the Mission, he went to Rome, where he employed himself in teaching the English language to the Romans, and in assisting, as far as was in his power, his own countrymen that visited the capital of the Christian world and the students in the English College. He died there Dec. 12, 1803, aged 77 or 78. Mr. Green was a gentleman of very considerable abilities, on which account his company was much sought for, especially among his countrymen.*

GREEN, JOHN, a Priest in Yorkshire. On October 10, 1745, he was brought before the Quarter Sessions for the West Riding on suspicion of being a Papist, and was committed to York Castle as " a Popish Priest and one disaffected to his Majesty." How long he was detained, or what became of him after, or where he died, I have not been able to discover, unless he be the same as *Lawrence* Green or as *Richard* Green who died in London, April 24, 1750. Both were Secular Priests.

GREEN, JOHN JOSEPH, O.P., was a native of Liverpool. He became a Dominican and took the degree of Bachelor in the faculty of Sorbonne. In 1735 he was chosen the 7th Rector of their College in Louvain, and in 1742 [he returned to England, where] he laboured with a truly apostolic zeal in the vineyard committed to his charge ; suffered a long imprisonment for his faith, and at last died at Liverpool, April 5, 1750, aged 48. (*Synopsis Fundationis Collegii Sancti Thomæ Lovanii*).

GREEN, STEPHEN.—He studied at Rome, and on his return to England was placed at Greenwich. He was a member of the Chapter and was a zealous and painstaking missionary. " His last illness was occasioned by a visit to the hulks at Woolwich, and was confirmed by the unreasonable importunity of an Irishman calling him, when unwell after the visit, to attend a person about Shadwell or Wapping. He said his last Mass on St. Stephen's Day, took to his bed of a typhus fever, and suffered till Jan. 31, 1815, when, having received all the Sacraments, he closed an exemplary life, spent in active zeal and missionary labour, by a death, we have reason to hope, precious in the sight of the Lord." Such is the testimony borne of him by Reverend Joseph Hodgson, V.G. of the London district.

GREEN, WILLIAM SCOTT, D.D., was born Nov. 16, 1696, and in 1711 went over to Douay, where he was received June 1. Being gifted with extraordinary talent, he made rapid progress in his studies, and was appointed to teach the Classics even before he became an alumnus or had taken the college oath. Having completed, with great applause, his usual course of studies, he was ordained priest, and soon after was called to fill the Chair of Divinity. About the same time he took the degree of D.D. in the University of Douay. When he came on the Mission he was for some time chaplain to Edward, Duke of Norfolk. But his presence being deemed necessary at Douay, he returned to teach Divinity there in Oct., 1749, and on the death of Dr. Thornburgh, he was appointed President of that house, June 3, 1750, and governed it with great prudence and ability, till within a few months of his death, when he resigned the office to Mr. Tichbourne Blount. He died there on Dec. 1, 1770. (*Douay Diary*). Mr. Green was a gentleman of great learning and solid piety, and was every way qualified for the important office of President. He was well supported in the administration of the temporals by Mr. Francis Petre, *alias* Squib, the Procurator or Vice-President ; and in the studies, by able professors of Divinity, Philosophy, and the Classics, as were Mr. Lodge, Mr. G. Kendall, and Mr. Bannister, S. T. P., Mr. Jas. (Bp.) Talbot and Mr. Holmes, P.P. ; Mr. Hugo Kendall and Mr. William Beeston in the Classics. The consequence was that

---

* The draft adds: "Born 1725: with Card. of York, *credo*; taught Rhetoric in 1750 and Divinity in 1751."

the College, in which there were, in 1751, 147 seniors and students, flourished
under his administration, and sent forth many able men, zealous Missionaries.
Dr. Green excelled in the pulpit, and left many valuable sermons behind him,
which* he bequeathed by way of legacy to the late Mr. Charles Fryer, *alias*
Foxwell, who had been his principal attendant during his last illness. Mr.
Thomas Eyre, of Ushaw, relates of Mr. Green that, " he never heard a sermon
but immediately after he penned down on paper the text, divisions, method of
treating it, most striking thoughts, etc."   He adds : " I repent again and
again that I never did this when I had such fine opportunities [such as you at
present have ; but alas ! those opportunities will never more return."]   Dr.
Green was a member of the Chapter, and Archdeacon of Worcester, and
Gloucestershire.

GREENE, RAYMOND, O.P., D.D.   He was born in Oxfordshire about the
year 1655, and when of proper age became a Dominican.   He was remarkable
for his quietness and uncommon abilities ; so that he had no sooner completed
his course of Divinity than he was appointed to teach Philosophy and then
Divinity at Louvain.   In 1686 he accompanied the Provincial to the General
Chapter held in Rome, when, on account of the manner in which he defended
his Universal Divinity, he was honoured by the General, Father Antonius
Cloche, with the title of *Presentator [sic] of the Order of St. Dominic.*   Having
finished his Divinity Lecture, he came on the Mission and remained some years
in the care of a Congregation.   In 1712 he was chosen the third Rector of the
College of his Order in Louvain, where he probably took his degree of D.D. At
the end of his triennium he was chosen Confessor to the Dominicanesses at
Brussels, called from the street where they lived *The Spellikins*, and was four
times confirmed in that office.   Seven years before his death a fit of the palsy
deprived him of the use of one side, which he bore with admirable patience and
resignation, and departed this life in the College at Louvain on July 28, 1740
[1741], in the 86th year of his age, the 68th of his profession, and 62nd of his
priesthood.   Father Greene had been twice Prior of Bornheim, and once Provincial of his Order in England, and was much esteemed and beloved by all who
knew him. (*Dominican Obituary*).

GREENLEAF ——, a secular priest who lived in Lancashire, of whom I only
hear that he wrote " Historical and Controversial Entertainments."   If I
remember right, the MS. was at Fernyhalgh, near Preston, where it is probable
that he was a missionary.

GREENWAY, JOHN, studied a few humanity schools at Douay, whence he
removed with a colony to Valladolid.   There he was ordained priest, and
afterwards taught Divinity, and was Vice-President under Mr. Shepherd.
When he came back to England, he was appointed to a new mission established
at Gloucester, where he was much respected by Dean Tucker, and by all who
knew him, both Catholics and Protestants.   For some years he took young
gentlemen for the purposes of education, and thus was enabled, without being
burdensome to his friends or the public, to erect a chapel in that city.   On
Nov. 21, 1800, while dining at Mrs. Stanford's, he had an attack of apoplexy, of
which he died on the 29th, and was buried Dec. 3, in his own chapel.   Mr.
Greenway was a gentleman of great talents, and of solid learning and piety,
but laboured under great disadvantages in conversation on account of his
deafness.   He left many MSS. at his death on various subjects, but none of
them have yet been given to the public. [An uncle of his wrote a poem in
which he described the lives of all the Presidents of Douay College.   *Ita* Dr.
Milner, Aug. 28, 1816, at Oscott].

GREENWELL, THOMAS, was educated at the College of St. Peter and St.
Paul in Lisbon, and on his arrival in England was called to the charge of the
Catholic Congregation at Stella Hall about the year 1737 ; and there performed

---

* The draft adds - " Which, in the opinion of the late Thos. Eyre, will be better adapted to this
mission at large than most others."

all the offices of a good pastor till about the year 1748 [or 1750], when William, Lord Widdrington, thought proper to present Mr. Turner, S.J., to the place of chaplain at Stella. On his removal Mr. Greenwell was obliged to retire to Blaydon, where he continued to devote himself to the service of his neighbour, and was chiefly supported by the voluntary contributions of his friends and of his flock till 1753, when being called to attend one John Cook, of Winlaton, who lay ill of a fever, he himself caught the infection, and after a few days' illness died of the same, on Thursday, Aug. 23. [Buried in Blaydon Church, Aug. 26].

GREENWILL, DENNIS J., S.J., priest. He was installed Dean of Durham, Dec. 14, 1684. "He was deprived Feb. 7, 1690, on the accession of William and Mary, and retiring into France in attendance upon King James, died there at Paris, April 7, 1703, and was buried in the lower end of St. Innocents' Churchyard in that city." (Willis' *History of Durham*, v. 1., p. 25).

GREENWOOD, GREGORY, O.S.B., of a good family of Brise Norton, near Witney, Oxon. He lived about forty years at Coughton Court, a seat of the Throckmorton family, in Warwickshire. He was chosen Provincial of Canterbury in 1733 [draft " in 1725, and re-chosen in 1729 and 1733."].

GREGSON, BERNARD, O.S.B. He was President, Nov. 1706, of the Congregation of English Benedictines.

GREGSON, VINCENT, O.S.B. He lived many years respected and beloved at Weston, near Olney, in Bucks., and died there Oct. 18, 1800. He was well skilled in medicine, and attended the poor in the neighbourhood *gratis*, while Mr. Throckmorton supplied them with medicines.

GRENE, *or* GREEN, WILLIAM, was a native of Staffordshire. He studied at Lisbon, and took the College oath and habit June 30, 1676. After he had received the order of priesthood he taught the Classics, and defended his universal Philosophy with great applause under Professor Maudesley, Nov. 3, 1682. In 1686 he was made Procurator of the College, and in 1692 the Confessarius, and in April, 1698, came over to the Mission, labouring for nearly thirty years. He died Oct. 3, 1727. (*Lisbon Register*).

GRIFFITH, JAMES. He lived at Newport, Salop, in the family of Mr. Talbot, of Longford. When old and infirm he had Mr. Gordon, a Carmelite, with him, upon his own expense and for his own use. "The proceeding was odd," says Mr. Berington, G.V., to Bishop Stonor, "but I could not refuse giving him approbation." On which that body (the Carmelites) contrived to have Mr. Gordon succeed him there ; but his stay was not of long duration. Mr. Griffith died at Longford, Feb. 23, 1740 (O.S.).

GRIFFITHS, JOHN. [Born Sept. 19, 1753]. He was sent young to Sedgley Park and, when of proper age, to Douay College, where he went through his Classics, etc. When a colony was sent to Valladolid he was charged with it, and there finished his course of Theology. On his arrival in England he was placed at St. George's in the Borough, and performed all the duties of a good pastor many years in that laborious Mission. He died Nov. 3, 1815, aged 62, after receiving all the rites of the Church. He was truly a zealous Missionary, and was much respected and beloved by all who knew him. [Among Dr. Kirk's drafts we find the following notice : "Be pleased to remember in your sacrifices our departed Brother, Rev. John Griffiths, aged 62 last Sept. 19, who has gone before us with the sign of Faith, and reposes, I trust, in the sleep of peace. He died this morning at one o'clock, having received all the Sacraments, and by mutual agreement is entitled to one Mass from each of his Brethren of the Secular Clergy.—I have the honour to remain, etc., Joseph Hodgson."]

GRIMBALSTONE, EMERIC, lived many years in the family of Mr. Clifton, of Lytham in the Fylde. He died April 18 [8], 1786. He was chosen a member of the Chapter April 11, 1763, and Archdeacon Nov. 19, 1771. [The draft adds : " A Mr. G. lived at Wycliff after Dr. Holden."].

GRIMBALSTONE, WILLIAM, was educated at Douay. He lived upward of thirty years at Wrightington in Lancashire, and died there Feb. 1, 1770.

GRYMES, RICHARD AMBROSE, O.P., D.D.   He took the habit of St. Dominic at Bornheim, April 9 [19], 1665.   Some time after his ordination he came on the Mission, and was made Preacher in Ordinary to Queen Catherine, Queen Dowager of Charles II.   I find him in Rome in 1695, where, through the interest of Cardinal Howard, the English Dominicans had obtained possession of the Convent and Church of SS. Peter and Paul on the Caelian Hill.   He was in great estimation, and filled successively all the honourable offices of his Order.   In 1709 he succeeded to Father Dominic Williams as Rector of their College in Louvain, and in 1712 was chosen Prior of Bornheim ; and at the end of the usual term of three years he retired to the College of Louvain to prepare himself for death, which happened Feb. 18, 1719, in his 75th year, at which time he was in possession of the title of Baronet of Montrose (*Montis Rosarum*) in Scotland.   (*Dominican Obituary* and *Synopsis Fundationis Collegii Lovaniensis*).

GUMBLESTONE, or GOMELDON [RICHARD].   He was the son of a jeweller, and became first a Catholic, and then, *it is said*, a Carmelite.*   His life, however, seems to have been a disgrace to his profession, whatever that were, whether a religious or layman.   Yet he is said to have had a zeal for religion, and was one of those who raised his voice against Jansenism, when that charge was wickedly brought against the Bishops and Clergy of England in the beginning of the 18th Century.   " A chief man employed," says Mr. Andrew Giffard,† " to bring accusations against us is a young debauchee, who has spent his patrimony *vivendo luxuriose cum meretricibus*, and now dares not show his head for fear of arrests.   He is a visionaire, who, according to his own words, often sees heaven open, but oftener converses with hell ; for he saies the Divil sits by his bedside many nights, and they talk and converse familiarly for several hours."   Mr Gomeldon drew up a paper of accusations against Mr. Piggot, " a most laborious and zealous priest," as Mr. A. Giffard styles him, and handed it about the town, and sent out into the country a paper entitled " Several of Dr. Short's tenets " (copy in Ushaw College), and affirmed that he heard the Doctor speak them all.   In this he seems to have been guided more by his prejudices and ignorance than by the love of truth, for he made no difficulty to declare that the Doctor's *memory was an execration to him* before he knew him ; and did not dare, when solemnly called upon, to swear to the truth, as Dr. Short actually did to the falsity of these propositions, immediately after communicating at the hands of Father Carter, a learned and venerable Benedictine.   What reparation he ever made, if any, and how and where he died, I have not discovered.

GWILLIM [*vere* TERRET *or* TYRWHIT, HENRY, S.J.], was born in London. At the age of 19 he was sent to Rome, and was admitted into the College by Father Lucas, the Rector, Oct. 18, 1691.   Having studied his Classics, probably at St. Omers, he began Philosophy, but in April 1692, he quitted the College to go to Naples and there entered the novitiate of the Jesuits.   I have not met with any further news of him. [See Foley *Records* VII. ii. 767].

GWILLIM, JOHN, was educated at Lisbon, and being ordained came on the Mission, and for many years lived at Holywell, where he died April 3, 1763.

HAGGERSTON, SIR CARNABY, third Bart., only son of William Haggerston, eldest surviving son of Sir Thomas, who, dying before his father, Sir Carnaby succeeded his grandfather.   He married Elizabeth Middleton, of Stockeld, Yorkshire, who died at York, Dec. 16, 1769 ; by whom he had three sons :— Sir Thomas, his successor ; William Constable of Everingham ; and Edward of Ellingham, Northumberland : and three daughters, one of whom married Thomas Clifton of Lytham.   Sir Carnaby died in 1756.

---

* See Gillow *Dictionary* III. p. 65, and Zimmerman, *Carmel in England*, p. 380 *n*.
† *Letter to Mr. Dicconson*, May [April] 3, 1710, in Ushaw College.

HAGGERSTON, SIR THOMAS, of Haggerston Castle, Northumberland, second Bart., was son of Sir Thomas (who for his services and sufferings of his family in the royal cause was created Bart. by Charles I.) and his wife Alice, daughter and heiress of Henry Banaster, of Bank, co. Lancaster. Sir Thomas married Mary, eldest daughter of Sir Francis Howard, of Corby Castle, Knt., and had by her nine sons and one daughter. Of these Henry, John, and Francis embraced religious lives, and William, his eldest surviving son, married Anne, daughter of Sir Philip Constable, of Everingham, Yorkshire, Bart., and had three daughters and one son. He afterwards succeeded to the title and estate of his grandfather. Sir Thomas, after the death of his first wife, married Jane, daughter and heiress of Sir William Carnaby, of Farnham, Northumberland, Knt., by whom he had no issue. In the reign of James II., he was made Governor of Berwick Castle, and Feb. 19, 1687, his house was burnt down, when he lost most of his writings and sustained above £6,000 damage, himself, wife, and family narrowly escaping.

HAGGERSTON, SIR THOMAS, fourth Bart., was eldest son of Sir Carnaby, third Bart. In 1754 he married Mary, daughter of George Silvertop, of Minster-acres, who died May 22, 1713, on a journey from Bath to London. By her he had three sons and two daughters. Sir Thomas died Nov. 1, 1777, and was succeeded by his eldest son, Sir Carnaby, who married Frances, second daughter of Walter Smythe, younger brother of Sir Edward Smythe, of Acton-burnel, Bart.

HALES, SIR JOHN, of Woodchurch in Kent, fourth Bart. and son of Sir Edward Hales, who was created by James II., while in France, Earl of Tenter-den in Kent, and Frances, his wife, daughter of Sir Francis Windebank, of Oxon., Knt. " His grandfather, Sir Edward, in his younger days, risqued his person and fortune in endeavouring to rescue Charles I. from his imprisonment in the Isle of Wight," as related by Lord Clarendon. Sir John married first Helen, daughter of Sir Richard Bealing, of Ireland, secretary to the Queen Dowager of Charles II., by whom he had two sons, (1) John, who died in his infancy, (2) Edward, who married Mrs. Parker, granddaughter of Sir Richard Bulstrode, Knt., who died at St. Germains, Oct. 1711, aged 102. Sir John died in 1744, and was succeeded by his grandson, Sir Edward Hales, fifth Bart., who married, first, Barbara, daughter of Sir Thomas Webb, Bart., and second, the relict of Mr. Palmer, of Ireland. He died Aug. 30, 1802, aged 78, without issue. (*Betham*, 130).

HALFORD, JOHN, was educated at Douay College. He distinguished himself by his application, piety, and good conduct. After teaching Classics for some time, he came on the Mission and resided at Tor Abbey, in Devon, and was much respected and beloved by all who were acquainted with him. He died at the house of his brother-in-law, at Henley-upon-Thames, Oct. 1, 1805.

HALFORD, SISTER MARY BENEDICT, O.S.D. " When she made her first communion at Boulogne," says Father Brittain, " she had an ecstasy. This I learned, on a certain occasion, from herself." She led a very pious life, and was novice Mistress in the Convent of our Dominicanesses at Bruxelles. She died at Bruxelles Aug. 28, 1792, aged 36, professed 10 years.

HALL, FRANCIS, *alias* FITZHERBERT, son of Roger Hall, was born in London. At the age of 18 he was sent to Rome, and was admitted into the English College Oct. 11, 1680. He was ordained Priest Feb. 11, 1685, and in May, 1687, left the College to proceed to England, and to labour on the Mission. He died in 1728.

HALL, LAWRENCE, O.S.F. He died at Louth, Mar. 12, 1783.

HALSEY [HALSALL] GEORGE, S.J., was son of James Halsey and Ann Bowker, his wife. He was born in Lancashire on Sept. 17, 1714. In 1732 he went to Rome, and by order of Cardinal de Via, the Protector, was admitted, Aug. 17, into the College, then under the administration of Father Percy Plowden. He took the oath of Alexander VII., May 10, 1733, and was ordained priest July 20, 1738. After remaining seven years in the Clergy College, he obtained from Clement XII. a dispensation from that part of his oath which precluded him entrance into any religious order, and on Aug. 28, 1739, went to Watten and became a Jesuit. This is one out of more than 200 instances, in which the young men, after studying years in a Clergy College under the administration of the Society, afterwards became Jesuits. The same often occurred in the Clergy College at Valladolid.

HALSEY, GEORGE, son of John and Susanna Halsey, was born Aug. 6, 1751, in Herefordshire. Though his father was a Catholic, he was brought up by his mother, who was a Protestant ; but being brought back to the Catholic Faith in 1762, he was sent to Bruges, where he passed five years in the study of the Classics. In 1769 he went to Rome, and was admitted into the College by order of Cardinal Lante, the Protector, May 3. Being found to be a youth of considerable abilities, he was placed by Father Hothersall, the Rector, on one of the *free funds*, by which means he was left at liberty to enter afterwards into religion without the necessity of a dispensation. As he received his early education under the Jesuits, and afterwards discovered a partiality for them, he probably would have entered among them, had not the suppression taken place in Aug., 1773. On Sept. 10, 1774, he publicly defended Divinity in the Sodality of the College before Cardinal Corsini, the Protector, much to the satisfaction of his Eminence and a crowded audience. On April 15, 1775, he was ordained priest, together with Mr. Robert Broomhead, and both left the College soon after their ordination. Mr. Broomhead proceeded to England, but Mr. Halsey stopped some time at Douay to continue his studies there. On his arrival in England he was placed at Midhurst, where he lived, much respected, and died April 25, 1834, in his 83rd year.

HAMMERTON, PETER, *alias* YOUNG, S.J. At the age of 22 he went to Rome, was admitted into the College Oct. 21, 1660, by Father John Stephens, whose true name was Poyntz. On May 7 following he left the College and entered into the Society of Jesus. In 1709 he was Provincial in England, and is called by Mr. Andrew Giffard "a Jesuit of worth and piety," who, when the English Clergy were falsely accused of Jansenism, bore honourable testimony to their orthodoxy. In that year Bishop Giffard, together with his G.V., Dr. Jones, "made a visit to Father Hammerton and desired him freely to declare if he knew of any priest in the district who might be justly accused or suspected of Jansenism." The said Rev. Father, as a person of worth and integrity, answered, that he *knew not, nor heard of any such person in his Lordship's whole district.* And further added, *that he was newly returned from his visit to the northern parts, and that he neither had heard, nor did know any person in that district, who could be accused of the said opinions of Jansenism.*
[See *Clergy's Circular Letter* of Nov. 29, 1709. "Yet endeavours were used," says Mr. A. Giffard (letter to Mr. Dicconson, June 30, 1710 ; original at Ushaw) "to decry this testimony of Father Hammerton. The account that I find of these endeavours is given by Mr. D—— in his journal in these words : June 11, 1710. In the morning, etc. . . Jan. p. 44."—*Original Records of Jansenism,* p. 143. From Father Sabran's letter of complaints to Cardinal Caprara it appears that Fathers Med and Hammerton were directed by him to call on Bishop Giffard.]

HANKINS, JOHN. He resided at Sunderland till his house and chapel were plundered by the mob in 1743. He was then placed at Witton Shields, and remained there till 1772, when he retired to Douay, and died in 1782 at St. Omers. (*Mr. Cotes*).

HANSBIE, JOSEPH, O.P., D.D. He was a native of Yorkshire, and became a Dominican. In 1715 he was chosen the fourth Rector of their college in Louvain, where he also taught Philosophy and Divinity. He was three times Prior of Bornheim and as often Provincial* of his order, and was held in great

---

* Provincial of the Dominicans in 1724.

estimation by his Brethren and others, "making himself all to all that he might gain all to Christ." He died in London, June 5, 1750, in the 76th year of his age, 54th of his profession, and 52nd of his priesthood.   (*Synopsis Fundationis Collegii Lovaniensis*, and *Dominican Obituary*).

HARBERT, JOHN, *alias* VANE.   He was educated at Lisbon, and when he came on the Mission, resided in London, and was the active agent of his Alma Mater.   He was also a member of the Chapter, and [a relation, probably a nephew, *cancelled*] of the Mr. Vane, who, after having received orders in the Church of England, became a Catholic, and going to Lisbon was afterwards there made priest.   He died Oct. 22, 1733.

HARDCASTLE, ——.   He studied at Valladolid, and came on the Mission about the year 1670.   In 1693 he resided with Mr. Messenger at Fountains Abbey, near Ripon, in Yorkshire.

HARDESTY —— [? *vere* TEMPEST, JOHN] S.J.   He lived at Aston, near Stone, and died sometime before November, 1752.

HARDWICK, GEORGE, was educated at Douay, and began his Divinity there October 1, 1737.   In 1742 I find him in the Mission at Yeldersley, in Derbyshire, and about 1751 he succeeded Mr. Alban Butler at Paynsley, the seat of Lord Langdale.   In 1759 he removed to Wingerworth, the seat of Sir Henry Hunloke, Bart., and lived there much respected and beloved till 1787.   He died Nov. 27 in the 79th year of his age.   Mr. H. was a Capitular Oct. 12, 1762, and on Oct. 16, 1770, was chosen Archdeacon.

HARNAGE, HENRY, of a good family in Shropshire, was son of Edward Harnage, of Bellswardine, Esq., by his wife Mary, daughter of —— Minn, of Somerton, Oxon, Esq.   His parents were both Catholics.   He was born in March, 1650.   Having studied his Latin and Greek Rudiments, he went over to Lisbon College in Jan. 1667 ; and having finished his Philosophical and Theological course, he returned to England in May, 1678.   Shropshire, which gave him birth, was also the theatre of his apostolic labours.   For many years he lived at Madely, together with Mr. Pigg, under the patronage of the powerful family of the Brooks of Madely Court, one being the house chaplain and the other attending the Catholics of the neighbourhood.   The testimony borne to them by Mr. George Barret, the Archdeacon of Shropshire and Herefordshire in 1693, was that "they were both learned and virtuous, of long standing in the Mission, and great pains-takers in the Harvest."   (*Chapter Collection* I., 397).   He was secretary to Bishop Giffard while he remained Bishop of the Midland District. He was also a member of the Chapter, and in Jan. 1700 (N.S.) was chosen Archdeacon of Shropshire and Herefordshire.   He died at Madely Jan. 7, 1736-7, "after a holy and devout life."   He left at his death a considerable benefaction to the Clergy.   (*Lisbon Register, Miscel. VI.* 1063, and *Clergy Obituary*).

HARNAGE, THOMAS, of Douay College, died in 1720.   He is named by Dodd in his *Flores Cleri Anglicani*, but not in his *Certamen utriusque Ecclesiæ*. He was brother to Henry, and second son of Mr. Harnage.   Their sister Dorothy married —— Clough, of Mindtown, Salop., Esq.   Mr. Harnage was uncle to Mr. George Bishop.

HARRISON, ALICE, called also Dame Alice.   " She was born at Fulwood Row, near Preston, was well educated and brought up to the profession of the Church of England.   She was converted by reading Catholic books.   She remained firm, was severely persecuted, corporally chastised, and when this would not reclaim her, turned adrift by her father.   She was encouraged by the priest at Fernyhalgh, probably Mr. Melling, to open a school near Fernyhalgh, on the top of the hill near the chapel (and Ladywell).   She had a numerous school.   Children flocked to her from the neighbourhood, from Preston, the Fylde, Liverpool, Manchester, London, and all parts of England.   She admitted scholars of all religions to the amount of between 100 and 200.   She had one other assistant called Mary Backhouse.   The scholars boarded, some with the

Dame, others in the cottages and farmhouses of the neighbourhood.   They paid
1s. 6d. per quarter to the Dame for schooling and £5 per annum for board and
lodging, and always stopped to say a *Pater, Ave,* and *Credo* at our Lady's Well.
The Rosary, Litanies, etc., were said every day in the school.   Those children
who were not Catholics were at liberty to absent themselves on this occasion, if
they pleased.   All the people in the neighbourhood of Fernyhalgh were Catholics
at that time, and both encouraged and protected the little Dame.   Dame Alice
lived to a great age, and was in her decline indebted for a comfortable retreat
to the respectable family of the Gerards.   Mr. Gradwell (see Mr. R. Southworth's letter on her) had these particulars from Mr. Peter Newby, and Miss
Singleton, of Preston, an old lady who had been her scholar.   Miss Singleton
afterwards, for many years, boarded several of her scholars.   She was buried
at the Catholic burying-place, Windleshaw, near St. Helen's.   (See *Catholic
Magazine and Review,* II. 476).

HARRISON, JOHN, studied at Douay, and soon after his ordination came on
the Mission, and was placed at Cottam.   In 1745 his house and chapel were
attacked by the mob, whom "he resisted with intrepidity"; but both were
burnt down by the ruffians.   He then removed to Townley, and served that
mission for thirty years and as long as he was able.   When infirmities in-
capacitated him for labour he retired to the house of his brother Laurence in
Preston, and died in Friargate about Jan. 16, 1780.

HART, *alias* HATHERLEY, JOHN, was a distinguished member of the
Chapter, and in the General Assembly held in 1684, was chosen Archdeacon of
Norfolk and Suffolk.   He died in 1695.

HARTLEY, GEORGE, was nephew of Thomas and William.   After studying
some time at Sedgley Park, he went to Lisbon, where he was ordained priest,
and on his return to England was placed at Spetchley, the seat of Robert
Berkeley, Esq., whence he removed in 1803 to Harvington, where he died June
26, 1806.   He succeeded Mr. Cornethwaite.

HARTLEY, THOMAS, was eldest son of Richard Hartley and Elizabeth
Taplin, his wife.   He was born near Banbury, June 26, 1740 (O.S.), and in 1754
was sent to Rome, where he was received into the College [on July 15] by
Father Henry Sheldon.   He was ordained priest Dec. 22, 1764.   On the
following April [25] he left the College to proceed to England.   He succeeded
Mr. P. Beeston at Wolverhampton on May [16] 1768, and Mr. Syers at Sedgley
Park in 1772.   After some time he removed to Moseley, the seat of Francis
Whitgreave, Esq., and there died July 11, 1781.   Mr. Hartley was a most
respectable clergyman, and an excellent Catechist.   He was buried at Bush-
bury.

HARTLEY, WILLIAM, brother of Thomas, was born [in Oxon, or near
Banbury, Warwickshire] July 26, 1742.   He was admitted into the English
College at Rome Nov. 20, 1756 [ordained Dec. 20, 1766].   He left the College
April 18, 1767, in company with Mr. Robert Tindall, and soon after his arrival
was placed at Cobridge, in the Potteries, where he remained many years, and
then removed to Sixhills, in Lincolnshire, where he died in 1794.   [William
Hartley died at Hainton 1794, July or later.   .   .   .   Thomas and William at
Longbirch, 1772].

HARVEY [JOHN] MONOX, *alias* RIVETT, son of Henry Harvey, by his wife
Margaret Rivett, was born in Norfolk in 1698 or 1699.   He became a Catholic
and at the age of 25 went to Rome, where Father Levinus Browne, the Rector,
received him into the College, by order of the Cardinal Protector, March 13,
1724.   He was ordained priest by Benedict XIII., Sep. 18, 1728, and on April
6 following left the College together with Mr. Nicholas Mason.   He resided in
London, "was a zealous and successful preacher," and was enabled by good
management to open a school for Catholic children, which he constantly
attended to instruct them in their religious duties.   "His success induced
several other priests to set up schools, which soon became famous through the

good management and strict discipline observed by their governors, and were resorted to by the children of the Catholic gentry that did not cross the seas, and of rich merchants and tradesmen. Many also came over from Maryland, Barbadoes, etc., to these schools. The principal of these was Twyford, where upwards of 100 boarders were educated, in 1733, under the care and direction of Father Fleetwood." Such is the account given by the anonymous author of the *Present State of Religion in England in a Letter to a Cardinal*, in 1733, p. 19. Betham, in his *English Baronetage*, says Sir Philip Monnoux, Bart., who died in 1707, married Dorothy, daughter of William Harvey, of Chigwell, in Essex, Esq. Probably Mr. Monox Harvey was of this family, as he bore the name both of Sir Philip and his lady. The Annals of the Roman College call him *Moxon*. He died in London, Dec. 22, 1756.

HATTERSKY [HATHERSTY*] JOSEPH, S.J., was son of Richard Hattersky and Elizabeth Grogan, Catholics. He was born in London Oct. 15, 1735 (N.S.). In 1749 he was sent to Rome and was admitted, Jan. 9, among *the Alumni* in the English College by Father Christopher Maire, the Rector. It is remarkable that he was allowed to remain on the College Funds *four years and a half* without taking the usual College oath; and at last, Aug. 2, 1753, he entered among the Jesuits. His first destination was for the English Mission, but it was afterwards changed by his Superiors and he went to Maryland. Here is another of the many instances in which young men were educated for several years on the *Clergy* Funds, and then became *Jesuits*, in consequence of their having the administration of the Clergy College. This was often the subject of complaint of our Bishops in their letters to His Holiness and to Propaganda. But such was the influence of the *Almighty Father*, as Mr. (Bishop) Dicconson called the General of the Jesuits, that their complaints were not listened to, or, at least, were not redressed. (*Annals of the Roman College*).

HAUGHTON, *or* HORTON, JOSEPH, was educated at Douay. When he came on the Mission, he resided chiefly in London, was a member of the Chapter, and on July 13, 1732, was chosen Archdeacon [but resigned some years before death]. He died in London, Dec. 2, 1764, in the 90th year of his age.

HAWARDEN, EDWARD (I) D.D., descended from a respectable family near Farnworth in Lancashire. He was sent very young to the English College in Douay, and in every stage of his academical course displayed those great talents with which the Almighty had gifted him. He received priest's orders June 7, 1686, and in the same year, if not sooner, he was appointed Professor of Philosophy, having previously taught the Classics. As his abilities were found to be far above the common, Dr. Paston, the President, determined to promote him, as soon as an opportunity offered, to the chair of Divinity ; and that he might be the better qualified for that situation, he took the Degree of Batchelor of Divinity in that University. In the meanwhile, Bishop Giffard being appointed Principal of Magdalen College, and most of the Fellows having been ejected for resisting the will of James II., it was determined by that Prince to give one college in Oxford to the Catholics, who had been the founders of them all, —————— only excepted. A colony was therefore sent from Douay to Magdalen College, at the head of which was Licentiate Hawarden, who was selected for the express purpose of teaching Divinity in that College. He accordingly left Douay Sept. 21st, 1688. On Oct. 5, Thomas Smith, Richard Goodwin, and Ralph Crathorn followed him to study Divinity there, and Edward Waldgrave to study Logic. Their stay, however, was but short in consequence of the expected (*sic*) revolution ; and Smith and Crathorn returned to Douay Oct. 31, and Mr. Hawarden with Mr. Shod [? Short], who had been admitted Fellow, Nov. 16, when the chair of Divinity was exchanged for that of Douay College, which Mr. Hawarden held for not less than seventeen years, with great credit to himself, and to the satisfaction of those who employed him, and of those who studied under him. Dr. Robert Witham, after

---

* Foley in his *Records* always calls him Hathersty.—P.R.

the death of Dr. Paston, was his associate, and the second Professor of Divinity. Soon after his return to Douay Mr. Hawarden took the degree of D.D.

When one of the Royal Chairs of Divinity became vacant in 1702, the reputation which Mr. Hawarden had acquired was such that he was solicited by the Bishop of the Diocese and by the principal members of the University, town, and province, to become a Candidate for it. It was the wish of Dr. Hawarden to pursue his studies in the retirement of his own College ; yet the applications were so numerous and so urgent, as well as so flattering to himself and to his college, that he at last, but reluctantly, consented.   As others concurred with him for the honour of the Chair, each one was obliged to give public exhibition of his abilities before the Provisors and Judges appointed to pronounce on their merits, and to name the successful candidate.   Some account of this *concours* is given by Dr. Meynell in a letter to Mr. Tunstall at Brussels, which I adjoin the more readily as the abilities displayed by Dr. Hawarden on this occasion seem to have raised that opposition and persecution which he afterwards experienced.   His letter is dated July 4, 1702.*   " In my last," he says, " I think I came to the citation of both parties to Tournay, and the engagement 'twixt Henricus de Cerf and Mons. Dumont.   On Friday morning we were in hopes to have seen a second part to the same tune 'twixt Cerf and Mr. Dumont, especially there having been a formal challenge, But Cerf did not appear. . . Saturday there was a Batchelor defended his third These for Licentiate. Delcourt being out of town (cited to Tournay), Cerf not very well, we supposed the clairvoyant Dr. Amon, that renowned King's Professor, would preside *pour la première fois*.   In fine, Dr. Hawarden went to see and put an argument, which fairly poked† both defendant and moderator.   All that Amon could say for himself was, " *Videris tibi ipsi scientificus*, and *velles videri aliis scientificus ; sed non es valde scientificus*," and desired the Doctor to dispute no further ; for neither he, or his defendant would answer a word : and accordingly both retreated to the middle of their pulpits and there kept silence a while ; and then Amon called up another Batchelor.   The Students did shout and hoot and laugh at a strange rate.   The Batchelor had not put two syllogisms till the Doctor took up the argument, and presently laid them as flat as before ; which was now a new occasion of laughter to the school, who showed very little respect to their new Professor."

These and similar proofs which Doctor Hawarden gave of his abilities and talents made it no ways doubtful that he would obtain the chair from impartial judges ; but there was at that time a party in the University that, like Dr. Amon, had frequently been foiled in the schools by Dr. Hawarden, at the head of whom was Adrian Delcourt, the Vice-Chancellor.   By extraordinary exertions this party succeeded, and at the conclusion of the *Concours* the chair of Divinity was awarded to another.   Such defeats as these here noticed are not easily forgiven, and other means were dictated by the *odium theologicum* to bring Dr. Hawarden down from the proud eminence he had obtained in the public estimation.   At that period the disputes on Jansenism ran high ; and it was whispered abroad that Dr. Hawarden was not free from the infection, yet so privately as not to appear in any tangible shape for some years.   " During all the time he was at college," says Mr. (Bishop) Dicconson, " his enemies could not, nor durst, attack him on the point of Jansenism ; " nor did they till he had actually left the College in 1707.   An intrigue, however, was carried on underhand with one of the students, named Poyntz, for the purpose of discovering the sentiments of Dr. Hawarden on these subjects, and in particular in order to get possession of his *Dictates*.   These he surrendered to them in 1704 ; but though closely examined they were not found to teach or to defend the doctrines of Jansenius, or of his abettors, nor does any specific objection appear to have been brought against him before the year 1710.   " In that year," says

---

* Original in Ushaw Collection.
† To "poke," French *pocher, i.e.* to pocket, to put into the sack. A scholastic term for defeating an adversary.

Mr. (Bishop) Dicconson, " in the discourse I had, on June 28, with Dr. Delcourt in the presence of Mr. J. Rigby, S.T.P., and of Mr. L. Green, *alias* Word, he affirmed that Dr. Hawarden had said things not right in the *Concours*. But when I reasoned the case and said what he declared of his own belief of *the fact* (of Jansenius' book) Dr. Delcourt answered that he had said something by which he showed that he would not condemn those who did not. To which I said that Dr. Hawarden being pressed to declare whether the four Bishops were among the *filii iniquitatis* or no, he waived the question, only saying that he was not *Judex episcoporum*.* On another occasion Dr. Delcourt said that Dr. Hawarden maintained that the Church was not infallible "in obscure grammatical facts ;" which, if true, was no proof that he denied her infallibility in Dogmatical facts. To these accusations and insinuations, when they saw the light, Dr. Hawarden replied that he had expressly condemned the *Cas de Conscience*, that he had, without any hesitation, declared his acceptance of the Constitutions of Innocent X., Alexander VII., and of Clement IX. ; that he had written a treatise expressly to prove that the five Propositions were all in the *Augustinus* of Jansenius ; and that he detested, and always had detested the errors of Jansenius, and all others condemned by the Apostolic See. . . ."†
When Dr. Hawarden was asked, " *An Jansenismum unquam probaveris ?*" the venerable man replied, " *Ne dormiens quidem* ; *nam vigilanti tale fascinus excidere non potuit*."

It has been said that Dr. Hawarden left Douay in 1707. He then came on the Mission, and was placed at Aldcliffe, near Lancaster, where the Daltons then resided. This mission included Lancaster, where no priest could then live with safety. Such, however, was the high opinion that Dr. Smith, Bishop of the North District, had of him, that, wishing to have him nearer to his own person, he placed him at Gilligate in Durham, and when he made his will in 1709 appointed him one of his trustees, and left him £10 for life on condition of his continuing to reside in the North. Soon after his arrival in England he was chosen a member of the Chapter, and in 1710 an Archdeacon, and and also the *Catholic Controversy Writer*. On this latter account it probably was found necessary that he should reside in London in order to have an eye to the works written against us, and that he might have the convenience of books necessary to answer them. He therefore quitted Durham sometime after 1719, and repaired to London. It was here that he had, by the desire of Queen Caroline, the Consort of George II., a conference with Dr. Clarke, in the presence of her Majesty, of Mrs. Middleton, a Catholic lady much in the confidence of the Queen, and of Dr. Courayer. Dr. Samuel Clarke denied the self-existence in the Blessed Trinity of the Son, and of the Holy Ghost ; maintained their derivation from, and subordination to the Father, and the personality and distinct agency of each person of the Holy Trinity. "When they met, Dr. Clarke, in very guarded terms, and with very great apparent perspicuity, stated and explained his system. After he had finished, a pause of some length ensued. Dr. Hawarden then said that he had listened with the greatest attention to what had been said by Dr. Clarke, that he believed he apprehended rightly the whole system ; that the only reply which he should make to it was—asking a single question ; that if the question were thought to contain any ambiguity, he wished it to be cleared of this before any answer was returned ; but desired that when the answer should be given it should be expressed either by the affirmative or negative monosyllable. To this proposition Dr. Clarke assented. ' Then,' said Dr. Hawarden, ' I ask : Can God the Father annihilate the Son and the Holy Ghost ? Answer me yes or no.' Dr. Clarke continued for some time in deep thought, and then said it was a question which he had never considered. Here the conference ended. A searching question it certainly was. If Dr. Clarke answered ' Yes,' he admitted the Son and the Holy Ghost to be mere creatures : if he answered ' No,' he admitted each to be absolutely God." Such is the account given of this celebrated conference by

---

* Letter in Ushaw Collection.
† See his solemn *Declarations* made to Bishop Smith, *Ibid*.

Mr. C. Butler (*Historical Memoirs* IV. 430) as frequently related to him by his uncle, Mr. Alban Butler, and by Mr. Winstanley, Professor of Philosophy in Douay College.   This conference must have happened some time before 1729, and caused Dr. Hawarden to publish in that year his *Answer to Dr. Clarke and Mr. Whiston*.   Dr. Hawarden died in London April 23, 1735.   " He was," says Dodd, " a person of consummate knowledge in all ecclesiastical matters, scholastic, moral and historical ; and to do him justice, perhaps the age in which he lived could not show his equal."

Besides a body of Divinity of near 20 years' labour, preserved in MSS. in Douay College, he published the following works : 1. *Charity and Truth, or Catholics not uncharitable in saying that none are saved out of the Catholic Communion.*   2. *Catholic Grounds ; or a summary and rational of the unchangeable Orthodoxy of the Catholic Church.*   3. *The true Church of Christ, showed by concurrent testimonies of Scripture, and Primitive Tradition, in three parts, etc.*, *being an answer* to *Mr. Lesley's Case Stated, etc.*   4. *An Answer to Dr. Clarke and Mr. Whiston concerning the Divinity of the Son of God and of the Holy Spirit, with a summary account of the Writers of the three first Ages.*   5. *Discourses of Religion ; between a Minister of the Church of England and a Country Gentleman, wherein the chief points of Controversy between the Church of England and Rome are truly stated and briefly Discussed.*   6. *The Rule of Faith truly Stated, in a New and Easy Method.*   7. *A Treatise of Usury, MS.*   8. *A Translation into Latin* of Father Dormer's *Defence of Usury*.   This was sent to the Congregation of the Index, and the *Defence* was condemned.   9. *A Treatise to prove that the Five Propositions were in the " Augustinus" of Jansenius.*   10. *Some Queries relating to a book entitled, " A Compassionate Address to Papists," etc., in five Letters in an answer to " The Case Re-stated," and " The Church of Christ Shewed."*   Cornhill, 1717.   It consists of 48 octavo pages ; the conciseness of the style, and the numerous questions, are very much in Dr. Hawarden's manner, and seem to bespeak him to be the writer.

HAWARDEN, EDWARD (II.), was educated at Douay, where he was General Prefect for several years, from 1761 to his coming over.   When he left the College for the Mission, he was placed at Wrightington, and lived there till the time of his death, Dec. 17, 1793.

HAWARDEN, JOHN, was educated at Douay, where he taught Poetry in 1752 and Rhetoric in 1753, and came on the Mission about the year 1754 or 1755. Lancashire [? at Stockton], which had given him birth, was also the scene of his labours, and where he died May 27, 1770.

HAWARDEN, THOMAS, also a priest, died in Lancashire, in April 1746. [Thomas Hawarden, V.G. to Bishop Dicconson in 1742].

HAWKINS, JOHN, O.S.B.   Son of Mr. Hawkins, of Nash Court, Co. Kent. He became a Benedictine, and after travelling with Mr. Bodenham, of Rotherwas in Herefordshire, lived with him some time as his chaplain.   When his confrere, Mr. Lewis, married, Mr. Hawkins remonstrated with him on the impropriety of his conduct, but soon after followed his example and married the sister of Dr. Burney.   His life, even while he was abroad with Mr. Bodenham, had not given much edification, and those who knew him best were little surprised at his conduct.   Through the means of his wife he became acquainted and great with North, then Bishop of Worcester, where he lived after his apostasy, and when he was translated to Winchester gave him a living in Hampshire, which he soon exchanged with a nephew of [Dr. Louth] for one in Essex, as his first was in the neighbourhood of Sir H. Tichborne, who had been his scholar, but on account of his proving unfaithful to his religious vows refused to notice him.   When Mr. Wharton left Worcester he addressed a letter to the Catholics of Worcester from America.   This letter Mr. Hawkins published, and afterwards wrote in defence of it his ponderous work entitled *An Appeal to Scripture, Reason, and Tradition, in support of the Doctrines contained in a Letter to the Roman Catholics of the City of Worcester*.   This appeal was answered by Rev. Joseph Berington, in 1785, in his *Reflections addressed to Rev. John Hawkins*.   Soon after he married, Mr. Hawkins wrote *An Essay on Celibacy*.

HAWKINS, THOMAS, *alias* PARKINS, S.J., was son of Thomas Hawkins and Joan Saxby, his wife ; was born at Slindon, in Sussex, Dec. 21, 1722. He studied his Classics at St. Omers, and at the age of 19 was sent to Rome and was admitted into the English College there by Father H. Sheldon, Nov. 5, 1741. On July 29, 1742, he took the oath of Alexander VII. and was ordained priest Feb. 12, 1747. In that year, and after living more than five years on the funds of the Clergy College, he obtained a dispensation from part of his oath and entered among the Jesuits at Watten, and in 1759 became a professed Father. He lived several years at Swinnerton, but left that place some time before Feb. 1765. I find that a person of the same name died in 1785.

HAYDOCK, CUTHBERT, was brother of Gilbert, and born at Cottam Hall. He studied at Douay, and being ordained priest, lived for some time in Lancashire. He afterwards was placed at Worksop Manor, where he lived forty years, respected and loved by all who knew him. Worksop Manor was burnt down in 1761, and it was the common remark that Mr. Haydock never looked up after, and died Jan. 11, 1763, in the 79th year of his age. Mr. Haydock was chosen a member of the Chapter on March 17, 1734 (O.S.). His elder brother, it is said, was master of the horse that occasioned the death of William III. Their aunt married Mr. Shuttleworth, of Hodsock, and thus themselves were first cousins of Mr. George Shuttleworth, of Hodsock Park. [The draft adds : Cuthbert Haydock, from Lancashire, defended Logic under Laurence Rigby, May 27, 1705. Joseph Hatherley defended Logic with Haydock].

HAYDOCK, GEORGE LEO, was brother to James and born at Tagg. He was a scholar of Mr. Banister at Mowbrick Hall, and afterwards went to Douay, where he was indefatigable during the whole course of his studies. At the beginning of the French Revolution he made his escape [a little before the gentlemen of Douay were imprisoned] in company with Mr. Davies [then Professor of Grammar and an excellent master], a native of Monmouthshire, and afterwards missionary at Chepstow. On his arrival in England he remained some time at Old Hall Green, together with Messrs. Thompson, Thomas Gillow, Thomas Penswick, Charles Saul, etc., and then removed with them to Crook Hall, where he studied Divinity, and defended his *Theologia Universa* with great applause in 1798. He afterwards taught Humanity about two years, and during his stay at College read incessantly the Fathers, Divines, and Biblical Commentators. He then went on the Mission to Ugthorpe, and is still living (1836) but has no pastoral care. He wrote the Prefaces and Notes of the greater part of the folio Bible, in three vols., printed by his brother Thomas at Manchester. [Mr. D. Rayment assisted in the New Testament to keep pace with the proofs].

HAYDOCK, GILBERT [born March 18, 1682, O.S.], was son of William Haydock, of Cottam, and his wife, Joanna Anderton, of Euxton, in Lancashire. He was sent early to Douay, and applied closely to the Classics, Philosophy, and Divinity, and made equal progress in virtue and piety, so as to be a pattern to all. In 1708 he was ordained priest and sent on the mission in the following year, where his apostolic zeal and labours were attended with the happiest effects in the conversion and care of souls. In 1716 (while in prison, my memoirs say) he was appointed chaplain [in succession to Mr. Lynds], to the Augustine Dames of St. Monica in Louvain, where he arrived Aug. 1, and filled that station till his death, greatly to the satisfaction and edification of those religious ladies, who, in their Mortuary Bill, bore this testimony to his merit, " that he was a holy, pious, and exemplary clergyman, and eminently exact in every duty. In the celebration of the divine mysteries his fervour and piety frequently manifested themselves in a copious profusion of tears, and his charity to the poor in abundant alms. In a word, he was the mirror and pattern of every virtue becoming a Christian and a clergyman." He ever bore a tender devotion to the Blessed Virgin, and every year, after a spiritual retreat of eight days, made a pilgrimage to her chapel of Monte Acuto [Montaigu]. [He was taken ill on the Feast of her Nativity, after saying Mass, and died on the Feast of her Name]. After an illness of fifteen days, which he bore with the most examplary patience, and spent in preparing himself for eternity, he departed this life on Sept. 22, 1749, in the 68th year of his age, and 42nd of his priesthood.

HAYDOCK, JAMES, was born at Tagg, near Preston, of respectable parents. He studied at Douay [was Professor of Syntax], and was ordained priest at Arras in 1792. He soon after came on the Mission, and was domestic chaplain to John Trafford, Esq., and had the care of the congregation around Trafford House about fifteen years. He then removed to Lea, near Preston, where he caught a fever in attending the sick of his congregation, and died a martyr of charity April 25, 1809. Mr. Haydock was a learned, laborious, and zealous Missionary. He was buried in the cemetary of New House Chapel, where a neat monument is erected to his memory. He was some years prefect of the study place at Douay, and taught Catechism, in which branch of his duty he excelled.

HEATLY, WILLIAM, O.S.B., was born at Dunkenhalgh, in Lancashire, in 1723. He became a monk at Lambspring, and took the name of Maurus. Having been ordained priest, he was sent upon the Mission, but returned to Lambspring, where he was chosen Abbot of the Monastery, Jan. 26, 1762, being then 39 years old. On June 1, 1802, and at the age of 79, he was suspended from his office and authority by Dr. Brewer, the President of the English Congregation, of which the monks at Lambspring were members, after having been Abbot forty years. He died Aug. 15 following. An undue severity and long confinement inflicted on one of his monks is said to have been the cause of his deposition.

HENEAGE, ELIZABETH WINDSOR, was daughter of —— Brown, Esq., of Newport, in the Isle of Wight, who is said to have been received into the Church by Bishop Thomas Talbot, while he lived at Brockhampton [Ita Mr. Edward Eyre, of Longbirch]. In 17— she married James Windsor Heneage, of Cadeby, Esq., in Lincolnshire, by whom she had two daughters, one of whom married Basil Fitzherbert, of Swinnerton, Esq., and the other William Brockholes, of Claughton, Esq. At the death of her husband, Feb. 19, 1786, she became possessed of upwards of £1,000 per annum, of which she spared little for herself, but was lavish of it to the poor and distressed, wherever she made acquaintance with them. She built and endowed two chapels at Cowes and Newport, in the Isle of Wight, and most of those built elsewhere after the year 1780 partook of her charities. She died, Dec. 10, 1800, at her house in Newport, Isle of Wight.

HESKETH, CATHARINE, daughter of William Hesketh, of Mains, Esq. She was thirteen years Abbess of the Benedictine Dames of Ghent, whom she conducted over to England when they were disturbed in their peaceable retreat at the French Revolution. They took a house in Preston, where she died Nov. 24, 1809, in the 81st or 82nd year of her age and 54th of her religious profession. She was buried in the Catholic Chapel at Fernyhalgh, where an elegant marble tablet was inscribed to her memory by William Fitzherbert Brockholes, of Claughton. After her death the Dames purchased Caverswall Castle, near Stone in Staffordshire, where they now are [i.e., in 1820. Since 1855 they have been at Oulton].

HESKETH, ROGER (I.), son of Gabriel Hesketh by his wife Anna Sympson, was born in Lancashire in 1643. He went over to Lisbon with his elder brother George, and, when ordained, was made Procurator of the College in 1667, and Confessarius in 1672. In Jan., 1676, he began to teach Philosophy, and Divinity in Sept., 1677. On Dec. 6, 1678, he was appointed Vice-President, and continued to fill that office till he was recalled by Bishop Leyburn in 1686. He left Lisbon, April 29, but not till he had taken his degree of D.D. When Dr. Watkinson wished to resign the government of Lisbon College, Dr. Hesketh was judged a proper person to succeed him, and received from the Chapter the patent for that purpose. In 1694 he was chosen a member of the Chapter, and in 1710 assisted at the General Chapter, at which Dr. Robert Jones, the Sub-Dean, presided, in the place of Dr. Perrott, the Dean, whose infirmities prevented his coming. In this Assembly a Declaration was agreed to, expressive of their abhorrence of Jansenism. It was signed by the Dean (Dr. Perrott) Dr. Jones (the Sub-Dean) and by twenty-six others, in person and by their deputies. It was afterwards sent to Rome with a letter signed by Dr. Perrott, Dr. Jones, and Mr. Wolfe (*alias* Brown), the Secretary (see *Records of Jansenism*). Dr. Hesketh wrote *A Treatise on Transubstantiation*, quoted in Dodd's *Certamen* and *Flores*. (*Register of Lisbon College*).

HESKETH, ROGER (II.) *alias* TALBOT, S.J., son of William Hesketh and Mary Brockholes his wife, was born in Lancashire in July, 1729. Being sent to Rome in 1750, he was admitted into the College as a Convictor Nov. 3, by Cardinal Lante, when he began Philosophy in Aug. 23, 1752. He left the College to go to Watten, and became a Jesuit. (*Annals of the Roman College*).

HEYDON, ROBERT, D.D., was a native of the diocese of Gloucester. After two years' study of Divinity at Douay he went to Paris in Sept., 1707 [where he was ordained at Whitsuntide, 1708], and in Oct., 1712, came on the Mission, in the hopes of bringing his father over to the Catholic Church. In 1715 he returned to St. Gregory's, and, after his two *examens*, entered his license the following January, and on August 6, 1718, took the cap of Doctor. On Sept. 8 he returned to the English Mission ; but in what place he exercised his pastoral duties, or where or when he died, I have not been able to discover.

HICKIN, PHILIP, son of John and Joan Hickin, was born in the neighbourhood, if not at, Wolverhampton. At the age of 21 he was admitted into the English College at Rome by Father Lucas, Oct. 18, 1691, and on Jan. 29, 1696, was ordained priest, and soon after came on the Mission. In 1710 he succeeded Mr. Francis Fitter at Oscott, and died there, Feb. 20, 1735, (O.S.) [had £15 per annum at Oscott].

HIGGINS, WILLIAM, was a native of Warwickshire. At the age of eighteen he was admitted into the College at Rome, by order of Cardinal Howard, Oct. 24, 1685. When ordained he came on the Mission, in 1692, and lived at Dutton, in Cheshire, with Lord Gerrard, yet made excursions to assist the Catholics in the neighbourhood. At a meeting of the Chapter held May 2, 1693, present twenty Capitulars, "he gave an account of the bad state of the Roman College under the Jesuits." Of this repeated representations were made to Rome, and memorials were sent by the Bishops, praying for the restoration of the College to the Secular Clergy, for whom it was founded, and for whom it was administered by the Jesuits, who had thus the means of securing some of the most promising youths for their own body, and at the expense of the Clergy.

HILL, AUGUSTIN, O.S.F. In 1692 he lived with Sir H. Tichbourne, near Winchester.

HILLS, ROBERT (*alias* HYDE), was a zealous Missioner, who lived at Winchester, and died there, Jan. 15, 1745, (O.S.). He was a member of the Chapter [elected Archdeacon of ——, May 23, 1729], and bequeathed £500 to it.

HINDE, FRANCIS, was born at Corby, in Lincolnshire, about the year 1726. He went over to Douay College with his countryman, Peter Beeston, and after some years' study there, went through his license at Paris, and then came on the Mission, where I find he succeeded Mr. Hardwick, at Paynsley, in Staffordshire, and, soon after, Mr. James Layfield, at Oscott. In 1764 he lived with Bishop Hornyhold at Longbirch, but soon after was, for some years, chaplain to the Augustine Nuns, at Bruges ; which place he quitted to become Vice-President of St. Omers. Lastly he became chaplain to a Mrs. Rachell [? Rackett, Rackell], in London, whom he survived fifteen years, and died at Somerstown, Dec. 5, 1810 [at the age of 85]. This account I have from Reverend Robert Beeston, of Eastwell.

HINDE, GEORGE. Having studied Divinity at Douay and taught Philosophy, he went to St. Gregory's, at Paris, and succeeded Mr. Umfreville, *alias* Fell, as Procurator of the Seminary. This office he filled for six years, but never became an Alumnus there. He then went to Brussels, but in April, 1735, resumed his office of Procurator. In January, 1741, he became confessor to the English Nuns at Rouen, where he died in April, 1752. (*St. Gregory's Register*).

HITCHCOCK, WILLIAM NEEDHAM, O.S.B., was born in Bucks. At the age of 19 he went to Rome, and was admitted into the College in the Rectorship of Father Stafford, Sept. 20, 1644. He was ordained priest at St. John Lateran's, March 20, 1649, and left for England, April 17, 1651. The Annals of the College say : *pacifice se gessit, et post triennium factus est Benedictinus, Duaci.* See his letter in Dodd, Vol. III., 392, there signed F. W. H.

HODGES, ——, was an Englishman, but not educated in any of our Colleges. He had a small benefice in Portugal, and no obligation to come on the Mission ; yet he was here several years off and on ; much abroad, and died abroad, "about the beginning of 1748 (N.S.)."

HODGSON, ALBERT, of Leighton Hall and Yelland Hall, near Lancaster. His estates were valued in 1716 at £327 9s. 3d. per annum.

HODGSON, FRANCIS, was educated at Douay, and when on the Mission, lived some years at Cliff with George Witham, Esq., and assisted the poor in the moors and in Cleveland. He lived some time in Bishoprick, but in 1692 returned into Yorkshire, where he was the Procurator of his Brethren of Yorkshire, Northumberland, and Durham, and lived at Hardenhill,* near his friend Bishop Smith, whom Francis Tunstall, of Wycliff, had received into his house at the Revolution, and whose charity made the Bishop consider his house as his home.† My memoirs say he lived many years at Wycliff, but resigned on account of old age, and retired to Hutton Hall. By his will, dated Feb. 22, 1725, he left £800 to his executor, Mr. Marmaduke Tunstall, for the benefit of the poor Catholics in his neighbourhood, and at and about Sunderland-by-sea, and South Shields. He died, May 24, 1726. He was "a very virtuous, advised, and pious man, and the true and trusty friend of Bishop Smith." Another Mr. Francis Hodgson, from Douay, died . . . April, 1733.

HODGSON, JOSEPH. After studying some time at Sedgley Park, he was sent to Douay, and reached the College Dec. 18, 1769. His progress in learning and piety was the admiration of all ; and after he had finished his course, he was made professor first of Philosophy and then of Divinity. The latter office he filled when the French Revolutionists had seized the College, and transferred the Superiors and the students first to Arras, and then to Dourlens. Mr. Hodgson used often to say that " he was the last of all to quit the College." At his arrival in England he was placed in the arduous mission of St. George's Fields, and for many years laboured hard in that portion of the London Mission. He afterwards removed to Castle Street, and was V.G. to Bishop Douglass, and afterwards to Bishop Poynter, and at the same time had the spiritual care of the school at Brook Green, Hammersmith, where he died, Nov. 30, 1821, respected and beloved by all who knew him. Mr. Hodgson was a good Classical scholar, a profound and sound Divine, and a zealous Missioner. He left, in MS., *A Narrative of the Seizure of Douay College, and of the Deportation of Seniors, Professors, and Students to Dourlens.* It was published in the *Catholic Magazine*, Vol. I. But. in justice to Mr. Hodgson, it must be said that it was never intended by him for publication, and was left by him in a very unfinished state ; yet it contains many interesting facts.

---

* In his draft, Kirk, quoting an older memoir, writes, " ' Lived at Hardenhill, near ye Lad Smith.' I suppose he means the Bishop."

† The draft says that Bishop Smith, by his will, "left £20 to the poor about Wycliffe and Cliff, and one guinea to each of the Superiors of the Benedictines, Jesuits, and Franciscans in his district."

HODGSON, PHILIP, of Tone, in the parish of North Middleton, Co. Northumberland. His estates valued at £238 per annum in 1716.

HODGSON, RALPH, of Lintz, in the county of Durham, was born about the year 1730. He was descended from an ancient and respectable family long established in that county. He received the early part of his classical education at Douay College, and finished his studies at Paris. He married one of the daughters and co-heiresses of Roger Strickland, Esq., of Catterick, in Yorkshire, nephew of Sir Roger Strickland, who was Admiral of the Fleet in the time of Charles II. and James II., whose fortunes he followed to France. Mr. Hodgson died in 1773, leaving issue Catherine, his only daughter and heiress, married to Thomas Selby, Esq., of Biddleston. He wrote *The dispassionate Narrative* [*of the conduct of the English Clergy in receiving from the French King and his Parliament the administration of the College at St. Omer, late under the direction of the English Jesuits*, London, 1768]. [The above details were communicated to Kirk by Thos. Selby, Jun., in a note dated Biddleston, Aug. 14, 1815].

HOLDEN, JOSEPH, D.D., was a native of Lancashire, probably of Standish. While Superior of the Seminary, he purchased houses in the Rue des Fours for the Seminary, but the Attorney ran away with the purchase money, which involved the Doctor and Seminary in difficulties and debts. His MSS. were seized by his creditors, among the rest a valuable Course of Divinity, which was adopted by one of the Bishops of France in his Seminary. Edward, Duke of Norfolk, called the Good Duke, was a considerable benefactor to the Seminary on this occasion. [Dr. Holden was succeeded by Dr. Charles Howard, the Duke's Chaplain, at Norfolk House]. When Dr. Holden was presented by Bishop Stonor, the Archbishop's confirmation was obtained with some difficulty, as " some busy people had whispered to the Archbishop that Dr. Holden was to be suspected for his principles, or want of submission to the decrees of the Church." But Dr. Holden abundantly cleared himself before Mons. Robinet, one of the G.V. of the Archbishop, by signing his submission to all the decrees in question, which satisfied both the Archbishop and his Vicar. The finances of the Seminary were in a bad state when Dr. Beer resigned, and did not improve in Dr. Holden's time, so that he was obliged to take pensioners, such as the late Sir Charles and his brother, Mr. Edward Jerningham, Mr. Ralph Standish, and others, who had no intention to take degrees, or even to enter into the ecclesiastical state. The same plan for the same reason was continued during the Superiority of Drs. Howard and Bew. (*St. Gregory's Register*, and *Catholic Magazine* III. p. 100).

HOLDERNESS, DUNSTAN, O.S.B. He was Prior of Dieuleward, and died June 25, 1782. See Dr. Marsh's account of Benedictine Priors, etc., in MS., *Collectanea Anglo-Catholica*.

HOLDFORT, THOMAS FRANCIS, *alias* HUNT, D.D. After studying his Rhetoric at Douay, he passed three months in a French Community, and was received at St. Gregory's, Sept. 12, 1724. In Sept. 1730, he was made priest, and took the Doctor's cap, March 16, 1734, and on May 9 departed for England for the Mission. He died at Lady Holt, or Harting, in Sussex, May 7, 1770. (*St. Gregory's Register*).

HOLFORD, PETER, was second son of —— Holford, Esq., of Holford, near Warrington, in Cheshire. He was sent to Christ Church College, Cambridge, for the purpose of taking Holy Orders. He accordingly applied himself to the study of Divinity, but being dissatisfied with the reasons assigned for the ground of the Reformation, he ventured to propose his difficulties to some clergymen of the establishment, and even to the Bishop of London. Their answers, he told me, instead of allaying, increased his difficulties, till at length he determined to leave his home and his friends, and, unknown to them, went to London with his sister, Elizabeth Holford. Here they introduced themselves to Bishop Challoner, by whom they were instructed, received into the Church, and confirmed.   They then went abroad, and having placed his sister in a convent, he thought of entering the army in order to support himself and her, their parents having turned their backs on them.   But the dangers of that state of life having been represented to him by his friends at Douay, he lived some time retired at Cambray.   On his return to England, a commission he received from Miss Carrington, a nun, daughter of —— Smith, Lord Carrington, to her sister Constantia Wright, widow of —— Wright, of Kelvedon, Esq., brought him acquainted with that lady, whom he afterwards married, and thus became possessed of the estate of Lord Carrington, at Wootton, in Warwickshire [and of Aston, near Ludlow], to which she was heiress.   By this marriage he had two children ; one died young, and Catherine Mary married Sir Edward Smyth, of Actonburnel, Bart., by whom she had one son, the present Baronet.   Mr. Holford had a cultivated mind, was a sincere convert, and an exemplary Catholic.   He died at Actonburnel, July 17, 1803, which day was also the anniversary of Mrs. Holford.   His sister died at Wootton, April 28, 1814, aged 81. Mr. Holford had an uncle, who also quitted his home, and was never heard of afterwards ; yet Mr. Holford thought he became a Catholic, and priest.   (This was Peter Holford, *alias* Lostock, who went to Lisbon and became a priest, and died at Paris, Aug. 31, 1722.)   Mr. Holford more than once told me that his father used to say that he, Peter, once entered his study and walked through into an adjoining room, but was not to be found, though he followed him.

HOLLAND, JOHN [? THOMAS], *alias* MARTINDALE, was a native of Lancashire.   At the age of 23, was admitted into the English College at Rome, Oct. 25, 1689, during the Rectorship of Father Lucas ; but before he took the College oath, left in April, 1690, and entered among the Jesuits.   Probably the same as Thomas.   (*Ann. Coll. Angl. Rom.*).

HOLLAND, THOMAS, S.J., lived at the Bar, in York, about 1710.   Mr. Mannock speaks thus of him, " Neither Mr. Holland . . . ." See *Records of Jansenism*, p. 128.   He was succeeded at the Bar [*i.e.*, Convent] by Edward Sadler, S.J.

HOLMAN, GEORGE, of Warkworth, Esq.   He was son of Michael Holman (who died Oct. 19, 1673, aged 43), and of Eleonora, daughter of George Gascoigne, Esq.*   He married Lady Anastasia Stafford, daughter of Lord Stafford, who was beheaded in 1680, when the nation was mad with Oates' Plot [and by her he had William, educated at Douay].   Mr. Holman died in 1703.   He was remarkable for his charities.   Among others, he gave 20,000 livres to form the establishment of St. Gregory's, at Paris.   Mr. Gother was his Chaplain, and lived with him at Warkworth.   Mrs. Holman died, May 28, 1719, aged 73.

HOLMAN, WILLIAM, son of George and Lady Anastasia Holman.   By the advice of Mr. Gother he was sent to Douay [ran from Douay, Sept. 20, 1704, about the end of Grammar], and at the end of Grammar, went to Harcourt College, at Paris, with his tutor, Mr. Lee, a young gentleman and a convert. On his return to England, he settled at Warkworth, and having no children, he bequeathed [about 1745] his estate to his nephews, Francis and Roland Eyre, of Hassop, sons of his sister, Mary Holman, who had married Mr. Eyre, of Hassop, Co. Derby.   Roland sold his moiety soon after he came into possession, and the other moiety was also sold after the death of Francis Eyre, Esq., when the fine old mansion of Warkworth Castle, near Banbury, built in 1592, was taken down and the materials sold.   (See Epitaph in *Rec. Miscell. Geo. I.*).

HOLMES, *or* HELMES, EDWARD, was educated at Douay, and after teaching Poetry and Philosophy, came on the Mission.   [He was an excellent scholar].   He lived many years at Manchester, where he was charged with the care of that mission, which then was small [scarcely amounting to seventy

* The draft adds, " By his wife Dorothy. . . . George had a brother Michael, if not an elder brother. , . . See the Epitaphs of Eleonora and Will. Holman in Minutes Book I., in *Rec. Miscel. George I.*"

souls], and also with that of the surrounding villages. He died there, Oct. 16, 1773.

HOLMES —— [? HOLME, EDWARD], O.S.F.　He was confessor to the nuns at Aire, in Artois.　He afterwards came over to England on the Mission, and conformed.　As a reward of his apostacy, a living was given him in Essex, but he died the day he preached his first sermon.　This happened about 1775. *Ita* Dr. Milner told me.—J. K.　(See also, *The Franciscans in England*, p. 253, by Father Thaddeus, O.F.M.—P. R.).

HOOKE [LUKE, JOSEPH], D.D.　He was son of Mr. Hooke, the author of the *Roman History*, in 4 Vols. 4to.　"Perhaps," says Mr. C. Butler, " the best modern history of that interesting people."　After taking his degrees in the Sorbonne, he was raised to the Chair of Divinity, and was one of the three Doctors who incautiously approved of the famous thesis of Abbé de Prade, which made so much noise in Paris and throughout France, was proscribed by the Parliament of Paris, condemned by the Archbishop, and by the Bishops of Montauban and Auxerre, and the University of Caen.　On Jan. 27, 1752, the Sorbonne censured ten propositions of the Abbe de Prade, and erased his name from the list of Bachelors.　Benedict XIV., in the March of that year, condemned his Thesis, and excommunicated the author of it, who fled into Holland, and there published an apology, "tres-insidieuse et remplie de sophismes seduisans," says Dr. Elloy.　On April 6, 1754, the Abbé signed a solemn retractation, in which he says, among other things, that " his life was not long enough to deplore his past conduct, and to thank the Almighty for the favour he had done him!"　This retractation he sent to the Pope, to the Sorbonne, and to the Bishop of Montauban.　The Bishop of Breslau wrote to the Pope in his favour, and bore testimony to his sincere repentance, to his orthodoxy, and to his excellent dispositions.　Benedict XIV., in consequence of this, took off the excommunication and obtained of the Sorbonne that he should be re-established in his degree or place of license.　The Bishop made him a Canon of his Cathedral and one of his Archdeacons.　The Abbé died at Glogau in 1782.　As for the three Doctors who had approved of the These, they were severely reprimanded by the Parliament of Paris ; the Sorbonne publicly reproached them for their inconsiderate signature ; and all lost their places.　But though Dr. Hooke vacated his Divinity Chair, yet, notwithstanding the opposition of M. de Beaumont, the Archbishop, he was named to the Chair of Hebrew in 1774, and was appointed Librarian to Mazarin College. It is difficult to understand how three professors of the Sorbonne could have approved of such a These, unless it be that, presuming on the orthodoxy of the candidate, they signed without reading what was submitted to them.　They indeed excused themselves by saying " that they had not read it, because it was printed in very small type."　Dr. Hooke died in Paris, after publishing his *Principia Religionis Naturalis et Revelatæ*.　Dr. Brewer gave a second edition, with many additions and notes.　(MS. letter of Dr. Elloy of the Sorbonne).

HOOKE, NATHANIEL.　An eminent historian of great abilities and high rank in the republic of letters, but of whose long life little or nothing is at present known.　From a modest but manly letter addressed to the Earl of Oxford, dated Oct. 17, 1722, it appears that in his youth he had some considerable losses in the South Sea infatuation.　"I endeavoured," he says, "to be rich, and imagined for a while that I was.　I am in some measure happy to find myself at this instant but just worth nothing.　If your Lordship, or any of your numerous friends, have need of a servant, with the bare qualifications of being able to read and write and to be honest, I shall gladly undertake any employment that your Lordship shall not think me unworthy of."　(See Butler's *Memoirs*, c. 43).　From the intimacy which subsisted between him and Pope, and from the style of his writings, compared with that of his contemporaries educated at Douay, and in other foreign establishments, I suspect that he may have studied with Mr. Pope at Twyford School, near Winchester.　It is not improbable that this same friend first got him introduced to the Earl of Oxford, which was previous to the date of the above letter. By whatever means he got introduced, Mr. Hooke, from that period to his death, "enjoyed the confidence and patronage of men not less distinguished by virtue than by titles." Among these were the said Earl of Oxford, the Earl of Marchmont, Mr. Speaker Onslow, Fénelon, Pope, Dr. Cheyne, Dr. King, the celebrated principal of St. Mary's Hall, Oxford, etc., to say nothing of the Dowager Duchess of Marlborough, from whom, in 1742, Mr. Hooke is said to have received £5,000 for writing his account of her conduct from her first coming to the Court to the year 1710. Mr. John Whiston says: "When the Duchess of Marlborough died, she left £500 a year to Mr. Hooke and David Mallet to write the history of the late Duke." It does not, however, appear that this was ever written. Mr. Hooke possessed no small share of Mr. Pope's esteem and friendship, and this friendship continued to the close of the life of our English Homer, when Mr. Hooke gave a signal proof of his attachment to Pope, by introducing a priest to assist him on his death-bed, in spite of the known aversion of Lord Bolingbroke to such interference. "The priest had scarcely departed," says Bishop Warburton, "when Bolingbroke, coming from Battersea, flew into a great fit of passion and indignation on the occasion." In his last will Pope left him £5 to be laid out in a ring, or any other memorial of him. Mr. Hooke survived his friend many years, and died himself in 1763. He left two sons, Thomas, a Divine of the Church of England, and the celebrated Doctor of Sorbonne. Dr. Warburton describes him as "a mystic and a Quietist, and a warm disciple of Fénelon." He was certainly partial, and deservedly so, to the great Fénelon ; but it does not follow from this partiality that he also approved of his system of *Quietism*, especially after his works on that subject had been condemned by himself, as well as by the Pope. In 1801 a tablet was erected to the memory of Mr. Hooke, in the churchyard of Hedsor, Bucks, at the expense of Lord Boston.

Mr. Hooke's works are : 1. *A History of the Life of the late Archbishop of Cambray ; translated from the French of Sir Andrew Ramsay.* Dedicated to the Earl of Oxford. 12mo., 1723. 2. *Travels of Cyrus ; translated from the French of Sir Andrew Ramsey.* 4to, 1739. 3. *The Roman History ; illustrated with maps and other plates.* Vol. I. Dedicated to Mr. Pope, and introduced by "Remarks on the history of the Seven Roman Kings, occasioned by Sir Isaac Newton's objections to the supposed 244 years of the Royal state of Rome." 4. *An Account of the Conduct of the Dowager Duchess of Marlborough, from her first coming to Court to the year 1710. In a letter from herself to Lord ——.* 8vo, 1742. "Though his reward on this occasion was considerable, yet the reputation he acquired by the performance was much greater." 5. *The Roman History.* Vol. II., 4to, 1745. This he dedicated to his worthy friend Hugh, Earl of Marchmont. The Capitoline Marbles, or Consular Calendars, discovered at Rome during the Pontificate of Paul III. in 1545, are annexed to this volume. 6. *Observations on the accounts given by Abbé de Vertot, Dr. Conyers Middleton, and Dr. Thomas Chapman, on the Roman Senate,* 1758. These were with great propriety inscribed to Mr. Speaker Onslow. 7. *The Roman History.* Vol. III. This was printed under Mr. Hooke's inspection, before his last illness, but was not published till after his death. 8. *The Roman History,* Vol. IV., was published in 1771, and, it is believed, by Dr. Gilbert Stuart. 9. Mr. Hooke also revised, in 1733, a translation of "The History of the Conquest of Mexico by the Spaniards, by Thomas Townshend, Esq." Two vols., 8vo. (*Illustrations of the Literary History of the 18th Century,* by John Nichols, F.S.A. Vol. II., p. 606 ; III. 50, 302, 633 ; VI., 632 ; IV. 463 ; V. 642, 395, 6 ; II. 712).

HORNBY [? ROBERT], S.J. He resided with Mr. William Dormer, at Idsworth, Hants.

HORNE, JAMES, *alias* GREEN, son of Henry Horne, a Protestant, and Elizabeth Smith, a Catholic, was born in London, Nov. 3, 1725. Having studied in part his Classics in London, at the age of 16 he went to Rome, and was admitted into the College, then under the administration of Father Sheldon, by order of Cardinal Pico de Mirandula, Sept. 30, 1741. Having completed his Divinity course, he was ordained priest Feb. 21, 1750 ; and on the 13th of the following April he departed for England, where he was made chaplain to the Venetian Ambassador.   He was also a Capitular and the Secretary to the Chapter.   He was an intelligent collector of coins and medals, and few private gentlemen had a better collection of them.   Mr. Horne had a younger brother named Henry, *alias* Green, born in London, Jan. 4, 1731, (O.S.), who also studied and was ordained at Rome.   [Baptised and confirmed by Bishop Petre, admitted at Rome by Father Christopher Maire, Oct. 13, 1745 ; ordained Mar. 15, 1755].   He lived in London, and died there, Jan. 12, 1769.   Mr. James Horne lived to a great age, and was the oldest missionary in London, when he died at his chambers in Furnival's Inn on Feb. 16th, 1802.   He compiled the Directories for many years, and in his youth wrote *The Wooden Bowl*.   [Kirk elsewhere attributes this to the next-mentioned William Horne].   (*Diary of Roman College*).

HORNE, WILLIAM.   He received his education at Rome [and was cousin to Mr. Green, at Rome].   Lived many years on the Mission in London.   Was a member of the Chapter, and an antiquarian.   He died, Nov. 13, 1799.

HORNYOLD, RIGHT REV. JOHN, Bishop of Philomelia, and Vic. Apost. of the Midland District, was born in the early part of the last century, Feb. 19, 1706, being a descendant of the ancient family of the Hornyolds, of Hanley Castle, situated between the Severn and the Malvern Hills.   He was, in his early years, destined for a worldly profession ; but, approaching to manhood, he felt a strong vocation to the ecclesiastical state, which he followed by betaking himself to that nursery of missionary martyrs and other distinguished clergymen, the English College of Douay.   He was admitted Aug. 7, 1728 ; took the oath, Dec. 24, 1730.   Here he applied himself to the exercises of a pious and studious life, with a fervour proportioned to the solidity of his vocation, when his religious design seemed on the point of being frustrated by an unfortunate accident.   One of his companions, incautiously waving a firebrand in the hour of recreation, struck our Prelate's left eye with it, and, for some time, deprived him of his sight.   By the blessing of God, however, he recovered the perfect use of his right eye, and continued to pursue his studies with that success which his writings shew.   Being ordained Priest, and sent on the English Mission, he was first stationed at Grantham, in Lincolnshire, where he found an ample field for the exercise of his zeal and fortitude.   No difficulties or dangers could withhold him from the discharge of his pastoral and religious duties.   Hearing that one of his flock at a distance was in danger of death, he flew to his assistance in the midst of a terrible storm, and swam his horse through a river swollen with a flood, with imminent danger of being drowned. On another occasion, the constables coming to seize upon him as a Catholic priest, just when he was finishing Mass, he could barely save himself by substituting a female cap for his flowing periwig and throwing a woman's large cloak over his vestments, and in this disguise throwing himself, in a corner of the room, into the attitude of prayer.

His neighbourhood to Irnham, then the seat of the ancient and religious family of Thimbleby, brought him acquainted with the several members of it. One of these, having married Mr. Giffard, of Chillington, in Staffordshire, and becoming a widow, chose Mr. Hornyold to reside with her as her chaplain at the neighbouring seat of Longbirch, where she resided.   Here, upon the death of the Rev. Mr. Brockholes, of Chillington, General Vicar to Bishop John Talbot Stonor (whose residence was first at Watlington Park, and next at old Heythrop, both in Oxfordshire), he was appointed to that important office by his said Bishop, solely in consideration of his eminent virtues and talents, as the latter declared.   Not long after this, the Bishop having obtained the consent of the above named lady (whose memory for her benefactions to the Mission and to Douay College, ought ever to be cherished by English Catholics) selected him for his coadjutor in the episcopacy, and consecrated him Bishop of Philomelia by virtue of a bull from Benedict XIV., dated Dec. 22, 1752, and he was consecrated, Feb. 10, 1752-3.   His ordinary residence continued to be at Longbirch, both during the lifetime and after the death of Mrs. Giffard, though he was most assiduous in making his pastoral visits throughout the whole of the district, and even in supplying the places of the clergy who, for various causes, were occasionally absent from them. He was indefatigable in preaching the word of God, both at home and abroad, and such was his faith and fervour in the discharge of his duty, that his eyes at those times generally overflowed with tears. It has been observed that our Prelate did not exempt himself from the ordinary functions of a missionary in consequence of his episcopal dignity and duties. A remarkable instance of this occurred, which he took pleasure in relating as a proof of the mercy and providence of our heavenly Father. Making one of his pastoral visitations, on a time, on horse-back, and coming to a division of the road, where each path led to the same place, he could not, with all his force and management, make his horse go the way he was desirous of travelling ; he let the beast, therefore, go the other road. He had not proceeded far in this, when he found a poor traveller lying on a bank, and near expiring. Approaching to him, and inquiring of the sick man what he could do to relieve him, the latter exclaimed : "I want a priest ; for God's sake procure me a Catholic priest!" On this, Bishop Hornyold assured the dying man that he himself was a Priest, and also a Bishop. It is needless to describe the joy of the penitent, or the charity and zeal of the confessor ; let it suffice to say, that having received the sick man's confession, and administered the Holy Viaticum and Extreme Unction to him (for the administration of both of which Sacraments it was the merciful providence of God that he should be at this time provided), he remained with the poor object of his pastoral care until he witnessed his happy end.

During the life-time of Bishop Stonor, that is, till the year 1756, our Prelate had the satisfaction of witnessing the establishment of the Rules of the Mission, in obtaining which the former was chiefly instrumental, through the agency of the Rev. Mr. Dicconson, afterwards Bishop in the North. These Rules put an end to a world of dissension and confusion which had previously existed. He had also, during the same time, the mortification of witnessing the passing of the Marriage Act, which all the English Prelates and other eminent Divines of that period considered as a greater grievance, on account of the sacrileges and other evils which it occasions, than all the penal laws put together. The Legislature meant nothing hostile to the Catholic Religion by that Act, but it could not then relieve us, as the existence of Catholic priests was not acknowledged by the laws. Bishop Hornyold, as well as several of our clergy, were sometimes molested by these laws, particularly on one occasion, when the military from Breewood were bent on seizing and prosecuting him, during which time the Bishop remained concealed in one of the Longbirch barns. He kept up a close correspondence with the Venerable Bishop Challoner, and occasionally remitted money to him to supply his wants. He also corresponded with the learned Alban Butler, who belonged to his district, and with several other distinguished men. Several letters from the two above-mentioned personages are still preserved. In 1744 he published his first work, being an exposition of the Decalogue, or ten commandments. This was so generally approved of that he received something like official thanks from Oxford for the publication. It was not to be expected, however, that he should be thanked from that quarter for his other works, which appeared in succession, on the Sacraments and on the Creed. These are his only compositions which are known to have been printed ; but he left a great many others in MSS., chiefly Sermons.* After two or three fruitless efforts in other parts, the Rev. Mr. Errington, with the concurrence of Bishop Challoner, established, in the year 1763, that most useful school of Sedgley Park, in order to educate, on the most economical plan, a considerable number of Catholic boys, in the middle ranks of life. The founder and proprietor dying in 1768, his representatives in London showed themselves unwilling to charge themselves with so hazardous a business, as this large

---

[* *Real Principles of Catholics*, or *Catechism for the Adult*, in 1749 ; *Feasts and Fasts Reduced*, in 1777.]

establishment was, and solicited Bishop Hornyold to undertake the management of it.   He complied with their wish, and the school flourished under his guidance.   In the meantime, he purchased some land for the benefit of his successors, and rebuilt the chapel and house at Oscott for their residence, whenever the lease of Longbirch should expire.

Though occupied with such weighty concerns, and engaged in such serious studies, as likewise with prayer, meditation, etc., and though he was most abstemious and mortified in his way of living, he was cheerful and good humoured, as his friends in general testify, and particularly those clergymen who, in succession, were his chaplains; for his custom was, as far as was practicable, to take the young priests, who were sent on the Mission, into his house, and there to prepare them for undertaking the important duties of pastors.   At length, finding his health decay, and that he was incapable of travelling, he pitched upon the Hon. and Rev. Thomas Talbot, whose brother had been made, eight years before, coadjutor to Bishop Challoner, to be his coadjutor.*   This choice was a thunderbolt to the humble Mr. Thomas Talbot, and the united efforts of all the Catholic Prelates, of Alban Butler, and of the most respectable characters in England, could not for a long time overcome the objections and repugnances he felt to rise above the condition of a poor, laborious missionary.   Pregnant proofs of this are upon record.   Being at length unable to withstand so violent an assault and such powerful means as were employed against him, he was forced to submit, and, in 1766, he was consecrated Bishop of Acon.   As to Bishop Hornyold, he continued to bear his infirmities and sufferings with the utmost patience and the most cheerful resignation to the adorable will of God, till Dec., 1778, when he died the death of the Saints, and went, we trust, to receive that never-fading crown which the Prince of Pastors has prepared for them who feed the flock of God, not by constraint, but willingly, according to God (1. Peter v. 2.).   He was buried in Breewood Church, where an humble stone records his name.   He left several legacies for pious and charitable purposes, and among the rest, £100 to Douay College.   (Obituary notice signed J. Milner).

HORNYHOLD, JOHN, of Blackmore Park, son of Robert and Bridget Windsor.   He married Mary, eldest daughter of Sir Pyers Mostyn, of Talacre, second Bart., by his wife, Frances Selby.   Mr. Hornyhold died, April 26, 1771, and was buried at Hanley.

HORNYHOLD, ROBERT, of Blackmore Park, only son of Thomas Hornyhold, by his wife, Margaret, daughter of Robert Gower, of Colemers.   He married Bridget, daughter of Anthony Windsor, Esq.   By a petition to Charles II., certified by the names of Shrewsbury, Cleveland, Plymouth, etc., it appears that Mr. Hornyhold brought a troop of horse into the field, and put himself at the head, under the Earl of Cleveland.   Being vanquished, he was forced to fly from his country; and his estates were sequestered by the Parliament, and £3,000 of timber was sold from his estates to repair the losses of one Alderman Elevin, of Worcester, a Rebel.   Mr. Hornyhold died Aug. 3, 1712, aged 54, and was buried at Hanley.

HORNYHOLD, THOMAS, son of John Hornyhold.   He married Mary, only daughter of Richard Townley, of Townley, Esq., by whom he had three children, Thomas, Charles, and Bridget.

HORRABIN, THOMAS, was born at Garstang, in Lancashire.   After studying some time at Douay, he formed part of the colony sent to Valladolid with Mr. Shepherd, the new President, where he completed his Divinity and was ordained priest.   In 1777 he returned to England, where his activity and ability in transacting business soon recommended him to the notice of his Brethren, and he was appointed agent to the College of St. Omers, and afterwards of Old

---

* The draft states that he had previously applied for James Talbot, but "this application, though supplemented by Letters addressed to Prince Charles and his brother, the Cardinal of York, was unsuccessful, probably because a similar application was made at the same time by Bishop Challoner, who designed to have Mr. J. Talbot for the London district."

Hall Green, as also of Sedgley Park, and Sion House at Lisbon. All these agencies, besides the commissions of numerous individuals, he executed with great punctuality and dispatch, and with real disinterestedness and cheerfulness. Yet, notwithstanding the numerous occupations of his agencies, he gave spiritual assistance to many Catholics who placed themselves under his direction. At last, worn out with labour, and after receiving with great piety the rites of the Church, he departed this life on March 6, 1801, "in a sweet composure, and apparently without an agony," and was buried, by his own direction, in the parish church of St. Andrew's, Holborn, on the 13th. Mr. Horrabin was a member of the Chapter, and few of his character were more beloved and respected than he. *Multis ille bonis flebilis occidit* was a common observation at the time of his death. [*Mr. Hodgson, Obituary*].

HORTON, *or* HAUGHTON, JOSEPH, was educated at Douay. He was chosen an Archdeacon of the Chapter [July 13, 1732]; was many years a missionary in London, and died there, Dec. 2, 1764, in his 90th year.

HOTHERSALL, WILLIAM, S.J., born July 19, 1725. He entered his noviceship, Sept. 7, 1744, and in 1762 was admitted a professed Father. Father John Booth was dismissed the College in 1766 by an order of the Secretary of State, for publicly acknowledging Prince Charles in the Hall of the College and in the church. Father Hothersall was appointed his successor, and continued to hold the situation of Rector till Aug. 17, 1773, when the Society was suppressed by Clement XIV., and he was dismissed. For some time he remained in Rome, but having obtained leave to go to Liège, he was allowed to retain his pension, and afterwards came over to England, where he lived in the family of Lord Wenman, whose lady, a daughter of Lord Abingdon, was a Catholic. At her death he retired to Oxford, and lived with his *confrère*, Mr. Lesley, senior, and died there.

HOUGHTON, CHARLES, born in Lancashire. He studied his humanities with the Jesuits, at Bruges, whom he left to go to Douay, where he was ordained·priest, and served the Mission for many years at Manchester ; afterwards travelled with Mr. Battersby into Italy, which gave great offence to his Bishop, from whom he had not leave to quit his post, and was suspended, [and was never the same man afterwards]. On his return he went to Carlton, in Yorkshire, and died at York, Sept. 7, 1797.

HOUNDSHILL, MARTIN. He was educated at Lisbon. On his return to England, he was stationed in Yorkshire. " On Nov. 18, 1745, he was taken before Richard Wilson and John Sawyer, Justices of the Peace. On his examination, he said he had not been at his parish church, nor received the Sacrament of the Lord's Supper for the preceding twelve months, and refused to take the oaths appointed in William and Mary. He was therefore committed to York gaol, and remained a prisoner thirteen months." For many years he assisted the Catholics at Arundel, in Sussex, probably after his release. He afterwards retired to Lisbon, and was chaplain to the nuns of Sion House ; but his health not allowing him to continue there, he returned to England in 1783, and a few days [14] after his arrival died suddenly in London, Aug. 9, 1783.

HOW, MR. AND MRS., lived at Boscobel, 1711. He seems to have served in the expedition sent against the Duke of Argyle in time of James II. Mr. Thomas How, jun., at Boscobel, in 1725.

HOWARD, AUSTIN, O.S.B., succeeded Father Shirburn as President of the English Benedictines, in 1697.

HOWARD, CHARLES, D.D., fourth son of Bernard Howard and Ann Roper, born in 1717. In April, 1736, was admitted at St. Gregory's, Paris, and June 8, 1737, took the Seminary oath, and was ordained Dec. 22, 1742 ; Jan. 1, 1744, he entered his license, and took the Doctor's Cap, March 17, 1746, at the expense of the Seminary. Aug. 19, 1746, he accompanied Dr. Thornburgh to Douay, where he remained till the following June, when, with the consent of Bishop Petre, and at the request of the Duke of Norfolk, he went to Rome. At the

end of Dr. Holden's second sexennium, Bishop Stonor, the Senior V.A., presented to the Archbishop of Paris Dr. Joseph Strickland, Dr. Umfreville, and
Mr. John Strickland to succeed him.   The Archbishop chose Mr. Umfreville,
but he declined the office on account of age and infirmities, when Dr. Howard's
name was added to the former two, and, though the last named, was the person
pitched on by the Archbishop, in 1756, to succeed Dr. Holden as Superior of St.
Gregory.   In this situation he was thrice confirmed, but in 1782 his health
became so much deranged with a nervous disorder that he became unfit for any
business, and obtained leave to go to England, where, by the importunities of
his friends, he was prevailed on to give his demission.   He died at St. Omers,
Feb. 28, 1792.   He was a member of the Chapter.   [Charles Howard, D.D.,
had an annuity from the Duke of Norfolk of £40.   Agent to St. Gregory's in
1756 to 1766].

HOWARD, *alias* FORMBY, CHARLES, son of James Howard and Ann
Formby, was born at North End, near Ince Blundell, in Lancashire, in
1740.   He studied at Douay, and being possessed of considerable abilities, was
recommended by Dr. Green, the President, as a proper subject for St.
Gregory's, and was admitted by Dr. Howard, Oct. 18, 1760.   He received
priest's orders, Sept. 21, 1765; sustained his Sorbonick in Aug., 1768, his
Major the following July, and took the Cap in March, 1770.   In June he came
on the Mission, and was placed for a while at Linton-on-Ouse, near York, but
was soon after appointed to accompany Charles Talbot, Esq., after Earl of
Shrewsbury, and Mr. Charles Browne to Paris.   On his return, in 1774, he was
placed at Burton Constable, the seat of William Constable, Esq., and arrived there
Aug. 15.   This Mr. Constable was a complete Deist, if not Atheist.   "The
night before he died he said, 'for my part, I believe in nothing,' was taken
speechless soon after, and died next morning without any assistance from me,
or others."   *Ita* Dr. Howard to me at Burton Constable.   Dr. Howard was a
very learned, agreeable, and pleasant gentleman, and was very dignified in his
manners and conversation.   He died at Marton, near Burton Constable,
Jan. 12, 1821.   (*St. Gregory's Register*).

HOWARD, EDWARD, NINTH DUKE OF NORFOLK, was born June 5,
1686.   Studied at Douay with his brother.   After he had passed his logic, he
went with his brother Philip to Paris, under the care of Mr. James Doyley,
whom their brother, the Duke of Norfolk, had chosen for their governor while
pursuing their studies in that city.   He was the third, and Philip the fifth,
brother.

HOWARD, EDWARD, S.J., born Dec. 29, 1740; entered the novitiate,
Sept. 7, 1759.

HOWARD, EDWARD, joined the Jacobite army a day or two before the surrender at Preston, in 1715.   Was committed to the Tower.

HOWARD, FRANCIS, S.J., born May, 1724, entered his noviceship Sept. 7,
1740, and made his four vows in 1758.

HOWARD, HENRY, of Corby Castle, was son of Philip Howard.   He also
studied at Douay, with the English Benedictines, and thence went to the
Theresian Academy at Vienna, where he was the only English student in that
renowned seat of learning, and where he was several times introduced to
the Empress Maria Theresa, and honoured by her notice.
He published : 1. *Strictures on Mr. Raine's St. Cuthbert.*   2. *Remarks on the
Erroneous Opinions entertained respecting the Catholic Religion*, 1825.   3.
[*Historical References in Support of the Remarks*, 1827].

HOWARD, HENRY, second son of Lord Thomas Howard, of Worksop, and
Elizabeth Saville.   He studied at Douay with his three brothers, Thomas,
Edward, and Philip.   He defended Universal Philosophy, July 28, 1704, under
Laurence Rigby, by the name of Paston, with great applause, in the presence
of the Bishop of Arras, the Governor of Douay, and all other people of quality
and distinction in the town ; "and such was the press to get in, that it was found

necessary to have a guard of soldiers at the door." He was ordained priest in Advent, 1709, and in Jan. went to Paris by order of his Mother, to enter the Seminary of St. Magloire, but much against his own will, it being his wish and the intention of Dr. Paston to employ him in teaching ; but quitted his design of St. Magloire, and of Bons Enfans, to enter with the Pères de la Doctrine Chrétienne. Father Plowden, S.J., told him that house was little better than St. Magloire, and that there is no place free from suspicion but St. Sulpice "and no medium between a supposed Jansenist and a Jesuit." Ep. Var. III. 87.*
In May, 1710, he went to live in the Seminary of St. Gregory's, but in July came over to England with his brother Richard, from Rome. In 1720 he was chosen Coadjutor to Bishop Giffard, with the title of Episcopus Ecclesiae Uticensis, by bull dated Sept. 30, and by another of Oct. 2, V.A., *cum futura successione*, but died the same year, on Nov. 22. He was a Capitular.

HOWARD, HENRY STAFFORD, Earl of Stafford, eldest son of Viscount Stafford and of Mary Stafford, Baroness de Stafford. His father was beheaded and attainted in 1680, (" Lady Alethea Talbot, the mother of Lord Viscount Stafford, was a Protestant," says Lord Shrewsbury to me, " as well as her husband ;" then how came Lord Stafford to be a Catholic ?) during Oates' Plot. An attempt was made in the 1st of James II. to reverse the attainder. The Bill passed the Lords, and was read twice in the Commons. His Lady was, however, summoned to attend the Convention of James, in 1685, as Baroness of Stafford, and seated among the Peeresses by descent, according to the antiquity of the old Stafford Barony. She was afterwards created a Countess in rank for life, and dying in 1693, was interred in Westminster Abbey, next to the tomb of her ancestor, Eleanor de Bohun, wife of Thomas Plantagenet, Duke of Gloucester. Her eldest son, Henry, was created Earl of Stafford the 4th of James II., in the lifetime of his mother, and on her decease in 1693, succeeded to the Baronies of Stafford. He died, April 19, 1719, leaving no issue by his wife Charlotte, daughter of Philibert, Count of Grammont. His third brother Francis, accompanied James into France. He had six sisters, Alethea, Isabella, Ursula, Anastasia (who married George Holman), and Helena [and Mary]. Alethea, Ursula, and Mary became nuns at the Spelicans at Brussels. Isabella married John Paulett, Marquis of Winchester.

HOWARD, HENRY CHARLES, of Greystock and Deepdene, nephew to Cardinal Howard, eldest surviving son of Charles Howard, Esq. (fourth son of Henry Frederic, Esq., of Arundel), and Mary Tattershall. On the death of his father in 1713¾, he became possessed of Greystock. He married Mary, daughter of John Aylward, Esq., descended from the Aylwards of the county of Waterford, by whom he had three sons and three daughters. Mr. Howard died, June 10, 1720. His second and eldest surviving son succeeded to the title of Duke of Norfolk, on the death of Edward, the ninth Duke, in 1777.

HOWARD, JOHN, S.J., born Oct. 26, 1718. Entered his noviceship, Sept. 7, 1737, and was made a professed Jesuit in 1755. He was President of the Academy at Liège, and died, Oct. 16, 1783.

HOWARD, JOHN STAFFORD, second son of Viscount Stafford. He married Mary, daughter of Sir John Southcote and, secondly, Teresa, daughter of Robert Strickland. At the revolution, he followed King James to St. Germains, and by an act (original at Cossey) dated July 30, 1696, he was sworn and admitted into the place and quality of Comptroller of the Household, "to have and to hold the same place with all the fees, salary, perquisites, privileges, and advantages thereto belonging." The Act bears the signature of James R., and is undersigned, " By His Majesty's command, Middleton." It is addressed to James Porter, Vice-Chancellor of the Household. He was afterwards made Vice-Chamberlain, while his Lady was one of the Maids of Honour to the Queen. He died in 1714, leaving by his first wife : 1. William

---

* There were several Father Plowdens alive about this time. Whichever is here meant, his alleged dictum, *if* truly reported, was a joke ; though Kirk does not seem to have seen it. I have not yet been able to make out the reference Ep. Var. III. 87.—J.H.P.

Stafford Howard ; 2. John Paul Stafford Howard ; 3. Mary Stafford Howard, who married Francis Plowden, by whom she had Mary, married to Sir George Jernyngham, who died in 1785 ; 4 and 5. Louisa and Xaveria, who became nuns, at Paris, in the English Convent, Faubourg St. Antoine, called the Blue Nuns.

HOWARD, JOHN PAUL STAFFORD, fourth Earl of Stafford, second son of John Stafford Howard and Mary Southcote. In his youth he was sent to Douay, where "he distinguished himself," says Mr. Dicconson, " by his application and piety, and at the end of the first year of Divinity defended the Treatise *de Incarnatione* with great applause, as he had done in Universal Philosophy the year before." He left the College, Sept. 26, 1704. He travelled into Italy, and resided some time at the Court. [But below, William Stafford Howard is said to have made the defence.—J.H.P.]

HOWARD, MARY STAFFORD, daughter of John Stafford Howard, and Mary Southcote. She was Maid of Honour, at St. Germains, to the Queen Dowager of James II. She married Francis Plowden, who sometime after succeeded his father-in-law as Comptroller of the Household, at St. Germains. Mrs. Plowden died at Paris in 1765, leaving one son, Francis, called the Abbé Plowden, and two daughters, Mary, the only surviving child and heir, who married, in 1734, Sir George Jernyngham, and died in 1785 ; and Louisa, who died unmarried, in 1784.

HOWARD, PHILIP, of Corby Castle. Was educated by the Monks at Douay, and thence went to the Academy at Turin. He wrote, *The Scriptural History of the Earth and of Mankind, compared with the Cosmogonies, Chronologies, and original traditions of Ancient Nations* ; an extract and review of several modern systems, with an attempt to explain philosophically the Mosaic account of the Creation and Deluge, and to deduce from this last event the causes of the actual structure of the Earth. In a series of letters with notes and illustrations. 4to, London, 1797. (See his *Preface*).

HOWARD RICHARD, fourth son of Lord Thomas Howard and Elizabeth Marie Saville. He studied at Douay. He afterwards was sent to Italy, and entered the Seminary of Monte Fiascone, and was there in 1703, at Bishop Witham's consecration. In 1707 he went to the Academy, near the Minerva in Rome, which had been opened a year before for young noblemen. At the end of 1709 he was made a Canon of St. Peter's and a prelate, with the title of Mgr. Howard de Norfolk, and in 1715 was chosen secretary to the Chapter of St. Peter's. His brother Thomas, Duke of Norfolk, settled an annuity on him in 1708 of £200 per annum, to support his dignity. In June, he brought a Cardinal's hat to Paris for Mgr. Polignac [having begun his journey, Mar. 29, 1713], and then accompanied his brother Henry to England. He returned to Rome, and died there, Aug. 22 (O.S.), or Sept. 6 (N.S.), 1722, and was buried in St. Peter's Church. His personal estates at his death amounted to scudi 6022·62. Through his means Bishop Witham obtained for Dodd the *Relatione* of Panzani. Dodd calls him "an eminent Prelate of singular candour and scrupulosity."

HOWARD, THOMAS, eighth Duke of Norfolk. Married, May 26, 1707, Maria Winifrida Francisca, sister of Richard Sherburn, of Stonyhurst, Esq., and daughter to Sir Nicholas Sherburn.

HOWARD, WILLIAM STAFFORD, second Earl of Stafford, eldest son of John Stafford Howard [? Vice-Chamberlain to the Queen at St. Germains], by Mary Southcote. He studied at Douay College, where he distinguished himself in the Classics, and in his *defensions* of Philosophy and of the Treatise *De Incarnatione*, which last he defended under Mr. Mayes, July 22, 1704, and on Sept. 26 following he left the College. He married his cousin Anne, daughter of George Holman, of Warkworth, and of Lady Anastasia. On the death of his uncle Henry he succeeded him, in 1719, as Baron and Earl of Stafford. He died in Jan. 1733-4, leaving issue : 1. William Matthias, who succeeded his father in his titles, and died in 1750. 2. Lady Mary, who married in 1744, the Comte de Rohan Chabot, and dying in 1769, was buried in West-minster Abbey. 3 and 4. Anastasia and Anne, who both entered among the Blue Nuns, at Paris. On the death of Lady Anne, in May, 1792, Lady Anastasia became the sole survivor of her brother, William Matthias, and her uncle, John Paul, Earl of Barons of Stafford, and died in Paris, April 27, 1807, aged 85.

HOWARD, WILLIAM MATTHIAS STAFFORD, third Earl of Stafford, and only son of William, second Earl, and Anne Holman. He married, in July, 1743, Henrietta, daughter of Richard Hamilton, but had no issue by her. He died Feb. 28, 1750 (O.S.).

HUDDLESTON, JOHN, son of Henry Huddleston, of Sawston, Esq., by his wife, Mary Bostock. He was born, Dec. 27, 1693. He was admitted into the College at Rome by Father Powell, the Rector, Oct. 16, 1711. He was ordained priest, March 27, 1717. When it was afterwards discovered that he had been ordained before he was of the proper age, he was suspended till the beginning of Jan. 1718. In the following April he departed for the Mission. For some time he resided with the Whitgreave family at Moseley, but in 1730 was placed at Lynn, in Norfolk, whence he removed to Hainton, where he lived in the family of Mr. Heneage, and died there in his 80th year, Jan. 3, 1773. He is said to have been " a gentlemanlike man, and a worthy character."

HUDSON, CHARLES, *alias* WRIGHT, son of Sir Benjamin Hudson and Mary Staveley, arrived at Douay, Oct. 1705.

HULL, WILLIAM, received his education at Douay. In 1780 he was placed at Hathrop, near Fairford, in Gloucestershire, and assisted the Catholics in the neighbourhood till 1793, when he was appointed to succeed the late Rev. Thomas Eyre at Stella Hall, and entered on his charge, March 11. He died at Stella Hall, July 22, 1835.

HUMBERSTONE, HENRY [*alias* HALL], S.J. He lived [probably] at Worcester, in the time of James II., and made himself known by a sermon preached there, April 18, 1686 : " On the sign of the Cross." Ezech. ix. 5, 6. " Go ye after him through the city, and strike : let not your eye spare, nor be ye moved with pity. Utterly destroy old and young, maidens, children, and women ; but upon whomsoever you shall see Thau, kill him not, and begin ye at my sanctuary." The sermon gave some offence, and caused people to say, on hearing the text, " Here must needs be a bloody sermon." The author printed it to convince the public that it was not what it appeared to be. *A Sermon preached at Worcester, April* 18, 1686 . . . *by H. H., of the Society of Jesus.* 1686. See *Catholic Sermons*, Vol. 2, p. 61.

HUNLOKE, SIR HENRY, of Wingerworth, co. Derby, second Bart., son of Sir Henry (who was knighted on the field of battle at Edgehill by Charles I., and was afterwards fined, for his loyalty, £1,458 by the sequestrators), and his wife Marian, daughter of Dixey Hickman, of Kew. He married Catharine, only daughter and heiress of Sir Francis Tyrwhit, of Kettleby, Lincolnshire, by whom he had seven sons and six daughters. His eldest daughter, Elizabeth, married George Heneage, of Hainton, and his youngest, Marian, was Abbess of the English Benedictines, at Pontoise. Sir Henry enjoyed the title and estate sixty-seven years, in which time he very much improved it. He lived and died in the universal esteem of his country, and was buried at Wingerworth, Jan. 6, 1715. The father of Sir Henry was famed for his loyalty and service to his King. In 1642 he lent to Charles I. a considerable sum of money, even at a time when there was little probability of its being ever repaid. Soon after, he levied and accoutred, at his own expense, a complete troop of horse, and at the memorable battle of Edgehill, though not 22 years old, he so signalised himself by his uncommon valour, conduct, and courage, that the King knighted him on the spot, and soon afterwards created him Baronet. Not long after, in a bold attempt upon the enemy near Bestwood Park, Notts., he received a cut on his elbow, which so disabled his right hand that it hung useless in a scarf to his dying day.

HUNLOKE, SIR THOMAS WINDSOR, third Bart., and third son of Henry by his wife, Catharine, daughter of Francis Tyrwhit. He married Charlotte, sixth daughter of Sir Robert Throckmorton, Bart., by whom he had issue four sons and seven daughters. He succeeded his father in 1715, and, in 1726, took down the old seat and erected a stately freestone building on a pleasant hill, adjoining the park. His lady died at Wingerworth, Dec. 31, 1738, and Sir Thomas, Jan. 30, 1752.

HUNLOKE, SIR HENRY, fourth Bart., son of Sir Thomas and his wife, Charlotte (as above). He married, Dec. 21, 1769, Margaret, eldest daughter of Wenman Coke, of Longford, co. Derby, by whom he had four sons and eight daughters. He died, Nov. 16, 1804.

HUNT, EDWARD, *alias* COLEBECK, studied at Douay. On his return to England, about 1680, he resided with Mr. Edmund Perkins, at Winckton, near Christ Church, Hants, where "he took extraordinary pains, as became a faithful Missioner." He died the end of Aug., 1726. (*Chapter Records*).

HUNT, THOMAS FRANCIS, D.D. He was educated at Douay, whence he went to St. Gregory's, at Paris; went through his Licence at the Sorbonne, and received the Doctor's Cap. On his return to England, he was chosen Archdeacon of the Chapter, July 14, 1736, and lived probably in or near London. He died at Harting, in Sussex, May 7, 1770.

HUNTER, FRANCIS, *vere* HARDWICKE, was a native of Yorkshire. In 1663 he went to Rome, and was admitted into the English College, Oct. 16. He was then 16 years of age. Having completed his studies, he came upon the Mission, in 1669; but in 1678 he returned to Rome, and having obtained a dispensation for that purpose, he entered among the hermits at Camaldoli, near Rome, and was in such estimation among them, that in 1685 he was chosen General of the Order. This account I copy from the Annals of the English College at Rome, p. 125, kept by the Rector, *pro tempore*. But Dr. Gradwell, though he applied to Cardinal Zurla, himself of Camaldoli, at my request, could obtain no knowledge of such General of the Order, or of him. (*Annals of the English College, Rome.*)

HUNTER, THOMAS, S.J. He entered the Society, Sept. 7, 1684, in the 18th year of his age. In 1701 he was Professor of Logic, at Liège. He succeeded Mr. Saltmarsh as Chaplain to the Duke of Norfolk, after his marriage with Maria, daughter of Sir Nicholas Sherburn, of Stoneyhurst. He died, Feb. 21, 1725.

He wrote: 1. *The Modest Defence*, in answer to Dodd's *History of Douay College*, about 1718. "It is civil, modest, and persuasive," says Mr. Charles Butler, in a letter of April 5, 1804, in *Collectanea Anglo-Catholica*. II., p. 367. 2. An answer to the twenty-four letters entitled, *The Secret Policy of the English Society of Jesus;* containing a letter to the author of the same, and *Five Dialogues*, in which the chief matters of fact contained in those letters are examined. MS. at Stonyhurst, and in Mr. Charles Butler's collection. "It is certain," says Mr. George Oliver, of Exeter, at the beginning of the Stonyhurst copy, "that Mr. Dodd was a dishonest historian, very deficient in Christian charity, and a stranger to the feelings and language of a gentleman." See observations on the Fifth Dialogue in my papers. [Probably uncle of George and Thomas Hunter, S.J.; George was professed in 1748, and Thomas in 1753. A Mr. Hunter, S.J., was priest at the Bar in 1763 to 1766; ditto at Wesby in 1745, succeeded Mr. *Lee* or *Leigh* (Roger)].

HURST, JOHN, studied at Douay. In 1762 he was chosen to conduct a small school at Betley, in the north of Staffordshire. When Mr. Berington undertook to establish the school at Sedgley Park, Mr. Hurst, after remaining at Betley twelve months, removed with his pupils, in all twelve, to Sedgley Park, at Lady Day, 1763, and for a time presided over the new establishment, till Rev. Hugo Kendall's arrival. He was then stationed in Norfolk, and for many years had charge of the congregation at and about Thetford. He died at Scarisbrick, in Lancashire, in Jan., 1792.

HURST, WILLIAM, brother of John Hurst.   He was a native of Lancashire, and was educated and ordained at Douay.   When St. Omers was made over to the secular Clergy, Mr. Hurst was sent thither to teach the humanity school, but soon after removed to Paris to be Confessor to the Austin Nuns, at the Fossée.   He was also the active agent there for Douay College, and the Clergy in England, till the French Revolution broke out, when he was arrested as a priest and a British subject, and sent to the Abbaye prison, under the sanguinary reign of Robespierre.   After some time he was brought back to the convent, but detained there under arrestation, in which state he died, rather suddenly, Nov. 27, 1793.   Mr. Hurst was a plain-spoken and upright man : was well-beloved and esteemed by all who knew him ; and had he not lived in the midst of, and witnessed the horrors of the revolution, might have lived many years.

HUSBAND, WILLIAM, was educated at Douay, where he arrived, July 7, 1759.   After teaching Rhetoric for some time, he came upon the Mission in 1770, and was placed at Salwick Hall, in Lancashire, where he died of the small-pox, Aug. 10, 1779.

HUSSEY, GILES, fifth son of John Hussey, of Marnhull, co. Dorset, where he was born, Feb. 10, 1710 or 1708.   After studying some time at Douay, he removed to St. Omers.   It is asserted that he was intended for trade, but his inclinations leading him more to painting, he was placed under Mr. Richardson, with whom he stayed but a short time, and afterwards studied under Damini, an Italian painter of history, in England.   With him Hussey travelled to Bologna in 1730, where the master robbed his pupil, and left him without money or clothes.   In this state of indigence he was relieved by an Italian nobleman, and was afterwards enabled by his relations to proceed to Rome, and arrived there in 1733.   After he was forsaken by Damini, he became the pupil of Ercole Lelli, an artist of considerable merit, and celebrated for his skill in anatomy.   At Rome, he was so much noticed by his countrymen there, that on his return to England, 1737, he found both his character and his reception to be very favourable to his future prospects in life.   (*Edwards' Anecdotes of Painters.*) Yet his success was by no means equal to his hopes and the expectation of his friends.   Whatever were his views while in Italy, he had not attended to that line of art which can alone ensure lucrative employment to the painters in this country, viz., portraiture.   The consequence was that he soon found himself in circumstances by no means affluent, so that, having struggled for some years against a train of difficulties, he quitted the profession, and settled with his youngest brother, a Benedictine, at Marlborough, at that time in possession of the patrimonial estate, who received him with great kindness.   They lived some time together, till the death of the elder brother left Mr. Giles Hussey as the next in full possession of Marnhull.   After residing some time upon his native soil, as the last surviving heir of his brother, he retired to Bearston, near Ashburton, co. [Devonshire], the residence of his nephew, Mr. Rowe, to whom he resigned the estate of Marnhull.   In this situation he amused himself with the cultivation of a small garden, in which, while digging, he dropped down suddenly and expired, in the year 1788.

"Mr. Hussey," says Mr. Nichols (*Literary Anecdotes of the 18th Century*, VIII., 190), " was of a middle stature, remarkably well made, and upright even to the last ; he had ever been intensely studious, which, with his religious and serious cast of mind, had introduced an habitual gravity of countenance and deportment. Yet, at times, no man could appear, and be, more easy, lively, jocund and diverting ; and that in such a manner and degree, as to make him remarkable for his humour to divert and please.   When young he must have been hand-some. . . .   His eye was blue, clear, quick, intelligent and piercing.   He looked you through and through, especially when he thought the person, or character, worth his notice and attention. . . .   By habitual temperance, carried almost to excess, Mr. Hussey enjoyed firm and uninterrupted health. Previous to his possessing Marnhull estate, a small annuity of £50 was his whole revenue.   When hearing of the uncommon distress of a respectable but reduced family, he appropriated nearly the whole of his revenue during one year to their assistance, and literally spent only £3 upon his own diet, which, to effect his charitable purpose, he made to consist merely of rice and water. (This fact is noted by Sir H. Lawson, who had it from a person of the first respectability, and who was well acquainted with Mr. Hussey).   His application to study was indefatigable and unremitting.   He used to say he was never fatigued, and that he could apply ten hours a day to study, without being languid and weary.   He had a natural turn for Geometry, and in all things he discovered an intuitive power of mind. . . . Let us not lament his profession of religion (the Catholic) for it made him a good man.   Though a perfect devotee, he had charity for others ; and though a saint himself, he commiserated sinners. . . .   His humility was equal to his modesty. . . .   In short, he had as few faults and weaknesses, to weigh against his virtues and excellences, as in general have fallen to the lot of imperfect humanity."   Mr. Hussey was a member of the Gentleman's Society, at Spalding, and is styled in their list, *Pictorum Princeps.*   A numerous collection of his pencilled portraits are now at Lulworth and Wardour Castles, and at Brough Hall.   Many also were in the possession of Matthew Duane, Esq , some of which were purchased at his sale by Mr. West, who, on one of them, observed, " that he would venture to show it against any head, ancient or modern ; that it was never exceeded, if ever equalled ; and that no man had ever imbibed the true Grecian character and art deeper than Giles Hussey." *Anecdotes of 18th Century.*   In politics, Mr. Hussey was favourable to the exiled family, and Prince Charles Stuart was a favourite subject of his pencil drawings. A very fine portrait of Mr. Hussey, drawn by himself, is carefully preserved at Lulworth Castle.   A sister of Mr. Hussey married a Mr. Rowe, whose son, John Rowe, succeeded to the family estate of Marnhull, and assumed the name of Hussey. (Mr. Butler's *Memoirs*, ch. 43.)

HUSSEY, THOMAS, D.D., and Bishop of Waterford.   Studied at Salamanca, and there took the degree of D.D.   Was chaplain to the Spanish Embassy. Being a gentleman, of good address, and well acquainted with the politics of England and Spain, he was sent with Mr. Cumberland to Spain.   He was well acquainted with Burke and Grattan, and through their means and the recommendation of the Duke of Portland, was made the first President of Maynooth College, and then Bishop of Waterford.   There he had a controversy with the Protestant Bishop of Waterford respecting Catholic soldiers going to church. His pastoral letter to the Catholics of his diocese gave great offence to Government, and caused the Ministry to recall him to England.   He died, July 11, 1803, aged 63.   Bishop Hussey was an eloquent preacher.   (See Mr. C. Butler's *Hist. Memoirs*, chap. 43.)   After the death of Bishop James Talbot in London, the Committee of English Catholics came to the resolution to depute Dr. Hussey to Rome, to explain to his Holiness the situation of affairs here respecting the nomination of Bishops, and, in particular, the appointment of a V.A. for London District.

Dr. Hussey published : 1. *Pastoral Letter.*   2. *Sermons.*

HUSSEY, THOMAS [*alias* BURDET], was son of John Hussey, of Marnhull, and his wife, Mary Burdet.   He was born at Marnhull, in Dorsetshire, Oct. 28, 1697.   After studying five years at Douay, his father wanted him home, and placed him in a mercantile situation, in which he continued reluctantly for nearly twelve years; after which he went to Rome, and was received into the College on trial, by order of the Cardinal Protector, in Jan. 1726.   On March 13, 1729, he was ordained Priest at St. John Lateran by Benedict XIII., and on May 10, 1730, went to Antwerp, to be chaplain to the English nuns in that city.

INGHILBY, CHARLES, son of William Jackson Inghilby and Mary Newton, his wife.   Was born in Yorkshire, June 18, 1694.   He was admitted into the Roman College by Father Powell, the Rector, Oct. 16, 1711.   Was ordained priest, April 16, 1718, and left for English Mission the following May.   Where he lived, or when he died, I do not find.

INGHILBY, SIR CHARLES KNIGHT. Sergeant of Law, of Austwick Hall, in the parish of Clapham [Yorks]. Had an estate in the West Riding and North Riding. On the death of Sir Richard Allibon, of Gray's Inn, he was requested to accept the office of Clergy Lawyer, in 1690.

INGLETON, JOHN, D.D. Died at Paris, Jan. 29, 1739 (N.S.), before his sexennium of Presidency was elapsed. He came to Douay from Paris to receive priest's orders, Sept. 4, 1685; returned to Paris, Oct. 2. Dr. Ingleton was designed, in Feb., 1693, to be a chaplain at St. Germains, which his inclination seemed to lead him to. He wrote the letter to Dodd, Jan. 3, 1719; also Nov. 23; 1718, to *Mr. Heskett, Prêtre Anglais au Coll. à Douay.* He was chosen by the late King, James II., for sub-preceptor to his son. Took degrees at the Seminary before 1693. Dr. Betham was preceptor to James' son; was chaplain at the death of James II., and conveyed the body to the (? monks) with an oration. Educated at Douay, President of St. Gregory's. (*See Catholic Magazine* III., 99.)

JACKSON, ANTHONY. He lived at Old Elvet, in Durham. Was V.G., and died there, Aug. 24, or Sept. 3, 1741, a very old man. He signed the rules drawn up by Bishop Smith, May 13, 1690.

JAKEMAN, FRANCIS, *alias* MAXFIELD, born in Staffordshire, in March, 1698. His parents were Protestant, but he became a Catholic, and was sent to St. Omers, and thence to Rome, in June, 1721, where he went through his course of Philosophy and Divinity. He was ordained sub-deacon by Benedict XIII., March 17, 1725, and priest, May 26 the same year. May 5, 1728, he left the College for England, and was placed at Madeley, in Salop, but soon removed to Shrewsbury, which mission he attended for many years, till age and infirmities obliged him to retire to Longbirch, where he died the end of March, 1778, aged 80. (*Annales Collegii Romani.*) [At Madeley, in 1728; at Salop, Sept. 1731; prch. Sept. 1730; 1757-9-60-62-68-69-71-73-75. In 1775 Mr. Clough was paid £12 12s. for attendance at Salop; alive March 25, 1776. His legacy to Mr. Varley paid by Mr. Clough, 1782.]

JAKEMAN, GEORGE. He succeeded Mr. Downs, at Hathersedge, in April, 1730, but left Dec. 1739, to come to Wolverhampton, where he died, June 17, 1740.

JAMES III., generally known by the name of *The Chevalier de St. George.* He married, in 1719, Maria Clementina Sobieski, eldest daughter of Prince James Sobieski, of Poland, the son of John III., King of Poland. She was descended from the illustrious House of Newburgh. By this marriage he had two sons—Charles Edward (whose history has been so ably given by Mr. Home in his account of the rebellion, in 1745), and Henry, who was created Cardinal of York. The Chevalier de St. George died at Rome, Dec. 30, 1765. (*Life of James II.*, Vol. 2. 617.)

JEFFERSON, ROBERT, returned from Douay in 1696 or 1697. He lived with Dr. Witham, at Preston, but died in Yorkshire, May 25, 1735.

JENKINS, AUGUSTIN, S.J. Born Jan. 12, 1747. Novice, Sept. 7, 1766.

JENKINS, PETER, S.J. Born Sept. 21, 1735. Novice, Sept. 7, 1753. Professed in 1771. (See the *Directory* for 1819.)

JENKINSON, CHRISTOPHER. Of a respectable family in Wyersdale, near Garstang. In 1693 he went over to Lisbon, and was admitted into the College, May 20. He defended his universal Philosophy, under Mr. George Slaughter, July 13, 1701, after which he taught the classics. Being ordained priest, he was chosen Procurator of the College, Sept. 22, 1711. On June 12, 1715, he came on the Mission, when he assisted the Catholics in and about Wyersdale, and officiated as the circumstances of those persecuting times permitted at his father's house in Wyersdale, and Scorton, Nately, the seat of the Leyburnes, etc. He died, Sept. 2, 1723, much respected and regretted by his flock. (*Lisbon Register.*)

JENNISON, AUGUSTIN, S.J., *alias* SAMFORD, brother of James Jennison, and also member of the same Society, and whose sister was mother to the Potiers.   He lived some years at Wardour, where a familiarity with his maid having given offence, he was reprehended by his noble patron, Lord Arundel, but without effect, for soon after he married her.   He then retired into Scotland, where he obtained some situation in the Church, and retained it for some years.   The remorse, however, of his conscience was so insupportable, as he afterwards acknowledged, that his life was a *hell upon earth.*   One day, on mounting his pulpit, he felt such inward reproaches that he was unable to speak, and was actually conducted to his home as a dumb, if not a dying, man.   That same evening he went to Edinburgh, and laid open his case to Bishop Hay, who, like an experienced physician, advised him to remove without delay to the distance of 100 miles or more from her who had occasioned his fall.   Mr. Jennison followed his advice, and proceeded immediately to England, Everingham, and London, and thence to Lulworth, intending to throw himself at the feet of Mr. Clinton, who, at that time, was much followed as a spiritual director. But his ancient confessor shut the door in his face, and could not be prevailed upon to admit him.   Upon this he returned to London, and had recourse to Bishop James Talbot, who received the prodigal son, like a tender father, and being satisfied of the sincerity of his conversion, advised him to retire to the College at St. Omers.   He here wrote a letter to his partner in guilt, and exhorted her to repentance.   By this she became acquainted with the situation he was in, and finding that Bishop Talbot had been his adviser, she threatened him with prosecution, till he engaged to allow her £100 per annum for life. Soon after, she married and settled in Winchester, where she received another letter from Mr. Jennison to the same purport with the former, through the medium of Mr. (Dr.) Milner, who did all in his power to bring her to a sense of her duty.   But he being connected with the College, he could seldom be allowed to see her; and at last she died raving, and without any assistance.   (This account I had from Dr. Milner.)

In making the above allowance of £100, Mr. Potier says Bishop Talbot told him he was assisted principally by some friends in Hampshire (Mr. Sone,* etc.). The gentlemen of the Society also contributed liberally on the occasion.   At St. Omers, Mr. Jennison took the name of Samford, and led a rigid and austere life of penance, and diffused a sweet odour of virtue to all around him.   For some time he judged himself unworthy to approach the altar in his former character of priest, and when he was at last induced, by the advice and persuasion of his director, to offer up the sacrifice of the Mass, the corporal was frequently bathed with his tears.   "His occupations at College, though perhaps not the least meritorious, were certainly such as are generally thought to have little claim to respect or esteem.   He taught the lowest classes, attended the boys in their hours of recreation, and had occasionally the care of the sick.   In these employments, at a late time of life, surrounded by boys, who are always thoughtless and not unfrequently petulant, he found abundant opportunities of exercising those virtues of humility and self-denial which, in the true spirit of penance, he looked upon as his glory and his crown.   When the French soldiery, on the breaking out of the revolution, broke into the College of St. Omers, and threatened destruction to the inhabitants, Mr. Jennison, rejoicing in the opportunity which was offered to him of standing forth the champion of that religion which he had before so grievously outraged, presented himself to them with an undaunted courage; and when asked his name, " My name, gentlemen," he said, "my name is a great, glorious name; my name is the name of the illustrious Doctor of the Church, the great St. Augustin, the firm defender of the Catholic Faith, and the terror of unbelievers."   He died soon after like a true Christian penitent, on Jan. 22, 1799.

JENNISON, JAMES, S.J.   He was descended from the Jennisons of Walworth, in the Bishopric of Durham; born May 14, 1737.   He was educated

---

* Mr. Sone was a wealthy miller near Havant.   On his death he left £10,000 to Bishop Douglass to build a College to replace Douay.   St. Edmund's was built out of this money.—E.B.

among the Jesuits, and became a member of the Society. He entered his noviceship, Sept. 7, 1755. For several years he was itinerant chaplain to Mrs. Porter. Happening to be on a visit to Mr. Webb Weston's at a time when Bishop James Talbot was there for the express purpose of settling what would be a proper salary for a priest, boarding himself, and living in a ready-furnished house, rent-free, and the good Bishop having in the simplicity of his heart fixed upon £50 per annum, Mr. Jennison on that occasion wrote his well-known *Oeconomia Clericalis*, in which he proves that £50 per annum is quite inadequate to the support of a priest in the above circumstances. (MS. of Rev. John Potier, whose mother was first cousin to Mr. Jennison.)

JENNISON, JOHN, S.J., born July 30, 1729, entered his noviceship, Sept. 7, 1745, and was professed in 1763.*

JERMYN, HENRY, BARON DOVER, of Dover, in Kent, Baron Jermyn of St. Edmundsbury, in Suffolk, younger son of Thomas Jermyn, Esq., of Rushbrooke, in Suffolk, by Rebecca, afterwards the wife of Viscount Brouncker, President of the Royal Society, was introduced by his uncle, Henry Jermyn, Earl of St. Albans, to the Court of King Charles II. The Earl was Master of the Horse, and Chamberlain of the Household to the Queen Mother Henrietta, and—according to Sir John Reresby (*Reresby's Letters*), Mademoiselle Bavière (*Mademoiselle Bavière's Letters*), and others—was clandestinely married to the Queen. His nephew became the intimate companion of James, Duke of York, and was privy to his marriage with Anne Hyde. The intrigues of his youth in the profligate Court of Charles are known to all the readers of Grammont. Soon, however, disgusted with the Court, Henry Jermyn retired to his house at Cheveley, in Cambridgeshire. St. Evremont visiting him there says : "We were kindly received by a person who, though he has taken leave of the Court, has carried the civility and good taste of it into the country." On the accession of King James to the throne, His Majesty appointed Henry Jermyn one of the Lords of the Bedchamber and a Commissioner of the Treasury, and gave him the command of the Royal Guard, creating him Baron Dover. The monarch, after his abdication, added the title of Earl of Dover to the honours conferred upon this personage. On the death of his elder brother, Thomas Lord Jermyn, in the year 1703, Henry, Lord Dover inherited the Barony of Jermyn. The family of Jermyn of Rushbrooke adhered in general to the Catholic religion; and Henry, Lord Dover, the last of this ancient house, died in the faith of his ancestors, and at his house in Cheveley, in Cambridgeshire, April 6, 1708. At his Lordship's request, his body was conveyed to Flanders and interred in the church of the Carmelites there, at Bruges. Judith, Lady Dover, his widow, the daughter of Sir Edward Poley, of Badley, in Suffolk, Kt., dying in 1726, was interred at her request with her husband. John Ives, F.S.A., in a MS. containing notes and monumental inscriptions relating to Suffolk families, says : "He was informed by the monastery that the monks, some years afterwards, opened the coffins of the Earl and Countess of Dover, which are deposited in a recess under the high altar, and found the bodies dried but uncorrupted. They had been buried in their ordinary apparel, which was very rich, and they had gold watches by their side, which (having satisfied their curiosity) the monks replaced and closed up the tomb." On the south side of the high altar is a marble monument, on which is the figure of Henry, Lord Dover in a Roman habit, cumbent on a Sarcophagus. The following epitaph is inscribed : "In Memoriam prænobilis viri domini Henrici Jermyn, Hæreditario Jure Domini Baronis de Burgo Sancti Edmundi in Comitatu Suffolciæ in Magna Britannia, et etiam Jure creationis per litteras patentes Serenissimi Jacobi Secundi Magnæ Britanniæ Regis, Domini Baronis et denuo Comitis Dubrensis in Comitatu Cantii. Fuit adhuc Juvenis, Jacobo tum Duci Eboracensi, Equorum Magister et postea Serenissmæ Majestati a Secretis Consiliis, unus e Dominis Baronibus interioris Cubiculi, unus etiam e Dominis Thesauri regii

---

* His mind eventually became affected, and he died in an asylum at Liege, Dec. 27, 1793. Foley).—J.H.P.

Commissis quaestoribus, locum tenens Generalis Exercituum ; et legionis equestris Satellitum ad custodiam Regis Legatus, nec non Dominus locum tenens Regis in Comitatu Cantabrigiæ.—*Obiit Sexto Aprilis Anno* 1708." Sir Thomas Gage is in possession of an original portrait of Henry, Lord Dover, who was connected by various alliances with the Gage family. There are also portraits of Lord Dover at Rushbrooke.   The male line of the ancient family, Jermyn of Rushbrooke, became extinct in the person of Lord Dover. His elder brother, Thomas, Lord Jermyn, left five daughters, his coheirs and the heirs general of the family of Jermyn : Mary, the eldest daughter, married Sir Robert Davers, Bart. ; Henrietta Maria married Thomas, younger son of Sir William Bond, Bart. ; Penelope married Gray Grove, Esq., of Park Hall, Salop ; and Merelina married first, Sir Thomas Gage, Bart., and second, ——. Sir Ambrose Jermyn, an ancestor of Lord Dover, was seized of the splendid Abbey of St. Edmundsbury. It is now vested in Frederick William, Earl of Bristol, by descent from the eldest coheir on whom it was settled by Lord Dover. N.B.—This account is taken from the pedigree of Jermyn at Rushbrooke, and family documents in possession of Sir Thomas Gage.

JERNEGAN, SIR FRANCIS, of Cossey, third Bart., son of Sir Henry Jernegan, and Mary, daughter of Benedict Hall, of High Meadow, co. Gloucester.   He was born in 1693, and married Anne, daughter of Sir George Blount, of Soddington, Bart., by whom he had : 1. Sir John, his successor ; 2. Sir George ; 3. Charles, M.D. ; 4. Henry ; 5. Francis, who became a Jesuit, and died in 1739 ; 6. Edward ; 7. Anne ; 8. [Richard] ; 9. Mary.   He died, Aug. 20, 1730, aged 80, and his lady, Feb. 13, 1735. (*Betham*, 223.)

JERNEGAN, SIR GEORGE, fifth Bart., second son of Sir Francis, was born June 2, 1680.   He passed the greater part of his life on the Continent, and was in his 54th year when he married, in 1733, Mary, eldest daughter, and at length heiress, of Francis Plowden, by Mary, daughter of the Hon. John Stafford, younger son of William Lord Viscount Stafford, beheaded in 1680, By this lady Sir George had four sons : John, who died of the small-pox at Stonor, aged 22 ; William, his successor ; Edward, the author of many elegant publications in verse and prose ; Charles, a general officer in France, and Knight of Malta, and Mary.   Sir George died at Cossey, Jan. 21, 1774, in the 94th year of his age.

JERNEGAN, SIR JOHN, fourth Bart., born at Cossey, Sept. 6, 1678. He succeeded his father, Sir Francis, in 1730, and married Margaret, daughter of Sir Henry Bedingfield, of Oxburgh, Bart., and dying without issue at Bath, June 14, 1737, was succeeded by his brother, Sir George.

JERNYNGHAM, CHARLES, son of Sir George Jernyngham, was born at Cossey in 1742.   He entered, early in life, the service of France ; became successively Colonel of the Regiments of Navarre and Buckeley, and was made Marshall de Camp in 1784.   At the Revolution he was stripped of the whole of his property placed in that kingdom, and compelled to return to England.   At the peace of Amiens, in 1802, he returned to France, to recover his property if possible ; but all his efforts were vain, and on the breaking out of war, in 1803, he was detained prisoner with the rest of his countrymen till the King's restoration.   It has been the lot, perhaps, of few individuals to enjoy the esteem and friendship of so many distinguished persons of both kingdoms, as was that of the Chevalier Jernyngham.   He was remarkable for the extent and elegance of his acquirements and literary accomplishments, the singular obligingness and courtesy of his manners, and the generous and noble qualities of his heart.   He was Knight of Malta, and of the Royal and Military Order of St. Louis.   He died at Cossey.

JERNYNGHAM, CHARLES, third son of Sir Francis Jernyngham, and Anne Blount. At the end of Philosophy, he left Douay College and went to St. Omers, but soon returned to Douay, and went to study Physic at Montpellier, where he applied himself closely and took his degree of M.D. He married Elizabeth Roper, daughter of Philip Lord Teynham, who died Nov. 14, 1736,

s.p.   He then married Frances, daughter of Rowland Bellasyse, brother of
Lord Viscount Fauconberg. He died at Cossey, April 28, 1760, in the 73rd year
of his age, *s.p.*, and lies buried in the chancel of the church. (*Betham*, and
Diary of Douay College.)

JERNINGHAM, HENRY, *or* JERNYGAN, the original name, was fourth
son of Sir Francis, and brother of Charles, M.D.   He was an ingenious artist,
a goldsmith, and jeweller, in Russell Street, London.   Vertue has given us a
fine engraving of a curious silver cistern made by him, and which was disposed
of by lottery about 1740.   The price of a ticket was 5s. or 6s., and the
purchaser had a silver medal into the bargain, valued at about 3s.   There
were, it is said, about 30,000, and the medal induced many to become
purchasers.   Mr. Jernygan died, Nov. 8, 1761, and was buried in the churchyard of St. Paul's, Covent Garden, with this inscription on his tomb, by Mr.
Aaron Hill :

> " All that accomplished body lends mankind,
>   From earth receiving he to earth resigned ;
>   All that e'er graced a soul from Heaven he drew
>   And took back with him as an angel's due."

He married Mary, daughter of Nicholas Jonquet l'Epine, and by her had five
sons and three daughters.   Hugh, his fifth son, entered among the English
Franciscans, at Douay, and remained there till the Revolution sent him and his
confrères to England.   He died at Dover in 1793.   His three daughters, Mary,
Elizabeth, and Edwardine, took the veil in the house of the English Augustine
Nuns at Bruges, but came to England with the community in 1794, and settled
at Hengrave, near Bury, in Suffolk.   The community afterwards returned to
Bruges.   (John Nichols' *Lit. Anecdotes*, II. 513.)

JERNINGHAM, NICHOLAS, fourth son of Henry, last named, and of Mary,
daughter of Nicholas Jonquet l'Epine, of London, merchant.   In his youth he
was sent early to Douay College ; and after he had finished his academical
course, and declining the priesthood, for which it is said he was intended, he
returned to England.   On the death of Mr. Carte, Mr. Jerninghan married his
widow, and by that means came into the possession of all the valuable papers
of that indefatigable historian.   But these being the property of his wife, she
left them to him only for his life, and, after his death, to the University of
Oxford.   Mr. Jerninghan, however, delivered them to the University for a
valuable consideration, said-to be £50.   They are now lodged in the Bodleian
Library.   Whilst they were in Mr. Jerninghan's possession, the late Lord
Hardwicke is said to have paid £200, and Mr. Macpherson £300 for the perusal
of them ; and out of these and other papers the latter gentleman compiled his
history, and state papers, as Sir John Dalrymple did from the same and from
the recollection of what he read every day in the Scotch College, at Paris.   Mr.
Jerninghan died in 1785.

JERNYGHAN, SIR WILLIAM, sixth Bart., and heir of Sir George, fifth Bart.
In June, 1767, he married Frances, eldest daughter of Henry, eleventh Viscount
Dillon, of Ireland, by whom he had issue three sons and two daughters : George
William, who married, Dec. 26, 1799, Frances, youngest daughter and coheiress
of Edward Sulyard, of Haughley, co. Suffolk ; William Charles, formerly in the
Austrian Service, and then in the English, (in the former, during the hard and
perilous campaigns from 1792 to the treaty of Campo Formio, he signalised
himself by distinguished bravery and judgment) ; Edward, of Lincoln's Inn ;
Mary, who died an infant ; and Charlotte Georgina, married in June, 1795, to
Sir Richard Bedingfield.   Sir William inherited, through his mother, maternally
descended from the noble family of Stafford, the Baronial Castle of Stafford,
with several other considerable estates in the counties of Salop and Stafford,
formerly a part of the vast possessions of Edward Stafford, Duke of Buckingham, beheaded 13th of Henry VIII., and which afterwards were restored, with
the Barony, to his son, Henry, Lord Stafford.   At the death of Lady Anastasia

Stafford, a nun, at Paris, and niece to the last Earl of that name, Sir William also became sole heir to the remaining honours of that noble family. He died July 14, 1809. He was succeeded by his son, George William, who was afterwards created Baron Stafford.

JOHNSON, JAMES, was educated at Douay. He taught Poetry from 1771 to 1774, and afterwards Divinity for several years. When he came on the Mission, he was placed at Pontop, "where he had an open field," says Mr. Thomas Eyre, "for the exercise of his talents and patience, and was truly a laborious, zealous, and worthy Missioner." He died at Pontop, Nov. 9, 1790.

JOHNSON, JOHN, was educated at Douay. The character given to him by Dr. Paston, the President, was that "he was an incomparable good man ; a true friend of the house, but excessively timorous." When on the Mission, he was a chaplain at Chillington, and on the death of Mr. Thomas Giffard, the last of the Chillington branch, he retired with Mrs. Giffard to Longbirch, and was chaplain there till her death, June 16, 1739. He was in great esteem among his brethren [chosen Archdeacon, March 27, 1714], was a member of the Chapter [1723], and administrator for many years [from May 26, 1711] of a fund for superannuated and disabled clergymen, called from his name, Johnson's fund. He left £200 for a priest at Linton-on-Ouse, near York (probably his native place) to increase the fund made there by Mr. Appleby.

[A Mr. John Johnson, *alias* Morgan, was chosen V.G. of Staffordshire, Shropshire, and Cheshire in 1685, on Mr. A. Giffard's declining it. A Mr. —— Moore, from Rome, had been at Longbirch in 1692.]

JOHNSON, ROBERT, was educated at Douay. Soon after his ordination he was made president of the preparatory school at Esquerchin, near Douay, and "was deemed a rigid disciplinarian." He came on the Mission between 1765 and 1768, which he served many years in Lancashire. In his old age he retired to Dodding Green, where he died, June 2, 1799, leaving £1 1s. to every one a priest who at College had felt the weight of his rod.

JOHNSON, *vere* MIDDLEHURST, THOMAS, son of John Middlehurst and Elizabeth Culcheth, his wife. He was born in Lancashire on March 7, 1732 (O.S.) ; was admitted into the College at Rome under Father Christopher Maire, Jan. 21, 1746. He was ordained Nov. 24, 1754, and departed for the Mission, Feb. 24, 1755. He lived many years as chaplain to —— Strickland, of Sizergh, Esq., and was tutor to his son, the late Thomas S. Standish, with whom he travelled to Rome, and resided with him in the Mazarine College. On his return he continued chaplain to the family, and had the care of the Catholics about Kendal, to which place he afterwards retired in consequence of blindness and the infirmities of old age. He died there, April 16, 1817, aged 87. He was a member of the Chapter, Nov. 19, 1776. Mr. Johnson was generally supposed to have written many of those discourses on the Creed, Sacraments, etc., which were published by his successor at Longbirch, Mr. (Bishop) Hornyold. Some of them I have seen in MS. by Mr. Johnson.

JOHNSON, THOMAS, *alias* TAYLOR. He lived many years as chaplain to Mrs. Roddam, at Staindrop Bishopric, and after her death, and till his own, with her daughter, Mrs. Ledger. He died, Feb. 4, 1750. [There was one Mr. Johnson at Lindley, 1741-1747.]

JOHNSTONE, ——, O.S.B. He informed Bossuet, in 1686, of the discovery made by Dr. Wake of alterations in his "Exposition." Mr. B. *Confessions*, p. 14. Dr. Johnstone, or Jonson, published in 1687, by order of James II., a work to quiet the consciences and fears of those who possessed Abbey-lands. See, in folio B. extract of a letter of July 29, 1736. Mr. William Eyston, in his MS. account of Authors quoted in his *Poor Little Monument*, says he was M.D. and Fellow of the Royal College of Physicians, in London. The title is, *The Assurance of Abbey and other church lands in England to the present possessors cleared from the doubts and arguments raised about the danger of resumption.* London, 8vo, 1687. He published other things, MSS. This M.D. and the

monk are sometimes confused, and may be the same person.   In some memoirs
I have seen the work ascribed to a Benedictine.

JONES, EDWARDS.   President of Lisbon College.   (See *Catholic Magazine*
Vol. V.)

JONES, JOHN [? PHILIP], S.J., was born July 7, 1721 ; entered his noviceship, Sept. 7, 1739, and was professed in 1757.   He lived in London, and is said
to have published, or caused to be published, the *Life of Clement XIV.*, in
letters, in 1785.   His *confrère*, Mr. Talbot, was also thought to have been concerned in the publication.   [See above, under Cordell.]   Mr. T. Bellamy wrote
against it.   Mr. Jones died, Aug. 10, 1800.   See Mr. Conolly's testimony in
MS. *Collectanea.*

JONES, PHILIP, was educated at Douay.   He lived many years at Holiwell,
and died there, Aug. 10, 1800.   He was a "highly respectable man," and
member of the Chapter.   [He was made Canon, Sept. 20, 1766, and March 14,
1775, Archdeacon.]   He left a fund for Holiwell, in the hands of Mr. Gildart, his
executor, who, by the advice of Bishop Sharrock, transferred it to Monmouth,
where it was more wanted than at Holiwell, there being already another chapel
there and but a small congregation.

JONES, ROBERT, D.D.   He was in great estimation among his brethren,
and much respected by all who knew him.   He was a member of the Institute,
and their chief Superior in London, when it was abolished by Bishop Giffard, to
whom he was Vicar-General *in Solidum*, and also to Bishop Witham, in 1712.
He was also a member of the Chapter [having been chosen Canon, June 2, 1690]
and had the title of Archdeacon of London, Westminster and Middlesex.
When the General Assembly was held in 1710, and Dr. Perrott, the Dean, was
too infirm to assist at it, Dr. Jones, as being the Senior Canon, was called to the
chair, and presided.   At this Assembly, which met Sept. 19, 1710, eighteen Archdeacons assisted, and twelve Canons, in person or by deputies.   As Dr. Perrott
had petitioned to have a Sub-Dean appointed to assist him, Dr. Jones was
chosen Sub-Dean on Sept. 3.   Little was done in this Assembly, except filling
up some vacancies, and settling some money concerns, and trusts, till the eighth
and last session, held Sept. 23, when it was ordered that the Sub-Dean be requested to write a letter to the Cardinal Protector in the name of the Dean and
Chapter assembled to be sent with the Declaration and sealed with the great
seal of the Chapter.   " The Declaration, containing their abhorrence of
Jansenism, in order to clear themselves of the calumnies laid to the English
Clergy, was read, agreed to, and signed by all unanimously."   It begins : *Cum
grave sit homini orthodoxo*, etc.   (*Chapter Collection*, I. 525).   The Acts were
then read and signed by all present, *i.e.*, by sixteen, for themselves and the
absent Brethren, for whom they were deputed to act.   Dr. Jones died in 1714.
As a curiosity worth preserving I here add the Roll of Chaptermen as it stood
in the General Assembly, held Sept. 19, 1710.   Mr. John Perrott, D.D.,
President of Lisbon College, Dean of the Chapter, and V.G. *in Solidum* : 1. Mr.
Edward Kynne, Archdeacon of Worcester, Gloucester, Warwick and Leicester
shires ; 2. Mr. Robert Jones, D.D., V.G. *in solidum*, Archdeacon of London,
Westminster and Middlesex, Sub-Dean and President of the Assembly ; 3.
Mr. Francis Thwaytes, Archdeacon of Essex, Hants. and Beds. ; 4. Mr.
William Reynolds, Archdeacon of Oxford, Berks. and Buckinghamshire ; 5.
Mr. Martin Giffard, Archdeacon of Cornwall, Devonshire and Dorsetshire ;
6. Mr. John Browne, Archdeacon of Norfolk and Suffolk, Secretary ; 7. Mr.
Roger Kynaston, Archdeacon of North Wales ; 8. Mr. Charles Corne, Arch-
deacon of Monmouthshire and all South Wales ; 9. Mr. Ferdinand Asmal,
Archdeacon of Northumberland, Cumberland and Durham ; 10. Mr. Sylvester
Jenks, Archdeacon of Surrey and Kent ; 11. Mr. Henry Haenage, Archdeacon
of Shropshire and Herefordshire ; 12. Mr. Thomas Yaxeley, Archdeacon of
Lincoln, Rutland and Nottingham shires, Treasurer ; 13. Mr. Christopher
Witham, Archdeacon of Yorkshire ; 14. Mr. John Stamford, Archdeacon of
Derby and Cheshire ; 15. Mr. John Vane, Archdeacon of Hampshire, Wiltshire

and Somersetshire ; 16. Mr. William Pegg, Archdeacon of Northampton, Cambridge and Huntingdonshire ; 17. Mr. Peter Saltmarsh, Archdeacon of Sussex ; 18. Mr. Edward Hawardin, Archdeacon of Lancashire and Westmorland.   Canons : 2. Mr. Gerard Saltmarsh ; 2. Mr. Roger Hesketh, D.D. ; 3. Mr. John Morgan ; 4. Mr. Reginald Williams ; 5. Mr. W. Martin ; 6. Mr. Francis Lovel ; 7. Mr. John Medcalfe ; 8. Mr. Simon Ryder, D.D. ; 9. Mr. Benjamin Petre ; 10. Mr. Ralph Claughton ; 11. Mr. J. Ingleton, D.D. ; 12. Mr. Robert Witham, D.D.

KEMBLE, WILLIAM, O.S.F. He lived at Tusmore, whence he came to Birmingham, where he was much respected and beloved, and where he died, July 31, 1801.

KEMPE, GEORGE. Of a good family. It does not appear in what College he studied, but on the Mission he was in great estimation among his Brethren. In 1676 he was chosen Archdeacon of Surrey and Kent, and, in 1692, resided with the Dowager Duchess of Norfolk, at the College in Yorkshire. In 1694 he assisted at the General Assembly of the Chapter, held July 9, at which were present Dr. Perrott, the Dean, five Vicars-General, sixteen Archdeacons, and nine Canons, in person or by their deputies. In the third Session it was resolved that "the election of officers to keep up the integrity of the Chapter according to its first institution should still, as hitherto, be exercised, but that they are not to exercise any ordinary jurisdiction which shall interfere with that of Lord Bishop Leyburn." Resolved also, "that the jurisdiction of the VV. GG. and of the *Vicarii Forarii*, instituted by the present Bishops, is to be reputed to cease upon the cessation of the Vicariate, by the death or otherwise, of the Lord Bishops, and that the Chapter reassumes the exercise of its Jurisdiction." In the fourth Session it was resolved "to address a second letter to the three resident Bishops, and a committee of seven was appointed to draw it up." The committee consisted of Dr. Perrott, Mr. Serjeant, Mr. Allibon, Dr. Jones, Mr. Thwayts, Mr. Gother, and Mr. Morgan ; and Dr. Perrott, Dr. Jones, Mr. Gother, and Mr. Serjeant were deputed to wait on Bishops Leyburn and Giffard with the Address. In this Address (which see in the Records of the Chapter) they point out the ill effects which they humbly conceive will necessarily follow in the respective vacancies their Lordships will leave at their deceases . . . for the prevention of which their holy predecessors of blessed memory thought it absolutely necessary to institute a Chapter, for the continuance of ordinary Episcopal jurisdiction, *sede vacante, donec pluribus in Anglia Episcopis Catholicis constitutis, plura in regno erigantur Capitula ;* they therefore, with all due respect, supplicate their Lordships effectually to solicit the See Apostolic for the establishment of such a succession of Ordinary Episcopal jurisdiction.

In the fifth Session, held on July 14, on the report of the above committee of seven, the Assembly resolved that the Chapter *Sede Vacante* hath " *omnem illam dignitatem, potestatem, and authoritatem quae Decano, et Capitulo jurecommuni vel ordinaria Ecclesiastica consuedudine debentur,*" according to the express words of the Constitutive Breve ; and, secondly, that in reference to extraordinary faculties, since it is unsafe to follow a probable opinion, especially when the validity of the Sacraments may be concerned, nor such faculties can nor ought to be made use of but as shall be obtained from the See Apostolic or the authority thereof. In the sixth and last Session, the acts of the Assembly were read, and then signed by the following persons :—

John Perrott, Dean.—Joannes Hollandus (Serjeant), pro meipso et D. Joanne Gildono.—Thomas Powell, for himself and Mr. Edward King.—John Parsons, for Mr. Thomas Coldham.—William Wilmot, deputy for Mr. George Barrat.— G. Kempe, for myself and Mr. Edward Cody.—David Norris, for myself and James Forrester.—Robert Woodroffe, deputy for Mr. Robert Fitzherbert.— Thomas Churchill.—Job Allibon.—Roger Kynaston.—Robert Jones.—John Gother, for myself and Dr. John Betham.—William Colston, for myself and Mr. Roger Anderton.—Francis Thwayts, for myself and Mr. William Byflet.—James Price.—William Reynolds. — Philip Lewys. — Gerard Saltmarshe. — Roger

Hesketh.—John Morgan, for myself and Mr. Daniel Fitter.—John Ward, Secretary, for myself and Mr. Richard Frank.

Mr. Kempe died in 1698. (*Chapter Records.*)

KENDALL, GEORGE, D.D., was educated at Douay, of which University he was made a Doctor. He lived at Fernyhalgh, and also was missionary at Manchester. After passing twenty years in the Mission, he went over to Douay, in 1754, and for many years taught Divinity there. He was a member of the Chapter. In the latter part of his life he laboured under a malady which affected his intellect, and he was removed to Lille, where he died, Jan. 4, 1766.

KENDALL, HENRY, lived at Croxdale, and then at Our Lady's Well, at Fernyhalgh, near Preston, where he died, Oct. 29, 1752.

KENDALL, HUGO, younger brother of Richard Kendall, and educated at Douay, where he taught Poetry, 1738, and Rhetoric, 1751. [Mr. Banister succeeded him in 1752, when Kendall probably came over.] When the school that had been opened at Betley in 1762, in the North of Staffordshire, was removed in 1763 to Sedgley Park, Mr. Kendall was appointed the first President, and established it on the plan that had been followed at Twyford School, and which his brother had adopted at Standon. As the penal laws against Catholics were yet in force, and were occasionally put in execution, Mr. Kendall had many difficulties to contend with, and great fears were apprehended that he would not be able to stand his ground, yet by his prudence, respectability, and conciliating manners, he overcame them all, and so far gained the esteem of his landlord, Lord Dudley, and Ward, that on one occasion, if not on more than one, he condescended to visit and to dine with him in the company of Thomas Gifford, of Chillington, Esq., who patronised the school, and of Bishop Hornyold. On another occasion he is said to have borne testimony to the inoffensiveness and respectability of Mr. Kendall, when his own conduct was blamed in Parliament "for letting him his house for a Popish School." During the riots of 1780, serious apprehensions were entertained that it would meet the fate of the Chapels, etc., in London, and threats were thrown out to that purpose. No mischief, however, was done, yet the alarm did not fail to considerably affect the health of Mr. Kendall, who had long suffered from gout and other infirmities incidental to his age. He died at the Park, July 2nd, 1781. Mr. Kendall was "a venerable and much esteemed clergyman." He was also a member of the Chapter, but on account of ill-health he sent in his resignation about four years before his death.

KENDALL, RICHARD (SENIOR), died at Arundel Castle, Feb. 7, 1747 (O.S.).

KENDALL, RICHARD (JUNIOR), born in Lancashire. Was educated at Douay, where he distinguished himself by his application and sterling piety. He defended his Universals under Mr. Laur. Thimelby, Aug., 1705, together with Robert Heydon, Gilbert Haydock, and Charles Jernyngham, and defended them both in Greek and Latin, to the admiration of all present. After serving the Mission some years in London, he was appointed Chief Master, afterwards President, of the school established at Standon, in Herts, within ten years after the dissolution of the celebrated school at Twyford, near Winchester, on the same plan, " and like it was chiefly calculated for the use of the Catholic nobility and gentry in their tender age." Feb. 6, 1771, he was chosen Dean of the Chapter, on the appointment of Dr. Walton to be coadjutor of Bishop Francis Petre in the North. He died in London, Dec. 10, 1780, the memorable year of the riots. Mr. Kendall was a zealous missionary and warm advocate of his *Alma Mater*, as well as a great benefactor.

KENDALL, ROBERT, died in Lancashire, April 19, 1746.

KENNEDY, FRANCIS, was many years Confessor to the nuns at Rouen, and died there July 3, 1791.

KENNEL, HENRY, lived fifty years in the Chumley [Cholmeley] family at Bransby, in Yorkshire, and died there Feb. 6, 1742 (O.S.).

KENNEL, HENRY, lived fifty years Chaplain in the Chumley [Cholmeley] family at Bransby, in Yorkshire, and died there, Feb. 6, 1742 (O.S).

KEYNES, [or KANE], JOHN, S.J.   He and others of the Society were introduced into Lime Street Chapel, " when calumny had caused Messrs. Giffard, Dymock, and Tootle to be turned out as Rigorists and Jansenists." Mr. Keynes was Provincial in 1687. (*See* Mr. A. Giffard's account in *Records of Jansenism.*)

KIRBY, GEORGE, eldest son of Thomas Kirby and Margaret Hornsley, Catholics, was born in London, Oct. 12, 1739, (O.S.).   On Dec. 19, 1753, he was admitted into the College at Rome, F. H. Sheldon being then the Rector, and was ordained, Dec. 17, 1763.   On May 1, 1764, he left the College and came on the Mission. He died in London, July 23, 1784.

KIRBY, HENRY, son of Henry Kirby and his wife, Elizabeth Fulborn, who were both in the service of the Court of St. Germains, where he was born, Feb. 26, 1712.   In 1720 he was received into the English College of Rome by special licence of Cardinal Gualtieri, as he had not studied his classics, none being admitted, *by the rules*, till they were ready to begin Philosophy or Rhetoric. He received confirmation from Benedict XIII., June 6, 1728 ; took the College oath, May 22, 1729, and was ordained, Feb. 13, 1735, by a dispensation for thirteen months.   On June 4 of that year he proceeded to the Mission.   He lived many years in the Heneage family at Cadeby, in Lincolnshire, and died there, May 17, 1767.   He is said to have been " as free from guilt as a child ; had a good taste for music, and was a good preacher." (MS. of Rev. William Harris, of Osgodby, Lincolnshire.)

KIRK, JOHN, son of William Kirk and Mary Fielding, his wife, both Catholics.   He was born at Actonburnel, near Shrewsbury, April 13, 1760, and baptised on the 14th by the Rev. —— Elliot, O.S.B. ; was also confirmed there by Bishop Hornyold.   On April 25, 1770, he was placed at Sedgley Park, and in Feb., 1773, he was sent to Rome, where he was admitted into the English College, June 5, by Cardinal Corsini.   Father William Hothersall was then the Rector, and continued till Aug. 16 or 17 of that year, when the Society of Jesus was dissolved, and he was succeeded by Monsignor Foggini.   On Sept. 22nd 1776, he took the College oath ; began Philosophy, Nov. 10 ; preached before the Pope on St. Stephen's Day, Dec. 26, 1776, and was ordained sub-deacon, June 14, 1783 ; Deacon, June 5, 1784 ; and Priest, Dec. 18 of the same year, by Cardinal Corsini in his private chapel in his palace at the Lungara.   He left the College, May 31, 1785, for Pisa ; and after a stay of a fortnight with Signor Bottieri, formerly his Professor of Philosophy in the English College, and then Principal of Ferdinando College in the University of Pisa, he proceeded to Leghorne, Genoa, Nice, Avignon, Lyons, and Paris, where he rested at the Seminary with Dr. Bew for about ten days, and then at Douay as many more, till the Assumption, when, after High Mass, he left with Mr. John Gillow for St. Omers, where they dined.   They slept at Calais, landed at Dover, and slept next day at Canterbury, Aug. 17, and on the 18th reached London.   My number of *admission* in the *Annales* is 1,465.   On Sep. 28, he accompanied Bishop T. Talbot to Sir Richard Acton's, at Aldenham, and remained with him till Dec. 17.   Jan. 24, 1786, he was placed at Sedgley Park, and Feb. 23, 1788, at Pipe Hall, but returned to the Park again, Dec. 18, 1792 ; and, April 27, succeeded Mr. Southworth as President of that establishment.   At the request of Bishop Berington he left the Park, Nov. 11, 1797, to live with him at Longbirch as his Chaplain and Secretary, and continued there after his death till Bishop Stapleton came down, when he was appointed to the new Mission established at Lichfield, and arrived there Oct. 9, 1801.   The Coton and Hopwas congregation was then united to that of Lichfield, where he bought land in 1802 and built the present house and chapel, the latter of which he enlarged in 1835 and greatly improved.   In 1829 he bought freehold land at Tamworth and built a house and chapel for a priest, who resides there, and has the care of that congregation which no longer belongs to Lichfield. [He died, Dec. 21, 1851, aged 91.]

KITCHEN, EDWARD, *alias* MARSDEN, was educated at Douay.   In 1773 he came on the Mission, and was placed at Lartington, the seat of Henry Maire, Esq. (on Mrs. Maire's leaving Lartington, Oct. 1, to live at Headlam), where he continued much to the satisfaction of Mr. Maire and his congregation till Mr. William Gibson, the President of Douay College, was chosen Bishop of the Northern District, when he succeeded him, in 1790, in the beginning of the French Revolution.   In consequence of illness, he came over to England in 1792, and resigned his post to Rev. Mr. Daniel.   He retired to Lartington, and died there, Jan. 3, 1793, and was succeeded by the Rev. Benedict Rayment.

KNARESBOROUGH, JOHN, born in Yorkshire, Dec. 4, 1672.   His family resided at Farnham, between Knaresborough and Ripon [at which latter place his mother was living in 1706], and was possessed of considerable property, as appears from their composition for recusancy, which amounted, in 1708, to £6 13s. 4d.—a considerable sum in those days.   Mr. Knaresborough was sent to Douay, and took the College oath, Sept. 16, 1691.   In Oct., 1694, he began to teach the Classics, and on Feb. 12, 1699 [?], was sent on the Mission with this character, *praestanti ingenio præditus.*   After remaining some time in Lancashire, he settled in his native county, and I find him in York in 1704, where he seems to have continued till his death, which happened Nov. 9, 1724.   Mr. Knaresborough was a zealous Missionary, and of great learning and perseverance in his researches.

He wrote a work entitled : *Sufferings of Catholics,* of which 5 vols. 8vo, fairly copied, are in MS. in the MS. library of Burton Constable.   This work was of great use to Dodd, who added some marginal notes, and to Bishop Challoner, in his *Lives of Missionary Priests,* considerable parts of which are copies from Mr. Knaresborough.   The work is said to contain the lives of all who suffered from 1573 to 1654, with general histories of the reigns.   Yet in these *five volumes are wanting* the lives of *all* who suffered in Elizabeth's reign, though Vol. I. contains an account of the laws enacted against Catholics ; lists of Bishops, Deans, heads of Colleges deprived, priests and laymen who suffered. In another volume, called *in Folio,* is the rough draft of Mr. Knaresborough's lives of all from Cuthbert Mayne to Campion, Sherwin and companions inclusively.   In this *Folio* are the rough copies of Mr. Knaresborough's letters, and many original ones.   Several vols. of Mr. Knaresborough's *Sufferings* are wanting at Burton Constable.   If I recollect right, one or more I found at Fernyhalgh, near Preston, probably borrowed by Dodd, or his relation, Mr. Tootell, who lived there.   [Knaresborough's collections are now in the possession of Lord Herries, at Everingham. There is a transcript of the *Sufferings of Catholics* at Ushaw College.—J. H. P.]

KNATCHBULL, ROBERT, S.J., of a good family in Kent.   Was appointed Rector of Ghent in 1766, and was the last of that house.

KNIGHT, CLARE, R.M. Abbess at Cambray.   Died Oct. 30, 1792, aged 52 ; religious life, 35 years.

KNIGHT, RICHARD, S.J., only surviving son and heir of William Knight, of Kingerby, in Lincolnshire, Esq., was born July 24, 1720.   He entered the Society of Jesus, July 11, 1739, and was professed in 1757.   He settled his estates at Irnham, in Lincolnshire, upon his only sister Lucy, the wife of Sir Thomas Rookwood Gage, fifth Bart. of Hengrave.   He founded the chapel at Lincoln, and died there, Dec. 6, 1793, eminent for his sanctity.   There is a portrait of him at Coldham Hall, Suffolk.

KYNASTON, ROGER, son of Raphael Kynaston, was a native of Shropshire, and at the age of 21 was sent to the College in Rome, and was admitted, Oct. 14, 1670, by Father Edward Courtney.   He was ordained Priest at St. John Lateran's, April 13, 1675, and left the College July 10, 1676.   " In 1692 he had been sixteen years on the Mission, and had the character of being a zealous and industrious Missionary."   He was a member of the Chapter, and, in 1687, succeeded Mr. Robert Edwards as Archdeacon of North Wales.   He died July 30, 1712.

KYNNE, EDWARD, succeeded, Mar. 24, 1683, Mr. John Kynne, as Arch-deacon of Worcestershire and Gloucester, and in that capacity assisted at the General Assemblies of the Chapter in 1684, 1694, 1703, and 1710; but died [in 1711] before the next was held in 1714.

LACY, FRANCIS, *alias* ELLSTON *or* EYSTON, son of Henry Lacy and Mary Eyston. At the age of 19 he was admitted into the College at Rome by Cardinal Barberini, in the rectorship of Father Postgate, March 15, 1705, when he began Philosophy. In 1710 or 1711 he was ordained Priest, and left the College, April 13, 1712. He served the Mission in London for upwards of sixty years, and was the Senior Capitular. He died in London in the 90th year of his age, Dec. 3, 1774.

LANCASTER, JAMES, *vere* LEMOTTE, S.J., son of James Lemotte and Mary Robinson, both Catholics, was born in Lancashire, in June, 1712, and after studying his Classics in that county for four years, he was admitted among the Alumni of the English College at Rome, Oct. 11, 1727. May 1, 1728, he took the oath of Alexander VII., but afterwards obtained a dispensa-tion from Clement XII.; and after remaining in the College nearly seven years he left it, July 6, 1734, and on the 7th he entered his noviceship at Watten, and was made a professed Father in 1750. (*Annals of the Roman College.*)

LANCASTER, LOUISA FRANCES, Superioress of the Augustinian Nuns at the Rue du Fossé, St. Victor. She stood her ground at the Revolution, being protected by Le Brun, the third Consul, and died May 22, 1808, aged 84, after governing the house forty-two years.
[Oswald Lancaster died at Dunkirk, Nov. 4, 1753.]

LANGDALE, MARMADUKE, second Baron Langdale, Lord of Holme, co. York. He succeeded his father in the Barony in 1661. He married Elizabeth, daughter of Thomas Savage, of Beeston, Cheshire (brother of John, Earl Rivers), by whom he had issue Marmaduke, who succeeded to the title, and two daughters. He died in Feb., 1702, (O.S.).

LANGDALE, MARMADUKE, third Lord, eldest surviving son of Marmaduke the second Lord Langdale, by his second wife, Elizabeth, daughter of Thomas Savage, of Beeston, co. Cheshire. He married Frances, only daughter of Richard Draycott, of Painsley, co. York, son of Sir Roger Draycott and Joan Aston, of Tixall. He died at York in 1718, and left one son, who suc-ceeded him; Elizabeth, married to Peter Middleton, of Stockheld, co. York; and Mary, married to Nicholas Blundell, of Crosby, co. Lancaster.

LANGDALE, MARMADUKE, fourth Lord, only son of the above and Frances Draycott. He married Elizabeth, daughter of William, Lord Widdrington, who died, Jan. 7, 1765, by whom he had Marmaduke, Alathea—who died young—Dorothea, wife of Sir Walter Vavasour, of Haslewood, and Elizabeth. Lord Langdale died in 1771.

LANGDALE, MARMADUKE, fifth Lord, only son of the fourth Lord and Elizabeth Widdrington. He married Constantia, daughter of Sir John Smythe, of Actonburnel, by whom he had a son and four daughters, which son and Constantia both died young. Elizabeth married Robert Butler, of Ballyragget, in Ireland. Mary married Charles Phillip, Lord Stourton, and Apollonia married Hugh, fifth Lord Clifford. Lord Langdale died in 1777, and leaving no male issue, the title became extinct. Lady Stourton alone had issue, and thus the Langdale and Draycott property became vested in the Stourton family. [Lady Constantia Langdale died in London, Nov. 24, 1792.]

LANGDALE, MARMADUKE, S.J., of a good family, was born Oct. 28, 1748. He entered his noviceship, Sept. 7, 1766, and was stationed at Wigan, in Lancashire, where he died, Nov. 3, 1786.

LANGDALE, PHILIP, of Houghton, co. York, son of Lord Langdale, I believe. He married —— Acton, of Aldenham, sister of Sir Richard Acton. He died, June 14, 1814, aged 90, when the estates of Sir Richard Acton came to the Chevalier Acton, of Naples.

LAW, JOHN, of Lauriston, in Scotland, son of William Law, of Lauriston, and Jean Campbell, born April 21, 1671. He was appointed Comptroller General of the Finances of France, Jan. 5, 1720. He died at Venice, Mar. 21, 1729, aged 58. He married Lady Catharine Knollis, third daughter of Nicholas, third Earl of Banbury. His son John was Cornet of the Regiment of Nassau, Friesland.

LAW, WILLIAM, brother of John, was born Oct. 24, 1675; was made Director-General of the India Company in France. He died, 1752, aged 77, and was buried in the chapel of the Scots' College, at Paris. His son John, born at Paris, Oct. 15, 1719, was made Governor of Pondicherry, Maréchal de Champ, etc., and died at Paris about 1797, and his recond son, John Francis, was Commander-in-Chief of the French East India Company's troops at Pondicherry.

LAWSON, SIR HENRY, of Brough Hall, second Bart., was eldest surviving son of Sir John Lawson (who was created Bart. by Charles II. in 1665 in consideration of his unshaken loyalty and great sufferings) by his wife, Catharine, second daughter of Sir William Howard, of Naworth, and sister of the Earl of Carlisle. It was by the interest of the Earl of Carlisle that Sir John, the first Bart., repurchased the family estates from Oliver Cromwell and the Rump Parliament, which had been confiscated for this family's loyalty to the King. The price was upwards of £9,000, to raise which sum sundry estates were sold off in Northumberland and Durham. During the confiscation, for some years the family was allowed to rent and to live upon one of the farms near Brough Hall. Sir Henry married Elizabeth, daughter of Sir Robert Knightley, of Off Church, co. Warwick, and had by her two sons and three daughters. Anne, the second daughter, married Mr. Witham, of Cliff, and Elizabeth, Stephen Tempest of Broughton Hall. Sir Henry died in 1725. His brothers, William and Thomas, who died at a very advanced age, in 1750, were ecclesiastics (Jesuits, I suppose), and most of his five sisters were nuns at Ghent.*

LAWSON, SIR JOHN, third Bart., eldest son of Sir Henry and Elizabeth Knightley, succeeded his father in 1725. He married Mary, eldest daughter of Sir John Shelley, of Michel Grove, Sussex, Bart., and had by her ten children, of whom three sons and two daughters, Mary and Bridget, survived, and who became nuns at Bruges, O.S.F., and died 1783 and 1787. His second son, Thomas, was a Jesuit, and died in London in the 87th year of his age. His third son, John (who died in London, 1791, aged 69), married Elizabeth, daughter of Thomas Selby, of Biddleston, by whom he had Thomas and Henry, O.S.B., and John, M.D., and Elizabeth, wife of John¡Webbe Weston. Sir John died at York, Oct. 19, 1739, aged about 50, and was buried at Catterick. His widow survived him till 1759.

LAWSON, SIR HENRY, fourth Bart., eldest son of Sir John Lawson and Mary Shelley, succeeded his father in 1739. He married Anastasia, youngest daughter of Thomas Maire, of Lartington Hall, co. York, and of Hardwick-near-the-Sea, Durham; and of Mary, daughter of Richard Fermor, of Tusmore, Oxon. She died, Nov. 5, 1764, leaving four children: Mary, who became a nun at Bruges; John, who succeeded him; Catharine, wife of John Silvertop; and Henry. Sir Henry died in Oct. 1781, aged 69.

LAWSON, SIR JOHN, fifth Bart., eldest son of Sir Henry Lawson and Anastasia Maire, born Sept. 13, 1744. Studied at St. Omers and Bruges. He married, Aug. 1, 1768, Elizabeth, youngest daughter of William Scarisbrick, of Scarisbrick, Lancashire, by whom he had: 1. Anastasia, wife of Thomas Strickland, of Sizergh; 2. Elizabeth, who married, in 1789, John Wright, of Kelvedon Hall, Essex; and 3. Henry, who died an infant. After the death of his first wife, he married Monica, daughter of Miles Stapleton, of Drax and Durwick Hill, residing at Clints, near Richmond, co. Yorks. Sir John died after a few days' illness, June 27, 1811. "While amiability of disposition, un-

---

* See the more precise pedigree in Foley's *Records S.J.*, v. 708.—J. H. P.

bounded hospitality, great liberality of sentiment, warm and affectionate feeling for the distresses of the comfortless and afflicted, are looked upon as virtues which adorn our nature, so long will the memory of Sir Jo. Lawson roll down the stream of time, revered and respected."

In his title and estate he was succeeded by his only brother Sir Henry Lawson, whose Lartington and Durham estates devolved on his sister, Mrs. Silvertop, widow of John Silvertop, Esq., of Minsteracres, co. Northumberland. Sir Henry, born Dec. 25, 1750, had previously (in pursuance of the last will of his maternal uncle, John Maire, of Lartington, by virtue of the Maire of the King's sign manual in 1771, when he succeeded to the estate of the Maire family) assumed the name and arms of the Maires. He married first, in 1773, Monica, youngest daughter of Nich. Stapleton, of Carleton, Esq., and secondly, in 1801, Catherine, only daughter of Henry Fermor, of Worcester, Esq., but had no issue by either.

LAWSON, THOMAS, SENIOR, S.J., was seventh son of Sir John Lawson, the first Baronet, of Brough Hall, by Catharine, daughter of Sir William Howard, of Naworth Castle, and sister of Charles, first Earl of Carlisle. He lived some time as Chaplain with his brother, Sir Henry Lawson, and, I believe, also with his nephew, Sir John Lawson, who died in 1739. Father Lawson died at Watten, in 1750.

LAWSON, THOMAS, JUN., S.J. He was second son of Sir John Lawson, of Brough Hall, third Bart., by Mary, daughter of Sir John Shelley [born Mar. 20, 1720; noviceship, Sept. 7, 1736; professed, 1754]. He died in London, July 11, 1807, *aetatis* 88. Father Lawson was uncle of Thomas and Henry Lawson, O.S.B., sons of John, third son of Sir John Lawson, third Bart., and Elizabeth Selby, and brothers of Dr. Lawson, of York.

LAYFIELD, CHRISTOPHER, younger brother to James Layfield. He was educated at Douay [began Philosophy Oct, 1, 1738], and when he was on the Mission, was placed at Tixall, [was there in 1751; a Mr. Layfield was at Sorden in 1745], in the family of Lord Aston, and died there, much beloved and respected, Sept 27, 1761.

LAYFIELD, JAMES, son of Richard Layfield, by his wife, Elizabeth Atkinson, was born in Lancashire, Sept. 8, 1707 (O.S.). After studying his Classics in England, he was received into the College at Rome by order of Cardinal Gualtieri, in the rectorship of Father Eberson, June 21, 1722. He was ordained Priest by Benedict XIII., together with Mr. Liddle, Mar. 16, 1726, and left the College, Sept. 9, 1728, to be confessor to the nuns at Liège. When he came on the Mission he was stationed at Wolverhampton [helped at Harvington in 1750, and in 1751, as executor to Mr. Williams. Was chosen Canon, Nov. 29, 1752], but afterwards settled at Oscott, where he died, Feb. 5, 1756. He was a member of the Chapter, and was much esteemed by all that knew him.

LECKONBY, JOHN, *vere* WHITE, son of John White and Alice Southern, born May 18, 1710. After studying the classics three years at Lancaster, he was admitted into the College at Rome, Oct. 5, 1727. He was ordained Priest on March 21, 1733, and left the College, Sept. 23, 1734, but remained half a year at Douay to finish his course of Divinity, or at least to prepare himself the better for the Mission. He lived at Brailes, with only £33 per an., and died in Feb., 1778. (*Annals of the Roman College.*)

LECKONBY, LUCAS, *vere* WHITE, elder brother of John, born Oct. 17, 1708, (O.S.). He was received into the College at Rome, June 20, 1724. He was ordained Sept. 9, 1731, and left for England on the 14th of the same month and year. Hence it appears that he was not quite 23 when ordained, and in less than a week afterwards was sent on the Mission ! I do not find his name in any Clergy catalogue. (*Annals of Roman College.*)

LECKONBY, THOMAS, S.J. born Oct. 15, 1717. Entered his noviceship, Sept. 7, 1736, and was made a professed Father in 1754. After remaining a few months (four months, thirteen days) at Swinnerton, in the Fitzherbert family, he removed to Callaly, near Alnwick, in 1748. A Mr. Leckonby was placed at Pontop about 1748, and lived there till Feb., 1778, when he died. He seems to have been a member of the Secular Clergy.

LEE, GEORGE HENRY, second Earl of Lichfield, eldest surviving son of Sir Edward Henry Lee (created Earl of Lichfield), and Charlotte, daughter of Charles II. and Barbara, Duchess of Cleveland. Born March 19, 1689. He married Frances, daughter of Sir John Hales, of Woodchurch, Kent, and by her had four sons and six daughters: George, born May 21, 1718, who succeeded to the title; Charlotte, married Robert, Visc. Dillon*; Mary, wife of Cosmas Nevill, of Holt; Harriet, wife of Lord Bellew; and Anne, married to Lord Clifford of Chudleigh. Lord Lichfield died Feb. 16, 1742 (O.S.).

LEEMBY, MR., lived at Croston, and at Pontop, or Tanfield. Rev. Edward Kenyon supposes White and Leemby to be the same person. Mr. Peter Browne says, "Mr. John White lived many years in Lancashire, and died at Euxton Hall, Feb. 7, 1778." He and Mr. Eyre disagreed.

LEIGH, PHILIP, S.J., *alias* LAYTON, son of Alexander Leigh. At the age of 20 he was admitted into the English College at Rome, Oct. 16, 1671, during the administration of Father John Clark, and was placed on one of the free funds, where he was not obliged to take that part of the oath of Alexander VII. which forbids the entrance into a religious order without leave of Propaganda. He was ordained Priest, April 13, 1675; and March 21, 1678, he defended *Universal Divinity* with great applause, and on the 27th of that month, after having lived six and a half years in the College, he went to Watten, and became a Jesuit. (*Annals of the Roman College.*)

LEIGH, ROGER, S.J., son of James Leigh and his wife, Alice Catterall, was born March 15, 1708. He entered his noviceship Sept. 7, 1728. He lived some time at Westby Hall, near Kirkham, Lancashire. During the latter part of his life he was very infirm, and lived with his nephew, Mr. Thomas Latham, of Wigan, Lancashire, where he died, Jan. 29, 1781.

LESLEY, ——, S.J.—He gave a new edition of the Mozarabic Liturgy at Rome in 1755, with curious notes, and shows that it was the old Spanish Liturgy, used probably from the beginning in the Church of Spain, with some additions, which St. Leander adopted for the use of the Goths. (Mr. Butler's *Life of S. Isidore*, February 4th.)

LESLEY, WILLIAM, a Scotch clergyman, and agent for the Scotch clergy in Rome, and was frequently employed as agent for Douay College, both by Dr. and Bishop Leyburn. He was a gentleman of great merit. He remembered the time of the Bishop of Chalcedon, and was alive when Bishop Witham was agent there.

LESTER, FRANCIS, S.J., son of Francis Lester and Rachael Taverner, Protestants, born Nov. 2, 1704. At Lisbon he became a Catholic by the reading of pious books, and was admitted into the English College there, where he remained two years, but in 1725 went to Rome, and was received among the alumni of Benedict XIII. in April, and was confirmed by that Pope June 6, 1728. On account of his health, he was advised by his physician to go into Flanders, where he obtained, Nov. 2, a dispensation from part of the oath of Alexander VII., which he had taken, and became a Jesuit. (*Annals of the Roman College.*)

LEVESON, EDWARD, S.J.—Published *A Sermon on Untimely Repentance*, preached before Lord Petre in his chapel at Ingatestone Hall, on Passion Sunday, April 1, 1688.

---

* This Lord Dillon conformed. He told Rev. Francis Bishop of Heythrop, while dining with him at Ditchley, that he had changed in order to get Ditchley. Mr. Ralph Sheldon also conformed, and gave as his reason that he "found it troublesome to follow conscience and inclination." Mr. Pinhard, in a letter to his father, says: "Lord Kingland returned to the Catholic Faith."

LEWIS [? THEODORE, *alias* FRANCIS SHELLEY, S.J.], resided with Mr. Ch. Wells at Brambridge, near Winchester, in 1692.

LEWIS, PHILIP, was chosen Archdeacon July 9, 1694.

LEWIS, O.S.B.—He was a native of Herefordshire, and studied among the Benedictines at Douay, where he took the degree of D.D. He lived for some years as chaplain to —— Howard, of Corby Castle, Esq. He was a good performer on the violin, and indulged his musical inclinations further than was consistent with his duties and in spite of the remonstrances of his superiors and confessors. His passion at last led him astray, and caused him so far to forget his solemn engagement and religious vows that he married Mr. Howard's maid. On this occasion his *confrère*, Mr. Hawkins, wrote to reprimand him, but soon after followed his example ; so far Dr. Milner states. Mr. Lewis, on his marriage, retired into Herefordshire, and for a while went regularly to hear Mass at Miss Mornington's chapel, as he said he had not changed his religion. His marriage was very unexpected, and greatly surprised his friends. He afterwards retired to Bridgenorth, where he lived many years, and about 1804 was found dead in his bed.

It probably was on the occasion of his, or some similar apostacy, that Bishop Challoner wrote to Bishop Hornyhold thus : " I truly condole with you on the afflictions which the scandalous behaviour of some of your subjects has brought upon you, than which nothing I am persuaded could be more sensible to your charitable heart. Would to God we had not all too much experience of this most dreadful of all evils, I mean the apostacy, or scandalous lives of Priests, often followed by final impenitence and miserable deaths, of which in my long time I have seen or known many instances. Our Lord have mercy on us all, and keep us by His powerful grace, that those that stand may not fall, and that such as are now fallen may open their eyes to see their misery, and to be effectually brought back to this our Father of mercies. In Him I am,
　　　　　　　　　　　　　　　　　" Honoured and dear Sir, etc.,
" Dec. 26, 1775.　　　　　　　　　　　　R. CHALLONER."

LEY, STEPHEN, was a Capitular, and in April, 1657, was chosen V.G. of Cheshire, Stafford, Derby, Notts, Rutland, Lincoln, Warwick, Leicester, Gloucester, and Worcestershire, and as such assisted at the General Assembly of the Dean and Chapter in 1657. But in order to make way for Dr. Michael Jennyns to come into the Chapter, he voluntarily divided his district at that Assembly, and the Doctor was made V.G. of the four latter counties. But after Dr. Jennyns' death, Mr. Ley was unanimously requested at the General Assembly in 1667 to reassume what he, out of his goodness, had divested himself of. Mr. Ley died in 1671. (*Chap. Records.*)

LEYBURNE, GEORGE.—At Painsley Dec., 1727 to 1736 ; died Jan. 24, 1736 (O.S.). Was Mr. Brockholes' executor. Left £100 to C. P. [From Kirk's draft.]

LEYBURNE, JOHN (I suppose he was nephew to Bishop Leyburne), of Nateby, near Garstang, co. Lancaster. He took part in the Rebellion of 1715, and his estates, which were valued at £317 6s. 5d., were forfeited to the Crown.

LEYBURNE, NICHOLAS, succeeded Mr. Brown at Norbury and Roston, 1720 : left in 1731½ ; died May 20, 1739. A Nich. Leyburne V. Pres. of Douay Coll. in 1697-1699. [From Kirk's draft.]

LIDDEL, JOHN *vere* Verhuyck, son of Ant Verhuyck and Elizabeth Liddel, born in London Sept. 30, 1688 ; received, aged 22, in Roman Coll. by order of Card. Caprara, Fr. Powell Rector, was ordained April 20, 1715, and in April, 1717, left for England. Mr. Liddell died in London June 25, 1738.

LIDDELL, THO.—Educated at Lisbon in 1766. Succeeded Mr. Hartley at Wolverhampton in 1771 to 1775. Served the mission many years in the North and Midland Districts : went from Wolverhampton to Liverpool for his health ; died at Liverpool May 12, 1775. [Kirk's Draft.]

LIDDELL, THO.—Priest at Lartington till 1713; died at Lisbon July 29, 1724. [Kirk's Draft.]

LINDOW, JOHN.—In his youth he was placed with, if not apprenticed to, a cabinet maker, but feeling an inclination to the Church, and discovering a good capacity, he was sent to Douay by Bishop Challoner, where he fully justified the opinion formed of him by his spiritual directors.   When ordained he was employed in London, and in a MS. letter of Rev. Thomas Walsh, preserved at Ushaw, and written in 1778, the following character is given of him : " He labours strenuously, and Mr. Miller (Bishop) thinks that no wrong is done to anyone by saying that he does more good than any in these parts.   What he wants in address he makes up by strength. He acts *opportune et importune*, and his burning charity, for I can call it no otherwise, is crowned with the most consoling success.   His apartment at night I have seen to be the asylum of consolation, good counsel, hope, and edification to the pious."
Mr. Lindow lived many years with Bishop Talbot, and afterwards with Bishop Poynter, in Castle Street.   He was many years a member of the Chapter [Archdeacon, Oct. 16, 1770], and on the death of Mr. P. Brown, succeeded him as Dean.   When worn out with his missionary labours, in his old age he retired to Old Hall Green, the original plan of which was given by him, and died there Dec. 9, 1806.

LITTLETON, ——. A Popish Priest, escaped after the battle of Preston by putting on a blue apron and passing himself off for an assistant or journeyman to an apothecary. [Kirk's Draft].

LLOYD, SYLVESTER LEWIS, O.S.F.— He published *General Instructions by way of Catechism*, in which the " history and truths of religion, the Christian morality, Sacraments, prayers and ceremonies, and rites of the Church are briefly explained by Holy Scripture and tradition.   Translated from the French, and carefully compared with the Spanish approved translation, by S. Lloyd," London, 1723.   It was condemned by a decree of the Index approved by Benedict XIII., Jany. 15, 1725.

LODGE, JOHN, left Douay College [with Charles Berwistle] for the Mission, June 27, 1707,   He lived in Yorkshire, and died there Mar. 26, 1741.

LODGE, JOHN.—[Began Poetry in October, 1738], taught Philosophy and Divinity [in 1751] at Douay, and was much esteemed by Dr. Green, the President.   When he came on the Mission he was placed at Sheffield, in Sept., 1758, and continued there many years.   In 1786 he succeeded Mr. Clavering at Durham, where, as Mr. Eyre writes, he spun out a frail life till Nov. 3, 1795, when he died, aged 74.
Mr. Lodge was a member of the Chapter [Archdeacon in 1770], and in such estimation with his brethren, and his Bishop, Francis Petre, that the latter named him as one of the three [third on the list] that he wished for his Coadjutor.

LODGE, MILES, was educated at Douay.   In 1693 I find him in the family of Sir —— Gascoigne, Bart., and he assisted the Catholics in that neighbourhood, and about Barnbow and Red-Hall belonging to Lady Saville.

LOMAX, JOHN.—In Jan., 1725, I find him living at Lord Dover's in Cambridgeshire [Jan. 27, 1725], and in 1727 at Moseley, or Tong Castle. He died April 29, 1732.

LONSDALE, JOHN, was educated at Douay.   He lived many years at York, and succeeded Mr. Thomas Daniel in the agency of the clergy of Yorkshire, when Bishop Walton resided with him.   From York he removed to Linton-on-Ouse, and about 1799 he retired to Dodding Green, near Kendal, in Westmoreland, where, after a long and painful illness, he died, on Oct. 8, 1802. Mr. Lonsdale was a most respectable, able, and zealous missionary.   He was a member of the Chapter, and had the title of "Archdeacon of Hants, Wilts, and Somersetshire."

LORIMER, FRANCIS, son of Michael Lorimer and Ann [?] Writte, his wife, was born in Monmouthshire, July 24, 1708 (N.S.). In 1723 he was admitted into the College at Rome by Cardinal Gualtieri, the Protector ; was ordained Priest March 21, 1733, and left the College on April 15 of the same year. He lived some years at Talacre, the seat of Sir —— Mostyn, Bart., in Flintshire, and died there, Sept. 30, 1765. (*Annals of the Roman College.*)

LOSTOCK, PETER.—See Lisbon *Diary*, Vol. VI., Miscel., and *Cath. Mag.*, Vol. III., p. 148. He died Aug. 31, 1722.

LOVEL, ——, was Professor of Philosophy in Douay College for some years. He laboured on the Mission in Leicestershire and Derbyshire [? chosen a Capitular in 1703]. He published *A View of Mr. White's Principles in his Book of the Middle State of Souls.* London. 12mo. 1712.

LOWE, WILLIAM *or* ANTHONY, son of Samuel Lowe and Alicia Spencer, was born in London, March 19, 1734 (N.S.). Both his parents were Protestants, but on the death of his father, his mother married a Catholic and educated her son a Catholic. In 1748 he embarked to go to Rome, but was taken by the Algerines to Algiers, where he remained for eleven months ; he was then allowed to depart, and was received in the English College at Rome by Father Christ. Maire, Jan. 9, 1749. He was ordained Priest Feb. 18, 1758, and in April of the following year left the College, and was sent to Gravelines to be Confessor to the Poor Clare nuns there. In the engagement with the Algerine vessel he received a wound, from which he remained lame during life. He died during the French Revolution, in 1795.

LUCAS, SIMON, was a native of Hanley in Arden, Warwickshire. He went first to Douay, and soon after was one of the colony that removed to Valladolid, where he was ordained Priest. For a short time he was assistant to Mr. Hugo Kendall at Sedgley Park, and then was made one of the Chaplains at Warwick Street, London. He afterwards became Chaplain to Mrs. Windsor Heneage of pious and charitable memory, and lived as such with her in the I. of Wight [at Newport], her native place, who by his advice created and provided for two chapels, one at Newport, the other at Cowes. He died at Old Hall Green, Jan. 31, 1801. Mr. Lucas was an interior man, and of great prayer and contemplation. Several small spiritual tracts, which were printed and distributed gratis by his worthy patroness, are thought to have been written and translated by Mr. Lucas. (Mr. Hodgson's *Obituary*).

LUND ANTHONY, was educated at Douay, where he taught Rhetoric from 1761, then Philosophy from 1764, and finally Divinity from 1768. He lived many years at Fernyhalgh, near Preston, where he died Sept. 20, 1811.

LUND, GEORGE [? JOHN], born at Barton, in Lancashire, was educated at Douay. His first mission was at Swinburne Castle, Northumberland, whence he removed to Lartington, Yorkshire. In 1759 he was placed at Cottam, in Lancashire, where he lived, respected and loved, for fifty-three years, and died there, June 28, 1812, aged 81. He was buried in his chapel, where a neat monument was erected to his memory. He was Rural Dean of the Amounderness Hundred, and was esteemed a good preacher, says Mr. Gradwell.

LUPTON, THOMAS, was born March 27, 1775, at Claughton, the estate of James Brockholes, Esq., and was the son of his gardener. He was sent to Douay College by that most religious and charitable gentleman. In the French Revolution he was sent with others to Dourlens, whence he made his escape and came over to England. He finished his Divinity Course at Crook Hall. He then succeeded Mr. Kenyon as assistant to Mr. Broomhead, in Rook Street Chapel, Manchester, where he was one of the most distinguished and valuable missionaries of his time. His health being much impaired by his labours, he left Manchester and retired to Garswood, where he is still living, 1838, and in tolerable good health.

LYNDE, GEORGE, was educated at Rome, but on his return remained some time to continue his studies at Douay College. In 1677 he went to Louvain as socius to Mr. Johnson, Confessor to the Austin nuns, and after his death succeeded him in that capacity, and died there, Feb. 15, 1715, aged 68.

MACCARTHY, or M'CARTAY, JAMES, was born in London, but probably Irish. At the age of 15 or 16 he went from Florence to Rome, with a recommendation from the Grand Duke of Tuscany to the Pope, who allowed him to be admitted into the English College, May 15, 1714, though under the required age and proficiency in learning.

The said Grand Duke paid for him 60 scudi per annum, until he began Philosophy, in 1717. In the following year he took the College oath and became an alumnus. On March 11, 1724 he was ordained Priest, and on June 9 he left the College, and went first to Florence, and afterwards to England. He lived Chaplain to Mr. Parkins, at Ufton Court, near Reading, son of ———— and Miss Fermor, the heroine of Pope's *Rape of the Lock*. Being sent in 1741 by his Patron to make a matrimonial proposal to the only daughter of Lord Stowell, he was told by the lady that if he had asked for himself he might have succeeded. His vanity was flattered by the preference given to him, and yielding to the temptation, he went off with her to London, and thence into the neighbourhood of Windsor, where they resided. In about six months after this marriage, perceiving one day, as he took off his stockings, a black spot on one of his legs, he became greatly alarmed, and within a few hours was a dead man. A short time before his fall he preached a sermon against scandal, and admonished his congregation not to be scandalized even if their Pastor himself should misbehave himself. (*Diary of Douay College*). See Mr. Milner's account of him.

MACKWORTH, THOMAS, son of Thomas Mackworth and Mary Pilkington, born in London. At the age of 20 was received at Rome by Father Powell, April 5, 1712 (N.S.), when he came from Lisbon College on finishing his Classics. Ordained April 11, 1716. Departed for England April 21, 1718. Was at Painsley from Sept. 1722 till 1726. Was troubled by Roger Warner, to whom, as forced unjustly, Mr. Miller [? Dr. Milner] paid from common purse £30. On July 20, 1723, went abroad. Thomas Mackworth died Jan. 11, 1733 (O.S.). "The Duke of Norfolk sent a page of his called Mackworth to Douay College in 1712."

MADRINE ——, studied at Rome. He first resided with Mr. Lacon of Linley, in Shropshire, but in 1693 removed, it appears, into Staffordshire. "He was a clergyman," says a MS., "of good esteem and credit."

MAINWARING, ——. "One Mr. Mainwaring," says Mr. Thomas Berington, "is late dead at Bromingham. After he had been a few years on the Mission he changed his coat for a Parson's gown, had a benefice in Bromley, in Staffordshire. Cozen Fleetwood, after some time, I guess about 20 [years] ago, shewed him into the right side of the Pale, but he did not shew much signs of a thorough Penitent ; performed no functions, lived in idleness ever since. It was required of him to live retired for a year, to dispose himself for working in the vineyard, but never would come to a resolve of going to any place from the said retirement. I want to be informed whether he had proper help at his death." He adds (March 4, 1739): "Mr. William Maire, Senior, who formerly lived at Hammersmith, and had been many years *non compos*, died on the 23rd ultimo."

MAIRE, CHRISTOPHER, S.J., of Hartbushes, Co. Durham. This was a younger branch of the Maire family, of Lartington. He entered the Society of Jesus, and became very eminent as a mathematician, and was employed by Benedict XIV., along with Father Boscovich, in making a survey of the Pope's estates in Italy, which was published in a most accurate map on a large scale. He died at Ghent at a very advanced age, about 1765 or 1766. He had three brothers priests, Peter, Soc. Jesu, William and Henry, of the Secular Clergy, and two sisters Poor Clares, at Dunkirk. Also two other brothers, John and George. The latter married the sister of Giles Hussey of Marnhull, Co. Dorset,

Esq., by whom he had three sons, viz., John Maire, a druggist in London, who died a bachelor, and Edward and George Maire, Priests, Soc. Jesu, the latter of whom, a most worthy Missioner, and excellent scholar, lived many years at Aston, in Staffordshire, and after undergoing an operation for the stone, at Stafford, died there in 1796. He was born March 21, 1738, was made a professed Father in 1772. His brother Edward was born Nov. 7, 1726, and was made a professed Father in 1760. In 1762 he went as Confessor to the Bar at York, but left in 1762 [sic] to live in London, where he died, April 13, 1797. See an interesting account of Giles Hussey of Marnhull in the 8th vol. of Nicholls' *Literary Anecdotes of the Eighteenth Century*, p. 177, and p. 189. " The latter account from the Late Sir H. Lawson."

MAIRE, HENRY, brother of Christopher and William, was educated at Douay. On his return to England he lived with Mr. Thornborough at Leyburne, and after that for some time with Mr. Skelton, a Priest, at Raventops or Raventofts. His next place was Cliffe-upon-Tees, where he helped Mr. Nicholas Clavering [who was preceded by Mr. Chambers], and assisted the Catholics thereabouts, and on the Durham side of the river, and where he died suddenly Nov. 5, 1775. [Kirk's drafts briefly mention the following members of this family:

Maire, Mrs., went to Headlam, Oct. 1, 1773.

Maire, Mrs. Henrietta, late from Ghent, died at Lartington, Oct. 8, 1794, aged 90.

Maire, Mrs. Ann, of Hardwick, widow of Francis Maire, *obiit* May 6, 1783.]

MAIRE, WILLIAM, BISHOP OF CINNA. William was the fourth son of Thomas Maire of Lartington, Esq., and of Mary Fermor, his wife, daughter of Richard Fermor, of Tusmore, Esq., by Frances, daughter of Sir Basil Brook, Knight, by Frances, his wife, the sister of John Mordaunt, Earl of Peterborough. William, their son, was educated at Douay College, where he taught Philosophy, and received the order of priesthood. He returned to England July , 1735. [*Douay Diary*, ii., 227].* For some time he lived among his relations, and served the poor Catholics in Richmond, as occasion required, till the death of his great-uncle, William Maire, when he succeeded him in Gilesgate; but in 1741 he resigned that charge for that of the Congregation of Old Elvet, Durham, which was void by the death of Mr. Jackson. In the same year he was appointed V.G. of Durham and Northumberland by Bishop Dicconson, and Special Vicar by Bishop Petre, Aug. 10, 1757. In 1759 he had been a member of the Chapter. In 1767 he was chosen Coadjutor to Bishop Petre in the North, and was consecrated with the title of Epūs Cinnensis by Bishop Challoner, assisted by Bishop James Talbot, on Trinity Sunday, in 1768. His bulls bear date Oct. 1, 1767.

But Mr. Maire had now laboured many years in the punctual discharge of arduous duties, and his health was then visibly on the decline. For which reason, as soon as he had received consecration, he quitted Durham, and retired to Lartington, the seat of his eldest brother, John Maire, Esq., where he died in great sentiments of piety, July 26, 1769, and was buried in the family vault in Romaldkirk Church. Bishop Maire was well versed in sacred and profane literature, and was not less remarkable for his piety and zeal. Bishop Maire was brother of Anastasia, the wife of Sir —— Lawson, and uncle of the late Sir John and Sir Henry Lawson, Baronets.

He published for the instruction of the younger clergy of his flock *A Treatise of the Imitation of the Youth of Jesus Christ*, translated from the French.

MAIRE, WILLIAM, of the Lartington family, was educated at Douay, and on his return from College succeeded Mr. R. Rivers at the College in Gilesgate, Durham. He lived in the house of his brother, Ralph Maire, Esq., whose daughter, Mary Maire, left the house to the Clergy. Mr. William Maire died in Gilesgate, March 6, 1760, and was succeeded by his grand-nephew, afterwards Bishop Maire.

---

* MS. note by Canon Tierney.

MAIRE, WILLIAM, brother to Christopher, after being ordained Priest at Douay, served the Mission in or near Durham and after at York, and died there July 10, 1733. I find in a MS. that William Maire, a Priest, was drowned at York, June 30, 1733; probably the same, June 30 being the O.S., and July 10 the N.S.

MALBURN, JOHN, D.D., of Seville, flourished in 1698.

MALONY, JOHN BAPTIST, was a native of Ireland, but exercised Missionary faculties in London. An information having been lodged against him by Pain, the famous trafficker on the penal laws, he was tried at the Old Bailey for being a Priest, and, as he openly confessed himself in court to be a Priest, the jury were under the necessity of finding him guilty, and he was accordingly sentenced to perpetual imprisonment. For this conviction, Pain, the carpenter, received from the Sheriff of the county £100, as the reward assigned by law for his information. " Malony was a man of morals," says Burke, in his speech at Bristol, in 1780, "neither guilty nor accused of anything noxious to the State. He was condemned to perpetual imprisonment for exercising the functions of his religion, and after lying in jail two or three years, was relieved by the mercy of government from perpetual imprisonment, on condition of perpetual banishment."

[His trial came on at Croydon, in Surrey, when his own handwriting, in which he declared he was a Priest, was produced against him; and, being convicted, he was sentenced to perpetual imprisonment. He was imprisoned in the new gaol, Southwark; but afterwards, on his petition, was removed to the King's Bench.]

MANLY, FR., *alias* SELBY, eldest son of Sir Thomas Manley, of Brentwood, in Essex, left Douay in Logic, April 20, 1705.

MANLEY, JOHN. Chosen Archdeacon, March 16, 1729-30. President of Lisbon, and killed there, Nov. 1, 1755, by the fall of the steeple at the English College, caused by the earthquake. He was preparing to sing High Mass.

On May 3, in the following year [1756], died there Thomas Brooke, chosen Archdeacon of ——, March 16, 1729.

MANN, THEODORE AUGUSTUS, commonly called Abbé Mann, was born about the year 1735. It is said that at an early part of his life he went into Spain, and served there in a military capacity. His good sense and orderly conduct attracted the notice of General Wall, the Minister, who honoured him with particular marks of his favour and friendship. But, preferring study and retirement to a military life, at the age of 25, or thereabouts, he entered among the English Carthusians, at Newport, and sometime after was chosen Superior of the House. His health was here much impaired, and he had to struggle with a complication of bodily sufferings, which obliged him to quit the unwholesome situation. When the Emperor Joseph began his reformation in the Netherlands, the convent of Newport was one of those which were dissolved. On quitting Newport, Mr. Mann removed to Brussels, where his merits soon became known and raised him to stations both of honour and emolument. He was made a Canon of Courtrai, and Secretary first and then President, if I mistake not, of the Imperial Academy of Science at Brussels. In 1777, he came over from Flanders as a sort of Agent of Prince Charles of Lorraine, Governor of the Netherlands, and presented to the Royal Society and to that of Antiquaries, the *Mémoires de l'Academie Impériale et Royale des Sciences et des Belles Lettres de Bruxelles*, and from that time he became a frequent correspondent in the *Gentleman's Magazine*. (See *Gentleman's Magazine* for 1787, p. 461). In 1793, he was admitted an honorary member of the Society of Antiquaries. I do not find at what period of his life he became a Catholic, but probably it was while he lived in Spain. When the French Revolution broke out, it produced such a sensation in Brussels that he says in a letter to Mr. Thickness, "he could liken it to nothing more aptly than to a violent sea, breaking in and over-passing all its boundaries, produced by a storm, or an earthquake at a distance, in the sea." As the storm approached, the Abbé found himself obliged to retire, and in 1797 I find him at Lautmortitz, in Bohemia. In 1814, Mr. Nichols, of the *Gentleman's Magazine*, had not heard of his death.

His works are : 1. *Abrégé de l'histoire de la Ville de Bruxelles, et de ses environs.* 1788, 2 vol., 8vo. 2. *Recueil des Mémoires Académiques, de M. L'Abbé Mann.* 1792, 8vo. 3. *Mémoires sur les grandes Gelées et leurs Effets.* Gand. 1792, 8vo. 4. *Description of what is called a Roman Camp in Westphalia, in the " Archæologia."* Vol. 13, p. 16, with a plate. 5. *A short chronological account of the Religious establishments made by English Catholics on the Continent. Ibid.*, pages 251. " I do not reckon him an able Divine," says Mr. Thomas Eyre, " however great abilities he is otherwise possessed of." (*Letter at Ushaw.*)

MANNING, JOHN, was son of John Manning and his wife, Elizabeth Usher, both Catholics. He was born in London, Nov. 4, 1731, and in Nov., 1749, was received into the College at Rome by the Rector, Father Christopher Maire, by order of Cardinal Lante, the Protector. In March, 1756, he was ordained Priest, and left the College the May following. He was a Missionary at Derby, where he succeeded the unfortunate Mr. Taprell, about 1773. When Mr. Slaughter died at Longford, near Newport, Salop, in 1781, Mr. Manning succeeded him. He died in July, 1783.

MANNING, ROBERT, studied at Douay. For some time was Professor of Humanity, and after teaching Philosophy for three years he went to Paris to take his degrees. But when it was discovered that his parents were not English, nor he himself born in England, which the rules required for admission into St. Gregory's Seminary, he was remanded, and soon after came on the Mission, where he lived many years in the family of Lord Petre, in Essex ; and where, besides the exercise of his functions, he spent his time in publishing several books of controversy, much esteemed by the learned, especially on account of his easy and flowing style ; but more so for the solidity of arguments, and Christian manner of writing. He died in Essex, March 4. 1730, (O.S.).

His works are : 1. *Moral Entertainments.* 3 vol., 8vo. Dedicated to Lord Petre, Baron of Writtle. 2. *Modern Controversy ; or, A plain and rational account of the Catholic Faith.* In 3 parts, 8vo, 1720. 3. *England's Conversion and Reformation Compared.* 8vo, 1725. 4. *A Single Combat ; or, A Personal Dispute between Mr. Trapp and his Anonymous Antagonist.* 5. *The Roman Catholic Religion ; or, Popery shown to be the very Religion of the Bible, and consentient with Antiquity,* in reply to *An Answer to " England's Conversion and Reformation Compared."* Published in 1728. MS. at Ushaw. 6. *The Shortest Way to End Disputes about Religion.* 7. *The Case stated between the Church of Rome and the Church of England.* 2 vols., 1721.

MANNOCK, FRANCIS, S.J., nephew of John Mannock, O.S.B. He was third son of Sir William Mannock, Bart., by his wife, Ursula, daughter of Henry Neville, *alias* Smith, son of Sir Thomas Nevill, of Holt. He [Francis] lived many years at Swinnerton, and, in 1739, undertook the spiritual charge of the Bar Convent, York ; and, after more than 48 years' labour in the vineyard, died there in 1748. Mr. Mannock was a very zealous and laborious Missionary ; yet his zeal for orthodoxy seems sometimes to have led him so far as to accuse— unintentionally, I have no doubt—of Jansenism several who were not guilty of it. Among others, there was Mr. Rivers, a clergyman of York, afterwards Lord Rivers. He collected from the praxis and conversation, as he says, *plurium*, seventy-seven propositions which he wished Bishop Stonor and Bishop Pritchard to send to Rome, that they might be condemned. They regarded the ignorance of the mysteries of Religion, the character of the Sacrament of Penance, the profanation of the Sunday, and the misapplication of the words of Scripture ; and the misconstruction put on the decrees of the Church, and in particular the censure passed on sixty-five propositions by Innocent XI.* The Bishops answered that all the propositions were not censurable ; that *pleræque*

---

* See them in the *Records of Jansenism*, etc

had already been condemned ; that *pleræque* of them were nowhere to be met with in print, and were unworthy of notice ; and that the accusations were too vague and general, and no one knew when or by whom they were advanced, as they were not fathered on any one. He succeeded better, however, with Bishop Williams, who, without entering into the merits or demerits of the propositions, gave a general approbation of the measure in June, 1738, and in the following year transmitted them to the Internuncio at Brussels, with such a letter as Mr. Mannock himself penned, at the desire of the Bishop, to accompany them.* What became of them afterwards I am unable to say, but I do not find that they were ever condemned. The seventy-seventh proposition—*Modus audiendi Missam utilissimus Rusticis qui legere non possunt, est recitare Rosarium B. M. Virginis*—was not sent to Rome.

MANNOCK, SIR GEORGE, S.J., son of Sir Francis Mannock, of Gifford's Hall, Suffolk, and Frances, his wife, daughter and heir of George Yates, of North Waltham. Born July 1, 1723. On Sept. 7, 1741, he entered the novitiate of the Jesuits and became a professed Father in 1759. On May 6, 1787, he was killed by the overturning of the Mail, at Dartford, while he was on his way to the Continent, where he wished to end his days.

MANNOCK, JOHN ANSELM, O.S.B., the fourth son of Sir Francis Mannock, of Gifford's Hall, Suffolk, Bart., by his wife, Mary, daughter of Sir George Heneage, of Hainton, Lincolnshire, Knight. It is related that he accidentally caused the death of his elder brother at Douay by the fall, or throw, from his window of one of the cannon balls fired into the town by Marlborough, during the siege in 1710. He then became a Benedictine. He lived nearly fifty years at Foxcoat, Warwickshire, whence he went to Kelvedon Hall, in Essex, the seat of John Wright, Esq., where he died, Nov. 30, 1764.

He wrote : 1, *The Poor Man's Catechism.* Published by Rev. George Bishop. 2. *The Poor Man's Controversy.* 3. *The Poor Man's Companion, or some Moral Collections upon the Commandments.* In 3 books : vol. 1, 4to of 545 pages ; vol. 2, on the Creed, Our Father, and Sacraments, in 3 books, pp. 624 (MS. at Downside.)

MEMORANDUM : I have printed the substance of this memoir of John A. Mannock in an Introduction to Dolman's new edition of the *Poor Man's Catechism*, June, 1848. [*MS. note by Canon Tierney.*]

MANNOCK, WILLIAM, son of William Mannock and his wife, Ursula [Nevill], was a native of Norfolk (or Suffolk : was he not related to the Mannocks of Gifford Hall ?). At the age of 16 he was admitted into the English College at Rome, Oct. 24, 1693, by order of Cardinal Howard. Having completed his course of Divinity, and before he attained the age required for the Priesthood, he left the College, March 19, 1700, and proceeded to Paris, and thence to Douay ; and after he had received Holy Orders at Liège, he returned to England, with the best of characters from his Superiors at Rome. He died at Windsor, March 9, 1748-9.

MANSELL, JOHN, S.J., was born January 8, 1709 ; entered his noviceship, Sept. 7, 1728, and became a professed Father in 1746. He lived many years at Lytham Hall, the seat of —— Clifton, Esq.

MANSFIELD, ROBERT, S.J. He succeeded Father Postgate as Rector of the English College in Rome, the end of 1698, or beginning of 1699. He built the new College and Sodality [chapel]. Many complaints being made against him by the Bishops, Clergy, and students (which see in Bishop W——'s Memorial), the Pope appointed Cardinal Francis Barberini to visit the College. He began his visitation, April 23, 1702.

MARKHAM, GEORGE, of Claxby, co. Lincoln, married, May 18, 1751, Mary, daughter of Brian Salvin, of Croxdale, co. Durham, Esq. He died, Feb. 22, 1760.

---

* See the letter and propositions in the Ushaw Collections.

MARMADUKE, [JAMES], an ingenious but not very fortunate bookseller in London. He wrote : 1. *Curious Remarks on the Douay Bible and on Dr. Challoner's revision of it*, MS. 2. *Languet's " Confidence in the Mercy of God."* Translated from the French by Mr. Marmaduke, who translated other works, published by himself.

MARSH, JOHN. He went to St. Omers and thence to Valladolid, where he was ordained Priest. He returned to England about the year 1660, and lived first in the South ; but, being banished London by Dangerfield, one of Oates's accomplices, he stayed sometime in Lancashire, and " then humbly betook himself to the most desolate and laborious place in Yorkshire, that is, to assist a great multitude of poor in the Moors, where, at one Easter, he had near 900 Communicants, and these scattered at great distances. His abode was chiefly at Egton-Bridge. He was a man of excellent wit, parts, and zeal." One John Marsh, died Feb. 28, 1732 (O.S.). They can hardly be the same person, as these dates would make John Marsh about 97. (*Chapter Papers.*)

MARTIN JOHN, was educated at Douay, and lived many years at Gosport, where he died, Feb. 14, 1788. He was a zealous and laborious Missionary.

MARTIN, THOMAS, *vere* WHITTAKER, son of Thomas Whittaker and Lucy Cooper, was born in London, Jan. 6, 1702. Was converted to the Catholic Faith by Father Peter Williams, S.J., and was sent to Rome in 1726. He was ordained Priest by Benedict XIII., March 13, 1729,, and left the College, May 10, 1730, to be Confessor to the Benedictine nuns at Brussels, after which he was placed at Woolhampton, Berks., where he lived about thirty years, and died there, June 22, 1778. Mr. Martin was a member of the Chapter.

MARTYN, FRANCIS. See *London and Dublin Orthodox Journal*, VII., 63.

MASON, THOMAS, O.S.B., was born in Lancashire of Catholic parents. In 1739 he went to Rome and was received into the College by Father Henry Sheldon, the Rector, at the age of 20. On Dec. 10, in 1741, he left the College to go to Lambspring, and there became a Benedictine.

MASSEY, WILLIAM, of Puddington, co. Chester, eldest son of Edward Massey by his wife, Alice, daughter of Richard Braithwait, of Barneside, co. Westmoreland, was born May 15, 1658. He was a zealous Catholic and warmly attached to the Stuart family while upon the throne, and after the Revolution. Having given his allegiance to James II. he did not conceive that anyone but the Prince who had received it could release him from the obligation thereby contracted. In 1715 he joined in that attempt, and is traditionally said to have fled home after the Battle of Preston, and to have effected his escape to Wirrall, in Cheshire, by a desperate attempt at swimming his horse over the Mersey below Hooton. He was seized at Puddington Hall and imprisoned in the Castle of Chester, and died shortly after, and was buried at Burton, Feb. 15, 1716-7 (O.S.). (Ormerod's *History of Cheshire*, II., 308.)

MASSEY, ——, succeeded Mr. Meynell as Confessor to the nuns of the Monastery of Bethlehem, in the suburbs of Paris, in 1696, and continued there till his death, on Aug. 11, 1715.

MASSEY, THOMAS, [*vere* STANLEY], S.J., of Puddington, was fourth son of Sir William Stanley, of Hooton, Bart., and Catherine Eyre. Born in 1715, and baptised Jan. 5, when Mr. Massey, of Puddington, stood godfather to him, and [Mr. Massey] dying without issue, he succeeded to his estates pursuant to his will, dated Feb. 6 of that year, and assumed the name of Massey.

MATHER, JAMES, was son of John Mather and his wife, Elizabeth Flint, of Newcastle-upon-Tyne. After he became a Catholic he studied Philosophy and Divinity in Paris ; and, after he had lived three years in the Community of the Curate of St. Sulpice, at the age of 26 was admitted into St. Gregory's, on one of the funds of the Seminary, and was ordained, June 5, 1746. After being an assistant to Dr. Holden in the temporal affairs of the Seminary for three years, and not being qualified to take degrees, he left the Seminary in Dec., 1747, to live in the parish of St. Margaret, and was curate of Menil, a small village near the town, and Priest of St. Germain in 1774, but on condition that he should repair to the English Mission whenever required so to do by the Superior of the Seminary. (*St. Gregory's Register.*)

MATTINGLEY, JOHN, S.J., was born in Maryland, Jan. 25, 1745. He studied in the College at Valladolid, but left it in 1766, and entered his Noviciate the same year. At the time of the suppression of the Society in 1773 he was Minister in the English College. At that time an annual pension was settled on him, and the Rector, Father Hothersall, and Father Porter, the Confessor, but in lieu of it Mr. Mattingley accepted a sum of money in hand, and came over to England, where he became tutor to some young gentlemen, and travelled with them. He was much respected and beloved, and died [Nov. 23, 1807].

MAUDESLEY or MOSELEY, WILLIAM, was a native of Lancashire. He studied at Lisbon, and took the College oath and gown July 12, 1693. Having received Priest's orders, he came on the Mission on Jan. 7, 1698. In 1710 he was recalled by his Superior to teach Philosophy and to be Confessarius, and in the following year was made Procurator. He also taught Divinity for some time, and was at last made Vice-President of the College, in Sept., 1716. In 1733 he left Lisbon to go to Goa, but died in his passage. (*Lisbon Register.*)

MAURICE, JAMES [*vere* PLUMMERDEN, [ROBERT], whose true name was Robert Plummerden, was son of Robert and Mary Plummerden, and born in London about 1664. At the age of nineteen was admitted into the College at Rome, then under Father William Morgan, by order of Cardinal Howard, Oct. 10, 1683. He was ordained at St. John Lateran's, June 12, 1688, and left the College May 30, 1690, and was appointed Confessor to the nuns, I think, Rue de Charenton, Paris. He died in 1751. In the Obituary he is called Robert Maurice Plummerden. He wrote *Additional Notes to Mr. Andrew Giffard's Letter of July* 7, 1710, detailing the complaints of the Clergy against the Padri, and assisted Dodd. Mr. Henry Howard (Bishop) says he was a "mighty good well-meaning man, and sincerely affected to the Clergy." (*Diary of Roman College.*)

MAXWELL, JOHN, S.J., born Jan. 8, 1709, entered his noviceship Sept. 7, 1728, and became a professed Father 1746. He lived many years at Lytham Hall, the seat of —— Clifton, Esq.

MAXWELL, WILLIAM, 5th EARL OF NITHSDALE.—He engaged in the rebellion of 1715, and was taken at Preston and sent to the Tower. He was tried in January following, and condemned to be beheaded, but made his escape, Feb. 23, 1715/6, the night before his execution, and got beyond seas, and died at Rome in 1744. His son William, Lord Maxwell, who would have succeeded to the earldom, had it not been forfeited, left a daughter and heiress, Lady Winifred, who married William Constable, of Everingham, Co. York.

MAY, JOHN, was born about 1622. He went first to St. Omers, and then to Valladolid, whence he returned to England about 1652. In 1690 he was about seventy years of age, and was then the oldest missionary in Yorkshire, where he resided, usually with Philip Langdale, Esq., at Houghton in the Woolds, but "was always an itinerant—some of his places were near 30 miles from the other, but most of his charge was within the East Riding. He was a learned and virtuous priest." (*Chapter Records.*)

MAYES, LAURENCE, son of Nicholas Mayes, of Freerage, near Yarm, in Yorkshire; at the age of fourteen he was sent to Douay, in July, 1687; was ordained Priest April 6, 1697, and some time after was made the Second Professor of Divinity; Dr. Hawarden was First Professor. In 1706 he was appointed agent to the Bishops in Rome, and left the College August 12 to go to Paris, where he remained till the middle of September. He there received instructions from Dr. Betham, who accompanied him to St. Germain's, and introduced him to the King and Queen. In his audience, the King (James III.)

insisted that, whenever the Clergy proposed anyone to Rome for Bishops, he should also be informed of it, this being the least they could do, though he did not pretend to the nomination of VV.A. in England. Learning from Dr. Betham, there present, that Dr. Witham, the former agent, had a letter of recommendation to the Pope, he gave one also to Mr. Mayes. After a dangerous voyage by sea, he arrived at Rome Oct. 25, and after two or three days waited on Cardinal Caprara, the Protector, who procured him an audience of the Pope, when he presented the letter of the King, and also that of Dr. Betham. In this, by mistake, Dr. Betham used the words *Sanctitas Tua*, instead of *Vestra*, which rendered the letter less pleasing and the answer to it less acceptable to Dr. Betham, "who wrote afterwards to Mr. Mayes to know what passed in this audience, for the answer to his letter, he said, seemed very cold." "Cardinal Caprara took Mr. Mayes to the English College, Jan. 23, 1707, and having called the students, ordered all the Superiors out of the room, and made Mr. Mayes sit down by him to hear their grievances, a thing the Jesuits highly resented and complained of to the Court of St. Germains, as if the Cardinal had erected a Clergy-tribunal over their heads, in the very College as the Cardinal himself, says Mr. Mayes, often took notice to him afterwards, and how angry the Jesuits were on this occasion" (*Mr. Mayes' Agency*, p. 10). Speaking of his agency, Mr. Mayes says : "It may be thought that some of the Memorials he presented are too low and cringing ; a right judgment of this depends wholly upon a due regard and attention to time and circumstances, but we must consider, (1) our obligations to the Holy See ; (2) our dependency upon it ; (3) the almost invincible prejudices of this Court at the time in cases of suspicion or accusation about doctrinal matters, as will appear by the history of the times ; in fine, the credit and industry of our enemies, and the authority of those persons who abetted and favoured them. We are apt to forget the dangers and terrors of a storm when the weather is cleared up, and we are got safe on shore " (*Introduction*, p. 11).

On the 12th of July, 1727, Mr. Mayes was appointed Preceptor to his R.H. the Prince of Wales, as he was called, by a patent signed *William Ellis*, and had apartments allotted to him in the Palace. In 1721 he had been made a Protonotarius Apostolicus, and for that purpose read the Profession of Faith before Monsignor Richard Howard, Canon of St. Peter's, June 2, 1721. He died in Rome Aug. 23, 1749, and was buried in the church belonging to the English College. Mr. Mayes was an intelligent and active agent for the Clergy, and was highly respected by all who knew him. He has left in MS. *The Clergy Agency from* 1706, in three vols; a treatise in Latin, *De Juramentis*, in 1720. It was presented to every Cardinal and foreign Ambassador in Rome ; the English Ministry were acquainted with the author.

MAYLAN, JOSEPH, was educated at St. Omers and Valladolid. He died in London, February 25, 1765.

MEDCALFE [or METCALFE, *alias* LAYTON *vere* LEIGH, PHILIP], S.J.— He was chosen Provincial of his Brethren about 1704. He was the gentleman to whom his successor, Father Sabran, addressed a letter in 170— from Liège, in Flanders, ordering him "to come over to him, for that he had a place of preferment to bestow upon him, and to bring all the accusations he could against the Clergy." This place of preferment the Clergy understood to be the Presidentship of Douay College, and that accusations were to be brought against themselves, designated by the letters Cl. "Mr. Medcalfe," says Mr. Andrew Giffard (letter to Dr. Paston, of July 7, 1710, original at Ushaw), "owned the letter to me, and complained of the injustice done him by Mrs. Thornton, who opened his letter, and when I urged to him that he was to gather and bring accusations against the Clergy, he muttered and knew not what to say, but that these accusations were against their own people. And upon another occasion, being pressed upon the same account, he answered that ' *the Jesuits were sometimes* called Clergy.' Hereupon," says Mr. Giffard (to Mr. Dicconson, original at Ushaw), " Mr. Medcalfe came up to London, endeavoured to get a pass ; actually to my knowledge money was paid to procure a pass to Flanders, for which he waited here above two months. But this being at the time of the Scotch invasion, no pass could be got ; so by that time their expectation of the College being defeated, Mr. Medcalfe stopped his journey.   Mr. Richard Levison and others of the Society waited here in town to go over with Mr. Medcalfe, upon the same design ; of which Mr. Levison, being reproached by Mr. Silliard, an auntient Clergyman, concerning the business and injustice of the design upon which he was going, the said Mr. Levison did not denie the thing, but only excused himself, that he must obey his Superior's orders."   What truth there may be in this relation I am unable to say.   I give it as I find it in Mr. Giffard's letter to Mr. Dicconson, then at Douay (original at Ushaw, and in Ushaw Collection).

Mr. Alban Butler, in the life of St. Winifred, Nov. 3, says that Father Metcalf, S.J., published in 1712 the life of St. Winifred, translated by Father Alford, *alias* Griffith, with some alterations, and additional late miracles.

MELLING, EDWARD, was born of Catholic and respectable parents in Lancashire.   His mother was sister to Mr. Christopher Tootell, so that he was first cousin to Dodd, whose true name was Hugo Tootell, and cousin also to Mr. John Shepherd, Dean of the Chapter, who died in 1761.   He studied at Douay, and, on the death of his uncle Christopher Tootell, in 1727, he seems to have succeeded him at Fernyhalgh, near Preston.   "Tradition," says Dr. Gradwell, "still speaks with affection of the learning, the labours, the piety and charity of Messieurs Tootell and Melling, the Pastors of Fernyhalgh." Mr. Melling died April 16, 1733.

MELLING, JOHN, was brother of Edward Melling.   He was sent to Douay, where it was remarked that his piety kept pace with his progress in his studies, particularly in Philosophy and Divinity.   For which reason he was judged a proper person to assist Mr. Gilbert Haydocke in the spiritual direction of the English nuns of St. Monica, in Louvain, in 1716.   "It is difficult to say with what diligence and discretion, and with what edification and satisfaction, of all who knew him, he complied with the duties of his situation, and of that of an exemplary Priest and thorough good man for the space of 29 years.   He died much lamented on the 10th of May, 1745 (N.S.) in the 58th year of his age, and 32nd of his priesthood, after an illness of three days.   Mr. Melling was much admired for his mildness, humility, and simplicity of manners ; for his modesty and gravity joined to a pleasing cheerfulness in conversation, and more particularly for that unaffected piety and strong sense of religion with which he daily celebrated the divine mysteries, and for which he was held by all in the greatest estimation."   (*Printed Obituary Letter.*)

MEREDITH [RICHARD], S.J.—He lived at Lincoln.   Was a very religious man, and esteemed a man of learning.   He died about 1760.

METCALF, JOHN. *alias* COLLINGWOOD, son of John and Eleonora Metcalf, of North Kelsey, in Lincolnshire.   At the age of 20 he was admitted into the English College at Rome by order of Cardinal Howard, under the administration of Father William Morgan.   He was ordained April 20, 1687, and left the College June 1, 1690, with this character : "*optime se in Collegio gessit.*" On Oct 6, 1704, he was chosen a member of the Chapter, and died in 1729.

METCALFE, JOSEPH, *alias* EGLESFIELD, born in Yorkshire, was sent to Douay.   On his return his residence was always at Nutt Hill, in Holderness, first with his parents, and after their death with his eldest brother's widow, but was principally supported by Mr. Henry Constable and his sister—uncle and aunt to Lord Dunbar.   "He was," says a contemporary who knew him well, "a virtuous and able man, exceeding prudent, and very active.   So that in all good respects I scarce know his fellow."   He died March 28, 1729. (*Chapter Records.*)

METHAM, ANTHONY, Priest, died at Douay, Dec. 7, 1694 (N.S.).   By his will, dated Feb. 16, 1693, he left to Mr. Francis Hodgson £600 to be disposed of by him in charities for the relief of the poor Catholics in Yorkshire and the Bishoprick.

METHAM, JAMES, defended Logic May 29, 1705, under Laurence Rigby. Being ordained Priest, he came on the Mission, and before he went to Douay he had a small school at Thory [*sic* ? Thorp], about six or seven miles from Cliff, and in 1692 Bishop Smith sent Mr. —— Hildreth to succeed him, probably on his leaving to go to Douay.

MEYNELL, ANTHONY, of a good family in Yorkshire. After his ordination at Douay he came on the Mission in 1676. In 1678 he accompanied Mr. George Witham to S. Gregory's, at Paris, and Jan. 1., 1686, they entered their license together, and March 4, 1687, he took the Doctor's cap, and made his "Resumpt" Sept. 22, 1696. When Dr. Betham was called over to England in 1685, and was made one of the King's Preachers in Ordinary, he left the economy of the Seminary to Mr. Meynell, and upon his death succeeded him as President of the Seminary. "After having given," says the Seminary Register, "a most wonderful example of patience and fervour during a long and painful sickness, and undergone many dolorous operations for an imposthume in his breast, to the astonishment of all that were about him, happily departed this life on Sept. 18, 1698, in a manner suitable to the holy and penitential life which he had led for many years in the Seminary." He was buried in St. Stephen's Church before Our Lady's altar. In the preface to *The Poor Man's Manual* of 1705, the writer says : " Dr. Meynell's solid learning and exemplary piety drew a veneration from all that had the happiness to be acquainted with him."

MEYNELL, JAMES, of Meynells of Yarm. He was brother to Mrs. Scroope and to Mrs. Witham's father. He studied at Douay. He lived many years at Aldborough, Yorkshire, with his brother, if not also with his father, and died there before 1731.

MEYNELL, THOMAS, S.J., of the same family with James, and probably his nephew. He was born Oct. 29, 1737. Entered his noviciate Sept. 7, 1756, and became a professed Father in 1772. He lived in London. While at Dr. Nicholl's he fell from his chair and died suddenly.

MEYNELL, WILLIAM, S.J., born May 3, 1744. Entered his noviciate Sept. 7, 1761.

MILFORD, *or* MITFORD, JAMES, was nephew to Roger Milford. He studied at Douay, probably on the fund established by his uncle, and on his coming to England, succeeded Mr. Edesford at Thropton, Northumberland. He had the character from one of his contemporaries of being " a laborious missionary and a very pious, inoffensive man, and was much esteemed by all." He died at Thropton, March 12, 1750. Mr. Milford was uncle or grand-uncle to the present Lord Reddesdale, whose family name is Mitford.

MIDFORD, ROGER [*or* MITFORD]. He was tutor and Chaplain to Francis, Earl of Derwentwater, and travelled with him to Rome. " It was here," says Dodd, in the MS. of his history, " that the original of Father Hitchcock's letter (Dodd, iii, 392) fell into Mr. Midford's hands." Dodd adds " that Father Hitchcock owned himself to be the writer of this letter, when he was charged with it, by the President of Douay College." In the MS. History it is signed *Francis William Hitchcock.* In the reign of James II., Mr. Midford was appointed by Bishop Smith, G.V. for Durham and Northumberland. He died at Dilston, the seat of his patron, the Earl of Derwentwater, on May 25, 1697, and was buried in Corbridge Church. He was not unmindful of his Alma Mater, Douay College, where he established a fund for the education of a student, and another for a Priest in the parish of Rothbury ; nor of the poor Fathers at Thropton-upon-Coquet. In his charities he was much assisted by a Mrs. Clare Ord, a relation of the Radcliffe family.

MILLER, JOHN. For many years he had the charge of the Catholics in and about Wolverhampton. He was in great esteem among his brethren, and was joint administrator of "the Common Purse" with Mr. Coyney, till disabled by a stroke of the palsy. In 1705 he underwent an operation for the stone, in London, which he did not long survive.

MILNER, RIGHT REV. DR. JOHN, whose family name was Miller, the
son of Joseph and Helen Miller, was born in London in 1752. His education
commenced at Sedgley Park and Edgbaston, from whence he removed to
Douay to finish his studies. In 1777 he was ordained Priest, and immediately
returned to London, where he remained some time in Gray's Inn. In 1779 he
quitted the metropolis to assist the French prisoners at Winchester, amongst
whom a malignant fever had broken out ; and towards the close of the same
year was appointed Pastor to the Catholic Chapel in that city. Here his attachment to the study of Ancient Ecclesiastical Architecture led him to an attentive
observation of the venerable remains of Catholic Antiquity with which
Winchester abounds. The learning and skill he displayed in that science procured for him the honour of an admission as a Fellow into the Royal Antiquarian
Society, on March 8, 1790, and his subsequent researches and communications
to the Society have greatly enriched its *Archæologia.*

In 1798 he published his *History, Civil and Ecclesiastical, and Survey of the
Antiquities of Winchester.* This work provoked the publication of the *Reflections
on Popery,* by Dr. Sturges, Prebendary of Winchester Cathedral, the credit of
whose religion he (Dr. Sturges') considered as impaired, in proportion as the
ancient glories of Catholicity and its venerable institutions were exalted. In
reply, Dr. Milner published those immortal *Letters to a Prebendary,* which have
so intimate a connection with his last and greatest work, either of which is
sufficient to rank him amongst the most learned, ingenious, and able defenders
of the Catholic Faith.

From the dawn of that period when, thanks to the paternal auspices of our
late Most Gracious and Venerable Sovereign, the Catholics of this Empire began
to be relieved from the oppressive weight of that barbarous, unjust, and penal
code, borne for centuries by their fathers, Dr. Milner was ever alert to repel
the aggression of the enemies of the Catholic Faith, or to smooth all obstacles
to Catholic emancipation, when the over-eagerness of its friends endangered
its safety and independence. Once, however, assenting to an ill-concerted
measure of conciliation with statesmen, who, abusing his confidence in their
integrity, artfully wrested it into a consent on his part to a royal *veto,* which
his faithful soul ever abhorred. From thence, on this topic, he displayed an
impetuosity which rendered him impatient and suspicious even of those who
were his equals in dignity and fidelity ; whilst their prudence, which is the first
and the guardian of the cardinal virtues, was thus occasionally superior to his
own. It is said that there are specks on the sun ; no one will take offence at a
speck on the halo of the wise and good, but such as vainly pretend that absolute
perfection is attainable by man.

But if, on the other hand, the wisdom of Dr. Milner failed in duly appreciating
in his brethren a becoming moderation and management, on the other hand, a
seeming toleration of, and inattention to, the progress of Radicalism, excited
unwisely the doubts of some who knew him only by the *public* expression of his
sentiments, and the malevolent strictures of others who hated him because they
hated his religion. Happily his admirable and well-timed Pastoral Letter to
his Clergy in 1819 (see *Catholic Spectator* for Jan. 1823) placed his political
principles in their just point of view. In that Pastoral he exposes the views of
the "professed Reformers," warns his flock against "the spreading infection
of turbulency and revolution," and with his native force inculcates the wisdom
and duty of subordination, and the "close alliance there is between Revolution
and Infidelity."

On the death of Bishop Stapleton, Dr. Milner was appointed to succeed him
as Vicar Apostolic in the Midland district, with the title of Bishop of Castabala.
Impressed with a due sense of the awful duties of the Episcopacy, he for some
time refused to consent to that dignity, but was at length consecrated on
May 22, 1803, in his own beautiful chapel at Winchester, of which he was the
architect. The consecration was performed by Bishop Douglass, then
V.A., L.D., assisted by Bishops Gibson and Sharrock, and by Bishop Poynter,
Coadjutor of the London District. The consecration sermon was delivered by
the late Rev. Thomas White, who throughout life was among the most esteemed

and the most intimate of our Prelate's literary confidants. This pious and accomplished scholar took his text from Matt. xvi., 18, "Thou art Peter," etc., a text in our Prelate's regard seemingly predictive, as it ever was the inspiring and appropriate motto of his great ecclesiastical labours.

In the years 1807 and 1808, Dr. Milner visited Ireland, to enable him to form, from personal observations and intercourse, his opinion on the veracity of the charges brought against the Catholics of that country, as he himself says in his preface to the work which was the result of these researches, and has added greatly to his literary name, viz., *An Inquiry into Certain Vulgar Opinions concerning the Catholic Inhabitants and the Antiquities of Ireland.* At this period he was appointed Agent in England to the Irish Catholic Hierarchy. His solicitude for the interests of religion in both countries impelled him to visit Rome in 1814, where he remained for about a twelvemonth, during which time he was frequently admitted to an audience of H.H. Pope Pius VII., whose chair he had so victoriously defended against the Blanchardists, and received from that illustrious Pontiff the most valuable marks of the approbation of his ecclesiastical services. Notwithstanding the most faithful and diligent discharge of the laborious duties of the Episcopacy in so widely extended a district, he did not remit, but rather increased, as occasion seemed to require, his controversial labours, which at length were crowned by the greatest of his works, *The End of Religious Controversy,* first published in 1818. Of this work he has often said in our hearing, that it is the favourite and only spontaneous production of his mind, all his other works being written on the spur of the occasion. His *Vindication of the End of Controversy, from the Exception of Dr. Burgess and the Rev. Richard Grier,* was published in 1822. It embraces such felicitous illustratious and after thoughts as confer on the vindicating and the vindicated work the last perfection.

At length that period was approaching which was to close the mortal career of the venerable Prelate. Early in the month of March, 1826, aware of his approaching dissolution, after having settled his worldly affairs, in which he included a bequest of £100 to be divided between the poor, and the poorest of his clergy, he entered a pious retreat, to prepare his passage to the mansions of eternity. On Maundy-Thursday he received the Holy Viaticum, and on the Saturday following the Extreme Unction, and finally, after a lingering illness, which he bore with exemplary fortitude, he resigned his soul into the hands of his Creator with a serenity that a holy and well-founded hope alone could inspire, on April 19, in the 74th year of his age, and the 23rd of his episcopacy. His venerable remains, agreeably to his own desire, were interred without pomp in the chapel at Wolverhampton on April 27, upon which occasion a solemn Dirge was performed by the Rt. Rev. Dr. Walsh, his successor. The funeral discourse was delivered by the Rev. F. Martyn, who took his text trom Wis. x., 10, etc. The name of Dr. Milner belongs to Ecclesiastical History ; it belongs especially to that of this empire, connected so honourably as it is with every event of ecclesiastical influence that has occurred for nearly half of the last century in the United Kingdom. R.I.P. (*Laity's Directory,* 1827, pp. 64-66).

"A.D. 1752 die 14 oct. Baptizatus fuit Joannes Miller, filius Josephi & Helenæ Miller, conjugum (Patrini fuerunt Jacobus Brown & Anna Marsland) a me.　　　　　　　　　　　　　　　　　　"Gul. Errington Miss Ap."
(*Extract of the Register in No. 4, Castle Street, Holborn*).

"In London," says Mr. Thomas Walsh, in 1778, "he acquired a great reputation by his preaching, zeal, and extensive charity, led a retired life, and never quitted his solitude (in Gray's Inn) but to be greatly serviceable to his neighbour."

Cardinal Litta, in a letter to Dr. Milner in 1817 or 1816, says, "S. Congregatio te maxime reprehendit . . . severe arguit," for writing as he did against Dr. Poynter, etc.

MILTON, SIR CHRISTOPHER, son of Sir John Milton, a brother to the poet. His grandfather and grandmother were zealous Catholics, but his father and his son John both conformed, while Christopher remained a Catholic, and in the Rebellion was a zealous partizan of Charles I. He was bred up to the law, and was promoted by James II. to be a Baron of the Exchequer in April, 1686, and on the 25th was knighted. He died at Ipswich, and was buried there at S. Nicholas's Church. (*See Chalmers*).

MOLINS, ——, Priest. He lived in Lancashire some years, and was accused of Jansenism by Father Mannock. He denied the charge *in toto*. (See *Records of Jansenism*, p. 123, and Mr. And. Giffard's letter to Mr. Dicconson *Ibid*).

MOLINS, FRANCIS, Priest, died in London, May 20, 1742, possibly the same. He was chosen a member of the Chapter, July, 1736.

MOLYNEUX, CARYL (MOLINEUX, *or* MULLINEUX), 6th Viscount Molyneux, son of William, 4th Viscount. On the death of his brother Richard without male issue he succeeded to his honours and estates. He died at Croxteth, November, 1745, and was buried at Sefton. He was succeeded in his title, etc., by his eldest son, Richard, 7th Viscount, who was a Jesuit and contemporary with Father Grey (Earl of Shrewsbury) and Father Dormer, Lord Dormer.

[Here and in what follows, Kirk has been misled by the peerages into making two persons of William Molyneux, S.J., the seventh Viscount. The true pedigree may be seen in Foley, *Records, S.J.*, vii., 515. The analysis is as follows : William, the 4th Viscount, had four sons, Richard, Caryll, William, S.J, and Thomas. The first three succeeded to the title as 5th, 6th, and 7th Viscounts. William, S.J., released the estate to Thomas, who had married Maria Errington, a Protestant ; and their son, Charles William, became 8th Viscount, then conformed, and was made Earl of Sefton.—J.H.P.]

MOLYNEUX, MATTHIAS, *or* MULLINEUX, son of Christr. Mullineux and Alicia How, his wife. He was a native of Shropshire, and born Aug. 18, 1689, O.S. At the age of 15 he went to Rome, and was admitted into the College by Father Postgate, Nov. 19, 1704, and was ordained Aug. 28, 1712. He lived many years at Sixhills in Lincolnshire, was G.V. before Mr. Busby, and had the character of being " a zealous and learned man." He left a foundation for the Priests in that part of Lincolnshire. A person of that name died at Stonor, Oxon, Feb. 1, 1759.

MOLYNEUX, RICHARD, 5th Viscount Molyneux. — Of Sephton, son of William, 4th Viscount, was born in 1678. He married Mary, eldest daughter of Lord Francis Brudenel, eldest son of Robert, Earl of Cardigan. He died Dec. 12, 1738, without male issue, at Little Oulton, Cheshire.

MOLYNEUX, RICHARD, S.J.—Eldest son of Caryl, Lord Molineux and elder brother of Robert Molineux. On the death of Caryl Molineux, 6th Visc. Molineux, in 1745, the title and estates came to him, but satisfied with an annuity, made over the estate to his brother [Thomas] Molineux (*Debrett's New Peerage*). He lived many years in an obscure and poor Mission House, called Scoles, near S. Helen's Lane, and died there in 1759. (Rev. C. Plowden's letter to Mr. Talbot). Elsewhere I find that —— Molineux, S.J., succeeded Mr. Smith, a secular Priest, at Marnhull, the seat of —— Hussey, Esq. He served that family 30 years, but left in 1760, or rather, 1761, because his age permitted him not to take upon himself the charge of the Congregation.

[Richard Molyneux, S.J., is here, by the error described above, identified with William Molyneux, S.J. According to Foley, *Records*, vii., 514-516, there were no less than seven Father Molyneux's contemporaries at this time, so the error is not very surprising. Richard, born in London in 1696, went to Marnhull about 1750, and died at Bonham in 1766. William was born in 1683 or 1685, and died in 1759. (*Ibid*.).—J. H. P.]

MOLYNEUX, WILLIAM, 4th Viscount Molyneux, of Sephton, Lancashire, was son of Caryl, 3rd Viscount Molyneux. He died March 8th, 1717, *æt.* 62, and was buried at Sephton. His estates in 1715 were (valued) £2,346 16s. 2d. p. an. (*Debrett's New Peerage*).

MOLYNEUX, WILLIAM, 8th Viscount Molyneux, was second son of Caryl, 6th Viscount. On the decease of his brother Richard, S.J., the 7th Viscount, who had made over to him the estates, reserving only an annuity for himself, he succeeded to the title. He died unmarried* in 1758, when the title, etc., devolved to his nephew, Charles William, eldest son of Thomas, third son of Caryl, Lord Molyneux, who was born Sept. 30, 1748, and conformed in 1768. On Nov. 30, 1771, he was created Earl of Sephton. [*But see under* " Molyneux Caryll and Richard."—J. H. P.]

MONTAGUE, ANTHONY BROWNE, 6th Viscount Montague, only son of Henry, 5th Viscount, and Barbara Walsingham. He married, July 28, 1720, Barbara, 3rd daughter of Sir John Webb, of Hathrop and Old Stock, and by her had two sons and one daughter, Mary, born in 1735, and married in 1761 to Sir Richard Bedingfield. Lord Montague died Apr. 23, 1767, and his daughter the 24th of Sept. following. [Collins, *Peerage*, 1779, vi., 22.]

MONTAGUE, ANTHONY, 7th Viscount, only surviving son of Anthony, 6th Visc., and Barbara Webb; born April 11, 1728. In 1765 he married Frances, daughter of Sir Herbert Mackworth, and the relict of Lord Halkerton, by whom he had a son born in 1769, and Elizabeth Mary, born in 1767, who married in 1794 William Stephen Poyntz. "This Lord became a Protestant," said Dr. Milner, "and as none of those reasons appeared which generally induced Catholics to embrace a downhill reformation, he was generally supposed to have acted from conscientious motives. In 178-, when the Emperor Joseph shut up many religious houses, Lord Montague endeavoured to purchase a church belonging to one of them, and opened it for Protestants. During this negotiation he was taken seriously ill, when his former religious sentiments and the grace of heaven operating on his mind, he sent for Abbé Mann, but he never having exercised that part of his ministry, Mr. Robert Plunkett, from the English Benedictines (rather, perhaps, Dominicans), was called in to his assistance. Lord Montague was reconciled to the Catholic Church, and, having summoned the whole of his family and others into his bed-chamber, he publicly declared to them, and requested that his declaration might be made known to the public, that nothing but libertinism both in theory and practice had induced him ever to abandon the faith of his ancestors, which he now professed, and in which profession he was about to end his days. This he continually repeated to his lady and domestics." He died in 1787. (See *Gent. Mag.* for 1787, pp. 578, 593, 654, 861-4, 948-955.)

MONTAGUE, FRANCIS BROWNE, 4th Viscount Montague.—He was lineally descended from Sir Antony Browne, Master of the Horse to Henry VIII. and one of his executors, whose son was created Viscount Montague by Queen Mary. Lord Francis was eldest surviving son of Francis, 3rd Viscount (who was a great sufferer for his loyalty to Charles I., and " his goods and papers, etc.," says Collins, " were plundered and burnt at his houses ") by his wife Elizabeth, 4th daughter of Henry Somerset, 1st Marquis of Worcester. He succeeded his father in 1682. In 1687 he was appointed Lord Lieutenant of Sussex by James II. He married Mary, daughter of William Herbert, Marquis of Powis, but had no issue by her. He died in 1708, and was buried at Midhurst.

MONTAGUE, GEORGE SAMUEL BROWNE, 8th Viscount Montague, only son of Anthony, 7th Visc., and Frances Mackworth. While on his travels he attempted, with his friend, Mr. Sedley Burdett, to pass the waterfalls of Schaufhausen. Though the magistrates ordered guards to be placed to prevent the rash attempt, they found means to elude every precaution. As they were on the point of stepping into a small, flat-bottomed punt, " Lord Montague's servant stopped short, and, as it were, instinctively seized his master by the collar, declaring for the moment he should forget the respect of the servant in the duty of the man. His Lordship, however, extricated himself,

---

* But my MS. says he married Bridget, daughter of Robert Lucy, of Charlecote, Co. Warwick.

at the expense of part of his collar and neckcloth, and pushed off immediately with his companion. They got over the first fall in safety and began to shout and wave their handkerchiefs in token of success. They then pushed down the second fall, by far more dangerous, from which time they have not been seen or heard of. It is supposed that the boat, hurried by the assistance of the cataract, jammed them between the rocks." At the time this rash attempt cost Lord Montague his life, his magnificent mansion at Cowdray was burnt down by an accidental fire. This happened in 1793. (See *Gent. Mag.* of that year.)

MONTAGUE, HENRY BROWNE, 5th Viscount Montague, only brother of Francis, 4th Viscount, and on his death, in 1708, succeeded to his honours and estates. He married Barbara, daughter of James Walsingham, of Chesterford, Essex, by whom he had one son and six daughters:—1, Mary, who died unmarried; 2, Elizabeth, a nun at Pontoise; 3, Barbara, wife of Ralph Salvin; 4, Catharine, wife of George Collingwood; 5, Anne, wife of Anthony Kempe of Slindon; and Henrietta, wife of Richard Harcourt, who lived at Boulogne in France. Lord Montague died at Epsom, Surrey, June 25, 1717.

MOORE, JOHN, educated at Douay. Was a Missionary in Lancashire about 50 years, and died at Chipping Lawn, June 26, 1783.

MORDAUNT, GEORGE. Was 5th son of John, first Viscount Mordaunt of Avalon, and Elizabeth, daughter and heiress of Thomas Carey, second son of Robert, Earl of Monmouth, and brother of Charles, 3rd Earl of Peterborough and Monmouth. His uncle Henry, the 2nd Earl of Peterborough, was a Catholic, and probably sent his nephew George abroad, where he entered among the English Benedictines. Dr. Milner tells us: "He was supposed to have expected to be made Bishop, and, being disappointed, conformed and married:—1st, Catharine, 4th daughter and heiress of Sir Thomas Spencer, of Yarnton, Bart.; 2ndly, Elizabeth, daughter of Sir John Dayly, of Chislehampton, Oxon., Bart., by whom he had Anna Maria, married to Dr. Jonathan Shipley, Bishop of S. Asaph; and 3rdly, Elizabeth, daughter of Lieutenant-Col. Collyer, by whom he had two daughters: Mary, wife of Valentine Maurice, Esq.; and Elizabeth, wife of Sir William Milner, Bart. George Mordaunt died July 28, 1728.

MORDAUNT, HENRY, 2nd Earl of Peterborough, son of John, 1st Earl, by his wife, [Elizabeth, daughter of William, third Lord Howard of Effingham.] He succeeded his father in 1644. In the time of James II. he became a Catholic (as his father had been till he conformed to the Established Church), for which reason the Commons resolved in 1689 that he and the Earl of Salisbury should be impeached of high treason "for departing from their allegiance and being reconciled to the Church of Rome." But the impeachment was dropt. He married Penelope, daughter of Barnabas, Earl of Thomond, Ireland, by whom he had two daughters, Elizabeth, and Mary, who married Henry, Duke of Norfolk, divorced in 1700. His Lordship died June 19, 1697. He was succeeded by his nephew, Charles, 3rd Earl, who was not a Catholic, and whose brother, George, became a Benedictine, but afterwards apostatized and married.

MORE, CHRISTOPHER, S.J.—Born May 10, 1729. Entered his Noviciate Sept. 7, 1746.

MORE, family of SIR THOMAS (d. 1535). His son, John More, married Cressacre. (From the Bamborough Register, co. York, where the family estate is, which was left by the late Thomas More to his sister, Mrs. Eyston).
—— More, the son and heir of Thomas More, was baptized in 1557.
—— More, daughter of Thomas More, baptized 1558.
Johanna More, daughter of ditto, Aug. 9, 1562.
Magdalene More, daughter of ditto, baptized July 25, 1563, died Jan. 7, 1566.
Catharine More, daughter of ditto, baptized Dec. 10, 1564.
Thomas More, son of ditto, baptized Jan. 13, 1565.

Henricus More, son of ditto, baptized March 15, 1566.
—— More, daughter of ditto, baptized Sept. 15, 1568.
Cressacre More, son of ditto, baptized July 6, 1572.
Mr. Everard More, buried May 2, 1620.
Darcinallus Michael Bartholomæus More, filius Basilii More, buried Sept. 5, 1680.
Mary More, daughter of Thomas and Sarah More, baptized June 29, 1689.
Gervas More, son of Thomas More, baptized Nov. 3, 1691.
John More, son of Thomas More, baptized July 5, 1694.
Mrs. Anne More,   of Basil More, buried April 5, 1694.
Basil More, buried Nov. 7, 1702.
Maria More, daughter of Cressacre More, baptized Sept. 8, 1703.
Mrs. Elizabeth More, married to Mr. Hodgshon, of Southwell, July 18, 1721.
Christopher Cressacre More, buried April 25, 1729.
Basil More, son of Thomas More, buried Jan. 11, 1730.
The celebrated picture of Sir Thomas More's family was in the Manor-house of Basill Legh (now pulled down), and is now, says the late Mr. Thomas More, at Burford Priory, the seat of John Lanthall, Esq. A similar, if not the same picture, is now at Bamburgh Hall.
—— More, married Catharine, daughter of John Giffard, of Black Ladies, and sister of Peter (who succeeded to the Chillington estate), John, Walter, and Mary Giffard, who married John Parry of Twissey.
Thomas More, S.J., son of the above.
—— Medcalf, daughter of ditto.
Mrs. More, of Bruges, daughter of ditto, Superior of Augustinian nuns at Bruges.
—— —— S.J., son of ditto.

MORE, THOMAS, S.J., was son of —— More, Esq., and his wife Catharine Giffard, sister of Peter Giffard of Chillington, Esq., and daughter of John Giffard of Black Ladies, Esq. He was born Sept. 19, 1722, entered his noviciate July 29, 1752, and became a professed Father Aug. 15, 1766. At the time of the suppression of the Society, he was Provincial, and Bishop Challoner made him his V.G., with regard to his Brethren of the Society. Mr. More was much respected and beloved, and died much regretted at Bath in May, 1795.

MORGAN, DAVID. Educated at Lisbon. He lived at Bedhampton, Havant, where he built the Chapel and Presbytery. Mr. (Bishop) Thomas Talbot succeeded him and paid the debt he had contracted by his buildings. Mr. Morgan died there Nov. 4, 1758.

MORGAN, JOHN *alias* GRIFFITH, was a native of Merionethshire. He studied at Douay, and being ordained, came on the Mission about 1690. He is called in the Chapter books " an Itinerant Missionary," but resided with Mr. John Parry, of Twysog, in Denbighshire. In 1694 he was chosen a Capitular, and died Jan. 27, 1718 (O.S.).

MORGAN, JOHN, studied at Douay. He lived as Chaplain to Lord Aston at Tixall. Mr. Fitzherbert, Archdeacon of Staffordshire, etc., says of him that " he was learned, and well able to give advice to his Brethren."

MORGAN, RICHARD, S.J., born Feb. 26, 1746. He studied in the Secular College at Valladolid, but when the Jesuits were ordered out of Spain, he left the College and entered into his noviciate, Sept. 7, 1766. He lived many years with Mr. Dunn, at Preston, much respected and beloved, and died there much regretted.

MORGAN, WILLIAM, S.J., was a native of Flintshire. At the age of 25 was received into the College at Rome, Oct. 16, 1648, by Father Joseph Simons, the Rector, and next year he took the College oath, by which he obliged himself to receive orders, and proceed to the Mission. But after staying three years, he left the College and entered his noviciate at S. Andrew's on the Quirinal Hill. In 1682 or 1683 he was appointed Rector of the College in Rome.

MORGAN, WILLIAM, *vere* PRICHARD, son of John and Joan Prichard, of Monmouthshire. At the age of 21 was admitted into the English College at Rome, Oct. 10, 1683. On April 20, 1687, was ordained Priest, and left the College, July 1, 1690, with a good character from his Superiors.

MORNINGTON, ANN TERESA.—She retired from an ample fortune, which she made over to ——, and entered among the nuns of the 3rd order of S. Francis in 1780. At the Revolution she came over to Winchester, and died at the Abbey House there, Nov. 25, 1794, *æt.* 58 ; Relig. 14.

MORNINGTONS, ——, of Sarnesfield. "The family is of long standing in Herefordshire, and originally from the village of Mornington, but about the time of Richard II. Mornington married the heiress of Sir Nicholas de Sarnesfield, Knight of the Garter, and they continued in that place till towards the end of last century, when the family ended in two daughters, who both died single : the last a nun at Bruges and afterwards at Winchester, where she died some years after her sister, having during her life disposed of her [? share to her] relation *John Webb*, who had also come into the property, and taken the name of Weston, by the will of Mr. Weston, of Sutton Place, by Guildford. One of his sons, it is understood, is to take the name of Mornington after his death. (*Mr. Thomas Berington MS.*)

MOSSEY, THOMAS, of Puddington, fourth son of Sir William Stanley, of Hootten, Bart., and Catharine Eyre. Born in 1715, and baptised Jan. 5, when William Mossey stood godfather to him, and dying without issue, he succeeded to his estates pursuant to his will, dated Feb. 6 of that year, and assumed the name of Mossey.

Is this the same that became a Jesuit ? But the Jesuit is said, in the list of Jesuits, to have been born June 7, 1716. Entered his noviceship Sept. 7, 1732, and was professed in 1750. He was uncle to Mr. Weld, of Lulworth, and died there.

MOSSEY, WILLIAM, of Puddington, co. Chester, was eldest son of Edward Mossey, by his wife Alice, daughter of Richard Braithwaite of Borneside, co. Westmoreland, and born May 15, 1658. He was a zealous Catholic, and warmly attached to the Stuart family while upon the throne and after the Revolution. Having given his alliance to Jamus II., he did not conceive that anyone but the Prince who had received it could release him from the obligation thereby contracted. In 1715 he joined in that attempt, and "is traditionally said to have fled home after the battle of Preston, and to have effected his escape to Wirral, in Cheshire, by a desperate attempt at swimming his horse over the Mersey below Hootton. He was seized at Puddington Hall and imprisoned in the castle of Chester, and died shortly after and was buried at Burton, Feb. 15, 1715 (O.S.). (Ormerod's *Hist. of Cheshire*, II., 308.)

MOSTYN, CHARLES BROWNE, third son of Sir Edward Mostyn, 5th Bart., by his wife, Barbara Browne, who died at Clifton, Feb. 8, 1810, aged 83. "She was a lady of great sense, and went thro' life with great honour to herself and family" (*Letter of Mr. C. Browne to me*). Mr. Browne was born Nov. 21, 1753, and was sent to St. Omers to study. He married for his first wife Elizabeth Witham, of Cliff, and for his second Ann Mary Tucker, daughter of John Tucker, late of Calais, who followed King James and was outlawed. He was descended from an old genteel family in the county of Kent. Mr. Browne is father to the present Dr. Mostyn, Bishop in the North, and grandfather to the present Lord Vaux. He is still living (1841) and is in his 89th year.

MOSTYN, SIR EDWARD, 5th Baronet, of Talacre, eldest son of Sir George and Teresa Towneley. He succeeded his father in 1745, and in June, 1748, married Barbara, daughter and heiress of Sir George Browne, of Kiddington, by Barbara, daughter and heiress of Edward Henry Lee, 1st Earl of Lichfield. By this lady he had three sons :—1, Sir Pyers ; 2, Charles, who died an infant ; and 3, Charles Browne, born Nov. 21, 1753. Sir Edward died in 1755, and was buried at Kiddington, March 15. He was succeeded by his eldest son, Sir Pyers, born Dec. 23, 1749, who married Barbara Slaughter, by whom he had a son, Edward, the present Bart., born April 10, 1785.

MOSTYN, SIR GEORGE, of Talacre, 4th Bart., 3rd son of Sir Pyers and Frances Selby. On the death of his brother, Sir Pyers, who died unmarried, he succeeded to the title and estates, and married : 1st, Mary, daughter of Thomas Clifton, of Lytham ; and 2ndly, Teresa, daughter of Charles Towneley, of Towneley, by whom he had four sons and three daughters : Sir Edward ; Pyers, born Jany. 1, 1727, who died unmarried ; Charles, who died an infant ; and Thomas, who married Mary Catharine, eldest daughter of Henry Lord Teynham. His daughters were Mary, wife of Charles Talbot, of Horecross, father of Charles, Earl of Salop, and grandfather of the present Earl ; Teresa, who died an infant ; and Elizabeth, born July 21, 1733, wife of Henry Blundell of Ince.   Sir George died at Talacre, Sept. 30, 1746.

MOSTYN, SIR PYERS, of Talacre, Flintshire, 2nd Bart., and was eldest surviving son of Sir Edward (who was created a Bart. by Charles II., April 28, 1670) and his wife Elizabeth, daughter of Mr. Downs, of Bodney, Norfolk. He married Frances, daughter and co-heiress of Sir George Selby, of Wintingham, Durham, by Mary, daughter of Lord Molineux of Ireland, and had by her four sons, Edward, and Sir Pyers, his successor, who both died unmarried, Sir George, and Thomas ; and five daughters : Mary, wife of John Hornyhold, of Blackmore Park ; Frances, wife of John Dalton, of Thurnham ; Anne, wife of Thomas, Culcheth, co. Lancaster ; Winifred and Juliana, who died unmarried. Sir Pyers died 1720.

MUNSON, ALBERT, O.P. (als. ANDERSON). — This venerable religious suffered imprisonment during the plot of Titus Oates, and was condemned to death, but was pardoned.   (See *State Trials*).   At the Revolution he left England with King James, but returned soon after and resumed his missionary labours. He died in London, Oct. 21, 1710, at the advanced age of 91. (*Obituary of O.S.D.*).

NARY, DR. CORNELIUS.—He published : 1, a Controversial work against Dr. Denison ; 2, an English Translation of the New Testament in 1719 in Dublin. Examined by Dr. Robert Witham in 1727.

NASSAU, JOHN.—Studied at Douay. For some time served St. Patrick's Chapel in London with Mr. Gabb, who gives this character of him : " He was universally admired and esteemed by all who knew him, but by none more than by myself. As a Priest he was very zealous and devout, at the altar a seraph, in the pulpit an angel, and this surely bespeaks what he was in the tribunal. As a member of society, he was a completely well-bred gentleman, humble without meanness ; hilarity and good nature were discerned in his countenance, while a dignity of mind uniformly marked his whole comportment.   He had, however, so tender and delicate a constitution that he could preach but seldom, and was prevented laborious exertion."   He died in London, in the flower of his age, Jan. 4, 1807.   He wrote : "*The Cause of Roman Catholics pleaded in an Address to the Protestants of Ireland,*" 1792.

NEEDHAM, ——, seems to have been educated at Lisbon.   " This morning, Jan. 12, 1743 O.S.," says Mr. Thomas Berington, " Mr. Needham, who was master at Twyford, set out for Lisbon to teach there, and I hope now that house will be very well provided with very good masters, and that we shall find the benefit of it.   Had our Masters here no more regard for the house than Messrs. Stonor and Dicconson, it had broken up by this time."

NEEDHAM, CHARLES, was sent to Douay, where, after he had finished his course, he was employed in teaching Humanity. Being sent on the Mission, he lived many years at Torr Abbey, Devon, where he was much respected and beloved.   He was admitted a member of the English Chapter, and appointed Archdeacon of Lancashire and Westmoreland.   In the decline of life he surrendered his congregation to Mr. Michael Alford, and retired to London, where he died, Sept. 10, 1802, aged 88.

NEEDHAM, JOSEPH, O.S.F.—After having filled with credit the office of Provincial of his Order, he died in London, March 24, 1791, aged 74, in the 58th year of religious profession and 50th of his Priesthood.

NELSON, LADY THEOPHILA, second daughter of George, 13th Lord Berkeley and 1st Earl of Bolinbroke (Privy Councillor to Charles II. and James II., "eminent for his affability, charity, and generosity." Epitaph.*), by his wife Elizabeth, daughter and co-heiress of John Massingbeard, Esq. She married—1st, Sir Kingsmill Lucy, Bart. ; and 2ndly, Robert Nelson. Esq., author of *The Feasts and Fasts of the Church of England*. Lady Nelson became a Catholic in the beginning of the last century. This conversion made some noise in the world, and gave rise to the *Letters between Dr. George Hickes and a Popish Priest on a young gentlewoman's departure from the Church of England*, which were published under that title in 1705. (This Dr. Hickes was Dean of Worcester, but, refusing to take the oath to William and Mary, he was suspended in 1689 and deprived in Feb. following. On the 4th of Feb., 1694 N.S., he was consecrated among the non-jurors Suffragan Bishop of Thetford.) "He was a man of universal learning, and deeply read in the primitive Fathers of the Church, whom he considered as the last expositors of Scripture ; and was particularly skilful in the old Northern languages and antiquities."† He died Dec. 15, 1715. His lady died in 1705.

Mr. Robert Nelson was son of an eminent Turkey merchant. His mother was the daughter of Sir Gabriel Roberts, also a Turkey merchant. "Mr. Nelson was one of the most distinguished gentlemen of his own or any other time, distinguished by the highest polish of manner and the most genuine piety of heart. Richardson had him in his eye in his Sir Charles Grandison, and from him formed the character of Sir Charles." (*Life of a Boy*, Vol. I., p. 373).

NESTFIELD, JOHN, was educated at Douay, and was General Prefect there for some time. He lived many years upon the Mission in Santa Cruz, in the West Indies, and died there in 1777.

NEVILL, GEORGE, Lord Abergavenny, only son of George Lord Abergavenny, and Mary Giffard, was born April 21, 1665. On the death of his father in 1666 he succeeded to his title and estates, and married Honora, daughter of John Lord Bellasyse, of Worlaby, and having no issue by her, the title descended to the heir male of Sir Christopher Nevill. Lord Abergavenny died, March 26, 1694, (O.S.), and was buried in the church of St. Giles-in-the-Fields. *Was he a Catholic?*

NEVILL, HENRY, of Holt, co. Leicester, eldest son of William Nevill and Elizabeth, daughter of Sir Gilbert Kniveton, Mircaston, co. Derby, Bart. His grandfather was fined, in March, 1644, (O.S.), £6,000 for his loyalty and that of his two sons, who were engaged in the Royal cause ; and this at a time when "his whole estate did not exceed £3,000 a year." In consequence of which it became necessary to sell certain manors, lands, and tenements in the counties of York and Leicester. Mr. Nevill died, June 28, 1728, aged 85, leaving three daughters and coheiresses. Margaret, the eldest, married Baldwin Conyers, Esq., and died 1758 ; Frances married John Tasburgh, of Flixton Hall, Suffolk ; and Mary married Cosmas Miglioruccio, a native of Italy and Polish Count, who, in consequence of this alliance, assumed the name of Nevill, and died in 1726-7 (Nichols' *Leicestershire*, II., 730.)

NEVILL, *or* MIGLIORUCCI, COSMAS HENRY JOSEPH, born Feb. 1, 1706, (O.S.), was son of Count Migliorucci and Mary Nevill, coheiress of Henry Nevill, of Holt. He married, July 31, 1742, Lady Mary Lee, second daughter of George Henry, Earl of Lichfield, by whom he had four sons and four daughters. Mr. Nevill died in 1763, Sept. 20 (O.S.). "He was a pattern of prudence, piety, and every Christian and social virtue." *Ibid.* He was suc-

---

* *Collin's Peerage.*
† *Literary Anecdotes*, 18 Cent., Vol. I., p. 17. [Mr. Gillow denies that Hick's letters were addressed to Lady Nelson.—J. H. P.]

ceeded by his eldest son, George Henry Nevill, who, dying in 1767, the whole estate came to the second son, Charles, who was a Jesuit, and resigned it over to his next brother, Cosmas Nevill, F.S.A.   He married Miss Gardiner, sister to Rev. Dr. Gardiner, a noted preacher at Bath.   She became a Catholic and the pattern of every virtue.   By her he had two sons and two daughters, both living in 1840.

NEWTON, EDWARD, of Irnham, co Lincoln.   Died Jan. 31, 1795.

NEWTON, ROBERT, lived at Sixhills Grange, in Lincolnshire.   But when the Chapel was removed from Hainton, and a new one built at Sixhills, and the congregation of Hainton added to that of Sixhills, Mr. Newton, being unable to do the duty of two congregations, retired to Claxby, where I saw him, in a very infirm state, in Sept. 1799, and where he died not long after.   "Mr. Newton was a man of very strong sense, and of sound judgment," said Mr. Knight, of Sixhills Grange, with whom Mr. Newton lived many years.

NEWTON, VINCENT, died April 10, 1814, aged 88.

NICOLAS, JAMES, studied at Douay, where he defended Universal Divinity with great applause, July 18, 1764, under Mr. Banister.   He taught Philosophy from 1767, and Divinity from 1770.   Came on the Mission about 1773; was chosen a Canon of the Chapter in 1775.   He died in London, where he exercised his pastoral duties, May 2, 1777.

NICHOLS, JOHN, born of Catholic parents at Southampton, Oct. 14, 1754, was received into the College at Rome by Father Hothersall, Nov. 19, 1767, but left Dec. 3, 1771, and together with three other students of the College, Messrs. Sharp, Parr, and Creighton, entered among the Dominicans and were received by Father (Bishop) Troy, Prior of St. Clement's.   He afterwards went to Lisbon, where he taught Hebrew, etc.

NIXON, THOMAS, S.J., son of Cuthbert Nixon and Helen Baines, his wife, was born in Lancashire, Oct. 6, 1735, (O.S.): was admitted into the College at Rome by Father H. Sheldon, S.J., Nov. 14, 1750; and, July 14, 1754, bound himself to the Mission, that being the obligation annexed to the Free Fund, on which he was placed.   Aug. 18, 1756, he went to Watten, entered his noviliate Oct. 9 of that year, and was made a professed Father in 1770.

NOLAN, JAMES, by birth an Irishman.   He entered among the Lazarites and was a renowned preacher in Paris, but happening to visit a French Convent at some distance from Paris, an English lady whom he accidently met there, took a fancy to him and made known her passion to him.   Shortly after he accompanied her to England and married her.   Urged, however, and overcome by the sting of conscience, he sought to return to France, intending to retire to La Trappe, and money was given and collected by —— French, Esq., to enable him to put into execution his resolution.   He accordingly went over, but soon returned again to England and to the cause of his ruin, but not to that peace of mind he was in search of.   For, dissatisfied with himself, he often thought of changing, consulted with Mr. (Dr.) Milner, then at Winchester, but putting off his conversion from day to day, he at last had no time left further to mock the Almighty, and dropt down dead in the street in London.   He left some children.   (*Hactenus*, Dr. Milner).

NORRIS, JOHN, S.J., son of Andrew and Charity Norris, was born in London in 1672, and in 1691 was sent to Rome, and admitted into the College by order of Cardinal Howard, then administered by Father Lucas, Oct. 18, but on April 5, 1692, he quitted it, and repaired to the Noviciate of the Jesuits on the Quirinal, and entered the Society.   (*Annales Collegii Anglicani de Urbe*).

NORTON, MATTHEW, O.P.   "He was a native of Yorkshire.   His parents," says Mr. Nichols, "were Protestant, but going early in life into Flanders, he embraced the Roman Catholic Faith, and entering into the Dominican Order assumed the religious name of 'Father Thomas.   About the year 1764 he was appointed Pastor of a small congregation at Aston Flamville, and about

1770 he was called to the office of Prior of the Convent of Bornheim, on the Schelt, between Ghent and Antwerp, and in 1775 was appointed Rector of the College in Louvain, where he was regularly admitted D.D.   In 1777 a Society in Brussels offering three premiums, a gold medal and two silver ones, for the best disputations on agriculture, draining of ground, and breeding of cattle, he gained all the three.   He had also employed much of his thoughts on the management of bees, but on this head he was somewhat visionary.   Returning to his pastoral charge at Hinckley, he had the satisfaction of being admitted under the mild laws of the present auspicious reign (George III.) to open a small but regular Chapel for the celebration of his religious duties, which he performed with such inoffensive integrity, as gained him the esteem of those of every other Christian profession.   Naturally possessed of a sound understanding, extensive knowledge, and great mental requirements, he tenaciously adhered to a faithful discharge of the ministry, and endeavoured, as much as he was able, to promote the interest and advance the happiness of all with whom he had any concern.   During the last two years he underwent great sufferings, which he supported with the collected firmness and pious resignation of a Christian.   He died at Hinckley on Aug. 7, 1800, aged 69, and was buried on Aug. 10, at Aston Flamville, attended by a numerous assembly of friends of various denominations from the adjacent villages." (*Leicestershire*, iv., 473).

NUGENT, MARY ELIZABETH, only daughter of Robert Nugent (created Baron Nugent in 1766 and Earl Nugent in 1776), and of Elizabeth, relict of Augustus, fourth Earl of Berkeley, and daughter of Henry Drax of Charborough, co. Dorset—his third wife.   She married George Nugent, Earl Temple.   In 1800 she was created Baroness Nugent, with remainder to her second son, Lord George Grenville Nugent Temple.   She died March 16, 1812, and was succeeded in her title by her second son, Earl Temple, who in 1784 was created Marquis of Buckingham.

Her father, Lord Nugent, who had conformed, was reconciled to the Catholic Church at Easter, 1788, through the ministry of Rev. Joseph Wilkes, at Bath. He died Oct. following, Mr. Patterson became his Chaplain, who was afterwards Priest at Buckenham, Norfolk.   Lord Nugent inherited his grandfather's ambition for poetry, and wrote a poem entitled *Portugal*.   (See *Gentleman's Magazine*, May, 1788).   Many of the French Emigrés Clergy and several of our communities of nuns, that were obliged to leave France at the time of the Revolution, partook largely of the charity of Lady Nugent.

NUTT, PACIFICUS, O.S.F., died in Birmingham, Sept. 27, 1799.   Had many years the charge of the School and Congregation at Edgbaston, but in 178— removed to Birmingham, and built the Chapel there.   He was much respected by all who knew him, Catholics and Protestants.

O'LEARY, ARTHUR, O.S.F.   A Capuchin, died in London, Jan. 8, 1802. (See Mr. Butler's *Hist. Mem.*, c. 43).

ONIONS, THOMAS *alias* MARTIN, son of William and Ann Martin, his wife, was born in Staffordshire, May 8, 1740, and was sent to Rome, and admitted into the College by order of Cardinal Lante, by Father Sheldon, July 15, 1754. Having been ordained May 24, 1766, he left the College the following Sept. [19], and came on the Mission.   His residence was at Hassop, near Bakewell, in Derbyshire, the seat of Francis Eyre, Esq., where he lived till his death, in April, 1814, aged 74.   (*Annales Collegii Anglicani de Urbe*).

ORME, JOHN, son of Robert Orme and Ann Matthews, his wife, was born in London, Dec. 17, 1719.   Having attended for some time Mr. Harvey's school in London, he went to Rome, and was received in the College as an alumnus by order of Cardinal de Via, Aug. 12, 1732.   He received priest's orders Feb. 2, 1744, and on the 29th of Sept. of that year left the College and came on the Mission.   He lived many years at Buckland as Chaplain to Sir Robert Throckmorton, much respected and beloved by all who knew him, and died there May 16, 1792, and was succeeded by Rev. Joseph Berington.   Mr. Orme was a member of the Chapter [in 1778].   (*Annales Coll. Angl. de Urbe.*)

ORRELL, JOSEPH, son of James Orrell, Esq., and his wife, Anne Bayle, of Blackbrook, Lancashire. Having finished his first year of Philosophy at Douay, he went to Paris, and was admitted into St. Gregory's Seminary: but not being thought to have a sufficient capacity for a D.D., he returned to Douay, Aug. 27th, 1771, and there finished his course and was ordained Priest. He lived many years with his family at Black Brook, and died there March 25, 1820. [From *St. Greg. Regr.*]

OVERBURY, THOMAS, of Barton, co. Warwick, was a zealous Catholic, and had a good estate there which was valued in 1715 at £295 17s.

OWEN, HUGH, son of Robert Owen, was born in the Isle of Man. At the age of 20 he was admitted into the College at Rome by order of Cardinal Howard, Oct. 25, 1689. He was ordained Nov. 23, 1692, but remained in the College till Sept. 13th, 1696. On his return he stayed for some time at Douay before he entered on the Mission. He lived many years in Suffolk, and died there Oct. 19, 1741. [The draft adds: January, 1725, at Bury.] (*Annales Coll. Angl. de Urbe.*)

OWEN, JOHN was son of John Owen [his mother was Wallian (? Gwendo-line)] Gales. He was born Nov. 1, about 1676. By order of Cardinal Caprara he was sent into the College at Rome, then under Father Powell, S.J., Oct 9, 1709, being then about 33 years old. Having studied his Classics and Phil-osophy, he began his course of Moral Divinity immediately on his admission. He received priest's orders Sept. 19th, 1711, and left the College April 19, 1713. He lived many years at Llanarth, in Monmouthshire, and died there, Aug. 29, 1761, nearly 84 years of age. (*Annales Coll. Angl.*) [*cf.* Foley, *Records*, V., 459.]

OXBOROUGH, or OXBURG, HENRY, was a native of Ireland. In the rebellion of 1715 he joined them in Northumberland, and had the reputation of commanding the English under Lieut.-General Forster, and on a particular occasion it was sworn by Calderwood, who acted as Quartermaster-General to the rebels, that he had commanded a detachment of 200 horse. He was found guilty and suffered at Tyburn, May 14, 1716, when his head was placed on Temple Bar. After his condemnation he drew up a petition to the King, which it is thought was never received, setting forth that he was a gentleman who, as well by his religion as by other ties, had been trained up in an affec-tion to King James's family; that, being in London when the oaths of allegi-ance were administered, and having truly a scrupulous conscience, he removed into the North of England, when he was unfortunately persuaded to join the rebels; humbly imploring His Majesty's clemency and promising to become the most obedient of his subjects. While he remained in the condemned hole his time was wholly spent in preparing himself for another world, and he ap-peared truly penitent for the sins of his past life, and refused all manner of sustenance but bread and water. The day of his execution was spent in con-stant prayer till he arrived at Tyburn, where he saluted the spectators and delivered to the Sheriff of Middlesex the paper, which will be found, I believe, among the "Records" temp. Geo: II. He then applied himself to his devo-tions, which being finished, he threw his book to a friend, and the cart was drawn away. His estates in King's County, Ireland, were let at £507 17s. 7d. per annum. [*Faithful Register.*]

PAINE, JAMES PHILIP, S.J. (See *Catholic Magazine and Review*, V., 170.)

PALIN, RICHARD, of the family of Diconsdale, near Albrighton, co. Salop, was educated at Douay, and ordained about 1716. As soon as January, 1725, if not sooner, he opened a school for Catholic children at Rowneywood in the parish of Alvechurch, not far from Beoley, where the Sheldons had a good estate, and probably it was under their patronage that he took the bold step. I find no mention of him or his school there after 1740, and it is probable he left Rowneywood in that or the following year, and that his school was closed.

Mr. Palin died in December, 1750 (O.S.) [*Draft Notes.*—A Mr. Palin, Priest in 1706. A Rich. Palin, gent., in a deed of Nov., 1722, is called by Mr. Thos. B-r-n, of Albrighton, co. Salop, gent. At Rowney-wood, Jan. 7, 1725, and 1734 : Longley-wood, 1736-7-8—1740. Feb., 1750, Mr. Palin paid Mr. Brockholes £10, a legacy left to Mrs. Catharine Giffard by the late Mr. Palin. Brother of a nephew of Thomas Palin, gent., of Dearnsdale (?). In 1715 (estate assessed) £64 15s. per annum. Rowney Green, Parish of All Church, Counsellor Guest's (?) 1 mile from Beoley.]

PARKER, FRANCIS, was born about 1740 at Harvington, or rather, at Blundington, near Harvington, where a family of that name lived till near the end of last century. From Douay he removed to Paris, where he took the degree of Licentiate in Divinity. He then came on the Mission, and was many years Chaplain to Lord Arundell at [Irn]ham, in Lincolnshire, where he was much esteemed, both by that noble family and by a numerous congregation. In the latter part of his life a stroke of the palsy deprived him of the use of one side ; yet he survived the stroke six or seven years, but was incapable of performing any pastoral duty. He then retired to his friends in Worcestershire, and died there in Sept., 1779.

Draft : —— Parker, at Irnham, Lincs., about 1770 (-4-5-6) or 1780. Was the last Clergy Priest there. Mr. Brent and then Mr. Walton, S.J., succeeded. Mr. Parker, of Plowden, S.J.

Sebastian Redford, S.J., at Croxteth, May 30, 1753. Had lived at Holywell (credo).

James Parker, born April 3, 1747 (noviceship S.J. Sept. 7, 1766).

Thomas Parker, born Nov. 19, 1739 (noviceship, June 28, 1773).

PARKINSON, CUTHBERT, studied at Douay, defended de Incarnatione " extremely well," July 23, 1704. After one year of Divinity taught Compendium. When Master of Logic concurred Feb., 1707, for the Greek lesson at Douay. (*Letter of Bishop Dicconson* and *Records of Douay*, p. 71-78.)

PARKINSON, CUTHBERT [ANTHONY], O.S.F. [*Draft :* Wrote *Collectanea Anglo Minoritica, or a Collection of the Antiquities of the English Franciscans*, 4to, much admired by Mr. Hearne (Cole, V. 31, p. 179) and Dr. Rawlinson, and approved by Bishop Pritchard, who was buried at Rockfield, near Monmouth.]

PARKINSON, EDWARD, studied at Douay. When he came on the Mission he was placed at York, and was Chaplain to Bishop Smith, and when at the Revolution the Bishop retired to Wycliff, on the invitation of Mr. Tunstall, Mr. Parkinson accompanied him, and continued with him till his death. Bishop Smith had a high opinion of him, made him his V.G., [and in that quality is painted at the back of his chair, they say, at York], and executor or trustee to his will. He left him also a small annuity on condition that he continued to reside in the Northern District. Mr. Parkinson had the reputation of being " an eminent preacher, and a zealous Missionary." He died at Wycliff, April 7, 1735.

PARKINSON, RICHARD, was a native of Yorkshire, and son of William and Alicia Parkinson. At the age of 18 he was admitted into the English College at Rome, Aug. 23rd, 1699, by Father Mansfield. On March 14, 1700, he took the oath of Alexander VII., but after studying Philosophy and Divinity for four years he obtained a dispensation from that part of it in which he solemnly promised never to enter into any religious order, and was admitted into the novitiate of the Jesuits, at Monte Cavallo, Jan. 24, 1704. This made some noise in Rome, and a memorial, dated May 28, 1705, was presented to the Cardinal of Propaganda, by Mr. (afterwards Bishop) Gordon, who then acted as agent for the English Bishops and Clergy. In this he stated that, though the alumni promised upon oath that they never would enter any religious society or congregation without the special license of the Apostolic See or of Propaganda, yet there were in a certain Pontifical College at Rome those who asserted that anyone might take the oath with the express intention of applying to the Sacred Congregation for such leave as soon as possible, even notwithstanding the declaration of Alexander VII. and Propaganda, that every kind of interpretation was expressly forbidden except such as should be given in writing on application to the Holy See ; and, therefore, he asks whether such exposition of the oath be the meaning of His Holiness, and of the Congregation, and whether any Professor or any Regular could, with a safe conscience, authorise such an intention.   To this Memorial no answer was given than, *Unusquisque consulat suæ conscientiæ.*   (*Annals of Roman College.*)

Mr. Parkinson consulted several Divines, and among others Dr. G. Witham, then Agent at Rome.   His answer was, " that, considering the answers of those many he had consulted, and other reasons, it seemed to me more likely that he was called to that state of life, to wit, the Society of Jesus. . . .   All things considered, I feared he would never be at rest till he was a Jesuit, and so that it was best to let him take that course.   These were my thoughts, yet I could wish he would consult you again and Mr. James Gordon."   (Mr. W's. letter to Mr. Lesley, April 12, 1703.)   I find a Mr. Parkinson, S.J., in London in 1733, " a zealous and active Missionary."   [*Draft*: Richard Parkinson, *Miscel.*, V., p. 150, etc.]

PARKINSON, ——.   [*Draft*: Professor of Philosophy at Douay, and in Oct. 1707, succeeded Mr. Crathorn as Prefect of Studies.]

PARKINSON, THOMAS, *alias* GOLDEN, died in Lancashire, Feb., 1750, (O.S.), in consequence of a heavy stone slate falling on his head.

PARR, FRANCIS, O.P., *and* O.S.F.   His true name was Macdonald ; his father was a Scotchman, but he was born in London, June 7, 1752.   He was received into the College at Rome, Jan. 16, 1767, but on July [24] 1770, he went to Florence with two or three other students of the College, and became a Dominican [with Jas. Sharpe].   At the suppression of the Jesuits the Grey Franciscans succeeded them as Penitentiaries at St. Peter's, and on the death of Father Purcell, Father Parr obtained leave to enter among the Franciscans, and was made Penitentiary at St. Peter's, but returned to England, and thence went into Scotland.

PARRY, PIERCE, was son of John and Mary Parry, and was born in Wales in 1716.   In 1736 he went to Rome, and was admitted into the College, Sept. 17, by Father Joseph Marshall, S.J., the Rector.   He took the College oath of Alexander VII., May 1, 1737.   He succeeded Mr. Barnes at Oscott, Dec. 16, 1759, and was much beloved and respected by his congregation, who, on occasion of some complaint made by Bishop Hornyold, certified that they had no fault to find with him in regard to his pastoral duties, that he was assiduous in preaching and instructing his flock, and in visiting the sick, and earnestly entreated he might be allowed to remain.   This memorial, dated Jan. 23, 1764, is signed by all the heads of the congregation for themselves and their families, and had the desired effect.   After this Mr. Parry entered into an agreement with Rev. Arthur Vaughan, of Harvington, to give up part of his house at Oscott for the purpose of establishing there a boarding-school which he had established at or near Harvington, then under the direction of Miss Ainsworth.   She accordingly removed her school to Oscott.   After her marriage the care of it was then given to Miss Johnson, whose mother was a daughter of Sir —— Wrottesley, Bart.   When Mr. Pierce was disabled by repeated paralytic attacks to comply with his duties, he quitted Oscott, in 1785, and retired to Aldridge, where Mrs. Johnson took charge of him in a manner honourable to himself and best suited to his circumstances.   Mr. Parry died Dec. 30, 1792.   Mr. Berington succeeded him at Oscott in 1785.   (*Annals of Roman College.*)

PASTON, MARGARET, was daughter and heir of Edward Paston, of Horton, co. Gloucester.   She married Sir Henry Bedingfield, of Oxborough, who was created Bart. by Charles II., Jan. 2, 1660, (O.S.), in consequence of the losses sustained by his family in his own and his Royal father's cause.   These losses —on a fair calculation made at the desire of the King, and presented to him— amounted to the enormous sum of £47,194 18s. 8d.   When his Majesty replied with concern that he was unable to make him adequate compensation, Mr.

Bedingfield answered that all he begged of his Majesty was, that he might hope for the future to enjoy in quiet the little that was left.   Amidst all his losses he had the happiness of living nearly fifty years with a wife of extraordinary parts, piety, and prudence, (*Betham,* II., 201), who, besides the great fortune she brought, equalled him in all his merits, aided him in all his difficulties, and, when forced to fly beyond the seas, managed all his concerns with the greatest prudence ; so that Sir Henry declared with his dying words that she had been a wife who had never displeased him.   Lady Bedingfield survived him eighteen years.   "After 50 years' enjoyment of perfect felicity in the married state, passed 18 years' widowhood, in an absolute retreat, in the constant exercise of her devotions, and daily distribution of charity, and departed this life, Jan. 14, 1702, (O.S.), aged 84 years."   (Epitaph, Oxborough Church.)

PATERSON, ——, DR., Bishop in Scotland.   (See *Catholic Magazine and Review,* V. cliii.)

PEACH, HENRY, was educated at Douay.   He was a very zealous and active missionary in London, where he founded the Charity School.   He often sought to meet Mr. James Smith, the Apostate, but always in vain.   Mr. Peach died at St. Omers, December 24th, 1781.

PEARSON, WILLIAM, was born at Richmond in Yorkshire.   At the age of 19 he was admitted into the College at Rome by Father Babthorp, the Rector, Oct. 16, 1651.   He was ordained Dec. 17, 1656, and departed for England April 25, 1658.   I find another William Pearson, who studied at Rome and returned to England 1672.   In 1692 he resided with Sir William Tankard, Bart., at Bramton, and had the character from the Archdeacon [C.P.] of being "a temperate and regular clergyman."   (*Coll. Angl. de Urbe*).

PEARSON, THOMAS, *alias* ATHERTON, died at W. Hampton, Dec. 31, 1758.

PEGG, WILLIAM, was of a good family in Derbyshire.   He studied at Douay, and for some time lived with Mr. Heneage (whom see) in or near Madeley in Shropshire.   He afterwards succeeded Mr. Daniel Fitter as Chaplain to Mr. Fowler, of St. Thomas' Priory, near Stafford, at the same time that Bishop Witham resided in that family.   [In 1705 went with the family to London].   He was as much respected by his brethren and beloved as he was by his family.   He succeeded Mr. Francis Fitter as Administrator of the Common Purse of Stafford and four counties, Dec. 3, 1702, and died [about Nov. 21], 1711.   "He was very reserved," says Bishop Witham, "and unwilling to tell him anything concerning the Common Purse."   Mr. Pegg was a member of the Chapter and was chosen Archdeacon, Feb. 14, 1703 (O.S.)

PEGGE, KATHARINE, was daughter of Thomas Pegge of Yeldersley, Esq., co. Derby.   Being abroad, she had a son by Charles II. in 1647 called FitzCharles, to whom he granted the Royal Arms, with a baton sinister, vaire, and whom in 1673 his Majesty created Earl of Plymouth, Viscount Totness and Baron Dartmouth.   He was bred to the sea, and, having been educated abroad, was known by the name of Don Carlos.   Katharine Pegge, his mother, married Sir Edward Greene, Bart., of Samford, in Essex, and died without issue by him.

PEMBRIDGE, MICHAEL, O.S.B.—He lived many years at Bath, 1783, and afterwards as Chaplain at Tixall.   In the latter part of his life he retired to his Brethren at St. Gregory's at Acton Burnell, where Sir Edward Smythe received them on their expulsion from Douay in the French Revolution.   Here he died, Nov. 20, 1806.   Mr. Pembridge published :—1. *A Prayer Book;* 2. *Some other small tracts of devotion ;* 3. *A Devout Exercise preparatory to Death,* 1800. 4. He gave a second edition of Pastorini, with a preface and some account of the author.

PEMBRIDGE, PHILIP, lived at Graystock before 1780, where he gave general satisfaction.

PENINGTON, ALLAN, O.P., was son of Richard and Ann Penington. At the age ot 23 he was received in the College at Rome by Father Postgate, the Rector, October 24, 1693, and, having studied his Classics and Philosophy elsewhere, he began his course of Divinity; but in the following April, and before he had taken the College oath, he left the College and became a Dominican. (*Annales Coll. Angl.*).

PENKETH, WILLIAM, son of Robert and Alicia Charnley, his wife, was born in Lancashire. At the age of 20 he went to Rome, and was received in the College by Father Mansfield, the Rector, Sept. 12th, 1699; was ordained Aug. 10, 1704, and left the College April 15, 1706, to go to Paris and thence to England. I do not find where he lived, but that he died Dec. 25, 1762, with great sentiments of piety, in [dom. D. in England.]

A Mr. Penketh [*alias* Japper] translated *The Spiritual Combat*. His brother, John P. [*alias* Rivers], studied at Rome [received in Roman College Nov. 29, 1704] and was ordained at St. John Lateran's, April 19, 1710, and left June 23, 1712, to go into Flanders. Richard Penketh, D.D., of Seville, is mentioned by Dodd in his *Flores* to have flourished in 1699.

PENRICE, CHARLES, studied at Lisbon. He lived many years with Mr. Kynne in Worcestershire as his assistant, and that of the poor Catholics of the surrounding country. In 1692 he had lived there about five years. I find nothing of him after that time.

PENSWICK, THOMAS, BP., was born at Garswood of respectable parents. His father was steward to Sir Wm. Gerard, a most respectable man. He went to a school at Prescot, and afterwards to Mr. Newby's school at Haighton, near Preston, and then was sent to Douay. At the French Revolution he happily escaped from the College the day before the President and Students were taken to prison. After staying some time at Old Hall Green, he finished his Divinity at Crook Hall, and defended it well. Chester was his first Mission, where he built the New Chapel and served it some years, till he was appointed to the Chapel built on Copperas Hill, Liverpool. In that place he was much respected and beloved by all who knew him. In 1824 he was chosen Coadjutor to Bishop Smith in the North, and on his death, which happened July 30, 1831, he succeeded to the charge of that District. His labours at Chester and Liverpool were great, nor were they less when invested with the Episcopal dignity. In 1836 he sunk under them. He died in the bosom of his own family, at Ashton-in-Makerfield, Jan. 28, much regretted in death, as he had been beloved in life. He published: 1. *A Sermon preached at Chester*. 2. *Boudon on the Blessed Sacrament*, translated from the French [Mr. Gradwell].

PERKINS, FRANCIS, educated at Douay, died Mar. 13, 1760, at Mr. Matthews', Hants, aged near 90 years.

PERROT *alias* JOHN BARNESLEY, D.D. was a native of Worcestershire and a convert from Protestantism. (See *Catholic Magazine*, VI., 103). In 1670 he obtained leave to resign the Presidentship of Lisbon College and to return to England, in consequence of his growing infirmities. At the General Assembly of the Chapter in 1672 he was chosen Archdeacon of North Hants and Cambridgeshire, and on the decease of Dr. Ellice *alias* Waring, he was chosen, Sept. 18, 1676, to succeed him as Dean. "When the troubles and severe persecution of Catholics began, on Sept. 28, 1678, in consequence of Oates's Plot, most of the Clergy then residing in London," says Dr. Giffard (Bp.), "were forced, some to retire into the country and others to secure themselves beyond sea. Dr. Perrott, the actual and acting Superior of the Clergy, chose rather to hazard all dangers and suffer all inconveniences than quit his pastoral charge, which he continued to exercise, while no Superior of any other ecclesiastical body remained in town, keeping a constant correspondence with the Brethren in France, Flanders, and all the counties of England." (Bp. Giffard's *Minute*).

Dr. Perrott presided at the General Meeting of the Chapter held Feb. 25, 1681 (O.S.). In this meeting a letter was read from Dr. Gage, President of Douay, and formerly Agent at Rome, in which he intimated, "that by fresh intelligence, he was certainly informed that upon the arrival of Father Provincial of the English Jesuits at Rome, whither he and two others of his Brethren went to be present at the election of their General, very vigorous endeavours would be used to procure a condemnation of the Oath of Allegiance, and a severe censure (even to the taking away of all faculties) to be inflicted upon all that should not renounce it." The Meeting "ordered that Dr. Giffard, the Secretary, should write a common letter to be signed by Dr. Perrott and himself, to Cardinal Howard, acquainting His Eminence with the state of the English Catholics as to the Oath of Allegiance, that most of the nobility, Gentry, and Commonalty had either actually taken it, or at least, seemed so convinced and resolved, that they approved what others had done, and were ready to do the like when it should be required of them, their Pastors generally approving of it, and being further confirmed by the authority of a great number of the Sorbonne Doctors, such a prohibition and censure must near cause a schism. For the preventing whereof His Eminence's powerful assistance is humbly implored."

It is remarkable that the Internuncio at Brussels, Tarari, published a condemnation of the Oath of Allegiance in March, 1682 [See *Records of Chapter*], and on May 14, following, Mr. Cary's book *The Catechist Catechized*, written in defence of the Oath, was condemned by Innocent XI. [See *Rec. Miscel.*]. Dr. Perrott presided at a meeting of some of the heads of the Clergy in June, 1683, at which it was resolved to write a letter to Cardinal Howard, to acquaint His Eminence of their ardent desire of a Bishop, and to desire His Eminence's judgment and direction, whether it may be proper at present to move in order to the obtaining of one." He presided also in his capacity of Dean, at the General Assemblies, held in 1684, 1687, 1694, 1703. At the close of the latter he represented to them that it was now twenty-seven years since, at the request of the late Dean, Dr. Ellice, he was chosen Sub-dean by the General Assembly of 1670, and requested the same favour might be granted to him. The proposal, however, did not meet with the concurrence of some of the Assembly, but was acceded to in 1710. Dr. Perrott died in 1714, aged 83. (*Lisbon Catalogue and Chapter Records*).

PERRY, PHILIP MARK, D.D. He was born at Bilston, where he studied his rudiments [? then at S. and Naulare College in Paris], and then went to Douay in 1746. At the end of his second year of Philosophy, he was received into the Seminary at Paris, by Dr. Bear, July 28, 1742, and took the oath the following May. In April, 1744, he returned to England for the recovery of his health, where he remained till Nov. 22, 1746. He was ordained Priest Dec. 18, 1751 ; entered his license Jan. 1, 1752, and took the cap May 22, 1754, and in June [? Sept.] departed for the Mission [by Douay]. Heythrop seems to have been his first place, but in consequence of some misunderstanding with Lord S. [*i.e.*, Lord Shrewsbury], he quitted it, telling him "Your Lordship is master of your own house, but not of my understanding." [Went to Longbirch to Bishop Hornyhold]. When the Jesuits were expelled out of Spain, the English College at Valladolid, which had been in their administration, but had supplied the Mission with very few labourers, was given to the Secular Clergy, whose College it had always been. Dr. Perry was appointed the first Secular President. He had then laboured more than twelve years in the Mission, "*summo cum animarum lucro*," says Bishop Hornyhold, who adds that he was "*fidei, morumque integritate, scientiæ laude ac zelo animarum apprime commendabilis, atque ideo in Hispaniam ob ardua Cleri Anglicani negotia delegatus, vel potius compulsus a nobis, & VV. Fratribus & Co-episcopis nostris.*" This attestation is dated Longbirch, Nov. 28, 1767. Having governed the College with great credit to himself and benefit of those committed to his charge, he died at Madrid, whither the affairs of his College had called him, about Sept. 5, 1774 [died of ye ? body-louse]. [His portrait at Scotch College there (? Valladolid)].

His nephew, the Rev. John Perry, told the writer at Sedgley Park, Jan. 12, 1815, that "he had seen his uncle since his death, and that he appeared to him to prevent his taking evil ways." [*Draft notes :*—Some time at St. Omers. Then on Mission, 1774; at Longbirch two years, ditto at Aldenham; in 1777 to ? Wthm.]

Dr. Perry wrote : 1. *An Essay on the Life and Manners of the Ven. Robert Grosstete, Bishop of Lincoln,* from his own works and from contemporary writers, MS. 8vo. of 502 pp. 2. *The Life and Death of John Fisher, Bishop of Rochester, and Cardinal Priest of the Title of S. Vitalis, and Martyr,* MS. in 2 vols. 8vo. Vol. 1, pp. 614; vol. 2, pp. 558. The second vol. or book ends with chap. x. " Bishop Fisher's endeavours, which he added to his writings, for keeping out heresy from his university," *Opus imperfectum.* Both MSS. were in the possession of Bishop Cameron, and his successor at Edinburgh [*ex dono auctoris*].

PETRE, BENJAMIN, Episcopus Prusensis. The Petres, of Fidlers, were descended from Thomas Petre, third son of Sir John Petre, Baron Petre of Writtle, in Essex. Benjamin was sent to Douay, and when ordained came on the Mission, and for some time was Chaplain to the Earl of Derwentwater, at Dilstone. In 1710 he was chosen a Member of the English Chapter, and in —— Bishop of Prusa, in Bithynia, and Coadjutor to the Bishop Giffard, in London. In his old age he wished to have Dr. Challoner for his Coadjutor, but met with great opposition from the Superiors of Douay, from the Vicars Apostolic, and from the Cardinals of Propaganda, who all wanted him to succeed to Dr. Robert Witham in the Presidentship of Douay College. On this Bishop Petre declared " that as Dr. Challoner was the most proper person he could find among the English Clergy to be his Coadjutor, and to govern the district after his death, if they would not consent to his having him for his Coadjutor, he would leave it to those concerned to find out a proper person to govern the District, and that he himself would relinquish his charge and pass the remainder of his days in retirement." (Mr. B. *Life of Bishop Challoner,* p. 57). Bishop Petre lived respected and beloved to a great age, and died in King Street, Golden Square, at ten o'clock Friday morning, Dec. 22, 1758, in his 88th year. (See *Catholic Magazine,* No. XV., p. 121).

PETRE, EDWARD, S.J., was 3rd son of William Baron Petre and Catharine, daughter of Edward Somerset, Earl of Worcester. James II. made him a Privy Councillor, &c., &c. He wrote : " A letter from Rev. Father Petre, S.J., Almoner to the King of England, to Rev. Father La Chaise, Confessor to the most Christian King, touching the present affairs of England, dated St. James's, Feb. 9, 1687." In the answer, Father La Chaise lays down the method and rules he must observe with his Majesty for the conversion of his Protestant subjects, dated Paris, March 7, 1688, N.S. (Both printed in the *Third Collection of Papers,* 4to. See *Kennet,* Vol. III., p. 490). [Kirk does not notice that these pieces are apocryphal, political squibs in the fashion of that day.— J. H. P.]

PETRE, FRANCIS (I.), was son of John Petre, of Fidlers, Esq., and his wife, Elizabeth, daughter of ——, both Catholics. In March, 1677, he was sent to Lisbon, and took the College oath, Sept. 7, 1686, and in the following October dedicated his Thesis of Universal Philosophy to Bishop Leyburn, and defended it with great applause under his Professor, Fr. Robert Smith. He was ordained Priest Nov. 20, 1689, by the Cardinal Protector, and appointed to teach the Classics and Philosophy in 1692. In 1694 he was made Confessarius of the College, Procurator in 1695, and at last President [? Vice-President] in 1697. In this latter office, which he held till his death, he was much admired for his moderation and fatherly tenderness to all around him. He introduced many pious customs and wholesome regulations for the discipline of the College. On the 16th of March, 1699, he was attacked by a malignant fever, which he bore with great fortitude and resignation till the 24th, when he died, after having received all the rites of the Church. By his will he left 100,000 reals to the College without any obligation or condition whatever. He lies buried within the rails, and at the foot of the Altar called of the B.V. de Pace.

PETRE, FRANCIS (II.), *alias* SQUIB, son of Robert and Maria Petre, was born in or near London, Sept. 25, 1691. He was sent to Douay, and took the

College oath Nov. 3, 1709. He was successively Professor of Grammar, Syntax, and in 1720 was made Confessor, and in 1722 Procurator, and Vice-President in 1730, in which quality he died, Jan. 26, 1762, aged 70. He was Vice-President 32 years, Procurator 40. He never came on the Mission, but was an invaluable Procurator and Disciplinarian.

PETRE, FRANCIS (III.), of the family of Fidlers, and nephew of Bishop Benjamin. He was educated at Douay, and after his ordination came upon the Mission. In 1750 he was appointed by Benedict XIV. Episcopus Amoriensis and Coadjutor to Bishop Dicconson in the North. His bulls, which are at Ushaw, are dated July 27, 1750. On the death of Bishop Dicconson, which took place April 24, 1752, he succeeded him in the charge of the Northern District, and lived upon his own estate at Showley, Lancashire, where he died Dec. 24, 1775, in the 84th year of his age. He had been chosen Canon July 11, 1733. (See his Epitaph in *Catholic Magazine*, or rather, *Catholic Miscellany* I., 385). [William Fisher was his chaplain ; he (Petre) was buried in the extra parochial Chapel of Stede].

PETRE, ROBERT, 7th Lord, was only surviving son of Thomas, 6th Lord Petre, and Mary Clifton, and succeeded him in 1707. On the 1st of March, 1711 (O.S.), he married Catharine, daughter of Bartholomew, and sole heiress of her brother, Francis Walmesley, of Dunkenhalgh, Lancashire. His Lordship died of the small pox, March 22, 1712 (O.S.), leaving his lady pregnant, who, on the 3rd of June following, was delivered of a son, Robert James. After his death, Lady Petre married Lord Stourton, in April, 1733. (See her Character in Bernard's life of Bishop Challoner.)

PETRE, ROBERT JAMES, 8th Lord, only son of Robert, 7th Lord Petre, and Catharine Walmesley, was born June 3, 1712. He married, May 2, 1732, Anne, daughter * of James, Earl of Derwentwater, by whom he had one son and three daughters : 1. Catharine, married to George Heneage, of Hainton ; 2. Barbara, wife of Thomas Giffard, of Chillington ; and 3. Julia, wife of John Weld, of Lulworth. † He died in July, 1742. He rebuilt the Church of West Thorndon, and is said to have been a nobleman of great accomplishments.

PETRE, ROBERT EDWARD, 9th Lord, only son of Robert James, 8th Lord, aad Lady Mary Anne Ratcliffe. He succeeded his father in 1742, and on the 19th April, 1762, he married for his first wife Anne, daughter of Philip Howard, of Buckenham, brother to Edward, Duke of Norfolk, by his wife Henrietta, daughter of Edward Blount, of Blagdon, and by her had issue, Robert Edward, born Sept. 2, 1763 ; George William, born Jan. 10, 1766 ; Ann Catherine, born March 8, 1769 ; and Philip Hugh, Dec. 20, 1773. His Lordship married 2ndly [Juliana Barbara, daughter of Henry Howard, of Glossop], and died July 2, 1801, and was succeeded by his eldest son, Robert Edward, who died March 29, 1809, aged 46. He published [*A Letter to Dr. Horsley.*]

PETRE, THOMAS, 6th LORD, and Baron Petre, of Writtle, Essex, was third son of Robert, 3rd Lord Petre, by his wife Mary, daughter of Antony, Viscount Montague. His elder brother, William, 4th Lord Petre, was one of the five Catholic Lords committed to the Tower in Oates's Plot, and died there Jan. 5, 1683. He was succeeded by his next brother, John, 5th Lord Petre, and he dying unmarried in 1684, the honours of the Barony and estates devolved upon his brother Thomas. His Lordship was in 1687 constituted Lord Lieutenant and Custos Rotulorum of the County of Essex by James II. He married Mary, daughter of Sir Thomas Clifton, of Lytham, by whom he had one son and a daughter, Mary, who died young. His Lordship died June 4, 1707, and was buried at Ingatestone. (*Monumenta Anglicana.* See Jan. 5, 1706.)

PETRE, [ROBERT], S.J., *alias* SPENCER, was brother of Edward, the Privy Councillor. He was accused by Protestants of tearing the English Bible in

---

* Edmondson calls her Mary.   † Edmondson calls him Edward Weld.

his pulpit in Lime Street.   In 1699 he lived in Marylebone under the name of Spencer, and was at the head of all the Jesuit affairs then.   (See *Letter of the growth of Papacy.*)

PHILLIPSON, THOMAS, O.S.B.   (See *Catholic Magazine and Review*, Vol. III., p. 223 ; and also *Catholic Miscellany*, I., 423.)

PIAZZA, HIERONYMO BARTOLOMEO, O.S.D., was born at Alessandria della Paglia.   He became a Dominican and Lecturer of Philosophy and Divinity, and was one of the Delegate Judges of the Inquisition in Orsino in the Province of Ancona.   On his arrival in England, he was patronised by Sir William Dawes, Archbishop of York and Bart.; but on his death he settled in Cambridge, and taught Italian.   Mr. Cole, Vol. II., p. 106 and 107 of his MSS. in the British Museum, gives this account of him : " He quitted his native country, friends, and a good maintenance to come and live here in a begging condition, with the plague of a wife and a houseful of children to provide for. . . . At his first coming over, as is usual with proselytes of all denominations to engratiate themselves with those to whom they come over, and at the expense of those they forsake, he published in English and French *A History of the Inquisition in Italy*, printed in London, 1722, dedicated to the King, which, if any has escaped the fate they must come to, is a most ridiculous performance, even lower than one would have expected from a lay-brother, much more from one who calls himself a Doctor in Divinity and Philosophy.   It is stuffed with idle stories of what happened to some who were put into the Holy Office while he was concerned in it, and legendary tales of Saints, wrote in such a manner as was thought most proper to persuade that he was a true convert to the Church of England.   This book, as it never sold, he used to make presents of to such young gentlemen as then came to the University, and whom he thought were likely to make a proper return.   Such shifts and difficulties are people put to who forsake the substance for the gilded shadow. As he was a well-behaved and decent man, he was well respected by everybody in the University, who at times collected very handsomely for him.   He died very suddenly in 1741 [" being at my chambers but the evening of the day he died"].   There were six gentlemen of the University who had been his scholars, among whom was myself, that supported his pall."

PICKERING, FRANCIS, was born in Portugal, where his father was converted to the Catholic Faith, and suffered much and great losses on that account.   He was sent to Rome, where he studied about six years in the Roman Seminary, and afterwards lived for two years (from 1707 to the end of 1709) in the Ecclesiastical Academy of Nobles, greatly to the satisfaction of the Superior and edification of all the members of that establishment.   I find nothing more of him.

PICKERING, LANCELLOT, [son of John and Margaret Pickering, was a native of Westmorland.   At the age of eighteen was received into the College at Rome by Father Mansfield, Sept. 12, 1699.   Being ordained Priest, April 3, 1706, he quitted the College April 30, 1707, but remained some time in Paris, and came over in the beginning of 1713 to the Mission, and was placed at Lartington, Jan. 13 of that year, where he continued till Jan. 14, 1763, when he died, aged 83, and was succeeded by Rev. John Lund, and he by Mr. Gibson in 1768, and remained until October, 1773.   (*Annales Coll. de Urbe.*)

PICKERING, THOMAS, was a Carmelite Priest, of a gentleman's family near Ludlow.   In his early life he was in the clock and watch line, and was a good mechanic ; but quitted the world to enter into a religious life among the Discalced Carmes in Italy.   On his coming on the Mission he was placed in the family of the Willoughbys, of Ospley, near Nottingham, and lived there 53 years to the time of his "happy and edifying death."   He was a model of humility, says my author, who knew him well, "and was much respected by all who knew him."   The house which the English Carmes had at Tongres was mainly purchased by Father Pickering.

PIGGOT, CHRISTOPHER, was son of Christopher and Ann Piggot. At the age of 19 he was received into the College at Rome, on Feb. 21, 1694, by Father Postgate, the Rector. He was ordained Priest May 19, 1697, and on account of his health left the College the following September, before he had completed his Theological course. On this account he remained some time in a French Seminary in Paris, and then came on the Mission. Mr. Andrew Giffard says he " was a most laborious Priest, who helped the poor people in and about Southwark, and seldom returned home from his labour until 10 or 11 o'clock at night." He was a member of the Chapter, and died at Islington, May 14, 1735. (*Annales Coll. Rom.*).

In a letter to a Cardinal at Rome on the " Present State of Popery in England," dated Jan. 1, 1733, the writer says : " Father John Baptist Piggott was the means of reconciling many persons of distinction, besides others, to the Catholic Faith. He is said to have formed a community of converted gentle-women in a village north of London (probably Islington), who bestowed large sums of money yearly towards maintaining several poor Catholic families in London, and sent considerable charities to Colleges, Seminaries, and nunneries abroad. They also portioned several young women, who became nuns beyond seas." The writer adds that they were "examples worthy of the primitive Saints, and of which we have still daily examples in England," p. 18. Though he calls him Father, he also calls Dr. Challoner and another clergyman by the same name, as it is common in foreigners to do. He may also have mistaken his Christian name, or Mr. Christopher may have been called John Baptist, for the dates seem to indicate the same person.

I find a Father Piggot, a Jesuit, at Douay in 1707, very busy with Poynts in bringing the charge of Jansenism against Dr. Hawarden. (Query : Does any-thing they said above apply to him ? *Non credo*). [The draft adds : " Mr. Christopher Piggot, a laborious missionary, left £700 for a foundation for a student at Douay College."]

PIGOTT, NATHANIEL.—" He was called to the Bar in 1688. The Statute of 7th and 8th of William interdicted the Bar to Catholics, so that after Mr. Pigott no Catholic was called to the Bar till 1791, when it was again opened to them. For several years Mr. Pigott practised as a Chamber-Counsel. In the conveyancing branch of the law his eminence was undisputed. Several of his MS. opinions show his profound learning. He left a MS. *Treatise on Recoveries*, which was published after his decease, and has not been superseded by the valuable treatises on the same subject since published by Mr. Cruise and Mr. Preston." (Butler's *Memoirs*, Vol. IV., p. 460).

PILLING, JOHN AND WILLIAM, O.S.F., brothers, and natives of Lan-cashire. Both became Franciscans at Douay, and were much esteemed, especially in their province, for their learning and piety. John died at Osmotherly, Yorkshire, Jan. 12, 1801, and William at Lower Hall, near Preston, Dec. 4, 1801.

PINCKARD, *vere* ROBERT TYPPER. — He was educated at Douay, and was Procurator for some time. He lived many years in London, and was there the Agent of Douay College. He died at Douay, Jan. 24, 1766. He was admitted into the Chapter in 1743. He translated :—1. Gobinet's *Instructions of Youth ;* 2. *The Spiritual Combat.*

PINCKARD, JOHN, *vere* THOMAS, son of Evens Thomas, by his wife, Mary Scudamore, both Catholics. He was born at Kevengilth, in Glamorganshire, in the beginning of April, 1702. Having studied four years at Douay and then two years at St. Omers, he went to Rome and was received in the College by Father Levinus Browne, the Rector, by order of Cardinal Gualtieri, Nov. 30, 1724. [Amongst the Alumni, Dec. 10 : Began Logic and took the oath of Alex. VII., June 24, 1725]. He was ordained Priest Jan. 22, 1730, and in the following Sept. 22 departed for England. He lived first at Witton Shields [the Draft says this of Pinckard, Robert], and then in Holderness, where he died, July 1, 1754.

PINCKARD, ROBERT. (See TYPPER).

PLOWDEN, CHARLES, S.J., was born May 1, 1743, and entered the noviceship Sept. 7, 1759. He travelled with Mr. Middleton, and when at Rome he
called with Mr. Thorpe to see me at the English College. We walked together
for some time in St. George's Hall, and he quite scandalized me with the
manner in which he spoke of Ganganelli. There is no doubt that Mr. Plowden
had a principal hand in the *Life of Ganganelli*, which was published in London,
1785. Father Thorpe supplied the materials (J. T. is subscribed to the letters
printed), and Mr. Plowden arranged them. I brought a packet of letters from
Mr. Thorpe to Mr. Charles Plowden, and one or two other packets were
brought from him to Mr. Plowden by other students. The contents were so
scandalous that Bishop Milner said in my hearing at Oscott that Mr. Weld,
with whom Mr. Charles Plowden lived, insisted on the work being suppressed.
The copies were all bought up, and I have never seen or heard of a copy since
I saw it in Coghlan's shop in 1785. Mr. Cordell, of Newcastle, wrote some
observations on it. Mr. Conally, S.J., told me at Oxford, Oct. 17, 1814, that
" he once saw in a corner of Mr. C. Plowden's room a heap of papers, some
torn and put there, apparently, to be burnt. I took up one of them," he said,
" which was torn in two ; it contained anecdotes of, and observations against,
Ganganelli." Mr. Plowden died on his return from Rome in June, 1821. (See
Cordell, Charles, above.)

PLOWDEN, FRANCIS (I.), best known by the name of the Abbé Plowden,
was son of Francis Plowden, Esq., by his wife Mary, daughter of the Hon.
John Stafford Howard and of Mary, daughter of Sir John Southcote. Such is
the account given me by Rev. Robert Plowden, who adds, that the Abbé was
brother to Mary of the Holy Cross, Abbess of the English Poor Clares, at
Rouen. This, however, does not agree with the account given in her life by
Mr. Alban Butler, p. 29, where he says that " Mrs. Mary Plowden, widow of
Francis Plowden, Esq., told him that Sister Mary of the Cross was daughter to
Sir Robert Howard." The Abbess' father followed the fortune of James II.,
and was Comptroller of his household, while his mother was Maid of Honour at
St. Germains. In the Register of St. Gregory's, it is said that after he had
finished his Philosophy at Douay* he became a pensioner at St. Gregory's in
Sept. 1725. On Jan. 29, 1730, he took the Seminary oath, and was ordained
Deacon, June 7, 1732. At the end of his license in 1735 he obtained leave of
Bishop Petre to remain another year in the Seminary, but left it in April, 1737,
without taking his cap of Doctor, " on account," says the Register, " of some
scruples concerning the Constitution."
    Whatever expectations he might have had to the honour of the Church in
France, through the Court of St. Germains, he bid adieu to them all, and by
the advice of a celebrated Doctor of Sorbonne he came over to England.
After staying three years without any active employment in the Mission, he returned to France and took up his abode with the Fathers of Christian Doctrine,
and was placed at the bottom of the list of those who catechised the children
in the parish of Monsieur Menesvier. It seems the Curates of Paris always
appointed the Catechists in their respective parishes ; but, on the death of
Mons. Menesvier, his successor, Mons. Bonnetin, required Abbé Plowden to
present himself to Mgr. de Beaumont, Archbishop of Paris, for his approbation.
This Mr. Plowden refused to do, on the plea that such a step was contrary to,
and as a precedent might be submersive of, the received practice in Paris.
Being by this means eased of his burden, he contented himself with assisting in
private those who had recourse to him for his spiritual advice and in answering
the numerous consultations he received from various parts of the country. In
this manner and in close application to those studies which become an Ecclesiastic, he spent the remainder of his long life, and at last died, Sept. 5, 1778,
at an advanced age.

---

* Educated at Douay, but Fr. Robert Plowden says at St. Omers.

He wrote: 1. *De Sacrificio Missæ.* I think, in 3 vols. 8vo; a work much esteemed. 2. *A Memoir,* in favour of the College of St. Omers, called *Précis.* This was during the law-suit with St. Omers College in 1773, etc., respecting Watten. *Ita* Mr. John Eyre.

PLOWDEN FRANCIS, (II), born July 10, 1749, brother of Robert and Charles, entered his novitiate Sept. 7, 1766, but the Suppression caused him to leave and betake himself to the law. He wrote: 1. *The History of Ireland.* 3 vols. 4to. 2. *Jura Anglorum.*

PLOWDEN, MARIANA, daughter of Francis Plowden of Plowden Hall, Salop, Esq., and Mrs. Catharine Audeley, widow of Mr. Butler, was fourth Prioress ot the Augustinian Nuns of Louvain. She died Nov. 1, 1715, aged 78, in the 60th of her profession. She was succeeded, Nov. 15, by Delphina Sheldon [who was elected fifth Prioress, Nov. 12, 1715], daughter of Edward Sheldon of Barton, Oxon, and Mrs. Catharine Constable of Everingham, Yorkshire.

PLOWDEN, RICHARD, S.J. He succeeded Father Powell at Rome as Rector of the Clergy College, in 1712, and in 1715 or 1716 was followed by Father Thomas Eberson. Father Richard was afterwards [in Sept. 1723] Rector of Liège.

PLOWDEN, ROBERT, S.J., born June 27, 1740. Entered his noviceship Sept. 7, 1756, and was many years a zealous Missionary at Bristol. When Bishop Talbot died there, April 23, 1795, Bishop Berington wished to say Mass the next morning for the repose of his soul, in the Chapel, but Mr. Plowden *refused to let him.*

In 1814 he refused to read Bishop Collingridge's Lenten Instructions, and in 1815, though he read them from the pulpit, he pronounced them heretical, for which he was suspended. Mr. Stone, Provincial, went to Bristol.

He afterwards lived at Swinnerton, in Mr. Fitzherbert's family, and afterwards in London, where, I think, he died. He wrote: *On Theological Inaccuracy.*

PLUMMERDEN, THOMAS *alias* PRITCHARD. He went to Douay, and at the end of Philosophy, was received in St. Gregory's at Paris. Having obtained a dispensation [from a letter of Cardinal Colredo to Dr. Paston, of April 21, 1702] from a part of the College oath, to enter into a religious Order but not to quit the Mission, in Aug. 1701, he went to Septfons, but his health not permitting him to continue there he went to Douay, and was employed in teaching some of the lower schools. He taught *Little Figures.* I do not find that he ever came on the Mission, nor when or where he died. See an interesting letter he wrote from Paray, or Perrecey, in the *Paris Seminary Collection,* Vol. I., p. 169, and his Declaration, p. 165.

PLUNKETT, ——. Abbé Plunkett was a native of Ireland. He was an eminent Professor of Divinity in the College of Navarre at Paris, and also Moral Divine and Casuist. He was G.V. to the Archbishop, and was the chief author of the Theological and didactic part of *Pastorale Parisiense,* or Paris Ritual, a work in high estimation about the year 1760.

POLE, VEN. SISTER TERESA MARY, O.S.F., of the ancient family of Cardinal Pole. She died at Lierre, May 31, 1793, aged 97, Relig. 80. (See *Life of Cardinal Pole,* by Phillips.)

POLLET *vere* DAVIES, *alias* BLOUNT MYLES, " was born," he says, " and bred with the straying herd, that is the Papists," in the Diocese of St. Asaph. He was sent to Douay, but was dismissed, says Bishop Giffard, for misconduct. At the age of 23 he was admitted into the College at Rome, Sept. 28, 1686, by order of Cardinal Howard, and was ordained Priest April 17, 1688. He left the College Oct. 15, and was recommended to Bishop Ellis, then in Paris, by the Cardinal, and received missionary faculties from the Bishop. On his arrival in England he exercised his functions in co. Gloucester, Hereford, and Flintshire. He was also "Confessor, he says, and Chaplain to the Roman Catholic families at Hill-End, at Malvern, and Blackmore Park, the seats of the Bartletts, Russells, Hornyholds and others near the cities of Worcester and elsewhere." His various functions did not, however, prevent his repairing occasionally to London, " where, as he says, he often resorted to St. Peter's, Cornhill, as a private hearer and spectator of the all-melting power of the Gospel of Christ, preached by Dr. William Beveridge, then Rector of that parish ; which at last completed those holy impressions which he had formerly conceived at a farther distance of his Lordship's Apostolical preaching of the purest Christianity."

In short, he read his recantation, and " after a private conformity to the Protestant Religion for the space of six or seven years, and so putting his conversion to a private probation, as preparatory to a publick one," he published in 1705 his Recantation Sermon, to which he prefixed a dedication to Dr. Beveridge, then Bishop of St. Asaph's, and a preface to the reader. This dedication is replete with the most fulsome flattery of Queen Anne, " who seemed to have obliged the very heavens into her confidence, and whose battles the Lord of Hosts had made His own ; and of that Heaven-born monarch King William, who alone was deemed by the kind heavens worthy and capable of obliging the Episcopal Hierarchy and primitive reformed Christianity with such an ornament and spiritual worthy as Dr. Beveridge "; and, finally, of the Bishop of St. Asaph, " whose parish of St. Peter, Cornhill, in the middle ot the great city of London, could show, " while he was Rector of it, more devout Christians, more frequent communicants, more instructed youth, and more learned laity than all the Popish countries could reckon up deluded nunneries, superstitious convents, apostatizing monasteries, and idolatrous churches." In his sermon upon Rev. xviii. 4 he outstrips most of his contemporaries in his abuse of the Church of Rome, which, with him, must needs be the scarlet whore of Babylon, " leaving for another opportunity to carry on a just parallel between Sodom and Rome, as also betwixt the Sodomites and the Papists." Whether or not he ever performed his promise I have not been able to discover, but he makes no scruple of revealing in the most unblushing manner " the confession of one of his penitents—a gentleman of a considerable estate," and this confession he says he heard while he was on a mission to Worcestershire, and was then living in the same house as the gentleman ; and adds such other circumstances as could not but lead, at the time, to the knowledge of his person. Such was the liberty which this convert of Protestantism gave himself on his renouncing the errors of Popery !

In his preface he laboured hard to prove the sincerity of his conversion, which seems to have been much questioned, and answers the charge of his having frequently changed his name, which was originally Davies, then Blount, then Pollet, etc., by observing that " the frequent changing of names is so essential to the trade of Priests and Jesuits, here in England especially, that there is no possibility of carrying on that emissary employment without that necessary variety of multiplying denominations as well as Protean garbs and other innumerable shiftings of the Incognito seen in the rest of their invisible legerdemain conduct." As if a more obvious and truer reason for such changes were not found in the sanguinary code of Elizabeth and William, which punished with fines, imprisonment, and even death, any priest or Jesuit who should be detected within " this kingdom of rights and priviliges, of Reformed consciences."

POOLE, SIR FRANCIS, of Poole Hall, Cheshire. Bart., was third and only surviving son of Sir James Poole (created Bart. Oct. 25, 1677) by his wife Anne, daughter of Thomas Eyre, of Hassop. He married Frances, daughter of Henry Pelham, of Lewes, at which time he probably conformed, if before a Catholic, and was chosen M.P. for Lewes. He died Feb. 15, 1763. His mother was a Catholic ; his brother James married Meliora, daughter of —— Gumbleton, co. Kent, a Catholic, and he and his father Sir James are among the Jacobites of 1715 in the Report.

POPE, ALEXANDER, ESQ. Dodd had heard that he was a pupil of Mr. Bromley, once Curate of St. Giles', London, but who became a Catholic. (Dodd III., 459).

Mr. Hooke, the Historian, told Mr. Warburton "that the Priest whom he had procured to the last office to the dying man came out from him penetrated to the last degree with the state of mind in which he found his penitent, resigned and rapt up with the love of God and man." (*Essay on Pope*, II., 2,012. See C. Butler's *Mem.*, chap. 43).*

" When Pope attained his eighth year, he was placed under the tuition of one Taverner, a Catholic Priest who lived somewhere in Hampshire. From him he learnt the rudiments of the Greek and Latin tongues, and he made very considerable progress under the care of this instructor. From this private tutor he was sent to a Catholic School at Twyford, near Winchester, where he did not continue any considerable time, for within about a year he was removed from thence to a school near Hyde Park Corner, being about ten years of age, which school was probably kept by Mr. Bromley, whose pupil Mr. Pope is said to have been."

POSTGATE, RALPH, S.J., was born in the Diocese of Oxford, say the *Annals of the Roman College*. He studied Logic and Physics at Douay, and at the age of 23 was sent to Rome to complete his Philosophy and Divinity in 1671, and was admitted into the College Oct. 16, 1671. He was ordained Priest March 24, 1674, but before he set off for the Mission he was taken dangerously ill, and during his illness obtained from Pope Clement X. (Father Christopher Anderton being then Rector) a dispensation from that part of the oath of Alexander VII. which he had taken at Douay, and which precluded his entrance into any religious Order, and was admitted into the Noviciate of St. Andrew on Monte Cavallo (Quirinal), and soon after made his Profession. Thus was the Clergy deprived of the services of a noble young man after being for many years educated on their funds at Douay and Rome. In 1691, or beginning of 1692, he was sent by his Superior to Rome, and was twice Rector of the College there.

POSTLETHWAITE, JOHN. He was educated at Douay. After his ordination he came on the Mission, and lived many years at Leyburne in Yorkshire, where he died, Jan. 5, 1785.

POTTER, ——. A gentleman of Manchester, who, about sixty years ago, contributed considerabiy to the building of the Catholic Chapel in Rook Street, Manchester. Disputes concerning religion at that time ran high, and prejudices were very strong. It was on this occasion that Mr. Potter is said to have written a Catholic pamphlet with the ludicrous title of *A Ball of Wax against a Ball of Soap*. So says the Rev. Edward Kenyon, formerly Priest at that Chapel and then Pastor at Blessington.

POTTS, LUKE *alias* COOPER, was born at Throckley, near Newcastle, and was sent to Douay. Having been sent on the Mission he was placed at Ugthorpe, and had the care of the Catholics at and about Scarborough. On Dec. 16, 1745, he was taken up on suspicion of being a Popish Priest, and of secretly combining with others of the same religion against His Majesty's person, and on his examination, confessing himself to be a Priest, and refusing to take the oaths, he was committed to York Castle, as were also on the same account five other Priests, to wit Messrs. Anderson, Rivett, Wilson, Shelton, and Hundshill. They remained there till the Lent Assizes in the following March, when they stood trials. (See *State Trials*). Subscriptions were raised among the Catholics for their maintenance in prison, and to defray the expenses of their trials, in which the charity of Mr. Tunstall, of Wycliff, and of Mr. Cholmely were highly conspicuous. The day Mr. Potts was released from

---

* These notes are in Kirk's hand, and are followed by a paper on Pope, compiled by some person whose name does not appear, and which by reason of its length is unsuited for introduction here. It follows very olosely the *Life* by Bowles, with occasional references to Ruffhead and " British Biographies." The date 1809 is in the watermark of this paper, and gives approximately the date of the composition. No later authors are referred to. There is no reference in it to the priest introduced to Pope's death-bed. Kirk probably intended to draw up a shorter biography by its aid. The passage quoted above about Pope's education is the only one in which reference is made to the poet's Catholicism.—J.H.P.

York Castle he rode to Wycliff, a distance of about sixty miles. The fatigue was such that when he was sought for next morning, which was a great holiday, he was found kneeling at his table, with his boots and spurs on, where he had knelt down to say his prayers at night. In 1750, Mr. Potts succeeded Mr. James Mitford, at Thropton, and was in no way inferior to his predecessor in piety and zeal for the good of his neighbours. There he died, Aug. 16, 1787. [Mr. Potts began Philosophy about 1739].

POWIS, LUCY HERBERT, LADY. She was Superior of the Augustine Nuns at Bruges, where, in 1743, a book was printed with this title:—*Several Methods and Practices of Devotion appertaining to a Religious Life, collected together by the Right Hon. Lady Lucy Herbert of Powis, Superior of the English Augustine Nuns at Bruges*, 1743. She was succeeded by Mrs. More, of the family of Sir Thomas More, and she by another Mrs. Moore, of Wolverhampton (Superior in 1817), who is sister of Mrs. Devey, of Wolverhampton.

POYNTER, REV. WILLIAM, D.D., Bishop of Halia, and Vicar Apostolic of the London District. Was born at Petersfield, in Hampshire, on May 20, 1762. At an early age he was sent by the Venerable Bishop Challoner to Douay College, where, after passing the usual course of studies, and receiving the Priesthood, he was successively promoted to the Professorships of Literature, Philosophy, and Theology. At the most dreadful period of the French Revolution, our Prelate, with the Superiors and Students of the College, was imprisoned in the Castle of Doullens, on the very day on which Queen Marie Antoinette was immolated on the scaffold. In prison, as in the College, he was at once the monitor and model of every virtue: resigned and fearless amidst the horrors he incessantly witnessed, and in which he and his colleagues were constantly in danger of being involved. From the wrecks of the English Colleges of Douay and St. Omers were formed those of St. Edmund's and of Crook Hall, since removed to Ushaw. At St. Edmund's, under the Presidency of Dr. Stapleton, Dr. Poynter was chosen Vice-president, and succeeded the former in his office upon his being raised to the Episcopacy and being appointed Vicar Apostolic of the Midland District. A pious and ardent zeal for the progress of the students inspired and animated his every endeavour, and he persevered in a faithful and rigid discharge of his Presidential duties until the death of Dr. Douglass in 1812, to whom he had been appointed Coadjutor in 1803, and whom he then succeeded as Vicar Apostolic of the London District. During his Episcopacy the same pastoral solicitude was discernible in the spiritual direction of his district that he had previously displayed in the more local and limited charge of Superior of St. Edmund's. As honey is more attractive than vinegar, the firmness of his purpose was never announced with austerity, but with a gentle earnestness, which ruder tempers, habitually abrupt, sometimes mistook for a weakness of character. Abroad or at home, his worth was duly appreciated and universally acknowledged, excepting when, in the conflicting jargon of opinions, precipitancy pronounced judgment. Dr. Poynter won the admiration and esteem of all whose praise could stamp upon his name a character that would transmit it to posterity as that of " a great Prelate, who in his days pleased God." If the " evil word " went forth with blighting breath, to taint so venerable a name, its effects must be counteracted by the *good word* of one of the greatest Prelates of our time : "I deem it a conscientious duty to testify that the illustrious Dr. Milner, not very long before his death, declared to me respecting the Venerable Dr. Poynter, in words which, coming from any-one else, might be construed into flattery, but he was not accustomed to flatter —he declared, with emotions scarcely susceptible of description, that he entertained the most unbounded veneration for the virtues, piety, and edifying character of Dr. Poynter, and that he would give the universe to possess half his merit in the sight of God." (See the *Funeral Discourse delivered by the Rev. L. Havard at the Obsequies of Dr. Poynter*, p. 20). And we may add with truth, that " in the time of wrath he became an atonement," for those contradictions which give birth to the confessor's merit he bore with a confessor's patience. Severe indeed was that trial of his fortitude when he had unexpectedly to witness a *second* confiscation, by a British tribunal, of that British Ecclesiastical property which had *first* been confiscated by revolutionary France, and subsequently restored by virtue of the treaties of Paris and Vienna. This was a dreadful and unexpected blow, and could not but have been severe to a Pastor who so well knew and so keenly felt the extensive wants and scanty means of the Mission. Moreover, a life of sedentary occupation, too sedulously pursued, and increased far beyond the limits of the Episcopal duties of the London District, by his situation of Metropolitan Prelate, which made him, as it were, a centre of communication in the Catholic Ecclesiastical affairs of the transmarine possessions of this kingdom, gradually impaired a constitution that promised, but in vain, length of days. For some months previous to his death his sufferings were severe and unremitted, and his illness gaining strength, baffled the skill of the ablest members of the Faculty. During this severe trial the holy calmness and resignation, for which he had been so remarkable from his infancy, shone forth with brighter lustre, and the number of his days hastening to their conclusion, we trust we may say he entered "into the joy of the Lord" on the evening of Nov. 26, 1827, in the 66th year of his age, the 16th of his Apostolical Vicariate, and the 25th of his Episcopacy.

The remains of this much-lamented Prelate were deposited, on Dec. 11, 1827, in a vault under the high altar of St. Mary's Chapel, Moorfields, the first stone of which sacred edifice he himself had laid. The ceremonies on this mournful occasion, under the regulation of the Rev. Mr. Ryan, of St. Edmund's College, were of a most imposing and affecting description. Bishop Bramston, the successor of the deceased in the London Vicariate, was the officiating Prelate, and was assisted by Bishop Weld, the Rev. Dr. Griffiths, President of St. Edmund's, several of the professors of that College, and above eighty of the clergy of the London District. The coffin, richly decorated, was raised upon a black cataphalque, surrounded by lighted tapers, and bore the following inscription : "G.H.V.A.L. Illustrissimus et reverendissimus Dominus, Dominus Gulielmus Poynter, Episcopus Haliensis, Et in Districtu Londinensi Vicarius Apostolicus, Obiit die 26 Novembris 1827, Ætatis suæ 66, Requiescat in Pace."

In compliance with the wish expressed in the will of the lamented Prelate, his heart was conveyed to St. Edmund's College, to be deposited beneath the foot of the altar, where the Priest stands to begin Mass. It was enclosed in a case covered with rich purple velvet, and bearing the following inscription : "In hoc Collegio Catholico Fidei Seminario Unde nunquam fuerat Avulsum Cor suum Testamento Reponi mandavit Illmus ac Revmus Gul. Hal. V.A.L."

A detailed and interesting account of the obsequies is appended to the very eloquent Funeral Oration then delivered by the Rev. Lewis Havard, which was published for the benefit of St. Mary's Chapel, Westminster.

The episcopal duties of Dr. Poynter left him but little leisure for literary occupation ; he has, nevertheless, added the following learned and pious productions to the British Catholic Library :

Theological Examination of the Doctrines of Columbanus; contained in his third Letter on the Spiritual Jurisdiction of Bishops, and the difference between a Bishop and a Priest. Published in 1812.

A Sermon preached at St. Patrick's Chapel on Thursday, March 17, 1825, the Festival of St. Patrick, Apostle of Ireland and Patron of the Chapel, the Most Rev. Dr. Curtis, R.C. Abp. of Armagh, and other Prelates being present.

Reflections on British Zeal for the Propagation of Christianity and on the state of Christianity in England. By C.C.

Christianity; or the Evidences and Characters of the Christian Religion. 8vo, 1827.

The New Year's Gifts in the Laity's Directories from the year 1813 to 1828 inclusively.

Declaration of the Catholic Bishops, Vicars Apostolic and their Coadjutors in Great Britain, being a Defence of their Principles, in opposition to the calumnious Misrepresentations on which the legal disabilities of Catholics are founded.

[Upwards of 100,000 of this admirable Declaration were distributed gratis by the British Catholic Association].
New and improved editions of first and second Catechisms. R.I.P.

POYNTZ, AUGUSTIN, son of Thomas and Sarah Poyntz (Lane), was a native of London, and was sent to Douay. At the age of 25 he went to Rome, and was admitted into the Roman College by Father Postgate, July 11, 1705. He was ordained April 3, 1706, and left April 30, 1707, to go through France. " By reason of the ill management of his affairs here," says Mr. Bryan Tunstall in a letter to Mr. Gordon at Rome, dated Dec. 14, 1705, " Mr. President, after a great deal of kind usage and tender ways (to make him sensible of his duty), was forced to dismiss him about a year ago, but in a civil and obliging manner ; supplying him with all things necessary, tho' there was a great hazard of never being paid again. Whilst he was with us he had applied himself to the Jesuits, and, that he might be supported by them, had given several underhand informations of some things he thought might be for the purpose of making them believe he was a sufferer with us upon their account, and in defending their opinions ; whereas the reasons of his dismission were far otherwise. When in England he did not stick to say many unworthy and false things of us." The author of the *Modest Defence* says, p. 120: " Mr. Poyntz, in that answer he gave me in writing, denies that he was dismissed from the College, that he studied revenge, and that in the first place he made his application to the Jesuits. As to the first, he appeals to Dr. Paston, and says he left Douay by his consent at the pressing instances of his acquaintances in England, on account of the death of some of his friends, and of a Bishop in England, who offered to bear his expenses if he would return into France to receive Holy Orders. He was afterwards admitted at Rome, carried himself well during his stay, and then the Jesuits recommended him to a place where he has carried himself (1714) for several years with very great edification." In July, 1707, he went to be Confessor to the Augustin nuns at Bruges, on the death of their Confessor. " A long and close intelligence was held with one Austin Poyntz." (See Andrew Giffard's account, and Mr. Dicconson's in *Records of Douay College*, B. 39 ; also Dr. Hawarden.)

PRESTON, HENRY, was born in Lancashire, and sent to Lisbon by Bishop Russell. He studied his Classics and Philosophy under Mr. Roger Brockholes, and publicly defended the latter July 1, 1689. In the preceding April he had taken the College oath and cassock, and in October, 1692, was sent on the Mission, and lived many years in the family of Lord Montague, at Cowdray. On Feb. 3, 1712, he was chosen a Canon of the Chapter. He afterwards lived with Lord Fauconberg, but left his Lordship Dec. 16, 1706 [and was succeeded by one Cayne, O.S.B., sent by F. Corker]. Mr. Preston died July 11, 1733. (*Lisbon Register* ; *Miscell.*, p. 1082.)

PRESTON, List of persons taken at :—

English Noblemen and Gentlemen	...	...	...	75
Their Vassals and Followers, etc.	...	...	...	83
Private Men in the Church ...	...	...	...	...	303
				461
Scotch Noblemen and Officers	...	...	...	...	143
Vassals, Servants, and others	...	...	...	...	862
				1,005

Catholics taken.—Earl of Derwentwater, Lord Widdrington, Edward Howard, Charles Ratcliff, Charles Widdrington, Peregine Widdrington, Walter Tancred, John Thornton, John Clavering, John Clavering, William Clavering, Nicholas Wogan, John Talbot, Roger Salkeld, George Collingwood. Forty-eight persons were executed. (*Faithful Register.*)

PRESTON, JOHN, had his education at Merchant Tailors' School, in London, and was designed for St. John's College, Oxford ; but, becoming a Catholic, he went over to Lisbon College [aged about 22] and spent the remainder of his life in the service of that house. He taught Humanity during the whole time of his studying Philosophy and Divinity, and performed every other office required of him. He was held in great estimation by the Court of Portugal, and was appointed tutor to the young Prince of Brazils, afterwards Prince Regent of Portugal. He died at Lisbon, Feb. 8, 1780, and was buried in the College church. Dr. Barnard, the President, wrote his Epitaph :

" Hic jacet quod mortale fuit Johannis Preston Sacerdotis, viri simplicis ac timentis Deum. Is in omni litterarum genere versatus, acri judicio, varia in hoc collegio munia obeundo, annos II de L, non sibi sed aliis vixit. Instituendo regio principi electus, munus honorificum diu exequi non potuit. Paralysi correptus, flebilis omnibus ob. æt. an. LXVIII ; an. dom. MDCCLXXX, VI Id. Feb. ; R.I.P. ; Socii mœr. pos." (*Lisbon Register.*)

PRITCHARD, MATTHEW, O.S.F., Bishop of Myra. He taught Divinity at Douay [in 1704] and was a strenuous defender of the Church's infallibility *in eo quod est facti non revelati.* After the Revolution, and when Bishop Ellis had quitted England, Bishop Giffard governed the Western District for him, and in 1699 travelled through Wales to give confirmation. (*Letter to a Member of Parliament on the growth of Popery.*) Mr. Mayes, in a letter to Dr. Thomas Witham of Aug. 19, 1713, says that when Mr. Sylvester Jenks was named for the Western District, the Internunce at Brussels named also Father Pritchard, and that on the list there were ten Benedictines, one Carmelite, and one Dominican—so bent were they on securing that District to the Regulars. Mr. Pritchard was appointed and consecrated at Cologne [Whitsuntide, 1715] Bishop of Myra, in Asia. He lived at Perthere, two miles from Monmouth, a seat of the Lorimers. His Grand Vicars in 1739 were Dr. Carnaby, Mr. Roydon, and Dr. Holden. He died [May 22] 1750, aged 81. (See *Catholic Magazine*, X., 708.)

He wrote the preface to Dr. R. Witham's *Remarks on Dr. Fell's " Lives of the Saints,"* and a letter in Dr. Challoner's *Missionary Priests*, II., 432.

PROGERS, THOMAS, *alias* JOHN POWELL was chosen Archdeacon of South Wales, March 6, 1666, (O.S.), and Vicar-General of Shropshire and North Wales at the General Assembly, June 4, 1684. He died between 1700 and 1703.

PULTON, GILES, *alias* PALMER, S.J., son of Ferdinand and Julia Pulton, was a native of Northamptonshire, and born Sept. 7, 1694. After studying the Classics at St. Omers [for six years], he went to Rome, and was received into the College at the age of 20 [by Fr. R. Plowden, Oct. 16, 1714]. On the following May 1, he was placed on the Free Fund, and took the original College oath, which left him at liberty to enter a Religious Order. On April 8, 1719, he was ordained Priest, and on Sept. 24, 1721, left the College to go to Watten, where he entered his noviciate and became a Jesuit. He died in London in 1752. See Mr. Oliver's list of Jesuits in *Catholic Journal.* (*Ann. Coll. Angl.*)

PULTON, WILLIAM, son of Giles Pulton and Mary Reeve, his wife, was born in Warwickshire. At the age of 22 he was received into the College at Rome by Father Postgate, the Rector, Oct. 15, 1698. He there studied his Philosophy and his Divinity, and was ordained, June 2, 1703, and departed for England, April 25, 1704. I find him a Missionary in Notts. on Jan. 7, 1725. He died, June 25, 1726. (*Ann. Coll. Angl. de Urbe.*)

PURCELL, WALTER CHETWYND, of a good family near Albrighton in Shropshire. He studied at Douay, and came on the Mission about 1690. In 1692 he resided with his uncle, and assisted where necessity called for his labours in the neighbourhood. He died at Oscott, Aug. 25, 1720. He had the character of " a well-learned and virtuous Missionary." (See Mr. Oliver's *List of Jesuits* for Fathers James and Thomas Parker, Sebastian Redford, Philip Carteret, Brent, and Walton, S.J.)

QUENEL, JAMES. A French Priest from Normandy. At the beginning of
the French Revolution he became, from his character, the object of Revolutionary fury, and was wounded in his hand. He then made his escape to England
with his brother, and both lived for some years in Wolverhampton. James
then went to Worcester, where he taught French, and occasionally said Mass
there, and at Spetchley, till some scandal was taken at his conduct, when he
was forbid by Dr. Milner to say Mass till the scandal was done away. Instead
of this he married publicly and continued to live in Worcester. This was a
source of much uneasiness to his virtuous brother, who did not fail to remonstrate with him to repent ; the same was done also by Dr. Milner, who warned
him of the miserable end of several who had fallen like himself. The poor man
was not altogether insensible to their entreaties, and even promised to reform,
adding that a venerable old Priest, who had been his Confessor in France, had
appeared to him and remonstrated with him. In the meanwhile he continued
in his scandalous course of life, and at last dropped down dead in the street at
Worcester. *Ita.* Dr. Milner.

RADCLIFFE, ANTHONY JAMES, fourth Earl of Newburgh, and son of
James Bartholomew, third Earl, in 1788 obtained an Act of Parliament which
granted to him and his heirs male a clear rent-charge of £2,500 per annum out
of the estates forfeited by his grand-uncle, the Earl of Derwentwater, and
settled on Greenwich Hospital. These estates are said to exceed at present
£40,000 per annum. This Earl was born in 1767, and on June 30, 1789, married
a daughter of Sir Thomas Webb. *N.B.*—I fear there is some confusion and
mistake in the pedigree of the Radcliffes.

RADCLIFFE, CHARLES, third son of Francis, second Earl, and Mary
Tudor, and brother of James, third Earl of Derwentwater, was born in 1693 [at
Little Faringdon, in Essex]. He was educated with his brother at St.
Germains, and when 22 joined the rebels, in 1715 ; yet neither he nor his
brother, the Earl, are thought to have been admitted into the secret of it, being
no ways provided with proper arms for such an expedition. When they left
Dilstone [they were only attended by menial servants] they stayed some days
at Sir Marmaduke Constable's house before they joined the Prince. This
was the first time he appeared in the military world, and at Preston behaved
with much intrepidity ; but, with his brother, he was obliged to surrender to
Generals Carpenter and Wills. He was brought up to London, and conveyed
to Newgate. On May 16, 1716, his trial came on, when he was convicted of
high treason, and received sentence of death, but was remanded to gaol,
where he remained seven months, and behaved with great cheerfulness, often
doing acts of kindness to his fellow prisoners. On Dec. 11, following, he
escaped with many others from Newgate, and proceeding to the coast of
Sussex, got over to Boulogne, and thence to Paris. He there met Charlotte
Lady Newburgh, daughter and heiress of Livingstone, widow of Lord
Newburgh, whom he afterwards married and by her had several children
[particularly a son, who was taken with him in 1745]. In the meantime his
friends solicited a free pardon, and for the recovery of the estate and title forfeited by his brother's attainder. Not being successful, he obtained a commission in the regiment of the Duke of Berwick, which was intended to go over to
Scotland, in 1745, and he actually embarked on board the *Espérance* of Dunkirk,
but was taken on the coast of Scotland, together with his son and several
officers belonging to the Irish Brigades in the French service. On Nov. 21,
1746, he was brought into court, and his former sentence and record of his
conviction being read, he pleaded that he was not Charles Radcliff, but the Earl
of Derwentwater, as his nephew John was dead, and a subject of the French
King, from whom he had a commission. This was overruled, and the jury
brought in their verdict that the prisoner was the same Charles Radcliffe who
was convicted of High Treason, and broke out of Newgate in 1716. He was
beheaded on Little Tower Hill, Dec. 8, 1746 (O.S.) [Dec. 19, N.S.]. Mr.
Radcliff was a gentleman of extensive learning and great charm, natural
courage, and a zealous Catholic. "I die," he said in his speech, "a true,

obedient and humble servant to the Holy Catholic and Apostolic Church : in perfect charity with all mankind, a true well-wisher to my dear country that can never be happy without doing justice to the best and most injured King. I die with all sentiments of gratitude, respect, and love to the King of France, Louis, the well-beloved, of glorious name.   I recommend to His Majesty my dear family, and heartily repent of all my sins, and have a firm confidence to obtain the mercy of Almighty God, through the merits of his beloved Son Jesus Christ, our Lord, to whom I recommend my soul.   Amen."

One of Charles Radcliff's daughters married Francis Eyre, of Warkworth, which estate he had from Mr. Holman, while his elder brother inherited Hassop.

The eldest daughter of his wife Charlotte (by her first marriage with Thomas, Lord Clifford of Chudleigh) married James, Count de Mahony, who had a government in Sicily, and whose daughter married, about 1757, Prince Giustiniani in Italy.   This Charlotte was daughter and heiress of Charles, second Lord Newburgh (whose mother is celebrated in the poems of Lord Lansdowne), and by his death without male issue, she, according to the patent, became a Countess in her own right.   She died in Aug. 1755, when the title devolved on her eldest son, James Bartholomew Radcliff, third Earl of Newburgh, who had two brothers, Charles Radcliffe, and [James], and four sisters, Charlotte, Barbara, Thomasina, and Mary.   "It seems," says the *Cheshire Miscellany*, of 1750, p. 162, "that the Derwentwater estate was only confiscated to the crown for the life of Charles Radcliffe, but by a clause in the Act of Parliament passed some years since, which says that the issue of any person attainted of High Treason, born or bred in any foreign dominion, and a Roman Catholic, shall forfeit his reversion of such estates, and the remainder shall be for ever fixed in the Crown.   By which clause, the son of the unfortunate gentleman is absolutely deprived of any title or interest in that affluent fortune of that antient family to the amount of better than £200,000."

RADCLIFFE, FRANCIS, second Earl of Derwentwater, was son of Sir Francis Ratcliffe, first Earl.   He succeeded his father in April, 1696, and married Lady Mary Tudor, natural daughter of Charles II., by Mary Davis, by whom he had issue three sons and one daughter.   He died April 29, 1705. She died at Paris, Nov. 5, 1726 (See *Gentleman's Magazine*, Vol. lxiv., 521, *Monumenta Anglicana*).   His brother, Thomas Radcliffe, died abroad, Dec. 31, 1715 (See *MS. Records of Jansenism*, p. 90, for something respecting him).

RADCLIFFE, JAMES, third Earl of Derwentwater, eldest son of Francis, second Earl, and Mary Tudor [natural daughter of Charles II. by Mistress Mary Davis], was born in 1695.   His family had distinguished themselves in the wars with Scotland, and for their eminent services Sir Robert Radcliffe was made Knight Banneret in the field in the reign of Henry III.   Sir Francis Radcliffe was created Earl of Derwentwater by James II. on his marriage with Lady Mary Tudor.   This affinity, and the education of the —— son and his brother Charles at St. Germains, turned the bias of their minds to the Jacobite interest.   About the end of Sept., 1715, the Earl had notice that there was a warrant out from the Secretary of State to apprehend him, and that the messengers were at Durham to take him.   This determined him to join the Rebels, on or about Oct. 6, on a hill called the Waterfalls, in Northumberland, together with some friends and all his servants from his seat at Dilstone, mounted on his coach- and other horses, and all very well armed.   The Earl commanded the first English troop of horse, having under him his brother, Charles Radcliffe, and Capt. Shaftoe.   Yet, says Robert Patten, who was himself in the Rebel Army, it was thought that this Lord did not join so heartily or so premeditately in this affair as was expected ; for there is no doubt that he might have brought far greater numbers of men into the field than he did.   The great estate he possessed, the money he could command, his interest among the Gentlemen, and, what was above all, his being so well beloved, could not fail to have procured him many hundreds of followers more than he had, if he had thought fit ; for his concerns in the lead mines in Alstone Moor are very considerable, where several hundreds of men are employed under him and get their bread from him, whom there is no doubt he might easily have engaged. Besides this, the sweetness of his temper and disposition, in which he had few equals, had so secured him the affection of all his tenants, neighbours, and dependants, that multitudes would have lived and died with him.   The truth is he was a man favoured by nature to be generally beloved, for he was of so universal a beneficence that he seemed to live for others.   As he lived among his own people, there he spent his estate, and continually did offices of kindness and good neighbourhood to everybody as opportunity offered.   He kept a house of generous hospitality and noble entertainment, was very charitable to the poor and distressed familes on all occasions, whether known to him or not, and whether Papists or Protestants.

From Penrith they marched for Appleby.   None of any account joined them in this march, "for all the Papists on that side of the country were secured beforehand in the castle of Carlisle, to their great good fortune. . . . About Kirkby-Lonsdale some Lancashire Papists, with their servants, came and joined them, and marched in the line with them.   In Lancashire a great many Lancashire gentlemen joined them with their tenants, servants, and friends, and some of very good figure in the country, but still all were Papists.* . . . The Gentlemen Volunteers were drawn up in the Churchyard at Preston under the command of the Earl of Derwentwater, Viscount Kenmure, Earls of Wintoun and Nithsdale.   The Earl of Derwentwater signalised himself, stripping into his waistcoat he encouraged the men, by giving them money, to cast up trenches and animating them to a vigorous defence of them.   He then ordered Mr. Patten (the writer) to bring him constantly an account of all the attacks, how things went on, and where succours were wanted, which Mr. Patten did till his horse was shot under him."   After a vigorous resistance the Earl was taken prisoner, and being found guilty on his trial, was condemned to be beheaded.   In the morning of Feb. 24, 1715, (O.S.), he was conveyed from the Tower to Tower-hill with Viscount Kenmure (£60,000 had been in vain offered Walpole to save his life.   See Hist., VIII., 147-9).   Separate rooms were prepared for their private devotions, and they had liberty to see their friends. (See Bishop Giffard's letter to the Earl.)   After an hour's retirement Lord Derwentwater walked to the scaffold, where, after spending some time in prayer on his knees, he read to the people assembled the papers (See the *Records*), and which he delivered to Sir John Fryer.   After which he read aloud from his prayer-book : " Have mercy on me, O God, according to Thy great mercy and according to the multitude of Thy tender mercies, blot out my iniquity.   O Lord, Thy will be done.   The Lord giveth and the Lord taketh away, and blessed be the name of the Lord.   Thy will be done on earth as it is in heaven (thrice).   Give me patience that I may suffer as becomes a Christian and Thy disciple."   He then said, "I forgive all that are concerned in my execution, and I forgive all the world."   Then kneeling down, he laid his head on the block to see if it fitted him, and said again, " I forgive my enemies, and hope God will forgive me."   Then turning to the executioner, and telling him to strike when he heard him repeat the words " Sweet Jesus " the third time, he said : " Sweet Jesus, receive my spirit ; Sweet Jesus, be merciful to me ; Sweet Jesus——" and seemed to be going on, when the executioner at one stroke severed his head from his body, and taking it in both his hands, he elevated it at the four corners of the scaffold, saying, "Behold the head of a traitor.   God save King George."   His body was then wrapped in black bayes [baize] and conveyed by his friends to the house of Mr. Metcalf, a surgeon.   It was here embalmed, together with the head, and conveyed to Dilstone.   The Earl married Anna Maria [who died at Brussels, Aug. 17, 1723], daughter of Sir John Webb, by whom he had two sons and a daughter, married to Robert, Lord Petre.   In the Report given into the House of Commons in 1717 by the Commissioners, his estates, which were all forfeited to the Crown, were valued at £6,374 4s. 5d., an amazing income in those days, besides £5,993 12s. 5½d. of personal estate ; £1,200, the unpaid

---

* The draft says : " Most of them Papists.   At Preston they were joined by a great number of gentlemen with their tenants, servants, and attendants."

marriage portion of Lady Derwentwater ; and £2,000 due on the death of Sir John Webb.

The Charities of the Derwentwater family were great, and are still upon record, and will never be forgotten—to say nothing of those bestowed on poor families about Dilstone during life : Francis, the first Earl, who died, April 21, 1696, and his sister Barbara, left each £400 for the relief of the poor Catholics in Northumberland ; and their example was followed by Francis, second Earl, and his brother, Francis Edward Radcliffe. The latter was also a great friend and benefactor of Douay College. (*History of the Late Rebellion* and *Faithful Register.*)

RADCLIFFE, LADY MARY *and* LADY CATHARINE, were nuns at St. Ursula's, in Louvain. The first died Oct. 26, 1729, the second in 1744. " They both excelled in humility and religious virtue. They and their family bestowed great wealth on the Community." (*Obituary of the Convent.*)

RAMSAY, SIR ANDREW MICHAEL, Knight of St. Lazarus and F.R.S. Born June 9, 1686, and died May 6, 1743. He was also an honorary member of the Literary Society at Spalding, in Lincolnshire. He wrote : 1. *The Life of Cyrus.* 2. *The History of Marshal Turenne,* 1737. 3. *The Philosophical Principles of Natural and Revealed Religion, unfolded in Geometrical order.* Glasgow, 1751, 2 vols., 4to. 4. An edition of *The Life and Works of Fénelon.* (See *Dict. Hist.* VI., 106, and *Biogr. Dict. French and English*).

RAVENSCROFT, JAMES, was of a good family in Lincolnshire. He lived in Lincolnshire to a great age, and was in great estimation among his Brethren. In 1682 he was offered by the Chapter, of which he was a member, the Arch-deaconry of Lincoln, Rutland, and Notts., but declined the honour, and Mr. Foster was chosen. He was alive in 1692.

He wrote : 1. *A Treatise of living well*, by James Ravenscroft, Esq. A thick folio. 2. *A Treatise of dying well.* Also a thick folio. By James Ravenscroft, Esq. 3. *Fears and terrors of death*, by the same. A very thick folio. 4. *The Theatre of Afflictions and the Triumphs of Patience.* By the same ; 1,091 folio pages.

N.B.—The handwriting was very similar to that of Mr. Thos. Thwing, who suffered in 1680. All these MSS. are in the library of MSS. at Burton Constable.

REEVE, JOHN, studied at Douay, and when he came on the Mission was placed at Foxcote, the seat of Francis Canning, Esq. After remaining there some years he removed to Newport, and thence to Madeley, in Shropshire, where he died in Feb., 1813. He was said to be a good Mathematician, and was a zealous missionary.

REEVE, JOSEPH, S.J., was born May 11, 1733, entered his noviceship Sept. 7, 1752, and was made a professed Father in 1770. See *Mr. Oliver's Lists.* He wrote : 1. *Discourses, etc.* 2 vols. 2. *History of the Bible.* 3. *The History of the Church.* 3 vols. 4. *Miscellaneous Poetry* (Ugbroke). 5. Translated into Latin Addison's *Cato* ; Mr. Dryden's *Alexander's Feast* ; Mr. Pope's *Ode on St. Cecilia* ; Ditto his *Messiah* and his *Pastorals*, and *Quatuor vertentis anni tempestates* (Anglice, the Seasons). (See *Catholic Spectator*, vi *n.* 425, if I be not mistaken).

REID, THOMAS, a Scotchman, educated at Rome in the College of his countrymen, and was ordained there. He left the College about 1765, and after staying a few weeks at Paris, came on the Mission. The theatre of his apostolical labours for more than half a century was at, or near, Gordon Castle, in Banffshire, among the numerous tenantry of the Duke. Sir James Gordon, Bart., of Letterfourie, near Cullen, was in his congregation. Mr. Reid died in 1816, or 1815. He wrote : *Sermons on the Nativity*, which were, and are, much admired.

REYDON, THOMAS (I) *alias* CORNFORTH. In Sept., 1708, with Bishop Smith's consent, he went from Douay to Notre Dame des Victoires, in Paris, to spend one year there to make him more fit for the Mission. In 1720 he attended Bishop Witham in his visitation in Lancashire as his V.G., for above two months, on his progress and in his sickness, which would allow him, he says, no respite, and took up a great part of the night. (*Ep. Var.*, VIII., 155). "In the late years of trouble and plunder," (he says, April 25, 1724), "there was little convenience and much hazard in lodging papers; where many writings were carried off, lost, or destroyed; where I had a large portion of personal difficulties increased by restraint and confinement; where most of my quarters and chief stages were disturbed and incumbered with the actual possession of the Commissioners (*i.e.*, for forfeited estates), their bailiffs, and tenants. What a number of miles was I obliged to travel! What a fatigue of riding to my separate quarters, not only in several distinct parishes, but also in several counties! And yet I was retarded and tethered by other indispensable attendances! Hard lot! When I reached home (if I may call it home, where, God be my comfort, I scarce ever rest three nights successively in the same bed), I had but a scantling of time to search into holes and snatch up materials. Harder still, a triple disadvantage was the result of these distant abodes, of these motions, and of my hurry. My answer was retarded; essential evidences were forgot, and left behind in haste; and, after all, my answer on the important subject would not only come too late, but also seemed to me imperfect and defective!" Letter to Dr. R. Witham. (*Ibid.*, p. 144). (On what occasion was this letter written? See *Bp. Dicconson's Diary*, Nov., 1716, and *Records of Douay College*, pp. 69-71.)

" On Oct. 3, I travelled from Kendal by Wycliff to Piercebridge, over the rugged roads of our hills, and your Stainmore, above forty-six miles in one single, and that one no long, day. On the 4th I waited on you at Cliffe "; p. 156. " My Journal," he says, " lodges me at Aldborough; Nov. 24, 1714, carries me to Cliffe, and back on the 26th. Again to Cliffe and back on Dec. 1. On the 2nd to Richmond : on the 3rd to Danby, the residence of my cousin Cornforth ; removes me on the 7th to York. What was the business of these motions? I was to consult you at Cliffe "; p. 146.

Mr. Reydon was nephew to Mr. Faceby, who left him £100 for the education of his nephew, secured to him on lands at Aldborough. Mr. Reydon and Mr. Cornforth were Executors to Mr. Faceby. In his old age he retired to Doddin Green, near Kendal [Westmoreland], where he died, Oct. 30, 1741. Mr. Thomas Berington, Dean of the English Chapter, says : " Mr. Reydon was a diligent and laborious missionary, a man of good judgment and capacity, and universally esteemed." Mr. Reydon was a member of the Chapter.

REYDON, THOMAS (II), nephew of the preceding, went to Douay in Aug. 1720. After he was ordained Priest, he taught Philosophy and Divinity for several years, and then came on the Mission. Lancaster was the seat of his labours, and on April 11, 1763, he was chosen Archdeacon by the Chapter Consult. Like his uncle he retired in his old age to Dodding Green, where he died, Oct. 16, 1764.

RICHARDSON, RICHARD, studied his Philosophy and Divinity at Rome, and came on the Mission about 1670. In 1692 he had been twenty-two years in England, eighteen of which he had lived in North Wales, and resided mostly at Beachfield, in Flintshire. I find no account of his death, but that he was "a faithful clergyman of an upright life and conversation, and a laborious Itinerant." (*Chapter Records.*)

RICHMOND, WILLIAM, Priest, lived in the family of the Towneleys of Towneley, near Burnley, Lancashire. He wrote : An *Account of the Behaviour of the Catholic Prisoners in York Castle*. (See *Missionary Priests*, I., 429; MS. in Towneley Library.)

RIDDLE, ROBERT, *alias* CAREY, was a native of Northumberland. At the age of 20 he was admitted into the College at Rome by order of Cardinal Francis Barberini, Oct. 4, 1664, Father Christopher Anderton being Rector. Being ordained Priest, he left the College, June 8, 1669, to go into Flanders. He lived many years at Newcastle-on-Tyne, and also at Dilstone, the seat of the Earl of Derwentwater, and at Swinburne Castle.

RIDDLE, THOMAS, son of Mr. Riddle, of Swinburne Castle, was taken prisoner at Preston.

RIGBY, JAMES, *alias* BARKER, D.D., son of Alexander Rigby, and his wife, Margaret Jameson, was a native of Lancashire. At the age of 19 he went to Douay, where he was admitted, March 5, 1691. At the end of Philosophy he went to Paris, and was received into the Seminary in Aug., 1694 ; but for some reason or other he was expelled by Dr. Meynell, the Superior, Aug. 7, 1697. By articles of agreement between Mr. Lutton and Dr. Thomas Witham, who succeeded Dr. Meynell (which articles were signed by Bishops Leyburn, Giffard, and Smith), Mr. Rigby was re-admitted into St. Gregory's in June, 1700, with the consent also of Dr. Betham.   In Sept. he returned to Douay to teach Philosophy, and entered his Licence at Paris, Jan. 1, 1704, and took his Cap, May 12, 1706.   In June following he succeeded Mr. Mayes at Douay as Professor of Divinity [on the death of Dr. Paston, President of Douay], in 1714. Mr. Dicconson says, in his *Journal*, that the Padri at Watten [*i.e.*, the English Jesuits] talked of Dr. Barker " as the only fit man to be President of Douay " ; on which account Dr. Dicconson wrote to Dr. Ingleton at Paris, by the advice of the other Seniors, to stand firm against Dr. Barker, and to procure orders to be sent from St. Germains to Cardinal Gualtieri, the Protector, to keep the election within the limits of those named from England.   Dodd observes in his MS. that Dr. Betham added a clause to his constitutions of the Seminary in Paris, that no one dismissed should be made President, though re-admitted upon submission, and that this was made on Dr. Barker's account.   Soon after this he came on the Mission ; resided in London, and was chosen a member of the Chapter, and Archdeacon, March 10, 1711, (O.S.).   Dr. Barker died, Sept. 23, 1731.   Dr. Ingleton says Dr. Barker was a man of excellent principles, and corresponded with Father Eyre, S.J.   He was thought to be the author of the *Memorial to Cardinal Altieri* against Douay College and St. Gregory's.   (See also *Visitation of Douay College*, and Bishop Smith's letter of Feb. 23, 1707.)

RIGBY, JAMES, O.S.F., was son of John Rigby and his wife, Ann Spence, both Catholics. He was born in Lancashire, in Feb., 1705, and was admitted into the College at Rome by Father Levinus Browne, the Rector, June 27, 1724. On Jan. 7, 1725, he took the oath prescribed by Alexander VII., and was ordained, Jan. 22, 1730. He afterwards obtained a dispensation from that part of his oath which precluded his admission into religious orders, and Nov. 20, 1730, left the College and entered among the English Franciscans at Douay. After which I find no trace of him. (*Annales Coll. Angl. de Urbe.*)

RIGBY, JOHN, D.D., was younger brother of Dr. Thomas Rigby.   At the end of Rhetoric he went from Douay to Paris, Aug. 1773.   He was then 19, and entered his Licence, Jan. 1, 1782, was ordained at Easter, and defended his " Sorbonic," Oct. 23.   After Dr. Howard had resigned his situation at the Seminary, a delay of some months took place in the appointment of a Superior, till at last Dr. Whittington was appointed.   But while he was preparing to leave Heythrop, he was summoned to take a much longer journey, and died Feb. 16, 1783.   This unexpected stroke threw the gentlemen of the Seminary into their former perplexities, out of which they had so happily, they say, extricated themselves by obtaining the object of their choice in Dr. Whittington.   Among the Doctors of the house, then unemployed, no one appeared to them to be anyways qualified to make the Seminary flourish, except Dr. Strickland, who having been refused in 1755, little probability remained of his being appointed.   Dr. C. Berington had been formally appealed to, and positively refused to come ; and Dr. Bellasyse had just undertaken the education of Lord Petre's eldest son. As no presentation came from England (except as above), the only expedient which was thought of by the Archbishop and his advisers was to leave things as they were, and to empower Mr. John Rigby, then B.D., and in the second year of his License, to act to all intents and purposes as Superior, till some one else could be procured.   The scheme appeared the more plausible, as, " in consequence of Dr. Howard's indolence

and neglect, the temporals of the House were much encumbered both with
debts and arrears ; so that by having no other Superior, the expense of keeping
one would be spared, and the Seminary better enabled to retrieve their totter-
ing affairs." Mr. Rigby accordingly received, March 13, 1783, a commission
in form from the Archbishop to act as Superior till another could be procured.
On the 21st of that month he presented to the Archbishop a state of Seminary
debts, which were found to amount to the sum of £48,824 [livres, I suppose.—
J. K.]. The arrangement thus made was approved of by Bishop James Talbot.
On March 6, 1784, J. Rigby made his "Vespérie" at Navarre, Dr. Plunkett
President, and on the 8th his "Doctorerie," at the Archbishopric. [Bishop's
Palace, I suppose.] The term of his residence in the Seminary was now
expired, but the Archbishop informed him that he should obtain Bishop Talbot's
consent for the continuance of the present scheme, or a presentation in form
which should include his name. Bishop Talbot renewed his approbation of the
present system, leaving the other to his Grace's choice. Things thus remained
on the former footing, and, in May, Dr. Rigby came over to England, with an
intention to return, leaving Dr. Bew, then Procurator, to supply his place. But
being advised by Bishop Talbot to accept of the mission at Lancaster, he
resigned the charge of the Seminary to Dr. Bew, and succeeded the Rev.
James Tyrer in the charge of the Lancaster Congregation, and continued its
Pastor till the day of his death, which happened on June 10, 1818 [16, 1817].
John Rigby was a most accomplished scholar, an excellent missioner, and a
great benefactor to the Mission. He built the fine Chapel and Chapel-house in
Dalton Square. (*St. Gregory's Register.*)

    He wrote : 1. *A Catechism*, divided into chapters of equal length. The
matter was excellent, and the plan good ; but Bishop Matthew Gibson did not
like to adopt it in lieu of " The Douay," a small Catechism for his Diocese. 2.
He translated from the Italian Muratori's work, *Della Regolata Devozione* ; but
it remained, I believe, in MS.

    RIGBY, LAURENCE. After teaching a course of Philosophy at Douay, he
went to St. Gregory's, June 7, 1705, entered his Licence, and at the end of it
took the Cap. When Dr. Hawarden left Douay, Dr. Rigby succeeded him,
Oct. 1707, as Professor of Divinity. He was afterwards made Vice-President
of the College. In 1713, he came on the Mission. In 1715, Bishop Giffard sent
him over to Paris to succeed Dr. Thomas Witham, when it was expected the
latter would resign on account of his health; but he continued Superior till 1717,
when Dr. Ingleton succeeded him. On his return he was made V.G. to
Bishop Witham, who presented him in 1718, and again in 1724, as a proper
person to be his Coadjutor. He was also a member of the Chapter. He lived
many years at Wycliff, and died there in 1731. (*St. Gregory's Register.*)

    RIGBY, THOMAS, D.D., was son of Richard and his wife, Mary Winstanley,
whose family was distinguished for its constant attachment to the Catholic
religion, and for its labour and sufferings in the cause. He studied at Douay
to the end of Rhetoric, and arrived at St. Gregory's on Aug. 13, 1771 to prosecute his higher studies, and took the oath Dec. 27, 1772. He was ordained
Priest here in 1776, and took the Doctor's Cap in 1782, and came on the
Mission the same year. London was the theatre of his labours, which were
both great and successful, in the conversion of many sinners and strayed sheep.
On the death of Mr. Julians he was made Chaplain of Lincoln's Inn Fields
Chapel, and for twenty years he catechised there every Sunday evening at
6 o'clock. When Dr. Howard was persuaded to resign his situation as
Principal of St. Gregory's, Paris, he did it on the expressed condition that Dr.
Thomas Rigby should be his successor. He was accordingly presented by
Bishop James Talbot, the Senior Clergy Bishop, together with Dr. Thomas
Wright and Dr. Charles Berington. The step, however, proved disagreeable
to some persons in Paris, and they prevailed on the Archbishop to return the
presentation and desire a new one might be sent to him. It is probable this
opposition arose from a certain roughness and a degree of peremptoriness in
the Doctor's manner, which was rather unpleasant, though well meant. He

was a strict disciplinarian.   After a long and most useful course of missionary labour, and in the office of Vicar-General of the London District, he died Jan. 24, 1815, aged 68.   Dr. Thomas Rigby was a sound Divine, a good Canonist, and an affectionate, zealous, and charitable Pastor.   He published *Catechetical Instructions*, in 4 vols.   (*Paris Register.*)

RIVERS, JOHN, *vere* PENKETH, was a native of Lancashire.   He was educated at Rome.   In 1697 he had lived about fifteen years on the Mission and was then at Gilesgate, Durham.   He was esteemed by his Brethren "a man of good parts."

RIVERS, RICHARD, was many years incumbent at Gilesgate, Durham, where he died, Dec. 13, 1731, "universally beloved," says the late Mr. Eyre, President of Ushaw.   Richard Savage, *alias* Rivers, of Rock Savage, co. Chester, went over to Douay College, 1650 or 1649.   Query : Were these two one and the same ?

RIVET, JOHN, lived at Ugthorpe, Yorkshire.   In 1745, " he was taken up as a Popish Priest, and for keeping a school for the education of children in the Popish Religion, and on examination confessing the same, and refusing to take the oaths, was committed to York Castle.   (See *State Trials.*)

Monox Harvey, *alias* John Rivet, a Priest, died in London, Dec. 22, 1756.

ROBERTS, JOHN, lived at Holywell, and died there, Jan. 6, 1753, aged 88.

ROBINSON, ANDREW, S.J., was born Aug. 1, 1751 [1741].   He entered his noviceship, Jan. 26, 1763.   His first place on the Mission seems to have been Swynnerton, and his second Spetchley.   On the death of Mr. Beanham, he succeeded him at Grafton, and then Mr. Sanders at Worcester.   (See *Mr. Oliver's List.*)

ROBINSON, *vere* VEZZOSI, JOSEPH, son of Michael Vezzosi, a Florentine, and Ann Robinson, his wife, was born in Rome.   At the instance of Prince Charles, grandson of James II., he was admitted into the English College, Oct. 19, 1731, by special license, as both his parents were not English, which the rules required, nor was he born in England, nor of the proper age to be admitted, not having completed his 12th year.   He took the original Catholic oath, which did not exclude him from becoming a Religious.   He was ordained Priest on Sept. 8, 1743, and on the 17th of the same month he proceeded to Watten, after having lived twelve or thirteen years on the Clergy Funds, and on Dec. 26 of the same year entered his noviceship.   He became a professed Father in 1734.   See *Mr. Oliver's List.*   (*Annales Coll. Angl. de Urbe.*)

ROBINSON, *vere* VEZZOSI, STEPHEN, (the elder brother), born in Tuscany in 1716, and like his brother being recommended by Prince Charles, and a dispensation having been obtained, was admitted into the English College, March 11, 1737.   On Feb, 2, 1744, he was ordained, and on Sept. 3, he left the College to be Confessor to the nuns at Hooghstraet.   He afterwards came on the Mission, and laboured in it for twenty-four years, dying at Shefford, in Bedfordshire, Feb. 8, 1781.   (*Annales Coll. Angl.*)

ROE, JOHN.   Longbirch, *July 6th*, 1838.
MY DEAR SIR,

     I hope you will excuse the request I am making.   Will you have the kindness to write a short account of Uncle Roe ?   It might be sent to *Andrews'* and the *Edinburgh* ; and I think *Andrews'* has a greater circulation.   Perhaps such things might do for Mr. Tierney, if he insert such things in his continuation of Dodd.   Uncle Roe was born on Feb. 1, 1757.   He left Douay College for the Mission on Aug. 28, 1784, having been ordained, I think, the Whitsuntide before.   He came to Black Ladies in the Spring of 1790, so that he was forty-eight years resident there.   The first years of his missionary career you know better than I do.   I know he was at the Park twice, and also at Bugden, but the dates I don't know.   Uncle is the third of my relations who have died in less than a year !   He is the last of my relations in that generation, and I have reason to thank God for sparing him so long.   Henry feels his loss much.

He and I are much obliged by your letter of condolence. Dr. Walsh intends writing to Mr. Giffard and proposing Henry. I wish he could have called at Chillington. The funeral was respectable ; 5 under-bearers, 6 pall-bearers, 4 of them priests, 1 officiating priest, and Henry and myself as mourners ; a hearse, 2 mourning coaches and a chaise ; a large concourse of people. Great part of the Congregation at Mass in the morning. Buried at White Ladies, near Mr. Stone, as he particularly requested. White Ladies is now a very decent, venerable, and truly Catholic Cemetery. May he rest in peace. *Sublatum quærimus invidi.* Kind compliments to Mrs. and Miss Kirk. I am, dear sir, yours truly, [The signature of this original letter is torn off. Mr. Joseph Gillow has queried in pencil: "By Rev. Robert Richmond?"] (See *Catholic Journal,* VII., 63.)

ROELS, CHARLES, S.J., was Procurator at Liège in 1730, succeeding Mr. Vaughan. In the correspondence (MS. at Aston, Staffordshire) on the debts of Liège, "Mrs. Stafford" signifies Staffordshire District or St. Chad's College, which included three or four Jesuits ; and Madame de la Fossé," Liège ; "my Mistress," the Society or Liège ; and "my Master," the Provincial. (See Mr. Oliver.)

ROGERS, N., O.S.B. On the death of Mr. Wilson, Mr. N. Witham, O.S.B., succeeded him in the charge of the Catholics at and about Stella Hall, in 1725. But being advanced in years, and not able to undergo the fatigues of that mission, he was succeeded in 1726 by Mr. Rogers, who did not remain more than three or four years, after which he quitted that station to attend the family of Sir Edward Gascoigne, Parlington, in Yorkshire. Rev. N. Hutton succeeded him at Stella.

ROLES, LUDOVIC, S.J., born Nov. 22, 1752, entered his noviceship, Sept. 7, 1753. (*See Mr. Oliver.*)

ROOKWOOD, AMBROSE, born Sept. 20, 1664, sixth son of Ambrose Rookwood, Esq,, of Coldham Hall, in Stanningfield, Suffolk, had the command of a brigade in King James II. service, and followed that Monarch to St. Germains. He came over to England in 1695, with Sir George Barclay, and was involved in the conspiracy called the Barclay Plot. He was tried by a Special Commission (See *State Trials*), in the King's Bench, April 8, 1696, together with Major Lowick and Charles Cranborne, for High Treason in conspiring the death of His Majesty, King William. He pleaded not guilty, and requested his brother (Thomas Rookwood, of Coldham Hall) might come to him in prison, and that he might be allowed the use of pen, ink, and paper, which were granted. After an adjournment his trial proceeded. He was assisted by his Counsel, Sir B. Shower, and Mr. Phipps. From the evidence of Captains Porter and Harris, of his Brigade, it appeared that he was privy to the plot, and had attended several secret meetings ; that at one of these meetings he remonstrated with Sir George Barclay against killing the King, who, turning to him, said he must obey his orders, as he held a commission for the purpose, and was his superior officer. That Rookwood on this and other occasions declared he was sent over to obey Sir George Barclay's orders and he was resolved to do so. The chief point on evidence against him was that he had delivered some written orders from Sir George Barclay, containing a list of those persons who were to be under his own immediate command in the attack upon his Majesty's person. Ambrose Rookwood, Major Lowick, and Charles Cranbourne were each attainted, and suffered death the 29th of the same month of April in which they were tried. The following address (An original printed copy is in possession of Sir T. Gage, Bart.) was printed and distributed after the death of Ambrose Rookwood :

"A true copie of the paper delivered by Brigadier Rookwood to the Sheriff at Tyburn, the place of execution, April 29, 1696 :—Wills of dying men were ever sacred and as such ought to be fulfilled. The sufferer, a man of deeds more than words, by way of will made to the people, consigned his thoughts to paper to be published. To this paper, as he told the said Sheriff he referred himself, and that he might not fail of his intent, some days before his execution he had transmitted a copy of it to a friend, who, since the Sheriff has so long failed of his trust and duty, resolves to supply it by doing this. Take it, therefore, in print. Mr. Sheriff cannot but own it to be the same word for word."

THE PAPER.—"Having committed the justice of my cause and recommended my soul to God, on whose mercies, through the merits of Jesus Christ, I wholly cast myself, I had once resolved to die in silence ; but second thoughts of my duty to others, chiefly to my true and liege Sovereign King James, moved me to leave this behind me. I do therefore with all truth and sincerity declare and avow I never knew, saw, or heard of any order or commission from King James for the assassinating of the Prince of Orange and attacking his guards, but I am certainly informed that he had rejected the proposals of that nature when made unto him. Nor do I think he knew the least of the particular design of attacking the guards at his landing, in which I was engaged as soldier by my immediate commander (much against my judgment). But his soldier I was, and as such I was to obey and act. Near twelve years I have served my true king and master, King James, and freely now lay down my life in his cause. I ever abhorred a treacherous action even to an enemy. If it be a guilt to have complied with what I thought, and still think, to have been my duty, I am guilty. No other guilt do I own. As I beg all to forgive me, so I forgive *all* from my heart, even the Prince of Orange, who as a soldier ought to have considered my case before he signed the warrant for my death.   I pray God to open his eyes and render him sensible of the much blood from all parts crying out against him, so to prevent a heavier execution hanging over his head, that what he inflicts on me." London, printed in the year 1696. [In the hand of Mr. John Gage.]

ROPER, CHRISTOPHER, fifth Lord Teynham, was eldest son of Christopher, fourth Lord Teynham, by his second wife, Philadelphia, daughter of Edward Knolles, of Grove Park, Herts.   On Jan. 16, 1687, he was made Lord Lieutenant and Custos Rotulorum of Herts., by James II. He married Elizabeth, daughter of Francis Brown, third Viscount Montague. At the Revolution he retired to Brussels, and there died the same year.

ROPER, CHRISTOPHER, seventh Lord Teynham, was second son of Christopher, the fifth Lord Teynham. He died in 1697, unmarried, and was succeeded by his next brother, Henry, eighth Lord Teynham. This Lord abandoned the faith of his fathers, and conformed to the Established Church, in or about 1720. In Jan., 1723, he was appointed one of the Gentlemen of the King's Bedchamber in the place of James Stuart, Earl of Bute. On May 16 of that year he shot himself through the head with a pistol, at his house in the Haymarket, and died immediately, aged 46. While he remained a Catholic he married, first, Catharine, daughter of Philip, Lord Strangford, by whom he had three children [Philip, Henry, and Elizabeth], and secondly, Mary, daughter of Sir John Gage, of Firle. (*Historical Register.*)

ROPER, JOHN, sixth Lord Teynham, was son of the fifth Lord and Lady Elizabeth Brown. He died unmarried in 1689.

ROUT, JOHN.   He was educated at Douay College, and when he came on the Mission he resided mostly with Mr. Arundel at Guildford, but helped many poor Catholics scattered over the county to a great distance.   He had the character of being "a virtuous and laborious Clergyman."   I find no mention of him after 1693.

RUSSELL, MARTIN, O.S.D.   He was an officer of the army of Charles I., and fought at the battle of Worcester.   He afterwards entered among the English Dominicans, and some time after his ordination he was sent by Father Howard (afterwards Cardinal), his Provincial in 1664, to Tangiers, in Africa, which had been given in dower by the King of Portugal to his daughter, the wife of Charles II., to assist the garrison in their spiritual wants ; but he returned in 1668, when he was made Prior of Bornheim [by Fr. Howard]. He afterwards came on the Mission, and laboured hard for many years [about forty-six years] in Shropshire, where he suffered much, and in prison, for his religion. " He died on Sept. 8, 1711, at the advanced age of 80, and was buried at Stanton-Lacy, about two miles north of Ludlow." (*Dominican Obituary.*) [He was of the family of the Russells of Little Malvern.]

RYDER, SIMON, D.D.,was a native of Staffordshire. Having finished his third year of Divinity at Douay, and being then deacon, he went in Oct., 1692, to Paris, and on the College Seminary funds, April 27, he made his " Expectative" and " Aulect." He returned to Douay, Sept. 24, 1697, and after teaching Philosophy and Divinity for two years each, he entered his Licence at Paris, and took the Doctor's Cap, March 6, 1704, and on the 8th left the Seminary to come on the Mission. He lived many years at Mawley, in Shropshire, the seat of Sir Walter Blount, Bart. On the death of Dr. Perrot, in 1714, he was chosen Dean of the Chapter, in the General Assembly held in London. This Assembly opened on Oct. 12, and thirty-four members were present at it. After settling its own internal concerns, and filling up some vacant places, it was unanimously resolved in this meeting that " the books of Mr. John Serjeant containing sharp and severe reflections upon his Brethren of the Chapter, as likewise the written answer of Mr. Sylvester Jenks containing sharp repartys to the said books, be suppressed and destroyed, and that the donation of Mr. Jerome White, made Archdeacon of Lincoln, Notts, and Rutland, in 1672, for a " controversial writer," be applied in future to Dr. Edward Hawarden as Controversial Writer. Dr. Ryder also presided in quality of Dean at the General Assembly in 1717. In the begining of Aug., 1731, he went into the country, as he usually did since he became infirm, meaning to pass a few months there ; but he fell ill, and after the second Sunday in Advent, was unable to say Mass. Yet he returned to London, and died there, May 31, 1732. (*Chapter Records.*)

SABRAN, LEWIS, S.J. With regard to the allegation that the Jesuits took steps to obtain possession of Douay College, Father Hunter, in his *Modest Defence*, p. 129, says : " They (the Superiors of the Jesuits) declare they neither directly nor indirectly had any design upon Douay College to wrest it out of the hands of the Clergy ; that they had no hand in the information made against the doctrine taught in the College. In particular the person who wrote the letter to one of his subjects in the North to call him over to a post of concern, declares most solemnly *in verbo Sacerdotis*, that he never had the first thought of any such design (of making him President of Douay), nor any other of his subjects which he knows of. . . The said Superior (p. 132) who then entering upon his office, called over this gentleman to be his helper and secretary . . . has made the following declaration:—' There had been severa disputes betwixt some Jesuits and some Clergymen in the North about books, which the latter recommended and the others looked upon as unsound in Faith, and about some principles and practices used by some Clergymen, which seemed to the Jesuits there to savour of erroneous novelties. Entering into my imploy, I desired to be informed of the grounds of these disputes, and of their certainty. It was my duty and design to direct those under my care how they should proceed in such debates, with as great regard to peace and charity as the preserving of the tenets and practices of religion could allow of.' "

Father Sabran was tutor to William Fuller, Gent., a noted spy and renegado in Flanders, and chaplain to the Chevalier S. George. This Fuller says he accompanied Mrs. Gray, the pretended mother of the Chevalier, to Dover in a coach and six, with the Marchioness Powis's woman and himself, and was there met by her brother, Father Gray, a secular Priest at Calais, who accompanied her to the Benedictine Nuns at Paris ; that Mrs. Gray made her escape, Feb. 1690, from the English nuns, but was taken three days after to St. Germains and there murthered to prevent the discovery. The whole story is treated as a forgery in " Fuller's proof, etc., made out to be no proof." (See *Records of Jansenism* p. 64, his letter to Father Metcalf, p. 81, and his justification, pp. 87-150 ; and *Records of Douay College*, p. 115. Also *Modest Defence*, p. 129.)

SACKVILLE, LOUISA ELIZABETH, a young lady who became a nun in the Abbey [of the Holy Sacrament, in Paris . . . and died in 1742]. (See Butler's *Lives of the Saints*, July 19.)

SALKELD, THOMAS, probably of the family of Salkeld of Whitehall, Cumberland. He studied at Douay, but being among those who rebelled against Dr. Paston in the beginning of Divinity, he was dismissed with some others. From a letter of Cardinal Howard's to Dr. Paston, it should appear that application was made for his admittance into the English College at Rome, but that he could not be received there, says Dodd in his *Adversaria*, because he had been a Jesuit. (Not probable.) He then went to Paris, where he obtained a recommendation from Dr. Thomas Hall to Dr. Watkinson, of Lisbon, who received him into his College. Here he completed his course of Divinity, which he dedicated to the Cardinal Protector, and defended it with great applause, July 28, 1693. (*Lisbon Register Miscel.*, VI. 1,086.) On Dec. 16, 1694, he was sent on the Mission, where he laboured hard and successfully in gaining souls to Christ, and died in 1708.

SALTMARSH, GERARD, *alias* IRELAND, son of Edward and Geraldine Saltmarsh, his wife, was born in Yorkshire of a good family about 1651. On Oct. 6, 1671, he was admitted into the College at Rome. He was ordained at St. John Lateran's, April 4, 1676, and on April 27, 1678, he left the College for England. I do not find where he laboured on the Mission for several years; but about 1700 he was appointed tutor to the young Duke of Norfolk, Thomas, and accompanied him in that capacity to the Academy at Turin, and remained with him there for about a year, and was much respected for his probity, zeal, and piety. He then went with the Duke to Rome, and made the tour of Italy with him. After an absence of four years they returned by Douay to England in April, 1705, when he was made Chaplain to the Duke's mother, at Worksop, and was in high esteem among his Brethren. In 1706, when Mr. Andrew Giffard refused the Western District, Mr. Saltmarsh was recommended from England, and as he had only left Rome about a year before, his merits were well known there, and he was unanimously chosen by the Cardinal and Propaganda to supply his place. Mgr. Olivieri, the Secretary of Propaganda, promised Mr. Mayes, the Clergy Agent, that he would immediately send the Brief of his appointment of which the letter gave notice to the Bishops. (Mr. Mayes' Agency, I., 215. "The King was so far gone," etc., D.D., p. 72.) But in consequence of some vague and unfounded accusations, preferred against him by Mgr. Bussi, the Nuncio at Cologne—from which, however, he cleared himself—the appointment did not take place. The accusation soured Mr. Saltmarsh, and as he also thought the Bishops had not been sufficiently active in his defence, he became discontented, and in 1715 he joined Bishops Stonor and Strickland in their attempt to remove Dr. Thomas Witham from St. Gregory's and to procure Dr. Stonor to be Coadjutor to Bishop Giffard, without his knowledge. In this, however, they failed. Mr. Saltmarsh, who also went by the name of Ireland in troublesome times, was also a member of the *Institutum Clericorum in communi viventium*, till it was dissolved by Bishop Giffard, and also a member of the Chapter. He died Jan. 26, 1732, (O.S.). (*Annales Coll. Angl.*)

His younger brother, Peter, *alias* Every, went to Rome at the age of 25, and was received into the College, Oct. 10, 1683. He was ordained at St. John Lateran's, April 13, 1686, and on April 12, 1690, left to go into France, and thence to England. I do not find where he exercised his missionary faculties, but that he was, like his brother, a member of the Chapter. He died, Feb. 2, 1724, (O.S.) (*Annales Coll. Angl.*)

SANDERS, FRANCIS [*alias* BAINES], S.J. He was Confessor to James II. at St. Germains and wrote his life, which was abridged by Father Bretonneau, S.J., and printed in English by Thomas Meighan. It is rather a panegyric of his virtues than an historical detail of his life. (See Mr. Oliver's List for these).

SAVAGE, JOHN [fifth and last] LORD RIVERS, was son of Richard Savage and Alice, daughter of Thomas Trafford, of Bridge Trafford, and grandson of John Savage, Lord Savage, of Rock Savage, who was created Earl Rivers in 1639. He studied at Douay, and having been ordained Priest left the college Dec. 11, 1689. From a letter of Mr. Mayes to Mr. Paston (Nov. 30, 1709) it appears that John Savage had employed a foreign ambassador and also the Bishops to procure him a dispensation to marry, urged to this no doubt by Lord Rivers. The petition lay two years at Rome unregarded, which is the Italian way of refusing. In 1710, Mr. Savage lived in York as missionary, at the time that T. Mannock, S.J., lived there in the family of Mr. Fitz[? herbert]. A conversation which Mr. Rivers had with Mr. Fitz—— gave rise to a string of accusations which Father Mannock brought against Mr. Rivers and sent to Father Kennet to be delivered to Father Culceth, the Provincial, to be sent over ; "a copy of which writing having been sent to Mr. Rivers, his answer was that it contained as many lies as lines." Mr. Rivers was held in great estimation by Bishop Smith, who judged him to be a fit person to succeed him, and Bishop Giffard placed him on the list for the North and East District in Sept., 1711.

Lord Rivers, a few months before his death, sent for Mr. Rivers, *alias* Savage, and made him live with him. At his death, in 1712, he left him his heir for life to £6,000 per annum, and the Lord Treasurer and Duke of Salop, Ambassador at Paris, his executors. He succeeded also to the title of Earl Rivers. His Protestant friends and the lawyers induced him to take the oath of allegiance. When Bishop Giffard returned to town from the country he pointed out to him the impropriety of such conduct ; then Lord Rivers cast himself at his feet, lamented what he had done, deceived by others, and protested he never intended to quit his religion. He then repaired to Lord Oxford, the Treasurer, and complained that he had persuaded him to take such a step and protested that rather than do anything contrary to his duty as a Catholic he was ready to part with his inheritance, and even with his life. He made the same declaration to others in the ministry (*Rom. Col.* II. 32). To avoid the further solicitations of his Protestant friends, and the Penal Laws, Lord Rivers went over to Douay under Dr. Witham, the new President, and thence, in 1716, went to Louvain and frequently preached in the Chapel of the English Augustinian Nuns. He was chosen Chanoin of Sachin, in the diocese of Tournay, where, or at Liège, he died, Feb. 26, 1737. He was a Capitular. (See *Extinct Peerages*.) "After his death the estate descended to Lady Penelope Barrymore, only legitimate daughter of Richard, Earl Rivers. His [*i.e.* Richard's] base daughter, Bessy Savage, married to Frederic, Earl of Rochford, had £60,000, while her base brother Richard, the celebrated and unfortunate poet," had little from the Earl. (Ormerod's *Cheshire;* see "Frodsham.")

SCARISBRICK, ROBERT, of Scarisbrick Hall, Co. Lancaster. The annual rents of his estate amounted to £388 3s. 7d.; but the Commissioners valued his estates at £1,349 18s. 7d., and his personal estate at £1,932.

SCROOPE, SIMON, of Danby, Co. York, married Mary Anne, daughter of Robert Sheldon, of Steeple Barton, Oxon., by his wife Mary Anne Elliot.

SEAFORTH, WILLIAM, LORD. His estates let in 1715 at £517 10s.

SERJEANT, JOHN, was born at Cockerham, near Lancaster. He was sent to Douay and after his ordination came over to England in 1745, when it is said he met the Prince's troops at Preston. However that may be, he was seized and taken to Lancaster Castle. On his liberation he was placed at Scorton, near Garstang, and continued there for fifty years, much beloved and respected by his congregation and neighbours. Here he died, Aug. 31, 1795, and was buried at Cockerham, his native place.

He wrote : 1. *Turk and Pope*. 2. *Some unpublished pieces of Controversy against the Vicar of Garstang*.

SEWALL, NICHOLAS, S.J. (See *Catholic Magazine and Review* V. 36).

SHAFTOE, WILLIAM, of Bevington Hall. His estates in 1715 let at £714 per annum. These were forfeited, as also a mortgage on them of £2,000, which the Commissioners said was settled for Popish or superstitious uses.

SHARP, JOHN, D.D., Canon and Ecolatre of St. Martin's Church in Liège, Missioner and Protonotary Apostolic 1734. This is printed under an engraving of an Angel holding a cross in his left hand and pointing with his right to a crown on the upper part of it ; over all these words are : *Tolle crucem, si vis coronam.* This is the only account I have ever seen of him.

SHARPE, JAMES, O.S.D., born in London of Catholic parents, Sept. 26, 1752, was received into the English College Jan. 16, 1767, but went to Florence, July 27, 1771, and entered among the Dominicans. Mr. Parr and Mr. Nichols left the College at the same time and for the same purpose. Mr. Sharpe afterwards came on the Mission and resided some time at Coventry, where he was much esteemed and beloved, and where he died of a putrid fever caught in attending the sick, Feb. 28, 1801. Parr, after remaining some years among the Dominicans, entered among the Conventuals and was made the English Penitentiary of St. Peter's after the death of Father Purcel. He did not remain there long, but returned to England and then went into Scotland. (*Annales Coll. Angl.*)

SHARROCK, GREGORY WILLIAM ; JOHN JEROME ; JOHN ; WALTER, ALL O.S.B. Gregory William, O.S.B. and V.A. of the Western District, was born in Friar Gate, Preston, Mar. 30, 1742. Mar. 6, 1755, he went to St. Gregory's, Douay, and became a Benedictine. Some time after he was ordained he came on the Mission and for some years lived with Mr. Jones of Lanarth. In 1781 he was made Coadjutor to Bishop Walmesley with the title of *Episcopus Thelmessensis,* and on his death succeeded to the Western District. He died at Bath, Oct. 7 or 27, 1809, in his sixty-seventh year, and forty-ninth of his Religious profession.

John Jerome, O.S.B., was born at Walton-le-dale, near Preston, Feb, 5, 1750. He became a Benedictine at Douay, and was Prior of St. Gregory's at the time of the French Revolution, when he was sent to Dourlens with his monks and the seniors and students of Douay College. When released from prison he came over to England, and was probably received by Sir Edward Smythe, Bart., at his seat at Actonburnel, near Salop, together with his monks, where he continued until his death, which took place April 1, 1808. " Mr. Sharrock," says Dr. Gradwell, " was a very learned, pious, and amiable man," a character which he truly deserved. I knew him well. Bishop Walmesley offered to make him his Coadjutor, but his humility caused him to decline that honour.

John was born at Walton-le-dale, April 19, 1754, and became a monk at St. Gregory's, Douay. When on the Mission he lived at Longhorsley, near Morpeth, in Northumberland, and died there.

Walter, the fourth brother, also became a Benedictine, but not a Priest. He was a lay brother at Ampleforth, not a member of St. Gregory's, Douay, but of Dieuleward, in Lorraine, whence the monks of Ampleforth came. (See the *Directory,* or *Catholic Journal* of 1807.)

SHELDON, EDWARD, O.S.B., was second son of William Sheldon, of Beoley, Esq., and Elizabeth, daughter of William Lord Petre. He became a Benedictine at Douay ; and on the death of his elder brother, Ralph Sheldon, in 1684, without issue, the estates devolved on Father Sheldon ; but having renounced the world, and refusing to take possession of them, they came to his cousin and next male heir, Robert, grandson of Ralph Sheldon, of Steeple Barton, Oxon, Esq. (See Nash's *Worcestershire.*)

SHELDON, DAME FRANCES, O.S.B., at Cambray. Died at Salford, July 14, 1808.

SHELDON, HENRY, S.J., was brother to Ralph, S.J., and fourth son of Robert Sheldon, who died June 16, 1736, and was buried at Beoley. Henry became a Jesuit, was Rector at Rome from 1737 to 1743, and again from 1750 to 1756, and in 1745 was Provincial of his Order. " Probably not being in the secrets," writes to me the late William Sheldon, of Gray's Inn, " he unluckily began his circuit in the North. Suspicion arose, and the Government seized all his papers in London, and they were delivered over to Dr. [John] Douglas (afterwards Bishop of Carlisle, and last of Salisbury), for examination. He told me upwards of forty years since that he found no treason or anything leading thereto, but complaints of misconduct and irregularities in some of the juvenile missioners, &c." Mr. Henry died at Rome.

SHELDON, RALPH [alias ELLIOT], S.J., second son of Robert Sheldon, of Weston and Beoley, Esq., and of his wife, Mary Anne, daughter of John Elliot, of Gatacre Park, Salop, Esq. He became a Jesuit, was Rector of the College in Rome, and died at Liège. (See Mr. Oliver.)

SHELLEY, THOMAS, was educated at Douay. He was Confessor to the Blue Nuns at Paris, but being obliged to leave during the Revolution, he came over to England, and died at Wolverhampton, which seems to have been his native place, Jan. 8, 1807.

SHEPHERD, JOHN, son of John Shepherd and Brigitta Wilkinson, his wife, both Catholics. He was born in London, Feb. 19, 1714, and after studying four and a-half years Humanity at Douay, was admitted into the College at Rome Aug. 6, 1731, but left April 17, 1732, on account of some difficulties respecting the College Oath. He then went to Lisbon, where he finished his Philosophy and Divinity, and being ordained, came on the Mission. He lived many years in the family of Lord Montague at Cowdray, and about 1758 settled at the Convent at Hammersmith. He was a member of the Chapter, and also the Secretary, and on the death of Mr. Richard Kendall, in Dec., 1780, he was chosen Dean in 1781, and died in London, March 11, 1789, in the 74th year of his age. Mr. Shepherd was uncle to Dr. Slaughter, who was his executor. (Annales Coll. Rom.)

SHEPHERD, THOMAS, alias COLDHAM. In 1667 he was 1st Professor of Divinity at Douay, while Mr. Paston, afterwards President, was second. But left Douay 1668, in consequence of some disagreement with Dr. Leyburn, the President. (See Factum.) When Dr. Perrot resigned the Presidentship of Lisbon College it was offered to Mr. Shepherd, but he declined it. At the General Assembly of the Chapter, 1672, he was made V.G. of Warwickshire, Worcester, Leicester, and Gloucestershire. At this Assembly Dr. H. Ellice, the Dean, presided, and three V.G.'s assisted (three Vicariates being vacant), and seventeen Archdeacons (two vacant) and eight Canons, but nine of that number only by their deputies. In the Assembly Mr. A. Holt read from his journal an account of the most remarkable passages and transactions during the three years of his agency at Rome. It was resolved that the Feast of St. George in England, and St. David in Wales, should be kept each as Duplex Majors; that Mr. Carr, the original founder, should be chosen Superior of St. Gregory's, Paris; that a letter should be written to the Internunce at Brussels requesting him not to give faculties for England to Aliens, contrary to a late decree of the Cardinal Protector; that the Brethren should pray particularly for the good success of His Majesty's forces, and recommend the same to the people; that rules should be drawn up by certain Brethren for the Seminary at Paris; that Mr. Holt's letter concerning the authority of the Chapter be revised by Dr. Godden and Mr. Sergeant, and sent to the VV. GG., and Archdeacons in the country. (Chapter Collection, I., 87). That "the Brethren should endeavour to make what friends they could at our own Court, as it appeared the Regulars did; that the name of Vicar-Apostolic be not admitted as endangering the existing Government, and the reasons be drawn up why such title cannot be admitted, and Mr. Ph. Howard (afterwards Cardinal Howard), the Lord Almoner to Her Majesty, be made acquainted therewith." (Ibid, p. 211.) The Assembly, with the call of which the King was acquainted by Dr. Godden, closed with the fifth session April 26. Mr.

Shepherd assisted at the General Assemblies of 1676, 1684, 1694, but died before the Assembly of 1703. Mr. Shepherd was one of the three presented by the Dean and Chapter to succeed Dr. Leyburn at Douay in 1675. (*Chapter Records.*)

SHEPPARD, JOHN, a native of Lancashire, and a near relative of the Tootells and Mellings, whom in his Obituary he calls his cousins. In 1694 he went to Lisbon, and was received into the College Aug. 30. He studied his Classics under Mr. Vane, Philosophy under Mr. George Slaughter, and Divinity under Mr. Edward Jones, the President. On Dec. 21, 1761, he took the College Oath, and having received the Order of Priesthood, he came on the Mission in June, 1706. I find him in Lincolnshire in 1725, of which county, and those of Rutland and Notts, he was chosen Archdeacon in the Chapter on Feb. 12, 1723 (O.S.). Some time after he went to London, and had the charge, it appears, of the nuns at Hammersmith. In the General Assembly of the Chapter in July, 1755, on account of the age and infirmities of Mr. Thomas Berington, the Dean, he was chosen Sub-dean, and Dean on March 9 following, which dignity he enjoyed till his death in London, Oct. 27, 1761, at which time he was aged 83 years, 9 months, 10 days, of which he had spent 55 years in the labours of the Mission. (*Lisbon Register Miscel.*, IV., 1,074.)

SHEPPARD, JOSEPH (I.), was born in Lancashire and educated at Douay, where he taught the Classics. He headed the Colony that was sent to Valladolid when the Jesuits were suppressed in Spain, and on the death of Dr. Perry, in 1774, succeeded him as President, and died there Oct. 31, 1796. "He left a very indifferent character," says Rev. Blase Moray, who studied under him, "and brought the College into disgrace by his light behaviour."

SHEPPARD, JOSEPH (II.) was nephew of the President of Valladolid. He was born at Bolton, and was sent to Valladolid. On his return to England "he assisted Mr. Storey two or three years in his school at Tudhoe, and at the same time attended the desolate Mission of New House, or Eshe Land. He was afterwards sent to Bolton, his native place, where, from his childhood, says Rev. Richard Thompson, G.V., he had ever made it his prayer that there might be a mission established. At his coming thither it was a forlorn hope. He had no property, there were a few, and a very few only, of poor Catholics, and he had to raise an altar in a small, pitiful loft over a stable, to which he ascended by steps. Happily he had a mother, a widow, resident in Bolton. With her he had a home, and she cheerfully for years contributed her means for his comfort. The gift of faith was her reward, and that of his sister, whom he had the happiness to see received into the bosom of the Catholic Church some years before their deaths. By the death of his uncle at Valladolid, and afterwards of his mother and other relatives, he became possessed of a comfortable little property which, as it came to him, he laid out for the improvement of his mission. I believe he also promoted a permanent mission at Rochdale, which place, and also Bury, he had attended ever since 1794. His labours in these missions were great and unceasing till 1824, when he became, from a gradual decay, incapable of any duty, and died Jan. 28, 1825, much beloved and regretted by a numerous congregation, which, in a great measure, he had formed by his meritorious and unremitted labours.

SHERBURNE, SIR NICHOLAS, of Stonyhurst, Bart. He married Catharine, third daughter of Sir Edward Charleton, of Hesley-side, Northumberland, Bart., by Dame Mary, his wife, eldest daughter and co-heiress of Sir Edward Widdrington, of Cartington, in said County. His only son, Richard Francis, born Dec. 3, 1693, died June 8, 1702. Captain Talbot married another daughter of Lady Charleton. His son was a Priest and was proposed by the Jesuits for successor of Bishop Witham in the North. (*Epistolæ Var.* IX., p. 32.)

SHERWOOD, JOSEPH, O.S.B., Abbot of Lamspring. "He was," says Weldon, "a most industrious, indefatigable and successful man, in the temporals of the House, which owes much to his pious care. He built the new church at Lamspring and repaired other buildings, yet left fewer debts when he died than he found when he was chosen Abbot." He died at Hildesheim, June 26, 1690.

SHIMMEL, CHARLES, taught Poetry and Rhetoric at Douay; was of a delicate constitution and was obliged to come over to England for his health. He soon returned to complete his Divinity and came to the Mission about the year 1739. He lived at Chideock in Dorset, and died May 26, 1764, while on a visit to Mr. Williams at Bearscomb. Rev. Joseph Berington, who knew him well, deemed him "a perfect master of the English language, and one of the best Classical schollars of his age." Dr. Milner added that he wrote in English verse the *History of Douay College and its Presidents.*

SHIMMEL, RICHARD, *alias* TURNER, son of John Shimmel and his wife, Eleanor Turner, was a native of Shropshire. Having been converted to the Catholic Faith by Mr. J. Jones, Agent for Lisbon College in London, he was sent over to that College at the age of 18, in 1710, where he acquired much honour by his talent and close application to his studies. In May, 1715, he took the oath and gown, and on Dec. 31 in the following year was ordained Priest. Soon after his ordination he came on the Mission, where he laboured for many years in the vineyard, and died at Chideock, in Dorsetshire, Nov. 18, 1765, where Mr. Charles Shimmel was settled and was probably his relation, if not brother. Mr. Richard Shimmel was a gentleman of considerable abilities and acquirements, and wrote: 1. *Epigramma in Honorem S. Andreae Avellini,* to which was adjudged the first prize of the Count of Villar-Major. 2. *Dissertationes de praestantia et usu Numismatum,* which he presented to the College Library. (*Lisbon Register.*)

SHIMMEL, THOMAS, was born in Devon and studied at Douay, where he filled the office of General Prefect for some years. When on the Mission he lived many years at Glossop, in Derbyshire, with Nathaniel Eyre, Esq., and thence went to Cromsall, where he soon after died, Aug. 23, 1779.

SHIRBURNE, JOSEPH, O.S.B. After the death of Father Stapylton, in 1680, he was chosen President of the English Congregation of Benedictines, and was continued in that office by re-election till his death, April 9, 1697, at Paris, at the age of 69. He built the new church at Paris, and dormitory, and enriched the church with plate, etc. He got his benefice of Choisy annexed to the house as a perpetual rent, and procured that the Religious might be capable of benefices. (*Weldon,* p. 217.)

SHORT, ANASTASIA, O.S.A., Reverend Mother Sister [*sic*] Prioress, died at Louvain, April 12, 1793.

SHORT, ANNA MARIA. After the death of her husband, who was brother of Father William Short, she entered the Dominicanesses, called Spellicans, of Brussels, and "was renowned for her humility, meekness, and equability of temper. She was repeatedly chosen Prioress or Sub-prioress, and always beloved by all." "This truly amiable lady," says Father Brittain, in a letter to me of July 15, 1817, "once edified me much. I was (*ex officio*) inquiring of all what were their complaints, when her answer was, 'I have no reason to complain of any of the Community. I do not see anything blame-worthy in anyone except myself'; a sentiment worthy of admiration." She died Dec. 10, 1782, in the eighty-third year of her age and fifty-second of her Profession.

SHORT, MARY AGNES, was own sister to the very worthy and universally esteemed Father B. Short, O.S.D. In 1733 she entered among the English Dominicanesses at Brussels (*Mortuary Bill*), and almost from the time of her profession filled the office of Procuratrix or Mistress of Novices, as she afterwards did that of Prioress for 12 years, and to the day of her death, which took place Oct. 19, 1780, in the sixty-fifth year of her age, and forty-seventh of her Profession. Blessed with a mind capable of great things, she undertook the most arduous whenever the glory of God and the good of the Community required it. Her prudence, fortitude and perseverance, became particularly conspicuous when she erected a new house and church from the foundations. But tho' distracted by so many cares she well knew how to unite the better part of Mary with the duties of Martha. Properly strict in maintaining the discipline of the house, she governed it less by authority than by her gentleness and example. Humility, patience and charity were her favourite virtues. By these, and by a peculiar sweetness of manner, she gained the hearts of all, and making herself all to all had the praise of being a tender mother to all. Under a cruel dysentery and gangrene, which she bore with admirable patience, she retained her usual serenity and conformity to the will of God, exhorting her sisters, that were bathed in tears for that approaching loss, to cease to oppose themselves to the divine will and ardently sighing to be dissolved and be with Christ.

SHORT, RICHARD. He was educated at Douay. When Magdalen College in Oxford was made over to Bishop Giffard by James II., Dr. Hawarden and other Professors, among whom was Mr. Short—tho' not in orders—came over from Douay to take possession of it, but returned again Nov. 16, 1688. Mr. Short afterwards applied to medicine and became an eminent physician in London and spent both his money and his labours in assisting the poor. (See *Dodd*, III. 460.)

SHORTER, [JOHN], son of Sir John Shorter, Lord Mayor of London, became a Catholic. ["Sir John Shorter died Sept. 4, 1688, and Sir John Eyles was the next day appointed to succeed him by the king." *Chron. Brit.*—Haydn, *Book of Dignities*, 1851, p. 262.]

SHUTTLEWORTH, GEORGE. Nephew of John, and son of —— Shuttleworth and his wife, —— Haydock. He was educated at Douay and ordained Priest. Having received a handsome fortune, left him by his grandfather, he purchased Hodsock Park, near Worksop, of the Mellishes, which till then his family held as a lease, and lived there like a farming country gentleman. At the age of 72 or 3, tho' in the vigour of health, he was killed about 3 miles from Worksop, supposed by a fall from his horse; but tho' found alive he did not live to give an account of the accident. He died May 11, 1791. He left, by will, Hodsock Park to his second grand nephew, the late —— Shuttleworth, Esq.

SHUTTLEWORTH, JOHN (I), born of a respectable family in Notts; his father was a convert to the Catholic Religion, but before his conversion sent his two sons to Douay. John became a Priest, and on his return exercised his missionary faculties in his native county, probably near Worksop Manor, and died Jan. 29, 1739 (N.S.)

John's brother married a Miss Haydock. One of his daughters married [Thomas Peter] Metcalf, Esq., of Lincolnshire, whose son married Miss Teresa Throckmorton, by whom he had the late Thomas [who assumed the name] More and Mrs. Eyston, of Hendred, Berks.

SHUTTLEWORTH, JOHN (II), a native of Lancashire. Was educated at Douay and lived many years at Brinn, near Wigan. Is truly a zealous Missionary and has done much, both by his zeal and purse, for the good of Religion. He is still alive and hearty, Feb. 27, 1839. I find in *Faithful Register of the late Rebellion*, London, 1718, that a Mr. Richard Shuttleworth was a man of estate and very rough in his manners, and was executed for the Rebellion at —— Preston, Jan. 28, 1715 (O.S.) He was tried at Liverpool before Baron Bury, Mr. Justice Eyre and Mr. Baron Montague. His head was fixed on the Town Hall or Market Place at Preston.

SILVERTOP, JOHN, of Minsteracres, Co. Northumberland, married, in 1772, Catharine, daughter of Sir H. Lawson, fourth Baronet, and of Anastasia Maire, by whom he had three sons, George, Henry, and Charles. Died at Minsteracres, Dec. 26, 1801.

SIMPSON, BONIFACE, O.S.F., of Barton-Blunt, in Derbyshire, where he possessed a comfortable estate. He was sent young to Douay, where he distinguished himself by his talents and vivacity, and often told his companions that, however incredible it might appear, he would certainly become one day a Franciscan friar. He returned to England before he took any orders, where he led a dissolute life, indulging himself in many follies, especially drunkenness On one occasion he misbehaved himself so much on a Sunday that he was put into the stocks, but found means to extricate himself by setting fire with his pipe to some gunpowder with which he had filled the lock. Another time, as he was reeling homewards from a drunken bout, he fell under a cart and there remained till the fumes of the liquor had nearly evaporated, when an indignity offered him by a dog gave rise to some serious reflection, which ended in his going over to Douay, where he and a favourite coachman applied to the Guardian of the English Franciscans to be admitted upon trial. During his noviciate, refusing to exchange places with a confrère who was doing penance on his knees in the refectory, with a bone in his mouth, and whom he had made the object of his raillery, he resolved to quit the house, and actually proceeded to the door of the Convent, where the sight of the Crucifix caused him to reflect on the step he was taking and to submit to the penance enjoined him. He afterwards became an altered and good man and was ordained Priest, and lived many years in his Convent much beloved and respected by all who knew him. He often went to the English College on Sundays to claim the portion of pudding which Mr. Petre, the Procurator, had promised him in a bantering way, if ever he became, as he said he should, a Franciscan friar. He was generally called Merry Simpson. He died at Douay, Mar. 5, 1776.

SIMPSON, CUTHBERT, O.S.B., was a native of Lancashire. He lived about twenty-eight years at Coughton Court, the seat of Sir Robert Throckmorton. In 1784 he retired to Bath, where he died, Nov. 15, 1785. He was a zealous Missionary and much respected and beloved at and about Coughton.

SIMPSON, JOHN, was educated at Valladolid and came on the Mission about 1687. In 1693 he lived with Mr. Errington, heir apparent to Sir Miles Stapleton, at Qousq.,* where he had formerly taught a school. He afterwards lived many years at Newhouse, near Esh, Co. Durham, where he died Jan. 29, 1726. He had the character of being "a virtuous, sober man." (*Chapter Papers*.)

SKELTON, NICHOLAS, of a good family in Cumberland and was related to the Salvins and Scroops. On his return from Douay College the care of the Catholics in and about Lancaster was confided to him. In 1745 he was committed to Lancaster Castle as a Priest, together with Mr. Edward Barrow, and suspected of being concerned in the rebellion. But nothing being proved against them, they were soon liberated. Mr. Skelton was the first Priest, it is said, who fixed his residence in Lancaster, where he was much respected. He served that Congregation upwards of fifty years, and died Nov. 13, 1766. Mr. James Tyer succeeded him.

SKINNER, [JOHN], S.J., lived at Brinn, near Wigan. At his death, in 1708, he gave a golden cross to Sir William Gerard which, he affirmed, was given to the first one of his ancestors by Queen Elizabeth, whose descendant he was reputed to be, as well as the Mountjoys in Ireland. (Dodd's *Compend. Hist.* 2nd book, p. 14. This is my reference, but I cannot find the MS. at Oscott. *Have you got it? [Sic in MS.]*)

SKROOPHAM, JOHN. In the height of the Popish Plot, as it was called, he retired into Yorkshire, and was entertained for two or three years at Thorphall, near Selby, by a Mr. Dealtry, though he and his family were Protestants. During this time he seems not to have appeared in his priestly character, probably because he was engaged in a law suit, by which he recovered a small estate of about £40 a year. He afterwards lived about Pomfret, and assisted the poor Catholics in that neighbourhood. "He had," says a writer in 1693, "great wit, memory, and reading, and could with ease preach every Sunday and holyday, and did so when he had conveniency, but was subject to melancholy and spleen" (*Chapter Papers*). He lived some months with Bishop Smith.

---

* "Qousq." So both draft and fair copy. Under Nicholas Stapleton it is given as Conteland

SLAUGHTER, GEORGE, was born in Herefordshire of a respectable family. In June, 1683, he went to Lisbon College, and in April, 1688, took the oath and cassock. He taught the Classics there for two years, Philosophy for six, and Divinity, with short intervals, while he was able, till his death. On his return from England in 1710, whither some domestic affairs had called him, he brought with him from Bishops Giffard, Smith, and Witham a Patent of Vice-President. He died in the College Sept. 10, 1741 (N.S.), to which he had been a great ornament and support by his abilities and good management (*Lisbon Register Miscell.*, VI. 1080).

SLAUGHTER, JAMES, nephew of George, was born in Herefordshire in March, 1712. He was sent to Douay, and took the College oath Nov. 4, 1736, and began Philosophy Oct. 1, 1737. Soon after his ordination he came on the mission, lived many years at Longford and Newport, Salop, the seat of a branch of the Talbot family, and died there June 12, 1781. He was much respected among his brethren and acquaintances, and died much regretted. He was a member of the Chapter and an Archdeacon. He translated Lambert's *Manière d'Instruire les pauvres de la Campagne*, but never published it, I believe. The MS. is in my possession.

SMITH, FRANCIS, lived at Mr. Chester's at Bearscomb, Co. Devon, and died there Feb. 25, 1747-8, at an advanced age.

SMITH, JAMES, studied at Lisbon, and there received the order of priesthood (see account of himself in his first *Dialogue*). He became a Protestant, and having abilities and some interest, was made Rector of Eastbridge, and some time after Vicar of Alklam, with the Chapel le Ferne annexed to it. After his fall he never would meet a Priest. The Rev. Henry Peach sought every opportunity of meeting him, and once met him on horseback, but Mr. Smith turned back and rode off. Mr. Allen, of Lisbon, wrote to him on his fall, and a controversy was carried on between them, but was soon discontinued by Mr. Smith. But to vindicate his conduct he published *The Errors of the Church of Rome, detected in Ten Dialogues* (2nd edition, 1780). This was answered by *Popery vindicated from divers vulgar aspersions in some letters occasioned by the Dialogues of Rev. James Smith, a Priest, educated at Lisbon,* by "Pacificus," London.

"Smith of Dover," says Bishop Milner, "was one of those wretched priests who, wanting the grace necessary for living up to the strictness of their obligations, have attempted to escape their breach of them by abusing the Church which imposes these upon them. His puny embryo was stifled in the birth, and himself, soon after his fall, met with that awful end which has been the general fate, within our own memory, of this class of converts." Smith dropped down dead in Canterbury Cathedral about the year 1780.

SMITH, JOHN, *alias* WARHAM, was brother to Robert, and studied with him at Lisbon, where he was admitted an alumnus Sept. 30. 1665. He was appointed to teach Philosophy, Jan. 13, 1676, and on April 18, 1681, left the College and came on the Mission. He laboured in the vineyard for more than thirty years, and died at Cowdray in Sussex, the seat of Lord Montague, March 19, 1714.

When the College at Lisbon wanted a President, Dr. Watkinson being disabled, and was in danger of ruin, Bishop Giffard referred the choice of a successor to the sons of the House assembled in London. They unanimously chose Mr. Warham as the most deserving of the place, on account of his learning, prudence, and piety, and Bishop Giffard gave him his diploma and recommended him to the College at Lisbon. After two fruitless attempts to proceed to his destination, in which he was driven back by stormy weather, and aware of the opposition he should meet with in reforming abuses that had crept into the College, he resigned his dignity, and never could be prevailed on to go over. Mr. Ed. Jones was then appointed in 1707 in his place. (*Lisbon Register.*)

SMITH, JOHN, eldest son of John Smith, by Elizabeth Pointer, his wife. He was born in Norfolk, Nov. 4, 1739 [O.S.], and on his father's conversion was sent to the English College, Rome, July 15, 1754, and on May 26th, 1766, he came on the Mission.   He lived many years as chaplain at South Street, London, and died, April 28, 1817, in his 78th year.   He was generally known among his friends by the name of " Goldsmith," in consequence of having obtained a good prize in the lottery. (*Annales Coll. Angl.*)

SMITH, ROBERT, *alias* WARHAM, studied at Lisbon, and after his ordina-tion taught the Classics for three years, and then a course of Philosophy.   On Nov. 4. 1684, he was made Prefect of Studies, and April 20, 1687, Professor of Divinity and Confessarius.   He received his missionary faculties Jan. 2, 1693, and came over to England ; but I cannot discover where he lived nor when he died. (*Lisbon Register.*)

SMITH, THOMAS, studied at Douay, and was a missionary at Oulston, Easingwold, Yorkshire. He died at Angram, Nov. 2, 1755.

SMITH, WILLIAM, *alias* CARRINGTON, was son of Francis Smith, Esq., of Aston, Co. Salop, and of the family of Lord Smith Carrington, of Wootton House, near Henley-in-Arden.   At the age of twenty he was received into the College at Rome by Father Courtenay, Oct. 18, 1668. He was ordained Priest April 16th, 1672, and came on the Mission about 1674.   I do not find in what part of the country he was missionary, but only that he was chosen an Arch-deacon by the Chapter in 1714, and died May 21, 1722, aged about 77. (*Annales Coll. Angl.*)

SMITH, WILLIAM, was educated at Naples and ordained there.   After having laboured many years on the Mission, he retired to Florence about 1771, and after some stay there went to Rome, where he died, April 13, 1776.   It was his wish to have lived as a pensioner in the College, but the Italian Superiors would not listen to his application.   He was buried by Dr. Stonor, the Clergy agent, and his executor, at S. Querico, near which church he first had his residence.

SMITHSON, AUG., was educated at Douay, and came on the mission about 1663, and lived with Mr. Trappes at Nid, Yorkshire.   It is said of him that he had "no want of parts, but of charity a great want."   " He was a declared enemy of the Chapter," and this may account for the character given of him about the year 1693 by a Capitular.

SMYTHE, FRANCIS, second Lord Carrington, was eldest son of Charles, first Lord Carrington, and of Elizabeth, daughter of Sir John Caryll, of South Harting, Knt.   He succeeded to the title and estates of his father, who was murdered at Pontoise by one of his servants in 1664.   He married first Juliana, daughter of Sir Thomas Walmesley, of Dunkenhalgh, Knt., by whom he had a son who died an infant ; second, Anne, daughter of William Herbert, first Marquis of Powis.   His Lordship possessed large estates in the counties of Leicester, Warwick, and Salop, and dying April 7, 1701, *aet* 80, without sur-viving issue, his title and estates came to his brother Charles, fourth son of the first Lord Carrington, who married Frances, daughter of Sir John Pate, but dying in May, 1706, without male issue, the title became extinct ; but the estates in great part came to his kinsman, Francis Carrington, of Aston, Salop, who, in 1730, was seated at Wootten Wawen, Co. Warwick. (Nichols, *Leicestershire*, III., 33.)

SMYTHE, of Eshe and Acton Burnell.—Sir Richard Smythe, of Esh, Co. Durham, second Bart., eldest son of Sir Edward Smythe (created Bart. by Charles II., Feb. 23, 1660 [O.S.]), by his wife, —— Lee, daughter and co-heiress of Sir Richard Lee, of Langley, Salop, Bart.   He married a daughter of Mr. Carrington, and niece of Lord Carrington, by whom he had only one daughter—Clare.   Sir Richard died Dec. 17, 1736 (O.S.), and was buried in the church at Acton Burnell, the present seat of the Smythes, which came into the family by his marrying the daughter of Sir Richard Lee, whose son, Sir Humphrey Lee, died in 1652. They are buried in the same church of Acton Burnell, as is also an ancestor, who possessed Acton Burnell: *Nicholas Burnell, miles Dominus de Holgot, obiit* Jan. 19, 1382. *Cujus animae propicietur Deus. Amen.*

On the death of Sir Richard, without issue male, his brother John succeeded to the title and estate in 1736 (O.S.), and married Constantia, daughter of George Blount [and sister of Sir Edward Blount], of Soddington, Bart., by whom he had two sons, Edward and Walter, and one daughter, Constantia, who married Marmaduke Langdale. Sir John survived his brother three-quarters of a year, and died (as per epitaph) Sept, 17, 1737.

Sir Edward, fourth Baronet, eldest son of Sir John, married, first, Mary, daughter of Peter Giffard, of Chillington, by whom he had one son, Edward. He married, second, Mary, daughter of Lord Clifford, by whom he had three sons—George Walter, born in 1767 ; Hugh Philip, born in 1769: William, born in 1770—and one daughter, Elizabeth Mary Anne, born in 1774, who married Raymund Arundell. Sir Edward died Nov. 2, 1784. He was a gentleman of great honour and integrity, and truly exemplary in his manners, and was highly respected in his neighbourhood and by all who knew him.

His brother, Walter Smythe, second son of Sir John Smythe, of Acton Burnell, studied with the monks at Douay, and on his return married Mary, daughter of John Errington, of Northumberland, by whom he had four sons— Walter, born in 1757 ; John, born in 1758 ; Charles, born in 1760; Henry, born in 1760—and two daughters, Mary Anne, born in 1756, and Frances, born in 1762, who married Sir Carnaby Haggerstone, Bart. Mary Anne married, first, Edward Weld, of Lulworth ; second, Thomas Fitzherbert, of Swinnerton ; and, third, George, Prince of Wales, afterwards George IV.; and died at Brighton. [March 29, 1837.] Mr. Walter Smythe died Jan 14, 1788.

Sir Edward Smythe, fifth Bart., eldest son of Edward, fourth Bart., was born in 1758. After studying with the monks at Douay, he passed some time in the Academy of Turin, and then travelled through Italy, etc. On his return he married Catharine Mary, only daughter of Peter Holford, of Wootton, near Henley, co. Warwick, by whom he had the present Bart., Sir Edward, born in 1787. Sir Edward died April 18, 1811, aged 52, R.I.P. ; and his Lady, May 7, 1831, R.I.P. She was a descendant of the families of Smith and Carrington, of Wooten Wawen, Co Warwick ; her father, Mr. Holford; having married Constantia Carrington, after the death of her first husband, Mr. Wright, of Kelvedon. Among her ancestors one of the most famous was Sir John Smith, Knight, third son of Sir Francis Smith, of Wootten (descended from the ancient family of Carrington from Sir Michael Carrington, standard-bearer to King Richard I. in the Holy Land), who with his own hands redeemed in the battle of Edgehill the banner Royal, for which signal valour he received in the field the honour of Knighthood from the King. After that, in several battles, he gave singular testimonies of his loyalty and courage, especially in the fight of Bramdean, March 29, having gained here several wounds in pursuit of victory, he died at Andover, March 30, 1664, aged 28. He is buried in the Cathedral of Christ Church, Oxford. Sir Francis Throckmorton, Bart., the son of his sister, had a black marble stone with an inscription laid over his grave. "The Catholic nobility and gentry," says Dr. Milner, speaking of the battle of Cheriton Down, I. 406, "exerted themselves almost to the ruin of their families and fortune in the cause of honour and loyalty. Many of them were amongst the best of the royal officers and generals, particularly the above-mentioned Sir John Smith, Sir Arthur Aston, Sir Marmaduke Langdale, Sir Henry Gage, Col. Howard, Sir John Weld, Major-General Webb, Lord Viscount Dunbar, Lord Powis, Lord Arundell of Wardour, the Earl of Carnarvon, the Marquesses of Winchester and Worcester, etc. The whole number of noblemen and gentlemen of that religion who lost their lives in the King's service on this occasion, was 194, being two-fifths of the sum total of Royalists of the said description so killed." (*History of Winchester*, I., 406.) (Logan's *Analogia Honorum ;* Guillim's *Heraldry*, p. 159, and *History of Colleges of Oxford*, p. 470, 9th Ed.)

SOUTHCOTE, PHILIP, of Woburn Farm, Surrey, was grandson of Sir John Southcote, Knight, and his wife, Elizabeth Aston, eldest daughter of Walter, second Lord Aston, of Tixall.   He lived at Woburn Farm and married Anne, daughter of Sir William Pulteney of Misterton, Co. Leicester, Knight, the widow of Charles Fitzroy, Duke of Cleveland, who died Feb. 2, 1745, (O.S.) " The ancient residence of the Southcotes was called Abbey Place, which they are said to have quitted in disgust on being refused burial for one ot them in the chancel.   It was pulled down in 1750.   The chapel is said to have been very splendid.   The loss of this family was long felt in the parish, and a grateful remembrance of their extensive charities has been handed down to the present day.   During their residence no calamity or casualty happened to an individual, no unproductive season occasioned a scarcity, but ready assistance was given. The last Lady Southcote (daughter of Walter, second Lord Aston) is said to have been constantly stationed, at certain well known times, on her garden terrace, overlooking the road, prepared to hear every petition, and to answer every claim on her benevolence.   " Such," adds the present worthy Rector, " was the family to whom burial in the church was refused, because they were Roman Catholics."   (Manning's *Surrey*, II., 260.)

SOUTHCOTE, THOMAS, O.S.B.   He is probably the person of whom Bishop Warburton (*Literary Anecdotes*, V., 650) says : " Poor Mr. Pope received just such a favour from Southcot (a receipt that saved his life), and he never was easy till he got him a rich Abbey in Flanders, which he did by the interest of Sir Robert Walpole and his brother Horace, with the Court of France."   Father Southcote translated Quesnel's *Moral Reflections on St. John's Gospel*, published in 1709 ; but this was published four years before Clement XI. condemned the book in 1713.   He was President at the General Chapter of the Order in 1721, 1725, 1729, 1733, 1737.   (Father Hewlett's MSS., 116-121.)

SOUTHWORTH, RICHARD ; RALPH ; THOMAS ; *and* WILLIAM. Richard Southworth was the eldest of five brothers, who all went over to Douay with the intention of entering the Church.   Four of them were ordained, and at different periods came on the Mission, but the fifth died while pursuing his studies at College.   Richard went over about 1756, and distinguished himself by his application, regularity, and piety.   In 1769 he was made Professor of Philosophy, and in 1775 succeeded Mr. Wilkinson as Professor of Divinity, and Vice-President.   Before the Revolution broke out he came on the Mission, and was placed at Brockhampton, Hampshire, where he lived much respected and beloved by his flock, and died there, Nov. 19, 1817, thus outliving all his brothers.   Mr. Southworth was an able divine, having been Professor of Divinity for fourteen or fifteen years, and a most zealous and exemplary missionary.   He was in such estimation with his Brethren and with Bishop James Talbot, that the latter wished him to be his successor, a wish recorded in his will.   That he was eminently worthy of that dignity was universally acknowledged ; but as he had lived all his life at College he was thought deficient in some of those qualifications which were deemed necessary in the person that was to fill the station of Bishop of the London District.   Mr. Douglass, of York, was therefore recommended to Rome, and was consecrated in 1790. (See *Orthodox Journal*, V., 446, and *The Catholicon*, V., 250.)

Ralph Southworth was the second of the five brothers. He also distinguished himself at College, and soon after his ordination went to Louvain as second Chaplain to the Augustinian nuns.   At the Revolution, being driven from their house, Mr. Southworth accompanied them to England, where they purchased a house at Spettisbury, and settled there.   Mr. Southworth continued with them till his death, which occurred July 13, 1810, in the 64th year of his age.

Thomas Southworth, the third son, was born in 1749, and when young was placed with his brother William under the care of his relation, the Rev. Hugo Kendall.   In 1766 they both went to Douay, where, having distinguished themselves by their application and still more by their regularity of conduct and solid piety, they were ordained Priests.   In 1777 or 1778 Thomas was sent over to England for the purpose of assisting Mr. Kendall at Sedgley Park, and on his death in 1781 he succeeded him, and governed that house, with a short interruption of five years, until his death in ——, with great prudence and advantage to the school and to the Catholic body; for under him it continued to supply Ecclesiastical establishments, both abroad and at home, with some of their best instructed and most promising plants for the ministry, and I believe it may be said with truth that the greater part of the Catholic Clergy of the present day began their education at Sedgley Park under Mr. Southworth. On the Feast of Pentecost, in 1816, in consequence of some great exertions he had been obliged to make in the preceding week, and while he was hearing Mass, he fainted away and was conveyed to his bed. On the Thursday following he received all the rites of the Church, and on June 9 resigned his soul into the hands of his Creator, about three o'clock in the evening of Trinity Sunday, having retained the perfect use of his faculties till within ten minutes of his death. "I saw him on Friday evening," says Rev. Mr. Quick, "and I assure you that the few minutes which I had at his bedside gave me great edification and convinced me that the hand of God supported him, and that now in the very shades of death he fears no evil. When I told him that all his children and friends at Oscott were offering their prayers for him, I perceived that his illness had not taken away that sweet sensibility for which, during life, he had been distinguished, admired and loved."

William Southworth came on the Mission in 1780 and succeeded Mr. Wilson at Heathersedge, in Derbyshire, where he remained as long as his health enabled him to bear the fatigues of a mountainous district. He afterwards was charged with a small Congregation at Moseley, near Wolverhampton, and then with another on the borders of Norfolk and Suffolk; and, lastly, was Confessor to a small community of nuns settled first at Churchill, near Worcester, and then at Wyrley Pool, where he died on his return in the evening from visiting Lady Smythe, of Wootten House, rather suddenly, April 28, 1814. The four brothers were gifted with good natural abilities which they all had cultivated at College, and were all most worthy and zealous missionaries, and much respected and beloved by their friends and neighbours.

STAFFORD, JOHN JOSEPH, *alias* KELLY, ex-Jesuit, born Dec. 2, 1743. entered his noviceship Sept. 7, 1762. This is probably the person of whom the Rev. Edward Kenyon gives the following account. "The Church had to lament his apostacy from her sacred ministry. The last Catholic Mission he filled was at Croston Hall, the seat of John Trafford, Esq. The writer is not informed how many years he served that place. It was, however, the scene of his fall. Unexpectedly he left the house of his patron and preached his recantation sermon in the parish church of that place. It was reported to Mr. Trafford that he, surely in the confusion of his mind, began his degrading address with the sign of the cross. He was afterwards, thro' the influence of Dr. Masters, the then Rector of Croston, appointed to the living of Whitworth, a place noted as the residence of Dr. John, a famous bone-setter. He served this place to his death and studiously avoided any communication with his old associates, or any other of the Catholic Clergy. The character he had at Rochdale, the place of his residence, was that of a punctual observer of the rites of the established Church, and he led a rather retired life. The late Rev. Richard Morgan, of Preston, informed the writer that when his Superior at Liège it was extremely difficult to keep him from the perusal of such authors as favoured the cause of infidelity." He died at Rochdale about the beginning of this [*i.e.* the nineteenth] century.

STANFORD, JOHN, son of John Stanford, Esq., probably of Salford. At the age of 17 he was received in the College at Rome, Oct. 16, 1671, and was ordained, Dec. 17, 1677. In the following April he left the College and came on the Mission. He lived many years at Wingerworth, Derbyshire, the seat of Sir Henry Hunloke, Bart., where he died, Jan. 27, 1736-7. He was many years Administrator of the Clergy Common Fund, but "a sorry accountant," says Rev. T. Brockholes, G.V., "and being unable to satisfy his assistant, Mr. Johnson, of Longbirch, in a huff gave up the administration and the fund to

Bishop Stonor, *violenter reclamantibus fratribus*, who were the subscribers to it, and who, therefore, refused to leave their thirds to it at their death, which, according to the rules, they were bound to do." This happened in 1725 or 6.

STANDISH, RALPH, of Standish, Co. Lancaster, was a gentleman of very good repute and plentiful fortune. He married into the family of the Duke of Norfolk. He was found guilty of high treason at Westminster. At his trial, June 16, 1716, he pleaded that he came to Preston about a suit then pending in the Palatine Court of Lancaster, and was there detained, as many others were who came to market. This, however, did not appear to the Court to be the case and the jury found him guilty. He had the character of being one of the most peaceable Roman Catholics. He was afterwards pardoned. His estates set at £671 10s. 10½d., but were valued by the Commissioners at £1,363 19s. 10½d. These, with £152 18s. 8d. personalty, were forfeited to the King. (*A Faithful Register of the late Rebellion*, London, 1718.)

STANLEY, JOHN, "born of honest and Catholic parents in the county of Notts; was sent to Douay, where he so intensely applied to his studies that he was second to none, but surpassed many of his companions. Being made Priest he went to Louvain, where, with ardent zeal and great benefit to the nuns, he filled the post of second confessor for four years, and afterwards that of first for nearly twenty-one years. He died, Sept. 1, 1770, after having devoutly received all the rites of the Church, with a composed and serene mind often raised to God and his Saviour hanging on the cross, in the fifty-first of his age and the twenty-sixth of his Priesthood. Mr. Stanley was a gentleman of mild and affable disposition; was esteemed and revered by the religious, courted by the burghers and adored by the poor." (*Louvain Obituary*.)

STANLEY, SIR JOHN MASSEY, sixth Baronet, third son of Sir William Stanley and Catharine Eyre. On the death of his elder brother, Thomas Massey, he succeeded to the Puddington estates and assumed the name of Massey, and added the name of Stanley on succeeding to the Baronetcy and estates of Hooton, on the death of his nephew Sir William, in 1792. Sir John married Mary, daughter of Thomas Clifton of Lytham, and died at Hooton, Nov. 24, 1794, aged 84. He was succeeded by his eldest son, Sir Thomas, who did not survive him three months, dying at York, Feb. 19, 1795.

STANLEY, SIR ROWLAND (I.), of Hooton, in the county of Cheshire, second Bart., was second son of Sir William Stanley (who was created Bart., June 17, 1661, by Charles II.) and his wife Charlotte, daughter of Richard, Viscount Molyneux, of Sefton. He was born June 1, 1653. His elder brother dying an infant he succeeded to his father's title and estates, and married Anne, daughter of Clement Paston, of Norfolk, by whom he had three sons and eight daughters. Catharine, his youngest daughter, married Robert Blundell, of Ince. Sir Rowland died in May, 1737, aged upwards of 80.

STANLEY, SIR ROWLAND (II.), fourth Bart., was son of Sir Rowland Stanley (I.) He married Elizabeth, daughter and co-heiress of Thomas Parry, of Pyrthymeanmach, Flintshire, by whom he had Sir William Stanley, the fifth Bart., who died in London, May 29, 1792, leaving no issue by his wife Barbara, only daughter of John Towneley, of Towneley, and in him failed the direct male line of this ancient house. The old hall of Hooton was pulled down in 1778 and the present noble house was built.

STANLEY, THOMAS, of Garret Hall, in the parish of Leigh, Lancashire. His estates, which were forfeited, are valued in the Report of the Commissioners of Enquiry at £332 8s. 10d. per annum, besides a personal property of £6,044 1s. 2d.

STANLEY, SIR THOMAS STANLEY MASSEY, eighth Bart., son of Sir Thomas, the seventh Bart., by his wife Catharine, daughter of William Salvin, of Croxdale. He married Mary, daughter of Sir Carnaby Haggerston, Bart., by whom he had several children.

STANLEY, SIR WILLIAM, third Bart., the eldest and only surviving son of Sir Rowland ——, was baptized Nov. 11, 1679. He married Catharine, the daughter of Rowland Eyre, of Hassop, by whom he had seven sons and three daughters. His son Thomas took the surname of Massey, being adopted son of William Massey, of Puddington in Wirrall, Cheshire. "Sir William was a gentleman," says Betham, "of strict honour and generosity and hospitality." He died in July, 1740.

STAPLETON, GREGORY, Bishop of *Hierocæsarea*, was son of Nicholas Stapleton, of Carlton, Esq., and his third wife, Winifred White. He studied at Douay, where he was Procurator for many years. In 1785 he left to travel with young Mr. Stonor, of Stonor, Oxon. When Mr. Wilkinson resigned his place at St. Omers in 1787, and Messrs. Chamberlayn and Douglass refused to accept of it, Mr. Stapleton, on his return from the Holy Land, was chosen by the Council to succeed him as President, in which situation he continued till the College was dissolved by the French Revolution. Mr. Stapleton suffered peculiar hardships in prison, and underwent very insidious examinations before two deputies of the National Convention sent purposely to examine into a malicious letter, forged for the express purpose of calumniating and ruining several English gentlemen in St. Omers, Dunkirk, and other places ; Mr. Stapleton, and also Mr. Cornthwaite, the Procurator, were marked out in a peculiar manner. Happily Mr. Cornthwaite was not in France, so that Mr. Stapleton, had to bear the whole brunt of their malice. This happened prior to the general arrestation of British subjects in Oct., 1793, when he, with his masters and students, were arrested and confined in the College of the French Jesuits in St. Omers. After some time they were removed to Arras, where they were confined successively in three different prisons, one of which was peculiarly inconvenient for want of room. In May, 1794, they were removed to the Citadel of Dourlens, in Picardy, where the Secular Clergy and the English Benedictines of Douay were confined. In the following October Mr. Stapleton was allowed to return with his colleagues to St. Omers. Here he watched every opportunity of availing himself of favourable circumstances, and at last obtained a passport with leave to go to Paris, whither he carried a petition signed by every individual of his College, of the College of Douay, and English Monks, for leave to return to England, which was granted, and on Mar. 2, St. Chad's day, he, with the gentlemen and scholars of St. Omers, Mr. President Daniel, with the gentlemen and scholars of Douay, and Father Prior Sharrock, with his Community of St. Gregory's, at Douay, arrived in England. Immediately on their arrival steps were taken to provide a College for Secular Clergy, after unavailing offers of union, and a general college for the four districts, he was chosen First President of St. Edmund's College at Old Hall Green, in Herts, (and then a Member of the Chapter), and remained till he was appointed V.A. of the Midland District, and Bishop of *Hierocæsarea*. "This appointment was made," said Mr. McPherson, the Scotch Agent at Rome, "as a stop-gap, and to prevent the appointment of another person, whose appointment had long been solicited by the Irish Bishops, some in England, and by Sir J. Cox Hippesley." Mr. Stapleton was consecrated by Bishop Douglass, on March 8, 1801, and came down to Longbirch in Nov., 1801. In the following year he was prevailed on to go over to Paris to attempt to recover the lost property of our Colleges and Convents. (Mr. Hodgson's *Obituary*.) For some years he had laboured under a confirmed asthma, which was much increased by the fatigue he underwent in giving confirmation in several places during the spring before he left Staffordshire. In consequence of this he was much indisposed while in London, but having gone to Shooter's Hill on May 18, he had a good night's rest, and next morning set forward in good spirits. At St. Omers this heaviness and sleepiness returned, and Dr. Bew and Mr. Clegtown, who accompanied him, called in medical assistance. Three physicians attended, and all agreed in the propriety ot opening a vein, when better symptoms appeared. The stupor, however, continued, and at 10.30 at night he departed this life without a groan, on

May 23, in the inn called St. Catharine's, after he had received Extreme Unction from the hands of his old friend, Mons. Caycoque. The following invitation was printed and handed about St. Omers, and was brought to London. "Messrs et Dames,—Vous êtes invités d'assister au convoi de Mgr. Greg. Stapleton, Evêque de Hiero-Cæsarea, V. Apos. du District du milieu d'Angleterre, ci-devant Président du Col. An. de St. Omers, décédé à l'auberge de S. Catharine, le 23 mai, 1802, agé de 54 ans environ. Son corps sera conduit à l'Englise de S. Denis le 25 du dit mois a 4 heures après Midi, ensuite au cimitière de l'ancienne Eglise de S. Martin au Laert.—*Requiescat in Pace.*"

STAPLETON, NICHOLAS (I.), of Carlton, Co. York. He was the only son of Mark Errington, of Conteland, and Anne, daughter of Sir Gilbert Stapleton, Bart. On the death of her brother, Sir Miles Stapleton, without any surviving issue, in 1707, the title became extinct, and the estate vested in her and her husband, Mr. Errington, whose son, in consequence, took the name of Stapleton, and married Mary, daughter of —— Scroope, of Danby, by whom he had Gilbert, who died young, and Nicholas. Mr. Stapleton died in 1715.

STAPLETON, NICHOLAS (II.), was the only surviving son of Nicholas and Mary Scroope. He married first, Charlotte Eyre, by whom he had four daughters. Second, Mary Bagnall, whose son and daughter died infants. Third, Winifred White, by whom he had Thomas, the late possessor of the estate, who claimed the title of Viscount Beaumont, as descended from Joanna, eldest of the two sisters of Francis Lovel, and eldest of the two daughters, and at length co-heiress of Joanna, only daughter of John, first Viscount Beaumont, whose only surviving son and heir, William, the second Viscount Beaumont, died without issue. This claim was determined a few years since, and again in the last session of Parliament. (Burke, *Dormant and Extinct Baronages* II., 42.)

STEPHENS, JOHN. "A Roman Catholic," says Chalmers on Dugdale. In the time of James II. he was a Collector of the Excise in Wales, and after the Revolution he followed the fortune of his master, and became a captain in the Army. He is well known to the learned world by his valuable continuation of Dugdale's *Monasticon*, and numerous translations, chiefly from the Spanish and Portuguese. In the library of Burton Constable, I remember to have seen a MS. (M. 266) with this title : *A Journal of my travels since the Revolution, containing a brief account of all the wars in Ireland, impartially related, and what I was an eye-witness to, and delivered upon my own knowledge, distinguished from what I received from others.* At the bottom of which is printed and pasted on it : "The author of the above was Mr. John Stephens, a Roman Catholic," as above.

STEVENSON, PAUL, was educated at Douay, and came over to England about 1675. "He was an able and witty man," says my author, "and in the reign of James II. was made Public Preacher in the Clergy Chapel at York." At the Revolution, in 1688, he was sent to prison, and on his being released he resided with Sir Walter Vavasour, at Hazelwood, and had the spiritual care of the Catholics in that neighbourhood. He was alive in 1693. (*Chapter Papers.*)

STONE, MARMADUKE, S.J. (*Catholic Magazine and Review*, V., clxix.)

STONOR, CHRISTOPHER, was son of Thomas Stonor, Esq., and Winifred Roper, daughter of Lord Teynham, and nephew to the Bishop. He became a pensioner at St. Gregory's in 1739, and entered his License Jan. 1, 1742. When Dr. Bear retired to Douay, in July, 1742, he committed the Seminary to Mr. Stonor's care, and also its temporals, till a Superior should be appointed, and he governed it till the arrival of Dr. Holden, Nov. 28. Mr. Stonor was ordained Dec. 21, 1743, and took his cap March 24 of the following year, and in April came over to England, having finished his course at his own expense.

In 1748 he was sent to Rome by his uncle as the Clergy Agent there, was admitted into the family of the Cardinal of York, and had an apartment in his palace, with an allowance of £60 per annum. He was afterwards made one of the Pope's Chamberlains, and Prelato di Mantellone, which honourable situation he held many years, till the infirmities of age obliged him to relinquish it. He was then made a Prelato di Mantelletta, and leaving the Pope's palace at Monte-Cavallo, where he had handsome apartments, he retired to a house in Strada Giulia, near to the Church della Morte, that he might have his eyes constantly fixed on that awful period for which he had been long preparing himself by a life becoming, what he really was, a good Christian and an exemplary Prelate. He died Feb. 12, 1795, at an advanced age. Monsignor Stonor was well versed in sacred and profane history, and particularly in the ecclesiastical history of the Church, and his own country ; had a most retentive memory, and was looked up to by the Romans as a Prelate of great respectability, piety, and learning. When Bishop Stonor applied to Rome for a Coadjutor, Dr. Stonor was the second in the list presented. Mr. Hornyhold was the first named, and was appointed Coadjutor, *cum futura successione*. Mr. Smelt was his executor, and succeeded him as Clergy Agent.

STONOR, JOHN TALBOT, Bishop of *Thespiæ*, and V.A. of the Midland District, was son of John Stonor, of Stonor, and Lady Mary Talbot, daughter of Francis, Earl of Shrewsbury. He went over to Douay in Sept., 1691. He defended Physics under Robert Witham, April 3, 1696, took the College Oath May 20, and defended Universal Philosophy July 18. In September he was received in St. Gregory's at his own expense, but left in Feb., 1698, and came over to England.   While here he seems to have thought of remaining, and even of entering into the state of marriage, for I find among Dodd's papers that in a letter of Oct. 23, 1698, to Dr. Paston, President of Douay, he complained that he was backward in obtaining a dispensation from the College Oath, that his agents were insignificant, that he had been ill-used, whereas he deserved better, that he had a considerable match in agitation, and waited to be released, that he was advised to apply himself to others for a dispensation, and that the consequences of a denial might prove dangerous. (Dodd's *Adversaria*, see *Catholic Allegiance*.) Whatever may have been the cause, he afterwards retraced his steps, and in Oct., 1705, returned to Paris to resume his studies, and qualify himself to enter the Church, in conformity with his College Oath. In July, 1709, he passed M.A., was ordained Priest at the mid-Lent Ordination, 1711, entered his License Jan. 1, 1712, and in May, 1714, took the Doctor's Cap, and came on the Mission Aug. 29 of the same year. In 1716 he was consecrated Bishop of *Thespiæ*, and succeeded Dr. George Witham as V.A. of the Midland District, when the former succeeded Bishop Smith in the Northern District. In that same year a design was formed to place him in London, and in the meanwhile a bull was granted to him to exercise, says Dodd, jurisdiction *in omnibus locis subjectis Epo Madaurensi, durante defectu, absentia aut impedimento ejusdem Madaurensis, et non alias*. Dr. Witham, President of Douay College, says this bull was granted by misinformation of Thomas Strickland. Three persons chiefly, viz. : Dr. Strickland, Dr. Stonor, and Mr. Gerard Saltmarsh (as above), represented Bishop Giffard as *incapax* ; while the generality of the clergy made and signed a declaration to the contrary. The Internuncio (probably Sartini, who succeeded Grimaldi in 1713), finding Strickland had imposed on him, dropped him, who then applied himself to Fathers Tellier and Galliard, Jesuits at Paris. They recommended him to Cardinal Bissi, and Bissi recommended him to Cardinal Fachini, at Rome. With these and Dr. Stonor's recommendation he goes to Rome pretending that he had all the clergy's recommendation, and it was by this means he obtained the bull, called " of inspection." He designed himself to be Bishop, but Rome never grants Coadjutors unless the incumbent asks for one. In the meantime the Internunce at Brussels declared in a letter to Dr. Witham, President of Douay, that it was not a bull of Inspection, of Aug. 16, 1676: "Que c'estoit avec beaucoup de pein qu'il entendoit que quelques donnèrent à ce bref le nom de bref d'inspection, dans le craint qu'on pourrait supçonner qu'un pouvoir supérieur à Mgr. de Madaura estoit donnez à Mons de Stonor, que rien n'étoit plus contraire à l'intention de sa Saintété," &c. The journal of Douay gives this character of Strickland (see below Dodd's *Adv.*). Bishop Stonor lived at Old Heythrop, and died there, March 29, 1756, in the 76th year of his age, and was buried at Stonor. " Bishop Stonor," says Mr. Berington, " had a mind naturally nervous and penetrating ; had enjoyed the advantages of an Academical education in the schools of Paris, and brought to his native country a stock of learning which few possess, and the endowments of a superior character. But a certain harshness, it appears, rendered those endowments less acceptable. He was, besides, unbending in his purposes when once they were formed, and imperious when their execution was resisted. It was he who planned and conducted the measures for the overthrow of the immunities of the Regulars," which obtained the Brief of Benedict XIV. in 1745, for the regulation of the English Mission. He also laboured hard, together with Bishop Petre, of L., to recover the English College at Rome, and in *Summa Abusuum* pointed out the evils arising from its being governed by Jesuits instead of the Clergy, to which originally the government had been confided by Gregory XIII. Mr. (afterwards Bishop) Dicconson was sent to Rome for the purpose, but was unable to succeed in opposition to the overwelming influence of the Society. (See his *Letters and Diary*. Also *Paris Registers* and *Catholic Gent. Magazine*, II., 44, where it is said he died at Stonor ; my papers say at Old Heythrop. See *Catholic Magazine*, III., 104.)

Bishop Stonor wrote *A Devout Exercise for Sundays.*

STOREY, ARTHUR, born at Cartington Hall, near Rothbury, Northumberland, was son of William Storey, and Anne, his wife. Having studied three years at Mr. Simon Boardley's school in Lancashire, he went to Douay, and at the end of Rhetoric removed to St. Gregory's, at Paris, where he studied Divinity under Abbé Plunkett, an eminent Theologian, and after V.G. of Paris. On March 12, 1764, he took the Seminary Oath, and on Sept. 19, 1767, was ordained Priest by Christopher de Beaumont, the Archbishop of Paris. For two years he was Chaplain of the Augustin Nuns at the Fossés, Rue S. Victor, and being B.D., prepared himself for his License, but in consequence of a bad state of health it was judged necessary he should try his native air. He came over to England in Oct., 1769, and had the Mission of Singleton, in Lancashire, for two years, and was then made domestic Chaplain to William Salvin, of Croxdale, Esq. Some time after he established a respectable school at Tudhoe, and presided over it for twenty-seven years. When the students of Douay were released from prison, and were allowed to come to England, Mr. Story gave up Tudhoe to those who belonged to the Northern District and retired to Robert Hall, where he remained four years, and then removed to Garstang. He died July 25, 1825, aged 82, while on a visit to his nephew at Thirsk, or at Stockton-on-Tees. (*St. Greg. Register.*)

STOURTON, CHARLES, fourteenth Lord Stourton, son of Charles (the third son of William, Lord Stourton) and of Catharine, daughter of Richard Frampton, of Bitson, Dorset. In April, 1753, he married Catharine, daughter of Bartholomew, and sole heiress of Francis Walmesley, of Dunkenhalgh, the relict of Lord Petre. His Lordship died March 11, 1753, and left issue. His sister Mary married Jordan Langdale, of Cliffe.

STOURTON, CHARLES PHILIP, sixteenth Lord Stourton, was son of William, fifteenth Lord Stourton, and Winifred Howard. He was born Aug. 22, 1752, and in 1775 he married Mary, second daughter and co-heiress of Marmaduke, Lord Langdale, by whom he left a large family. His Lordship died April 29, 1816, aged 64.

STOURTON, EDWARD, twelfth Lord Stourton, was son of William, Lord Stourton, and Elizabeth, daughter of Sir John Preston, of Furness Abbey, Lancashire. He married at Paris a daughter of Robert Buckingham, who had followed James II., but had no issue by her. In consequence of the penal aws he sold, in the reign of Queen Anne, the manor of Stourton, Wilts, which gave him his title of Baron Stourton, and also the advowson of the parish church of Stourton and the manor of Stourton-Caundle, Dorset, to Sir Thomas Meres for the sum of £19,400. He died at Paris in Oct., 1720. Two of his daughters became nuns at Liège. He was succeeded by his brother Thomas, thirteenth Lord, who died without issue, Mar. 24, 1743 (O.S.)

STOURTON, WILLIAM, fifteenth Lord Stourton, brother of Charles, four-teenth Lord Stourton. On Oct. 11, 1749, he married Winifred, daughter of Philip Howard, of Buckenham, by his wife Winifred Stonor, and, in 1753, succeeded his brother Charles, fourteenth Lord Stourton. He died Oct. 3, 1781.

STRICKLAND, JOHN, brother of Joseph Strickland. He studied at Douay, and after defending Universal Divinity, taught Humanity for two years, and in 1747 was sent by Bishop Petre to St. Gregory's, being already a Priest. In Dec., 1749, he went to assist the nuns at Rouen in place of Mr. Edward Daniel, and in Dec., 1753, to the Poor Clares at Dunkirk, but returned to Paris to supply Dr. Perry's place, July, 1754. In April, 1756, he left the Seminary to go to England, being then B.D. only. He was chosen a member of the Chapter, and some time after Archdeacon of Essex, Herts and Bedfordshire. Where or how long he laboured on the Mission I do not find. "He was eccentric in many things," says Mr. Hodgson, "but especially in fasting, which he would prolong for a considerable time and suddenly surprise his friends by the quantity of food he took immediately after his fast. He spent several years at Louvain where he assisted the nuns, and afterwards led a kind of heremitical life in the south of France. In the beginning of the French Revolution he lived some time at Lyons. In 1802, Dr, Rigby, of Lancaster, found him in Paris, looking like a Jew with a long beard." He died there in May, 1802.

Mr. Mannock Strickland, his father, studied at Douay, was a Conveyancer in London, and wrote a Law Tract on the claim of the Jesuits to the property of the Earl of Shrewsbury, a Jesuit. (*St. Gregory's Register.*)

STRICKLAND, JOSEPH, son of Mannock Strickland and Mary Wright, of London, was born in 1724. Having finished his Philosophy at Plessis College he was admitted into the Seminary at Paris, May 9, 1744, and took the oath Sept. 8, and was ordained Dec. 21, 1748. He made his "Sorbonic" Aug. 3, 1751, and having obtained leave of absence from the Faculty of Sorbonne and permission from Dr. Holden in October, he was, by the desire of Bishop Stonor, made preceptor to Mr. T. Stonor, eldest son of Thomas Stonor, of Stonor, Esq. In May, 1752, he took the Doctor's cap. By the rules of the Seminary, the senior V.A. in England every six years presents to the Archbishop of Paris (Beaumont), a D.D. or a Licentiate in some University for principal. At the end of Dr. Holden's sexennium, Bishop Stonor, as senior V.A., presented, in 1755, to Dr. Beaumont the Archbishop, Dr. Joseph Strickland, Dr. Umfreville, and John Strickland, B.D. and then entering his license; but "*Josephum Strick-land,*" he said, "*prae caeteris commendo.*" The Archbishop, however, passed Dr. Strickland over and appointed Dr. Umfreville, but he, on account of his infirmities declined the honour, and Bishop Stonor again wrote to the Arch-bishop and expressed his concern that Dr. Strickland was not appointed, and at the same time assured him that nothing but calumny could have prevented his complying with his request, and therefore bore ample testimony to the soundness of his doctrine and submission to the decrees of the Church, and especially to the Bull *Unigenitus*, and again presented him for Superior of St. Gregory's together with Mr. John Strickland and Dr. Howard. According to established usages the Archbishop, it seems, ought to have made his choice of one of the two remaining nominees of the first presentation, but passing over them both he offered it to Dr. Howard, who accepted the office and took possession. Some time after this Dr. Strickland came on the Mission and lived at Stonor with his former pupil, and died there, Aug. 22, 1790. (*St. Gregory's Register.*)

STRICKLAND, SIMON, studied at Douay and was ordained Priest at Arras. He was Missionary at Askew, near Bedale, Yorkshire, and died there, Mar. 21, 1782. He was a Capitular.

STRICKLAND, THOMAS JOHN FRANCIS (the Abbé Strickland), Bishop of Namur, was son of Sir Thomas Strickland, of Sizergh, and Jane, daughter and co-heiress of John Moseley, of Uskelf, Co. Worcester, Esq. After four years Divinity at Douay, he was admitted into St. Gregory's at his own expense, Jan. 9, 1703. On April 4, 1704, he went to S. Sulpice, but returned to St. Gregory's in 1711, and took the Doctor's cap, April 2, 1712, and left the Seminary Dec. 16. I do not find that he ever acted as Missionary in England, but served a chapel in the Church of S. Sulpice in Paris, and had an Abbey in Normandy. In 1717 he went a second time to Rome—recommended by the Internuncio at Brussels, the Duke of Norfolk, and Bishop Stonor—and pressed hard for the Catholics to be allowed to take an oath of submission to George I. The answer of the Congregation di S. Officio was *consulant Theologos.* Dr. Witham gives this character of Dr. Strickland in the Douay Diary. "Non erat difficile conjicere Breve hoc, quod vocant Inspectionis, obtentum fuisse artibus et falsis suggestionibus Domini Stricklandi. Erat hic juvenis Doctor ingenio praeditus acerrimo, foelicissima memoria, mira lingua praesertim Gallicae volubilitate, inter conversandum omnes in sui admirationem trahebat. Diceres hominem scire omnium scripta Patrum, omnes omnino historiæ et theologiæ difficultates, in omnibus praesentis temporis controversiis expertissimum ; in rebus politicis perspicacissimum, ipsumque non minus omnes magni nominis personas quam res et scripta cognoscere. Verum multo plura se scire jactitabat, quam revera sciebat, insolita quadam impudentia, falsa et dubia pro veris et indubitatis ubique spargebat. Qui per dies aliquot ejus utebatur conversatione evidentem judicii imbecillitatem, prudentiae et experientiae defectum, turpissimam vanitatem in illo notabant." (Dodd's *Adversaria.*) By a letter of Bishop Smith to Dr. Paston of April 11, 1709, it appears that some evil reports had been spread respecting Mr. Strickland, and that the Superior of S. Sulpice, where he then lived, was requested to manage him and try if he were fit for orders. (Dodd's *Adversaria.*) The upshot was favourable to him and he returned to the Seminary. He was chosen Bishop of Namur, and governed that diocese about ten years. (*Paris Register;* Berington's *Panzani,* p. 408 ; *Cath. Mag.* III., 104 ; Coxe's *History of the House of Austria.*)

STYCKE, JOHN, *alias* HAWKINS, studied at Lisbon, as appears from a letter of Mr. Thomas Berington, of Sept. 29, 1744. He came on the Mission in 1744, and lived in Lincolnshire in the family of Thomas Heneage, of Hainton Esq., and where he seems to have died, March 9, 1764.

STYCKE, ——, a native of Staffordshire, but on the Mission he took the name of Bridgwood. He lived many years at Bellamore, a seat of Lord Aston of Tixall, and attended the Catholics thereabouts, and at Hore Cross, and Pipe Hall, near Lichfield.

SUMNER R [ICHARD] AND JAMES. (*Cath. Miscell.* I., 336.)

SUMNER JOHN. (*Catholic Magazine and Review,* V., cii.)

SUSSEX, ANNE, COUNTESS OF, daughter, by Charles II., of Lady Castlemain, who, after her separation, was created Duchess of Cleveland. She married Lord Dacre, afterwards Earl of Sussex, grandfather of the Lord Dacre who died in 1786. She died in 1721. (*Ita,* Rev. Thomas Potts.)

SUTTON, JOHN, of Sutton Place, Co. Surrey. He married Elizabeth, daughter of George Penruddock, Hants, and heiress to her brothers, who died childless.

SWARBRICK, JAMES, *alias* SINGLETON. At the age of 19 he was admitted into the English College at Rome Oct. 3, 1673. He was ordained April 9, 1678, and left to go to Flanders May 15, 1680. Was a native of Lancashire. A Priest of this name was a missionary at Great Singleton,

Lancashire, and died in Lancaster Castle in 1716, "where he had been confined for his priestly character." (*Annals Roman College.*)

SWINBURNE, EDWARD AND JAMES, brothers of Sir William, the second
Bart. They were taken at Preston, and their trial came on June 4, 1716. It
was proved that James was with the rebels at Hexham and Preston, and on the
day of the action rode out of the town towards Ribble Bridge, and was not
seen after till he was dismounted and taken in the churchyard. His counsel
endeavoured to prove him a lunatic, and brought forward two witnesses to
establish the point, one of whom was Edward Shaftoe, an old grey-headed
gentleman, a relation of Mr. Swinburne and a King's evidence. This plea was
overruled, so the jury found him guilty. On the trial of his brother Edward
Mr. Patten declared that when he joined the rebels with eighteen persons,
at the "Hugh Head Inn," at Wooler, the prisoner told him *he was welcome
with his troop*, and need not fear being well received. By the testimony of
others it was proved that he had accompanied the rebels in their march, and
at Preston rode out with his brother, and was taken with him. The case
admitted no doubt, and he was found guilty. His estates, which were
forfeited, brought in £305 annual rents. Edward was a very handsome
gentleman, and of good parts. He died in Newgate. James, through long
confinement, and, some say, an hereditary distemper, became pensive and
melancholy, and died in 1728. (Patten's *History of the Rebellion*, London,
1745.)

SWINBURNE, HENRY, of Hammersley, third son of Sir John, the second
Baronet, was born in 1743, at Capheaton. He studied with the English
Monks at Douay. He resided much in high life at the Courts of Madrid,
Naples, &c. He married Martha, daughter of John Baker, of Chichester,
Solicitor to the Leeward Islands, a lady of great learning. Hamsterly, or
Hammersley, in Bishoprick, was his residence. Late in life he had an
appointment from Government in Trinidad, and died there, April 1, 1803. He
told Mr. Eyre, of Ushaw, that in his works there were many reflections
respecting religion, Monks, &c., which though he thought them true at the
time he wrote them, he had since been convinced were false, and acknowledged
that an ambition in his early life to be considered liberal and free from religious
prejudices induced him to write those reflections which he afterwards so
regretted." (Dr. Gradwell.) He wrote : *Travels into Spain. Travels into
the two Sicilies.* His eldest and favourite daughter died at Rome and was
buried in the Church of the English College. (See her Epitaph.)

SWINBURNE, SIR JOHN (I.), of Capheaton, Northumberland, son of John
Swinburne (who on account of his loyalty had a Baronetcy patent granted
him by Charles I., but it was not taken out), and Anne, his wife, daughter of
Sir Charles Blount, of Maple Durham. Sir John was created Bart. Sept. 26,
1660, and married Isabella, daughter and heiress of Henry Lawson, of Brough,
by Catharine, his wife, daughter and co-heiress of Sir William Fenwick, of
Mildon, Northumberland. By his lady he had twenty-four children, of whom
Catharine, Margaret and Isabella became nuns at Cambray, and Alathea at
———. Sir John re-built the castle at Capheaton, and a handsome vault in the
Church of Whelpington. He died June 19, 1706. (*Betham* III., *Appendix*.)

SWINBURNE, SIR JOHN (II.), third Bart., was son of Sir William and Mary
Englefield. He married Mary, daughter of Sir Henry Bedingfield, of Oxburgh,
who died in 1761. By her he had four sons and seven daughters ; of these
Sir John and Sir Edward succeeded to the title. Henry, the third son,
travelled in Spain and Sicily. Teresa married Edward Charleton, of Hesley-
side. Mary married Edward Bedingfield. Isabella married Thomas Crathorne, of Ness, Yorkshire, and Anne became a nun at Montargis, in Gatinois.
Sir John died at Bath in 1744 or 5, and was succeeded by his elder surviving
son, John, who died at Paris in 1763, *sine prole*, and was succeeded by his
brother Edward, fifth Bart.

SWINBURNE, SIR WILLIAM, of Capheaton, second Bart., was the nineteenth child and eldest surviving son of Sir John and Isabella Lawson. In 1699 he married Mary, daughter of Anthony Englefield, of Sunning, Berks, by whom he had three sons and one daughter, Mary, who died young. (1) John, who succeeded his father. (2) Matthew, born in 1700, married in 1738, Eleanora, daughter and heiress of Mr. Thirlwall, of Thirlwall Castle, Northumberland. (3) Thomas, who married Mary, daughter and heiress of Anthony Meaburne, of Pontop, Durham, and relict of Thomas Thornton, of Nether Witton, who died in 1786, leaving one daughter, Mary, and one son, Thomas, who married the daughter and heiress of Mr. Spearman. Sir William died April 17, 1716.

SYERS, JOSEPH, studied at Douay, and when he came on the Mission lived some time at Sedgley Park, where he had the care of the children till 1770 or 71. He then went to London, was Chaplain to Bishop Challoner for many years, and died at Twickenham, June 26, 1807.

TALBOT, HON. CHARLES, second son of George Talbot (commonly called Earl of Shrewsbury), and Mary Fitzwilliam, was brother to George, Earl of Shrewsbury, and father of the late Charles, Earl of Shrewsbury. He lived at Hore Cross, Needwood Forest, and died, April 11, 1766, aged 44. He was buried in Yoxall Church. He married first, Mary Allwyn, daughter and co-heir of Robert Allwyn, of Trayford, Sussex, and second, in 1752, Mary, eldest daughter of Sir Pierce Mostyn, Bart., and Dame Teresa, his wife. By her he had three sons, Charles, born March 8, 1753, who succeeded to the estates and title on the death of his uncle, George, the fourteenth Earl of Shrewsbury. (Charles also dying April 6, 1827, without issue, was succeeded by his nephew, John, fifteenth Earl of Shrewsbury, the present Earl, son of John Joseph Talbot and Catherine Clifton, of Lytham.) George Joseph, born Nov. 23, 1765 (sic), John Joseph, father of the present Earl, born June 9, 1765, also Frances, Barbara, Catharine, Mary, Teresa, Juliana, Elizabeth, Teresa, Anne Mary, and a posthumous daughter married, Charlotte Mary, born Oct. 4, 1766. An elder daughter called Anne, born March 9, 1754, died July 4, 1755.

TALBOT, FRANCIS, of Witham Lodge, Essex, fifth son of George, (commonly called the Earl of Shrewsbury), and Mary Fitzwilliam, and brother of George, the fourteenth Earl, and Bishops James and Thomas Talbot. He married Anne Belasyse, daughter of Thomas, Earl of Fauconberg, and had many children by her. Mr. Talbot died Nov. 26, 1813, aged 86.

TALBOT, GEORGE, third son of Gilbert Talbot and Jane Flatsbury. He married in 1719 Mary, daughter of Thomas, Viscount Fitzwilliam, of Merrion, in Ireland, she died Dec. 20, 1752, and by her had seven sons: George, Charles, John, James and Thomas (Bishops), Francis and Gilbert. Three daughters: Barbara, married to James, fifth Lord Aston ; Mary, married Charles Dormer, son and heir to John Dormer, of Peterly, Bucks ; and Lucy. who became a nun. This Mr. George Talbot was usually called Earl of Shrewsbury, his eldest brother, Gilbert, the real Earl, being a Jesuit. He died Dec. 23, 1733, before his brother Gilbert, and was buried at Albrighton, Co. Salop.

TALBOT, GEORGE, fourteenth Earl of Shrewsbury, was eldest son of George Talbot and Mary Fitzwilliam, and born Dec. 11, 1719 (O.S.) On the death of his father in 1733, he succeeded to the estates of the house of Shrewsbury, and in 1743 to the title at the death of his uncle, Gilbert (Father Grey). He married, Nov. 21, 1753, Elizabeth, daughter of the Hon. John Dormer, by whom he had no issue. He died July 21, 1787.

TALBOT, GILBERT (alias GREY), S.J., was son of Gilbert Talbot, Esq., the fourth son of John, tenth Earl of Shrewsbury, by Mary, daughter of Sir Francis Fortescue. He studied at St. Omers, and afterwards entered into the Society of Jesus, and took the name of Grey. On the death of his cousin, Charles, twelfth Earl of Shrewsbury (who had been created by King William

April 30, 1694, Duke of Shrewsbury and Marquis of Alton), Feb. 1, 1717 (O.S.), Father Grey succeeded to the title and estates, as the thirteenth Earl of Shrewsbury, but reserving only a small pittance to himself, made over the family estates to his brother, George Talbot, who was hence commonly but erroneously called the Earl of Shrewsbury. The Rev. C. Plowden gives the following account of Father Grey in a letter to the present Earl of Shrewsbury : "I lived with several others who had known him, and who used openly to speak of him as a man of prayer, of great humility, and charity to the poor. Old Father Scarisbrick used to commemorate his coming from Ghent to the Mission in wretched second-hand apparel, which happened to be allotted to him by a lay brother. Another who knew him, mentioned to me his stripping off his own clothes to give them to the poor. He lived many years at Dunkenhalgh, in the Lancashire Hills, always among the poor, as Chaplain to Lady Stourton, and living with the Steward. He enjoyed her Ladyship's confidence. I have often heard that his advice prevented her from yielding to the importunity of her second husband, who pressed her to settle her Dunkenhalgh and Walmesley property on his family, to the prejudice of her own grandson, Lord Petre. I find in a mortuary register that he once belonged to St. Omers College, that he died on July 22, 1743, in London. I always understood that Father Grey was brought up at St. Omers, that after his course there he made himself novice at Watten, passed thence to Liège and Ghent, and so to the Mission ; that he made a full renunciation of his birth-rights to his younger brother, &c., reserving, as was usual in such cases, a trifle to himself. Instances of heirs of opulent families becoming Jesuits were not rare. I have known several. A few years after their first vows they made their renunciation, commonly with a small reserve. But even this reserve was to be renounced before they made their solemn profession, and it was this private act of Father Grey, which after his death occasioned an unpleasant dispute and a Chancery suit between the Shrewsbury family and the Superiors of the Jesuits, which being prosecuted on the principle of the Penal Laws, the Jesuits of course were worsted, and gained nothing but the ill-will of the noble families of Talbot and Dormer, which had always been remarkably friendly to them. Father Grey lived estranged from his family as well as from the rest of the world, but I have never heard that any dispute or difference existed between them. I have always heard that Father Grey, renouncing his small property or *peculium*, as it was called, made an assignment of it to the Provincial of the Jesuits, and added a clause by which he also assigned to him whatever property might accrue in future to him. Many years after this act property to a considerable amount (I never heard how much or by what means) did fall to Mr. Grey as the eldest of the family, and it was claimed by the Provincial, to whom the original deed had been legally transmitted. Hence the dispute, in which Mr. Grey, I believe, was not concerned. I often heard this affair spoken of, when I was young, with warmth on both sides. Sixty years ago I read a printed Factura in 4to in support of the Jesuit's claim in the affair of Father Grey, and I was told it was the work of their Provincial, Father Carteret." * [Letter to Lord Shrewsbury, then Mr. Talbot, dated Stonyhurst, June 4, 1820.]

It was on the death of Father Grey's brother, in 1733 [?], to whom he had ceded the family estates, the above claim was put in by the Provincial. Mr. Booth, a Catholic councillor, wrote two papers on the subject. His opinion was "that though the letter of the Statute for the Distribution of the Estates of Intestates prefers Father Grey to the other relations, yet he cannot avail himself of this Statute without also availing himself of those laws which immediately upon the Reformation set all the Religious Orders at large, cancelled their vows, and repealed not only their disabilities but also their very profession, and made it void. I think that Father Grey cannot, con-

---

* It appears clearly from this and other phrases above that Fr. Plowden was writing from memory, or from tradition. This was a pity, as he has fallen into several errors, and misled Dr. Kirk, also Br. Foley, *Records*, vii., 754.—J.H.P.

sistently with the principles of a Catholic, and consequently cannot without doing violence to his conscience, claim any share of, or at all interfere in the disposition of this estate." Dr. Fell was consulted by Mr. Booth in his answer, who says, Sept. 3, 1743 : " The reasons alleged by you are invincible as to England. . . . Whoever he is who has taken up the affirmative, he cites several decrees of the civil and canon law which are either not to the point or have been disused." P. 28.

" It is strange casuistry that any body of men should pretend to be exempt from prior general laws made to restrain their power. It sounds no less strange that Catholic laws should be looked upon as an oppression of the Religious and Protestant laws as favourable of them." (*Ibid.*) " That professed Religious should inherit from a layman *ab intestato*, I humbly conceive cannot be proved by the practice of any Catholic country." (*Ibid.*) *

The Statute alluded to by Mr. Booth was an Act of Parliament obtained by the Duke of Shrewsbury to settle the family property ; who passed over Father Grey in his will, and left everything to his younger brother. It is recited in that Act, " that the said Gilbert is resolved not to marry, and being desirous to pay a due observance to the intentions of the said Duke expressed in the said settlement and will, had persuaded the said George Talbot, his younger brother, to marry the Hon. Mary Fitzwilliam," &c. The object of procuring the Act of Parliament appears to have been to secure property to the Protestant heirs in case the said George Talbot had no male issue. The Bishop of Salisbury was the nearest Protestant heir, and is named as such in the Act. It was also for the purpose of holding out a bait to the young Catholic heirs, whoever they might be, to become Protestants by inserting a clause which placed the whole property at their disposal in case of conformity to Protestantism.

I find amongst my papers an account that Francis Talbot, twelfth [? eleventh] Earl of Shrewsbury, left by his will *satis obscuro et informi* 16,000 English crowns to the Society of Jesus, 2,000 to *Virgini Lauretanæ*, 1,000 to *Virgini Hallensi*, 1,000 to *Virgini Montis Accuti, hæc duo Sacella* in *Comitatu Brabantiae* about the year 1660. The Duke, who was the thirteenth [? twelfth] Earl, refused to pay the sums. About 1718 the Jesuits demanded payment from the Catholic Lord. *Post disceptationem aliquam*, the case was referred to Bishop Stonor, who *statuit ut ¼ pars totius summae et non amplius penderetur*. (*Roman Collection*, II., p. 533, or Mr. Mayes' Agency.) This " ¼ pars " £1,000, was paid on condition that the Society should always keep a Priest at Grafton, near Bromsgrove, a seat of Lord Shrewsbury.

TALBOT, GILBERT, was a native of Northumberland, and son of Captain John Talbot, an Irish Gentleman, and of Mary Charleton, daughter of Sir Edward Charleton, of Hesleyside, Co. Northumberland. At the age of 23 was received as a Convictor at Rome, Nov. 28, 1704. He was ordained Priest Sept. 19, 1711. He was nearly related to the Duchess of Norfolk (Sherborn), and in 1726 he was mentioned at Rome as proper to succeed Bishop Witham " by the interest of the Jesuits," Dr. R. Witham says, " and had great recommendations from the nobility of England, but wanted qualifications necessary for a Bishop, and I hear has done nothing at all of a Missioner's office." (*Ep. Var.* IX., 32.) " He died lately in London " (says

---

* The above quotations are, of course, only the pleadings of an advocate, and are interesting under that aspect, however unpraiseworthy in themselves. Thus, for instance. the claim is said to be that of *inheritance ab intestato*, whereas in reality there was a will, as mentioned below, *which still exists*, but which Father Talbot could not bring into court because of its Catholic clauses, and was therefore obliged to rely on other arguments. The sneer about Jesuit casuistry, from a Catholic advocate, is, therefore, to say the least of it, in decidedly bad taste. But the important point to notice is that both Father Plowden (who had only his memory to guide him) and the Rev. John Kirk (though he had Bp. Stonor's award before him) mistake the facts. It was not Father Talbot's will, but that of his predecessor, which was under dispute, as the award clearly shows. The origin of the affair goes back a long way. Sir George Wintour had borrowed the money of the Jesuit Mission to redeem his forfeited estates, in 1652. He made restitution by his will, but his real estate proved insufficient to discharge its obligations. Hence further complications, which were protracted until the award above mentioned.—J.H.P.

Mr. T. Berington, March 5, 1747), "he had no obligation, neither did he labour on the Mission, and had little correspondence with us, but seemed rather a member of the *Padri* than a Clergyman."

TALBOT, JAMES, V.A., and Bishop of *Birtha*, was son of George Talbot, Esq. (brother of Gilbert Talbot, the thirteenth Earl of Shrewsbury and S.J.), and of Mary, daughter of Thomas, Viscount Fitzwilliam, was born in 1726. He was sent to Douay in 1737 or 8, and after he had finished his studies travelled through France to Italy, together with his brother, Thomas, with Rev. Alban Butler. On his return, 1749, he taught Philosophy, and then Divinity, and at the same time went through his License. He it was who purchased Esquerchin as a Preparatory School for the College, and presided over it. While he presided there, and at the age of 33, Bishop Hornyhold wished to have him for his Coadjutor, and as he obstinately declined the honour, he applied to the Pope, Clement XIII., requesting, *ut severo mandato ei in virtute obedientiæ praecipiat, ne munus a Deo impositum in se suscipere detrectet.* Another letter was written to Prince Charles Stuart, and a third to his brother, the Cardinal of York, entreating them to recommend the affair to his Holiness. All these applications proved fruitless. When Bishop York applied in 1756 for a Coadjutor about three years before Bishop Hornyhold, there were several in the Congregation of Propaganda, says Dr. Stonor, the Agent at Rome, that would give Mr. James Talbot the preference, but there were one or two persons, too respectable to be named, who insisted upon having one of the VV. AA., a Regular. He was, however, chosen Coadjutor to Bishop Challoner, and on his death succeeded to the charge of the London District. In 1771, upon the information of one Payne, he was indicted for exercising the office of a Popish Bishop, and was tried at the Old Bailey : but as the Government in general, and the Lord Chief Justice Mansfield in particular, decidedly set their faces against such prosecutions, Bishop Talbot was acquitted, as were all the other Priests who were tried, except an Irish Priest named Malony, who openly confessed himself in court to be a Priest and was sentenced to perpetual imprisonment, which was afterwards remitted on the condition of his transporting himself. Bishop James Talbot died at Hammersmith, Jan. 26, 1790, in his 64th year. Bishop Talbot was gifted with a happy facility for preaching and pulpit eloquence, and in the opinion of Mr. Alban Butler, in learning, prudence, and piety in zeal and respect for the Apostolic See, he yielded to none. Mr. Burke, in his speech at Bristol, speaking of Bishop Talbot's indictment, says indignantly : "A brother of the Earl of Shrewsbury, a Talbot, a name respectable in this country, whilst its glory was any part of its concern, was hauled to the Bar of the Old Bailey among common felons, and only escaped perpetual imprisonment either by some error in the process, or that the wretch who brought him there could not correctly describe his person."

TALBOT, THOMAS JOSEPH, Bishop of *Acon*, son of George Talbot, and brother of James, was born Feb. 17, 1727. Bishop Giffard stood godfather to him, and in his will, dated July 17, 1728, he says : "To my godson, Thomas Joseph Talbot, I leave my ring with a purple stone. I hope God has designed him for a good Churchman, and in order thereunto I earnestly desire of Lord and Lady Shrewsbury,* that at the age of thirteen they will send him to Douay College, intimating to the President, Vice-President, and other Seniors, that I hope they will always consider him most particularly recommended to them by me." Conformably with this request of the good Bishop, which seems to have something prophetic in it, he was sent to Douay, where his application, regularity, and solid piety gained him the esteem of all his superiors and fellow students. Having finished his course, he and his brother travelled through France and Italy with Mr. Alban Butler, and when the latter was

---

* They were commonly called so, though the real Lord Shrewsbury, Father Grey, S.J., was living.

placed at Norwich Mr. Thomas Talbot resided some time with him. About the year 1754 he succeeded Mr. David Morgan (at Brockhampton, near Havant, Sussex), who had got into difficulties in building his house and chapel, and was removed to another situation. Mr. Talbot paid off all the incumbrances, and on account of the great services done to the clergy thereby, he was chosen a member of the Chapter in the General Assembly, July 8, 1755. In 1758 Bishop Challoner put his name on his list for Coadjutor, together with James Talbot and Dr. Walton. When St. Omers was taken from the Jesuits in 1762 (I think, see Hodgson's account), Mr. Talbot was chosen President, and as soon as he could he got the burden transferred to his friend, Mr. Alban Butler. Being thus at liberty, Bishop Hornyhold seized the favourable moment and requested he would consent to be his Coadjutor, but having resigned the office of President, nothing, he said, should induce him to undertake the greater responsibility attached to the office of Bishop. And if ever man were sincere in saying *Nolo Episcopari*, most assuredly Mr. Talbot was ; nor could the most earnest entreaties of Bishop Hornyhold induce him to recede from his resolution. It was therefore necessary to employ other means, and his friend, Mr. A. Butler, and Bishop Challoner were engaged to write to him the most pressing and earnest letters, and those not succeeding, a request, or rather a command from Rome, was necessary to cause him to acquiesce. He was consecrated Bishop of Acon in March, 1766, and appointed Coadjutor to Bishop Hornyhold, whom he succeeded in the charge of the Midland District at the end of 1779. In 1795 he was persuaded to go to Bristol for the benefit of his health, and took his Coadjutor, Mr. B., with him, and died there, Feb. 23, *aet.* 68. Bishop Talbot was a prelate of solid and unaffected piety, and was greatly respected by his clergy and all who were honoured with his acquaintance, and a great friend to the poor. He published a small treatise *On Almsdeeds*, translated from the French, but written originally, I believe, in Spanish.

TANCRED, SIR WILLIAM, second Bart., only son of Sir Thomas (created Bart. by Charles II.), and his wife, Frances, co-heir of Christopher Maltby, of Cottingham. Having no issue by his first wife, Dorothy, daughter and co-heir of Robert Wilde, of Hunton, he married, second, Elizabeth, daughter of Charles Waldgrave, of Stanning Hall, Norfolk, second son of Sir Edward Waldgrave, of Hever Castle, Kent, by whom he had six sons. (*Betham*, II., 332.)

Sir Thomas, third Bart., was son of Sir William and Elizabeth Waldgrave. He married Elizabeth, daughter of William Messinger, of Fountains Abbey, by whom he had four sons, all of whom died young but Thomas, the third son. Sir Thomas died Jan. 19, 1744.

Sir Thomas, the fourth Bart., married Judith, daughter of Peter Dalton, or Dallon, of Greneston, in Tipperary, by whom he had four sons and nine daughters. He died in June, 1759.

Sir Thomas, fifth Bart., son of the above. He married in Sept., 1776, Penelope, daughter of Thomas Ashton, of St. Mary-la-Bonne, and died at his house in May-Fair, and was succeeded by his son, Sir Thomas, the sixth Bart., born in 1780.

TAPRAL, ——, studied at Douay, where his talents and abilities were much admired. He lived from 1753 to 1776 at Derby, where he had to attend the Catholics there, at West Hallam, Barrow, and other places, far distant one from the other. About 1776 he unfortunately married a Miss Townshend, of a respectable family and good connections, &c. This was the subject of great astonishment and deep regret to all who knew him, and who had till that time much respected him. The circumstances indeed weighed heavily on his mind, and at last broke his heart. In going to the church to read his recantation he is said to have rested his head upon his arm against a tree in deep thought and apparent remorse of conscience. After his marriage he practised Physic at Marston Montgomery, in Derbyshire, where he died suddenly, and was buried there.

TAVERNER, ——, for some time had the care of the Catholic School at Twyford. He afterwards lived in the family of the Holmans, at Warkworth, near Banbury, and died there, in August, 1745. He probably succeeded Mr. Gildon, at Twyford, who died there in 1736.

TAYLOR, ALEXANDER, son of Joseph Taylor and Dorothy Worswick, of Lancaster. After the end of Rhetoric he left Douay and was received in St. Gregory's, Paris, July 3, 1744, aged near 20. He was ordained Sept. 20, 1749, and in October came on the Mission. For some time he was Chaplain and Secretary to Bishop Stonor, but in 1758 I find him at Oscott, and then at Wolverhampton, from Aug. 1, 1762, till March, 1775, where his sermons were much admired. About this time an accusation was brought against him that instead of real wine of the grape he had used raisin wine at the altar. In his defence Mr. Taylor said that he was not able to judge of the genuineness of wine, and therefore depended on the judgment of others, and supposed that what was provided for the altar was such as it should be. His plea, however, was over-ruled, as at various times the wine left in the cruet had been carefully collected and pronounced to be raisin wine, and it was, moreover, well known that Mr. Lewellen, who provided the wine, was a maker of raisin wine. Bishop Hornyhold therefore suspended Mr. Taylor, yet offered to restore him his faculties in some other Mission. Mr. Taylor replied that if he were guilty he ought not to be employed anywhere, but if innocent he ought to remain where he was. Mr. Taylor, therefore, left the chapel house and took lodgings in town. Endeavours were made to draw him to the Church, but in vain; for as long as Mr. Kendal lived, who was his director, he attended regularly the chapel at Sedgley Park. But soon after his death he retired to Moseley, near Birmingham, where he ceased to attend the Catholic Chapel, but never, it is said, frequented the Church. Some years after his removal from Wolverhampton "he dropt down dead," Bishop Milner says, "as he was stepping into a stage coach." There were not wanting those who thought Mr. Taylor, even if guilty, had been rather hardly used, and it is a fact that after Bishop Hornyhold's death, Bishop Talbot sought opportunities to meet Mr. Taylor, which the latter studiously, it is said, declined. Those who believed him guilty, for the reasons assigned above, were confirmed in their opinion by his known saving disposition and penuriousness, but his friends replied that the Priest's allowance was so scanty that it was necessary for him to be as saving as possible. All, however, who knew Mr. Taylor regretted the loss of him and his absenting himself from chapel.

TAYLOR, JAMES, nephew of Christopher, and son of Thomas and Elizabeth Taylor, born July 1, 1761. After remaining some time at Sedgley Park, he went to Rome in 1776, and was placed on the free fund of Pippi. He applied himself to his studies, and displayed a great turn for Mathematics. He was, however, subject to fainting fits, and left the College Sept. 15, 1783, to go to Douay, where he finished his course, and for some time lived at Bugden on the Riding Mission, as it was called. He afterwards became Chaplain to Lord Shrewsbury and lived at Heythrop, and finally with Sir Edward Hales, at Hales Place, near Canterbury, where he died March 5, 1806, much respected and beloved.

TEASDALE, VINCENT, O.S.D. AND S.T.D. This gentleman "was renowned and beloved by all for his humility, piety, and very gentle and genteel manners." "I knew him," says Father Brittain, "for many years, and in him more virtues than are mentioned in his obituary." He was fourteen years on the Mission, and eighteen years Confessor to the English Dominican nuns at Brussels, and was thrice Prior of Bornheim, where he died on Jan. 5, 1790, aet. 87, Professed 67, Jubilarian 18. (*Dominican Obituary.*)

TEMPEST, JANE, sole heiress of Sir Thomas Tempest. She married William, Lord Widdrington, April 7, 1700. Her charities to the poor were considerable during her life, and the Catholics in the neighbourhood of Stella Hall reap the benefit of them to this day.

TEMPEST, JOHN, probably son of Thomas Tempest, by his wife, Ann, only child of Henry Scroop, of Danby. Being ordained Priest (Jesuit), he went on the Mission in the East, and on his return, about 1731, resided with Robert James, Lord Petre, at Thorndon, where he died, Feb. 22, 1737. From a letter to his father from Salonica, extant in Whitaker's *History of Craven*, and from the epitaph erected to him by Lord Petre, he appears to have been a man of talents, piety, and learning, and of great suavity of manners.

TEMPEST, STEPHEN, of Broughton Hall, Co. York, was son of Stephen Tempest (who was above seventy years Lord of the Manor of Broughton, and Captain of Horse at the Revolution, and died in 1742, aged 88), and of his wife Elizabeth, third daughter of Richard Fermor, of Tusmore. He died Aug. 12, 1771. He was author of *Religio Laici*, "a sensible tract, which every country gentleman may peruse with advantage." "This must be understood with one material exception," says Dr. Whitaker (*History of Craven*, p. 81). "In speaking of duels, the author appears to think the law of charity is satisfied if the party challenged make all reasonable explanations, interpose the mediation of friends, &c., but if these and all other attempts at reconciliation fail, then the Christian may lawfully *fight*. This is a compromise between religion and honour, which the former will not admit. If an explicit precept is given in Scripture, and surely there cannot be a precept more explicit than 'avenge not yourselves,' shame, distress, and death itself must be encountered rather than infringe it. On no other consideration shall we be acknowledged by Christ as his disciples."

His wife lived happily with him for fifty-one years, and died Dec. 29, 1738, aged 73, full of faith, hope, and charity. She is said to have been happily formed by Providence for all the duties of a wife, a parent, and mistress of a family, to have been gifted with a prudence and wisdom above her sex, and not to have fallen short of the incomparable character of Solomon's *mulierem fortem* in Proverbs xxxi.

THOMPSON, CHARLES, S.J., born Sept. 5, 1746. He entered his novice-ship Sept. 7, 1766. After the Jesuits left St. Omers Mr. Thompson came over to England, lived some time, my author thinks, in Lord Stourton's family, then at Gifford's Hall, for seven years as Chaplain to Anastasia (Brown), Lady Mannock, who died at Windsor, April 18, 1814, and lastly succeeded Rev. John Gage at Bury St. Edmund's, where he lived five years, and died at Mr. Plowden's in Bristol of a liver complaint, April 6, 1795. "Mr. Thompson was a most excellent Priest." (See Mr. Oliver's *Catalogue*.)

THOMPSON, LANCELOT. At the end of his third year of Divinity left Douay to go to Paris, in Oct., 1698, and after passing "Bachelor of the Sorbonne with very good applause and credit" he returned to Douay to teach Logic in company with Mr. Dicconson, the Procurator, "who had been with his brother at St. Germains to pay the compliments of the College to the King and Queen on his birthday, June 21." (*Mr. Dicconson's Journal.*)

THORALL OR THOROLD, EDMUND, S.J., a native of Oxon. He became a Jesuit and resided at Powis Castle, where he served the poor Catholics of Northamptonshire and of the Welsh borders of Shropshire.

THORNBURGH, WILLIAM, younger son of —— Thornburgh, Esq., of Leyburne, in Yorkshire. On the death of Dr. Robert Witham several were proposed to Propaganda as proper to succeed to the Presidentship, to wit, Mr. Squib (*alias* Petre), the Vice-President and Procurator, Dr. Thornburgh, Mr. Seath and Mr. Francis Petre, nephew of Bishop Petre. But the Agent of the Clergy represented to the Congregation that "Dr. Thornburgh was judged in England the best qualified, as being *nobile di nascità*, D. of Douay, and universally esteemed by the College and Catholic nobility, especially of the North." He was accordingly appointed President, and arrived at Douay July 18 or 28, 1739. The College flourished exceedingly under him. His Seniors and Professors were Mr. Petre, Vice-President and Procurator, Dr. Green, *alias* Scott, First Professor of Divinity, Thomas Reydon, Second Professor of Divinity, J. Wilkinson, Alban Butler, Professor of Physics, Turberville Needham, Professor of Logic, Charles Needham, of Rudiments, Hugo Kendall, of Poetry, Joseph Barnes, of Rhetoric, John Roberts, *alias* Basville, of Syntax, Edward Worthington, *alias* Ball, of Grammar." Oct. 1, 1738, there were 17 Divines, 16 Philosophers, 10 Rhetoricians, 10 Poets, 15 Syntaxians, 13 Grammarians, 33 Rudiments, Seniors 9, and Professors 18—in all 131 [*sic.* ? 141]. His health or business brought him over to England about the beginning of 1750, and he died at his brother's house in Yorkshire, March 4, 1750 (N.S.).

THORPE, JOHN, *alias* MASTERS, was son of John Masters, and a native of Hants. At the age of twelve he was sent, in 1692, to Lisbon, and March 30, 1697, took the College oath and gown. Having completed his Philosophy and Divinity course he defended them both with great applause, and Dec. 23, 1702, he received Priest's Orders. He then taught the Classics four years, and afterwards Philosophy. He had also the charge of the library, of the studies, and of the infirmary, in all of which he introduced more order and method than hitherto had been observed. As his health was injured by his close application he obtained leave to go on the Mission, and left the College Sept. 22, 1711. After this I find no trace of him. (*Lisbon Register, Miscell.* II., 1087.)

THORPE, JOHN, S.J. He was born Oct. 21, 1726. Entered his noviceship Sept. 7, 1747, and became professed Father in 1765. He was penitentiary at St. Peter's, Rome, at the time of the suppression of the Jesuits. After the suppression he continued to live in Rome, and was the active agent for the Academy at Liège, that set up a claim to the vineyard of the Magliana, belonging to the English College. In this capacity, and to prefer this claim to the Pope, he went to the Vatican, and not being willing to lose his place and turn to be admitted to an audience, he brought on a retention of urine, which was the immediate cause of his death, April 12, 1792. Mr. Thorpe was a most respectable and religious man, and a great connoisseur of painting. [For his connection with the Life of Clement XIV. see "Cordell," and "Plowden, Charles."]

THROCKMORTON, GEORGE (I.), third son of Sir Francis Throckmorton, of Coughton Court, and his wife Anne, daughter and heiress of John Monson, Esq., of Kinnersley, Co. Surrey. His parents endeavoured by early instruction to ground him in the principles of the Catholic Religion, and to persuade him from those errors in faith and corruption in morals to which youths, especially in the higher walks of life, are too often exposed. (*Life of Sir George Throckmorton,* printed in 1706.) With that in view he was placed under the care of the Fathers of the Oratory, in the College of Julie, in France, and no pains were spared to answer the proposed end. After residing some time at College he travelled into Italy in the company of Sir Francis Andrews, and under the conduct of a virtuous and religious man (Father Francis), and on his return had the reputation of being one of the most accomplished young gentlemen of his time. His vanity, however, increased by the flatteries of friends, soon led him into all kinds of extravagance and folly till the age of 27, when the earnest remonstrances and pious examples of two sisters who had renounced the world [Ann was a nun in the Fossez, and Elizabeth a Poor Clare at Rouen], and his own reflection on two providential escapes from the most imminent danger, caused him to enter into himself, and by the all-powerful grace of Almighty God produced in him a most extraordinary and entire change of life. From this period he became a new man, and choosing Paris for his residence—which had been formerly one of the principal theatres of his follies—he there lived "a public and living example of penance and a perfect model of a true and sincere conversion." Prayer, alms-deeds, and fasting were now the eminent good works in which his soul found her greatest delight. "The deep sense he had of his own great wants, the high esteem he had of God's grace, and the entire confidence he placed in the promises and merits of Jesus Christ hindered him from ever thinking the time long which he spent in prayer. . . . He regularly recited the greatest part of the Canonical hours, and never would absent himself away from the duties of his parish church, which he looked upon as the fold in which he was to be secured from the roaring lion with the rest of the flock; and as the part assigned to him in the spiritual war and combat he had to undergo and sustain him against his enemies. The mortification and holy severities which he practised against himself were regulated by those two great maxims of the Holy Fathers in general, and of St. Gregory in particular, which he had deeply imprinted in his soul : that contraries are to be cured by contraries, and that unlawful pleasures are to be expiated and punished by pain, and the retrenchment of even those that are lawful. . . . His frequent infirmities he received as a fatherly chastisement from the hand of God ; yet he was sensible that all exterior mortifications avail but little unless they be animated and accompanied by the real and interior mortification of our own passions. His piety and devotion were sincere, free, easy, quiet, and serene, without noise or trouble to others." All the time that could be spared from the church service, private devotions, and other necessary duties, was employed in visiting, comforting and relieving the poor and those who were in prison, to whom he imparted such instructions, exhortations, and pecuniary relief as their spiritual and corporal wants required.

Having passed more than three years in these and other exercises of piety, he was visited by a long and painful sickness, "which he bore," says Dr. Thomas Witham, "in his life with great alacrity and resignation, and gave us many most edifying examples of patience, obedience, and self-denial. He continued his ordinary exercises of reading and prayer till within two or three days of his death, and enjoyed a perfect presence of mind and liberty of judgment to the very last." He died on Palm Sunday, April 6, 1705 (N.S.), in the 35th year of his age, after having first received, with great piety and sense of devotion, all the rites of the Church from the hands of his parish Priest. He was buried among the poor in St. Stephen's churchyard, as he himself had expressly desired ; but his heart was embalmed and conveyed to the English nunnery of the Fossez de S. Victoir, where Anne, his eldest sister, was a religious. Mr. Throckmorton's conversion was as sincere as it was extraordinary. He rose every morning about four and continued in prayer about half-an-hour, when he recited Lauds and Prime of the Divine Office, and spent some time in spiritual reading, which was performed by another during his meals. After working in his garden with three or four people who came for that purpose, which work always began and ended with prayer, he repaired to the church, where he heard Mass, with a modesty, attention and devotion that edified all present. The remainder of the morning and noon was spent in reciting the Divine Office, in visiting the poor or his sisters and nieces at the Fossez, and some church, where he poured forth his soul in fervent prayer. About six he returned home, and after supper his little family listened to half-an-hour's spiritual reading, which ended with night prayers. About half past eight all retired to bed except himself, who generally remained in prayer and on his knees and in the dark till about ten, when he went to bed, or frequently, without taking off his clothes, laid himself down upon his bed imagining it to be his grave, which thoughts, as he himself owned to me, says Dr. Witham, he had always present for some years when he lay down on his bed. This account of Mr. Throckmorton is taken from a short discourse delivered on the occasion of his death by Dr. Thomas Witham, Superior of St. George's Seminary, at Paris.

THROCKMORTON, GEORGE (II.), son and heir of Sir Robert Throckmorton. He married Miss Paston, an heiress. "He was," says Mr. Cole, MS. Vol. 44, p. 315, in British Museum, "a most agreeable and amiable man, a most admirable husband, father and neighbour, a delightful son, had a large and well-chosen library, and understood the value of it. He was so beloved in his neighbourhood that on his death at Bath of the smallpox, which took place Dec. 29, 1762, I never knew any person so universally lamented. His widow was a most amiable and virtuous lady, and never were two people more happily united in tempers and manners than they were." He left four sons :

John, George, and Charles (who all three succeeded to the title and estates), and William and Teresa, who married Mr. Metcalf, the mother of the late Thomas Metcalf, who assumed the name of More, and Mrs. Eyston.

THROCKMORTON, SIR JOHN COURTENAY, fifth Bart., son of Sir George Throckmorton (and grandson of Sir Robert), and Anna Maria Paston. Was born July 27, 1753. His father dying at Bath, Dec. 30, 1762, he succeeded to the title and a considerable portion of the family estates on the death of his grandfather, in 1791, at which time he quitted Weston, which had been settled on his brother George, and repaired to Buckland. On Aug. 19, 1782, he married Mary Catharine, daughter of Thomas Giffard, of Chillington, by his first wife, Barbara, daughter of Robert Lord Petre. He and his brothers were educated with the monks at Douay. Sir John died Jan. 3, 1819, and was succeeded by his brother, George, and then by Charles. The following epitaph was written by Rev. Joseph Berington : " Hic Jacent Commixtæ Proavorum cineribus mortales Exuviæ Johannis Throckmortoni Baronetti, viri ornati benevoli modesti, virtutis nobilitate,* ingenii viribus, morum gravitate insignis, qui duris Regni legibus ob avitum Numinis cultum, rebus inesse publicis prohibitus, in studiis Artium liberalium, in fovendis Patriæ institutis, in rerum rusticarum oblectamentis, in levandis egenorum curis, in amicorum colloquiis, in officiis probi hominis erga omnes, vitam egit, sibi jucundam, multis utilem, suis charam.   Vixit annos 66, menses 5, dies 6.   Mortem obiit Jan. 3, A.D. 1819. R. I. P."

THROCKMORTON, SIR ROBERT, third Bart., eldest surviving son of Sir Francis Throckmorton, second Bart., by his wife, Anne, daughter and heiress of John Monson, of Kinnersley, Surrey, son of Sir William Monson, Knight, Vice-Admiral of England in time of James I. Born at Moor Hall, near Coughton, Jan. 10, 1662. On the death of Sir Francis, Nov. 7, 1680, he succeeded to the title and estates of his ancestors, being the heir general of Abberbury, Basford, Spinney and Weston, heir of Bosum or Bosun. He resided chiefly at Weston, Co. Bucks, where he lived in great hospitality and much esteemed by all. In the second of James II. he was put in the Commission of the Peace for Warwickshire, Worcester, and Bucks, and in the fourth of ditto was commissioned to raise a troop of horse, which he performed at his own charge in which he expended upwards of £1,000. In 1687 he built a chapel at Coughton Court wherein Divine service was held till on the Thursday, called the *Running Thursday*, it met with the fate of all the new erected chapels, being pulled down by a mob from Alcester. He married Mary, second daughter of Sir Charles Yates, of Buckland (who died in July, 1728), sole surviving sister and heiress of Sir John Yates, and had issue three sons, of whom Robert, the third, alone survived and succeeded him, and seven daughters : Anne, wife of John Petre, of Fidlers ; Mary, wife of James Fermor, of Tusmore ; Elizabeth and Catharine, nuns at the Fossez, Paris ; Charlotte, wife of Sir Thomas Windsor Hunloke ; Apolonia, wife of Sir Edward Blount, of Soddington ; and Barbara, wife of Peter Giffard, of Chillington. He almost new built his house at Weston, and in conjunction with some others built a new school house there, endowing the Vicar with an additional £25 per annum for ever, provided the Vicar teaches in the said school his tenants' children, and lastly he gave funds for ever for maintaining five poor decayed tenants. Sir Robert died at Weston March 8, 1720, aged 58. Lady Throckmorton died in 1728. Her mother, Lady Mary Yates, was eldest daughter and co-heiress of Humphrey Packington. She married Sir John Yates, of Buckland. She settled £50 per annum on the Divinity and Philosophy Professors at Douay, i.e., £15 to each of the Professors of Divinity, and £10 to each of the two Professors of Philosophy. She enjoyed her Harvington estate and the Manor of Chaddesley Corbett, Co. Worcester, 65 years, and died, June 12, 1696, aged 86, and is buried in the church of Chaddesley Corbett. In the epitaph it is said : " She was eminent for her great piety to God and charitable liberality towards all sorts of poor." (*Betham*, 486.)

---

* The motto alluded to is *Virtus sola Nobilitas.*

THROCKMORTON, SIR RORERT, fourth Bart., son of Sir Robert and Mary Yates, born Aug. 21, 1702.   He married first, Lady Teresa, daughter of William Herbert, Marquis of Powis, who died at Weston.   By her he had two sons and one daughter, Robert, who died in France, unmarried ; George, who married in 1748, Anna Maria, only daughter of William Paston, of Horton, Gloucestershire, by his wife, daughter and heir of John Courtenay, of Molland, Devon, by whom he had six sons and three daughters : Robert, John Courtenay, George, Charles, Francis, and William ; Mary, Anne ; and Teresa, who married, Aug. 28, 1789, Thomas Metcalf ; Mary Teresa, Sir Robert's daughter, married Thomas Fitzherbert, of Swinnerton, and died at Bath, Feb. 26, 1791.   On the death of his first wife Sir Robert married, in Jan., 1737 (O.S.), Catharine, daughter of George Collingwood, of Eslington, Northumberland, executed in 1715.   She died in 1761 and was buried at Buckland, Aug. 3.   By her he had two daughters who died infants, and Barbara, married to Thomas Giffard, of Chillington.   By his third wife, Lucy, daughter of Jones Haywood, of Maristow, Devon, who died Nov. 30, 1795, he had no issue.   Sir Robert, soon after the marriage of his son, George, settled at Buckland, Bucks, which estate he inherited from his mother, where he built the present handsome house, and much beautified the place, and died there, Dec. 8, 1791, in his 90th year, and was buried at Coughton, under the tomb erected in that church by his ancestor, Sir Robert Throckmorton, Kt.

THWAITES, FRANCIS, *alias* SMITH, was born in Leicestershire, and was admitted into the College in Rome, Oct. 11, 1658.   He was ordained Priest at St. John Lateran, March 8, 1664, and in the April following departed for England.   He lived in London, was a member of the Chapter, and in 1692 was chosen Archdeacon of Essex, Herts, and Bedfordshire, in which honorary character he succeeded to Dr. (Bishop) Bonaventure Giffard.   In 1714, as Dr. Perrot, the Dean, was dead, and no successor had been then appointed, Mr. Thwaites, as Senior Capitular, presided at the General Assembly of the Chapter held in London, when Dr. Ryder was chosen Dean.   He was in great estimation among his brethren, and died May 6, 1723.   He assisted at the General Assembly of the Chapter in 1694, 1703, 1710, 1714 and 1717.

Before Quesnel's *Reflections* were condemned by Clement XI. St. Matthew was translated by —— Whittenhall, Esq., uncle of Mr. Thwaites.   After his death Mr. Thwaites and Mr. Southcote, O.S.B., completed the translation, and Mr. Thwaites published St. Mark and St. Luke in 1707, six years before the condemnation appeared.   (*Annales Coll. Angl. Rom.*)

TICHBORNE, SIR HENRY, sixth Bart., son of James Tichborne, of Frimley, Surrey, married Mary, daughter of Michael Blount, of Maple Durham, by Mary, daughter of Henry Tichborne, fourth Bart.   He was born Sept. 6 1710, and on the death of his grandfather, Sir Henry, succeeded to his estates in 1743 [and to the title in 1748, after the death of John Hermengild Tichborne, fifth Baronet (brother of Henry Young Joseph, fourth Baronet), who was Priest of the Society of Jesus].   He died July 16, 1785.

TICHBORNE, SIR HENRY, seventh Bart., only son of the former.   He married, in 1778, Elizabeth, daughter of Mr. Plowden, of Plowden, Salop, and had issue ten children.

TICHBORNE, SIR HENRY JOSEPH, fourth Baronet, of Tichborne, Hants, son of Sir Henry Tichborne and his wife, Mary, daughter of William Arundell, brother to Thomas, Lord Arundell of Wardour, was born in 1666. In 1689 he married Mary, daughter of Anthony Kemp, of Slindon, and by her had three sons—Henry, Henry John, and John—who all died young before him, and three daughters : Mary Agnes, who married Michael Blount, of Maple Durham, and died May 20, 1777 ; Frances Cecily, who married George Brownlow Doughty, of Snarford Hall, and died Aug. 20, 1765, aged 72 ; and Mabella, who married John Webb, eldest son of Sir John Webb, of Hathrop, and died Sept., 1727.   He succeeded his father in 1689, and died in July, 1743, *aet.* 77.   (*Betham* I., 203.)

TILDESLY, EDWARD, of the Lodge, Lancashire. He was taken at Preston, and put on his trial at the Marshalsea, May 15, 1716. The King's Counsel attempted to prove that he was a party in the rebellion of 1715, and had entered Preston at the head of his troops with his drawn sword. In his defence Anna Maria Tildesley, his housekeeper, swore that on the Friday morning a great number of armed men came to his house and in a threatening manner said they would have him with them ; and after having confined the prisoner, and taken what the house afforded, they actually took him away with them, and that he afterwards attempted to make his escape from them, and for that purpose it was agreed that he should go away in woman's clothes, which were accordingly provided for him by a relative of his, and his size. Sir George Warburton and some other gentlemen being called to speak to his general character, deposed that they never heard him speak with disrespect of the Government, and that he was a facetious but inoffensive old man. The jury admitted the plea and acquitted him.

TOUCHET, GEORGE, O.S.B., was uncle to Lady Eleanor or Helena Touchet, and brother to James, Earl of Castlehaven. He was second son of Mervyn, ninth Lord Audley, and Elizabeth Barnham. He became a Benedictine. By the death of his elder brother, James, the tenth Lord Audley, in 1684, without issue, George was debarred from succeeding to the title, being a monk, and the title descended to Mervyn, the third son. His brother, James, published *Memoirs of his engagement and carriage in the Irish Wars.*

TOWNELEY, CHARLES, younger brother of Richard Towneley, was born in 1690 and died in 1713. His sister, Ursula, was a nun at Louvain. John, brother of Richard and Charles, was born in 1697 and died in 1782. Is this the same as Col. John Towneley who published *Hudibras* in French verse in three vols., 12mo, London, 1757? The publication was superintended by Mr. Turberville Needham, and illustrated with notes by Larcher and with engravings from the designs of Hogarth. (See *Biogr. Dict.*)

TOWNELEY, CHARLES, son of Richard Towneley by his wife, Margaret Paston, was born April 19, 1658. He married Ursula, daughter of Richard Fermor, of Tusmore. He died in 1711. He had two brothers, John and Richard, and two sisters, Margaret and Cecily, nuns at the Fossez, Paris. John became a monk, and Richard, born in 1664, a Carthusian at Newport.

TOWNELEY, FRANCIS, was probably brother of Richard [see *infra*]. In 1727 he entered as a volunteer, and in 1728 obtained a commission in the French Service. He was at the siege of Phillipsburg, and near the Duke of Berwick when his head was shot off, and in several other actions and sieges, and is said to have always behaved well and with honour. About 1740 he quitted the service and returned to England. When Prince Charles entered England he unfortunately joined him between Lancaster and Preston, and at Macclesfield received a commission from him to raise a regiment of foot, and afterwards, at Carlisle, a regiment of horse, when he was appointed Commandant of the place, but obliged to surrender it and himself at discretion. It was proved also at his trial, at Southwark, July 13, 1746, that from Manchester he marched with the rebels to Macclesfield and Derby, and thence back to Carlisle, where he was made Commandant of the place by Prince Charles. After about ten minutes' consultation the jury brought him in guilty. He was executed on Kennington Common on July 30, 1746, and his head fixed on Temple Bar. (See *A genuine account of the behaviour, etc., of Francis Towneley, etc.*)

TOWNELEY, JOHN, was son of Charles Towneley. His portrait (as are all the portraits of the preceding), is at Towneley, and on it is this inscription : "This John the 6 or 7 yere of her Majesty now reigning for professing the Apostolicall Religion," &c., as you had it in my letter, Nov. 4.

TOWNELEY, RICHARD, son of Charles Towneley, and his wife, Mary, daughter of Sir Francis Trapps Birnand, of Harrowgate, was born in 1628. He married Margaret, daughter of Clement Paston, of Berningham, Co. Norfolk. He died Jan. 30, 1706 or 1707.

TOWNELEY, RICHARD, of Towneley, Co. Lancaster, was born in 1687 [query, grandson of Richard Towneley and Mary Trapps]. He married Mary, daughter of William, Lord Widdrington, who died in July, 1721. He joined the rebels in 1715, and was taken prisoner at Preston. At his trial on Tuesday, May 15, 1716, in the Marshalsea, his counsel stated in his defence that he left his house at Towneley, not to join the rebels, but to prevent being secured by the Militia of the county, who were then assembling to secure Papists and persons reputed to be disaffected to the Government, that the Militia came to Towneley and swore they would shoot him, and actually fired a pistol into his and Mrs. Towneley's bedroom ; that from Towneley he proceeded to Rochdale, and thence to Kirkham, as he found on enquiry at home that it was out of the question to return, but on the way he was surrounded by a party of Highlanders and carried prisoner to Preston. And when the King's Counsel observed that his flying from the King's forces and Militia, who intended doing him no harm and would have protected him, argued guilt, Mr. Towneley himself said this might be very true in regard to others, but Roman Catholics on such occasions were usually taken up and their horses and arms were seized and themselves confined, so that at the best it was very chargeable and troublesome to them, to avoid which they usually retired till the noise was over, and then returned with safety to their houses. After deliberating about half-an-hour the jury brought in a verdict of *Not Guilty.* He died at Towneley, Aug., 1735.

TOWNELEY, THOMAS, of the Towneleys of Towneley, Lancashire. At the beginning of Divinity he went from Douay to the Seminary of the Bons Infans, and after staying about half a year he entered St. Gregory's June 27, 1690, but left it July 12, 1694, to live at the Seminary of S. Magloire. Some time after he came on the Mission and lived at or near York, and assisted at the meeting of the Yorkshire Clergy, with Bishop Smith, July 13, 1698. On the death of Bishop Witham, Messrs. Rigby and Carnaby, the Grand Vicars, presented Mr. Towneley to Rome as a proper person to succeed : *operarium sedulum et laboriosum, ex familia nobili, insigni pietate, zelo, et prudentia praeditum, Sacrae Sedi per omnia specialiter addictum,* and acceptable to clergy and laity. Bishop Giffard, as Senior V.A., had presented three others, but consented to their sending their presentation. Mr. Towneley died in Lancashire March 4 (Mr. T. Berington says the 9th), 1736 or 7. They wrote in the name of their brethren and entreated the early appointment of one to preserve the discipline of the two last VV.AA., and advantages arising from their regulations and dispositions, *i.e.,* the donations to the Secular Clergy by Laity and Secular Clergy for their support and pious use. They state reasons for having only a Clergy Bishop, instead of whom, Bishop Williams, a Dominican, was appointed.

TOWNSON, JOHN, O.S.B., of Lambspring. He wrote *An Account of the Foundation of that Abbey and Church.* The MS. is at Ampleforth.

TUNSTALL, PETER BRYAN, was fourth son of Francis Tunstall, Esq., by ——, daughter of Thomas Riddell, of Swinburne, Esq., who was a younger son of the Wycliffe family. Bryan was sent early to Douay, and after his ordination, was many years General Prefect. In 1710 he was sent Agent to Brussels, principally to obtain from the Nuncio impartial visitors of the College, in which he succeeded. He went again thither in 1713. When on the Mission he resided at York at the chapel house in Blake Street. In 1741 he was appointed V.G. for Yorkshire by Bishop Dicconson, and was also Agent for the Clergy of Yorkshire, succeeding in that office Mr. Addison, *alias* Hildreth. He was a member also of the Chapter, and died at York, June 1, 1742.

TUNSTALL, WILLIAM, of Wycliff, was born to a splendid estate. In 1715 he was made Paymaster-General or Quartermaster-General to the forces. He was taken at Preston. His trial came on at the Court of Admiralty, Southwark, May 30, 1716 (O.S.). When the first Juryman was sworn Mr. Tunstall told the Court he would save them any further trouble by throwing himself on his Master's mercy and owning his indictment, which being read to him, he owned himself guilty of being taken in arms, but not of any design of murdering the King, which never entered his head. Upon this his Lordship advised him to draw up the statement of what he had to say in a petition, and he would recommend it to the King. During his confinement he amused himself with writing verses, which met the applause of good judges, and show that though old and under sentence of death, yet he did not despond. I do not find that he suffered death. (*Faithful Register of the late Rebellion.*)

TURNER, JOHN, S.J., was charged with the care of the Catholics at and about Stella in Bishoprick from about 1748. When the estate passed into the hands of Mr. Eyre, of Hassop, he placed his kinsman, Mr. Thomas Eyre, there in 1775. On his quitting Stella, Mr. Turner was invited to Salisbury by Everard Arundell, Esq.

TURVILE, CARRINGTON FRANCIS, of Aston Flamvile, eldest son of William and Catharine Turvile, was born March 9, 1689. He possessed a property at Aston of £587 11s. in 1730. He died at Brussels, Oct. 29, 1749, and was buried in the old church of the English Benedictine nuns in that city. His son, George, died in 1735.

TURVILE, CHARLES FORTESCUE, of Husband's Bosworth, was son of Charles Fortescue and Frances Bodenham. He married Elizabeth Login, daughter of —— Login, of Idbury, Oxon, by whom he had Francis and Mary Alathea, who both dying unmarried, the estates of Husband's Bosworth and Idbury became vested in the late Francis Fortescue, then of Aston Flamvile. Mr. Charles Fortescue died about 1732. His will is dated April 25, 1730, but was proved March, 1732 (O.S.).

TURVILE, FRANCIS FORTESCUE, son of William Turvile and Mary Bolney, his wife, was the representative of the ancient families of the Turviles of Thurleston, Nenhall, Normanton, Turvile, and Aston Flamvile, all in Leicestershire. On April 9, 1780, he married Barbara, daughter of Charles Talbot, of Hore Cross, and sister of Charles, Earl of Shrewsbury. By the will of Elizabeth Fortescue he became possessed of all her estates in the counties of Leicester, Oxon, Notts, and Bucks. He died at Leamington, July 13, 1839, aged 89.

TURVILE, WILLIAM (I.), of Aston Flamvile, eldest son of William Turvile and Catharine, his wife, daugher and co-heiress of Sir Francis Englefield, Bart., was born May 25, 1667. He married Frances, daughter of Charles Fortescue, of Husband's Bosworth, Co. Leicester, and died in 1702.

TURVILE WILLIAM (II.), was born July 13, 1692. According to the *College Annals* (but no mention is made of him in Nichol's *Pedigree*), he was son of William Turvile, who died in 1702, and Frances Fortescue. He was sent first to St. Omers, and at the age of 21 to Rome, where he was ordained April 16, 1719, and left the College for the Mission, June 4, 1719. He lived some years at Moat Hall, Co. Salop, and then succeeded Mr. Bowes, *alias* Lane, at Hathrop. One of his congregation, by name Davies, taking offence at Mr. Turvile for allowing a woman, through necessity, to supply the place of clerk in his chapel, laid an information against him for being a Priest. The Justice of the Peace, who was a neighbour, and as such wished to live on friendly terms with Mr. Turvile, told him he had no time to attend to him and dismissed him. After a few days he called again, but was put off a second time. Meeting with no better success in his third and fourth application, he at last desisted, and Mr. Turvile continued unmolested till his death, which took place Dec. 13, 1765. He was succeeded by a Mr. Chester, *alias* Lolli, from Douay ; but of a physician of souls he soon became a physician of bodies, to the great scandal of his congregation. He was afterwards a bankrupt and a prisoner in the Fleet, where Bishop Walton says "he died penitent," April 13, 1779. Mr. Hall, one of his successors at Hathrop, adds : "He died a true and sincere penitent."

TYLECOTE, JOSEPH, *alias* EDWARDS, O.S.D. and D.D., was of a good family at Nailstone, Co. Leicester. The Rev. Father Brittain, who performed his whole course of studies under him at Louvain, gives the following account of him : " The Rev. Mr. Tylecote, *alias* Edwards, during my studies at Louvain fell so sick that he was dying. We all went to his room in the College, where he appeared the picture of death. He had quitted his bed, and was by his desire lying on a blanket on the floor. He, however, exerted himself and spoke to us in his usual extremely candid style. He related for our edification the outlines of his life. During his nervous and pathetic discourse some of us were so affected that we fainted away. His family, he said, were all Protestants. He studied surgery in London, and went to sea to practise as a surgeon in the Navy, but was there afflicted with invincible sea-sickness, tending to ruin his constitution. He therefore ere long quitted the sea. His prevalent passion, he owned, had been from his childhood an insatiable thirst for know-ledge ; never at rest till he could fathom every part of mechanics, anatomy, &c. This unbounded passion for knowledge led him into presumption. Hence he began to reject and disbelieve whatever he was unable to fathom or fully comprehend. Thus he lost all faith, becoming an absolute Freethinker. ' While the rest of my family,' said he, ' were going on *bona fide*, as they had been educated, in the Protestant religion, I deemed the whole fabric of religion to be baseless. I need no other proof,' said he, ' of the gratuity and efficacy of Divine grace but what I am convinced of from my own experience. I alone of all my family were enlightened and conducted to the Catholic Faith, when I deserved this grace the least of all. I had not, indeed, during my presumptuous incredulity ever given into the too common vices of excessive drinking or impurity. For those I ever abhorred, not from any motive of virtue, but of antipathy, as vile, filthy, beastly vices, as obstructive to my predominant passion for learning and knowledge. The first event that somewhat moved me and shook my incredulity was when I assisted an officer who died at sea who said he saw continually a crowd of horrid spectres before his eyes ; nor could we appease him, but he expired amid these horrors. He had been a freethinker and free liver. Afterwards we were shipwrecked on the Irish coast, when I and some of our officers went about the coast to recover some things lost from the vessel and picked up by the poor inhabitants. Here we came to a poor long thatched cottage, entered, and found a respectable Priest employed in catechising and instructing a number of poor, bare-legged children. He told us that as Easter was near, when the people came to confes-sion they would be admonished to restore whatever they might have taken, and then we might expect to meet with some restitutions. We invited this good Priest to dine with us on board, and from time to time he came. He told us he lived on potatoes daily except Sundays. I found him to be a well-informed man, as knowing and clever as myself, and I asked him how he could pass his life in such misery, while many less able than he in England and elsewhere enjoyed respectable livings. He answered : ' Then who will instruct these poor creatures? I look for my reward and comfort not here, but hereafter.' This was to me,' said Father Tylecote, ' a still more striking argument than the alarming death I mentioned, for I saw that this Priest was sincerely and fully convinced of the truths he was teaching. I afterwards quitted the sea, which began to ruin my health, and settled as a surgeon in my native country. Still I had the same passion for science, and a neighbouring missionary Priest lent me St. Thomas of Aquin's *Whole Sum of Divinity*. This was to me a treasure, for I had heard so much of the great Doctor, Thomas Aquinas. This large book I with glee immediately carried home, thinking that I should soon penetrate and see through his proofs of the foundations of Faith. I eagerly began to examine his arguments in order : the existence and nature of God ; Revelation, Trinity, &c., all proved from Scripture and reason. I found beyond my expectation his proofs solidly grounded, his succeeding arguments being regularly and clearly deduced from the leading principles he had already demonstrated. I relished his steady and sedate mode of reason-ing, for I idolized right reason. I therefore with pleasure pursued the golden chain of his reasoning, and seemed myself to learn from him how reason properly employed leads to Truth.   Thus I was proceeding till at length one day, by the grace of God and the lights of the Holy Spirit, I shut the book and exclaimed : "The Christian religion is founded and true."   I then needed not five minutes to know where to seek for it.   I quitted my profession, went to Bornheim, and made my religious profession there in St. Dominic's Order of Preachers.'

"Now though I cannot vouch for the identical words, yet such was the sum and subject of his discourse at that time when he escaped death, and lived for many years after.   The Rev. Mr. Tylecote's character was through life rational.   This came from his habitual love and pursuit of knowledge and truth.   He was naturally cheerful, entertaining and affable to all : not stiff or reserved.   A certain forbidding stiffness and air of importance, he used to say, were the marks of weak heads or of a deficiency of knowledge.   Such men keep you at a distance, lest you should discover their want of capacity or knowledge.   As all the sciences naturally assist each other, our Rev. Rector frequently excited us to improve in every, even the least, art and science, to cultivate the orthography and pronunciation of our own language, too much neglected in the universities at that time, writing, arithmetic, and the like less noble though more useful arts.   . . .   The sole flaw I ever heard him reproached with was a fondness for arguing, even in convivial assemblies.   His ardour for knowledge betrayed him into this error.   However, he was not overbearing or dictatorial in such discussions, but open to conviction, not offended when contradicted, even by his disciples, being a zealous candidate for truth.   But if flattered to his face he was visibly hurt, deeming this an insult to his sound judgment and penetration, as if easily imposed on.   Even in his devotions he was generally guided and supported by reason alone, and owned to us that he seldom or never felt the unction or spiritual sweetness of devotion.   He died undaunted and rational as he had lived."   So far Father Brittain.

Father Tylecote was Professor of Philosophy and Theology for eleven years, and presided over the College of Louvain thirteen years, where he built a chapel, and enriched the library with philosophical instruments, and improved it with many useful books.   He afterwards came on the Mission, and was charged with the congregation of Hinckley, near his native place, and there he died, universally respected and regretted, Sept. 4, 1781, in the 59th year of his age, the 29th of his religious profession, and the 28th of his priesthood.   (*MS. in my hands.*)

TYPPER, ——.   I find his name in 1709 and 1750, but no particulars except that he seems to have been employed in the edition of the Bible.   In November, 1743, Mr. Thomas Berington writes : "You desire my opinion and that of others about the intended edition of the Bible.   The best light I can give is to let you know the parties concerned in the birth, and then you may judge for yourself better than I.   Mr. Typper has been pregnant some time, and is now in labour ; Dr. Challoner, *lambendo formabit* ; Needham, *Bibliopola in lucem edet.*"   *Tres ex Clero seculari magnis sane meritis piisque in Dei vinea laboribus insignes.*   Messrs. R. & C. approved the same, but added, with Bishop G.'s consent, Laurence Mayes and Mr. Townley.

USHER, JAMES, was a Belfast merchant and traded to Chester with Irish linen.   He became a Catholic and, I believe, a Priest, and settled at Kensington Gravel Pits, where he opened a school.   When the cry was loud against the growth of Popery, he wrote his admirable work, entitled *A Free Enquiry*, &c., in which he was assisted by Mr. Walker,* his usher, who wrote the article on Anti-Christ, and, not being a Priest, said in reply to the charge that the work was written by a Catholic and a Priest, that he was not a Priest.   "This," continues Dr. Milner, "was the first work that openly defended Catholics, but in the character of a *Free Thinker*.   (See Mr. Butler's *Memoirs*, chapter 43).

---

* See Walker, John, below.

VALENTINE, JOSEPH, son of Robert Valentine, an Englishman, and Julia Baletti, an Italian ; was born in Rome, March 5, 1713, and was confirmed by Clement XI., June 15, 1721. On Oct. 16, 1729, he was admitted into the English College, and was ordained Feb. 12, 1736, and in April, 1738, departed and came to England. He lived many years at the Hay, near Madeley, Salop, in the family of John Giffard, Esq., whose daughter Barbara married —— Slaughter, Esq., father of the late Doctor Slaughter and the late Lady Mostyn. He appears to have left the Hay, perhaps on the death of Mr. Giffard, in 1759, and went to Shrewsbury, where he died, Feb. 21, 1761.

VANE, JOHN, *alias* HERBERT, *alias* JONES.—His parents were Protestants, and he was sent to one of the universities and took orders in the Church of England. At the Revolution, " being scandalized at the doctrine and practice of his Church, which maintained it was lawful to depose a King," he became a Catholic, and was received into the Church by Bishop Giffard, who had been apprehended at the Revolution and was then confined in Newgate. In the latter end of 1688 he went over to Lisbon, and in November, 1692, took the College oath and cassock. In 1693 he defended Universal Philosophy, and dedicated his Thesis to the Dowager Queen Catharine. After he was ordained Priest he taught the Classics for three years, and in July, 1694, defended some treatises of Divinity under Mr. Roger Brockholes. On April 10, 1699, he left the College and was appointed agent of his College in London, where he resided. He was chosen member of the Chapter in 1703, *nemine contradicente,* and laboured hard in the missionary duties, and particularly among the poor. Mr. Smith, the Jesuit, reported that Mr. Vane had been a Jansenist, but that he had caused him to retract his errors. The same Father Smith told others that Mr. Vane was relapsed into Jansenism. . . . The Superioress of the nuns at York reported that Mr. Vane was suspended from his function for the crime of Jansenism, which is a notorious bare-faced lie, for all the world knows that he was never suspended, nor in danger thereof. Mr. Vane has several times writ to the said Superioress to prove or retract what she had said, but she has nothing to say for herself ; but her silence and confusion bear witness to her guilt. (Mr. A. Giffard to Mr. Dicconson, June 30, 1710). Mr. Vane died Oct. 22, 1733. (See *Records of Jansenism,* pp. 15, 20 ; and *Lisbon Register*).

VARLEY, THOMAS, studied at Douay, and was many years missionary in London and Agent for Douay College. In 1776 he was chosen a Capitular, and Dean of the Chapter on the resignation of Mr. Lindow. He was much respected by his brethren, and in his capacity of Agent was highly serviceable to the College of Douay. He died Nov. 27, 1806.

VAUGHAN, ARTHUR, went over to Douay in 1738 or 9. He succeeded Mr. George Bishop at Harvington, in Worcestershire, in 1752, and continued there till his death, which took place July 17, 1792. He was much respected where he was known. He published :—1, *The Triumphs of the Cross,* or life of Mary of Egypt, a Poem. 2, *The Ghost of Sansom Fields,* on the occasion of Mr. Wharton's S.J. leaving the chapel at Sansom Fields, Worcester, and the Catholic Religion. 3, *Madan's *Thelypthora burlesqued,* a MS.

VAVASOUR, SIR WALTER, of Hazelwood, 3rd Bart., son of Sir Walter Vavasour, 2nd Bart., by his wife Ursula, daughter of Thomas Viscount Fauconberg. He married Jane, daughter of Sir John Crossland, Knt., but had no issue by her. He died Feb. 16, 1712 (O.S.). His grandfather, Sir Thomas, was created a Bart. on April 24, 1628. For his recusancy he paid the composition of £150 per annum to Charles I. (*Betham,* 355).

VAVASOUR, SIR WALTER, 4th Bart., son of Peter Vavasour, M.D., 5th son of Sir Thomas, the 1st Bart., by Elizabeth his wife, daughter of Philip Langdale, of Langthorpe. Sir Walter died in Lancashire, May, 1740, aged 80.

---

* *Thelypthora,* or *A Treatise on Female Ruin,* published in 1780 by Martin Madan (1726-1790), advocated polygamy. It provoked a flood of literature in reply, among those who joined issue with Madan being his relative, the poet Cowper with " Anti-Thelypthora, a Tale in Verse " (1781). [See Dict. Nat. Biog. xxxv., 290.]

VAVASOUR, SIR WALTER, 5th Bart., nephew of Sir Walter, the 4th Bart., was son of Peter, who was another son of Dr. Peter Vavasour, and died Jan. 9th, 1735, aged 68. He married Elizabeth, daughter of Peter Vavasour of Willitoft, in the East Riding of Yorkshire, by whom he had one daughter, who died young. After her death, he married, in April, 1741, Dorothy, eldest daughter of the Lord Langdale, by whom he had three sons : Walter, born Jan. 16, 1744, who succeeded his father as 6th Baronet, and married, in Sept., 1797, Jane, daughter and heiress of William Langdale, of Longthorpe ; 2nd, Thomas, 7th Baronet ; 3rd, Peter. Sir Walter, 5th Bart., died April 13, 1766.

V————, T————, O.S.B.—He published *A Daily Exercise of the Devout Christian, containing several moving practices of piety in order to live holily and die happily*, 6th Edit. in 1743, Dublin. In his dedication to the Hon. Henry Tichborne, Bart., son of Sir Richard, he mentions the custom of the family to give a great Dole to all comers on the 25th of March. N.B.—A very fine picture representing this Dole is, or was, at Mapledurham.

VINTNER, *or* VINTER, ROBERT, was educated at Douay, and Missionary at York. " He was an able, discreet and portly man, but so fat, unwieldy and infirm in 1691 that he was obliged to confine himself to York, Cholmly, and Bransby, and two or three families thereabouts." In 1700 he was chosen Archdeacon, but soon afterwards resigned. (*Chapter Records*).

WALDEGRAVE, LORD, of Chewton. He was educated a Catholic and lived some years as such, but conformed in 172—; and June, 1723, was appointed one of the Lords of the Bedchamber, in the room of Charles Lennox, Duke of Richmond, deceased.

WALDEGRAVE, NICHOLAS, was a native of Norfolk, and nephew to Bishop Russell, who sent him to Lisbon College, where he was admitted May 1st, 1683. After he was ordained Priest, he went to Coimbra to study the Canon Law. On the death of his uncle, who left him his heir, he returned to Lisbon, and Oct. 3, 1697, was made Procurator of the College, where he died Dec. 13, 1734. (*Lisbon Register*).

WALKER, AUGUSTINE, O.S.B., was Confessor to the Benedictine Dames at Cambray. At the Revolution he was sent to Compiègne, and died there in prison, Jan. 13, 1794. The same, I suppose, as was President of the Congregation of Benedictines, and lived at Douay in 1785. He had also been Procurator at Rome for several years, and was succeeded by Mr. Waters. (Dr. Marsh's *Biography of Presidents of the English O.S.B.* in the *Collect. Ang., Catholic*).

WALKER, JOHN, was sometime on the stage, where he acquired some reputation in serious characters. On becoming a Catholic he quitted it, justly considering, says Dr. Milner, how difficult it was to attend to the duties of his religious calling in a life of so much dissipation. Garrick had a good opinion of him; and he is supposed to have written his *Cadwallader*, in which Mr. Walker performed a principal part. He had also a high opinion of Mr. Garrick, and was once applied to to edit his works; which his esteem for Mr. Garrick prompted him to undertake, but was deterred by conscientious motives and the levities that occasionally are interspersed in them. He then became an assistant to Mr. Usher, and while there contributed towards *The Free Enquiry*. The *Letter on Antichrist* is entirely Mr. Walker's, who wrote also :—*A Critical Pronouncing Dictionary ; Elements of Elocution*; *Rhyming Dictionary*, and other works.—(Dr. Milner's account of him.)

WALMESLEY, CATHARINE, Lady Stourton, daughter of Bartholomew Walmesley of Dunkenhalgh, Co. Lancashire, and of Dorothy, daughter of John Smith of Crabbet, Co. Sussex. By the death of her brother, Francis Walmesley, without issue, and of her two sisters, Juliana and Mary, she became the sole heiress of the large estate of Dunkenhalgh. On March 1, 1712, she married Robert, Lord Petre, and after his death, Charles, Lord Stourton, in April 1733. She died in 1785 "a beneficent and amiable woman," says Dr.

Whitaker in his *History of Whalley*, p. 391. After James II. published his
second Declaration, her father, " who was then a young man and newly returned
from abroad, seized upon the chapel of Langho, cast out all the pews from the
chancel, &c., fitted it up for the service of the Church of Rome, and actually
had Mass performed in it March 1687-8. On this intrusion Mr. Price, Vicar of
Blackburn, petitioned the King, who referred the consideration of the case to
Chancellor Jeffries, and he, by a short decree dated June 16, 1688, ordered the
chapel to be restored to its proper owner." "This will prove," adds Dr.
Whitaker, p. 424, "that however the indulgence might be abused, neither
James nor his ministers were deaf to the voice of Justice, even against a
Catholic."
   QUERY.—Is there no mistake in their being married so soon as 1712?
   Her charities were boundless, and they chiefly passed through the hands of
Bishop Challoner and Mr. Short, O.S.D., who was her chaplain. I believe
their house at Bornheim was built in great part with Lady Stourton's money.

   WALMESLEY, C. RICHARD [Gillow and D. N. B. call him Charles], consecrated Bishop December 21, 1756, coadjutor to Bishop York, till he resigned
and went to Bath; died November 25, 1797, *æt.* 75 or 76. . . . Born 1722.
When he applied for a coadjutor he presented three O.S.B.'s to Propaganda.
This Propaganda did not like, and therefore wrote to Mr. Challoner to desire
an answer to the following three queries :—

   1. Does Mr. Walmesley really want a coadjutor? 2. What is the character
of the three presentees? 3. Is there no Secular fit to be presented?
   To all which queries the old gentleman replied in order:—
   1. That he did not think Mr. Walmesley really wanted an assistant. 2. That
the presentees were all unknown to him and his. 3. That a Secular would
never be agreeable to Mr. Walmesley, nor would any Secular choose to be an
assistant to him. From all which he concluded it better to put a *niente* on his
petition. — Bishop James to Bishop Thomas Talbot, original at Longbirch.
(See *Cath. Gent. Magazine*, vol. 1, p. 796, and *Orthodox Journal*, No. 69, p. 65;
also C. Butler's *Memoirs*, c. 43).

   WALTON, WILLIAM, D.D., Bishop, Episcopus Trachonensis. Studied at
Douay, and began Divinity under Dr. Green Oct. 1, 1736. After he was
ordained he taught first Philosophy and then Divinity for many years, during
which he took the degree of D.D. in that university. In 1748 he and Dr. Green
examined and approved of Dr. Challoner's edition of the New Testament.
London was the theatre of his missionary labours, where he was much respected
and looked up to by his brethren. He was Clergy Agent for the Midland district and Capitular; in 1757 was chosen "Controversial Writer," in that
capacity succeeding Dr. Challoner, and in 1762 was chosen Dean of the
Chapter, on the death of Mr. Thomas Berington. He was much in the confidence of Bishop Challoner and Bishop Maire, who frequently took his advice
on the most important subjects, and in 1758 Bishop Challoner placed him the
second in his list for his coadjutor. In 1779 he was appointed coadjutor to
Bishop Francis Petre, in the North, and was consecrated *Episcopus Trachonensis.* By the desire of Bishop Petre he lived in Lancashire, that he might be
near to him, who lived at Showley. At the death of Bishop Petre he took up
his residence with Mr. Lonsdale, at York, where he arrived December 12, 1770,
and remained there till his death, Dec. 26, 1780.
   Bishop Walton was a gentleman of great learning and piety, and possessed
a thorough knowledge of the world and mankind. He was principally concerned with Bishop Challoner in the reduction of the Feasts and Fasts, which
was authorised by Brief of Pius VI., dated March 9, 1777. He published a
work on the *Miraculous Powers of the Church*, in answer to Dr. Conyers
Middleton.

   WARD, JOHN, *alias* ROGERS, was son of Thomas Ward, the author of
England's Conversion, and other works. He studied at Valladolid, and returned
to England in 1658 or 1659. He was chosen a member of the Chapter, and in

1683 Archdeacon of Hants, Wilts and Somersetshire. He assisted at the General Assembly of the Chapter in 1684, 1687, and 1694, and preached as Secretary at the latter. "He lived many years in Hants," he says of himself, "but about 1687 was sent to Oxford to assist the Dean of Christ Church, and in 1692 he lived in London and supplied the place of Secretary to the Chapter in the absence of Dr. Betham." When Bishop Giffard was appointed Principal of Magdalen College in Oxford, Mr. A. Giffard, his brother, was appointed Vice-President and Mr. Ward Bursar; but their stay was of short duration. Mr. Ward died in London, March 9, 1723. He wrote a long history of the affairs of the English Chapter, from the fall of religion to his own time; a MS. in folio, kept among the Records of the Chapter, from which Mr. John Serjeant collected his account and defence of the Chapter in 1703. QUERY.— What did he do at Christ Church? Is it not a mistake for Magdalen College?

WARD, ROBERT, studied at Valladolid. On his return in 1683 or 1684 he taught, for about a year, some boys at —— Quosque,* in Yorkshire, but soon went to York, and on the death of Mr. Salkeld succeeded him in the family of the rich and virtuous widow, Mrs. Westby.

WARRILOW, WILLIAM, S.J., succeeded Mr. John Walsh, S.J., at New-castle-upon-Tyne, whose chapel in Gateshead had been burnt down in the year 1745, as the Duke of Cumberland was passing through with his army to the North. Mr. Walsh then came to Newcastle and had his chapel in a small house in the Close. The chapel was afterwards removed to Westgate Street by Mr. Warrilow. The Jesuits had had there an establishment nearly 150 years, yet, after Mr. Warrilow's death, no one was sent to succeed him, and they removed the Fund and everything belonging to the place—even the poor box. "Both I," says Mr. James Worswick, "and the congregation remonstrated in vain. The business had been left to the decision of Mr. Walsh, who had removed to Durham, and Sir John Lawson, who recommended that the Jesuits should give the Clergy £500 to supply the place. But not a farthing have I received for the additional burthen of that congregation." Mr. Warrilow died Nov. 13, 1807. "His talents as a preacher," says Mr. Worswick, "were admired."—(Letter to me.)

WATKINSON, MATTHIAS, was born in London in July, 1634. In 1647 he joined his father in Lisbon, who, having suffered much on account of his religion, had left England, that he might attend to his spiritual and temporal concerns with more quiet, and on Dec. 7 was admitted into the college. Having gone through his course of Philosophy and Divinity he was ordained Dec. 7, 1658. In 1661 he was made procurator, and in the same year dedicated a Theological Thesis to Queen Catharine, at which Dr. Godden presided. In 1664 he was chosen Professor of Philosophy and *Confessarius* of the house; Vice-President in 1668, and May 9, 1672, he succeeded Dr. Barnesly, *alias* Perrot, in the presidentship of the College. In consequence of some misunder-standing between him and Bishop Russell, who had been an alumnus and professor, and was still a benefactor to the house, and was allowed apartments in the College, he requested and obtained leave of the Chapter to return to England, but was prevailed on by the Inquisitor-General to remain. To this the Chapter consented. But when his health was much impaired by his intense application to the numerous duties of his station, the burden of his office was laid upon Mr. Edward Jones, by an express injunction of Bishops Giffard, Smith, and Witham, in 1706, and though he continued to enjoy the dignity of President he led a private life in the College. On March 29, 1709, he had a paralytic stroke, which reduced him almost to the last extremity, and being followed by a second on the same day of the same month of the following year, he died on the 30th in the 77th year of his age. He was buried in the Church of the College, within the rails and at the foot of the Crucifix altar. His library, with all his furniture and silver candlesticks, he left to the College.

* See above under Simpson, John, and Stapleton, Nicholas (I.), where, however, Conteland is an error for Ponteland.

Dr. Watkinson was in great estimation among his brethren, both at Lisbon and in England, of which a better proof cannot be had than his being continued in the presidentship for near 40 years, the usual term being six years. He was chosen a member of the Chapter and V.G. June 4, 1684.—(*Lisbon Register.*)

WEATHERBY [? *vere* BROWNE, THOMAS]. He resided for some years in the North of England, but on Aug. 12, 1688, Bishop Leyburne requested he might go to assist Mr. —— near Winchester, probably at Twyford School. Thomas Browne, *alias* Weatherby, died in April 1728.

WEBB, JAMES, was educated at Douay, and left the College for the Mission, Sept. 12, 1757. He lived in London, where he was apprehended on the information of Payne, a carpenter, who, as the counsel observed, had been all his life a common informer. He was brought to his trial at Westminster, June 25, 1768, before Lord Mansfield. On an objection being made by Counsellor Mansfield his lordship observed that himself and the other judges were agreed in opinion that the 11th and 12th William III. are so worded that, in order to convict anyone on them, it is necessary that it be first proved that he is a Priest, and then that he had said Mass. This Payne was unable to do, and it was observed that all the things sworn to by him to have been done by Mr. Webb in Virginia Street Chapel might have been done by a person who is not a Priest. He was therefore acquitted. When Mr. Webb's trial was ended, that of Mr. Hyacinth de Magallaens came on. But as nothing more appeared against him than against Mr. Webb, he also was acquitted. Mr. Webb died in London, April 15, 1781.—(*Life of Bishop Challoner*, p. 137.)

WEBB, of Odstock, Wilts. Sir John Webb, of Odstock, Wilts (2nd Baronet), son of Sir John Webb, 1st Baronet, created Baronet by Charles I., "as a reward," says the Patent, "of his family having both shed their blood in the King's service, and contributing, as far as they were able with their purses, in his defence." His mother was Mary, daughter of Sir John Caryll, of Harting, Sussex, Knight. On the death of his father he succeeded to the title and estates, and married Mary, sole heiress of her brothers, John and William Blomer, of Hathrop, Gloucestershire, by Frances, daughter of Anthony Browne, Viscount Montague, by whom he had one son. Sir John died in 1700, and was succeeded by his son, Sir John, the 3rd Baronet. He married Barbara, daughter and coheir of John Lord Bellasyse, Baron of Worlaby, and son of Thomas Bellasyse, Lord Viscount Fauconberg, by his third wife, Lady Anne, daughter of Sir John Powlett, and Marquis of Winchester and sister of Charles, Duke of Bolton. By this lady, who died March 28, 1740, he had two sons and four or five daughters. (1), John, who married Mabella, daughter of Sir Henry Tichborne ; (2), Thomas ; (3), Anna Maria, wife of James Radcliffe, Earl of Derwentwater, and died in 1723 ; (4), Mary, wife of James, 1st Earl of Waldegrave ; (5), Barbara, wife of Antony, sixth Viscount Montague ; (6), Winifred, wife of Sir Edward Hales, of St. Stephen's, Kent. Sir John died at Aix-la-Chapelle, in Oct. 1745, and was succeeded by his son, Sir Thomas (4th Baronet). He married Anne, daughter and coheiress of Thomas Gybson, of Welford, Hants, by whom he had two sons ; (1), Sir John, who succeeded him as 5th Baronet ; (2), Joseph, who married Mary, daughter of John White, of Canford, in 1776, by whom he had two sons, Joseph, who died young, and Thomas, who succeeded his uncle ; and Anne, wife of Anthony James Radcliffe, Earl of Derwentwater.

Sir Thomas died June 29, 1763, and was succeeded by his son John (5th Baronet), who married the second daughter of Sir John Moore, of Fawley, Bart., by whom he had one daughter, married to Anthony Ashley Cooper, Earl of Shaftesbury. This Sir John died April 25, 1797, aged 65, and was succeeded by his nephew, Sir Thomas Webb, who married Charlotte Frances, daughter of Charles, twelfth Viscount Dillon.—(Betham II. 19, 20.)

WEBBE [SAMUEL, the elder], a composer of sacred music and Organist at Lincoln's Inn Fields Chapel.—(See *Cath. Gentleman's Magazine*, No. 8 ; at the end of Charles Butler's *Essay on Music* and his *Historical Memoirs*, c. 43.)

WELD, JOHN, of Lulworth Castle, Co. Dorset. He married Julia, third daughter of Robert James, eighth Lord Petre, and of Lady Mary Radcliffe, daughter of James, Earl of Derwentwater, who died June 16, 1772.

WELD, WILLIAM, son and heir of John Weld, of Lulworth. He married Elizabeth, daughter of Richard Sherburne, of Stonyhurst, son and heir of Sir Nicholas Sherburne, by whom he had : — Humphrey Weld, who married Margaret, only daughter of Sir James Simeon, Bart., of Aston Hall, near Stone, Staffordshire, by whom he had Edward Weld, who married Teresa, daughter of John Vaughan, of Courtfield, Co. Monmouth, and died July 21, 1754, æt. 40, leaving besides other children :—Thomas Weld, who married, in 1772, Mary, eldest daughter of Sir John Stanley, of Hooton, Bart., by whom he had 15 children ; Thomas, the eldest, born in 1773, married Lucy, second daughter of Thomas Clifford (Sir Thomas Clifford). After her death he entered into Holy Orders, was made Bishop and afterwards Cardinal, and died in Rome.

WELDON, JOHN, of Raffin, P.P.C. He wrote *The Second Nativity of Jesus the Accomplishment of the First.* Translated from the Tract of a French Capuchin, Antwerp, 1686.

WELDON, RALPH BENEDICT, O.S.B., was professed at the English Priory of St. Edmund, at Paris. He wrote *Chronological Notes,* "containing the rise, growth, and present state of the English congregation, of the Order of St. Bennet, drawn from the Archives of the houses of the said Congregation at Douay, Dieulewart, Paris, and Lambspring, where are preserved the Authentic Acts and original deeds." (Mr. William Eyston's Catalogue of Author's MSS.) The original work in folio MS. is at Ampleforth. His dedication of it to Father Gregson, President of the English Congregation, is dated from the Convent of St. Edmund, at Paris, May 25, 1709. A small 4to copy is at Down-side, consisting of 233 pages. In the beginning is written : "These Chrono-logical Notes collected by Mr. Ralph, *alias* Bennet Weldon, a Benedictine Monk of Paris. Transcribed A.D. 1713." The folio work is a different thing, or rather an enlargement of the other. It is entitled "Collections of Dom Ralph Weldon, O.S.B., Paris, 1707"; or, "Memoires des Constitutions" Benedictinorum Anglorum. [Has been printed in 1882, with title *A Chronicle of the English Benedictine Monks,* &c., being the Chronological Notes of Dom B. Weldon.]

WELLS, DAVID, of Burback, Co. Leicester, F.S.A. He was son of David Wells, who had acquired a decent competence in the wine trade. He was born near St. Nicholas' Church, at Coventry, Aug. 1, 1733, and the beautiful steeple of that church, one of the earliest objects of his youthful admiration, impressed on him a zealous ardour for the study of antiquities, which, with a turn for natural history and an innate attachment to music, he continued to cultivate through life. His father allowed him the privilege of improving his natural abilities by an education on the Continent ; an indulgence which, on the part of the son, was not misused. He availed himself of every opportunity of studying men and manners, as well as books, and returned to enjoy the estate bequeathed to him by his father, with reputation to himself and to the universal satisfaction of his neighbourhood, where he constantly resided, and particu-larly to the poor, among whom he diffused the blessings of a moderate independence with a kind and judicious hand. On Feb. 4, 1790, he had attained the summit of his ambition by being enrolled a member of the Society of Antiquaries of London, and gave early proofs that he would have been a credit to that respectable body by a curious paper on *Stone Seats in Churches,* which found admission into their *Vetusta Monumenta* III., plates IV. and V. To the papers of the *Gentleman's Magazine,* from April 1784 till his death, he was an able and constant contributor. He died of a putrid fever May 1, 1790, and was buried at Burback, May 3. Having no issue by his wife, Elizabeth Lockley, of Boscobel, the whole of his property, amongst which was a variety of curious articles in various branches of study, and no small collection of natural curiosities, descended to his nephew, Ambrose Salisbury, who sold it by public auction in 1795. The Burback and Hinkly property consisted of nearly 430 acres. Mr. Wells was a gentleman ot polished manners and extensive erudition. He published (1) *On Stone Seats in Churches*; (2) *An Essay of Rood-Lofts*, printed in the Archæologia; (3) *Letters, Essays and Observations*, published in the *Gentleman's Magazine*. He printed a list of them for the use of his friends a little before his death. They amount to 90. A few other articles under the signature of "Observator," by Mr. Wells, appeared (some ot them posthumously) in subsequent volumes of the Magazine.

Mr. Nichols dedicated to him his *History of the Villages of Aston Flamville and Burback*, and there acknowledges himself "indebted for much that is valuable in it to the truly original suggestions, judiciary observations and critical remarks of Mr. Wells." This history appeared in his 43rd No. ot *Bibliographia Topographica Britannica* (John Nichols, F.S.A., *Leicestershire*, IV. 460, with Wells's portrait, *Ibid.*, Pl. lxix.

WELLS, GERTRUDE, O.S.B., sister of David Wells. She became a Benedictine, and with the rest of the community came over to England in the beginning of the French Revolution, and settled at Hammersmith, where she died, Nov, 3, 1807, aged 84, and in the 62nd year of her religious profession.

WEST, THOMAS, S.J., born Jan. 1, 1720, entered his noviceship Sept. 7, 1751. He lived some time in the family of Mr. Fitzherbert, at Swinnerton, and afterwards at Ulverstone-in-Furness. In his old age he retired to Mr. Strickland's, at Sizergh, near Kendal, and died there, much beloved and respected where known, July 10, 1779, in the 63rd year of his age. He, according to his request, was buried in the chapel belonging to the Strickland family in Kendal Church. He wrote (1): *The History and Antiquities of Furness Abbey*, dedicated to Lord Cavendish, 4to.; (2) *A Guide to the Lakes of Cumberland, Westmoreland, and Lancashire.*

WESTON, JOHN WEBBE, of Sutton Place, Co. Surrey, and Somersfield, Co. Hereford. He married Elizabeth Lawson, daughter of John, the third son of Sir Henry Lawson, second Baronet, and of his wife, Elizabeth Selby, who died in 1791, leaving a numerous family.

WHARTON, MICHAEL, born near Kirby Stephen, near Gray Rig. He was educated at Lisbon, and lived many years at Yealand, near Burton, Westmoreland, and died there Dec. 10, 1809. He was a very respectable Missionary, and Rural Dean of Lonsdale Hundred.

WHARTON, PHILIP, Marquis of Wharton, son of Thomas Wharton, who was raised to the dignity of Marquis by Queen Anne, 1715, and was a nobleman of "great sagacity and spirit, and a complete statesman." Philip succeeded his father in all his titles and abilities. "With attachment to no party," says Walpole, in his *Royal and Noble Authors*, "this lively man changed the free air of Westminster for the gloom of the Escurial; the prospect of King George's Garter for the Pretender's, and with indifference to all religion, the frolic lord, who had written a ballad on the Archbishop of Canterbury, died in the habit of a Capuchin." In 1717 (O.S.) he was created Duke of Wharton. Some time after he left England, became a Catholic, entered into the service of the Chevalier St. George, and was a volunteer in the Spanish Army before Gibraltar, in 1727. He retired at last into a monastery of Benedictines—I think in Spain—and there died, without issue in 1734. (Burke's *Dormant and Extinct Barons*, II. 588.)

WHETENHALL, JAMES, son of Henry Whetenhall, of East Peckham, Kent, and of Letitia Tichburne, was born in 1702. His parents were both Catholics. After studying his Classics at Douay, he was sent to Rome by Bishop Giffard, and was received in the College by Father Eberson, Jan. 18, 1722, and ordained Dec. 21, 1726, by Benedict XIII., at St. John Lateran's. On May 2, 1728, he left the College and went to Ghent, where he was Confessarius to the English Benedictine Dames for the space of forty-four years. "Religiosas curae suae commissas," says the Obituary, "et verbo et exemplo ad virtutis et perfectionis studium incitare sedulo laboravit. Mundi strepitus exosus, tempus quod a sacris functionibus supererat, domi fere sibi et Deo vacans impendebat." He suffered much illness for the last four years of his life, which he bore with great patience and resignation to the Divine Will. He died, March 2, 1773, at Ghent, in the 71st year of his age and the 46th of his Priesthood.

WHITE, JOHN, *alias* LECKENBY, son of John White and Alice Southard, or Southworth, was born in Lancashire, May 18, 1710 (O.S.), and studied his Classics there three years. In 1727 he was received in the English College at Rome. He received minor orders from Benedict XIII. in 1729, and was ordained Priest March 21, 1733, and left the College September 23, 1734. In 1748 he went to Pontop, "where he lived," says Mr. Thomas Eyre, "till February 7, 1778, when he died."

(Mr. Leckenby lived at Creston and at Pontop or Tanfield. Rev. Edward Kenyon supposes White and Leckenby to be the same person. Mr. Peter Browne says: "Mr. John White lived many years in Lancashire, and died at Euxton Hall, Feb. 7, 1778." He and Mr. Eyre disagree.)

WHITE, LUCAS, elder brother of John, was born October 17, 1708 (O.S.) Entered the College at Rome June 27, 1724, was ordained September 9, 1731, and left for the Mission on the 14th—five days after he was ordained. He lived many years in Lancashire, at Euxton or Alkston, or at both places, and died in July, 1765. Dr. Gradwell says "He was an able Missioner, and had the reputation of great skill in physic."

WHITE, RICHARD, *alias* JOHNSON. He was Confessor to the Augustinian nuns, at Louvain; for twenty years socius to Mr. Barnes and Confessarius thirty-six. He died there, Jan. 12, 1687, in the 84th year of his age. He had the character of being "pious, wise, prudent, peaceful, learned, and good-humoured." Was much beloved, not only by the Community, but by all who knew him. "He spent his whole time," says his Obituary, "in studying, writing, preaching, and catechizing his flock. Some few years before his death he was disabled by the palsy in his tongue, hands and feet from saying Mass or hearing Confessions, but failed not in his judgment, memory, or understanding. He left in MS. 100 *Catechistical Instructions;* 300 *Sermons on all sorts of subjects; A Paraphrase of the Veni Sancte Spiritus, the Pater Noster and Ave Maria;* two *Books of Meditations,* and another of *Instructions* for several occasions, in all which," continues the Obituary, "he has left us a lively picture of himself; for he ever practised exactly what he taught to others."

WHITE, THOMAS, educated at Douay. For some time he was Chaplain at Warwick Street, London, but when Dr. Milner was chosen V.A. of the M.D., in 1802, he succeeded him at Winchester, where he was much respected and beloved, and where he died, April 9, 1826, only ten days before Dr. Milner. Mr. White was a zealous Missioner and an eloquent preacher. He left behind him :—(1) *A Sermon* at the consecration of Dr. Milner ; (2) *Two vols. of Sermons* edited by Dr. Lingard ; (3) Some occasional pieces.

WHITEHALL, ANDREW, from Douay. He was a zealous labourer among the poor on the border of Staffordshire and Derbyshire. He lived at Norbury, an estate belonging to the Fitzherberts, of Swinnerton, and died in the beginning of 1682.

WHITGREAVE, JOHN & JAMES, S.J. Brothers of —— Whitgreave of Moseley, Esq. Both lived at Moseley, and died there ; John, Feb. 17, 1725, and James, July 15, 1750. Both were buried at the Parish Church of Bushbury.

WHITGREAVE, THOMAS, of Moseley, Co. Stafford, son of Thomas Whitgreave, who concealed Charles II. in his house after the battle of Worcester. He married Isabella, daughter of William Turvile, of Aston Flamville, and his wife, Isabella, daughter and coheiress of Sir Aston Cockaine, of Pooley, Co. Warwick, Bart. He died Sept. 10, 1728, and his wife July 19, 1742.

Both are buried at Bushbury, his Parish Church. (See his father's Epitaph among the *Records*.)

WHITNALL, ——, a native, it seems, of Kent, where he had a small estate. He began *The Translation of Quesnell's Reflections*, which Mr. Thwaites and Father Southcote, O.S.B., finished and published, but before the original was condemned at Rome.

WHITTINGHAM, THOMAS, D.D., son of Thomas Whittingham and his wife, Frances Tanks, was born at Cadsall, near Wolverhampton. He went to Douay in 1751, and after defending his Universal Philosophy there with great applause, and where he had taken the lead in all his schools, he went to Paris in September, 1758, and was ordained Priest September 24, 1763. On January 1, 1766, he entered his license, and took the Doctor's cap March 21, 1768. In April he came on the Mission. His residence was at Heythrop, in Oxon, the seat of the Earl of Shrewsbury. When the Archbishop of Paris, in 1782, returned the first presentation made to him by Bishop James Talbot, on Dr. Howard's surrendering his office of Superior of St. Gregory's, and a second was sent him with the names of Dr. Joseph Strickland, Dr. Wright and Dr. Whittingham, the latter became the object of his choice, and he was appointed Superior of the Seminary. Although he was highly acceptable to the gentlemen of the Seminary, yet, knowing that Bishop Talbot, who had particularly recommended Dr. Wright, disapproved of the choice, he at first refused to accept of the offered honour. He was, however, afterwards persuaded to accept of it, but, unfortunately for the Seminary, and to the great regret of all that knew him, he died on February 16, 1783, *æt.* 45, while he was preparing for his departure from Heythrop. Dr. Whittingham was a learned and zealous Priest, and was much beloved and respected at Heythrop, and in the neighbourhood. He was a member of the Chapter.—See *Cath. Mag.* II. p. 102-7. (*St. Gregory's Register.*)

WIDDRINGTON, PEREGRINE, youngest son of William, fourth Lord Widdrington. In 1745 he had the misfortune to join Prince Charles, and was made Aide-de-camp to General Forster. He was taken prisoner at Preston and sent to Newgate, whence he was taken into the custody of a King's Messenger, in order for a pardon. But his health having suffered by a long imprisonment, he died Feb. 4, 1748 or 9. He is said to have been "a man of the strictest friendship and honour, with all the good qualities that accomplished a fine gentleman ; he was of so amiable a disposition and so engaging that he was beloved and esteemed by all who had the honour and happiness of his acquaintance, being ever ready to oblige and to act the friendly part on all occasions, firm and steadfast in all his principles, which were delicately fine and good as could be wished in any man ; he was both sincere and agreeable in life and conversation." (Monument in Mitton Church in Dr. Whitaker's *Whalley*, p. 450).

WIDDRINGTON, ROBERT.—I suppose he was a Priest, for in the beginning of the eighteenth century he resided at Widdrington Castle, and assisted the Catholics in and about Alnwick. On his retiring to Biddleston the same were assisted by Mr. Henry Widdrington, who resided at Callaly till 1729, when he died, and Mr. Kingsley, of Ellingham, supplied his place. (*Papers of the Rev. Thos. Eyre*, of Ushaw College.)

WIDDRINGTON, WILLIAM LORD, son of William, third Lord Widdrington, and of Alathea, daughter and co-heiress of Charles, fifth Viscount Fairfax, of Ireland, by Abigail, daughter of Sir John Yates, Knt. His was the second troop of English that joined the Scotch when they entered England in 1715. Mr. Errington, of Beaufront, was his Captain. He was taken at Preston and sent to the Tower, but received the benefit of the Act of Grace. His annual rents amounted to £4,904 6s. 10½d., besides the unwrought colliery of Stella, which was computed at £250 per annum, and personal property amounting to £7,129 17s. 4d. "From a nice principle of grateful attachment to that family which had been the fountain of honour to his own house, Lord Widdrington took part in what was called the Rebellion of 1715, wherein his equally mistaken sons, Charles and Peregrine, also participating, they were made prisoners at Preston, and at length arraigned May 3, and found guilty of High Treason July 7, 1716. But in 1717 they and several more had the Royal pardon. An act of clemency the expectation of which, observed his Lordship in answer to the articles of impeachment, had induced divers noblemen and gentlemen to a voluntary submission, for, continues the noble Lord, nature must have started at yielding themselves up to a certain and ignominious death, when it must be acknowledged that it was not impracticable for many of them to have escaped, and it was possible so great a number grown desperate might have obtained further success, and thereby prevented the so speedy suppression of that insurrection." He married first, Jane, daughter and heiress of Sir Thomas Tempest, of Stella, and secondly, Mrs. Graham, with a considerable fortune. His Lordship died in 1743 at Bath, leaving one son, Henry, and two daughters, Alathea and Anne. (Burke's *Dormant Baronage* III., 743.)

WILKINSON, WILLIAM, after teaching Philosophy and Divinity at Douay, succeeded Mr. Fr. Petre as Procurator and Vice-President in 1762, and Mr. Alban Butler as President of St. Omers in 1773. The latter office he resigned to Mr. Greg. (Bp.) Stapleton in 1787, and came to England. It was principally through his and Mr. Joseph Berington's means that Mr. Tichbourne Blount was chosen President of Douay, and Mr. Alban Blount excluded, which caused the latter, as Mr. Berington told me, to make such opposition in his thesis (Mr. Berington's), which was levied more at Mr. Blount, the approver of the thesis, than at Mr. Berington. Mr. Wilkinson died at Bath, March 24, 1803.

WILLIAMS, EDWARD DOMINIC, O.P., D.D., AND BP. He was a native of Monmouthshire. He entered among the Dominicans and took the habit at Bornheim Oct. 28, 1664, with the name of Dominic, and made his profession Sept. 27, 1665. He studied Philosophy at Rome, where Cardinal Howard had procured for those of his Order the Convent of St. John and St. Paul, on the Celian Hill, and Divinity also partly there and partly at Naples. In 1674 he was chosen Prior of Bornheim. Father Bing having purchased, in 1696, a College at Louvain with money left for that purpose by Cardinal Howard, and this College having been admitted to all the privileges of that University, Father Williams, after having filled the office of Provincial of his Order, was chosen first Rector of the College in 1697, which he governed twelve years. For nine years of this time he taught Philosophy and Divinity. In 1724 he was sent by Father Hansbie, the Provincial, to Rome, together with Father Martin, to solicit some favour of Benedict XIII., who had been a Dominican, and to remonstrate, it is said, against some proceedings or acts of Bishop Petre, Coadjutor to Bishop Giffard.

While there he was mentioned to the Chevalier as a proper person for a mitre, who recommended him to the Pope. He was accordingly appointed and consecrated Bishop of Tiberiopolis by the Pope, Dec. 30, 1725, and was sent to England in quality of V.A. to succeed Bishop Witham in the North. As he came among them unasked for and without their knowledge, it is not surprising that he was unacceptable to the generality of the Clergy, who had petitioned for one of their own body. Yet, when he became better known, I do not find that they made any complaints against him. For he was exact in all the duties of his high station, and was particularly noted for his compassion and charity towards the sick and the poor in general. He strongly recommended to his Clergy the duty of catechising their congregation. (See article, Reydon.) His Grand Vicars were Dr. Carnaby, in Bishopric, Mr. Reydon, in Lancashire, and Dr. Holden, in Yorkshire, all of the Secular Clergy. His residence was at Huddleston, a seat of Sir Thomas Gascoigne, in Yorkshire, where he died April 3, 1740 (O.S.), in the 73rd year of his age and the 54th of his Profession, and 49th of his Priesthood, and 14th of Episcopacy. (*Synopsis fund. Col. S. Thomae Aq.*, Louvain, and the *Dominican Obituary*.)

WILLIAMS, FRANCIS, *alias* GULIELMI, O.S.D. AND D.D.   He had been Prior of Bornheim, and in 1688 he was Provincial of his Order, and in that quality signed the Resolution.   He died in London, Sept. 11, 1688.   (See Mr. Mayes' Letter in Book II. of his agency.)

WILLIAMS, REGINALD, was a native of Montgomeryshire, received into the College at Rome Oct. 6, 1677.   He was ordained Jan. 25, 1682, and left the College April 10, 1684.   He was a Capitular, and in 1714 assisted at the General Assembly of the Chapter, when he was chosen Archdeacon of North Wales.   In 1732 he presided at the General Assembly as the Senior Capitular, when Mr. Douglas Day was chosen to succeed Dr. Ryder as Dean.   He lived many years in Oxfordshire and afterwards in Wales, where he died April 17th, 1737, aged 79.

WILLOUGHBY, EDWARD, of Aspley, near Nottingham.   He married Margaret. . . . He died at Aspley, Oct. 17, 1792, in the 85th year of his age, and his wife in Nov., 1795, aged 82. (See *Hist. of Nottinghamshire.*)

WILLOUGHBY, EDWARD, a Carmelite, son of Edward Willoughby and Sarah Bird, was born in London, June 24, 1766, and was sent to Rome with his elder brother George, by Signor Bonomi's agency, an Italian architect, in 1775. He was then only nine years of age, and began his education by learning to read and write, to such a low ebb was the College reduced, the Bishops refusing to send students while it was governed by Italians.   On account of bad health he applied but little to his studies, and in Sept., 1783, he was sent home.   Afterwards he entered among the Carmelites at Tongres ; was ordained and came on the Mission, and lived with his grandfather and grandmother at Aspley, near Nottingham.   After their death he conformed, printed his recantation sermon, and soon after went to America.   I heard at Douay, in 1785, that he had been there a few days before, when his behaviour was far from edifying.   Vanity was his great fault, as his aunt, Mrs. Fanny Willoughby, told me.

WILMOT, JOHN, *alias* B.D., was educated at Rome, and on his return was secretary to Bishop Leyburne.   He wrote : *Controversial Discourses relating to the Church, being an answer to Dr. Sherlock's Discourse concerning the nature, unity, and communion of the Catholick Church.*   By B.D., Douay ; 8vo., 1697. Mr. Wilmot died in 1719.

WILMOT, WILLIAM, lived at Holywell, and in 1694, though not a member of the Chapter, was sent by Mr. George Barrett (Archdeacon of Shropshire and part of Herefordshire) as his deputy to the General Assembly of the Chapter.   This was the most important of all the General Assemblies of the Chapter on account of the matters treated of, and resolutions passed at it.   A full account is given of it in my MS. at Chap. VIII. (J.K.)   Mr. Wilmot died at Holywell Aug. 2, 1720.

WILSON, JOHN, O.S.B.   He assisted the Catholics about Stella Hall, Northumberland, in the beginning of the eighteenth century, under the patronage of the Tempest and Widdrington families.   In the year 1715 he was seized as a Roman Catholic Priest, and was hurried to Durham Gaol.   " It was in the recollection of many," says Rev. Thomas Eyre, "that on his way he passed through Winlaton on horseback with the feet tied under the horse's belly.   When set at liberty he returned to his flock, and never quitted them till he was called to the reward of his labours, on Friday, June 22, 1725, at Blaydon."   He was probably the author of *The Creed Expounded*, by J. W., M.O.S.B., but published after his death.

WILSON, THOMAS, whose true name was Clarke, was born at or near Stourbridge, and was sent to the College at Rome, and after he was ordained came on the Mission, and was placed in the family of Lord Aston, at Tixall, where he lived many years, and was esteemed a good and zealous missionary. He afterwards retired to Stafford, in 1754, where he died far advanced in years, March 9th, 1766.   He was succeeded at Tixall by Mr. Christopher Langfield.

WILSON, THOMAS, was educated at Douay, and returned to England about the year 1740, when he was charged with the congregation at and about Hathersedge, in the Peak of Derbyshire. In 1745 he was apprehended and sent to York Castle on Nov. 5, "as a reputed Popish Priest and dangerous to the peace of the Kingdom," but after a confinement of some months was released and returned to his flock at Hathersedge, where he spent the remainder of his days in peace, and died much respected and beloved, December 12, 1779.

WINDER, PETER, was born at Caton, near Lancaster, and in 1661 went to Douay. He was then 16 years old, and for some time was servant to Dr. Kellison, the President. Afterwards pursuing his studies, he was ordained Priest, and sent on the Mission. Mr. Dodd says in the MS. account of him that he knew him when he was a very old man, in the reign of James II.

WINSTANLEY, EDMUND, was educated at Douay, where he taught Philosophy for a short time. When he came on the Mission he was made Chaplain to the Duke of Norfolk. He afterwards lived at Mapledurham, in the family of Mr. Blount, and died there, Dec. 18, 1783. In 1771 he was admitted into the Chapter, and was Archdeacon of Worcester and Gloucestershire.

WITHAM, ANTHONY, went from Douay to St. Gregory's, Sept., 1703, to finish his Philosophy at his own expense. Having finished his quinquennium he passed M.A. in May, 1709. In July, 1712, he went to the Poor Clares at Rouen to recover his health. He afterwards came on the Mission and lived with Henry Heneage, at Cadeby, near Louth, and died there March 21, 1763.

WITHAM, CHRISTOPHER, brother of the Bishop and of Dr. Robert Witham. He studied at Douay, and came on the Mission in 1686 or 7. I find him residing with his father and mother at Cliffe in 1693, where he assisted the poor Catholics in that neighbourhood, and was esteemed a very pious and regular Priest, and preached often. He died Sept. 5, 1754. He was a Capitular and an Archdeacon in the Chapter. (*Chapter Records.*)

WITHAM, GEORGE, D.D., *alias* MARKHAM, Episcopus Marcopolitanus. He was son of George Witham, of Cliffe, Esq., and Grace, daughter of Sir Marmaduke Wyvill, Bart., of Constable Burton, and was born in 1655. Having studied Philosophy and part of his Divinity at Douay, he went to Paris in 1678 and took the Cap of D.D. in 1688, and in Aug. returned to Douay to teach Divinity. After teaching the course he came on the Mission, lived with his sister and brother-in-law, Mr. and Mrs. Palms, near York, and was made G.V. by Bishop Smith. In 1694 he was deputed to Rome by the Vicars Apostolic in consequence of some misunderstanding with the Benedictines, and obtained the Decrees in *Dodd*, III., p. 529, and *Panzani s Memoirs*. He went a second time in 1701. In 1702 he was appointed V.A. for the Midland District of England to succeed Mr. Giffard, who was translated to London on the death of Bishop Leyburne. His bulls are dated Aug. 12, 1702. He then went to Monte-fiascone and resided in the Seminary, where he found Mr. Richard Howard, afterwards made Canon of St. Peter's. Here he was consecrated on April 15, 1703, by Cardinal Barberigo, with the assistance of the Bishops of Bagnoria and of Sutri. On his way to England "he visited the Legate at Bologna, Cardinal d'Adda, who had been Legate in England, and who sent his remembrance to the two Bishops in England, whom he called his sons, because he had consecrated them." He then continued his journey in company with Mr. Tunstall and his tutor, Mr. Syliard, through Venice, Vienna, Prague, Saxony, Hanover and Holland, and arrived in London June 22 (O.S.). His residence in the Midland District was at St. Thomas's Priory, the seat of —— Fowler, Esq., where he was known by the name of Markham. After the death of Bishop Smith in 1711, the Northern District remained vacant for about five years, and was governed by Bishop Giffard as the senior Bishop, who appointed Mr. Robert Witham his V.G. for that District. In 1716 Bishop Witham was translated to the Northern District. His bulls of translation are dated March 16, 1716, and his faculties March 19. Here he resided principally, with his own family, at Cliffe, and here he died April 27, 1725 (N.S.) *subita morte praereptus.*

Bishop Witham wrote : (1) *Discursus brevis de praeviis ad Fidem Christianam,* *et de methodo eam inveniendi,* MS. of 39 folio pp. (see *Miscel.* viii., p. 1). (2) *Methodi Catholicae Vindiciae,* MS. fol. 16 pp. (3) *A Catholick Thesis, he* *who denies all infallibility in knowing what Christ taught can have no* *Christian Faith,* MS. (*Ibid.*). (4) *Explicatio versus* 11 *and* 12, *capituli* 7, *Genesis.* "*Rupti sunt fontes Abyssi magni,*" MS. (5) *An Answer to Dr.* *Tillotson's Discourse against Transubstantiation.* 27 fol. pp. MS. On this he received, in a long letter of 21 folio pages, the congratulations of a person of quality, dated July 25, 1701, from Monte Citorio, where he was making a spiritual retreat. (6) *Dubia quædam proposita Viris doctis circa methodum* *tractandi cum Protestantibus, ut viis moderatis et pacificis ad Ecclesiæ Catholicæ* *reducantur unitatem,* MS. (7) *Conferentia de delectu opinionum in materia* *morali,* MS. (8) *A weekly exercise for the use of a good Christian.* MS. imperfect. (9) *Prudential Directions.* All these MSS. may be seen in *Miscel.* viii. I know not whether any were published. (10) *Panzani's Memoirs,* a translation from the Italian. Bishop Thomas Smith had, and probably Dr. Briggs has, the MS. (See *Cath. Mag.* III., 103.)

WITHAM, JAMES, O.S.B. He was son of John Witham, of Cliffe, Esq., and nephew to the foregoing. In 1725 he went to live at Stella, and served that Mission under the patronage of the Tempest and Widdrington families, but being advanced in years was unable to undergo the fatigues of the Mission, and in 1726 was succeeded by Mr. Rogers, also O.S.B.

WITHAM, ROBERT, D.D. He was the seventh son of Mr. Witham, of Cliffe, and brother to the Bishop, and was born in 1667. He was educated at Douay with two of his brothers, and defended Universal Philosophy under Dr. Hawarden, July 30, 1688, and the treatise *De Incarnatione* under his brother, Dr. George Witham, in Oct., 1689. On Sept. 22, 1694, he was ordained Priest, and after teaching two courses of Philosophy and three years Divinity, as second Professor (Dr. Hawarden being the first), he came on the Mission in 1698 or 9, and lived at Cliffe. On the death of Bishop Smith, in 1711, he was made V.G. of the Northern District by Bishop Giffard, the senior Bishop, and filled that office till the death of Dr. Paston, in 1715, when he was nominated President of Douay College by the joint consent of the Propaganda (there being no Protector), the Bishops and Chapter agreeing to it. At that time the College was 40,000 florins in debt, and Mr. Witham, then only Licentiate in Divinity, refused to go over till it was reduced to 14,000. He reached Douay Oct. 28, 1715, having in his company John Savage, Earl Rivers (a Priest), who went over with a design to reside there. At that time there were ninety-two persons in the College, and in 1717 they were increased to 115. On Sept. 4, 1716, the English College presented a petition, signed by the King's Commissioners who visited the University, to the Rector, that they might be admitted to their ancient right of teaching public lessons. But they were opposed by the Faculty of Divinity, then only three in number, Dr. Elcourt, De Morque, and Amand. Their answer was replied to by the College and signed by the Commissioners. On which D'Elcourt wrote to the Internuncio at Brussels that it was against the interests of the Mission that they should teach. (*Manebat alta mente repostum.* See Art. Dr. Hawarden.) He governed the College for nearly 23 years, and died there, May 18, 1738. "He was a good Divine," says Mr. Thomas Berington, the Dean of the Chapter, "and indefatigable in teaching, preaching, &c." The College flourished under his direction, was happy in having able professors, and sent many learned and zealous Priests on the Mission.

Dr. Witham published : (1) *The English Translation of the New Testament* *by Cornelius Nary, C.F.P.D., examined and compared with the Latin Vulgate* *and the Greek,* by R. W., D.D., an. 1727. 4to of 22 pages. (2) *Annotations on* *the New Test.* In two vols., 8vo. Douay, 1730. (3) *Observations on Dr.*

Fell's Lives of the Saints, which he sent to Rome for the purpose of procuring a condemnation of them, with what success I know not. I saw them in MS. in the College Library. (See *Dodd* III., p. 488.)

WITHAM, THOMAS, D.D., was cousin to the Bishop. Having finished his Philosophy at Douay he went to the Seminary of Bons Enfans, at Paris, for about half a year, and entered that of St. Gregory, Sept. 19, 1680. After making his Tentative, Aug. 3, 1689, he came over to England and was made King's Preacher in ordinary, but returned again in Feb., 1689, and entered his License, Jan. 1, 1690, and April 5, 1692, took the Doctor's Cap. In May, 1692, he went to Douay, where he was desired by Dr. Paston to be Confessarius to the house and to read a private lesson on Moral Divinity. On this occasion Bishop Smith tells Dr. Paston that "if they at Douay will please God, profit their neighbour, and gain applause to themselves, they must strive to imitate his preaching, for I can assure them," he adds, "no person was more esteemed than he. He was sufficiently known for his great talent in preaching and directing of souls." Preface to *Poor Man's Manual*, 1705, 5th edition.

At the call of Bishop Smith he went on the Mission to Newcastle-on-Tyne, but on the death of Dr. Meynell he was chosen Principal of St. Gregory's, and arrived there April 29, 1699. In September, 1706, he fell ill, and relapsed again in Oct., and was about a year in recovering. In October, 1711, he was again presented by Bishop Giffard to the Archbishop, and was confirmed for six years. In May, 1712, he went to Douay with Mr. Henry Howard, *alias* Preston, and Dr. Strickland, and thence to the Poor Clares at Dunkirk. Three days after his arrival he received a letter from Mr. William Dicconson at St. Germains, confirmed by another by Dr. Ingleton, that complaints had been carried to Rome about him concerning the respect due to the Pope's decrees, and that it was to be apprehended that the Court of France, then zealously bent for the Constitution, would remove him. He was therefore desired not to return, and remained there till towards the last week of August, and having cleared himself with the Internunce of Brussels went to Newport, and stayed with the Carthusians till Sept. 1, on which day Lewis XIV. died. He then returned to Dunkirk, but in the meantime Dr. Laurence Rigby was sent over to secure the Community. There being, however, no danger by the death of the King of France, he was desired to return, which he did Dec. 6, and was continued in his place by the Cardinal's (Noailles) order, and at the desire of Bishop Giffard. After governing the Seminary with exemplary piety nearly eighteen years, he resigned his office June 8, 1717, and retiring into Flanders, died at Dunkirk, Jan. 8, 1728 (N.S.), so says my author, but Mr. Eyre, of Ushaw, says positively that "Thomas Witham died Dec. 28, 1727 (O.S.), at Preston-upon-Skerne, near Stockton." If so, and the dates are the same, he probably succeeded Mr. John Booth, who died there Oct. 1, 1722. Dr. Witham wrote : *A Short Discourse upon the Life and Death of Mr. George Throckmorton*, in 1706 or 5, second edition, with additions by another hand in 1710. MS. in Buckland library. (*St. Gregory's Register.*)

WOODROFFE, ROBERT, born in Staffordshire of respectable parents. In January, 1692, he was admitted a Convictor in Lisbon College. Having completed his course of studies and being ordained Priest he took the oath of the Mission with the promise annexed to it, July 17, 1680, and returned to England. His residence was at Yeldersley, in De'byshire, and he attended the poor Catholics at and about Norbury and Roston, where he was much esteemed as a preacher and a zealous exemplary missionary. (*Lisbon Register and Miscel.* VI., p. 1,074.)

WORSWICK, ROBERT, *alias* Butler, son of Robert Worswick and Elizabeth Butler, born March 31, 1714, was educated at Douay. In Oct., 1738, he went to Paris, and was ordained Sept. 19, 1744. Having passed B.D. in that University, he was allowed to come to England in Dec., 1744, on account of his health. He was some time on the Mission at Singleton, in Lancashire, and afterwards settled in Manchester, where he died Aug. 17, 1752.

WORTHINGTON, THOMAS, O.P. He was Chaplain to Bishop Williams in the North. He became a celebrated Professor of Philosophy, Divinity, and Scripture at Louvain. Was five times chosen Prior of Bornheim, four times Provincial of his Order, and having passed more than thirty years on the Mission, he died *Mediae Villae* (Middleton, probably), in Yorkshire, Feb. 25, 1754, in the 85th year of his age, the 63rd of Religion, and the 60th of his Priesthood. Was much lamented by all who knew him. He wrote : *Annales FF. Praedicatorum Prov. Angliæ restauratae,* a collection from the *Annals of Flanders* of Father Coomans, O.S.D. (*Dominican Obituary.*)

WRIGHT, JAMES, was son of Mr. Abraham Wright, a minister of the Church of England, and sometime Vicar of Okeham, Co. Rutland. He was born at Yarnton, Co. Oxon, and entered in 1666, without being educated at the University, into the Society of New Inn, near London, whence he removed three years after to the Middle Temple, where he spent some time, and became a Catholic. If he would have complied with the times and taken the oath, he would have been one of the Benchers of the Temple, and met with other encouragements. He died at his chambers in the Temple in 1716. (Wood's *Athenae*, part 2, col. 642.) He wrote several things in prose and verse. Among others : (1) *The History and Antiquities of the County of Rutland,* illustrated with Sculptures, London, 1684, a thin folio. (2) *An Epitome of the Monasticon Anglicanum,* London, 1693. (William Eyston's *Catalogue of Writers,* MSS. at Hendred.) (See Chalmer's art., *Wright.*)

WRIGHT, JOHN, was born at Irnham, in Lincolnshire. He studied at Douay, and for some time taught Philosophy there. In 1784 he came on the Mission and lived at Newport, Co. Salop, till 1796, when he removed to Longbirch, and lived with Bishop Berington. He had long been subject to epileptic fits, of which, however, he generally had sufficient notice to call for assistance. He is supposed to have had one of these on Sunday, July 23, 1797, as he was found dead in the morning with his head hanging over the side of the bed. Mr. Wright was a respectable clergyman, and was much esteemed both at Newport and at Longbirch, and loved by his congregation.

WRIGHT, THOMAS, son of Thomas Wright and Martha Clary, of Norwich. He studied Humanity at Douay, and being observed to be gifted with excellent abilities, was sent to Paris in 1761, where he studied Philosophy and Divinity. Having defended his Tentative in Sorbonne, Jan. 5, 1767, he went to teach at St. Omers, and was ordained at Arras in December following. In July, 1769, he returned to Paris, and entered his License in Jan., and took the cap Mar. 21, 1771, and in April came on the Mission, and was placed in the family of George Heneage, of Hainton, Esq., where he was held in great estimation by the family and a numerous congregation. When Dr. Howard retired from St. Gregory's, Bishop James Talbot, who as senior V.A. had the right of presentation, particularly recommended Mr. Wright to the Archbishop of Paris to be his successor, though named in the second place. He, however, required a second presentation, and chose Dr. Whittingham. On the death of Mr. Heneage Dr. Wright left Hainton, and was charged with the care of the Catholics at and about West Ham, in Essex. He died May 26, 1699. He was a member of the Chapter. (*Paris Reg.* See *Cath. Mag.* III., 107.)

WYNTER, ANDREW, O.P., was a native of Brecon, in Wales, and Preacher-General of his Order. In 1730 he succeeded Father Burgess as Rector of their College in Louvain, and in 1735 was chosen Prior of Bornheim, and again Rector of Louvain in 1742, in which capacity death found him, March 19, 1754. He was succeeded by Antoninus Thompson, a native of Brussels, though of English parents, who was the first admitted Alumnus of the College, and governed it with great praise to the age of 80 and upwards. (*Synopsis Fund,* &c.)

YATE, LADY MARY. She was buried in the church of Chadsley Corbet, Co. Worcester, within a mile of Harvington. On a mural marble tablet is this inscription : " D. O. M.—Here lies the eldest daughter and co-heiress of

Humphrey Packington, Esq., Lord of the Manor of Chadsley Corbet, and the incomparable widow of Sir John Yate, of Buckland, Knight and Baronet. The Lady Mary Yate, of pious memory, whose loss is too great to be forgotten. She lived for the common good, and died for her own, and could not have died if the prayers of the poor had prevailed. Her prudence in the management of a bad world was allwaies aiming at a better. Her justice was more than exact in paying all she owed, even before it was due. Her fortitude was built upon her Faith, a rock which no storm could move. Her temperance was grounded on her hope and charity, which raised her heart so much above the world that she used it without enjoying it. She bestowed it liberally upon those who needed it, lived in it as unconcernedly as if she never loved it, and left it as easily as if she had allwaies despised it. Ripe for Heaven and as full of virtues as of daies, she died in the 80th year of her age, June 12, in the year of our Lord, 1696, after having been Lady of this Manor 65 years.— Requiescat in Pace. This, as a dutyfull tribute, was erected by her daughter, Appolonia Yate." Lady Yate lived at Harvington Hall. Within the moat and adjoining the Hall is the Priest's house, where Dodd lived and wrote his *History* and his *Apology*.

YAXLEY, JOHN, left Douay about 1682 and came on the Mission. He lived at Coxhoe, near Durham, which was the ancient family seat of the Kennets, and was Chaplain to Lord Seaforth, who went in Sept., 1726, to thank the King for his pardon. Mr. Yaxley was G.V. and a Capitular in the North, and died at Coxhoe, Nov. 15, 1731. Mr. Chambers, a very old Missionary, lived with him at Coxhoe in 1697. Mr. Yaxley, in 1723, was for publishing a *Mandatum de Condemnatione Usurae*, but it was suppressed by the advice of his brethren, and even of Bishop Witham.

YAXLEY, THOMAS, *alias* GRANGE. A branch of the Yaxley's, or Yoxlers, of Yoxler Hall, Suffolk. While at College at Douay he was thought to be too rigid a disciplinarian, on which account Drs. Betham and Meynell advised Dr. Paston to part with him. He then came on the Mission, and lived in the parish of St. Andrews, Holborn, was G.V. to Bishop Giffard, and also an Archdeacon in the Chapter. He died March 19, 1721 (O.S.).

FINIS. APRIL 7, 1841.

APPENDIX.

The following documents are samples of the excellent collection of Papers put together by the Rev. J. Kirk as materials for his "History" and his "Biographies." It is not too much to say that their value for all interested in the history of Catholicism in Lancashire can hardly be over-estimated. They are now preserved in the Archives of Oscott College, with the title, "Kirk Papers, Collectanea Anglo-Catholica," Vol. III. (pp. 1121, 1122).

I.—THE REV. R. GRADWELL TO THE REV. J. KIRK, 1816.

CLAUGHTON, 11 Nov., 1816.

DEAR SIR,

If I have delayed answering your enquiries, it is only with a view of collecting better information than I was at first possessed of. I sent you per last *Catholicon* some curious things relating to Mr. Tootel and Mr. Melling. I have since learned some further particulars. Christopher Tootel had a brother also a Priest. He was at one time Missionary in Lancashire. In my old register of the Fund I find a Hugh Tootel who was a missioner in these parts in 1683. I have an old *Imitatio Christi* which appears to have belonged successively to Joannes Tootel and Christophorus Tootel. I am inclined to think that John was uncle and Hugh the brother of Christopher. It is remarkable that in one part of the register the fund gave in 1683 Hugoni Tootill "pro victu Dni Metcalf—£1 0s. 0d."; and in another part of the said register I find Hugo Hesketh entered among the members of the fund. The year of this last entry is not specified, but it is written in a hand that does not appear in the register later than 1704. But as there were ten members added between Hugo Hesketh and 1704, it is reasonable to suppose that Hugh was entered a member between 1690 and 1700. I am minute in these statements, that you may compare them with your own notes. Further, Cr. Tootel had a sister who married a Mr. Melling. The offspring of this marriage were (perhaps among others of whom I can learn nothing) Rev. Edward Melling, who, I now know, was Priest at Fernyhalgh, and died there and was buried in the neighbouring church of Broughton; 2nd, another son, who was confessor to the nuns of Louvain, and died there; 3rd, a daughter, who married a Mr. Daniel. This daughter was grandmother of Rev. John Daniel, President, and Rev. Edward Daniel; 4th, another daughter, Helen, who married Mr. Jenkinson, of Wyersdale in this neighbourhood. It is from the present Mr. Jenkinson, her son, a most respectable man of an old Catholic family, that I have learnt these particulars, who traces a relationship between the Tootels and Mellings and the present Catholic families in Lancashire—Daniels, Penswicks, Jenkinsons, and Gradwells. The present Lancashire families of the name of Melling, one gentleman of which families was Priest at Hazlewood, and died there a few years ago, were no relations of Rev. Ed. Melling of Fernyhalgh. The Tootels and Mellings, who are the objects of your enquiries, were all born and lived in the neighbourhood of Preston; and, as far as I can learn, the Priests of

those names were all educated at Douay. Rev. Edw. Daniel was a relation.
He was missioner at Scorton, near Garstang, before the year 1745. He was
too busy in the rebellion, and forced to decamp. He first went abroad, then
returned to Hornby, or Robert Hall, and was last at Scarborough. Tradition
still speaks with affection of Cr. Tootel and Edw. Melling, their learning, their
labours, their piety and charity. This is all the information I have been able
to gather by a very diligent enquiry. I mean to consult the funeral register of
Broughton Church ; and it is possible that the papers which I sent last month
to the *Catholicon*, by becoming popular in the neighbourhood of Fernyhalgh,
may elicit some other particulars. If this be the case I will inform you. The
" Itinerant Missioner," by C. Tootel, is a course of sermons and instructions
for Sundays and Holidays.

Rev. Chr. Gradwell was born in Lancashire, a distant relation of us, a near
relation of the Orrells. He was a Douay Priest, and many years missioner at
Sheffield. He taught Rev. Thos. Eyre his catechism. Mr. Eyre used to say
that he was a very good scholar, and always spoke of him with respect and
affection. My grandmother's double manual, in 18mo or very small 12mo, with
plates, appears to be the first edition both from title and preface. It was
printed by Mary Thomson, London, 1688, and dedicated to, I think, Lady
Powis.

Rt. Rev. Wm. Sharrock, O.S.B., was born in Friargate, Preston, 30 March,
1742 ; went to St. Gregory's, Douay, 6 May, 1755.

Rev. James Sharrock, O.S.B., his brother, was born at Walton, near Preston,
5 Feb., 1750. He became Prior of St. Gregory's, Douay ; was with us a
prisoner at Dourlens ; refused the mitre ; a very learned, pious, and amiable
man.

Rev. John Sharrock, O.S.B., brother, born at Walton, 19 April, 1754 ; Douay;
still living at Longhorsley, Northumberland.

Walter Sharrock, brother, born at Walton, O.S.B. Lay brother at Douay ;
still living at Ampleforth.

I enclose part of the papers which I have prepared for you, but only the
more ancient part. The first page consists of observations taken out of the
pay-list of the Fund. In pages 2, 3, 4 you have the whole list of members as
far as it goes in my first sheet, viz., to about 1760. I have some biographical
notices for you. Perhaps in the course of next year I may send a few of them
to *Catholicon*. I am always making memorandums in my pocket-book on such
subjects purposely for you as I learn them by enquiry and conversation. They
are too much to send by post. If you would wish to see the old register itself
you shall. I shall be always happy to render you any assistance in my power.

Mr. Lingard is going to re-write in his history (which down to Henry VIII. is
to go to press next spring) the whole history of St. Thomas of Canterbury. I
have seen Gandolphy's *Audi alteram partem*. Is he turning a firebrand or
losing his reason ? Mr. Lingard and Dr. Rigby have persuaded me to print in
a separate pamphlet my dissertation on Anti-Christ, which appeared in the
Catholicon. Mr. Brockholes sends his compliments, and hopes to see you
when next you come to Lancashire. Excuse the roughness of this letter and
sentientiousness. I must compress my observations within this half-sheet,
because two of these sheets weigh an ounce.

Yours very truly,

ROB. GRADWELL.

II.—Observations Extracted from the Registers of the Lancashire and Westmoreland Fund, and some Added from Private Intelligence from other Quarters. 1682-1769.

Same source, pp. 1127-1130. *Enclosure in foregoing.*

Dnus. Edvardus Andertonus sacerdos obiit 19 Mart. 1682-3.

Dnus. Hatherwaite obiit 1683.

Dnus. Thomas Ecclestonus decanus ruralis centuriæ Derbensis (Derby Hundred, Lancashire), gave £50 to the Fund in 1694.

Dnus. Thos. Weedonus dec. rural. Centur. Salfordiensis, gave ditto in 1704, again in 17 .

Dnus. Joan. Howes dec. rural. Cent. Blackburnensis, do. 1704.

Dnus. Jacobus Swarbricke sacerdos, qui diem obiit 1716 dum includeretur religionis causa in castro Lancastr. dedit £10 1716. Was priest at Gt. Singleton.

Dnus. Thos. Weedonus dec. ruralis ut supra appears to have died in 1719.

Dnus. Edv. Barlow, Vic. Gen., who lived at Park Hall, appears to have died in 1719. He was on the mission in 1676 : probably came on mission then.

Dnus. Christr. Jenkinson sacerdos, Priest of Lisbon, appears to have died in 1723. He was of a respectable family in Wyersdale, near Garstang, which family still lives there. He served the Catholics in those parts, and officiated alternately, or as the circumstances of those persecuting times permitted, at his father's house in Wyersdale and at Scorton, Nateby, &c. Nateby then belonged to the Leyburns.

D. Roger Brockholes, gave £10 in 1723.

D. Rich. Taylor, *alias* Sherburne, missioner of Claughton, gave £10 in 1726.

R. D. Thos. Anderton, do. 1728.

R. D. Gul. Mayre, *alias* Hawarden, do. 1728.

D. Geor. Crosby sacerdos obiit Duaci 1729.

Rev. Dom. Edvardus Melling obiit 17 April, 1732. Ecce !

Rev. Dom. Jacob. Gaunt obiit 26 Nov. 1734, at Salwick Hall.

Rev. Dom. Tho. Anderton was alive in Blackburn Hundred, 1735/6.

R. D. Gul. Winkley Dec. rur. Leyland, gave £20 in 1742.

R. D. Thos. Hawarden, Vic. Gen. (in Cent. Derb.), gave do. in 1748.

R. D. Geo. Boardley (Dec. rurl. Derbi), do. 1757.

Mr. Richard Barton, Priest, condemned and kept in prison in Lancaster Castle, causa religionis, from 1679 to 1684, received £10 per annum from the clergy fund during the whole of that period. He was living in 1701, but appears to have died that year.

R. D. Jacobus Gaunt obiit 1734 sacerd. in Lonsdale Hundred.

Rev. Luke White appears to have come on the mission in 1767. He lived at Euxton, near Preston. Was a very able missioner, and had the reputation of great skill in physic.

Rev. Charles Ingolby appears to have come on the mission in 1773. He lived in Blackburn Hundred.

Rev. Ed. Helme appears on the mission in 1773. He was missioner at Manchester several years. He had been professor of Philosophy at Douay, and was an excellent scholar. In his days the Catholic congregation of Manchester scarcely contained seventy souls.

Rev. John Davidson, at Salwick, gave £10 in 1774. A good Greek and mathematical scholar, modest and bashful.

Rev. Wm. Husband, at Salwick, gave £10 in 1779.

The fund of the secular clergy of the Archidiaconate, including Lancashire and Westmoreland, was instituted in the reign of Charles II. in 1672. In 1681-2 it included 37 brethren. In 1694 there were 30.

In 1685 and 1686 the annual meeting of the brethren was held at Claughton at Mr. Sherburn's. In 1709-1710 it was held at Park Hall. In 1688 at Preston. In 1705 at Fernyhalgh. In 1736, Aug. 31, the secular Priests of the counties of Chester and Cumberland were voted into the society of the fund, heretofore including only those of Lancaster and Westmoreland. The vote was unanimous, and is attested by Thomas Roydon, V.G., Nicholas Skelton, and John Cowban.

The original list of Clergy Priests who were members and subscribers to the aforesaid fund. It is in the handwriting of the then treasurer, and both the names of the subscribers, the rules, the accounts, &c., are written in the same beautiful hand down to 1704, when the list is continued by a different hand.

Peter Gifford, Vic. Gen., appears to have died in 1689.

Roger Anderton.

Thirston Anderton.

Thos. Hughson subscribed £10 in 1676, and £20 in 1691.

Geor. Crook.

Tho. Weedon subscribed £10 in 1675, and paid £200 in 1700. He was rural dean of Salford Hundred.

John Howes paid £10 in 1704.

Edw. Baldwin.

Rich. Penketh.

John Holden subscribed £10 in 1676.

Edw. Barlow subscribed £10 in 1676.

John Blackburn, Priest at Claughton.

John Tatlock paid £10 in 1692.

Peter Winder.

Henry Holden subscribed £20 in 1676.

Peter Gooden.

Nich. Sanderson.

Rich. Barton, op. fid. condemnatus.

John Jackson.

Edw. Blackburn subscribed £10 in 1680.

Francis Kirk, Priest at Hough, near New House, near Preston. Mrs. Grant, aunt of Rob. Gillow, Esq., boarded with him.

John Urmston.

John Kendal subscribed £10 in 1680.

James Swarbrick.

John Robinson.

Edw. Smith, *alias* Kitchen.

Nich. Banks.

Jas. Markland, *alias* Almond.

John Egerton paid £20 in 1691.

Wm. Gerard, *alias* Barton.

Nich. Metcalf.

Edw. Molineux.

Rich. Sales.

Tho. Eccleston paid £50 in Dec., 1694, Dec. rur. Derb.

Thos. Young.

— Hatherwaite, 1683, obiit.

— Marten.

Rich. Dorley.

Henry Long.

Edw. Anderton.

Matt. Harrison.

John Laiton.

John Blackburn.

Thos. Hayes.

Christ. Tootel.

Rich. Rivers.

Rich. Taylor.

Thos. Penketh paid £30 in 1735 for self and brothers, Chas. and Rich.

John Malburn.

Thos. Anderton.

A second list of the Priests belonging to the fund, beginning later than the former, but without date, and in the same handwriting. It is continued by different hands down to 1782. From 1754 it was kept, but in a slovenly manner, by Rev. John Carter, of Hollsforth, till 1782, then by Mr. Banister, Mr. Barrow, and Dr. Rigby unto this day.

Edw. Barlow, V.G., missioner at Park Hall.

Edw. Blackburn.

Francis Kirk.

James Swarbrick, Priest at Singleton.

John Kendal, brother of Hugo and Dr. George. Hugo was master at Sedgley, Geo. was at Fernyhalgh.

Rich. Taylor, *alias* Sherburn, at Claughton.

Chris. Tootel, V.G., at Fernyhalgh.

John Howse.

Rich. Penket.

Thos. Brockholes, probably meaning Roger, brother of Thos. and Chas., Thos. died missioner at Chillington.

Nich. Singleton.

Tho. Martin.

Tho. Weedon, rural dean of Salford Hundred, appears to have been on the mission from 1704 to 1719.

Roger Anderton.

Tho. Brooks, *alias* Young.

Thos. Eccleston.

Rich. Barton.

Edw. Molineux.

Christ. Laythorn.

Rich. Sales.

Wm. Gerard, *alias* Barton.

John Blackburn.

John Malbon.

Wm. Hawerden, G.V. in 1744.

John Pearson.

Hugh Hesketh. [Is not this Dodd? No date; but the name was written by the secretary who ceased to write in this register in 1704; there are ten names in that handwriting after Hugh Hesketh.]

Chas. Penketh.

James Charnley.

Tho. Royden.

John Knaresborough.

Thos. Wolful.

Geor. Bostoc.

Wm. Caton, Priest at Great Eccleston Lane, died at Cottam, with Thos. Holmes.

Thos. Taylor.

John Pearson.

The handwriting in which the above names are written does not appear in any part of the book after 1704.

Rob. Swarbrick, missioner at Singleton.

John Barton.

Tho. Anderton.

James Gerard.

John Wilkinson.

Geo. Ball.

Rich. Hitchmough. He fell, and was parson at Woodplumpton. He was cracked.

Wm. Winkley.

Tho. Smith.

Fran. Molins.

John Shepherd.

Edw. Hawerden, S.T.D., missioner at Aldcliffe, near Lancaster, where the Daltons then resided. His mission included Lancaster, where no Priest could then live with safety.

James Gant, missioner at Salwick Hall, Lancaster, a good man, died 1734.

Edw. Melling, nephew of Chr. Tootel, rural dean of Amounderness Hundred, Lancaster, obt. 17 Apr. 1732.

James Gorsuch.

Roger Brockholes, missioner at Claughton, died there in 1743.

Edw. Gilpin was missioner at Robert Hall, in Lancs.

John Swarbrick, missioner at Thurnham, near Lancaster.

John Lodge, *alias* Bates.

Cuthb. Haydock was afterwards at Worksop.

Laur. Rigby.

John Penketh.

Chris. Jenkinson, missioner in Wyersdale, Lancs.; born in Wyersdale, educated at Lisbon.

Wm. Fisher.

Nich. Skelton.

Charles Ingolby.

Tho. Lancaster.

Jos. Martin.

Jas. Skelton.

Thos. Hawarden.

James Gandy, missioner at Robert Hall, was from Liverpool.

Edw. Barlow.

Wm. Calvert.

Wm. Breres.

Tho. Townly.

Edw. Dicconson, Bishop.

Geo. Ball, Jun.

John Cowban, born in the Fylde, Lancs., was missioner some time at Exeter and at Cottam.

John Moore, missioner at Chipping Laund, Lancs.

Robert Kendall.

Geo. Kendall, S.T.D., missioner at Manchester [and] Fernyhalgh. Died abroad, insane.

Edw. Daniel, born in Lancs., missioner at Scorton [and] Scarborough.

John Carter, at New House in Lancs., had refuge in my grandfather's house at Clifton in 1745.

Geo. Boardley, born at Thurnham, Lancs., missioner at Mowbreck, Salwick, Moor Hall, &c.

Tho. Roydon, Grand Vicar, lived at Dodding Green, near Kendal.

Rob. Worswick, born in Lancs., was missioner some time at Singleton, then at Manchester; died there.

Jos. Barnes, missioner at Kendal.

John Serjeant, born at Cockenham, Lancs., educated at Douay, missioner at Scorton, Lancs., above fifty years; buried at Cockenham Church. He was author of *Turk and Pope* and some unpublished pieces of controversy against the Vicar of Garstang church town. Was one of the Priests confined in York jail in 1745 with Mr. Potts.

Emer. Grimbalston was missioner at Birchley in Lancs. under the Gerards.

Tho. Liddell, Douay, Priest. The first missioner who resided at Chester.

Wm. Pennington, missioner at Robert Hall, Lancs.

Thos. Penswick, born at Lytham in Lancs, missioner at Wycliffe. Lived with M. Tunstall, Esq.

Wm. Gant, missioner at Mowbrick. He afterwards became insane, and turned parson at Wray Green.

Rob. Worswick. [This name is in Mr. Carter's hand; the preceding gentleman belonged to the fund before 1754.]

Edw. Bell.

John Barrow, of saintly memory, missioner at Claughton.

Wm. Grimbleston, missioner at Wrightenton, Lancs.

Wm. Foster lived afterwards and died at Hazlewood. He promoted the study of Greek at Douay.

Peter Waring, missioner at Singleton, Park Hall, then at Chester.

John Cooling, missioner first at Singleton, then at Manchester, and died there.

Wm. Aldersey.

John Bamber, missioner itinerant in all Westmoreland and Cumberland, then at Durham in St. Giles's Gate, last at Sunderland by the Sea. He built the house and chapel at Sunderland.

Thos. Parkinson, perhaps at Blackbrook, killed there by a slate falling.

James Brown was natural son of Lord Nithsdale, who sent him to Douay. He was missioner at Manchester, then at Burscough many years till death.

John Davidson, born in Bishopric, missioner at Esh in Bishopric, then at Salwick, &c.

James Parkinson,

III.—Dr. R. Gradwell to Rev. J. Kirk.

Same source, pp. 1123-1126. Encloses the following.

CLAUGHTON, 2 March, 1817.

DEAR SIR,

Mr. G. Fitzherbert, who has been here since his return from India, leaves us to-morrow. He will pass through Staffordshire, perhaps through your city. I only learned this last night, but I have been endeavouring to prepare you a map and catalogue of all the Catholic chapels in Lancashire. Having been obliged to do it hastily and by candle-light, it is not so clear as I could wish; but it is pretty correct and, I think, compleat. Where the chapels do not belong to the secular clergy, I have mentioned to whom they belong. I have also pointed out by the cypher O a few places where chapels of note formerly existed, such as Sholley, Mowbrick, Salwick, Singleton, etc. These names will occur in your old manuscripts, and deserve a reference in the map. I have not time to give you a list of the incumbents and their predecessors at present. I have made some collections in this way, but have been so much occupied with other business all this winter that they are not yet in a fit state to give you satisfaction.

In the Catalogue of the ex-Jesuits which I sent you some time ago, it is expressly mentioned in the first page of the original from which yours is copied, that the third date is the Prof. The second date in Jos. Mosely is 1748 / 3 Vot / 1765. The name of Dame Alice was Harrison. The account Mr. Southworth has given you is accurate. She was born at Fulwood Row, near Preston; was well educated, and brought up to the profession of the Church of England. She was converted by reading Catholic books, and remaining firm, was severely persecuted, corporally chastised, and when this would not reclaim her, turned adrift by her father. She was encouraged by the Priest at Fernyhalgh, probably Mr. Melling, to open a school near Fernyhalgh at the house which I showed you. She had a very numerous school; children flocked to her from the neighbourhood, from Preston, the Fylde, Liverpool, Manchester, London, and all parts of England. She admitted scholars of all religions to the amount of between one and two hundred. She had another assistant called Mary Blackburn. The scholars boarded some with the dame, others in the cottages and farmhouses in the neighbourhood. They paid 1s. 6d. per quarter to the dame for schooling and £5 per annum for board, lodging, &c. She took all her Catholic scholars to prayers at the chapel every day, and always stopped to say a *Pater*, *Ave*, and *Credo* at our Lady's Well. The Rosary, Litanies, &c., were said every day in the school. Those children who were not Catholics were at liberty to absent themselves on this occasion if they pleased. All the people in the neighbourhood of Fernyhalgh were Catholics at that time, and both encouraged and protected the dame. Dame Alice lived to a great age, and was in her decline indebted for a comfortable retreat to the respectable family of the Orrels of Blackbrook.

These particulars I have learned from Mr. Peter Newby, who was her scholar, and from Miss Singleton, of Preston, an old lady who was once scholar of the dame, and afterwards for many years boarded many of her scholars.

I am in hopes of learning a few more particulars and anecdotes respecting this respectable woman, which I will communicate to you. In a few months I will send to the *Catholicon* some short memoirs of Rev. Charles Cordell, who was one of her scholars. I shall notice this circumstance. In consequence of which you may either write your queries respecting the little dame (she was a little woman), and I will answer them by a biographical notice, or you may draw up a notice yourself as you like best. Excuse the haste with which I am obliged to write this. It has been a very laborious Sunday. I shall be always happy to render you any assistance in my power. I have been pressed to write an answer to a virulent pamphlet lately published. I have begun it with reluctance, and I am afraid *pingui Minerva* in the *Catholicon*. This at such a time of the year when I have several sick to attend, &c., &c., has left me little time to assist your labours.

I am, dear Sir, truly yours,

ROB. GRADWELL.

Catalogue of Catholic Chapels in Lancashire.

Ulverston olim Exjt., lately by R. Rev. Dr. Everard, at present vacant.
Yealand.
Robert Hall, vacant at present.
Hornby.
Lancaster.
Thurnham.
Scorton.
Garstang.
Claughton.
Chipping, Exjesuit at present.
Stonyhurst, attached to it are Clithero, Coln, Dunkin Hall, Exjesuits.
Lee House, Franciscan.
Goosnargh, Franciscan.
Stid, near Ribchester, olim at Sholley.
Eccleston.
Poulton, olim at Singleton.
New House.
Fernyhalgh.
Alston.
Preston, Exjesuit.
Cottam.
Lea, olim at Salwick.
Kirkham, olim at Mowbrick.
Westby, Benedictine, olim Exjesuit.
Lytham.
Townley, French Priest.
Lower Hall, Friar Franciscan, vacant.
Brindle, Benedictine.
Blackburn.
Brownedge, Benedictine.
Southhill, olim Sladedelf, Exjesuit.
Euxton.
Croston, Benedictine, olim Sec. Cler.

Weldbank.
Fairhurst, Friar of some sort.
Scarisbrick, French Priest.
Burscough.
Ormskirk, Benedictine.
Lidyet, Exjt.
Moor Hall, or Boardley.
Ince Blundell.
Netherton, olim at Sefton, Bened.
Crosby, Exjt.
Formby.
Gill Moss, Exjt.
Standish, Bened.
Wigan, Exjt.
Ince.
Bolton.
Hindley, Exjt.
Wrightington, Bened., olim Sec. Cler.
Crosbrook.
Brinn.
Billinge.
Garswood.
Blackbrook.
St. Helen's, Exjt.
Portico, or Prescot, Exjt.
Liverpool, Benedictine and Sec. Cler. olim Exjt.
Woolton, Bened.
Appleton.
Southworth, Exjt. French Priest.
Warrington.
Culceth, Sec. Cler., vacant.
Leigh, Exjt.
Trafford.
Manchester.
Stockport.

IV.—THE FERNYHALGH LIST OF DECEASED PRIESTS, 1733-1739.

From the *Kirk Papers.* Same volume, p. 1131. This is an original document, with later notes by Rev. R. Gradwell in the margin, here printed in italics.

This list of deceased Priests from 1733 to 1739 was found at Fernyhalgh. Rev. Henry Gradwell is desired to send this paper to Rev. John Kirk, Lichfield.

R. GRADWELL.

Claughton, 28th Aug., 1817.

SACERDOTES DEFUNCTI.

1733.
Oct. 24.   Mr. John Vane, Capitular.

1733-4.
Jan. 11.   Mr. Thomas Mackworth.
Mar. 12.   The R. R. Bonaventure
                Giffard.
Mar. 20.   Mr. John Wilkinson.

1734.
May 12.   Mr. Francis Dod.
,, 31.   Mr. George Collingwood,
                Capitular.
June   Mr. William Moseley.
                Mr. Richard Bartlet.
                Mr. Francis Dodd.
Aug. 24.   Mr. Christopher Wytham.
Oct. 29.   Mr. James Gant.
Nov.   Mr. Richard Jameson, at
                Pemberton, near Wigan.
                Mr. William Prichard.
,, 26.   Mr. George Ball, senior.
Dec. 2.   Mr. Peter Brailsford.

1735.
Apr.   Mr. Edward Parkinson.
May   Mr. Edward Hawarden.
                Mr. Christopher Piggott.
July 14.   Mr. William Colvert.
,, 25.   Mr. Joseph Wolfe, Capitular.
Aug.   Mr. James Griffith.
                Mr. Robert Lane, *alias*
                Bows.*

1735-6.
Jan.   Mr. William Jones.
Feb.   Mr. Edward Barlow, *Park
                Hall, V.G.*
,, 20.   Mr. William Hickin.
Mar. 3.   Mr. Robert Borry.

1736.
April 28.   Mr. William Adison, at
                Aldbrough.
June 24.   Mr. John Sharp, *alias*
                Gunsong, at London.
                Mr. John Wolfe, Capitular,
July 20.†   mentioned by Mr. Day.
                Mr. Joseph Gildon, vid.
                Berin(gton).
Sept. 24.   Mr. Charles Higgs, in
                Cornwall.
Dec.   Mr. Gregory Grange, *alias*
                Yaxley, in the Christmass
                holy days

1736-7.
Jan. 7.   Mr. Henry Harneage,
                Capitular.
,, 24.   Mr. George Leyburn.
:, 27.   Mr. John Standford,
                Capitular.
Feb. 25.   N.S. 14th O.S., the Right
                Honble. John Savage,
                Earl of Rivers, Capitular.
,, 25.   O.S. Mr. Robert Swarbrick,
                Subscriber.
Mar. 9.   Mr. Thomas Townley, Sub-
                scriber.

1737.
Apr. 17.   Mr. Reginald Williams,
                Capitular.
Aug. 6.   Mr. James Augustin Jones.
Sept. 4.   N.S. at Lisbon } Tobias
                Mr. Berington } Gibbons.
                Oct. 11 }

1737.   Sacerdotes Defuncti.
Sept.   } Mr. Edward Jones,
Dec. 23 N.S.   } President of Lisbon.
1737-8.   Mr. Jonathan Elston, vid.
                Carnaby de Yorkshire.

1738.
May 18.   Mr. Robert Wytham,
                President of Douay.
June 28.   Mr. John Liddel.
May   Mr. Jonas Bourne, at
                Hexham *sine die.*
July 8.   Mr. Joseph Price.
Oct. 10.   Thomas Brockholes, senior,
                at Bugh, near Chorley,
                Subscriber.
Dec. 14.   Mr. James Dod, at Twick-
                enham, Governor to **Lord**
                Montaigue.

1738-9.
Jan. 19.   Mr. James Gorsuch, Rural
                Dean.
Jan. 29 N.S.   Dr. John Ingleton,
                President of St. Gregory's.
Jan. 29.   Mr. John Shuttleworth,
                Nottinghamshire.
1739.
May 20.   Mr. Nicholas Leyburn,
                Subscriber in Cheshire.
June 16.   Mr. John Johnson, in
                Staffordshire.

---

* *Query. Was not this Robert Lane, alias Bows, the author of " Practical
Reflections" ? R. Gradwell has heard Rev. Thomas Eyre say so. Mr. Bows was
a Douay Priest.*

† *This date is between Wolfe and Gildon, and might apply to either.*

V.—Dr. Gradwell to Dr. Kirk.

Dear Sir,

I send you a parcel of scraps and memorandums. I am sorry they are in such an imperfect state, but I have not now time to improve them. They are the result of my enquiries from well-informed persons and just what I wrote down in my pocket-book at the time, with a view of drawing up a few biographical lists and notices for you. Though they are slovenly and imperfect, some of them may perhaps be useful. I have, therefore, resolved to send these papers to you rather than destroy them. I shall either send them to you before my departure for Rome or desire my brother Henry, who is coming from Ushaw to succeed me at Claughton, to send them after I am gone. Perhaps I may have an opportunity of being serviceable to you where I am going; I shall be happy to do so. If I have an opportunity of passing through Lincoln I will contrive to stop a day with you. I wish every success to your history.

I am, dear Sir,
Yours truly,
R. Gradwell.

Claughton, 31st *August*, 1817.

In the *Original* list of the Jesuits the last column of dates has *Prof.* above it.

John Shepherd, born in Lancashire, was afterwards at Egton Bridge, Yorkshire.

John Harrison at Cottam. In 1745 his house and chapel burnt down. He resisted the ruffians with intrepidity.

Hugh Edmondson, born in Lancashire, missioner at Alston, near Preston, uncle of his successor, late Rev. Richard Edmondson.

James Morley, *alias* Wilson, missioner at Greystock, Alston, and Ugthorpe; turned insane, died in Asylum at York.

Philip Butler, missioner at Blackbrooke, Lancashire, built the chapel there; great friend of Bp. Petre; succeeded by Rev. John Orrell.

John Chadwick, born at or near Preston; V.G. missioner at Weldbank, built the house and old chapel; succeeded by Rev. Richard Thompson, V.G.

Francis Cliffe, missioner at Eccleston, Lancashire, a good preacher, failed in strength some years before his death; assisted and succeeded by Henry Parkingson.

Marmaduke Wilson, brother of Rev. Robert Wilson, *alias* Langstaff, born in Yorkshire, missioner—still living at Appleton, Lancashire, assisted by Thomas Pinnington.

William Fisher, was missionary at Sholley, Lancashire; retired in his latter years and died at Stid Lodge, Ribchester; succeeded by Mr. Wagstaffe.

Michael Wharton, Lisbon Priest, was born near Kirby Stephen at Grey Rig, rural dean of Lonsdale Hundred, very respected missioner at Yealand; succeeded by Basil Barrett.

Richard Talbot, missioner at Thornton, Yorkshire, born at Wheelton in Lancashire.

James Maudsley, *alias* Carter, born in Lancashire, educated at Douay, assisted and succeeded his uncle, John Carter, at Newhouse, Lancashire, assisted and succeeded by his nephew, Henry Carter.

Thomas Johnson, Dodding Green, Westmoreland.

William Gant, fell and turned silly.

Robert Johnson, at Kendal, has been blind several years. Could say great part of Breviary by heart.

James Barrow, born at Westby, studied at Rome, missioner at Ness in Yorkshire; died there, brother of John, Joseph, and Richard.

John Lund, born in Boston, Lancashire, educated at Douay, was missioner first at Swinburne Castle, Northumberland, then at Lartington, Yorkshire;

then at Cottam 53 years ; rural dean of Amunderness Hundred, good preacher ; died at Cottam, aged 81 ; buried in his chapel, neat monument to him.

ARTHUR STORY, born in Northumberland, educated at Douay, Theol. Licen., Paris, missioner at Singleton, Lancashire, Tudhoe in Co. Durham, Robert Hall, and now at Garstang.

JOHN MARSDEN, missioner at Chester, born at Stone Bridge in Barton, near Preston.

ROBERT BANISTER MOWBRECK, born at Hesketh, Bank, etc., etc.

WILLIAM HUSBAND, born in Lancashire ; Douay ; missioner at Salwick Hall, Lancashire, died of smallpox, caught by attending his sick.

JOSEPH ORRELL, born at Blackbrooke, Lancashire, missioner many, near 40, years at Singleton, now at Blackbrooke.

JOHN ORRELL, brother to the above gentleman, prefect at Douay, missioner at Blackbrooke, succeeded Mr. Philip Butler, his uncle ; was succeeded by Joseph Orell.

WILLIAM HALLIWELL, missioner at Greystock, Cumberland, the seat of the Duke of Norfolk, born in Lancashire.

CHARLES HOUGHTON, born at Preston, missioner at Manchester, then in Yorkshire at Carleton ; died at York while on a visit.

ROWLAND BROOMHEAD, born at Sheffield, missioner at Manchester, educated at Rome, at Manchester.

FRANCIS BLUNDELL, born near Ince Blundell, Douay, missioner at Stony-hurst.

ROBERT WILSON, *alias* Langstaffe, brother of Marmaduke, born in York-shire ; Douay, Paris ; missioner at Salwick ; good man.

EDWARD DANIEL, born at Kirkham, brother of John Daniel, president. Edward is the first missioner at Croston, Lancashire, now at Garswood.

JAMES LAWRENSON, born at Claughton, Lancashire ; Douay missioner, Chipping Lawn, now at Scorton, Lancashire.

WILLIAM DUNN, S.T.D., born at Brough, Yorkshire ; Douay, Paris ; 1st missioner at Blackburne ; died saying Mass there.

THOMAS CATON, born at Preston, educated at Lisbon ; missioner at Townley, Lancashire ; succeeded John Lund at Cottam, still living.

ROBERT SWARBRECK, born at Weeton, Lancashire, missioner at Euxton, Lancashire ; built the Priest's house ; died there, succeeded by John Bell.

EDWARD HAWERDEN, missioner at Wrightington, Lancashire, many years.

NICHOLAS SKELTON, missioner at Lancaster, was succeeded by Mr. Tyrer, and then by Dr. John Rigby. Mr. Skelton was related to the Salvins and Scroopes ; he was put in prison at Lancaster Castle in 1745, at the same time as Mr. Edward Barrow.

In Bishop Leyburn's Confirmation list published in CATHOLICON. The Lodge was Sir Thomas Tildesley's residence. It is in Myerscough, three miles S.W. of Claughton, two miles N. of New House. Nateby was the Leyburn family's residence, a mile north of Garstang. Leighton, or Layton, near Yealand, belonging to the Townleys, is ten miles N. of Lancaster ; Aldcliffe and Thurnham a little S.W. of Lancaster. Euxton never belonged to the Daltons, but to the Andertons, to whom it still belongs. Dame Alice buried at the Catholic burying place, Windleshaw, near Prescot. She was patronised in her old age by the Gerard family, not the Orrels.

Dr. Thomas and Dr. John Rigby born near Wigan.

Rev. James Haydock, born at Tagg, near Preston, educated at Douay, was professor of Syntax there ; ordained at Arras in 1792, went on the mission soon after, and was domestic chaplain to John Trafford, Esq., Trafford House, about 15 years ; he then went to Lea, near Preston. He caught a fever in attending the sick of his congregation, and died a martyr of charity 1808 or 9. He was a learned, laborious and very virtuous missionary. He was buried in the cemetery of New House Chapel, where a neat monument is erected to his memory. He was some years prefect of the study place, and taught catechism at Douay. He excelled in teaching the catechism.

Rev. George Leo Haydock, brother to the above, born *ut supra*, was a scholar of Mr. Banister at Mowbrick Hall ; then went to Douay in 178- ; was a most indefatigable student. Escaped when in Philosophy from France a little while before the gentlemen of Douay College were imprisoned (he escaped in company with Rev. William Davis, then professor of Grammar, an excellent master, native of Monmouthshire, missioner at Chepstow). Mr. G. Haydock then was a short time at Old Hall Green with Richard Thompson, Thomas Gillow, Thomas Penswick, Charles Saul, etc., his fellow students at Douay. He followed them to Crook Hall, studied his divinity there, and defended his *theologia universa* with great applause in 1798. He taught Humanity there perhaps two years, and read incessantly the Fathers, divines and biblical commentators. He then went on the mission to Ugthorpe, where he is still living. Mr. G. Haydock wrote the prefaces and notes for his brother Thomas's edition in 3 V. fol. of the Bible. But as the printing went on rapidly, I believe Rev. Bent. Rayment took the charge of annotating on the gospels, if not on the whole New Testament.

Thomas Haydock, brother of the above, studied at Douay, a little while at Lisbon, a year at Crook Hall. He did not take holy orders, but became a printer at Manchester and then at Dublin. He is still living there low in the world.

A sister of these three Haydocks went abroad to the Augustin Convent at (blank in MS.), and was professed there. She is, I believe, still alive with her community at Spettisbury.

Rev. Thomas Penswick, born in Lancashire, at Senley Green, near Garswood (his most respectable father was steward to Sir William Gerard, of Garswood), was at school at Prescot—then at Highton, near Preston, under Mr. Peter Newby, then at Douay till he escaped the day before we were put in prison, then at Old Hall a while, lastly for his Divinity at Crook Hall, which he defended well, then on the mission at Chester—built the present chapel, published a sermon there, removed to the new elegant chapel in Liverpool, Copperas Hill, where he still remains. I believe he translated Boudon on the Holy Sacrament published by Thomas Haydock.

John Penswick, his brother, educated at Sedgely Park, then went to Douay, was in prison at Dourlens, continued his studies from Poetry upwards at Crook Hall ; soon after his ordination went on the mission to Birchley Lane, where he still remains.

Thomas Gillow was born at Great Singleton, Lancashire, went to Douay ; in Philosophy escaped *ut supra* ; went a short time to Old Hall, finished his Divinity at Crook Hall, then went to be domestic chaplain to John Clavering, Esq., at Callaly, Northumberland, where he still remains. He wrote *Catholic Principles of Allegiance* ; he was schoolfellow with Mr. Thompson and Mr. Thomas Penswick.

Rev. Richard Thompson, our present V.G., was born at Scholes, a part of Wigan, was patronised by the late Rev. J. Chadwick, of Weldbank, and sent to Douay by him.

Rev. George Gibson, Right Rev. Matthew, Right Rev. William, Rev. Richard Gibson were all brothers born at Stonecroft, near Hexham. Thomas Gibson, missioner at Newcastle-on-Tyne, was their uncle.

Rev. Luke Potts was born at Throckly, near Newcastle. Soon after his arrival in England from Douay he was seized at Ugthorpe with Rev. John Sergeant and others and committed to York Gaol. Potts was missioner at Thropton, Northumberland.

Rev. John Coates, born at Aldwick (Douay Priest), was missioner at Netherwitton, in Northumberland ; lived to above 90, died at Thropton.

Henry Swinburne, Esq., born at Capheaton, in Northumberland ; educated at St. Gregory's, Douay ; resided much abroad in high life at the Courts of Madrid, Naples, etc., author of *Travels in Spain*, ditto in *The Two Sicilies*, etc. ; married Miss Baker, daughter of a rich merchant, a lady of great learning. Hamsterly, in Co. Durham, was his residence. He was appointed by Government to an office (I think in Trinidad), where he died 18—. He told Mr. Eyre that there were many reflections in his books respecting religion, monks, etc., which, though he thought them true at the time he wrote them, he had since been convinced were false, and acknowledged that an ambition in his early life to be considered liberal and free from religious prejudice induced him to write some reflections which he afterwards regretted.

Rev. Arthur Story, born at Cartington Hall, near Rothbury, Northumberland, educated at Mr. Boardley's school three years; then to Douay, till the end of Rhetoric, five or six years; then to the Seminary at Paris, seven years; made Bachelor of Divinity (studied Divinity under Abbé Plunkett, afterwards Grand-Vicar in Paris, an eminent theologian), ordained Priest there by Archbishop Christophe de Beaumont; was chaplain to the Augustin nuns at Fossees, Rue St. Victor, two years; came in 1769 to be missioner at Singleton, Lancashire, two years; then was domestic chaplain to William Salvin, Esq., Croxdale; then established a respectable school at Tudhoe, and presided over it 27 years; then missioner at Robert Hall, Lancashire, four years; now living at Garstang.

— Holden, D.D., of Sorbonne, and Superior of the English Seminary, born in Lancashire, educated at Douay; a very learned divine. While Superior of the Seminary (perhaps about 1750) he purchased houses in the Rue de Fours in Paris for the Seminary. The Attorney ran away [with] the purchase-money, which involved Dr. Holden and the Seminary in difficulties and debts. His manuscripts were seized by his creditors; among the rest a valuable course of divinity. It was adopted by one French Bishop in his Seminary. Thomas Duke of Norfolk, called the good duke, was a considerable benefactor to the Seminary on this occasion. Dr. Holden was succeeded by Dr. Charles Howard, then the Duke's chaplain at Norfolk House.

Charles Howard (the one still living) was born at North End, near Ince-Blundell, Lancashire; sent to Douay about 1753, went to the Seminary, Paris, at the end of Rhetoric; performed his Philosophy and Theology there, and took the degree of D.D.; was very learned; agreeable, pleasant and dignified in his manners and conversation; was missioner at York, and went thence to Marton, near Burton Constable, Yorkshire; has been about 43 years missioner.

Abbé Plunkett, an Irishman, was an eminent professor of divinity in college of Navarre at Paris; was afterwards Grand-Vicar of Paris; an eminent moral divine and casuist, and chief author of the theological and didactic part of the Pastorale Parisiense or Paris ritual, a work in high estimation about the year 1760.

Charles Howard, Esq., of Greystock, who afterwards became Duke of Norfolk, wrote a sensible book, entitled *Thoughts, Essays and Maxims*, chiefly religious and political, 12mo, London, 1768. Mr. Kirk may transcribe the character of the Duke of Berwick from this book into his history. It is in Mr. Brockholes's library.

VI.—SCRAPS AND MEMORANDA.

These are scraps and memoranda on pages evidently torn from a note-book, in the handwriting of Dr. Gradwell, some in pencil inked over. The sequence is far from clear. They have been pasted together and form pages 1134 and 1139-1140 of Kirk's Collectanea Anglo-Catholica, Vol. III.

Rev. Thomas Reid, a Scotchman, was educated at Rome, and became a secular Priest. He left Rome about 1765, and stopped at Paris a few weeks; he was proceeding to the mission in Scotland. The theatre of his missionary labours for nearly half a century was at ———, near Gordon Castle, in Banffshire, among the numerous Catholic tenantry of the Duke.

Sir James Gordon, Bart., of Letter Fourie, near Cullen, was in his congregation. He died a year or two ago. Mr. Reid was author of *Sermons on the Nativity*, etc.

Priests at Preston—Jesuits.

Mr. Porter, ————, Barnwell, Smith, Mr. Jenison, — Dunn, — Morgan.

Alston.

Hugh Edmondson, — Wilson, Richard Edmondson.

John Blackburn was owner of Buller's land.

Lady Stourton settled £20 a year for ————, Jesuit at Preston, and Mrs. Sandforth gave the house in Friargate. Mr. Leigh was one of the first, and baptised Mrs. Woodcock.

Mr. Harrison went from Cottam to Townley, and served as long as he was able ; died in Friargate with his brother, Laurence, in Preston.

Charles Houghton ran away from his mission and travelled in Italy with a Mr. Battersby ; collected paintings, etc., which were seized. Suspended for going without leave ; never was the same man afterwards.

John Harrison, Cottam, had chapel built in 1745.

Mrs. Kitchin, born at Ribbleton.

Southerds, ————, born in Catforth.

Priests at Manchester.

Dr. Kendall, after he had been missioner at Sutton, was some time Priest at Manchester, then at Fernyhalgh.

Mr. Brown was there some time, but went to Burscough.

Mr. Thomas Brockholes, brother of Rev. Roger [?] and of Rev. Charles Brockholes, was Priest at Manchester some years and left £100 to the place. He was afterwards at Chillingham.

Mr. Johnson afterwards at Dodding Green.

Mr. Salus, a Jesuit (about a year) ; both served there some time.

Mr. Hulme (who had been professor of philosophy at Douay and was an eminent scholar) was here several years.

Rev. John Orrell, who was general-prefect at Douay when the new refectory was opened in 177- ; served at Manchester two or three years, but then went to succeed his uncle, Philip Butler, at Blackbrooke.

Rowland Broomhead, born at Sheffield and educated at Rome, and Charles Houghton, born at Preston, came to Manchester in 1777. Charles Houghton went about 1797 to Carleton, and died there. About 1793 the new chapel opened and served by Mr. Kenyon. Manchester was Mr. Thompson's first mission in 1797 till the death of Mr. Chadwick, of Weldbank, when Mr. Thompson succeeded Mr. C.

Rev. Thomas Lupton, born at Claughton, 27th March, 1776, son of the gardener of James Brockholes, Esq., sent to Douay by Mr. Brockholes, and supported wholly by that most religious and charitable gentleman ; was a prisoner at Dourlens in 1793-4, but escaped ; finished his studies at Crookhall.

Mr. Broomhead and Mr. Lupton have been two of the most indefatigable and valuable missioners of our time.

James Mather, born in ————, went to Lambspring, became a monk, and died there.

George Duckett, born at Claughton, O.S.B. missioner at Strangeways, Lancashire, built the chapel at Hendley and died there of a dropsy soon after.

Edward Kitchin, born at Grims—gh, was a scholar of Richardson at Plumpton Gt.

Wigforth was a Priest, born in Ballam.

James Tyrer, of Lancaster, born at St. Helens, came about 1760.

Adam Tyrer, his brother, missioner in Wales.

Skreton very poor ; about £10.
Conyers at Eccleston, a Jesuit.
Weldon, an Irishman, Jesuit.
Nailor at Brindle.
Many French banished about 50 years ago at Liverpool ; Great Cowley Hill.
Richard Skelton died in 1766 ; had been 40 years a Westmoreland man.
Tyrer, born at St. Helens, died November, 1784.
Dr. Hawarden at Aldcliffe, near Lancaster.

Garstang Chapel (built in 1785).

Mr. Shuttleworth, Mr. Barnes, Mr. John Worswick, Mr. John Barrow, Mr. Arthur Story.

Scorton Chapel.

Jenkinson died in 1723, John ————, James Laurenson.
Forster, Walmsley, Daniel.—Daniel was too busy at 1745 ; went abroad and returned to Robert Hall or Hornby, then to Scarborough. He was a relation to the present Daniels and E. Melling. The rich Jenny Daniel, of Euxton, was his sister.

Thurnham.

Mr. Carteret, of the Carteret family, perhaps Lord himself.

Chapel in the Hall.

James Forster, first that resided.

Lancaster.

Nicholas Skelton, James Tyrer, John Rigby.

Priests at Claughton.

There was always a Priest there since the Reformation.
Rev. Mr. Walmsley, Rev. Mr. Blackburn.
Richard Taylor, alias Sherburne, born at Claughton, was alive 1711.
Rev. Roger Brockholes, brother of Rev. Thomas, junior, and Rev. Charles Brockholes, Douay Priest, died before 1745.
Rev. James Parkinson, born at Claughton, was a Douay Priest, and served this place 22 years ; died of a fever caught by attending his flock.
Rev. John Barrow, born at Westby, brother of several Priests, educated at Rome. On his return there in philosophy he was impressed at Portsmouth and served as common sailor on board a man-of-war seven years. Escaped at last by swimming. Finished his studies at Douay, came to Claughton 1766, died there February 11th, 1811. He was a man of vigorous faculties, but rough and singular temper. He was a good missioner.
Rev. Robert Gradwell, younger twin, born at Clifton, near Preston, January 26th, 1777 ; schooled there. Arrived at Douay, 30th September, 1791. Imprisoned with the rest, October 12th, 1793. Returned to England with the rest of the gentlemen of Douay and St. Omers Colleges, March 2nd, 1795. Finished his studies and ordained Priest at Crook Hall, December 4th, 1802. Taught rhetoric and poetry there seven years. Arrived at Claughton, July 22nd, 1809. He is the last of the Douay students who took to the Church.

At Westby Chapel, Lancashire.

Mr. Lee, Jesuit ; Mr. Hunter, Jesuit, 1745 ; Thomas Cuerden, Jesuit ; Mr. Butler, O.S.B., living there.

Lytham Hall Chapel.

Mr. Mansel, Jesuit ; Mr. Pope, O.S.B., went thence to Netherton ; Thomas Dawson.

Eccleston.

Mr. Caton, Francis Cliffe, Henry Parkinson.

Mowbrick Hall.

James Gaunt, Mr. Jones, Mr. Banister, Mr. William Irving, Thomas Sherburne.

Priests at Chester.

Thomas Liddell, — Cooling, Tindale (some time), Richardson, Marsden, John Lancaster, Thomas Penswick, John Ashurst.

Right Rev. William Sharrock was born in Friar Gate, Preston, 30th March, 1742 ; went to St. Gregory's, Douay, May 6th, 1755.

Rev. James Sharrock was born in Walton-le-Dale, 5th February, 1750. He became prior of St. Gregory's ; was a prisoner at Dourlens then, having refused the mitre of the Western district ; died at Acton Burnell.

Rev. John Sharrock, born at Walton, 26th May, 1756 ; became a lay brother O.S.B. at Douay ; still living.   These were all brothers.

Thomas Eccleston, of Eccleston, went to Ireland with James ; fought a duel and was wounded ; left the estate to Mr. Scarisbrick, to Thomas B. Scarisbrick of Scarisbrick ; became a Jesuit and was Priest at Eccleston ; wrote *The Way to Happiness.*

Rev. Mr. Eccleston, *alias* Gosswick, V.G.

Hornby Chapel (built by Mrs. Fenwick).

Thomas Butler, John Worswick, John Lingard.

Robert Hall (by Gerard family).

Gandy, Mr. Pennington, A. Story.

Yealand Chapel (built by the Townleys).

Michael Wharton, Basil Barrett.

New House Chapel (built by John Carter).

John Carter, James Maudsley, *alias* Carter, Henry Carter.

— Barnes, a great ornament of Douay College, was Priest at Kendal some years, but afterwards went to Sir — Blount's, and died there.

Before Mr. Hunter, Lee was at Westby, John White at Euxton, Luke White at Alston, Swarbrick at Thurnham, William Forster at Thurnham, — Moore at Thurnham, died at Bath.

Mr. Edward Melling, of Fernyhalgh, buried at Broughton, was half-brother of Mrs. Helen Jenkinson.   He was brother to the grandmother of Thomas, John and Edward Daniel ; and had a brother Priest, confessor at Louvain.

CLASSIFIED LISTS OF BIOGRAPHIES

AND

Indices of Aliases, Catholic Houses, Stations, Chapels, Convents, Schools, &c.

These lists are arranged under the following heads : (I.) BISHOPS ; (II.) CAPITULARS (*i.e., members of the old Clergy Chapter*) *and other* CHURCH DIGNITARIES ; (III.) SECULAR PRIESTS : (IV.) RELIGIOUS ORDERS ; (A) *Benedictines,* (B) *Carmelites,* (E) *Dominicans,* (F) *Franciscans,* (G) *Jesuits, etc.* ; (V.) PEERS, *according to both their titles and their family names ;* (VI.) BARONETS, *according to their family names ;* (VII.) LAYMEN ; (VIII.) NUNS AND LADIES ; (IX.) RELIGIOUS NAMES AND ALIASES ; (X.) APOSTATES ; (XI.) CATHOLIC HOUSES, CHAPELS, CONVENTS, *etc.*

I.—BISHOPS.

Berington, Charles, 16

Challoner, Richard, 42
Collingridge, Peter, O.S.F., 51

Dicconson, Edward, 63
Douglass, John, 66

Fenwick, Edward Dominic, 79

Gibson, Matthew, 97 ; William, 98
Giffard, Bonaventure, 100
Gradwell, Robert, 104

Hornyold, John, 125
Howard, Henry, 129 ; Richard, 131
Hussey, Thomas, 135

Maire, William, 155
Milner, John, 164

Paterson, Alexander, 178
Penswick, Thomas, 179
Petre, Benjamin, 181 ; Francis (III.), 182
Poynter, William, 189
Pritchard, Matthew, 192

Stapleton, Gregory, 218
Stonor, John Talbot, 220
Strickland, Tho. Jh. Fran. 223

Talbot, James, 228 ; Thomas Joseph, 228

Walmesley, Charles, 243
Walton, William, 243
Williams, Dominic, O.P., 250
Witham, George, 252

II.—CAPITULARS AND DIGNITARIES.

Allibon, Job, 1
Anderton, Roger, 2 ; Thomas, 4

Barnard, Gerard, 10 ; James, 10
Barnesley, John, 11
Barrett, George, 11
Beeston, Robert, 15
Berington, Simon, 20 ; Thomas, 21
Betts, John, 23

Bew, John, 24
Bishop, George, 26
Blackburne, Edward, 27
Bolton, Joseph, 30
Brockholes, Roger (I.), 34 ; Thomas, 35
Browne, James, 36 ; Peter, 37
Busby, John, 38
Buxton, George, 39
Byflet, William, 49

19

CAPITULARS AND DIGNITARIES—*continued.*

Vane, John, 241
Varley, Thomas, 241
Vintner, Robert, 242

Ward, John, 243
Watkinson, Matthias, 244
Wharton, Michael, 247

Whittingham, Thomas, 249
Williams, Reginald, 251
Winstanley, Edmund, 252
Witham, Christopher, 252 ; Robert, 253
Wright, Thomas, 255

Yaxley, John, 256 ; Thomas, 256

III.—SECULAR PRIESTS.

Adams, Thomas, 1
Addis, Joseph, 1
Addison, William, 1
Allen, Henry, 1 ; Jerome, 1
Anderson, Sir William, 2
Anderton, Bruno, 2
Angel, James, 4
Apedaile, George, 4
Appleton, James, 4
Archdeacon, Robert, 4
Archer, James, 4
Ashmall, Ferdinand, 7

Ball, Edward, 9 ; George, 9 ; John, 9
Bamber, John, 9
Barnaby, Thomas, 10
Barrett, Edward, 11
Barrow, John, 11
Barton, Richard, 12
Basset, Joshua, 12
Bates, John, 13
Bear, Matthew, 13
Beaumont, Edward, 13
Beeston, George, 15 ; Peter, 15
Bellasyse, Charles, D.D., 16
Benyon, Thomas, 16
Berington, Joseph, 17
Bernard, William, 23
Berry, Matthew, 23
Billinge, Thomas, 25
Blackburne, John, 27
Bloodworth, Thomas, 27
Blount, Walter, 29
Booth, John, 31
Bordley, Simon George, 31
Bostock, George (I.), 32 ; George (II.), 32
Bosvile, John, 32
Bower, William, 32
Bowes, Robert, 32 ; Stanislaus, 33 ; Stephen, 33
Bradshaw, John, 33
Brailsford, Peter, 33
Brand, John, 33
Brian, or Bryan, John, 34, 37
Bridgwood, Thomas, 34
Brockholes, Roger (II.), 35
Bromhead, Roland, 37
Bromwich, Andrew, 35

Browne, James, 36
Bullen, Robert, 38
Butler, Alban, 38 ; Philip, 38 ; Thomas, 39
Byon, ———, 40

Cardwell, John, 40
Carter, John (I.), 41 ; John (II.), 41
Catrow, Charles, 42
Chamberlayne, George, 43
Churcher, John, 44
Clavering, Ralph, 44
Clayton, Thomas, 45
Clifford, William, 47
Codrington, Thomas, 49
Cordell, Charles, 58
Corne, James, 58 ; John, 58
Cornethwaite, Richard, 58
Cornwall, J. M., 59
Cowban, John, 59
Coyney, Edward, 59
Crathorne, Francis, 59

Dalton, Marmaduke, 61
Daniel, Edward, 61 ; John (I.), 61 ; John (II.), 62 ; Richard, 62
Davies, Chas. or Samuel, 62 ; James, 62 ; Rowland, 63
Debord, John, 63
Digby [? Joseph], 64
Diggs, J. D., 64
Denmore, ———, 64
Dobson, Thomas, 64
Dodd, Charles, 65
Downs, Richard, 66
Doyly, James, 66
Dunn, Francis, 67 ; Peter, 67
Duvall, Edward, 67

Edisford, James [? William], 68
Edmondson, Henry, 68 ; Hugh, 68
Elston, John, 69
Errington, William, 70
Eustace, John Chetwode, 70
Eyre, Edward, 71 ; John, 71

Farmer, ———, 78
Fell, Charles, 79

SECULAR PRIESTS—*continued.*

SECULAR PRIESTS—*continued.*

Meynell, Anthony, 163 ; James, 163
Midford, Roger, 163
Milford, or Mitford, James, 163
Miller, John, 163
Molins, ——, 166
Moore, John, 168
Morgan, David, 169 ; John (II.), 169 ; William, 170

Nassau, John, 171
Needham, ——, 171
Nestfield, John, 172
Newton, Robert, 173 ; Vincent, 173

Onions, Thomas, 174
Orrell, Joseph, 175
Owen, Hugh, 175 ; John, 175

Parker, Francis, 176
Parkinson, ——, 177 ; Thomas, 177
Parry, Pierce, 177
Peach, Henry, 178
Pearson, William, 178 ; Thomas, 178
Pembridge, Philip, 178
Penketh, William, 179
Penrice, Charles, 179
Perkins, Francis, 179
Perry, Philip Mark, D.D., 180
Petre, Francis (I.), 181 ; Francis (II.), 181
Pickering, Francis, 183 ; Lancelot, 183
Pinckard, ——, 184
Plowden, Abbé, Francis (I.), 185
Plummerden, Thomas, 186
Plunkett, ——, Abbé, 186
Postlethwaite, John, 188
Potts, Luke, 188
Poyntz, Augustin, 191
Preston, John, 192
Pulton, William, 192
Purcell, Walter Chetwynd, 192

Reeve, John, 196
Reid, Thomas, 196
Richardson, Richard, 197
Richmond, William, 197
Riddle, Robert, 197
Rigby, John, D.D., 198
Rivers, John, 200 ; Richard, 200
Rivet, John, 200
Robinson, Stephen, 200
Roe, John, 200
Rout, John, 202

Salkeld, Thomas, 204
Saltmarsh, Gerard, 204
Serjeant, John, 205

Shelley, Thomas, 207
Sheppard, Joseph (I.), 208 ; Joseph (II.), 208
Shimmel, Charles, 209 ; Richard, 209 ; Thomas, 209
Shuttleworth, John (I.), 210 ; John (II.), 210
Simpson, John, 211
Skelton, Nicholas, 211
Skroopham, John, 211
Slaughter, George, 212
Smith, Francis, 212 ; John, 212 ; John, 213 ; Robert, 213 ; Thomas, 213 ; William, 213
Smithson, Augustine, 213
Southworth (4 brothers), ——, 215
Stanford, John, 216
Stanley, John, 217
Stevenson, Paul, 219
Storey, Arthur, 221
Strickland, Joseph, 222
Stycke, John, 223 ; ——, 223
Swarbrick, James, 223
Syers, Joseph, 225

Talbot, Gilbert, 227
Tavener, ——, 230
Taylor, Alexander, 230 ; James, 230
Thompson, Lancelot, 231
Thorpe, John, 232
Turvile, William (II.), 238
Typper, ——, 240

Usher, James, 240

Valentine, Joseph, 241
Vaughan, Arthur, 241

Waldegrave, Nicholas, 242
Ward, Robert, 244
Weatherby, Thomas, 245
Webb, James, 245
Whetenhall, James, 247
White, John, 248 ; Lucas, 248 ; Richard, 248 ; Thomas, 248
Whitehall, Andrew, 248
Widdrington, Henry, 249 ; Robert, 249
Wilkinson, William, 250
Wilmot, John, 251 ; William, 251
Wilson, Thomas (I.), 251 ; Thomas (II.), 252
Winder, Peter, 252
Witham, Anthony, 252 ; Thomas, D.D., 254
Woodroffe, Robert, 254
Worswick, Robert, 254
Wright, John, 255

IV.—RELIGIOUS ORDERS.

RELIGIOUS ORDERS—*continued.*

Bedingfield, Chas. Bonaventure, 15
Bernardine, ———, 23
Bishop, Henry, 26
Bix, Angel, 26

Chapman, Francis, 43
Clifton, Bernardine, 48
Codrington, Anthony, 49
Cross, Nicholas, 60

Englefield, Charles or Francis, 69
Eyston, Bernard Francis, 75

Frost, Peter, 88

Hill, Augustin, 119

Kemble, William, 143

Lloyd, Sylvester Lewis, 152

Needham, Joseph, 172
Nutt, Pacificus, 174

O'Leary, Arthur, 174

Parkinson, Cuthbert [Anthony], 176
Parr, Francis, 177
Pilling, John, 184 ; William, 184

Rigby, James, 198

Simpson, Boniface, 210

(G) *Jesuits.*

Alloway, John, 2
Anderton, Christopher, 2
Aston, William, 7
Atkinson, James or John, 8

Blake, James, 27
Booth, Charles, 30 ; Ralph, 31
Bracey, Edmund, 33
Brewer, John, 33 ; Thomas, 34
Browne, Levinus, 36

Carroll, John (Abp. of Baltimore), 41
Chamberlain, John, 42
Champion, John, 43
Clifford, Walter, 46
Clifton (Francis, Sen.), 48
Clinton, Alexander, 49
Collingwood, Robert, 52
Constable, John, 54 ; Robert, 56
Conyers, John, 57
Cuerdon, Thomas, 60

Dean, Thomas, 63
Dunn, Joseph, 67

Eccleston, Thomas, 68
Elliot, Nathaniel, 69
Eyre, Thomas, 71

Fairfax, Thomas, 76
Falkner, Thomas, 77
Fentham, Henry, 79
Flann, or Hanne, Charles, 86
Fleetwood, Walter, 87
Foxe, James or John, 88

Gage, John, 93
Galloway, Edward, 94
Greenwill, Dennis, 107
Gwillim, Henry, 108

Halsey, or Halsall, George, 109
Hammerton, Peter, 110
Hardesty, ———, 111
Hattersley, or Hattersty, Joseph, 113
Hawkins, Thomas, 117
Hesketh, Roger (II.), 119
Holland, John Thomas, 122
Hornby Robert, 124
Hothersall, William, 128
Howard, Edward, 129 ; Francis, 129 ;
  John, 130
Humberstone, Henry, 132
Hunter, Thomas, 132

Jenkins, Augustin, 136 ; Peter, 136
Jennison, Augustin, 137 ; James, 137 ;
  John, 138
Jones, John Philip, 142

Keynes, or Kane, John, 145
Knatchbull, Robert, 146
Knight, Richard, 146

Lancaster, James, 147
Langdale, Marmaduke, 147
Lawson, Thos., Senr. and Junr., 149
Leckonby, Thomas, 149
Leigh, Philip, 150; Roger, 150
Lesley, ———, 150
Lester, Francis, 150
Leveson, Edward, 150
Lewis, Theodore, 151

Maire, Christopher, 154
Mannock, Francis, 157 ; Sir George, 158
Mansell, John, 158
Mansfield, Robert, 158
Massey, Thomas, 159
Mattingley, John, 160
Maxwell, John, 160
Medcalfe, or Metcalfe, 161
Meredith, Richard, 162

V.—PEERS

(ACCORDING TO BOTH TITLES AND FAMILY NAMES).

VI.—BARONETS AND KNIGHTS
(ACCORDING TO FAMILIES).

Acton, 1
Anderson, 2
Anderton, 2

Bedingfield, 14, 15
Blount, 27-29
Brown, 35, 36
Bulstrode, 38

Clifton, 48
Constable, 56

Englefield, 69

Fleetwood, 86
Fletcher, 87

Gage, 90-94
Gascoigne, 94
Gerard, 96
Haggerston, 108, 109
Hales, 109
Hunloke, 132-133

Inghilby, 136

Jerningham, 139, 140

Lawson, 148

Mannock, 158
Milton, 165
Mostyn, 170, 171

Poole, 187

Ramsay, 196

Sherburne, 208
Smythe, 213
Stanley, 217, 218
Swinburne, 224, 225

Tancred, 229
Throckmorton, 233, 234
Tichborne, 235

Vavasour, 241

Webb, 245

VII.—LAYMEN.

Arne [Thomas Augustine], 5

Baddeley, Thomas, 9
Bartlett, Basil, 12; Edward, 12
Berington, John, 17; Thomas (I.), 22;
    Thomas (II.), 22; William, 22
Berkeley, Robert, 23; Thomas, 23
Biddulph, John, 25; Richard, 25
Blount, —— (of Orleton), 27; George,
    29
Blundell, Henry, 29; Robert, 29
Bodenham, Charles, 30
Booth, James [? Nathaniel], 31;
    Nathaniel, 31
Butter, Richard, 39
Byarley, Charles, 39

Caryll [John], 42
Charleton, Edward, 43
Charnock, Robert, 43
Chorley, Charles, 44; Richard, 44
Clavering, William and John, 45
Clifford, Arthur, 45; Henry, 45; Hon.
    Thomas, 46
Clifton, ——, 48
Collingwood, George (I.), 52
Conquest, Benedict, 52
Constable, Cuthbert, 52; M. C., 55;
    M. M., 56; Wm. (I. and II.), 57

Dalton, John, 60
Dicconson, Roger, 64; William, 64
                                    [68
Eccleston, Thomas, 68; Thomas Ralph,
Errington, Thomas, 70
Eyre, Adam, 71; Francis, 71; Henry,
    71; Roland, 71; Thomas (II.), (III.),
    72, 73; Vincent (I.), (II.), 73
Eyston, Charles, 75; George, 76; John,
    76
Fitzherbert, Thomas, 85
Fleetwood, Thomas, 87
Fowler, Walter, 88
Fuller, William, 89

Gage, Henry Walgrave, 92; Joseph
    (I.), 93; Joseph (II.), 93
Gascoigne, Richard, 94
Gawen, Thomas, 95
Gibson, George, 97
Giffard, John (I. and II.), 101; Peter
    (II.), 101; Thomas (I. and II.), 102
Hodgson, Albert, 120; Philip, 121;
    Ralph, 121
Holford, Peter, 121
Holman, George, 122; William, 122
Hooke, Nathaniel, 123
Hornyhold, John, 127; Robert, 127;
    Thomas, 127

LAYMEN—*continued.*

VIII.—NUNS AND LADIES.

NUNS AND LADIES—*continued.*

Radcliffe, Lady Mary, 196 ; Catharine, 196

Sackville, Louisa Elizabeth, 204
Sheldon, Dame Frances, 206
Short, Anastasia, 209 ; Anna Maria, 209 ; Mary Agnes, 209
Sussex, Ann, Countess of, 223

Tempest, Jane, 230

Walmesley, Catharine, 242
Wells, Gertrude, 247

Yate, Lady Mary, 255

IX.—RELIGIOUS NAMES AND ALIASES.

Alexis, Frère, *see* Graham, Robert
Alice, *see* Harrison
Anderson, *see* Munson
Atherton, *see* Pearson, T.

Baines, *see* Sanders, F.
Barker, *see* Rigby, J.
Barnesby, *see* Perrot
Baron, *see* Bostock
Barret, *see* Daniel
Beckett, *see* Fairfax, F.
Bede of St. Simon Stock, *see* Travers
Bernardine, *see*
Bishop, *see* Gifford, M.
Blount, M., *see* Pollet
Booth, Jos., *see* Dalton, M.
Browne, Thomas, *see* Weatherby
Burdet, *see* Hussey
Butter, *see* Worswick
Byfleet, *see* Gildon

Carey, *see* Riddle
Carnforth, *see* Reydon
Carrington, *see* Smith
Clare, *see* Eden
Clarke, *see* Wilson
Clerophilus Alethes, *see* Constable, John, S.J.
Coldham, *see* Shepherd
Cole, *see* Giffard
Colebeck, *see* Hunt
Collingwood, *see* Metcalf
Cooper, *see* Potts

D., B., *see* Wilmot
Davies, *see* Pollet
Dawson, *see* Debord

Earpe, *see* Dunn
Eccleston, *see* Gorsuch
Edwards, *see* Tylecote
Eglesfield, *see* Metcalfe
Ellston, or Eyston, *see* Lacy
Elliot, *see* Sheldon
Every, *see* Saltmarsh

Fitton, *see* Fisher
Fitzherbert, *see* Hall

Gardiner, *see* Carnaby
Giffard, *see* Fentham
Gildon, *see* Byfleet
Golden, *see* Parkinson
Gomeldon, *see* Gumblestone
Gorsuch, *see* Eccleston
Grange, *see* Yaxley
Green, *see* Horne
Grey, *see* Talbot
Griffith, *see* Morgan
Gulielmi, *see* Williams

Hall, *see* Humberstone ; *see* Diggs
Hatherley, *see* Hart
Hathersty, *see* Hatterskey
Hanmer, *see* Buxton
Hanne, *see* Flann
Hardwicke, *see* Hunter
Haskett, *see* Downs
Hawkins, *see* Styke
Herbert, *see* Vane
Hildreth, *see* Addison
Holland, *see* Eccleston
Hunt, *see* Holdfort
Hyde, *see* Hills

Ireland, *see* Saltmarsh

James, Mary of St. Margaret, *see* Gordon, James
Johnson, *see* White, Richard
Jones, *see* Vane, John

Leckenby, *see* White, John

Markham, *see* William George
Masters, *see* Thorpe, John
Maxfield, *see* Jakeman
Middlehurst, *see* Johnson, Thomas
Migliorucci, *see* Nevill
Mosley, *see* Mandesley

Palmer, *see* Pulton, Giles
Parkins, *see* Hawkins
Paston, *see* Howard, Henry (II.)
Paul of St. Francis, *see* Atkinson
Penketh, *see* Rivers, John
Perrot, *see* Barnesley

RELIGIOUS NAMES AND ALIASES—*continued.*

Philips, *see* Elston, John
Pits, *see* Atwood.
Plowden, *see* Dean, Thomas
Plummerden, *see* Maurice
Pollet, *see* Davies and Myles Blount
Powell, *see* Progers
Preston, Hugh, *see* Clifford, H.
Price, *see* Brian, or Bryan, John
Prichard, *see* Morgan, William
Pritchard, *see* Plummerden

Rivet, *see* Harvey
Rogers, *see* Ward, John
Romanus, *see* Chapman, Francis

Scarisbrick, *see* Eccleston, Thos. Ralph
Severison, *see* Gilpin, Thomas
Sheldon, *see* Elliot, Nathaniel
Shelley, *see* Lewis
Shepherd, Augustin, *see* Crathorne, Wm.
Shrewsbury, *see* Talbot, George
Singleton, *see* Swarbrick, James
Smelt, *see* Archdeacon
Smith, *see* Thwaites, Francis
Spencer, *see* Petre [Robert]
Squib, *see* Petre, Francis (II.)
Stanley, *see* Massey, Thomas
Staveley, *see* Brand, John
Stycke, Bridgwood, Thomas

Talbot, *see* Hesketh
Taylor, *see* Johnson, Thomas
Tempest, *see* Hardesty
Terret, or Tyrwhit, *see* Gwillim
Thomas, *see* Pinckard
Thompson, *see* Buxton, George
Tootell, Hugh, *see* Dodd, Charles
Thorold, *see* Thorall   [bert
Tunstall, Cuthbert, *see* Constable, Cuth-
Tunstall, *see* Constable, M.C.
Turner, *see* Shimmel, Richard
Typper, *see* Pinckard

Umfreville, *see* Fell, Charles

Vane, *see* Herbert John
Verhuyck, *see* Liddel, John
Vezzosi, Joseph, *see* Robinson
Vezzosi, Stephen, *see* Robinson
Vinter, *see* Vintner

Warham, *see* Smith, John and Robert
West, *see* Bostock, George (I.)
White, *see* Leckonby
Whittaker, *see* Martin, Thomas
Woodbury, *see* Barnard
Worthington, *see* Ball
Wright, *see* Hudson, Charles

Young, *see* Hammerton, Peter

X.—APOSTATES.

Aspinwall [Edward], 7
Austin, John, 8
Aylmer, William Augustine, 9

Billinge [Charles], 25
Bower, Archibald, 32

Chester, James, 43

Doran, James, 65

? Eden, James, 68

Fournier [Bernard], 87

? Geddes, Alexander, 95
Gumblestone, Richard, 108

Holmes [Edward] 123

MacCarthy, James, 154
Mainwaring, ———, 154
Mordaunt, George, 168

Nolan, James, 173

Piazza, Hïeron, 183
Pollet, *vere* Davies, 186

Quenel, James, 193

Smith, James, 212
Stafford, John Joseph, 216

Tapral, ———, 229

Waldegrave, Lord, 242
Willoughby, Edward, 251

XI.—CATHOLIC HOUSES, STATIONS, CHAPELS, CONVENTS, SCHOOLS, &c.

Under the penal laws, before chapels were tolerated, almost every large Catholic house became a station, at which Mass was said, sometimes regularly and for long periods, sometimes only rarely, or for a short time. It is interesting and important to ascertain, as well as we can, which those Catholic houses were. The main object of the following list is therefore to index those houses which were either presumably or avowedly Catholic at one time or another. It is, of course, not pretended that more than a small proportion were Catholic at the same time. Indeed, no positive assurance can be given that in every case the household was Catholic, though the master or the mistress was. Again, though the presumption is that the religion of the husband was that of the wife, and vice versa (for mixed marriages were then extremely rare), still this again is only a presumption, though one which must be made if our list is to be complete in regard to families into which Catholicism presumably entered at one time or other. The strength and weakness of the presumptions will vary extremely, and must be specially estimated in each case.

CATHOLIC HOUSES, STATIONS, CHAPELS, &c.—*continued.*

CATHOLIC HOUSES, STATIONS, CHAPELS, &c.—*continued.*

CATHOLIC HOUSES, STATIONS, CHAPELS, &c.—*continued.*

CATHOLIC HOUSES, STATIONS, CHAPELS, &c.—*continued.*

Rue Notre Dame des Vertues, 196
St. Germains, 50, 72, 136
St. Magloire, 130

Park Hall, 259, 260, 261, 262, 265
Parlington, 201
Paynsley, 147, 151, 154
Pemberton, 265
Peckham, East, 247
Perthere, near Monmouth, 192
Peterley, 76, 225
Petersfield, Hants, 189
Pipe Hall, 34, 145, 223
Plowden Hall, 77, 86, 235
Plumpton, Great, 270
Pomfret, 211
Ponteland, 219
Pontesbury, 22
Pontoise, 44, 79, 132
Pontop, 141, 150, 225, 248
Poole Hall, 187
Pooley, 248
Portarlington, 69
Porter's, Mrs., 138
Portico, 264
Portsea, 90
Poulton, 264
Powis Castle, 231
Prescot, 264 ; School, 179, 268
Preston, 15, 97, 104, 112, 118, 260, 264, 270 ; Mr. Dun's, 169 ; R. Morgan's, 216 ; Dr. Witham's, 136
Preston-upon-Skerne, 31, 254
Puddington, 65, 159, 170, 217, 218
Pyrthymeanmach, 217

"Qousq" (Yorks), 211, 244

Raventops, 155
Rawcliffe, 39
Red Hall, 152
Redheugh, 40
Redlingfield, 45
Rendcomb, 27
Richmond (Yorks), 155, 197
Robert Hall, 61, 221, 258, 261, 262, 264, 267, 269, 271, 272
Rochdale, 208
Rome, English College, 1, 2, 3, 4, 8, 9, 11, 16, 27, 33, 35, 36, 60, 62, 64, 69, 101, 104, 117, 147, 179, 207, 223
Roston, 151, 254
Rotherwas, 30, 116
Rothbury, 68
Rouen, Poor Clares, 5, 120, 144, 185, 222, 232, 252
Roundhay, 57
Rowington, 78
Rowneywood, 43, 175, 176

Rushbrooke, 138
Rushton Grange, 34
Ryton, 73

St. Alkmund's, 22
St. Columb's, 7
St. Edmundsbury, 138
St. Helen's, 103, 264
St. Stephen's, 245
St. Thomas' Priory, 33, 39, 73, 78, 82, 88
St. Omers, 4, 6, 7, 9, 10, 15, 30, 52, 57, 58, 64, 71, 74, 93, 108, 110, 117, 119, 129, 134, 137, 158, 160, 161, 170, 178, 181, 186, 189, 218, 225, 226, 229
Salisbury, 6, 238
Salwick, 63, 134, 259, 261, 262, 263, 264, 267
Samford, 178
Sawston, 30, 43, 132
Scarborough, 61, 188, 258, 262, 271
Scarisbrick, 68, 133, 148, 205, 264, 272
Scargill Castle, 57
Scoles, 166
Scorton, 61, 205, 258, 259, 262, 264, 267, 271 ; Hall, 81
Scorton Nateby, 136
Scotney, 23
Sedgley Park, 15, 27, 30, 37, 46, 58, 59, 70, 102, 107, 112, 120, 126, 128, 133, 144, 145, 153, 163, 180, 200, 215, 225, 230, 261, 268
Sefton, 166, 264
Septfons, 186
Seville, 155
Shadwell (or Wapping), 105
Sheffield, 37, 75, 104, 152, 258
Shepton Mallet, 33, 56
Sherborne Castle, 7, 93
Sherburn, 93
Shefford, 200
Showley, 182, 243, 263, 266
Shrewsbury, 58, 136, 241
Silkstead, 23, 24
Singleton, 103, 221, 223, 254, 261, 262, 263, 267, 269
Sixhills, 112, 166, 173
Sizergh, 141, 168, 223, 247
Sladedelf, 264
Sladwish, 103
Slindon, 72, 117, 168
Snarford Hall, 235
Snitterfield, 27
Soddington, 7, 27, 29, 136, 214, 234
Somersfield, 247
Somerton, 111
Southall Park, 70
South Hill, 264
South Shields, 49, 120
Southworth, 88, 264